OXFORD READINGS IN
THEOLO.͵

VOLUME 2

Oxford Readings in Philosophical Theology
Volume 2

Providence, Scripture, and Resurrection

Edited By
MICHAEL REA

OXFORD
UNIVERSITY PRESS

OXFORD
UNIVERSITY PRESS

Great Clarendon Street, Oxford OX2 6DP

Oxford University Press is a department of the University of Oxford.
It furthers the University's objective of excellence in research, scholarship,
and education by publishing worldwide in

Oxford New York

Auckland   Cape Town Dar es Salaam   Hong Kong   Karachi
Kuala Lumpur Madrid Melbourne Mexico City   Nairobi
New Delhi Shanghai Taipei Toronto
With offices in
Argentina Austria Brazil Chile Czech Republic France Greece
Guatemala Hungary Italy Japan South Korea Poland Portugal
Singapore Switzerland Thailand Turkey Ukraine Vietnam

Oxford is a registered trade mark of Oxford University Press
in the UK and in certain other countries

Published in the United States
by Oxford University Press Inc., New York

ISBN 978-0-19-923748-7

Printed in the United Kingdom by
Lightning Source UK Ltd., Milton Keynes

For Little Kris

Contents

III. MATERIALISM AND THE RESURRECTION
OF THE DEAD

List of Abbreviations

ABRL	Anchor Bible Reference Library
AGJU	Arbeiten zur Geschichte des Antiken Judentums und des Urchristentums
APAMS	American Philological Association Mongraph Series
AUSS	*Andrews University Seminary Studies*
CCSL	Corpus Christianorum, Series Latina
CTA	*Corpus des tablettes en cuneiforms alphabétiques découvertes à Ras Shamra-Ugarit de* 1929 à 1939, Mission de Ras Shamra, x (Paris: P. Geuthner, 1963)
GIBM	Greek Inscriptions in the British Museum
GNO	Werner Jaeger et. al. (eds.), *Gregorii Nysseni Opera*, 10 vols. (Leiden: Brill, 1960–90)
HNT	Handbuch zum Neuen Testament
ICC	International Critical Commentary
IG	Inscriptiones Graecae
IGR	Inscriptiones Graecae ad Res Romanas Pertinentes
JSNTSup	*Journal for the Study of the New Testament—Supplement Series*
JSOT	*Journal for the Study of the Old Testament*
JSPSup	*Journal for the Study of Pseudepigrapha—Supplement Series*
JTS	*Journal of Theological Studies*
LXX	Septuagint
NTS	*New Testament Studies*
NT	New Testament
OGIS	*Orientis Graeci Inscriptiones Selectae, Supplementum Sylloge Inscriptionum Graecarum*, ed. Wilhlem Dittenberger (Hildesheim/New York: G. Olms, 1986)
OT	Old Testament
PG	Patrologia Graeca (J.-P. Migne)
RILP	Roehampton Institute London Papers
SBLDS	Society of Biblical Literature Dissertation Series
SIG	Al. N. Oikonomides (ed.), *Sylloge Inscriptionum Graecarum et Latinarum Macedoniae* (Chicago: Ares, 1980)
WBC	Word Biblical Commentary

Introduction*

This is the second volume of a two-volume collection of readings in philosophical theology. Volume 1 treats the topics of trinity, incarnation, and atonement. The present volume focuses on divine providence, divine revelation and the inspiration of scripture, and the resurrection of the dead.

I. DIVINE PROVIDENCE

To speak of God's providence is to speak of the nature and extent of God's control over creation. All parties to the debates about divine providence agree that God is sovereign in some sense over creation and that God sees to it that creation unfolds according to some sort of plan. But what sort of control does God exercise, and how much depth is included in the plan? Answers to these questions fall along a spectrum. At one end lie views according to which God leaves a great deal to chance and to the decisions of free creatures; at the other end lie views according to which absolutely every matter of fact is the product of some divine decree. The essays in the first part of this volume discuss a variety of views along this spectrum.[1]

In the first essay, Thomas P. Flint contrasts the two views that have dominated the current discussion: Thomism (a view which might as easily be labelled 'Calvinism' or 'Augustinianism') and Molinism. Thomism, as Flint presents it, offers a maximally strong view of divine providence. God's control over his

* I am grateful to the Institute for Scholarship in the Liberal Arts at the University of Notre Dame for financial support that assisted in the production of these volumes, and to Luke Potter for help in assembling the manuscript and securing the permissions. I would also like to thank my wife, Chris Brinks Rea for help in selecting articles for Part II of this volume. Scattered portions of this introduction overlap bits of the second chapter of Michael Murray and Michael Rea, *Introduction to the Philosophy of Religion* (Cambridge: Cambridge University Press, 2008). I am grateful to Cambridge University Press for permission to use that material.

[1] The literature on divine providence is voluminous. For a good start into that literature, see James Beilby and Paul Eddy (eds.), *Divine Foreknowledge: Four Views* (Ithaca, NY: Cornell University Press, 1998); William Hasker et al., eds., *Middle Knowledge: Theory and Applications* (Frankfurt am Main: Peter Lang, 2000); and Clark Pinnock, et al., *The Openness of God: A Biblical Challenge to the Traditional Understanding of God* (Downers Grove, IL: InterVarsity Press, 1994). See also Thomas P. Flint, 'Divine Providence', in Flint and Michael Rea (eds.), *The Oxford Handbook of Philosophical Theology* (Oxford: Oxford University Press, 2009).

creation is absolute and, as some put it, *meticulous*. Nothing is left to chance; no contingent fact obtains independently of the will of God. For those unsettled by the possibility of God taking risks or leaving important matters like the destinies of our eternal souls in the hands of fallible free creatures, Thomism is maximally comforting. On the other hand, precisely because it takes everything out of the hands of fallible free creatures, Thomism leaves us wondering (even more than we would ordinarily) what to say in response to the problem of evil and the problem of hell. If God really disapproves of murder and desires that all go to heaven, and if (as Thomists say) *nothing* happens apart from the will of God, then why do murders take place and why does it seem as though there are people who will go to hell?

On Thomism, divine providence operates simply by divine decree: God foreordains everything that is to occur; and, accordingly, he foreknows everything that will occur. On Molinism, by contrast, divine providence relies in part on what has been called God's 'middle knowledge'. According to Flint, medieval philosophers prior to the sixteenth century distinguished between God's *natural knowledge*, which comprised his knowledge of truths that were both *necessary* and *independent of God's will* (such as truths of logic and mathematics), and God's *free knowledge*, which comprised his knowledge of truths that were *contingent* and *dependent* on his will (for example, ordinary truths about what objects and events exist in the world). The sixteenth-century Spanish Jesuit Luis de Molina, however, identified a third kind of knowledge—knowledge of truths that are *contingent* (like the objects of God's free knowledge), but nevertheless *independent of God's will* (like the objects of his natural knowledge). Since this sort of knowledge stands, in a way, 'in between' God's natural and free knowledge, it was referred to as 'middle knowledge'. The primary examples of truths that are objects of God's middle knowledge are truths about what free creatures *would do* in circumstances that are not yet or never to become actual. In other words, God's middle knowledge consists primarily of his knowledge of counterfactuals of freedom—claims like 'If Fred were to propose marriage to Wilma, Wilma would freely accept.' According to the Molinist, such truths are contingent—the counterfactuals true in the actual world might have been false. But they are nevertheless independent of God's will—it is, in other words, not up to God which counterfactuals are true.

By exploiting his awareness of what his creatures would freely do if they were to find themselves in various different circumstances, God is able to exercise a great deal of control over creation. Some outcomes that God might desire will be unobtainable, because it might just turn out that there are no circumstances under which one or another of his free creatures *would freely* do some particular thing that God wants him or her to do—again, the truth values of the counterfactuals of freedom are not up to God. But any *feasible* outcome— any outcome that is compatible with the particular range of necessary and contingent-but-not-up-to-God truths that God finds himself confronted with—will be obtainable by virtue of divine omnipotence together with God's exhaustive knowledge of the relevant truths.

Molinism is a powerful view with a great deal of theoretical utility. The fact that, on Molinism, God has extensive but not complete control of his creation allows Molinists to affirm a strong (even if not *maximally* strong) view of divine sovereignty while also offering some explanation for the existence of evil. (Perhaps, Molinists say, evil was simply unavoidable given God's desire to create free creatures and given the hand of counterfactuals of freedom that was dealt to him.) It also supports explanations for why hell might be populated. (Perhaps, for example, there are some people whom it was valuable to create but who were simply such that nothing God could have done would have resulted in their freely choosing a relationship with him.) It has also been invoked in the service of defending particular views about the inspiration of scripture (see the essay by Craig in Part II), and it has been put to work in buttressing a variety of other traditional Christian doctrines as well. Flint himself is one of the leading defenders of Molinism, and the paper under discussion here offers a variety of considerations in favour of the view.

That said, Molinism also faces some serious objections. Central to Molinism is the supposition that there are true counterfactuals of freedom. Many philosophers, however, are inclined to reject this supposition on the grounds that, in the case of counterfactuals of freedom with *false* antecedents, it is hard to see what could possibly ground their truth. For example: Suppose Wilma is free and would remain free if Fred were to propose to her. Suppose further that it is true that if Fred were to propose, Wilma would accept. What makes this true? Nothing about Wilma *guarantees* that she would accept. She is, after all, free—which, one might think, is just to say that she *might or might not accept* if Fred were to propose.[2] And if nothing about Wilma guarantees that she would accept, it is hard to see what else might guarantee this without interfering with her freedom. And so, again, it is hard to see what could possibly make it true that she would accept; or, in different terminology, it is hard to see what *in the world* could possibly *explain* the fact that she would accept.

This so-called 'grounding objection' is discussed in some detail in the two essays following Flint's. Timothy O'Connor presses the grounding objection against Molinists, and then goes on to argue that even if there were true counterfactuals of freedom, it is hard to see how God could possibly know them. Thus, he concludes, Molinism cannot reasonably be accepted. William Lane Craig, on the other hand, argues that the standard grounding objection against Molinism is a non-starter. On his view, the grounding objection depends on views about the ontology of truth and about the nature of 'truth-makers' that anti-Molinists have

---

[2] This claim by itself might be thought to provide grounds for rejecting the possibility of middle knowledge. See Peter van Inwagen, 'Against Middle Knowledge', *Midwest Studies in Philosophy* 21 (1997): 225–36.

not yet managed to articulate in clear enough detail. In the end, he concludes that 'it is evident that anti-Molinists have not even begun to do the necessary homework in order for their grounding objection to fly'.

Leaving Molinism aside, we turn now to David Hunt's 'Simple Foreknowledge' theory of providence—a view that I like to call *Responsivism*. This view is aligned with Molinism in embracing human freedom and in rejecting the idea that freedom is compatible with exhaustive divine foreordination (or, for that matter, physical determinism). It departs from Molinism in denying that providence operates by reliance upon middle knowledge. According to Hunt, simple foreknowledge plus exhaustive knowledge of what is currently, possibly, and necessarily true, is sufficient for God to exercise providential control over the world.

The main objection against Responsivism is the fact that *mere* foreknowledge seems to be providentially useless. In particular, it comes too late in the 'order of explanation' for it to serve as the *basis* of God's providential decisions. The reason, in short, is that knowledge of the future will include the consequences of God's acts; thus, once God knows for sure what will happen in the world, it has already been decided in some sense how he will act. But if it has already been decided how he will act, then God's *foreknowledge* cannot play a role in guiding his actions. The main purpose of Hunt's article is to address this objection; and he does so by trying to show how divine action might be guided by simple foreknowledge in conjunction with an exhaustively detailed 'contingency' plan—i.e., a complete working out of what is to be done in response to anything that might possibly occur. The contingency plan does not in any way depend upon knowledge of what *would* happen in non-actual circumstances. Rather, it depends solely upon God's knowledge of what is possible. Foreknowledge then provides God with the necessary additional information to, as it were, work his way through the tree of hypotheticals and determine how to act.

The final essay in Part I is Peter van Inwagen's 'The Place of Chance in a World Sustained by God'.[3] Chance events, according to van Inwagen, are (roughly) undetermined events that are not part of anyone's plan (not even God's). On the views discussed so far, it is hard to see any clear sense in which anything in the world could count as a chance event. On Thomism, everything that happens is the product of divine decree. On Molinism, not everything is determined; but, even so, God makes use of his exhaustive knowledge of counterfactuals to ensure that he gets *precisely* the feasible outcome that he desires. On

---

[3] The essay by van Inwagen is intended to provide partial coverage of the position known as 'open theism'—a package of views that includes the claims that the future is open, God takes risks, and God lacks complete foreknowledge of future events. Van Inwagen's essay most relevantly supports the first two of these claims, though van Inwagen himself also endorses the third (explicitly, in 'What does an Omniscient Being Know about the Future?' [unpublished MS]). The claim that God lacks complete foreknowledge is typically supported by arguments whose proper treatment would demand an entire additional section in this volume (at least). For a start into this literature, however, see John Martin Fischer (ed.), *God, Foreknowledge, and Freedom* (Stanford: Stanford University Press, 1989.) For an introduction to open theism generally, see Pinnock, et. al., *The Openness of God*.

Responsivism, God (apparently) has exactly the same range of control over the world as he does on Molinism, only without reliance on middle knowledge. Van Inwagen, however, works out a view according to which some things that happen are no part of God's plan and, indeed, were not even foreknown by him. Van Inwagen rebuts several reasons theists might offer for resisting this picture of divine providence, and he goes on to note that God might in fact have good reason for leaving his creatures to some extent at the mercy of fortune. One use to which this supposition might be put is in solving the problem of evil—a problem that is far more difficult to solve on the supposition that God exercises the sort of strong sovereignty over creation that Thomists, Molinists, and Responsivists accept.[4]

II. DIVINE REVELATION AND THE INSPIRATION OF SCRIPTURE

Many religious believers take themselves to be in possession of texts that are inspired by God. Many also think that divine inspiration amounts to something like divine *authorship*: the scriptures in some sense are or contain the very words of God. Not surprisingly, then, many believers take their sacred texts to speak with some degree of authority in their lives. Such beliefs, however, raise serious philosophical questions. What does divine inspiration amount to? How does it work, and under what conditions is it rational to believe that a text possesses it? What is the 'unit' of inspiration? Is it each individual word of an inspired text that is inspired, or each paragraph, or the canon as a whole, or the propositional content of the canon at some level of abstraction, or what? What sort of character must an inspired (or divinely authored) book possess? Can it contain sentences that, naturally interpreted, assert falsehoods? If so, can it also contain sentences that assert falsehoods about spiritual matters? Can we, for example, sensibly believe that the book of Leviticus (which is both part of the Hebrew Bible and of the Old Testament) is divinely inspired but wholly misleading about God's attitudes toward various moral issues like slavery and homosexuality? And what sort of authority ought we to accord a book that we take to be divinely inspired? When biblical assertions are highly counterintuitive, ought we to revise our intuitions, reject the relevant biblical assertion as false, interpret the biblical assertion as metaphor, or something else? Alas, the questions might go on and on.

These issues are vitally important. They impinge upon a wide variety of religious controversies and just a moment's reflection reveals that they are near the heart of almost all of the major religious conflicts that occupy our attention today. It is therefore highly curious that they have received (comparatively) so little attention in the philosophical literature. Leaving aside historical figures, the

---

[4] See also Peter van Inwagen, *The Problem of Evil* (Oxford: Oxford University Press, 2006).

philosophical literature on the questions just raised consists of little more than a
handful of books and a smattering of articles.[5]

The first essay in Part II, by Richard Swinburne, takes up three central questions
about divine revelation: (i) Do we have reason to expect it? (ii) What would it be like
if it were given? (iii) What kind of historical evidence would show that we had got it?
On Swinburne's view, we do have reason to expect it, because we have reason to
believe in God, and we also have reason to believe that if there is a God, he would
want to reveal himself to his creatures (to show them how to live, to communicate
his love and desires for their lives, and so on). As to what it would be like, Swinburne
thinks that divine revelation would likely be communicated in a way that doesn't
aim to correct 'irrelevant' false scientific or historical presuppositions; and it would
likely also be communicated in a way that involves metaphor and analogy. In short,
it would be similar in some ways to adult communication with children. What this
means practically speaking, though, is that we can and must rely on reason, science,
and historical research to help us to interpret scripture. Where we spot apparent
falsehood, there we know that the revelation has gone metaphorical or is engaged in
some sort of cultural accommodation. The true content, however, is infallible.
Finally, our beliefs about the content of divine revelation will ultimately depend on
miracles of various sorts that serve to 'authorize' particular individuals, institutions,
or texts as the bearers, vehicles, or interpreters of divine revelation; or it will depend
on testimony from previously authorized texts, individuals, or institutions to the
effect that some additional text, institution, or individual is a bearer, vehicle, or
interpreter of divine revelation.

For all that he *does* say, however, Swinburne does not try to offer any sort of
theory about what divine inspiration consists in or how it works. The next two
essays, however, do address this issue. William J. Abraham argues that the way in
which God inspires a text is akin to the way in which an admired teacher might
be thought to inspire the texts of his students. Thus, for example, much of my
own thinking about the topic of epistemology has been inspired by the writings
and lectures of my dissertation supervisor, Alvin Plantinga. Plantinga would not
agree with everything that I have to say about epistemology; and he certainly can't
be blamed for authoring any of it. But when I say that it is 'inspired' by him,
I don't mean to say that he authored it or that he would endorse all of it. I don't
mean to say that I took his dictation or even that he told me (in any sense) what
to write. All I mean to say is that his influence is present; and if I claim 'strong'
Plantingian inspiration, all I mean is that his influence is *strongly* present, that my
thoughts are in a kind of alignment with his. Likewise, Abraham thinks, to say

---

[5] The main philosophical resources apart from those reprinted here are Stephen T. Davis, *The
Debate about the Bible: Inerrancy versus Infallibility* (Philadelphia, PA: Westminster Press, 1977) and
'The Inspiration of Scripture', in Flint and Rea (eds.), *Oxford Handbook of Philosophical Theology*;
and Richard Swinburne, *Revelation: From Metaphor to Analogy*, 2nd ed. (Oxford: Clarendon Press,
2007) and 'The Authority of Scripture, Tradition, and the Church', in Flint and Rea (eds.), *Oxford
Handbook of Philosophical Theology*.

that God inspired the scriptures isn't to say that God is their author or that God agrees with everything they assert; it isn't to say that the biblical authors received anything like divine 'dictation', or even that they were told what to write. Rather, all it means (or, better, all it *guarantees*) is that the scriptures bear God's influence—that in writing what they wrote, they wrote something that could sensibly be regarded as in alignment with God's thoughts.

This is a comparatively weak view of divine inspiration. It doesn't guarantee infallibility of content. It doesn't even guarantee infallibility on fundamental spiritual matters. Consider, for example, the doctrine of the trinity, by all accounts a fundamental doctrine, but one which is inferred from scripture, rather than explicitly taught therein. The passages from which the doctrine is inferred don't comprise a large proportion of the Bible as a whole. Thus, it is possible that the Bible as a whole is inspired in Abraham's sense, but that the biblical authors managed to garble things in just the places that lead us to detect a doctrine of the trinity—and this despite the fact that the doctrine of the trinity is fundamental to the Christian faith.

A stronger concept of divine inspiration is offered by William Lane Craig. Craig exploits the theory of middle knowledge to offer a way in which God might be able to guarantee that the Bible says exactly (or almost exactly) what he wants it to say without engaging in any *direct* revelatory activity whatsoever. If God has middle knowledge, then among the things he will know will be all of the facts about what free creatures *would say* were they to write about God, or the life of Jesus, or the history of Israel, or whatever under various kinds of circumstances (in prison, in exile, off on an island, in sickness or health, etc.). God would also know what would be done with these writings (depending upon when they were produced, to whom they were given, etc.). Armed with all of this knowledge, perhaps God could arrange for documents saying exactly the things he wants them to say to be produced under just the right circumstances to guarantee their effective transmission and subsequent adoption into the canon. (I say 'perhaps' because, of course, the relevant counterfactuals of freedom might not turn out to have the truth values that God needs in order to accomplish exactly what he wants.) If this is possible, then we can grant that the authorship and transmission of the biblical texts was a very human and non-miraculous (or, at any rate, not-visibly-miraculous) process that involved little or nothing at all like divine words from heaven. Yet we can also grant (as Craig and others have wanted to) that God is the author of scripture, and that the words in scripture are God's words to us.

Leaving aside questions about how inspiration takes place, we turn now to three essays that discuss the nature of the canon and the authority of scripture. The two issues are interrelated. One of the primary motivations behind William Lane Craig's view about how divine inspiration takes place is his desire to preserve a view according to which every passage of scripture is equally inspired, and thus equally authoritative. This is a common view; and it has a natural (widely endorsed) corollary: nothing outside of scripture is on a par with scripture either in its inspiration or its authority. Thus, many are inclined to believe (implicitly, even if not explicitly) that the canon is simply a collection of divinely inspired and authoritative texts, all of which are on a par. Many are also inclined to believe that the canon is complete, in the sense that it contains all of the inspired and authoritative texts that exist. The essays by Keller and Sundberg each challenge aspects of this common view (while also disagreeing with one another). The essay by Wolterstorff defends a view about what *unifies* the canonical works that might be construed as a qualified variation on the common view and that also offers an important challenge to some of the interpretive suggestions made by Keller.

According to Keller, what I have just called 'the common view' must be abandoned if we are to be rationally justified in treating the Bible as authoritative.[6] On his view, the 'locus of authority' is not the *passage*, as if the Bible as a whole derived its authority from being a collection of (equally) authoritative passages. Rather, his view is that the Bible as a whole is authoritative, but that individual passages might differ in the degree to which they have authority. This suggests a view according to which *presence in the canon* is what makes a text authoritative rather than the other way around. And, importantly, it is books, not passages, that are the fundamental units in the canon.

Moreover, he argues that, in order to assess the authoritative weight of a passage, we should begin by formulating an overall view about what is essential to Christian faith and practice. This done, we should then use that background view to help us to determine which passages to discount, which to reject, and which to count as fully authoritative. In arriving at our view about the essentials of Christian faith and practice, we should rely on a variety of sources—experience, our own reasoning, and the Bible as well. But, he argues, in relying on the Bible to help guide the formation of this overall view, we should *not* look to individual passages for guidance. Rather, we should take our guidance from a more holistic, biblically informed picture of what faith and religious life came to for each of the various writers of the books in the Bible. Again, it is *books*, not *passages*, that are the fundamental units in the canon.

If Keller is right, then the *canon* provides us with a determinate list of authoritative books; and it is up to us to determine *how* authoritative each one is, and which particular passages within each book are devoid of authority. Both features of this view will be contentious; and both are challenged in interesting ways by Albert Sundberg Jr. According to Sundberg, whether a book is *inspired* or *authoritative* is not something that is to be determined by individual believers. Instead, the canon itself is what helps us to determine what is inspired. On his view, the fathers of the early church handed us a variety of documents that were supposed to have been clearly written under the guidance of the Holy Spirit, and so inspired. *Some* of these documents, but not all, were collected into a canon that now forms the 'measure of inspiration'. If Sundberg is right, then the common view is false: the canon does not contain all of the inspired works; and, since inspired works are authoritative, it does not contain all of the

---

[6] Keller's views are further developed in chapter 6 of *Problems of Evil and the Power of God* (London: Ashgate, 2007).

authoritative works either. Likewise, Sundberg's view conflicts with Keller's: the *measure* of inspiration (and so of authority too) is not any view that we bring to the table, or even anything that we ourselves can discover as intrinsic to the text; rather, the measure of inspiration is simply concurrence with the canon.[7]

As noted earlier, Nicholas Wolterstorff offers another challenge to Keller's view. For Keller, again, the way to determine the degree of authority possessed by a passage in scripture is to interpret it in light of our views about what the *particular human authors* of the biblical texts saw as essential to faith and practice. According to Wolterstorff, however, our interpretation of a passage of any text depends in important ways upon what sort of *work* we take to be the whole of which the passage is a part. Are the passages of scripture merely parts of the individual human works that we call the 'books of the Bible'? Or are they also parts of a larger work, compiled not only by human editors but, in some sense, by God himself? Our answers to these questions make a significant interpretive difference; for if the books of the Bible are part of a larger divine work, then they have a kind of unity that they would otherwise lack—a unity that helps to determine how we should understand each one individually. On Wolterstorff's view, the books of the Bible do have precisely this sort of unity. All of this sits rather uneasily, however, with Keller's interpretive recommendations. Moreover, if Wolterstorff is right, there is (at least) an element of truth in the common view after all: the texts that comprise the Bible have together been authorized by God as *his work*. This fact lends each part of the Bible (properly interpreted) a kind of authoritative weight that it would not have on its own—and it is hard to see why the authoritative weight should be distributed unequally. Of course, this falls short of the claim that all parts of the Bible are equally authoritative; for some parts might acquire further authority from other sources. This is why Wolterstorff's view can, at best, be construed as a qualified variation on the common view. Nevertheless, it is a significant step closer to the common view than Keller's.

Finally, Part II concludes with three articles discussing the attitudes that religious believers ought to take toward the results of the discipline of historical biblical criticism. If its results were treated with the authority of the deliverances of any other science, historical biblical criticism would pose serious *prima facie* challenges to traditional religious belief. For example, summarizing what he calls the *liberal consensus*—which is supposed to be a consensus among historical biblical critics—Thomas Sheehan writes:[8]

In Roman Catholic seminaries . . . it is now common teaching that Jesus of Nazareth did not assert any of the messianic claims that the Gospels attribute to him and that he died without believing that he was the Christ or the Son of God, not to mention the founder of a new religion.

---

[7] Thanks to Chris Brinks Rea for valuable comments on this section.

[8] Thomas Sheehan, Review of Hans Küng's *Eternal Life*, *New York Review of Books* 31 (June 14, 1984), quoted in Michael Dummett, 'A Remarkable Consensus', *New Blackfriars* 68 (1987): 424–31.

Nor did Jesus know that his mother, Mary, had remained a virgin in the very act of conceiving him.... Most likely Mary told Jesus what she herself knew of his origins: that he had a natural father and was born not in Bethlehem but in Nazareth, indeed without the ministrations of angels, shepherds, and late-arriving wise men bearing gifts. She could have told her son the traditional nativity story only if she had managed to read, long before they were written, the inspiring but unhistorical Christmas legends that first appeared in the gospels of Matthew and Luke fifty years after her son had died.

Moreover, according to the consensus, although Jesus had a reputation as a faith healer during his life, it is likely that he performed very few such 'miracles', perhaps only two. (Probably he never walked on water.) (428–9)

To be sure, there is some exaggeration in saying that this represents a *consensus* among practitioners of historical biblical criticism. But there is truth enough in that claim that, if the results of historical biblical criticism were to be taken as the final word on what we ought to believe about the historical claims made by the Bible, traditional Christian faith would be in shambles.

The essays by Eleonore Stump and Alvin Plantinga, however, both argue that the results of historical biblical criticism depend heavily upon methodological and philosophical presuppositions that are eminently questionable and, in many cases, perfectly reasonable for a religious believer to reject. Taking a contrary position, Evan Fales argues against Plantinga for the conclusion that the threat to traditional Christian faith from historical biblical criticism is real, and that the moves Plantinga wants to make in order to deflect that threat are unsuccessful.

III. MATERIALISM AND RESURRECTION

Though it is curiously de-emphasized in many popular presentations of the heart of the Christian faith, the doctrine of the *resurrection* is absolutely central to Christianity. In the fifteenth chapter of Paul's first epistle to the Corinthians, St Paul declares that the sting of death is drawn *not* when the immaterial souls of believers are finally united in some ethereal heaven, but when the dead are raised and 'this mortal body' puts on immortality.[9] The resurrection of the body is affirmed in the earliest Christian creeds, and it is affirmed and discussed throughout the New Testament. The idea that the afterlife consists in eternal *disembodied* existence is present in other religious and philosophical traditions. (It was Plato's view, for example.) But it is not a Christian view.

Other religious traditions also teach doctrines of resurrection. The Hebrew Bible speaks of resurrection; and the New Testament tells us that belief in resurrection was a central point of contention between the Hellenistically minded Sadducees who disbelieved in resurrection, and the theologically more conservative Pharisees who believed in it. The Koran also anticipates resurrection. Thus:

[9] 1 Cor. 15: 50–8.

I swear by the Day of Resurrection, and by the self-reproaching soul. Does man think We shall never put his bones together again? Indeed, We can remould his very fingers! Yet man would ever deny what is to come. 'When will this be,' he asks, 'this day of Resurrection?' But when the sight of mortals is confounded and the moon eclipsed; when sun and moon are brought together—on that day man will ask 'Whither shall I flee?' No, there shall be no escape. For on that day all shall return to your Lord.[10]

In all three of the major theistic traditions, then, the idea that our dead bodies will one day return to life is present.

People sometimes speak as if philosophical problems pertaining to resurrection are of special concern to *materialists*—those who believe that human persons are material beings. This is probably because it is natural for materialists to think that human persons are identical to their bodies—so that if resurrection is impossible, then immortality is impossible. But there are versions of materialism according to which human persons are *not* identical to their bodies (see Lynne Rudder Baker's essay for one such view); and some of these versions will allow for *post mortem* survival via reincarnation rather than resurrection. So materialists as such don't *have* to be able to make sense of resurrection in order to preserve belief in an afterlife. Moreover, adherents of religious traditions (like Christianity) in which belief in resurrection is central will have to grapple with the problems pertaining to resurrection regardless of their stance on materialism. So it is simply a mistake to think that problems about resurrection are primarily problems for materialists.

Resurrection occurs when one and the same material body is restored to life after its death. As I understand it, a *person* is resurrected if, and only if, she is restored to life in (or as) *numerically the same body* that she had (or was) prior to her death. Getting a new body—not just a transformed body, but a numerically distinct one—is reincarnation, not resurrection. (Note that this terminology will not do for Baker, who wants to say that one and the same person is constituted by multiple bodies throughout her lifetime. For Baker, resurrection is a matter of one and the same *person* being restored to life.[11] I do not know what reincarnation would amount to on her view—which is one reason why I will persist in using terms the way that I have just suggested, rather than in a way that is more accommodating toward her view.) All of this is true for dualists as well as materialists: resurrection is a matter of being or being re-embodied in the same body; reincarnation involves being or being re-embodied in a numerically different one.[12]

[10] *The Koran*, trans. by N. J. Dawood, 2nd edn., (Baltimore, MD: Penguin Books, 1999), p. 412.

[11] Indeed, Baker says that 'the doctrine of the resurrection of the body *entails* that a person can exist without the body that she was born with' (my emphasis). I think that this is not the correct way to understand the doctrine of the resurrection; but that is not a dispute that can be pursued here.

[12] The topics of materialism, dualism, and the doctrine of the resurrection of the body are discussed together in a wide variety of places. Among the more interesting and useful resources are the following: Caroline Walker Bynum, *The Resurrection of the Body in Western Christianity,*

The central problem with resurrection is just that it is very hard to see what it would take to bring a dead body back to life. The problem isn't that we can't imagine corpses being resuscitated. We can. Rather, the problem is that it is hard to imagine the scattered parts of a decayed corpse, or any other parts, being put together in such a way as to *reconstitute* the living organism whose corpse it was. In the last essay in this Part, Peter van Inwagen raises the problem vividly by way of the following illustration:

Suppose a certain monastery claims to have in its possession a manuscript written in St. Augustine's own hand. And suppose the monks of this monastery further claim that this manuscript was burned by Arians in the year 457. It would immediately occur to me to ask how *this* manuscript, the one I can touch, could be the very manuscript that was burned in 457. Suppose their answer to this question is that God miraculously recreated Augustine's manuscript in 458. I should respond to this answer as follows: the deed it describes seems quite impossible, even as an accomplishment of omnipotence. God certainly might have created a perfect duplicate of the original manuscript, but it would not be *that* one; its earliest moment of existence would have been after Augustine's death; it would never have known the impress of his hand; it would not have been a part of the furniture of the world when he was alive; and so on.[13]

The problem, presumably, is that anything we can imagine God doing in this scenario would count not as 'resurrecting' the manuscript, but (at best) as creating a mere duplicate. Likewise in the case of resurrecting human bodies: once they have undergone decay, there is nothing that even God could do, on van Inwagen's view, to bring them back. Thus, he ultimately argues that, if resurrection is to be possible at all, God must (contrary to appearances) prevent our bodies from undergoing decay. His suggestion is that perhaps God replaces each body at the moment of death with a simulacrum, and then stores the body somewhere until the day of resurrection.

Not surprisingly, many have found van Inwagen's 'body-snatching' suggestion rather unpalatable. The question, however, is whether there are any viable alternatives. The challenge might be put this way: Suppose God creates or assembles a body, *RB*, at the end of days, with the aim of resurrecting St Peter. What would God have to do—what *could* God do—in order to ensure that *RB* is identical to the body Peter had at some point in his life? As van Inwagen notes, reassembling the particles that composed Peter's body at some stage of his life (say, at some moment *m* on his thirtieth birthday) won't suffice; for, after all, if

---

200–1336 (New York: Columbia University Press, 1995); Kevin Corcoran (ed.), *Soul, Body, and Survival* (Ithaca, NY: Cornell University Press, 2001); Hud Hudson, *A Materialist Metaphysics of the Human Person* (Ithaca, NY: Cornell University Press, 2001); John W. Cooper, *Body, Soul, and Life Everlasting* (Grand Rapids, MI: Wm. B. Eerdmans); and Peter van Inwagen and Dean Zimmerman (eds.), *Persons: Human and Divine* (Oxford: Oxford University Press, 2006).

[13] p. 104 below.

God were simultaneously to reassemble both the particles that composed him at *m* and the particles that composed him at some moment on his tenth birthday, *m**, we wouldn't think that God had resurrected Peter twice over. For the same reason, simply creating a body that resembles Peter's body at *m* and that has all of the same beliefs, desires, memories, and so on won't do either; for, again, God could just as easily create multiple bodies that resemble a variety of 'Peter-stages' in all of the right ways.

The next three essays in Part III take up this challenge in various ways. Dean Zimmerman argues (in effect) that *RB* would count as St Peter's body only if two conditions are met: (i) *RB* stands in *immanent causal relations*[14] with some pre-resurrection 'stage' of St Peter's body, and (ii) no other body stands in the same (or stronger) causal relations with a pre-resurrection stage of St Peter's body. One way for these conditions to be satisfied would be for God to engage in body-snatching, just as van Inwagen describes. But another way is for God to arrange for a certain kind of fission to take place. Suppose that, at the moment of Peter's death, God arranges for every particle of Peter's body to divide (amoebae-like) across a temporal gap. In other words, suppose that every particle splits into two—one of which exists at the moment immediately after the time of fission, and the other of which exists at the end of days, when the resurrection occurs. Suppose further that all of the particles that exist immediately after the time of fission compose a corpse, whereas the particles that exist on the day of resurrection compose a barely living body. The corpse is not at a candidate for being the body of St Peter—it is a corpse, after all, not a living body. Thus, the body that exists at the day of resurrection is the 'temporally closest candidate' for being the body of St Peter. Thus, conditions (i) and (ii) are satisfied: that body stands in immanent causal relations with Peter's pre-resurrection body; and, assuming there are not multiple living fission-products, no other body stands in the same causal relations with Peter's pre-resurrection body. Hence, that body is Peter's. Of course, it is only barely alive; but God can either immediately (and miraculously) heal it, or let it die and then immediately resuscitate it.

Lynne Baker takes a rather different approach. On Baker's view, as I have noted, a material person is constituted by different bodies throughout her lifetime. Thus, her view does not demand that the *same body* return to life in order for the same *material person* to return to life. Rather, all that is required for *RB* to count as St Peter's resurrection body is that *RB constitute* St Peter. In order for this to happen, the right sorts of continuity relations would have to be

---

[14] Immanent causation is, roughly, a causal relation that holds between states of the same persisting object. According to Hermann Lotze, in immanent causation, 'a state *a*1 of a thing a begins to bring about a consequent state, *a*2, in the same thing'. (Hermann Lotze, *Metaphysic (In Three Books: Ontology, Cosmology, and Psychology)*, 2nd edn., vol. i, ed. Bernard Bosanquet (Oxford: at the Clarendon Press, 1887), p. 116; quoted in Dean Zimmerman, 'Immanent Causation', *Philosophical Perspectives* 11 (1997): 433–71. Zimmerman himself offers a much more rigorous analysis.)

preserved between St Peter's pre-resurrection body and his post-resurrection body; but Baker offers a variety of suggestions as to how this might be possible. In the end, however, it seems that the problem is partly solved by terminological fiat; for there is nothing clearly built in to Baker's view that would allow us to recognize Peter's *post mortem* body as clearly a *resurrection* body rather than a *reincarnated* body. So far as I can tell, it is just by terminological stipulation that she guarantees that it is the former rather than the latter.

One possibility that seems largely ignored, or implicitly denied, in the essays by van Inwagen, Zimmerman, and Baker is that God might not have to do anything special at all to 'make it the case' that *RB* is identical to Peter's pre-resurrection body. This idea is defended in the paper by Merricks. According to Merricks, there are no criteria of identity over time—no (informative) necessary and sufficient conditions for an object *a* being identical to an object *b*. If this is right, then one looks in vain for an informative answer to the question, 'What would God have to do ensure that *RB* is identical to Peter's pre-resurrection body?' Any answer we might give to this question would be either false or equivalent to something like 'God would have to re-create Peter's body,' which, of course, tells us nothing very interesting at all.

The essays by van Inwagen, Zimmerman, Merricks, and Baker all take it for granted that materialism is viable; and two of them—the essays by Merricks and Baker—make a point of arguing that materialism is consistent with orthodox Christian belief. Indeed, both Merricks and Baker think that Christian theological considerations not only can be accommodated by materialism, but actually speak in favor of materialism. This is an issue of independent interest; for, as is well known, materialism is widely accepted in the academy and it is also widely regarded as inconsistent with traditional Christian belief. If that view is correct, and if materialism is indeed well motivated, then traditional Christian belief faces a real challenge from the philosophy of mind. Towards providing a counterbalancing response to the pro-materialist arguments of some of these other essays, then, I close this part of the book with an essay by Alvin Plantinga, which argues, both from a Christian perspective and on independent grounds, for the conclusion that materialism is false.

Part I
Providence

1

Two Accounts of Providence*

Thomas P. Flint

A few years ago, an adjunct Spanish teacher at a major midwestern university was facing significant financial difficulties. Hoping for some assistance, she attended a mass on the feast day of Our Lady of Guadalupe and prayed for help. Shortly thereafter, she was informed that she was the recipient of a financial award for which she had never applied; of which, indeed, she was unaware. The prize was an annual award given in honor of Our Lady of Guadalupe.

Stories such as this strike all of us as intriguing. But while many will view it as merely a happy coincidence that things turned out as they did, those of us who are Christians are inclined to see it as something more—or, at least, are tempted so to see it. We are inclined to think that God's hand was in evidence here. We are likely to speak of such events as not merely fortunate, but providential.

Of course, in saying that this event *was* providential, we do not mean to imply that other events are *not*. We tend to *call* providential those occurrences in which we find the presence of God especially evident, but as Christians we hold that all events are in God's hands. Providence extends over each of God's creatures, whether they or we recognize it or not. Generally, indeed, we *don't* recognize it. For most of us, few events serve to remind us of God's plan for his world, and we spend very few of our conscious moments thinking about divine providence. And this may very well be all for the good.

Still, if and when we *do* pause to think about it, providence provides a rich subject for philosophical reflection. In the history of Catholic thought, such reflection has led to two substantially different explications of the concept of providence. In this essay, I examine these two accounts. Section 1 sets forth the orthodox notion of providence, while section 2 clears the way for presentation of the two divergent explications. The two views are then described in sections 3 and 4. In section 5, I suggest that these opposed theological accounts may well be but the theological reflection of a familiar metaphysical dispute; the

* Reprinted from *Divine and Human Action: Essays in the Metaphysics of Theism*, edited by Thomas V. Morris. Copyright © 1988 by Cornell University. Used by permission of the publisher, Cornell University Press.

ramifications this appears to have regarding the resolution of the theological debate are then discussed. Section 6 provides a brief historical conclusion.

The reader should be aware of three points from the start. First, I am presupposing that it is the traditional, strong notion of providence—a notion the major characteristics of which will be described shortly—that the Christian is concerned to explicate. Many recent writers in the philosophy of religion have been led to abandon one or more of the elements of this classical Christian tenet. I do not here discuss arguments for or against the various dilutions of the concept that have been proposed, but merely assume that it is the robust orthodox notion of providence with which we are concerned. Even those who reject this notion would presumably retain some interest as to how it might be explicated.

Second, the two accounts of providence to be examined here will be those which have been best developed within the Catholic tradition—Molinism and Thomism. To a very large extent, the differences between these two schools map onto differences between Protestants—e.g., between Arminians and mainline Calvinists. Indeed, this essay suggests that *any* orthodox Christian will have only two genuine choices when it comes to providence: a view that is more or less Molinist, or a view that is more or less Thomist. Still, there are advantages to limiting our focus to the dispute among Catholics; for example, the discussion regarding the efficacy of grace is particularly fine grained and revealing in the writings of Thomists and Molinists. Hence, while much of what will be said here has obvious implications for the Protestant dispute, the spotlight will be on the two Catholic positions.

Finally, a note of warning to historians. The view of providence held by the Molinists can clearly be traced to Luis de Molina, the sixteenth-century Spanish Jesuit whose *Concordia* sparked the Catholic controversy over grace.[1] But whether what I shall call the Thomist account of providence is a view that Thomas himself would have endorsed is not nearly so clear. I suspect that he would have, but feel far from confident, and realize that the resolution of this thorny question lies well beyond my competence. Hence, the view labeled Thomist here can be confidently ascribed only to a large segment of Aquinas's intellectual heirs, not necessarily to their eponymous philosophical progenitor.

1. THE TRADITIONAL NOTION OF PROVIDENCE

There are at least three components to the strong notion of providence traditionally upheld by Christians. First, as the etymology of the term suggests, providence involves foresight. A God who is provident does not in any significant

---

[1] Luis de Molina, *Liberi arbitrii cum gratiae donis, divina praescientia, providentia, praedestinatione et reprobatione concordia* (hereafter *Concordia*). The first edition was published in 1588; a revised second edition appeared in 1595 and is the one that will be cited in this essay. A modern critical edition of the *Concordia* edited by J. Rabeneck was published in Madrid in 1953.

sense grow in knowledge as time passes;[2] everything that occurs was always foreseen—and foreseen with certainty—by him. Nothing does or can take a provident God by surprise.[3]

But foreknowledge alone hardly suffices to qualify one as provident, for such knowledge could conceivably be had by an utterly powerless or uncaring deity. For providence, then, two more elements are required. A provident God is one who not only knows what will happen, but in some sense or other actively controls what will happen; in Calvin's memorable phrase, providence 'belongs no less to his hands than to his eyes.'[4] Christians see God as sovereign over his world, as 'holding the helm of the universe, and regulating all events.'[5] To call God provident yet deny him such control would be, from the orthodox perspective, to contradict oneself.

Finally, providence presupposes that God employs his sovereignty wisely and morally. That is, it requires that God exercise his control with some end or purpose in mind, a good end attained in a morally exemplary way. In short, God has a plan in creation, and the execution of this plan gives evidence of his unsurpassable beneficence.

Much more is undoubtedly involved in providence, but I feel we can confidently view the three components thus far noted as those which are most central. For the most remarkable or telling attributes of God are, it would seem, his infinite knowledge, power, and goodness, and the three elements we have highlighted here merely indicate the way in which these three attributes are manifested by a God who is also a Creator.[6]

2. COMMON GROUND IN EXPLICATING PROVIDENCE

Virtually from the start of Christianity, the strong notion of providence that it affirms has been alleged to be at odds with certain evident facts about our world. Divine foreknowledge, we have been told, is incompatible with genuine human freedom. If God knew from the first moment of creation that Cuthbert would,

---

[2] Obviously, room must be made for the fact that Jesus *did* grow in knowledge; see Luke 2:52.

[3] That God has complete and perfect foreknowledge is not a matter over which orthodox Catholic theologians can disagree, since the First Vatican Council declared the thesis to be *de fide*. See Heinrich Denzinger and Adolf Schonmetzer, eds., *Enchiridion symbolorum*, 23d ed. (Freiburg: Herder, 1963), nos. 3001 and 3003, new numbering (1782 and 1784, old numbering). Many of the scriptural passages supporting this doctrine are cited by Molina in Disputation 52, sec. 8 of the *Concordia*.

[4] John Calvin, *Institutes of the Christian Religion*, bk. I, trans. John Allen (Philadelphia: Presbyterian Board of Christian Education, 1936), p. 222.

[5] Ibid.

[6] The threefold nature of providence suggested here has obvious similarities to that enunciated by Aquinas. See *Quaestiones disputatae de veritate*, Q. 5, A. 1.

say, buy an iguana in 1998, then (given God's doxastic perfection) it follows with certainty that Cuthbert will buy an iguana in 1998; but if it's thus determined by God's past beliefs that Cuthbert will do so, his doing so could hardly be free. Similarly, we have heard, the suggestion that this world has resulted from the providential activity of a loving God is incompatible with, or at least most improbable given, the evil we see in the world. Each of these charges is, I trust, familiar to contemporary philosophers; equally familiar, I hope, are the various recent discussions that show just how weak such charges really are.[7] Arguments of this kind give the reflective Christian no significant reason to doubt the genuineness of providence.

Still, questions of another sort *can* be asked—requests not for a defense of the concept of providence, but rather for an articulation or clarification of the notion. Such questions arise more naturally, I think, with regard to God's sovereignty and its connection with human freedom than with regard to his foreknowledge or beneficence, but the discussion of God's foreordination of free actions becomes so intimately connected with the discussion of his foreknowledge that it is somewhat artificial to view any particular element of providence as the one that necessitates clarification. In any case, our attempt to explicate the two major ways of answering such questions will be aided by our approaching them via the framework of possible worlds.

A possible world can be thought of as a maximal possible state of affairs—a state of affairs that specifies a complete history (from beginning to end) of how things might have been. Infinitely many such worlds *exist*, but only one *obtains* or is *actual*, for only one of these complete histories is true. Things *could* have been infinitely many different ways, but they *are* only *one* way.[8]

Now, according to the doctrine of providence, things are the way they are—this world, as opposed to each of the other possible worlds, is *actual*—because of God's creative activity. God knowingly and lovingly willed to create this very world. He didn't merely give a sort of initial impetus to things and then let them proceed on their merry (or miserable) way, not knowing, directing, or caring how things would turn out. On the contrary, his providence, his sovereignty, his control extend to each and every event that takes place. His is a particular, not merely a general, providence.

    [7] For discussions of the foreknowledge/freedom question, see Alfred J. Freddoso's introduction to Luis de Molina, *On Divine Foreknowledge: Part IV of the Concordia* (Ithaca: Cornell University Press, 1988); George I. Mavrodes, 'Is the Past Unpreventable?' *Faith and Philosophy* 1 (1984), 131–46; Thomas Talbott, 'On Divine Foreknowledge and Bringing about the Past,' *Philosophy and Phenomenological Research* 46 (1986), pp. 455–69; and Alvin Plantinga, 'On Ockham's Way Out,' *Faith and Philosophy* 3 (1986), pp. 235–69, reprinted in *The Concept of God*, ed. Thomas V. Morris (Oxford: Oxford University Press, 1987). Numerous responses to the problem of evil have been offered; the most impressive and influential, I think, has been that of Alvin Plantinga. See his *God, Freedom and Evil* (New York: Harper & Row, 1974), pt. 1, and *The Nature of Necessity* (Oxford: Clarendon Press, 1974), chap. 9.
    [8] For a fuller discussion of the notion of a possible world being employed here, see Plantinga, *The Nature of Necessity*, pp. 44ff.

There are two opposite and extreme interpretations of this thesis of particular providence that orthodox Christians have generally shunned. On the one extreme, one could hold that his world is indeed the result of God's loving activity, yet deny that that activity could possibly have been at all other than it actually was; rather, God's will was necessarily constrained (by his perfect knowledge and goodness, perhaps) to perform a certain creative action. Hence, while the actual world is the result of a divine act of will, that will should not be seen as free to will other than it did. At the other extreme, one might insist upon God's freedom in an utterly unlimited sense. That is, one might see every particular state of affairs that obtains, even a state of affairs such as four's being equal to three plus one, as being such that it was genuinely up to God whether or not it obtained.

On the first of these views, a view often ascribed (somewhat unfairly) to Spinoza and Leibniz, there is really only one possible world, and hence *no* divine freedom; on the latter view, which is often (and perhaps just as unfairly) labeled Cartesian, there is no such thing as an *impossible* world, and thus *unlimited* divine freedom. The first insists that whatever *can* be, *is*; the latter maintains that whatever *can* be, can *not* be. Each position has its attractive features, but each is clearly inconsistent with both orthodox Christian belief and widespread philosophical intuitions regarding modality, and hence the two are best seen as marking the boundaries beyond which the clearheaded orthodox Christian dare not stray.

A traditional and helpful way of marking the middle ground between the two extremes is in terms of God's knowledge. If God's will is free but limited, then presumably he is aware of this fact, and his creative act of will takes place in full cognizance of it. (By his creative act of will I mean his eternal decision to create a certain order of creatures in a certain set of circumstances, an unchanging decision that leads to a multitude of successive temporal acts—e.g., the creation of Adam at this time and place, the bestowal of this grace at this time to this person, and so on—which together can be thought of as constituting God's complete creative action.)[9] Hence, his knowledge of which worlds are possible— what the medievals called his knowledge of simple intelligence, or *natural knowledge*—provides the basis from which his act of will proceeds.[10] That free act of will in turn leads to the world that is actual, and to God's eternal and complete knowledge of that world—his knowledge of vision, or *free knowledge*.[11] Thus, God's natural knowledge is (in a sense) prior to his act of will, which is in turn (in a sense) prior to his free knowledge. The parenthetical qualifiers are needed lest we think of this priority as being a temporal one, for clearly there can never be a time when a provident God is ignorant of what he will do, or of what

---

[9] I intend for God's complete creative action to be understood as equivalent to what Plantinga thinks of as God's actualizing the largest state of affairs that he *strongly actualizes*. See *The Nature of Necessity*, pp. 173, 180–1.

[10] The term 'natural knowledge' is the one used by Molina; see the *Concordia*, disputation 49 and following.

[11] Again, 'free knowledge' is the Molinist term of choice.

world is actual. Still, there seems to be a clear analogy from the process of practical reasoning on the human level (where *action* temporally follows *choice*, which in turn follows *deliberation*) to that on the divine level, and thus talk of priority seems apropos.

So, prior to any act of will on his part, God knows which worlds are *possible*. Subsequent to his act of will, he knows which world is *actual*. On these points, all who subscribe to the strong notion of providence will agree. But this state of consensus begins to dissolve as soon as we ask our proponents of providence just how this transition or growth in God's knowledge is supposed to occur. More specifically, how does natural knowledge lead to free knowledge if God's creative act of will includes his willing to create *free* beings?

Freedom leads to a problem because it presupposes the ability to do otherwise. Suppose that Cuthbert will buy that iguana in 1998, and buy it freely. If so, then it must also be true that Cuthbert will have the power to refrain from buying it freely, for without such a power, the act would not be free.[12] So the situation or circumstances in which Cuthbert will find himself in 1998 will be compatible both with Cuthbert's freely buying an iguana and with his refraining from freely buying one.[13] But then it follows that there are two distinct sets of possible worlds that share the same Cuthbertian iguana-buying circumstances (circumstances that we shall call C): the set of B-worlds (B_1, B_2, B_3, and so forth) in which Cuthbert buys the iguana freely, and the set of R-worlds (R_1, R_2, R_3, and so forth) in which he freely refrains. Now it would appear that God, by his natural knowledge, would know that each of these worlds is possible; and let us further suppose that, by a creative act of will, he could directly bring it about that C obtains.[14] How would this knowledge and this act of will allow him to know whether a B-world or an R-world will become actual, since either type of world is fully compatible with that knowledge and that act of will? How can God have *free* knowledge, how can he exercise genuine providence, if he creates free beings?

The answer to these questions is evident: providence can be exercised, free knowledge can be present, only if God knows how his free creatures would freely act if placed in various different situations. For example, suppose that God knew that, if he *did* place Cuthbert in C, then Cuthbert would freely buy the iguana.

[12] Why is the 'freely' needed in this sentence? Why not say that, if Cuthbert does something freely, then he must have the power to refrain from doing it—period? The problem is that such conditionals appear to be disconfirmed by certain cases of over-determination made famous by Harry Frankfurt in his 'Alternate Possibilities and Moral Responsibility,' *The Journal of Philosophy* 66 (1969), 829–39. While Frankfurt's cases suggest that the ability to refrain from doing x is not a necessary condition of one's doing x freely, they leave intact the principle that, if one does x freely, then one had the power to refrain from doing x freely.

[13] The notion of a situation or circumstance is intentionally left vague throughout this section so as to allow both sides to affirm what is being said here—as, indeed, they would surely wish to do. As we shall see below, such vagueness needs to be eliminated before the distinctions between Thomists and Molinists can be clarified.

[14] This is, of course, most unlikely, since C will almost surely include some activity of agents other than God, and hence will not have been brought about directly and exclusively by him.

Given his knowledge of that counterfactual of freedom, God would know that, should he bring about *C*, a *B*-world would result. To know *which B*-world, he would have to know infinitely many other counterfactuals of freedom, about Cuthbert and about other free beings. And since God's providential activity does not begin in 1998, but has been present since the beginning of time, he must have known from eternity how *any* free creature he might create would freely act in *any* situation in which that being might be placed. Let us call any such counterfactual whose antecedent is complete—i.e., one that, like *C*, specifies the complete set of circumstances in which a creature is placed and left free—a *counterfactual of creaturely freedom*.[15] Provided that God has knowledge of all the true counterfactuals of creaturely freedom, there is no problem with either his exercise of providence or his possession of free knowledge.

Where, then, is the dissension among the advocates of providence? If all agree that the passage from natural to free knowledge requires that God know counterfactuals of creaturely freedom, why speak of there being *two* accounts of providence? Such questions are surely appropriate, and serve to remind us that the two accounts of providence we shall be examining are far more similar than their proponents are likely to remember in the heat of the battle. Still, there is ample room left for combat, and the battlelines are now fairly easy to draw.

Take any true counterfactual of creaturely freedom. Into which category of divine knowledge is this counterfactual supposed to fall? Does it constitute (i) part of God's natural knowledge? Or (ii) part of his free knowledge? Or (iii) does it fall into neither of these categories? While it might appear that there are three possible answers here, only two positions have in fact been defended. This is hardly surprising, for as we shall see, only two positions seem genuinely defensible. Those who answer along the lines of (iii) endorse the *Molinist* view of providence, while those who reject (iii) are led to the *Thomist* position. Whether Thomism is to be characterized more positively as an endorsement of (i) or (ii) is, as we shall see, a question to which no straightforward answer can be given.

Before we compare these two accounts, it would be wise for us to emphasize an oft-overlooked fact. It is sometimes suggested that the debate between Thomists and Molinists hinges on whether or not there are true counterfactuals of creaturely freedom: if there *are*, Molinism is true, while if there *aren't*, Thomism triumphs. But this is surely a misconstrual of the question. Properly understood, Thomism involves no rejection of counterfactuals of creaturely freedom; on the contrary, the Thomist will insist that there are such truths, and that God knows

---

[15] For a fuller discussion of such counterfactuals, see my 'The Problem of Divine Freedom,' *American Philosophical Quarterly* 20 (1983), 255–64. It is worth noting that, in addition to counterfactuals of *creaturely* freedom, there are also true counterfactuals of *divine* freedom—i.e., counterfactuals saying what *God* would freely do were he placed in various different situations. (See below, n. 21.) According to the Molinists, though, these latter counterfactuals need to be strictly separated from the former, for the latter *are* under God's control, while the former are *not*. See Molina, *Concordia*, Disputation 52, secs. 11–13.

them.[16] For the Thomist no less than the Molinist is a proponent of the strong notion of providence, and as my presentation suggests—and, in truth, as the literature on the issue amply confirms[17]—to deny God knowledge of counter-factuals of creaturely freedom is tantamount to denying him that providence which traditional Christianity requires. For the orthodox, then, there can be no question that God knows counterfactuals of creaturely freedom; the question concerns the status of that knowledge.[18] Let us now consider the two answers.

3. THE MOLINIST ACCOUNT

In order to motivate more clearly the Molinist contention that God's knowledge of counterfactuals of creaturely freedom is neither natural nor free, it would be best to highlight a couple of respects in which the contents of those two types of knowledge are crucially different.

By his natural knowledge, we have said, God knows which worlds are possible. This might lead one to think of God's natural knowledge as a knowledge of all *possible* truths—i.e., to think of the content of his natural knowledge as an infinite number of propositions of the form, *It is possible that p*. While not exactly incorrect, this may not be the most revealing way to think of God's natural knowledge. For natural knowledge is supposed to be that part of God's knowledge which he by his very nature believes—that part of his know-ledge which could not have been different from what it is. But to say that God *has to* know a certain proposition implies that that proposition *has to* be true. Thus, it seems natural to think of God's natural knowledge as a knowledge of all *metaphysically necessary* truths.[19] And since, as we have seen, the orthodox Christian denies that God has any control over such truths, natural knowledge

---

[16] Many Thomists, of course, do recognize that their position commits them to an acceptance of counterfactuals of creaturely freedom. For an especially clear example, see Franz Diekamp, *Theologine dogmaticae manuale,* vol. 1 (Paris: Society of St. John the Evangelist, 1932), p. 204.

[17] Many recent writers have denied that there are true counterfactuals of creaturely freedom. See Robert Adams, 'Middle Knowledge and the Problem of Evil,' *American Philosophical Quarterly* 14 (1977), 109–17; Bruce Reichenbach, 'Must God Create the Best World?' *International Philosophical Quarterly* 19 (1979), 203–12; and William Hasker, 'A Refutation of Middle Knowledge,' *Noûs* 20 (1986), 545–57. Not surprisingly, none of these writers would appear to endorse the strong notion of providence delineated above in sec. 1.

[18] That God knows counterfactuals of creaturely freedom is not quite an article of faith for Catholics, but it comes close. See Ludwig Ott, *Fundamentals of Catholic Dogma,* ed. James Bastible, trans. Patrick Lynch (St. Louis: B. Herder, 1964), p. 42. It is also worth noting that, when discussing his Catholic critics such as Banez (in Disputation 50 of the *Concordia*) and Zumel (in Disputation 53), Molina never seriously alleges that his opponents deny that there are true counterfactuals of creaturely freedom.

[19] Given an *S*–5 interpretation of metaphysical necessity, something is possible if and only if it's necessarily possible. Hence, one who knows all necessary truths will know all possible truths, and vice versa. So the two ways of conceiving of God's natural knowledge turn out to be equivalent.

can be defined as a knowledge of *necessary* truths whose truth is *independent of* (or *prior to*) any free act of will on God's part.

Free knowledge exhibits neither of these characteristics. Being that knowledge which God acquires as a result of his creative act of will, it includes only *metaphysically contingent* truths, truths that, since God could have prevented their truth by merely creating different situations for his creatures, different creatures, or even no creatures at all, are clearly *dependent upon* (or *posterior to*) God's will.

	Natural knowledge	*Free knowledge*
Truths known are:	(1) Necessary	(1) Contingent
	(2) Independent of God's free will	(2) Dependent on God's free will

The double distinction between natural and free knowledge can be graphically displayed as follows:

Given such a display, it soon becomes evident why the Molinists hold that God's knowledge of counterfactuals of creaturely freedom constitutes part of neither his natural nor his free knowledge. For truths of this sort—such truths as *If C were to obtain, Cuthbert would freely buy an iguana*—are, as the Molinist sees it, patently not dependent upon or posterior to God's will. If Cuthbert is genuinely free, Molinists insist, then it's not up to *God* what Cuthbert would do in C, but up to Cuthbert. Knowledge of such conditionals will surely guide God's providential activity, but their truth or falsity will not be under his control; hence, God's knowledge of them cannot be part of his free knowledge. But neither can it be part of his natural knowledge. For as we have seen, natural knowledge is knowledge of necessary truths. But counterfactuals of creaturely freedom, the Molinist maintains, are *not* necessary truths. Even if it's true that Cuthbert would freely buy an iguana if placed in C, it's surely possible that C obtain yet Cuthbert *not* freely buy the iguana; if this *weren't* possible, the Molinist will ask, what sense would it make to speak of Cuthbert's action being *free*? Since the relevant counterfactuals are only contingently true, it follows that they are not encompassed by God's natural knowledge.

So God's knowledge of counterfactuals of creaturely freedom stands between his natural and his free knowledge. It is more like natural knowledge in that the propositions known are true independent of God's free will; yet it is more like free knowledge in that the propositions known are only contingently true. Given the in-between status of this knowledge, it is hardly surprising that Molina chose to call it middle knowledge (*scientia media*).[20] Adding middle knowledge to our

[20] Throughout the first edition of the *Concordia*, Molina referred to God's knowledge of counterfactuals of creaturely freedom as a special part of his natural knowledge. It was not until the second edition that he spoke of middle knowledge, and even then, he forgot to make the necessary changes in certain places—e.g., in Disputation 49, secs. 11–15.

chart, we arrive at a graphic illustration of the Molinists' threefold division of divine knowledge:

	Natural knowledge	Middle knowledge	Free knowledge
Truths known are:	(1) Necessary	(1) Contingent	(1) Contingent
	(2) Independent of God's free will	(2) Independent of God's free will	(2) Dependent on God's free will

Given middle knowledge, the Molinist is able to offer a clear explication of each of our three components of the strong notion of providence. Prior to creation, God by his natural knowledge knows which worlds are possible. But given middle knowledge, he also knows which worlds are *feasible*—that is, for any creative act of will he might perform, even those acts of will which involve the creation of free beings, God knows which world would as a matter of fact (though not necessarily) result. For instance, since by his middle knowledge God would know whether or not Cuthbert would freely buy that iguana if placed in C, he would know prior to creation which type of world was feasible for him, a *B*-world or an *R*-world; knowledge of other counterfactuals would further inform him as to *which B*-worlds or *R*-worlds were feasible.[21] Since every feasible world contains a different divine creative act of will, it follows that, immediately upon deciding which complete creative action to perform, God knows which feasible world will be actual—i.e., he has *free* knowledge. And since the relevant act of will on God's part is presumably one that was always present (that is why it is potentially misleading to speak of God as *deciding* to create), the Molinist can say that middle knowledge allows God always to have had perfect and complete foreknowledge.

Sovereignty is also easily explicable given middle knowledge. Though God has no control over which truths he knows via middle knowledge, and thus no control over which possible worlds are feasible worlds, he has complete control over which feasible world will become actual, and he fully exercises this complete control by performing a particular complete creative act. Hence, the Molinist can consistently say that each and every contingent event that occurs is subject to divine sovereignty. If God had, say, wished to prevent Cuthbert's free purchase of that iguana, he could have done so—by seeing to it that Cuthbert was in a situation in which he would freely refrain from buying the iguana; or by directly causing Cuthbert to refrain (unfreely) from entering the pet store; or perhaps even by deciding not to create Cuthbert, or iguanas, at all. Hence, the whole

---

[21] For more on feasibility, see my 'Problem of Divine Freedom.' As noted there, the set of all the worlds that are feasible for God can be thought of as the *galaxy* of worlds with which God is presented, a galaxy that is necessarily a proper subset of the set of all possible worlds. In different possible worlds, God would be presented with different galaxies, and being presented with a galaxy can thus be thought of as what constitutes the situation or circumstances referred to in the antecedents of certain counterfactuals of *divine* freedom. (See above, n. 15.)

world truly *is* in God's hands: everything that happens was not only foreseen, but either intended or at least permitted by a deity who had full power to prevent it.[22]

Finally, middle knowledge makes it possible for the Molinist to explain just how it is that God's good plan for his world can be achieved with certainty. Given middle knowledge, God would have no doubt as to which worlds were feasible; nor would he have any doubt as to exactly what *he* would have to do—which creatures he would have to create (and when), which laws of nature he would have to institute and sustain,[23] which graces he would have to give which persons, and so on—in order to see to it that any one of these feasible worlds would become actual. We can thus think of God as surveying the feasible worlds prior to creation and choosing one of them—perhaps because of its special fittingness as an illustration of its creator's knowledge, power, goodness, mercy, and the like.[24] God's performance of the various actions that he sees via middle knowledge will lead to this world would thus amount to his executing his plan for creation, and the certainty of that knowledge would thus guarantee the success of that plan.

Two related points deserve mention here. First, the existence of evil poses no serious objection to this Molinist account of providence. Some of the worlds feasible for God—namely, those which contain no free creatures—surely contain no moral evil, and may well contain no evil at all; but such worlds just as surely exhibit none of the good moral qualities that presuppose genuinely free creatures. If God freely chose to create a world containing moral good—if that was one of the goods he wanted his world to include—he would have to restrict his choice to those feasible worlds containing significantly free creatures.[25] But since *which* worlds are feasible is *not* a matter that is under God's control, it could well turn out that *no* world containing such free creatures included moral good but no moral evil. Indeed, God might well have found that the only feasible worlds containing significant amounts of moral good, or particularly noble instances of it—triumph over especially great temptations, say, or striking cases of repentance and reconciliation—were also worlds that contained significant amounts of evil. If that were so, God might well still decide to create such a world, permitting the evil in order to obtain the good that he know would accompany it.[26]

---

[22] David Basinger has implicitly denied that the Molinists' God could have specific sovereignty. See his 'Christian Theism and the Free Will Defense,' *Sophia* 19 (1980), 20–33. I responded to Basinger in 'Divine Sovereignty and the Free Will Defense,' *Sophia* 23 (1984), 41–52.

[23] I am assuming here that God does have at least some degree of control over which natural laws will apply to the beings he creates. For another opinion, see Alfred J. Freddoso, 'The Necessity of Nature,' *Midwest Studies in Philosophy* 11 (1986), 215–42.

[24] There is a clear danger of anthropomorphism here; readers should consider themselves warned. Also, talk of fittingness probably cannot be pushed very far. *Any* feasible world would have to be fitting enough for God to create it; otherwise, it wouldn't be feasible in the first place.

[25] I follow Plantinga here in speaking of a significantly free creature as one who is free with respect to a morally significant action. See *The Nature of Necessity*, p. 166.

[26] The reply to the problem of evil given here stems from Plantinga; see the work cited in n. 7. I somewhat modified his version of the free will defense in my 'Divine Sovereignty and the Free Will Defense.'

Second, the manner in which predestination would operate is also explicable given middle knowledge. The orthodox Catholic position on fallen mankind lies squarely between the optimism regarding human nature evidenced by Pelagius and his modern humanist offspring and the corresponding pessimism evidenced by reformers such as Luther. According to the Catholic view, we humans retain after the Fall our ability to perform some good actions without any special divine assistance. But our true happiness is something we cannot attain solely through the use of our own natural powers: the end that we seek—the eternal life of the beatific vision—is not a natural end and cannot be achieved by natural means. The supernatural assistance that each of us requires to attain eternal life is known generically as *grace*, while the particular type of grace we need to perform those salutary acts that God has ordained will allow us to merit eternal life is known as *actual grace*.[27] Actual grace is in turn divided into *prevenient* (or *antecedent*) *grace*, which precedes and prepares the way for a free act of our will, and *cooperating* (or *consequent*) *grace*, which is concurrent with that free act of will.

Now since God wills that all of us be saved, and since salvation presupposes cooperating grace, it follows that God offers all of us enough cooperating grace for us to merit salvation. So everyone receives *sufficient grace*—i.e., grace that empowers one to perform salutary acts. Of course, this power is not always exercised; some of us do not (or at least *may* not) attain salvation. When cooperating grace does have its intended effect, though—i.e., when it leads to a salutary act—it is called *efficacious grace*.

As the Molinists see it, efficacious grace is not intrinsically different from sufficient grace: it is merely sufficient grace that 'works.' If a recipient of sufficient grace performs that salutary act which God intended that person to perform, the grace in question is *ipso facto* efficacious; if not, it is merely sufficient. But whether the person uses the grace for the purpose that God intended is *not* up to God, for it is a doctrine of faith that grace leaves a person free.[28] Efficacious grace, then, is essentially sufficient but only contingently efficacious, and its being efficacious is determined by us, not by God.

How, then, can God will that all be saved, yet predestine only some to glory? How can membership in the elect be up to him if his grace is resistible? Again, Molinists maintain, middle knowledge holds the key. As we have seen, God's universal salvific will requires that he grant everyone sufficient grace. But God can fulfill this requirement in various ways: he can create Cuthbert in numerous different situations, and those situations can include God's bestowing upon him varying degrees of grace (though always sufficient and never irresistible).

---

[27] Salutary acts are those acts of prayer, repentance, faith, and the like that bring one into the life of God—that justify and sanctify the person—along with those subsequent good actions generated by the love that accompanies this sanctification.

[28] The Tridentine enunciation of this doctrine was often referred to by Molina in Disputation 53 of the *Concordia*—see pt. 1, sec. 7; pt. 2, sec. 30; pt. 3, sec. 8; and pt. 4, sec. 14. For the actual declaration by the Council of Trent, see Denzinger, n. 1554 (814).

By virtue of his middle knowledge, God would know prior to creation how Cuthbert would freely react to any such bestowal of sufficient grace. Now suppose that there are feasible worlds in which Cuthbert cooperates with God's sufficient grace, thus rendering it efficacious, and thereby meriting salvation. If so, then God can predestine Cuthbert by choosing to create one of those worlds. God's election of Cuthbert would be free in such a case, for there might well be other feasible worlds in which the grace given to Cuthbert remains merely sufficient, and there surely are feasible worlds in which Cuthbert doesn't exist at all. Hence, predestination would be genuinely up to God even though the means by which he carries it out (grace) is resistible.[29]

By viewing God's knowledge of counterfactuals of creaturely freedom as genuinely middle knowledge, then, the Molinist is able to explicate his belief in the harmony between human freedom and God's providential activity. Few Christians, I think, can fail to be struck by the power of this ingenious account of providence, nor by the light it might shed on various related topics—prophecy, petitionary prayer, conciliar and/or papal infallibility, and the like.[30] Still, many proponents of the strong notion of providence have rejected, and some have even gone so far as to condemn, the Molinist view of providence. What is the source of their opposition to it? And what alternative picture of God's knowledge of counterfactuals of creaturely freedom have they championed in its place?

4. THE THOMIST ACCOUNT

While numerous objections to the Molinist account have been raised, I think it is fair to say that the fundamental criticism that Thomists have leveled against the Molinist explication of providence is that Molinism robs God of the supreme independence and power that he as First Cause is required to possess. If God is genuinely the First Cause, the source of all being, then all contingent beings and all contingent truths must be determined by his will. But if counterfactuals of creaturely freedom were, as the Molinists insist, contingent yet independent of God's will, *they* would limit, *they* would determine, *him*. As Garrigou-Lagrange puts it:

[29] A later variation on Molinism known as *congruism* held, in effect, that, even though grace is *not* intrinsically efficacious, God can save whomever he wishes—i.e., that, for any person (indeed, for any 'possible person'), God could bestow graces congruent to the situation in which the person is (or might be) placed that would effect that person's salvation. It should be evident that, while the congruist thesis is not incompatible with Molinism, it could at best be contingently true given Molinist presuppositions.

[30] As Alfred Freddoso and I have argued, Molinism also helps provide us with the means to fashion an adequate analysis of the concept of divine omnipotence. See our 'Maximal Power,' in *The Existence and Nature of God*, ed. Alfred J. Freddoso (Notre Dame, Ind.: University of Notre Dame Press, 1983), pp. 81–113.

God's knowledge cannot be determined by anything which is extrinsic to Him, and which would not be caused by Him. But such is the *scientia media,* which depends on the determination of the free conditioned future [i.e., the counterfactual or creaturely freedom]; for this determination does not come from God but from the human liberty, granted that it is placed in such particular circumstances; so that 'it was not in God's power to know any other thing . . . , but if the created free will were to do the opposite, He would have known this other thing,' as Molina says in the passage just quoted. Thus God would be dependent on another, would be passive in His knowledge, and would be no longer pure Act. The dilemma is unsolvable: Either God is the first determining Being, or else He is determined by another; there is no other alternative. In other words, the *scientia media* involves an imperfection, which cannot exist in God. Hence there is a certain tinge of anthropomorphism in this theory.

All the aforesaid arguments bring us to this conclusion: there is no determination without a determining cause, and the supreme determining cause is God, otherwise He would be determined by another. But this is nothing else than the principle of causality.[31]

For the Thomists, then, there are no contingent truths independent of God's will, and hence no middle knowledge; there are only natural knowledge and free knowledge. Where, then, would the Thomists place counterfactuals of creaturely freedom? At first glance, it would seem that they view them as part of God's free knowledge—as contingent truths dependent upon his will. Garrigou-Lagrange writes: 'St. Thomas admits only the knowledge of simple intelligence [natural knowledge], which is concerned with possible things, and the knowledge of vision [free knowledge] which, granted a decree, intuits future things. The knowledge of conditioned futures belongs by a reductive process to this latter.'[32] The 'reductive process' that Garrigou-Lagrange has in mind is undoubtedly something like the following. The Molinists insist that the counterfactuals of creaturely freedom are contingent truths. But no contingent truth can be true independent of or prior to God's will, for as we have seen, such a status would compromise God's divinity. Therefore, the Molinists' counterfactuals of creaturely freedom must be part of God's free knowledge.

Yet there is a curious anomaly here. When discussing his position and contrasting it with that of his Thomist opponents, Molina makes it clear that, as he sees it, the Thomists have to situate counterfactuals of creaturely freedom within God's *natural* knowledge.[33] And when we consider the matter carefully, such a conclusion seems quite plausible. Take Cuthbert and his iguana-buying. Suppose it is true that Cuthbert would buy the iguana were he placed in

---

[31] Reginald Garrigou-Lagrange, *The One God,* trans. Dom. Bede Rose (St. Louis: B. Herder, 1944), pp. 465–6. A similar remark is made by the commentator to the Blackfriars translation of Aquinas's *Summa theologiae* (New York: McGraw-Hill, 1963), Pt. 1, Q. 22, A. 4, pp. 104–5.

[32] Garrigou-Lagrange, *The One God,* p. 464. The same point is made clear by Diekamp; see the work and page cited in n. 16, as well as his *Katholische Dogmatik,* vol. 1 (Munster: Aschendorff, 1949), p. 200.

[33] *Concordia,* Disputation 53, pt. 1, sec. 10, and especially Disputation 53, pt. 3, secs. 6 and 10.

circumstances *C*—i.e. that *C → B*.³⁴ Now, according to the Thomist, God as First Cause determined that this counterfactual (rather than its negation) be true. Just as his creative activity brought into existence other contingent beings, and made true other contingent truths, so his creative activity guaranteed the truth of *C→B*. Indeed, the Thomist would insist that, given all that God himself has done, *C → B* could not fail to be true; God has made it true. If we allow G to stand for God's complete creative activity, then, the Thomists would insist that *G ⇒ (C → B)*.³⁵ But from this it follows that *(G&C) ⇒ B*.³⁶ Now, *C* is supposed to specify the complete circumstances in which Cuthbert finds himself at the time of his action. Since what God has done would surely constitute a part—yea, a most significant part—of the situation in which Cuthbert finds himself when he acts, it would seem that *G* must be considered part of *C*—i.e., *C ⇒ G*. But if *C ⇒ G*, then *C ⇒ (G&C)*; and since the Thomist is committed to *(G&C) ⇒ B*, it follows by transitivity that the Thomist is committed to *C ⇒ B*. That is, the Thomist is committed to saying that it is a metaphysically necessary truth that Cuthbert buy that iguana if placed in circumstances *C*. And since metaphysically necessary truths are known by God via his natural knowledge, Molina's contention seems eminently defensible.

Something is surely amiss here. Recall that, on the Thomist view, a counterfactual of creaturely freedom such as *C →B* is supposed to be a *contingent* proposition, a proposition whose truth or falsity is *up to God*. Yet Molina says (not implausibly, as we have seen) that the Thomist is committed to viewing the relation between *C* and *B* as a necessary one: *C → B* is true, but only because *C* *entails B*. How do we account for this discrepancy? Are the Thomists blind to the implication of their position regarding God's all-encompassing causal activity? Or is Molina's description of the view, and our argument in support of that description, misguided in some way?

The problem, I think, hinges on the question of what is to be included in the *circumstances* that the antecedent of a counterfactual of creaturely freedom specify. Thomists have generally been reluctant to allow that the *circumstances* in which a *free* action is performed could be *determinative* of that action. Kondoleon's statement is typical:

Propositions supposedly the objects of God's 'middle knowledge' would not be propositions involving a relationship of strict implication between the antecedent and the

³⁴ I use the single-line arrow to symbolize counterfactual implication, the double-line arrow for entailment (i.e., for metaphysically necessary material implication).

³⁵ I assume that *G* does *not* occur in every possible world—i.e., that God's complete creative activity in *this* world does *not* take place in many other worlds. Some Thomists might not like this way of speaking, since they seem to prefer to view God's activity as a constant across different worlds. See, for instance, James Ross, 'Creation,' *Journal of Philosophy* 77 (1980), 614–29, and 'Creation II,' in *The Existence and Nature of God*, pp. 115–41.

³⁶ Suppose *G ⇒ (C → B)*. From this it follows that *(G&C) ⇒ [C&(C → B)]*. But *[C& (C → B)]* entails *B*. Therefore, given that entailment is a transitive relation, it follows that *(G&C) ⇒ B*.

consequent, unless, of course, one were to acknowledge a determination of circumstances. In the latter case such a proposition as 'If God creates *x* and places him in circumstances *y*, then *x* will do *A*' would be true if *x* were determined to do *A* because of *y*. While such an explanation would give an adequate account of how such propositions could be true, it would be fatal to free will.[37]

So, according to most Thomists, the circumstances in which an agent is placed do not determine that agent's free actions. And yet, as we have seen, the core Thomist contention is that every contingent event and proposition, including those involving free agents, is completely determined by God; *my* action, even if free, is still determined by *God's* action. The way to reconcile these two positions and to resolve our present perplexity thus seems evident. The Thomist, unlike the Molinist, is not thinking of the circumstances (the condition, the situation) in which an agent acts as including every prior and concurrent divine activity. Exactly what is to be left out of the circumstances is not completely clear. But the Thomist account of predestination offers some definite hints.

On the Molinist view, predestination is executed via grace that is intrinsically sufficient but extrinsically efficacious. Thomists reject this scheme, for they see it as placing the ultimate source of one's election in one's own will rather than in God's:

Let us suppose that Peter and Judas situated in equal circumstances receive equal prevenient grace; then [according to the Molinists] God sees Peter consenting to accept that grace, and hence singling himself out from Judas who does not consent, not on account of the grace, for an equal grace is indifferently offered to each. Therefore it is because the will decides to accept the grace. Thus do all Thomists argue against Molina, and they thus affirm as revealed the principle that can be called 'the principle of predilection,' namely, that no one would be better than another unless he were loved more and helped more by God.[38]

For Thomists, then, grace that is efficacious is *intrinsically* efficacious; its efficaciousness is not determined by whether or not the human will cooperates with it, for it is not possible that the will *not* cooperate with it. God determines all contingent beings and events, and the way in which he determines us to salvation or damnation is by bestowing or withholding efficacious grace. Molinists, by denying intrinsically efficacious grace, implicitly deny God's determining role and reduce his power: 'The theory of the *scientia media* limits the divine omnipotence. For if God, by means of the *scientia media,* foresees that our will under certain conditions will refuse to be moved to perform some good act, then He is already incapable of moving our will so that in these conditions it freely consent to be moved to perform this good act.'[39]

---

[37] Theodore J. Kondoleon, 'The Free Will Defense: New and Old,' *The Thomist* 46 (1983), 19. For similar remarks on the determination of circumstances, see Garrigou-Lagrange, pp. 465, 470, and the commentary to Aquinas's *Summa theologiae* cited in n. 31.

[38] Garrigou-Lagrange, *The One God*, p. 463.

[39] Ibid., p. 466.

Now the general view of predestination that I have just described is pretty much what one would expect of the Thomists, given their emphasis on God's role as First Cause. But the manner in which this view is presented is, I think, revealing of the Thomist notion of a circumstance. For God's bestowal of grace is depicted by Garrigou-Lagrange as something *extra* given to Peter and Judas who are supposed to be 'situated in equal circumstances.' Similarly, if the conditions in which an agent is placed leave that being free, he implies, then an omnipotent God should be able to act so that the being 'in these conditions' does as God wills. What seems clear is that, in each of these cases, God's act of bestowing efficacious grace is viewed as something *external* to the circumstances, something that determines what the agent would do in circumstances that, *taken by themselves,* determine the agent to no particular course of action.

In the case of predestination, then, it seems that what the Thomist wants to exclude from the circumstances of action is any concurrent supernatural activity on God's part. More generally, I think, the Thomist wants to deny that any extraordinary divine action simultaneous with a creature's action should count as part of the circumstances in which that creature acts. All of God's *prior* actions constitute part of the circumstances, as do their ordinary, natural effects up to the time in question. But nothing out of the ordinary (i.e., beyond his constant conserving activity) that God does *at the time* the agent acts is to be thought of as an element in an agent's situation. Since God's bestowal of efficacious grace is *not* included in his ordinary activity, and *is* concurrent with the creature's action, it will not be found among the circumstances in which the action takes place.

If this depiction of the Thomists' view of circumstances is more or less correct, we can quickly resolve our puzzle concerning the Thomists' categorization of counterfactuals of creaturely freedom. Take again $C \rightarrow B$, our counterfactual about Cuthbert. If C is thought of as specifying circumstances *in the limited Thomistic sense,* then most Thomists will insist that the counterfactual is a contingent one that God can make true or false, and that hence is (if true) part of God's free knowledge. On the other hand, if C is thought of as specifying circumstances *in the unlimited Molinist sense* (i.e., as including *all* of God's activity, even that which is simultaneous with the action), then $C \rightarrow B$ will indeed be a necessary truth that God knows via his natural knowledge.

Each of these ways of circumscribing circumstances has something to be said for it, and I doubt that a compelling case could be made for taking either as the more appropriate.[40] So long as we are clear about which notion it is that we are using, we can employ that notion to distinguish Thomism from Molinism. Whichever sense of 'circumstance' we employ, God's knowledge of

[40] It is interesting to note that a similar disagreement over what is to count as a circumstance seems to lie at the base of the contemporary discussion of compatibilism. (Wilfrid Sellars brings this point to the fore quite clearly; see especially his 'Reply to Alan Donagan,' *Philosophical Studies* 27 (1975), 150.) One might take this as a sign that the debate over freedom and the Thomist/Molinist dispute are not totally separate. As we shall see, one would be wise so to take it.

counterfactuals of creaturely freedom will be an instance of middle knowledge according to the Molinist[41]; for the Thomist, there is no room for middle knowledge *however* circumstances are defined.

Since Thomists reject middle knowledge, they will also see no need for us to talk of feasible worlds. For the Molinist, no complete creative action that God might perform will be determinative of any particular possible world; many different worlds *could* result from any such action, and all of these worlds are possible. But, for any such action, God knows which of these worlds *would* result, and hence knows that only that world is *feasible*. For the Thomist, though, the distinction between possibility and feasibility collapses. As First Cause, God completely determines which world is actual. Any complete creative action he might perform is compatible with the actuality of only that possible world which it determines to be actual. Hence, there is a one-to-one correspondence between distinct divine creative actions and distinct possible worlds; and thus, the Thomist concludes, *any* possible world is such that God had the power to actualize it.[42]

It should be evident that the Thomist is able to offer a clear explication of the strong orthodox notion of providence. Since God fully determines which world is actual, the passage from natural to free knowledge is accomplished immediately upon his creative act of will. And since that act of will has eternally been present in God, he has eternally known exactly what was going to happen; that is, he possesses complete and perfect foreknowledge.[43] Since this foreknowledge stems from his all-encompassing causal activity, it is clear that all that happens is truly under his control; the Thomist God is an *active* sovereign who knowingly causes (directly or indirectly) all that occurs. But he is also a *good* sovereign. His creative power is equal to the actualizing of any possible world whatsoever, and he can and does choose a world which is indicative of its maker's wisdom and love.

It is on this last point—the goodness of such a God—that some of the strongest criticisms against the Thomist stance have been leveled. For given the Thomist account of providence, the existence of evil in general, and of the especially flagrant kind of evil which results in damnation in particular, would seem to be all but inexplicable. Surely there are possible worlds that contain free beings but no evil, or at least no moral evil, and surely some of these worlds exhibit a large amount and a wide variety of goods. If God is omnibenevolent

[41] It should be noted, though, that one need not embrace the law of conditional excluded middle in order to be a Molinist. If the sense of 'circumstance' employed gives us antecedents that are very thin in terms of content, the Molinist could consistently say that all such conditionals are false. All that is central to Molinism is that there be some conditionals of freedom that are true and known by God prior to his creative act of will.

[42] See Ross, 'Creation,' p. 614.

[43] It is worth emphasizing that, for the Thomists, it is God's status as First Cause, *not* his presence in eternity, that is primarily to be thought of as responsible for his foreknowledge; see Garrigou-Lagrange, *The One God*, pp. 456–7. Aquinas himself makes the same point in *Quaestiones disputatae de veritate,* Q. 5, A. 1.

and can actualize any possible world he wishes, why did he not actualize one of *these* worlds? And even if he *did* have a reason for actualizing a world with moral evil, why did he actualize a world in which some of his creatures become so immersed in evil as to warrant damnation? Given Thomist presuppositions, he could easily have prevented it: by simply offering efficacious grace to all, he could have seen to it that all were saved, and none reprobated. Why did he not do so? Where does God's universal salvific will fit in given the Thomist view?[44]

Troubling as such questions may appear, Thomists are not without replies. Frequently, such replies hinge on the notion that it is fitting or appropriate that God create a world whose inhabitants exhibit a variety of grades of being. Hence, it was fitting that God create not only immaterial, incorruptible beings, but material, corruptible beings as well. Since corruption is natural to such beings, it is not to be expected that God will always prevent the evil of corruption from befalling them, for there would be something almost contradictory in God's creating a being and then systematically frustrating its natural tendencies. Much the same goes for the moral agents God has created. Fallen human nature leaves us naturally inclined toward sin and perdition. For God to save even some of us is a purely gratuitous act on his part; by no means is he required to save *all* of us. In fact, a world in which only some are saved may well be a more fitting illustration of the divine nature, for not only are God's mercy and kindness made manifest through his saving of the elect, but in addition his justice—more specifically, his *vindictive* or *retributive* justice—is evidenced by his permitting some to remain in sin and subsequently punishing them with damnation. Nor, says the Thomist, need we deny that God wills that all of us be saved, for we can consistently say that God in his goodness offers sufficient grace to all. Those who are damned could have done otherwise and have no reason to curse God for their fate. True, they *would* have done otherwise if and only if God had given them intrinsically efficacious graces to do otherwise, but that fact in no way eliminates the fact that God in his goodness offered sufficient grace to all and thereby manifested his universal salvific will.[45]

Molinists push Thomists on many of these points, and some Thomists (like some Calvinists) end up conceding that there is an apparent harshness, a seeming arbitrariness, in God's salvific action. But Thomists will insist that this appearance is more than outweighed by the hard evidence of Scripture (e.g., the ninth chapter of Paul's letter to the Romans) and the philosophically demonstrable implications of taking seriously the belief that God is the First, complete and universal, Cause. Besides, the Thomist will remind us, Molinists have similar embarrassing questions of their own to deal with, even on the question of

[44] It is not quite *de fide* that God wills all to be saved; see Ott, *Fundamentals of Catholic Dogma*, pp. 188–9. Nevertheless, I am aware of no Thomist who would deny God's universal salvific will.
[45] The emphasis on vindictive justice is clearly present in Aquinas—see, for example, *Summa theologiae*, Pt. 1, Q. 23, A. 5—but has been pushed with evident relish by Thomists such as Garrigou-Lagrange; see *The One God*, p. 705. See also Kondoleon, 'The Free Will Defense,' p. 35.

predestination. For example, if Cuthbert is damned in the actual world, but saved in some other feasible world, does it not at least appear that God has arbitrarily excluded Cuthbert from heaven? How can the Molinist say that God truly *willed* that Cuthbert be saved if God created him in a situation that God knew—and knew with certainty—would result in Cuthbert's damnation, when he could just as easily have actualized one of those worlds in which Cuthbert is saved? The point of such questions is not to suggest that God would actually be cruel, or even less than perfectly good, on the Molinist scheme. Rather, they simply serve to remind us that no one who ascribes to the orthodox position regarding reprobation will find it easy to reconcile that doctrine with the belief in an all-loving God. For all of us, Thomists and Molinists alike, there is need here for faith.[46]

5. THE METAPHYSICAL FOUNDATION OF THE DISPUTE

The mention of faith should serve to remind us that the difference between Thomism and Molinism is not, properly speaking, a religious difference. Though Thomists have been wont to call Molinists semi-Pelagian innovators, and Molinists have returned the favor by labeling their opponents Calvinists, such colorful language is more a sign of the heat of battle than of genuine doctrinal difference. In truth, there is not one article of faith or biblical passage that either a Thomist or a Molinist will reject. And though the point could be argued, I think it is fair to say that neither party is dissembling: there simply is no way to resolve the dispute by appealing to Scripture or tradition.[47] What we are faced with, then, are two distinct and incompatible theological explications of a common religious faith.

Of course, the fact that there is no religious resolution available does not imply that the debate is hopeless. Might it not be that the theological divergence is traceable to a more fundamental divergence of some sort? If not a credal divergence, what kind of disagreement might account for the dispute?

One answer—an answer that has surely occurred to many readers by now, and that undoubtedly all but leapt at many when reading the Thomist explanation of how one denied efficacious grace nonetheless could have acted otherwise—seems particularly revealing. The dispute between Thomists and Molinists *is* rooted in a more fundamental dispute—a metaphysical dispute. All of their theological

[46] In an excellent discussion of the Wesleyan/Calvinist dispute, Jerry Walls has suggested that the ground-level difference between the two sides has more to do with the concept of divine goodness than that of human freedom. As this paragraph suggests, I have my doubts about this. See his 'The Free Will Defense, Calvinism, Wesley, and the Goodness of God,' *Christian Scholar's Review* 13 (1983), 19–33.

[47] Passages from Scripture that the Thomists emphasize include Psalm 135:6, Proverbs 21:1, 1 Corinthians 4:7, Romans 8:28–9:33, Philippians 2:13, and Ephesians 1:11 and 2:8–9. Among the Molinists' favorite passages are Wisdom 4:11, Sirach 31:8–11, 1 Samuel 23:1–13, Deuteronomy 30:15–20, and Matthew 11:21 and 23:37.

differences stem from a core philosophical difference regarding the necessary conditions of free human action.

Consider first the Molinist stance. What notion of freedom would most naturally lead to such a theological system? Clearly, I think, it is that which is commonly called libertarianism. The libertarian insists that the circumstances (even if broadly construed) in which a free agent acts are not determinative of the agent's action. But then, any proposition affirming that a free agent would act a certain way in a certain situation would have to be both contingent and (if the situation were inclusive enough) not under God's control. For if it weren't contingent, the *circumstances* would determine one's free action, while if it were under God's control, then *God* would be the ultimate determiner of one's free action, and neither of these consequences is compatible with the full-blooded libertarian assertion that nothing and no one other than the agent determines the agent's free action. As we have seen, one can uphold the strong concept of providence only if one agrees that there are true counterfactuals of freedom. Therefore, any libertarian who affirms providence will have to say that all such conditionals are contingent propositions known by God but not under his control. That is, the libertarian will have to embrace the concept of middle knowledge. And once middle knowledge is accepted, Molinism is all but inevitable.

So the path from libertarianism to Molinism seems clear. It would be gratifying if a similar trail to Thomism could be discerned. It would be especially gratifying if that trail set off from a view concerning human freedom. And it would most gratifying of all if that starting point were none other than that alternative to libertarianism known commonly as compatibilism. Now it might well seem that proponents of contemporary compatibilism who wished to endorse the strong concept of providence would indeed be led toward the Thomist position, for if physical determinism is true, it will presumably be seen by the theist as merely the means by which God determines all events, including free human actions. One might thus be led to think that the road from compatibilism to Thomism is as clear as that from libertarianism to Molinism. Unfortunately, things are not quite so simple, for at least two reasons.

In the first place, the preceding discussion of compatibilism ignores a crucial distinction. Some compatibilists maintain that it is *possible* that free human actions be physically determined, while some also maintain that it is *necessary* that such actions be physically determined. Those in the first but not the second group, whom we may call *soft compatibilists*, say that the truth or falsity of determinism is irrelevant to the question of human freedom; those in the latter group, the *hard compatibilists*, insist that a human action can be free only if it is determined.[48] While it may be true that hard compatibilists will be led toward a

---

[48] Most of the more strident classical compatibilists (such as Hume, Mill, and Schlick) were clearly hard compatibilists. In recent days, many if not most compatibilists (including Sellars, Lehrer, and Kenny, to name but a few) seem to have gone soft.

Thomist elucidation of providence, it is at least less clear that the same can be said for soft compatibilists.

Second, and more important, it is fairly clear that relatively few of those who have called themselves Thomists would accept either of the forms of compatibilism delineated above. As we have seen, Thomists generally reject the idea that human freedom is compatible with what they call a determinism of circumstances, and as several of them make clear, the upshot of this rejection is that human freedom could not exist in a world where all actions were determined by the laws of nature and the prior history of the world. In denouncing modern-day compatibilism, hard or soft, most Thomists have been as vociferous as the Molinists.

So it would be misleading to represent Thomism as the compatibilist view of providence, as opposed to the Molinists' libertarian view, for as we have seen, Thomism neither entails nor is entailed by what we generally call compatibilism. Still, I think it is fair to characterize Thomism as a compatibilist position, provided we expand the notion of compatibilism in a manner that I shall now try to explicate.

One clear way of characterizing the distinction between libertarian and compatibilist views of freedom is in terms of principles setting forth necessary conditions of human freedom. As a first approximation, one might suggest that the affirmation of

> (A) Necessarily, for any human agent S, action A, and circumstances C, if S performs A freely in C, then it is possible that S refrain from performing A freely in C

is what is definitive of the libertarian position, while compatibilism is characterized by the denial of (A). Unfortunately, such a suggestion is simply false; most compatibilists would have little trouble accepting (A). As they see it, one cannot plausibly consider the entire past history of the world as being part of the circumstances in which an action is performed.[49] And if not, then the circumstances in which a free agent acts are, even according to the staunchest defender of determinism, logically and physically compatible with that agent's having acted otherwise.[50]

The failure of (A) to discriminate between libertarians and compatibilists can easily be rectified by removing any ambiguity regarding the notion of circumstance. For consider:

> (B) Necessarily, for any human agent S, action A, and time t, if S performs A freely at t, then the history of the world prior to t and the laws of nature are jointly compatible with S's refraining from performing A freely.

---

[49] See the reference to Sellars in n. 40.

[50] I am assuming here that the determinist is one who believes that determinism is operative only if formulated at the level of microphysical entities and laws, not at the level of, say, minds and psychological laws. Those who espouse the latter kind of determinism—those whom Sellars refers to as *vulgar* determinists ('Reply to Alan Donagan,' 156)—might well have problems with (A).

I think that (B) does allow us to distinguish between libertarians and compatibilists, the former affirming and the latter denying this principle. Indeed, (B) *may* also allow us to set off some Thomists from their Molinist opponents. For while all Molinists would, I take it, affirm (B), some Thomists—namely, those who think God's all-determining activity operates exclusively through natural laws and bestowals of prevenient grace—might reject it.[51] Still, I suspect that most Thomists would have little trouble endorsing (B). For as they see it, the actions by which God determines our free actions are not prior to, but concurrent with, those actions. If Cuthbert performs some salutary action, the Thomist will insist, that action was determined by God's bestowal of intrinsically efficacious grace. But, as we have seen, such grace is generally viewed as cooperating rather than prevenient. It is present *when* one acts, but not *before* one acts; otherwise, one would have the dreaded determinism of circumstances. Analogous points could be made, from the Thomist viewpoint, regarding God's concurrence with Cuthbert's nonsalutary free actions: God's determining activity is not to be thought of as something that occurs temporally prior to Cuthbert's action. So, while (B) allows us to separate libertarians from compatibilists, it does not go far in distinguishing Molinists from Thomists.

Nevertheless, it seems clear that the kind of divine activity that the Thomists see as compatible with human freedom would not be deemed compatible by those with libertarian inclinations. For the heart and soul of libertarianism is the conviction that what an agent does freely is genuinely up to the agent to do freely or refrain from doing freely; no external circumstance, no other agent, does or even can determine what I do freely.[52] Physical determinism, which sees my actions as determined by physical laws and *prior* states of the universe, is clearly at odds with this core insight. But surely the Thomist picture of *simultaneous* divine determinism will strike the true libertarian as equally destructive of human freedom. And, indeed, if external determination *is* incompatible with human freedom, does it really make that much difference just how the determination is accomplished? Are the movements of a hand puppet any more under its own control than those of a windup doll? In sum, if we think of compatibilism in the broader sense as the view that a free action *can* be externally determined, does it not appear that Thomism is indeed ultimately rooted in compatibilism?

[51] See, for example, Thomas Loughran, 'Theological Compatibilism' (Ph.D. diss.: University of Notre Dame, 1986).

[52] A clear early statement of this libertarian intuition is found in the writings of that grand old man of libertarianism, Thomas Reid: 'If, in any action, [a man] had power to will what he did, or not to will it, in that action he is free. But if, in every voluntary action, the determination of his will be the necessary consequence of something involuntary in the state of his mind, or of something in his external circumstances, he is not free; he has not what I call the liberty of a moral agent, but is subject to necessity.' As the discussion following makes clear, Reid is using 'circumstances' in the broad Molinist sense; for him, a paradigm case of an unfree action would be one that was determined by an external agent. See his *Essays on the Active Powers of the Human Mind* (Cambridge, Mass.: MIT Press, 1969), p. 259.

If we wish to articulate this broader notion of compatibilism in terms of a principle along the lines of (A) and (B), the following would seem to do the trick:

>   (C) Necessarily, for any human agent *S*, action *A*, and time *t*, if *S* performs *A* freely at *t*, then the history of the world prior to *t*, the laws of nature, and the actions of any other agent (including God) prior to and at *t* are jointly compatible with *S*'s refraining from performing *A* freely.

The affirmation of (C) can, I think, be seen as virtually definitive of the libertarian position, and that position does indeed leave the advocate of strong providence little choice but to embrace Molinism. Suppose we call Compatibilism that broad notion of compatibilism which is constituted by the rejection of (C). It would be convenient if Compatibilism stood to Thomism as libertarianism does to Molinism; but, alas, things are not quite so easy. For just as there is a distinction between hard and soft compatibilism, so there is a distinction between hard and soft Compatibilism. Hard Compatibilists feel that free human action is not only *compatible* with divine determinism, but in fact *requires* it; soft Compatibilists refuse to make the latter and stronger claim. That is, while all Compatibilists agree in rejecting (C), they differ over a principle such as

>   (D) Necessarily, for any human agent *S*, action *A*, and time *t*, if *S* performs *A* freely at *t*, then the history of the world prior to *t*, the laws of nature, and the actions of God prior to and at *t* jointly entail that *S* performs *A* freely at *t*.

Hard Compatibilists endorse (D), while soft Compatibilists reject it along with (C).

With hard Compatibilism, we have indeed found a notion of freedom that, if endorsed, seems to lead the believer in providence inexorably toward Thomism. Soft Compatibilism, though, is more baffling. On such a view, there are some possible worlds in which God *does* determine our free actions and other possible worlds in which he *doesn't*. There may even be worlds in which some of our free actions are divinely determined, and some are not. What follows—Thomism or Molinism? Or does neither view follow? Should the soft Compatibilist perhaps be thought of as providing us the material to fashion a *third* account of providence?

Though I doubt that sure answers to such questions can be offered—after all, just what are the identity conditions for *accounts*?—I think we do ourselves little good by taking soft Compatibilism too seriously, or by honoring it as the root of a third explication of providence.

Why not take soft Compatibilism seriously? For one thing, because it seems to have so few advocates. Indeed, few Christians seem to have even considered such a stance, let alone endorsed it. And when we consider the position more carefully, it is easy to see why. After all, if God *can* determine Cuthbert's actions while leaving them fully free, why on earth would he fail to do so? For example, if God *can* offer Cuthbert the Thomists' intrinsically efficacious grace yet still leave

Cuthbert's actions as free and meritorious as such actions can be, what possible reason could he have for offering Cuthbert only the Molinists' extrinsically efficacious grace? Such considerations are, of course, far from logically conclusive; God could have reasons of which we are unaware. Still, they do lead us to wonder whether, if Compatibilism is true, there are any possible worlds in which God doesn't determine all of our free actions. If a theist is inclined toward Compatibilism at all, it is hard to see why he or she would reject hard Compatibilism.

Even if there were reasons to favor soft over hard Compatibilism, though, I doubt that we would want to view soft Compatibilism as grounding a genuinely distinct explication of providence. For if soft Compatibilism is true, then God can in effect choose which type of world including free human actions to create—one in which those actions are divinely determined, or one in which they are not, or one in which some are and some aren't. If God chooses the first kind of world, his providence will be exercised in precisely the way envisaged by the Thomists. If he chooses the second type of world, the Molinist picture will be exactly correct. And if he chooses the third, the Thomist explication will cover some events, the Molinist account the rest. In a sense, then, soft Compatibilists would not really be offering a third account of providence; they would merely be saying that it's up to God which of our two accounts will apply.

So I think we can safely ignore soft Compatibilism and view libertarianism and hard Compatibilism as the two views of freedom toward which a Christian might be drawn, metaphysical views that, given one and the same religious faith, generate radically different theological accounts of providence. If Scripture or tradition definitively favored one of these views of freedom, then the theological question could be answered; but, again, neither the Bible nor the Church appears clearly to address the metaphysical debate. And if that is so, then the dispute between Thomists and Molinists is resolvable only if the dispute between libertarians and Compatibilists can be settled on philosophical grounds.

What are the prospects of such a resolution? Consider first the debate between libertarians and compatibilists, a millennial contest replete, to be sure, with intricate arguments launched by each camp, but at least as noteworthy for the plethora of exquisite invectives it has inspired.[53] Such vituperative language is not

[53] Readers will, no doubt, have their own favorite examples of the salty language that has peppered this dispute; here, I shall recount only three especially memorable ones. Kant referred to the typical compatibilist stance as a 'wretched subterfuge' and chided such compatibilists for thinking that 'with a little quibbling they have found the solution to the difficult problem which centuries have sought in vain and which could hardly be expected to be found so completely on the surface.' His opinion was seconded by William James, who labeled compatibilism 'a quagmire of evasion.' On the other side, Schlick considered it 'one of the greatest scandals of philosophy' that one still had to expend time and energy discussing libertarianism, since the truth of compatibilism had long since been established by 'certain sensible persons' such as Hume. See Immanuel Kant, *Critique of Practical Reason*, tr. by Lewis White Beck (Indianapolis: Bobbs-Merrill, 1956), p. 96; William James, 'The Dilemma of Determinism,' *The Will to Believe and Other Essays in Popular Philosophy* (New York: Dover, 1956), p. 149; and Moritz Schlick, 'When Is a Man Responsible?', *Free Will and Determinism*, ed. Bernard Berofsky (New York: Harper & Row, 1966), p. 54.

without reason. For the arguments by which each side has attempted to prove its position, and thereby best its combatant, have never been very successful. While their failure could conceivably be the result of the stupidity or intransigence of one side or the other, I doubt that any honest observer of the dispute could come to such a conclusion. Rather, neither side has been converted because no demonstrative arguments for either position have been devised. The dispute between libertarians and compatibilists is ultimately a dispute over the necessary conditions for human freedom. Libertarians feel that something like (B) states such a necessary condition; compatibilists feel it does not. But neither side has offered anything approaching a proof of the truth or falsity of (B). In the absence of such a proof, the controversy stands little chance of abating.[54]

Are the chances for resolving the dispute between libertarians and Compatibilists any better? I see no reason to think so. Is it likely that either side can produce an argument for or against (C) that is anything more than a slight variation on one of the arguments for or against (B)? As we have already seen, the heart of libertarianism lies in the intuition that external determination of a free human action is impossible; how and when that external determination takes place is of little consequence to the true libertarian. But then, the switch from compatibilism to Compatibilism is unlikely to break the dialectical impasse. Libertarians will still insist, and Compatibilists still deny, that external determination robs agents of control over, and hence responsibility for, their actions. Compatibilists will still insist, and libertarians deny, that human actions that are not ultimately externally determined are random, out-of-the-blue, inexplicable happenings. In short, the debate will continue more or less unchanged, with little likelihood of a definitive conclusion.

If the prospects of proving or disproving either libertarianism or Compatibilism are as bleak as I have suggested, then so are the chances of resolving the dispute between Molinists and Thomists. For the two theological views are simply the images that naturally appear when a common religious faith is observed through divergent metaphysical lenses. If metaphysical consensus is unattainable, theological diversity is all but assured.

This is not to say that the Christian should maintain a tepid neutrality on these two pairs of views. Indeed, it seems to me that one can build a strong case for preferring the Molinist picture of providence to that painted by the Thomists. The libertarian assumption upon which Molinism depends seems clearly right to me: a free action simply cannot be determined by anything or anyone other than its agent. Furthermore, the Compatibilist position that undergirds Thomism leads to a disanalogy between divine and human freedom that strikes me as most

---

[54] Despite my conviction that libertarianism is true and that the arguments against it are weak, I doubt that the compatibilist alternative is demonstrably false. For a defense of compatibilism against a common libertarian attack, see my 'Compatibilism and the Argument from Unavoidability,' *The Journal of Philosophy* 84 (1987), 423–40.

peculiar. For though the Compatibilist will insist that *our* free actions are determined externally, the *Christian* Compatibilist can hardly contend that *God's* free actions are determined externally. So the Christian Compatibilist must admit that there are some free actions (namely, God's) that are free in the sense in which libertarians say *our* free actions are free. But if there is no incoherence in the notion of libertarian free action, are not most of the considerations favoring Compatibilism rendered otiose, at least for the Christian? How could one contend, say, that a self-determined action would be a random happening, or that the agent would not be responsible for an action not determined by his or her character, when one has no choice but to hold that *God's* free actions *are* self-determined, and are *not* determined by his character?

So it seems clear to me that the Molinist perspective on providence is by far the stronger of the two. Even so, it also seems clear to me that the case is insufficient to justify the hurling of anathemas at the Thomists. The reasons offered above for rejecting Compatibilism hardly amount to a conclusive refutation of that position. No dyed-in-the-wool Compatibilist will share my intuition regarding the core libertarian assumption on the necessary conditions of freedom. Nor, I suspect, would many Christian Compatibilists be moved by my distaste for the disanalogy between divine freedom and human freedom that Christian Compatibilism requires. While I think that Compatibilists would be mistaken in each of these reactions, I don't see how one could truly demonstrate to them the error of their ways. In sum, I doubt that there are compelling reasons for a Christian to endorse either libertarianism or Compatibilism. And if my suspicions are accurate, the dispute between Molinists and Thomists is destined to endure.

6. A HISTORICAL POSTLUDE

I end with a brief historical note. While it can be debated whether the concept of middle knowledge and the theological system that flows therefrom originated with Molina,[55] there can be no doubt that the appearance of his *Concordia* in 1588, by publicizing a position so at odds with the dominant (though, at the time, still developing) Thomist view, ignited a fiery and extended debate among Catholic theologians. Charges and countercharges were made to the bishops and the leaders of the Inquisition in Spain. Eventually, Pope Clement VIII appointed a commission to advise him as to whether or not the new Molinist position should be declared heretical. On three separate occasions, this commission recommended that various Molinist theses be condemned. Indeed, we are told that, as Molina lay dying in Madrid in April of 1600, rumors spread through the

---

[55] Molina himself insisted that only his terminology was novel; the concept of middle knowledge, he maintained, was present in the writings of the Fathers of the Church. See his *Concordia*, Disputation 53, pt. 2, sec. 22.

city that he had indeed been condemned by the pope, and that the works of the newly declared heretic were now warming the hands (though still not the hearts) of his Dominican detractors in Rome.[56]

But the rumors were false. Clement avoided making a final decision, choosing instead to have the issue debated before him and the commission by the theologians from the two sides. The disputations that followed lasted nearly four years (March 20, 1602—March 1, 1606), and in fact outlasted Clement, who died in 1605—grateful, perhaps, that he was not called upon to render judgment. His successor,[57] Paul V, had been present as a cardinal at the earlier disputations, and saw them through to their conclusion. In the end, the commission recommended that forty-two propositions of Molina be condemned.

The long-awaited papal decision finally arrived in August of 1607. Refusing to take the course of action consistently counseled by his commission, the pope declared that the Molinist position had not been shown to be at odds with the faith. Both Molinists and Thomists were to be allowed to promulgate their teachings, but each side was strictly admonished to desist from condemning the other. Any final decision on the matter, Paul declared, would come from Rome; until such a decision was reached, theological tolerance was to be shown by all concerned.

And so the matter rests to this day. No final decision was ever made, and none appears forthcoming.

If the thesis of this essay regarding the ultimate source of the dispute is correct, Paul's decision seems entirely appropriate. But is appropriateness all that we can discern therein? Might it not be that Molinists, and perhaps even Thomists, can justly discern in this story the workings of that very providence which each side upholds?[58]

---

[56] See the article on the *congregatio de auxiliis* in *The New Catholic Encyclopedia*, vol. 4 (New York: McGraw-Hill, 1967), pp. 168–71.

[57] Actually, Clement's immediate successor was Leo XI. But Leo's pontificate lasted less than a month. He was followed by Paul V.

[58] This research was supported by a grant from the American Council of Learned Societies under a program sponsored by the National Endowment for the Humanities. I owe thanks to many people for their help with this project, especially to Fred Freddoso.

2

The Impossibility of Middle Knowledge*

Timothy O'Connor

I

A good deal of attention has been given in recent philosophy of religion to the question of whether we can sensibly attribute to God a form of knowledge which the 16th-century Jesuit theologian Luis de Molina termed 'middle knowledge'. Interest in the doctrine has been spurred by a recognition of its intimate connection to certain conceptions of providence, prophecy, and response to petitionary prayer. According to defenders of the doctrine, which I will call 'Molinism', the objects of middle knowledge are all the true counterfactuals of the form, 'If C were to occur, then S would freely do A', where C specifies a particular set of circumstances. (Such propositions are usually referred to as 'counterfactuals of freedom'—hereafter 'CFs'.)[1]

In order to give a systematic account of the truth-conditions for CFs, contemporary Molinists[2] have by and large drawn upon important recent work clarifying the nature of counterfactuals generally. In particular, they have (following Alvin Plantinga, who gave new life to the doctrine) adopted the Stalnaker—Lewis possible-worlds account. On David Lewis's version, a counterfactual $p \mathbin{\Box\!\!\rightarrow} q$ is true just in case either (i) there is no world in which p is true, or (ii) there is a world W in which both p and q are true and (iii) there is no world W*

* Timothy O'Connor, 'The Impossibility of Middle Knowledge.' *Philosophical Studies* vol. 66 (1992): 139–66. © 1992 Kluwer Academic Publishers. Reprinted with kind permission from Springer Science and Business Media.

[1] The defenders of course assume that there are true propositions of this sort—lots of them. Can we be more precise? We can if we take the doctrine to be committed to the law of the conditional excluded middle (as applied to CFs), which states that for any p, q (where p is contingent), either $p \mathbin{\Box\!\!\rightarrow} q$ or $p \mathbin{\Box\!\!\rightarrow} \sim q$. ('$\Box\!\!\rightarrow$' is Lewis symbol for the counterfactual connective.) A Molinist who accepts this law will thus maintain as a special case that for any p, q, where p is contingent and q specifies some sort of free behavior of an agent (a choice, action, or freely-chosen inactivity), either $p \mathbin{\Box\!\!\rightarrow} q$ or $p \mathbin{\Box\!\!\rightarrow} \sim q$. In other to simplify an already complicated discussion, I will not press here any special problems associated with commitment to CEM for CFs, beyond those thought to be connected with the assertion that at least some such propositions are true. So for present purposes we may take the doctrine to involve acceptance of CEM (for CFs).

[2] See, e.g., Alvin Plantinga (1974), ch. 9 and Edward Wierenga (1989), ch. 5.

that is as similar as or more similar than W to the actual world and in which p is true and q is false.

With this framework in view (at least initially), I will try to assess the current status of two distinct questions: (1) Are there true CFs? and (2) Could God know true CFs if there are any? Obviously, Molinism must answer both questions affirmatively. Most of the discussion has focused on the first question.[3] I hope to show that this approach has been a dialectical mistake on the part of critics of Molinism, for the difficulties of giving an affirmative answer to question (2) are, I believe, far easier to state clearly and convincingly.

I begin in section II by examining William Hasker's attempt to provide a direct refutation of Molinism, and I argue that his attempt fails. In sections III–IV, I consider the two central objections to the view that there can be true CFs. I argue (in opposition to recent defenses of this view) that both of these objections pose irresolvable difficulties for the Molinist who accepts the standard Stalnaker-Lewis semantics for counterfactuals. I then turn in section V to Alfred Freddoso's proposal that this account of counterfactual semantics be abandoned. On the basis of his suggestion, I sketch an account of how the notion of 'truth' might be thought to apply to CFs. In the light of this alternative, it becomes clear that an effective criticism (one with a chance of persuading the Molinist, at any rate) must focus on question (2) above. In section VI, I discuss attempts to meet the challenge posed by question (2), and I try to show that these attempts are unsuccessful. I thus conclude that, despite certain theoretical attractions of Molinism for philosophical theology, we lack at present any legitimate basis for adopting or adhering to the theory.

II

Hasker has recently put forward a fairly complex argument, that purports to refute the claim that there can be true counterfactuals of freedom.[4] There are two main stages to the proof. In the first, we being by assuming for the sake of the argument that there are true CFs. We then ask who or what brings it about that they are true. The Molinist, Hasker believes, holds that the agent who is the subject of a particular CF brings it about *in those worlds in which the antecedent is true*,[5] by simply performing the action described in the consequent of the conditional. Hasker attempts to show, however, that this is mistaken—i.e., that

---

[3] This is true of both defenders of Molinism such as Plantinga and Wierenga as well as critics such as Adams and Kenny. See A. Kenny (1979), pp. 68–71, and Robert Adams (1987) and (1985).

[4] Hasker (1986) and (1989). My references are to the later version.

[5] Actually, this cannot be correct as it stands, since there are possible worlds in which the antecedent of a given CF is true, but the consequent is false. What is needed, I think, is the claim that the agent brings it about in the closest worlds to our own in which the antecedent is true. This revision is of no consequence to Hasker's argument.

the truth of the counterfactual (p $\square\!\!\rightarrow$ q) is independent of the agent's action. In the second stage of the argument, we go on to consider what the agent has it in her powder to do, given p. Clearly, she has it in her power to do the action identified in q (because she in fact does it). But does she have the power to render q false? Since p $\square\!\!\rightarrow$ $\sim$ q is a necessary condition for q's being false, her doing so entails the truth of p $\square\!\!\rightarrow$ $\sim$ q. But since this counterfactual is in fact false, it will be in her power to render q false only if it is also in her power to bring about the truth of the counterfactual. And since it was shown in the first part of the argument that she does not have this latter power, it seems that she correspondingly lacks the power to falsify q (i.e., to do other than what she in fact does). This outcome, however, contradicts the assumption that the action in question was free. So it seems that there cannot be true counterfactuals *of freedom*.[6]

Hasker's arguments for the claim that, even in a world in which p is true, the truth of a CF p $\square\!\!\rightarrow$ q is independent of the agent's action centers around the example of Elizabeth, a graduate student who is being considered for a research grant. We consider the following two CFs:

(1) If Elizabeth were offered the grant, she would accept it. (O $\square\!\!\rightarrow$ A)
(2) If Elizabeth were offered the grant, she would not accept it. (O $\square\!\!\rightarrow$ $\sim$ A)

As it happens, the offer is made and she accepts it. So we now wish to decide whether Elizabeth brought about the truth of (1) by accepting the offer or if, rather, its truth was independent of her action. It seems that the latter option must be correct if both of the following counterfactuals are true:

(3) If Elizabeth were to accept the grant, it would be true that O $\square\!\!\rightarrow$ A (i.e., A $\square\!\!\rightarrow$ (O $\square\!\!\rightarrow$ A)).
(4) If Elizabeth were not to accept the grant, it would be true that O $\square\!\!\rightarrow$ A (i.e., $\sim$ A $\square\!\!\rightarrow$ (O $\square\!\!\rightarrow$ A)).

(3), as we've seen, is true. But we must be careful, Hasker suggests, about quickly concluding that (4) is obviously false. For it must not be confused with

(5) If Elizabeth were to *reject* the grant, it would be true that O $\square\!\!\rightarrow$ A (i.e., (O& $\sim$ A) $\square\!\!\rightarrow$ (O $\square\!\!\rightarrow$ A)).

This is obviously false, but is a stronger claim that (4), in that the truth of (4)'s antecedent 'is consistent both with [Elizabeth's] rejecting the offer and with the offer's never having been made. If she rejects it, then "O $\square\!\!\rightarrow$ A" must be false,

---

[6] Some recent writers have attempted to resist this conclusion by rejecting the 'power entailment principle' upon which it relies, viz.,

If it is in A's power to bring it about that p, and 'p' entails 'q' and 'q' is false, then it is in A's power to bring it about that q.

(See, e.g., David Basinger (1987).) I will not enter into a discussion of power entailment principles, however, because the first part of his argument (as I argue in the text) is mistaken—Hasker has not satisfactorily shown that in a world in which p is true, the truth of a counterfactual freedom p $\square\!\!\rightarrow$ q is independent of the agent's action.

but if no offer is made, "O $\Box\!\!\!\rightarrow$ A" will still be true.' (p. 43) So we need to answer the question: 'If Elizabeth were not to have accepted the grant, would that have been (a) because she rejected it, or (b) because it had not been offered to her?' If (b), then (4) is true as well as (3), and it will have been shown that the truth of 'O $\Box\!\!\!\rightarrow$ A' is independent of Elizabeth's action, and thus that she did not in fact bring it about.

Since this question itself concerns a comparison of counterfactuals, we must decide it by comparing a world in which Elizabeth receives and rejects the offer with one in which the offer is not made to her. Which of them is more similar to the actual world (in which the offer is made to her and she accepts it)? Hasker argues that the truth of a counterfactual such as 'O $\Box\!\!\!\rightarrow$ A' is more important in assessing comparative similarity than is a particular contingent fact such as the offer's being made. Hence, all else being equal, a world in which 'O $\Box\!\!\!\rightarrow$ A' remains constant, though the offer is not made, is 'closer' to the actual world than one in which the truth-value of the counterfactual is changed. So it seems that (4) above is true after all.

Why does Hasker suppose that the Molinist must concede that the truth of a CF is more important in assessing similarity of worlds than any particular contingent fact? This conclusion is inferred from the following two claims:

(6) CFs are more fundamental features of the world than are counter-factuals backed by laws of nature.

(7) Counterfactuals backed by laws of nature are more fundamental features of the world than are particular contingent facts.[7]

Hasker takes (7) to be fairly evident, and I am inclined to agree. (6), however, certainly looks rather dubious at first glance. But, Hasker argues, the mere fact that the appropriate agents have control over the truth of certain CFs ought not to be taken to settle the matter. For a competing consideration is that God Himself is said to have *no* control over the truth of such propositions. Hence, we are left with, on the one hand, God's having control over laws of nature, but not over counterfactuals of freedom, and, on the other, human agents' having control over counterfactuals of freedom, but not over laws of nature. He suggests that

the upshot would seem to be that we cannot decide, on the basis of these considerations alone, whether counterfactuals of freedom are more fundamental than laws of nature, or vice versa. If anything, what seems to be suggested is that the two are roughly at a parity. (p. 47)

Now we need to ask what God's having 'no control over' the truth of a given CF, A $\Box\!\!\!\rightarrow$ B, say, comes to here. Hasker's argument might be persuasive if this claim implied, for example, that it would be simply impossible for God to prevent *B*, given that A obtained. If that were the case, then we could envision

---

[7] These formulations, with one minor change, are taken from Flint (1990).

the following sort of scenario: God deliberates about which world to actualize. B is a state of affairs that God very much wants *not* to obtain. So He is forced to conclude that He will have to forgo any world in which A obtains, no matter how desirable it might be in other respects, because there is simply no getting around the coming to pass of B, given A. But this is of course absurd. God could easily prevent the obtaining of B. Doing so, no doubt, would involve his nullifying or at least restricting in some way the agent's capacity to freely choose in those circumstances, but I take it that there are no cogent reasons for supposing that God would *never* do that under any circumstances. And, at any rate, the point is simply that it is not beyond God's power to do so. Thus, the truth of 'A $\Box\!\!\rightarrow$ B' itself crucially depends on the assumption that God has (or would have) no intention to intervene given the circumstances depicted by A. But then the original claim that God has no control over, e.g., 'A $\Box\!\!\rightarrow$ B', amounts to no more than the claim that God cannot alter the fact that B would result, as a matter of contingent fact, given A *and His own non-intervention*. But once this is recognized, it seems to me, it becomes apparent that Hasker's case for a 'parity' between CFs and counterfactuals backed by laws of nature falls flat.

Hasker, however, goes on to raise another consideration: the fundamental laws of nature appear to be probabilistic; hence, the particular counterfactuals they support are strictly only would-probably conditionals. As such, they are of a weaker logical type than ordinary counterfactuals (including CFs). This is illustrated by the fact that the truth of a would-probably conditional is consistent with the truth of its antecedent and the falsity of its consequent.[8] Hasker concludes from this that

the counterfactuals of freedom seem to be considerably more fundamental, with respect to explaining why things are as they are, than the laws of nature; a fortiori, they are more fundamental than particular facts such as that Elizabeth is offered the grant. (p. 47)

The Molinist, however, has a response readily available to him: though the laws of nature may strictly *imply* only would-probably conditionals, there are, nonetheless, true counterfactuals of the *ordinary* sort corresponding to these (at least in general, and certainly for those applicable to macro-scale phenomena, which are the ones relevant to our concern). Though the consequents of such counterfactuals are not fully determined, they would obtain, as a matter of contingent fact, given the antecedents. At least, we certainly should suppose this if there are true *counterfactuals of freedom*, whose consequents are made far less causally probable by their antecedents (in most cases).[9] Therefore, the

---

[8] Cf. Hasker (1990), pp. 119–20.

[9] Below I will challenge the tenability of the Molinist's program of converting would-probably counterfactuals into ordinary counterfactuals. But Hasker's argument is designed to show an *internal* inconsistency within Molinism, and so he must allow this further assumption, which is really implicit in the theory.

Molinist needn't suppose that the only true counterfactuals in the neighborhood, where causal laws are concerned, are of a weaker logical type than her CFs.[10]

If we wish to assess similarity of worlds, then, which sort of counterfactuals is 'more fundamental'—counterfactuals of freedom or counterfactuals that are largely grounded in the causal properties of physical objects? (Since we are assuming for the purpose of argument that there are true CFs, we must also grant (what the clear-headed Molinist will also maintain) that there are true counterfactuals associated with merely probabilistic causal laws.) It seems clear that the nod must go to the latter of these, for the following reason: in the case of the law-backed counterfactuals, the consequent is rendered exceedingly causally probable (particularly where it depicts a macro-phenomenon) given the antecedent; whereas facts about the agent's motivational state together with the circumstances given by a CF's antecedent only render it somewhat more probable—at most—that the consequent will obtain.[11] As far as I can see, Hasker's entire basis for resisting this straightforward conclusion resides in the considerations criticized above.

III

Having discounted Hasker's attempt to show that Molinism cannot be consistently maintained, we may go on to consider two objections that have been thought to provide a telling critique of the theory. The first of these has been urged by Robert Adams.[12] Adams objects that it is difficult to see what the truth of this particular sort of counterfactual proposition might consist in—there seems to be nothing which grounds their truth. Adams develops this objection through discussion of the following CF:

(8) If David stayed in Keilah, Saul would besiege the city.

Since (8) is endorsed as a counterfactual of freedom, we may suppose that the truth of its antecedent together with the relevant circumstances obtaining at

---

[10] The Molinist will maintain that there are true counterfactuals of the 'ordinary' type associated with probabilistic causal laws for the same reason she is committed to true CFs—it is required by the very strong conception of God's providence that she embraces. Now on the standard 'not-would-not' reading of would-probably conditionals suggested by David Lewis. 'If it were that A, then it would be that B' and 'If it were that A, then it would probably be that B' are inconsistent. (An account of this is given below.) So the Molinist must either deny that there are both true ordinary counterfactuals and true would-probably conditionals (with the same antecedents and consequents) associated with probabilistic causal laws, or endorse an alternative account of the would-probably variety. For some discussion of this, see Wierenga (1989) and Plantinga (1985).

[11] It could also be pointed out that various laws of nature are part of the very preconditions of true CFs (an agent obviously cannot even so much as act, let alone act freely, unless there are nomic connections between choice or volition and bodily movement), but the converse does not hold.

[12] Adams (1987), pp. 79–84.

the time in question would not causally necessitate Saul's besieging the city.[13] Now, in the actual world, David prudently elected to leave the city, and so the antecedent never obtained. But, given all that, Adams wonders in virtue of what state of affairs might this proposition be true?

It might be suggested that the truth of (8) *is* grounded in a categorical state of affairs—the character and intentions of Saul just prior to David's decision to leave Keilah. To evaluate this proposal, we should recall the conditions laid down by the standard semantics for counterfactual logic for assessing the truth of counterfactuals generally:

a counterfactual p $\square\mapsto$ q is true just in case either (i) there is no world in which p is true, or (ii) there is a world W in which both p and q are true and (iii) there is no world W* that is as similar as or more similar than W to the actual world and in which p is true and q is false.

The suggestion, then, might be that of the worlds in which David stays in Keilah, those closest to the actual world are worlds in which Saul besieges the city, and that they are closest in virtue of their greater similarity to the actual world with respect to Saul's character and intentions. Adams objects that if Saul's character is taken to underwrite the truth of not just the claim that he would *probably* besiege the city if David remained there, but also the stronger assertion that he would *definitely* do so, then we are embracing an analysis of truth for CFs that rules out the possibility that an individual might have acted out of character under certain circumstances. This gives us definiteness at the expense of plausibility (pp. 83–4).

Both Wierenga[14] and Kvanvig[15] argue that the crucial premise of Adams's argument admits of several readings, and the only one of these that leads to the desired conclusion essentially amounts to a denial that there are true CFs. So, they suggest, one can hardly expect the Molinist to be persuaded by the argument. Adams's claim that

(9) If David stayed in Keilah, Saul might not besiege the city

could be read as an assertion that it was possible that Saul so act, or that it was within his power to do so. But neither of these entails the falsity of (8). If, however, (9) is understood to be a 'might'-counter-factual, then it is equivalent (on the standard not-would-not reading of such propositions)[16] to

(9*) It is not the case that if David were to stay in Keilah, then Saul would besiege the city.

And while (9*) does yield the conclusion that (8) is false, it can be seen to be equivalent to a mere assertion that this is so.

---

[13] And, clearly, the truth of the consequent does not follow of *logical* necessity either.
[14] Wierenga (1989), pp. 141–3.
[15] Kvanvig (1986), pp. 133–4.
[16] In general, 'if it were that x, then it might be that y' comes out on this reading as 'it is not the case that: if it were that x, then it would be that y.'

I believe, however, that there is more to be said for accepting (9) at face value (i.e., as spelled out by (9*)) than either Wierenga or Kvanvig appear to realize. Kvanvig explicitly acknowledges (p. 134) that the assumed causal indeterminacy involved in Saul's action under the counterfactual circumstances implies that there is an objective chance of his refraining from besieging the city. But it is hard to see how one can deny that this entails (9). For we are not here considering the (epistemic) probability of a proposition such as (8) (a straight-forward CF) being true, but an objective causal possibility attached to the consequent of such a CF. (It may be, though, that we cannot speak of a determinate *probability* here, since presumably there is no well-defined probability distribution over the range of alternatives open to the agent at the time in question.) And the fact that there is such a causal possibility given all the causally-relevant factors seems inconsistent not merely with the denial that the consequent is logically possible under the circumstances, but also with the denial that it *might* occur.

One move open to the Molinist at this point is to try to tap the resources recently provided by David Lewis[17] for analyzing counter-factuals under the assumption (strongly suggested by currently-accepted physics) that the laws of nature are indeterministic.

Lewis has us consider the counterfactual scenario of Nixon's pressing a button (at, say, time t1) designed to trigger the launching of nuclear warheads. If indeterministic processes are in fact pervasive in nature, then there would be a negligible (but non-zero) chance that a quasi-miraculous sequence of improbable sub-atomic events would ensue, such that the warheads fail to launch and the world perfectly reconverges to the state of the actual world at some later time t2. This would have to include a 'cover-up' of all the traces of Nixon's action, mental state at t1, etc., down to the tiniest detail. But it needn't involve any violation of the actual laws of nature. This implies that:

> (10) If Nixon had pressed the button, there would have been some minute chance of a quasi-miracle.

Now perfect reconvergence to the actual world may seem to be a weighty respect of similarity.[18] Since it can be achieved without supposing a series of widespread, varied miracles (or even one small 'divergent miracle'), why doesn't our similarity analysis of counterfactuals commit us to supposing that such a reconvergence would occur, rather than the launching of the warheads and a subsequent state of affairs drastically different from the actual post-t1 history of the world? Lewis

---

[17] Lewis (1986).

[18] No doubt many readers would question the idea that similarity between worlds after the event given in the counterfactual supposition should be given any weight at all in determining closeness of worlds. (Lewis's adherence to the claim that it should stems from his reluctance to build an asymmetry between the directions of time into his analysis of counterfactuals, since this would put (as he sees it) undesirable a priori constraints on an account of the nature of causality.) But I needn't decide this question here, since my purpose is simply to investigate whether Lewis's general strategy for dealing with might-counterfactuals may be transferred to the problem involving CFs.

plausibly claims that what must be said is that this quasi-miraculous sequence 'would be such a remarkable coincidence that it would be quite unlike the goings-on we take to be typical of our world. Like a big genuine miracle, it makes a tremendous difference from our world. Therefore it is not something that happens in the closest worlds to ours where Nixon presses the button' (1986, p. 60). (As he notes, it is not just that such a sequence is extremely improbable, but rather that the chance outcomes conform to a pattern in a way which just doesn't occur in our world.) Hence,

> (11) If Nixon had pressed the button, there would not have been a quasi-miracle.

However, a problem seems to arise at this point, precisely analogous to the one we encountered with CFs. For (10) seems to imply

> (12) If Nixon had pressed the button, there might have been a quasi-miracle.

And (11) and (12) conflict on Lewis's original 'not-would-not' reading of 'might' counterfactuals, according to which (12) may be recast as

> (12*) It is not the case that: if Nixon had pressed the button, there would not have been a quasi-miracle.

((12*) is simply the negation of (11).) This prompts Lewis to suggest the following alternate reading in order to dissolve the conflict:

> (12**) If Nixon had pressed the button, it would be that: a quasi-miracle is possible.

On (12*), at least some of the closest worlds in which Nixon presses the button are ones in which a quasi-miracle actually occurs. But (12**) implies only that in all of these worlds it is possible that a quasi-miracle occurs. If this possibility is unfulfilled in all of these worlds, (12*) comes out false and (12**) comes out true. And whereas (11) conflicts with (12*), there is no such conflict between (11) and (12**).

Suppose that we accept Lewis's 'would-be-possible' reading to handle remote-chance cases of this sort (given a desire to retain a similarity theory of counterfactuals). Can the Molinist effectively bring this to bear on the dispute concerning CFs? I don't think so. For presumably the argument would proceed along these lines:

One may consistently grant Adams's point that an agent might act in a manner inconsistent with her character and intentions under counterfactual circumstances C. For this only commits us (employing Lewis's 'would-be-possible' reading), to maintaining that in the worlds closest to our own in which those circumstances obtain, it is possible (i.e., there is some chance) that the agent so act. But it remains true nonetheless that in those worlds the agent does not so act. So it is true that if C were to obtain, the agent would not act out of character, even though he might have.

The problem with this approach is that it proves too much. For it seems that we must say that CFs that indicate that (under ordinary circumstances) an agent will act in a way that corresponds to her character and previous intentions are always true. But if agents do not always so act in the actual world, why should we suppose that they would always do so under counterfactual circumstances? We are not here dealing with an exceedingly improbable sequence of events that smacks of a conspiratorial cover-up job, the likes of which are not found in our world (or so we believe). Rather, we have to do with the often enough observed phenomena of an agent acting in uncharacteristic ways, or simply changing his mind. So we clearly may not simply point to character and previous intention when asked to show what features of the actual world ground the truth of propositions about how an agent would freely behave. And once it is conceded that this is untenable as a general position, it seems that one must conclude correspondingly that putatively true CFs cannot be grounded through features of qualitative similarity between worlds.

Contemporary Molinists have acknowledged the force of this point by abandoning the attempt to ground counterfactuals in terms of categorical similarity between worlds in favor of *counterfactual* similarity. This suggestion has been endorsed, for example, by both Plantinga and Wierenga.[19] They each note that one group of counterfactuals that are used uncontroversially in comparisons of similarity are those that characterize the operation of causal laws.

But clearly this observation regarding causal laws is not enough to motivate treating CFs in a similar manner, since counterfactuals associated with causal laws are grounded either in the causal properties of existing objects (on non-Humean accounts) or in observed patterns of regularity, and neither of these considerations applies in the case of CFs. What's more, anyone who does hold CFs themselves to be more fundamental in comparisons of similarity of worlds than particular matters of fact such as an individual's character or intentions cannot escape Hasker's problem discussed in section II above.[20]

Finally, one may well wonder what the point of a possible-worlds account of CFs is if their truth is not grounded in non-counterfactual similarity relations. Plantinga urges that it is helpful nonetheless. For, similarly, although a proposition's being true in all possible worlds is not what *makes* it necessary or *explains why* it's necessary,

---

[19] Plantinga (1974), p. 178; Wierenga (1989), pp. 146–8.

[20] Indeed, Hasker formulates his refutation of middle knowledge partly on the assumption that its adherents are committed to the claim that CFs are more fundamental in such comparisons. We could then view his argument as not so much a direct refutation of Molinism as an attempt to show that the Molinist must abandon the attempt to provide a semantics for CFs in terms of similarity among possible worlds. As we shall see in the following section, such a move is available and is currently being developed. Finally, I should again note that some Molinists concede Hasker's conclusion that the truth values of CFs are not brought about by the actions of agents, but deny his further argument that this entails that our actions—which can always be described as the consequent of some counterfactual—are never free. I will not discuss such attempts here, but they strike me as extremely unconvincing.

it may still be extremely useful to note the equivalence of *p is necessary* and *p is true in all possible worlds*: it is useful in the way diagrams and definitions are in mathematics; it enables us to see connections, entertain propositions and resolve questions that could otherwise be seen, entertained and resolved only with the greatest difficulty if at all.[21]

However, this reply seems inadequate. The question being raised is not one of the usefulness of thinking of counterfactuals of freedom (assuming there are true CFs) as being true at some worlds and false at others. The possible-worlds framework itself is already justified, as Plantinga observes, by its utility in considering questions pertaining to the notion of metaphysical necessity. But why should we bother thinking of the *similarity* of worlds as depending in part on the truth values of their CFs? Why not just acknowledge that the values of CFs are, according to Molinism, just brute facts about each world, and so dispense with the theoretical formalism of talking about 'similarity' of worlds?[22] Retaining the machinery is apt to lull one into thinking that some sort of interesting account of the matter is being given, when in fact no explanation is being offered at all.

IV

Before turning to an alternative to the possible-worlds approach to providing a semantics for CFs, I want to consider a further, important objection to the applicability of this approach to resolving certain difficulties connected with God's creation decision. For, if sound, this objection will point to further constraints on a viable framework for understanding the theory of middle knowledge.

The objection was formulated independently by Robert Adams and Anthony Kenny.[23] On the Molinist view, God's decision regarding which world to create is guided by his middle knowledge, allowing him to order the world providentially (given the choices free human agents would make) in accordance with his will. So if God is to make use of such knowledge, it

must be prior, if not temporally, at least in the order of explanation (*prius ratione*, as Suarez puts it), to his decisions about what creatures to create. (Adams, 1987, p. 84)

In particular, his decision took account of the truth of

(13) If God created Adam and Eve, there would be more moral good than moral evil in the history of the world.

---

[21] Plantinga (1985b), p. 378.
[22] This theoretical device has a point when considering ordinary counterfactuals which super-vene on non-counterfactual facts about possible worlds.
[23] Adams (1987), pp. 84–6; Kenny (1979), pp. 68–71.

But there seems to be a difficulty here. For according to the possible-worlds account, the truth of (13) depends upon which world is actual (since it is true in some worlds, but false in others), but which world is actual depends upon which world God creates. It follows, it would seem, that the truth of (13) depends upon which world God creates. But since this latter fact has not been determined *prius ratione* to God's creation decision, neither has the truth of (13). Hence, it seems, God cannot base his creation decision upon his knowledge of propositions such as (13).

Plantinga attempts to dispose of this objection by showing that it is invalid. He invites us to consider this analogue:

(1*) The truth of *The Allies Won the Second World War* depends on which world is actual;

(2*) Which world is actual depends on whether I mow my lawn this afternoon;

therefore

(3*) the truth of *The Allies Won the Second World War* depends on whether I mow my lawn this afternoon.

The evident absurdity of this conclusion is taken to show that 'the relation expressed by the relevant sense of "depends" isn't transitive' (1985b, p. 376).[24]

My response to Plantinga's argument begins with the observation that the form of Plantinga's analogue is more general than the example Adams considers, in that Adams's example is concerned only with the dependency of what he terms 'deliberative conditionals', and not of propositions generally.[25] So if Adams's argument is in fact sound, we ought to be able to spell out the notion of dependency it employs in such a way that it is clear that the reconstructed version of the argument *is* valid, and that at least one of the premises in Plantinga's parallel argument is false when interpreted in this way.

I think the required explication may be put in the following way: A proposition such as (13) can have a determinate truth value at a (temporal or logical) moment t only if the categorical propositions concerning the actual world have determinate truth values at t. But this latter condition may be satisfied only if at t God has already decided which world to create. Hence, (13) is not determinately true or false before God has decided which world to create, and so God cannot base his decision upon knowledge of this proposition.

It is evident that the argument so construed is logically valid. Furthermore, if Plantinga's analogous argument is spelled out in the same way, we have as a second premise the claim that the categorical propositions concerning the actual

[24] Plantinga's criticism of Adams's objection is also endorsed (without further comment) by Wierenga (1989), pp. 119–50.

[25] Deliberative conditionals have the general form. 'If A were to do x, y would result.' We might further note that Adams grants that a possible-worlds theory can probably meet this sort of difficulty with deliberative conditionals in ordinary cases, though this needn't detain us here.

world have determinate truth values only if I have mowed my lawn this afternoon, a claim that is obviously false.

Yet some Molinists may respond to Adams's argument by maintaining that
categorical propositions concerning the world that God will create are true prior
to his decision to do so (although he cannot have knowledge of such propositions
prior to his creation decision).[26] (Indeed, it's not clear that a Molinist could
consistently *dissent* from this claim, since the clearest motivation for doing so—
the fact there are at that moment no *grounds* for the truth of such propositions—
is equally a basis for an objection to the Molinist position that there are
true CFs.) Consequently, they would not accept the second premise. I won't
try to rebut such a claim, since it is easy to transform Adams's metaphysical
objection into an epistemological one. For consider the fact that we cannot think
of God as knowing which world he would actualize *prius ratione* to his decision to
do so. Hence, he did not know, prevolitionally, which unconditional, contingent
propositions about some time in the history of the world were true and which
were false. But if he did not have this knowledge, then neither, it seems, could he
have had knowledge about propositions such as (13), since these vary from world
to world. How could God know, prior to his creation decision, which counterfactuals were true of the world that was going to be, if he did not know *which*
world was going to be?

It may help to further clarify this matter if we consider the following attempt
to reply to the argument on the Molinist's behalf. Granted that God does not
know which world is going to be actual prior to his decision to create, still,
mightn't he know which propositions are true at each possible world, including
the CFs? And if so, it seems he has all the knowledge he needs in order to base his
decision on the truth/falsity of propositions such as (13), since by choosing to
create a particular world W, he is knowingly choosing to create a world in which a
particular set of CFs are true.

The problem with this reply is that it fails to distinguish that which God
strongly actualizes in creating a world from that which he weakly actualizes.
Roughly put, the distinction is between the complex state of affairs that God
causes to obtain in creating a world and the more inclusive state of affairs that
would (happen to) obtain, were he to cause the first to obtain. Following
Plantinga, we may set this out more formally as follows:

God *strongly* actualizes a state of affairs S if and only if he causes S to be actual and causes
to be actual every contingent state of affairs S* such that S includes S*... God *weakly*
actualizes a state of affairs S if and only if he strongly actualizes a state of affairs S* that
counterfactually implies S. (1985a, p. 49)

---

[26] Kvanvig appears to take something like this line in responding to Kenny's formulation of the
objection, although I am not confident that I have clearly understood his position on this point. See
Kvanvig (1986), pp. 139–43.

Let us say that T(W) is the largest state of affairs that God strongly actualizes in creating a world W. T(W) obtains in a large number of worlds, many of which differ markedly from W. The issue as to whether God may have prevolitional knowledge of propositions such as (13) is essentially the issue of whether he may know that if he were to strongly actualize, e.g., T(W), W (and not some other world W*) would be weakly actualized—i.e., whether he prevolitionally knows

(14) G(T(W)) □→ W

But (14), Molinists allow, is true in some worlds but not in others (and presumably is true in only one of the worlds in which T(W) obtains—W itself). So, again, it seems that God must know which world is going to be actual in order to know whether (14) is true. But precisely this he cannot know prior, *prius ratione,* to his decision to create.

I can think of only one *formally* effective reply here, one which Plantinga may be endorsing, although this is not at all clear to me.[27] It might be suggested that the set of true CFs is precisely the same in all the worlds God could have (weakly) actualized. So even 'prior' to knowing which one was going to be actualized, and so prior to knowledge of unconditional contingent propositions, God knew precisely which CFs were true. The problem with this suggestion is that it seems, on the face of it, literally incredible. As Hasker remarks:

How are we to explain the alleged fact that the same counterfactuals of freedom are true in all the worlds God could actualize? These counterfactuals, according to the theory, are not necessary truths. . . . Is this not a deeply puzzling, even baffling state of affairs? (1989, p. 38)

V

In the detailed introduction to his translation of Molina's *Concordia,*[28] Alfred Freddoso attempts to extend Molina's own account of the theory of middle knowledge. His proposal involves a way of viewing the grounding of counterfactuals of freedom which hints at an alternative to the possible worlds semantics for ordinary counterfactuals. A central notion in Freddoso's account is that of a creation situation. For every possible world, there is a creation situation corresponding to it. The creation situation for a given world w (CS(w)) is the set that has all and only those propositions which God knows prevolitionally in w. These propositions[29] include the set of metaphysically necessary propositions N

---

[27] A passage which suggests this is pp. 377–8 of Plantinga (1985b). (Hasker (pp. 36–8) also interprets Plantinga in this way.)

[28] Freddoso (1988).

[29] Freddoso actually frames his account in terms of abstract 'states of affairs', but since he speaks of future contingent states of affairs as presently 'obtaining', a usage both critical to the question of what grounds CFs and potentially misleading. I will stick to propositions, which Freddoso acknowledges to be exactly isomorphic to his 'states of affairs'.

(which, of course, do not vary across worlds), and the set of true conditional future contingents (essentially our 'counterfactuals of freedom') in that world. The latter have the form *F(S) on H*, where S denotes a present-tense categorical state of affairs (involving the free choices of a creaturely agent), and the proposition asserts that S would obtain at a future time t if hypothesis H were to obtain at t.

A given creation situation is common to many distinct possible worlds. Indeed, the set of possible worlds that have the same creation situation as the one which God actually finds himself in corresponds to the range of alternatives available to him in creation. Freddoso labels this set of worlds the galaxy for CS(w).

We can see in this a pictorialized version of Plantinga's response to the puzzle discussed in section IV, viz., how is it that God can know prevolitionally which counterfactuals of freedom are true, if this depends upon which world is actual, and God does not know which world is in fact actual? For any complete set of counterfactuals of freedom, G, there is a unique set ('galaxy') of possible worlds which are such that all and only those CFs which are elements of G are true in those worlds. So all that God need know is which galaxy he happens to be in, though precisely which world is actual remains to be determined by his own free choice.

At the end of the last section, I expressed bafflement at the suggestion that the only worlds available to God to actualize happen to share the same set of CFs (as a purely contingent matter of fact). For no attempt was made to motivate the claim within the context of an account of how CFs come to have truth-values at a given world. So we need to consider whether Freddoso is able to provide an account that improves upon the attempts noted earlier to respond to the charge that CFs lack any grounds for their truth.

Freddoso develops a response to this claim by first noting that this objection is very similar to that advanced in favor of antirealism with respect to future contingent events. There is nothing in the present state of the world which corresponds to propositions about such events, nor are such future events a direct causal or logical consequence of presently obtaining facts together with the laws of nature. So, it is argued, there is at present no grounding of the truth of propositions asserting the occurrence of future events.

Freddoso suggests that realists concerning future truth may reply that there are now adequate grounds for the truth of a future-tense contingent proposition just in case there will be adequate grounds for the truth of its present-tense counter-part at some future time. I think it's clear, however, that this way of putting the matter is misleading and needs to be modified. The grounding of present-tense (contingent) propositions is some presently-occurring event or set of events. No such feature of the present grounds (contingent) future-tense propositions. (Rather, Freddoso is recommending that such a proposition be *said to have* grounds now if the corresponding present-tense proposition *comes to have* grounds in the future.) Hence, if the term 'grounds' is going to do the work for which it was originally intended, Freddoso's suggestion is just wrong, for there is not anything 'there' in the world which *is* its grounds. We may say rather that a future-tense contingent proposition p *is true* just in case its present-tense counterpart will have grounds at a future time.[30]

We may note further that even on Freddoso's own stipulation, it turns out that *no* propositions that are future contingent relative to t have grounds at t. For he claimed that there are now grounds for the truth of a future-tense contingent proposition p just in case

(15) there will be adequate grounds for the present-tense counterpart of p at some future time t.

—i.e., there are grounds for p just in case (15) is (now) true. But surely (15) is a future-contingent proposition if p is. And according to Freddoso, all true propositions have grounds, even future-contingent ones. So Freddoso is committed to

(16) p has grounds iff (15) is true

and

(17) (15) is true iff (15) has grounds

and

(18) (15) has grounds iff the present-tense counterpart of (15) will have grounds at some future time t.

It should be clear to the reader by now that we are off on an infinite regress. Attention to the nature of that regress should make it clear as well that it is not harmless. It has the form '*α* has grounds iff *β* has grounds, but *β* has grounds iff *γ* has grounds. . . .' At no point in the process is some element independently grounded by the state of the world. Obviously, if a ground is to be a ground, then all conditions for its being so must be satisfied. But this will not be the case where any condition c of the putative ground is such that every condition on *it* must satisfy some further condition.[31] Assuming that Freddoso would not wish to supplement his account with an unargued assertion that p (or some other element in the regress) just does have grounds, I conclude that the account unintendedly implies that *no* future-tense contingent propositions have grounds.[32]

---

[30] I might note that on my view, propositions, as opposed to typical linguistic expressions of them, have a tense-less structure, and do not vary in truth-value over time. But for the purpose of greater continuity with Freddoso's discussion, I will continue to speak of 'present-tense' and 'future-tense' propositions.

[31] Cf. the similar remarks by Alan Donagan in criticizing Roderick Chisholm's view that every time an agent acts, he causally contributes to an infinite series of simultaneous events. ('Chisholm's Theory of Agency', in E. Sosa, ed., *Essays on the Philosophy of Roderick Chisholm*. Amsterdam: Rodopi, 1979, p. 225.)

[32] I would hasten to add that a parallel problem does not arise for the claim (which I endorsed) that a future-contingent proposition *is true* just in case it will have grounds at some future time t. For

Given his own (problematic) account of the 'grounding' of future-tense propositions, Freddoso goes on to suggest that

> it seems reasonable to claim that there are now adequate metaphysical grounds for the truth of a conditional future contingent $F^t(p)$ on H just in case there *would* be adequate metaphysical grounds as t for the truth of the present-tense proposition p on the condition that H should obtain at t. At any rate, the argument leading up to this claim is exactly the same.... (p. 72)

In line with what I've said above, we may re-interpret this as the suggestion that a conditional future contingent $F^t(p)$ on H is *true* just in case there would be adequate metaphysical grounds at t for the truth of the present-tense proposition p were H to obtain at t.

This suggestion needs to be spelled out. First of all, (as Freddoso himself recognizes) H must include a complete description of the causal history of the world through but not including time t. For if CFs are true at all, it is undoubtedly the case that under even slightly different circumstances, agents would (as a matter of brute fact) act differently on occasion. It will be objected, of course, that there are two possible worlds sharing exactly the same causal history until time t, but in which (at t) an agent performs different actions. How can we maintain that there is an (ungrounded) fact of the matter abut which action the agent would have performed?

Well, for starters, suppose that God had chosen to create a different universe. For the purpose of simplicity and clarity, let us suppose that a) this world is to be completely causally deterministic, apart from human free choice, b) God's sole causal activity in relation to the world after creation is to sustain its continued existence, and c) no human free choices occur until time t. So God calls this concrete world into being. At t, the agent A is faced with a situation calling for a free choice. What would he have chosen? While it's true that there are many *possible* worlds sharing this description which diverge at t, there can only be one concrete world,[33] with but one of any set of mutually exclusive states of affairs obtaining at a given time. So if God had actualized this sort of universe, one—but only one—of these courses of action would have been undertaken. Which one?—Who knows? (I'll return to this in a moment)—but surely it cannot be denied that something would have occurred.

Consider now the universe God did in fact create. And consider the first free choice of some agent A at t. There are possible worlds identical in their causal history up to time t which diverge at t, due to the different choices available to A,

---

this biconditional is not intended to prescribe a procedure by which it may be determined whether a future contingent is *grounded*—it is simply indicating that it has no grounds now, but, if it is in fact true, it will have grounds at a later time. Nor is it prescribing how one may determine whether such propositions are true. One cannot make that sort of determination, I believe, precisely because there are as yet no grounds for its truth.

[33] I.e., large spatio-temporal entity, such as the one you and I are physically part of.

but only one of these alternatives was actually taken. But then it seems that $F^t(p)$ on H, where H describes in complete detail the *actual* history of our world until t, and p describes what actually occurred at t, is *true*. What's more, it always was true, on the omnitemporal view of truth. Similar remarks seem to hold for all CFs whose antecedents are completely specified, and whose antecedents and consequents actually obtain. (This very fact, that some of the conditional future contingents are not *counter*factual, prompts some to avoid the term 'counter-factuals of freedom', and speak of 'subjunctives of freedom' instead.) So this is one set of CFs or conditional future contingents whose members it seems plausible to acknowledge as true.[34]

I am not persuaded that we ought to treat conditional future contingents which are genuinely counterfactual as similar in this way to 'absolute'[35] future contingents. But I think it provides a coherent enough picture for ascribing truth to such propositions that one is unlikely to dissuade the convinced Molinist by engaging her in battle over this point. Rather, I think it forces the discussion back to the epistemological issue of whether it is reasonable to ascribe *knowledge* of such propositions to God, even if some of them may be said to be true in this way. Some may view this as an unwarranted and unhelpful concession to the Molinist,[36] but I think that it actually may help in the attempt to refute her theory, now that we have some sort of picture of how a Molinist might come to take various CFs as true.

I do not believe that the claim that God can know prevolitionally, with absolute certainty, which conditional future contingents are true is intelligible. If we are inclined to suppose that the recognition that some such propositions must be true is a natural extension of the omnitemporalist ascription of truth to absolute future contingents, we must concede nonetheless that they are intrin-sically unknowable.[37] More precisely, they are unknowable unless and until their

---

[34] Note that in the above attempt to show that one might have some reason to think that there can be true propositions of this sort (even in the case of genuinely contrary-to-fact conditionals concerning free human actions), all talk of similarity relations between possible worlds has been jettisoned.

[35] I am following Freddoso in using the term 'absolute' to refer to future-contingent propositions that have an unconditional (or categorical) structure.

[36] Compare Hasker's remark: 'It is important to see that the question is metaphysical, not epistemological. The question is not, How can we know that a counterfactual of freedom is true? It may be that we cannot know this, except perhaps in a very few cases, and although it is claimed that God knows them, it is not clear that the friend of counterfactuals (or any other theist, for that matter) is required to explain how it is that God knows what he knows.' (p. 29)

[37] Here and in the sequel, when I speak of the truth-value of such propositions as being 'unknowable', this is to be understood as an abbreviation for 'such that they cannot be known with absolute certainty, or infallibly'. For it seems that if we are willing to suppose that CFs can be true, it is reasonable to hold that we can know those which are not only fairly likely, but exceedingly plausible. I have in mind here examples like the one Adams gives concerning his butcher: If I were to offer him the price he has set for a pound of beef under ordinary circumstances, he would sell it to me. If either this CF or the corresponding one stating that he would not sell it to me is true, I take it that it's plausible to say that I *know* that he would sell it it me. But this is not infallible knowledge—it is quite possible (though rather unlikely) that I am simply mistaken.

antecedents (or the 'hypothesis' H in Freddoso's formula $F^t(p)$ on H) have been realized in the (concrete) world. Given that this condition has not been satisfied for any conditional future contingents prior (in the order of explanation) to God's creation decision, it follows that his decision was not informed by knowledge of any such propositions. (To put this in terms of Freddoso's picture that there is a unique galaxy of possible worlds having all the same true CFCs which comprise God's 'creation situation', I am claiming that God could not prevolitionally know which galaxy he was in.)

Support for this claim seems simple and compelling. God's infallible knowledge of a genuinely contingent proposition p involves or just consists of an immediate acquaintance with the grounds for p. Now in the special case in which a CFC's antecedent comes to be realized (at time t) and its consequent is in fact grounded, we may say that the CFC itself is grounded or has grounds at t. But then God cannot *prevolitionally* know any CFC, since there are no grounds to be directly acquainted with prior to his decision to create. There is simply nothing there in the world the direct awareness of which would constitute knowledge of p. (One cannot, after all, discern the truth of a contingent proposition by having a specially penetrating insight into the nature of the proposition itself!)

VI

As compelling as I believe this simple consideration is, I have yet to discuss the artful replies which Molinists have devised. Accordingly, I will here consider each of the three replies of which I am aware.

The first of these replies is the bold move of claiming that the tenability of the theory of middle knowledge stands or falls on the outcome of the battle over whether there are true CFCs. If there are, middle knowledge emerges victorious, as no account needs to be given of how God knows the things he knows, including true CFCs (if such there be). This position can easily seem appealing at first blush. Do we understand, e.g., just how it is that God's intellect immediately and completely grasps the entire state of the universe at any given time?

But the strength of this reply vanishes under scrutiny. There is nothing obviously unintelligible in supposing that there exists a mind which is not limited in its ability to be directly acquainted with the grounds of the truth of an infinite number of true propositions. In one sense of 'understand', of course, I do not understand this for a moment. But that is just to say that I have no clear idea of what the experience of such an intellect is like, or no clear grasp on the marvelous nature of such an intellect. But this is not the sort of puzzlement we have over the suggestion that any mind—even God's—could know ungrounded CFCs. We are not wondering about the lack of limitation on the number of propositions known, or the ability to be directly acquainted with circumstances of enormous spatio-temporal magnitude or complexity. Rather, the bafflement has to do with how one can be directly acquainted with what is not 'there'—there simply are no 'grounds' in the case of CFCs of which God's prevolitional intellect might be aware. If the Molinist adamantly insists that the excellence of God's intellect extends to the ability to know the truth-values of CFCs 'directly', apart from any grounds, I have nothing more to say to him. He is refusing to give an explanation where an explanation seems to be quite evidently required.

I take Molina's own view that God 'supercomprehends' the nature of his creatures so as to know the truth-values of CFCs to be essentially a claim of this sort. As Adams remarks, the appropriate response to this is that of Suarez, who 'pointed out in rejecting the theory of supercomprehension, [that] to comprehend something is already to understand about it everything that is there to be understood, and it is absurd to suppose that anyone, even God, could understand more than that.' (1987, p. 81)

Freddoso denies that Molina 'is making the absurd claim that by His middle knowledge God knows something that is not there "objectively" to be known. To the contrary, the states of affairs which God knows by his middle knowledge really obtain from eternity and the corresponding propositions are really true from eternity' (1988, p. 52). The reader might well be puzzled by Freddoso's statement that the state of affairs expressed by a CFC 'obtains from eternity'. But in Freddoso's usage, a CFC state of affairs obtains just in case its consequent would obtain if the antecedent were to obtain.

However, if it is said in this way that a true CFC 'obtains', this does *not* (in any intelligible sense) imply that there is something 'there "objectively" to be known'. This corresponds precisely to my earlier point that if (again, with Freddoso) one were to try to speak of a CFC whose antecedent is not realized as 'having grounds', this should not be taken to suggest that there is something there with which God's intellect is acquainted.

The second sort of reply has been made by Plantinga:

> . . . surely there are many actions and many creatures such that God knows what he would have done if one of the latter had taken one of the former. There seem to be true counterfactuals of freedom about God; but what would *ground* the truth of such a counterfactual of freedom? And if counterfactuals about God can be true even if their antecedents neither entail nor causally necessitate their consequents, why can't the same be true for similar counterfactuals about other persons? (1985b. p. 375)

Plantinga's purpose here is primarily to argue that CFs can be *true,* though ungrounded. But he attempts to do so by appealing to what we would intuitively want to say that God *knows.* So his remark seems equally applicable to the claim that God can know true but ungrounded CFs.

I think that some remarks of Hasker point the way towards a proper response to Plantinga's suggestion.[38] God's knowledge

---

[38] In the passage quoted, Hasker is speaking of the truth of CFs about God's actions being grounded. I am adapting it to the claim that God's *knowledge* of his actions under counterfactual circumstances is not ungrounded.

of such a counterfactual about [his] action is grounded in [his] conditional intention to act in a certain way. But humans, for the most part, have no such conditional intentions about choices they might be called upon to make—or, when they do have them, the intentions at best ground [knowledge of] '*would probably*' counterfactuals. (pp. 31–2, n. 25)

If God really does know with absolute certainty precisely how he would respond if certain circumstances were to obtain, this is because such knowledge of his is grounded in a) his fixed, detailed, conditional intentions to act in certain ways, and b) his knowledge that he cannot waver in his purposes. But this does nothing to show that he can have knowledge of human free actions under counterfactual circumstances, to which there are no analogues of (a) and (b). It might be noted further that to whatever extent it may be the case that humans develop at least some highly stable fixed intentions, this is a feature of their character which develops over time. God could not know prevolitionally what choices would be made in the early stages of a free creature's life which would contribute to the development of such intentions, and so he also could not know the resulting character of the intentions themselves.

Finally, I will comment briefly on a suggestion by Calvin Normore (which Freddoso quotes with approval):

Imagine that God's mind contains a perfect model of each possible thing—a complete divine idea of a particular or, if you like, an individual concept. Imagine that God simulates possible histories by thinking about how the being which is A would behave under circumstances C—i.e., he simulates C and 'sees' how A behaves. Now *if* there is a way in which A *would* behave in C, a perfect model should reflect it, so if conditional excluded middle is valid such a model is possible and God knows the history of the world by knowing that model, i.e., by knowing his own intellect and his creative intentions.[39]

Normore's picture strikes me as an ingenious attempt to show how God's middle knowledge might be grounded. Nonetheless, I think it clearly fails. For we were able to motivate the Molinist's contention that there is exactly one way that A would behave under circumstances C by appealing to the simple fact that there can be only one concrete world. If our world had been such that circumstances C obtained, A would have acted in some way or other—who knows which? It will be forever undetermined, given that C did not (and will not) in fact obtain. But, still, some action would have been undertaken, and a correct description of that action (whatever it would have been) is the consequent of a true CF which has C as its antecedent. (Or so we are granting the Molinist for the sake of discussion.)

Now Normore's picture suggests that God's intellect may construct a 'test run' which will necessarily result in the action characterized in the consequent of the 'true' CF. To suppose that this simulated world corresponds to how free agents would act—as a matter of brute fact—if God had brought about such a world is to suppose that there is something about the essence of all created entities

[39] Normore (1985). pp. 15–16.

(free agents included) such that they will inevitably act in a certain manner under certain circumstances.[40] For the 'divine simulator' produces what is itself a kind of world—if only an ideal one. What reason do we have to believe that the essence of A will act in the same way in every circumstance when instantiated in a concrete world as it does when 'instantiated' in the ideal world, existing only in the mind of God? I can think of only one—if the agent in question is not truly undetermined in choosing a course of action, and hence not truly free.

VII

The theory of divine middle knowledge cannot be reasonably maintained. Even granting a very generous interpretation of the notion of 'truth' which would license the application of this concept to propositions which will forever remain ungrounded, the project of making plausible the claim that God could know with absolute certainty which conditional future contingents describing the actions of free creatures are thus 'true' seems hopeless. It is to be hoped that this consequence will become more widely appreciated in philosophical theology, so that we may get on with the task of exploring and developing viable approaches to the concepts of providence, prophecy, and petitionary prayer.[41]

REFERENCES

Adams, Robert, 1985, 'Plantinga on the Problem of Evil', in J. Tomberlin et al., eds., *Alvin Plantinga* (Dordrecht: D. Reidel), pp. 225–56.

Adams, Robert, 1987, 'Middle Knowledge and the Problem of Evil', in *The Virtue of Faith* (New York: Oxford University Press), pp. 77–93.

Basinger, David, 1987, 'Middle Knowledge and Human Freedom: Some Clarifications', *Faith and Philosophy* 4 (July), pp. 330–6.

Flint, Thomas P., 1990, 'Hasker's *God, Time, and Knowledge*', *Philosophical Studies* 60, pp. 103–15.

Freddoso. Alfred, 1988, Introduction to Luis de Molina, *On Divine Foreknowledge* (Ithaca: Cornell University Press), pp. 1–81.

Hasker, William, 1986, 'A Refutation of Middle Knowledge', *Noûs* 20, pp. 545–7.

---

[40] Cf. Kvanvig (1986), p. 124: 'But what of the first requirement, that it be possible for God to know what will obtain even before he creates? In order to capture this constraint, it must be claimed that essences are such that, even before they are instantiated, they reveal what an instantiation of them would be like.' Again, the only apparent way to make sense of this suggestion that essences contain such counterfactual properties discernible by God involves supposing some deterministic mechanism or other in virtue of which the instantiated essence would act in a certain way under specific circumstances.

[41] I wish to thank William Hasker, Carl Ginet, and, especially, Norman Kretzmann for many helpful suggestions and comments on an earlier draft of this paper. I am also grateful to Steve Maitzen and Al Howsepian for discussion on the topic of this paper.

Hasker, William, 1989, *God, Time, and Knowledge* (Ithaca: Cornell University Press).

Hasker, William, 1990, 'Response to Thomas Flint', *Philosophical Studies* 60, pp. 117–26.

Kenny, Anthony, 1979, *The God of the Philosophers* (Oxford: Oxford University Press).

Kvanvig, Jonathan, 1986, *The Possibility of an All-Knowing God* (New York: St. Martin's Press).

Lewis, David, 1986, 'Postscript D to 'Counterfactual Dependence and Time's Arrow', in *Philosophical Papers*, vol. 2 (Oxford; Oxford University Press), pp. 63–6.

Normore, Calvin, 1985, 'Divine Omniscience, Omnipotence and Future Contingents: An Overview', in T. Rudavsky. ed., *Divine Omniscience and Omnipotence in Medieval Philosophy* (Dordrecht: D. Reidel).

Plantinga, Alvin, 1974, *The Nature of Necessity* (Oxford: Clarendon Press).

Plantinga, Alvin, 1985a, 'Self-Profile', in *Alvin Plantinga*, pp. 3–97.

Plantinga, Alvin, 1985b, 'Replies', in *Alvin Plantinga,* pp. 313–96.

Wierenga, Edward, 1989, *The Nature of God* (Ithaca: Cornell University Press).

3

Middle Knowledge, Truth-Makers, and the 'Grounding Objection'*

William Lane Craig

INTRODUCTION

Thomas Flint has observed that the so-called 'grounding objection' is in the minds of many philosophers 'the principal obstacle' to endorsing the Molinist doctrine of divine middle knowledge.[1] I share Flint's impression. What is ironic about this situation is not merely the fact that the many Molinist responses to the grounding objection remain largely ignored or unrefuted in the literature, nor yet again the fact that Molinist solutions to the objection tend to be far more sophisticated philosophically than the almost casual statements of the objection itself; rather the irony is that this allegedly powerful objection has virtually never been articulated or defended in any depth by its advocates. Contrary to Flint's claim that the objection 'is as easy to state as it is difficult fully to resolve,'[2] I hope to show that this objection is far from easy to state adequately—we shall see that Flint's own formulation is inadequate—and far from easy to defend.

No anti-Molinist has, to my knowledge, yet responded to Alvin Plantinga's simple retort to the grounding objection: 'It seems to me much clearer that some counterfactuals of freedom are at least possibly true than that the truth of

---

* © *Faith and Philosophy,* vol. 18 (2001). Reprinted by permission of the publisher.

[1] Thomas P. Flint, *Divine Providence,* Cornell Studies in the Philosophy of Religion (Ithaca, N.Y.: Cornell University Press, 1998), p. 123. The doctrine of divine middle knowledge (*scientia media*), first articulated by the Counter-Reformation theologian Luis de Molina in 1588, holds that God's decree concerning which world to create is based upon and, hence, explanatorily posterior to His knowledge of what every free creature He could possibly create would do in any appropriately specified set of circumstances in which God might place him. Thus logically prior to His creative decree, God knows the truth of propositions describing how some creature would freely act in a specific set of circumstances, *e.g., If Goldwater were to win the U.S. presidential election in 1964, he would order the invasion of North Viet Nam.* The doctrine presupposes that there are such true counterfactuals and that their truth is logically independent of the divine decree. For an outstanding introduction to and translation of a crucial portion of Molina's *Concordia,* see Luis de Molina, *On Divine Foreknowledge,* trans. with an Introduction and Notes by Alfred J. Freddoso (Ithaca, N.Y.: Cornell University Press, 1988).

[2] Flint, *Divine Providence,* p. 123.

propositions must, in general, be grounded in this way.'[3] What Plantinga understands—and grounding objectors apparently by and large do not—is that behind the grounding objection lies a theory about the relationship of truth and reality which needs to be articulated, defended, and then applied to counterfactuals of freedom if the grounding objection is to carry any probative force. Anti-Molinists have not even begun to address these issues.

What is the grounding objection? It is the claim that there are no true counterfactuals concerning what creatures would freely do under certain specified circumstances—the propositions expressed by such counterfactual sentences are said either to have no truth value or to be uniformly false—,since there is nothing to make these counterfactuals true. Because they are contrary-to-fact conditionals and are supposed to be true logically prior to God's creative decree, there is no ground of the truth of such counterfactual propositions. Thus, they cannot be known by God.

WARRANT FOR THE MOLINIST ASSUMPTION

Before scrutinizing this objection, it deserves to be underlined just how radical a claim it makes. It asserts that there are no true counterfactuals about how creatures would freely act under any given set of circumstances. This assertion is no mere ostensibly *undercutting* defeater of Molinism, but a putatively *rebutting* defeater. It makes a bold and positive assertion and therefore requires warrant in excess of that which attends the Molinist assumption that there are true counterfactuals about creaturely free actions. And the warrant for the Molinist belief that there are such truths is not at all inconsiderable: *First,* we ourselves often appear to know such true counterfactuals. Very little reflection is required to reveal how pervasive and indispensable a role such counterfactuals play in rational conduct and planning. We not infrequently base our very lives upon the assumption of their truth or falsity. *Second,* it is plausible that the Law of Conditional Excluded Middle (LCEM) holds for counterfactuals of a certain special form, usually called 'counterfactuals of creaturely freedom.' Counterfactuals of creaturely freedom are counterfactuals of the form *If S were in* C, S *would freely do* A, where *S* is a created agent, *A* is some action, and *C* is a set of fully specified circumstances including the whole history of the world up until the time of *S*'s free action. According to LCEM for any counterfactual $p \:\square\!\!\rightarrow q$, $(p \:\square\!\!\rightarrow q)v(p \:\square\!\!\rightarrow q)$. Molinists need not and should not endorse LCEM unqualifiedly. There is no reason to think, for example, that if Suarez were to have scratched his head on June 8, 1582, then either Freddoso would have scratched his head on June 8, 1982 or would not have scratched his head on

[3] Alvin Plantinga, 'Reply to Robert Adams,' in *Alvin Plantinga,* ed. James E. Tomberlin and Peter Van Inwagen, Profiles 5 (Dordrecht: D. Reidel, 1985), p. 378.

June 8, 1982. But it is plausible that counterfactuals of the very specialized sort we are considering must be either true or false. For since the circumstances *C* in which the free agent is placed are fully specified in the counterfactual's antecedent, it seems that if the agent were placed in *C* and left free with respect to action *A*, then he must either do *A* or not do *A*. For what other alternative is there?[4] *Third*, the Scriptures are replete with counterfactual statements, so that the Christian theist, at least, should be committed to the truth of certain counterfactuals about free, creaturely actions. The Church has never, until the modern age, doubted that God possesses knowledge of true counterfactuals concerning free, creaturely decisions; the whole dispute focused on whether He possessed that knowledge logically prior to the divine creative decree or only posterior to the divine decree. The Church's confidence that God knows such truths is rooted in the Scriptures themselves. To pick but one example, Paul, in reflecting upon God's eternal salvific plan realized in Christ, asserts, 'None of the rulers of this age understood this; for if they had, they would not have crucified the Lord of Glory' (I Cor. 2.8). By 'the rulers of this age' Paul means either the Jewish and Roman authorities such as Herod and Pilate who were the historical agents who instigated or carried out the crucifixion (cf. Acts 4. 27–28) or, more plausibly, the spiritual principalities and powers who rule 'this present evil age' (Gal. 1.4; cf. I Cor. 2. 6). In either case, we have here a counterfactual about creaturely free actions. So is Paul's assertion true or not? Will we have the temerity to say that Paul was wrong? Since the Church believes that Paul was inspired by the Holy Spirit to write these words, she accepts them as revealed truth from God. Thus, we have strong *prima facie* warrant for holding that there are true counterfactuals concerning what creatures would freely do under various circumstances.

In light of these considerations the grounding objector might retreat to the position that although there are now true counterfactuals about creaturely free acts, there are none logically prior to the divine creative decree. But then the grounding objector owes us a still more nuanced account of the grounding objection, since there seems to be no more ground now for many counterfactuals about creaturely free acts than there is logically prior to God's decree. Moreover, limiting the truth of such counterfactuals to a moment logically posterior to God's decree appears to make God the author of sin and to obliterate human freedom, since in that case it is God who decrees which counterfactuals about creaturely free acts are true, including counterfactuals concerning sinful human decisions. Thus, we have good reason for thinking that if such counterfactuals are now true or false, they must have been so logically prior to God's decree.

---

[4] Van Inwagen's objection that it might be the case that the agent would on one occasion do *A* and on a second go-around not do *A* actually supports the Molinist case, for these are two *different* turns and thus different sets of circumstances, and by Van Inwagen's own lights on each turn the agent would do something (Peter Van Inwagen, 'Against Middle Knowledge,' lecture dated April 12, 1996).

The point of these considerations is simply to underscore that the grounding objection, if it is to be successful, must, as a rebutting defeater, have more warrant than that enjoyed by the Molinist assumption that there are true counterfactuals concerning creaturely free actions. The Molinist is under no obligation to provide warrant for that assumption, since he is merely proposing a model which is intended as one possible solution to the alleged antinomy of divine sovereignty and human freedom. Nevertheless, if the model's detractors aim to defeat that solution by rebutting one of its elements, namely, the assumption that there are true counterfactuals about how creatures would freely behave under certain circumstances, then it is worth emphasizing the warrant that can be given for that assumption, since such warrant makes it all the more difficult to defeat that feature of the Molinist model.

THE GROUNDING OBJECTION AND
TRUTH-MAKER THEORY

So what can be said on behalf of the grounding objection? I have said that the grounding objection seems to assume a particular theory about the relationship of truth and reality. The theory presupposed by the grounding objection appears to be a certain construal or version of a view of truth as correspondence which has come to be known as the theory of *truth-makers*.[5] During the realist revival in the early years of the twentieth century various philosophers turned their attention to the question of the ontology of truth. Logical Atomists such as Russell and Wittgenstein thought that in addition to truth-bearers, whether these be sentences, thoughts, propositions, or what have you, there must also be entities in virtue of which such sentences and/or propositions are true. Various names were employed for these entities, such as 'facts' or 'states of affairs.' Among contemporary philosophers they have come to be known as 'truth-makers.'

A truth-maker is typically defined as *that in virtue of which a sentence and/or a proposition is true.* According to Peter Simons, 'Truth-maker theory accepts the role of something which makes a proposition true, that is, whose existence suffices for the proposition to be true. But it does not automatically pronounce on the ontological category of the truth-maker.'[6] 'Indeed,' he insists, '*anything*

---

[5] See the seminal article by Kevin Mulligan, Peter Simons, and Barry Smith, 'Truth-Makers,' *Philosophy and Phenomenological Research* 44 (1984): 287–321. An informative survey of the historical background of truth-maker theory may be found in *Historisches Wörterbuch der Philosophie*, ed. Joachim Ritter and Karlfried Gründer (Basel: Scwabe, 1971), s.v. 'Tatsache II,' by Peter Simons. See further John F. Fox, 'Truthmaker,' *Australasian Journal of Philosophy* 65 (1987): 188–207; Herbert Hochberg, 'Truth Makers, Truth Predicates, and Truth Types,' in *Language, Truth, and Ontology*, ed. Kevin Mulligan, Philosophical Studies Series 51 (Dordrecht: Kluwer Academic Publishers, 1992), pp. 87–117.

[6] Peter Simons, 'How the World Can Make Propositions True: A Celebration of Logical Atomism,' in *Sktonnosci Metafizyczna [Metaphysical Inclinations]* (Warsaw: Uniwersytet Warszawski, 1998), p. 119.

whatever is a truth-maker.'[7] But historically the orthodox view has identified truth-makers with such abstract realities as facts or states of affairs—more often than not, the fact stated as a proposition's truth condition, as disclosed by the disquotation principle. Thus, what makes the statement 'Al Plantinga is an avid rock-climber' true is the fact that *Al Plantinga is an avid rock-climber* or the state of affairs of *Al Plantinga's being an avid rock-climber.*

Now we immediately see the potentially misleading connotations of the term 'truth-maker' for such entities. For *making* sounds like a causal relation between a truth-bearer and some concrete object, but truth-maker theorists are quite clear that the relation is by no means causal. An entity *a* **makes a proposition** *p* **true** if and only if that *a* exists entails that *p*.[8] That truth-makers are usually conceived to be such abstract entities as facts or states of affairs underlines the point that a causal relation is not at issue here.

That the relation between a truth-maker and a truth-bearer is not causal is especially evident if we require truth-makers for negative existential statements like 'Baal does not exist.' According to Kevin Mulligan, Peter Simons, and Barry Smith, 'Not only Wittgenstein, but indeed almost all other philosophers who have investigated the relation of making true, have felt compelled in the face of the problems raised by negative propositions to adopt an ontology of truth makers as special, non-objectual entities having a complexity which is essentially logical.'[9] Obviously a fact like Baal's non-existence, which is sufficient for the truth that Baal does not exist, is not a cause of anything.

A proper understanding of truth-makers, then, invalidates at once the crude construal of the grounding objection expressed in Robert Adams's statement of the problem and again in Alfred Freddoso's and Thomas Flint's respective formulations of the grounding objection:

---

[7] Peter Simons, 'Existential Propositions,' in *Criss-Crossing a Philosophical Landscape,* ed. Joachim Schulte and Göran Sundholm, Grazer Philosophische Studien 42 (Rodopi, 1992), p. 257.

[8] Ibid. The theist must regard this characterization as untenable, however, since (unless one denies with William Alston that God has beliefs) God's beliefs then count as truth-makers for the propositions He believes. For God's beliefs are usually taken to be entities in a sense countenanced by truth-maker theory, often being characterized as 'hard' or 'soft' facts about the past. But taking God's beliefs as truth-makers seems to stand things on their head, since intuitively something is not true because God believes it, but God believes it because it is true. Moreover, if God's beliefs are explanatorily prior to the truth of propositions about human actions, then creaturely freedom would seem to be eliminated, just as divine freedom would be eliminated if counterfactuals of divine freedom were true explanatorily prior to God's decree. Bigelow states the truth-maker principle more acceptably: What Truthmaker says is: 'For each truth *A* there must be something *a* such that, *necessarily, if a exists then A is true*' (John Bigelow, *The Reality of Numbers* [Oxford: Clarendon Press, 1988], p. 127). Unfortunately this principle is false because it entails truth-maker maximalism (see below); but at least it captures the idea that truth-making is essentially a logical relation. Perhaps the truth-maker theorist should say that for any truth-bearer *A* which has a truth-maker *a*, *A* is true in virtue of *a* (or *a* makes *A* true) =$_{def}$ *a*'s existence entails that *A* has the value *true*.

[9] Mulligan, Simons, and Smith, 'Truth-Makers,' p. 315.

Counterfactuals of freedom ... are supposed to be contingent truths that are not caused to be true by God. Who or what does cause them to be true?[10]

... metaphysically contingent propositions ... require *causal* grounding in order to be true. That is, they must be *caused to be true* by some agent or agents, since it is not of their nature to be true.[11]

But if such conditionals are contingent, they might not have been true. Who, then, *makes* them true? Or, to phrase this question more carefully: Who or what actually *causes* the ones that are true to be true and the ones that are false to be false?

... neither God nor his free creatures cause counterfactuals of creaturely freedom to be true. ... The conclusion that seems forced upon us, then, is that nobody actually causes the counterfactuals in question to be true.[12]

The truth-maker theorist would take it as understood that nobody actually causes counterfactuals or any other sort of proposition to be true.[13] The demand for a cause of a proposition's being true is inept, unless the anti-Molinist is presupposing some very special causal theory of truth-makers, in which case he owes us an articulation of that theory and a defense, not merely of its adequacy, but of its superiority to customary truth-maker theories.

It might be said that the demand for a cause of the truth of true counterfactuals of creaturely freedom is a mere rhetorical flourish on the part of the anti-Molinist. But even if we give him the benefit of the doubt in this regard, the fact remains that the anti-Molinist still seems to be presupposing that in order to be true, counterfactuals of freedom must have truth-makers that either are or imply the existence of concrete objects. Not only does he owe us some explanation and justification for restricting truth-makers in this way, but such an assumption seems quite implausible. For we can think of other types of true propositions whose truth-makers neither are nor imply the existence of concrete objects. Consider, for example, the following statements:

1. No physical objects exist.
2. Dinosaurs are extinct today.
3. All ravens are black.

[10] Robert Adams, 'Plantinga on the Problem of Evil,' in *Alvin Plantinga*, p. 232. Cf. William Hasker's demand, 'Who or what is it (if anything) that *brings it about* that these propositions are true?' (William Hasker, 'A Refutation of Middle knowledge,' *Noûs* 20 [1986]: 547).
[11] Alfred J. Freddoso, 'Introduction' to *On Divine Foreknowledge* by Luis de Molina, trans. with Notes by Alfred J. Freddoso (Ithaca, N.Y.: Cornell University Press, 1988), p. 70.
[12] Flint, *Divine Providence,* pp. 123, 125. I should add that Freddoso and Flint are simply accurately reporting the objection as formulated by the detractors of middle knowledge.
[13] 'Making to be the case is of course not *causal*' (D. M. Armstrong, *A World of States of Affairs,* Cambridge Studies in Philosophy [Cambridge: Cambridge University Press, 1997], p. 115); 'The notion "makes it true that" has nothing to do with causality' (Peter Simons, 'Logical Atomism and Its Ontological Refinement: A Defense,' in *Language, Truth, and Ontology,* p. 159); 'A truthmaker should 'make' something true, not in a causal sense, but rather, in what is presumably a logical sense. ... the 'making' in 'making true' is essentially logical entailment' (Bigelow, *Reality of Numbers,* p. 125).

4. Torturing a child is wrong.
5. Napoleon lost the Battle of Waterloo.
6. The U. S. President in 2070 will be a woman.
7. If a rigid rod were placed in uniform motion through the aether, it would suffer a FitzGerald-Lorentz contraction.

Statement (1) could be true and statement (2) is true, yet they preclude truth-makers which are or imply the existence of the relevant concrete objects (such as dinosaurs). If such statements have truth-makers they would seem to be such things as the state of affairs of *there being no universe* or of *dinosaurs' no longer existing*. Some truth-maker theorists have maintained that such negative existential statements are true without having any truth-makers. For example, Mulligan, Simons, and Smith assert, 'it seems more adequate to regard sentences of the given kind as true not in virtue of any truth maker of their own, but simply in virtue of the fact that the corresponding positive sentences have no truth maker.'[14] But this assertion is self-contradictory. For a truth-maker is precisely that entity in virtue of which a sentence and/or proposition is true, and on their account a true, negative existential statement like 'Baal does not exist' is true *in virtue of the fact* that the corresponding positive statement 'Baal exists' lacks a truth-maker. Thus, this negative existential statement does have a truth-maker after all, namely, the fact that *'Baal exists' has no truth-maker*. A similar problem seems to attend D. M. Armstrong's attempt to eliminate truth-makers for negative existential statements on the basis of the second-order state of affairs of there being all the first-order states of affairs there are.[15] Presumably the idea is that if the state of affairs described by the corresponding positive existential statement is not included in the second-order state of affairs cataloging all the first order states of affairs, then the negative statement is true without having a truth-maker. But, we may ask, is it not then the case that the negative statement is true in virtue of the fact that the relevant positive state of affairs is not included in the totality of states of affairs or in virtue of existence of the state of affairs of the positive state's not being so included?

A further difficulty for such accounts is that the want of a truth-maker for an affirmative existential statement or the absence of a positive state of affairs from a second-order state of affairs does not always seem to constitute plausible grounds for denying truth-makers to a negative statement. Take (2), for example. The want of a truth-maker for 'Dinosaurs are alive today' or the absence of the relevant state of affairs from the totality of states does not seem to make it true that dinosaurs are extinct today. The same goes for 'Dinosaurs are still alive today,' for the negation of that sort of statement is notoriously ambiguous. The difficulty is that (2) seems to imply the positive assertion that dinosaurs were

14 Mulligan, Simons, and Smith, 'Truth-Makers,' p. 315.
15 Armstrong, *World of States of Affairs*, pp. 27, 135.

once alive and so needs more than just the lack of a truth-maker in order to be true. It seems to require as its truth-maker the fact that dinosaurs were once alive and now are not alive. In any case, even if negative existential statements are not made true in virtue of some fact or state of affairs, the anti-Molinist can hardly be encouraged by the prospect that we have here an exception to notion that true statements require truth-makers. If there can be true statements without any truth-makers of those statements, how do we know that counterfactual statements cannot be true without truth-makers?

Statement (3) is a universally quantified statement which as such does not apply merely to any ravens which happen to exist. Therefore, it cannot be true just in virtue of existing ravens' being black, much less in virtue of the black ravens there are. Statement (4) is an ethical judgement which implies neither that children exist nor that any are ever actually tortured. It is hard to see how ethical and aesthetic judgements can be made true apart from ethical and aesthetic facts being among their truth-makers.

Statements (5) and (6) are tensed statements about persons who no longer or do not yet exist (at least on a dynamic theory of time[16]) and so cannot have such persons among their truth-makers. Truth-maker theorists have yet to grapple seriously with problems posed by tense and temporal becoming. But in a recent discussion Barry Smith offers two proposals: either we 'need to introduce an explicit temporal dimension into our account of truthmaking, along the lines of: this liquid makes it true *at t* that it is odourless,' or alternatively, we 'might embrace a strictly presentist reading of "*x* makes it true that *p*". Some true contingent past and future tense judgments will then be such that, while their truthmakers do not exist, they did or will exist.'[17] These brief suggestions are merely programmatic; but the first seems to contemplate tenselessly existing truth-makers of tensed sentences along the lines of a static theory of time,[18] while the second appears to involve tensed truth-makers of tensed sentences such as might be postulated in a dynamic theory of time.[19] Smith's suggestion for this latter view is to assert that past- and future-tense statements literally have (present-tense) no truth-makers, although they either did or will. This suggestion

---

[16] According to a dynamic or tensed theory of time (often, in nomenclature borrowed from McTaggart, called an A-Theory of time), the distinction between past, present, and future is an objective feature of reality, whereas on a static or tenseless theory of time (often called the B-Theory of time), moments of time are not objectively past, present, or future but are ordered by the unchanging relations *earlier than, simultaneous with,* and *later than.* Moreover, on a dynamic theory, temporal becoming is real, and things come into being and go out of existence; whereas on the static theory temporal becoming is but a subjective feature of consciousness, and all things are equally real regardless of their temporal location.

[17] Barry Smith, 'Truthmaker Realism,' *Australasian Journal of Philosophy* 77 (1999): 274–91.

[18] See, for example, D. H. Mellor, *Real Time II* (London: Routledge, 1998), p. 34.

[19] Compare the tensed truth-conditions given by Graham Priest, 'Tense and Truth Conditions,' *Analysis* 46 (1986): 162–6; see further D.H. Mellor, 'Tense's Tenseless Truth Conditions,' *Analysis* 46 (1986): 167–72; Graham Priest, 'Tense, *Tense,* and TENSE,' *Analysis* 47 (1987): 184–7.

is problematic, however, because when the truth-maker of, say, a future-tense sentence like 'Bush will be inaugurated as our forty-second President' becomes present, then that statement, far from being true, is false, and the corresponding present-tense statement, 'Bush is being inaugurated as our forty-second President' is or becomes true. Thus, we should more plausibly say either that true past- and future-tense statements have no truth-makers at all, though their present-tense counterparts did or will have or that their truth-makers are the present-tense statements' having been or going to be true, or more simply the tensed facts stated as their tensed truth conditions, as disclosed by the disquotation principle. None of this is encouraging to the anti-Molinist, for again we find an important class of statements which either are true without having truth-makers or else have as their truth-makers abstractions like facts or states of affairs.

Finally, statement (7) is a true counterfactual about the aether of nineteenth century mechanics, which does not exist. One cannot say that the aether's properties serve as the truth-maker of (7), for the aether, being non-existent, has no properties. Of course, if the aether did exist, the aether would have properties, so perhaps one could say that what makes (7) true is the fact that in the most similar possible worlds in which the antecedent is realized, the indicative version of the consequent has a truth-maker—but this would be of no comfort to anti-Molinists who presuppose that truth-makers must be or imply the existence of concrete objects.

All of the above types of truths are matters of vigorous discussion among truth-maker theorists. These illustrations and the controversies they engender underscore just how naïve an understanding grounding objectors generally have of the nature of truth-makers. The idea that the truth-makers of counterfactuals of creaturely freedom must be literal people or any sort of concrete object is extraordinary.[20]

DO COUNTERFACTUALS OF CREATURELY FREEDOM NEED TRUTH-MAKERS?

Now, as I say, it is a matter of considerable debate whether true propositions do have truth-makers at all. Truth-maker theory is, after all, a minority position, associated in analytic philosophy with thinkers in the tradition of Logical Atomism. Simons admits that since Tarski's development of truth-theory without truth-makers, it has been widely held that there is 'no need' for

---

[20] And, of course, the same holds for counterfactuals about how creatures would freely act under various circumstances which are not, technically speaking, counterfactuals of creaturely freedom because the circumstances mentioned in their antecedents are not fully specified. So as to avoid pedantry, I shall henceforth not distinguish such counterfactual truths from counterfactuals of creaturely freedom.

truth-makers, such as Russell and Wittgenstein advocated.[21] In a recent critique, Greg Restall demonstrates that given the customary axioms of truth-maker theory, it follows that every true proposition is made true by every truth-maker there is, so that, for example, *Grass is green* is made true by snow's being white. In a monumental understatement, Restall muses, 'This is clearly not acceptable for any philosophically discriminating account of truthmakers.'[22] Perhaps these difficulties in truth-maker theory can be ironed out;[23] but the point remains that the doctrine is controversial and cannot just be assumed to be true.

In any case many truth-maker theorists themselves reject the doctrine of *truth-maker maximalism*,[24] the doctrine that every true statement has a truth-maker. I have yet to encounter an argument for the conclusion that counterfactuals of creaturely freedom cannot be among those types of truths lacking a truth-maker. Indeed, when one reflects on the fact that such statements are *counter*factual in nature, then such statements might seem to be prime candidates for belonging to that diverse class of statements which are true without having any truth-makers. Truth-maker theory, which is still in its nascence, has not yet, to my knowledge, been applied to such counterfactuals. But the analogy with past- and future-tensed statements is suggestive. Freddoso has argued that just as future-tense statements or propositions are grounded in the fact that a relevant present-tense proposition will have grounds of its truth, so a counterfactual of creaturely freedom is grounded in the fact that a relevant indicative proposition would have grounds of its truth. He explains,

A realist about the absolute future will claim that there are *now* adequate metaphysical grounds for the truth of a future-tense proposition Fp just in case there *will* be at some future time adequate metaphysical grounds for the truth of its present-tense counter-part p. . . .
But if this is so, then it seems reasonable to claim that there are now adequate metaphysical grounds for the truth of a conditional future contingent $F^t(p)$ *on H* just in case there would be adequate metaphysical grounds at t for the truth of the present-tense proposition p on the condition that H should obtain at t.[25]

On Freddoso's account, contingent propositions of the form Fp or $F^t(p)$ *on H* do have truth-makers, namely the fact or state of affairs that p *will have a truth-maker* or p *would have a truth-maker under the relevant condition* respectively.

---

[21] Simons, 'Logical Atomism,' p. 158. Bigelow is embarrassed by the 'linguistic magic' that guides truth-maker theory—'inferring the *existence* of certain things from the *truth* of certain claims: a way of calling things into existence by linguistic magic—*defining* things into existence' (Bigelow, *Reality of Numbers*, p. 7).

[22] Greg Restall, 'Truthmakers, Entailment, and Necessity,' *Australasian Journal of Philosophy* 74 (1996): 334.

[23] Restall proposes to solve the problem by an account of truth-makers in which he leaves his truth-makers undefined. The abstractness of the account only reinforces how ham-fisted is the handling of truth-makers by grounding objectors.

[24] This is Barry Smith's term.

[25] Freddoso, 'Introduction,' p. 72. A future-tense proposition may be understood as a proposition whose linguistic expression in English must involve the future-tense.

In his analysis of Freddoso's view, Timothy O'Connor maintains that it would be more accurate simply to say that future contingent propositions have no grounds of their truth, but that they are true just in case their relevant present-tense counterparts will have grounds of their truth.[26] That is to say, propositions of the form *Fp* have *truth-conditions* which may be satisfied even though they lack *truth-makers*. This revision of Freddoso's view is along the lines of Barry Smith's second suggestion for dealing with future-tense statements. Analogously, O'Connor proposes, we should reinterpret Freddoso's truth-makers for counterfactuals of creaturely freedom as giving truth-conditions for propositions of the form $F^t(p)$ *on H*, while maintaining that such propositions do not have truth-makers. Although O'Connor, as an anti-Molinist, is none too happy about this analogy between future contingent propositions and counterfactuals of creaturely freedom, he grudgingly acknowledges its coherence and chooses to attack Molinism elsewhere.[27] But the point remains that it is far from obvious

[26] Timothy O'Connor, 'The Impossibility of Middle Knowledge,' *Philosophical Studies* 66 (1992): 155–6 (this volume, p. 60). Thus, O'Connor provides a semantics more consistent with a dynamic theory of time than does David Paul Hunt, 'Middle Knowledge: The "Foreknowledge Defense",' *International Journal for Philosophy of Religion* 28 (1990): 7, who says that future-tense statements '*are* true in virtue of corresponding to an actual state of affairs, albeit one that lies in the future.'

[27] Ibid., pp. 158–9. O'Connor retreats from denying the *truth* of counterfactuals of creaturely freedom to denying their *knowability*. His denial is based on the assumption that 'God's infallible knowledge of a genuinely contingent proposition *p* involves or just consists of an immediate acquaintance with the grounds for *p*' (Ibid., p. 158). This is an astonishing claim. It entails that God is ignorant of all true contingent propositions which lack truth-makers. Why think that the way in which God knows true propositions is by knowing what are their truth-makers? O'Connor answers, 'One cannot, after all, discern the truth of a contingent proposition by having a specially penetrating insight into the nature of the proposition itself' (Ibid., p. 159). If O'Connor is correct in this assertion, then God will be ignorant not only of all contingent truths which lack truth-makers, but He will also be ignorant of all non-analytic necessary truths as well, since those also lack truth-makers, according to standard truth-maker theory. O'Connor's position is thus incompatible with classical theism. In any case, his justification for restricting God's knowledge to propositions which have truth-makers is wholly implausible. For given the ontology of truth presupposed by the theory of truth-makers, there really are entities, like propositions, which serve as truth-bearers. These are real property-bearing entities, and one of the properties they bear is truth (or falsity). This is a genuine property inhering in some, but not all, of these entities. Therefore, God most certainly can by an immediate inspection of the proposition itself discern whether it bears the property of truth or not.

Indeed, thinkers like O'Connor and Hasker, who admit the bivalence of counterfactuals of creaturely freedom or future contingent propositions (see Flint, *Divine Providence*, p. 130) but deny God's knowledge of the same, find themselves in an ultimately incoherent position. For what must they say concerning a present-tense proposition *q* to the effect that a particular future contingent proposition *Fp* or counterfactual of creaturely freedom $F^t(p)$ *on H*, is true? If *q* is now true, then, as a present-tense proposition, God must know it. Indeed, *q* seems to have an evident truth-maker, namely, the inherence of the property of truth in *Fp* or $F^t(p)$ *on H*. The state of affairs of *Fp's being true* is not only a contingent state of affairs which presently obtains in the world, but *Fp's being true* is literally an event, since *Fp* may change in its truth value once *p* becomes true, in which case *q* undergoes an intrinsic change from being true to being false. Thus, *if q*, God must know that *q* and, hence, know that *Fp* and $F^t(p)$ *on H* are true. But if He knows that these propositions are true, then He knows the facts which they state. Thus, anyone who agrees that the Principle of Bivalence governs future contingent propositions or counterfactuals of creaturely freedom and who holds that God knows all presently true propositions or is immediately acquainted with all existing truth-makers cannot on pain of incoherence deny that God knows the truth of future contingent propositions and counterfactuals of creaturely freedom. This conclusion presents a real crisis for thinkers like Hasker whose only escape from theological fatalism is to deny God's foreknowledge of true future contingent propositions.

that counterfactuals of creaturely freedom have to have truth-makers in order to be true. Anti-Molinists have not even begun the task of showing that counter-factuals of creaturely freedom are members of the set of propositions or statements which require truth-makers if they are to be true.

DO COUNTERFACTUALS OF CREATURELY FREEDOM HAVE TRUTH-MAKERS?

But suppose that future-tense statements and counterfactuals of creaturely free-dom do belong to that class of propositions or statements requiring truth-makers in order to be true. What is wrong with the facts or states of affairs proposed by Freddoso as the truth-makers of such propositions? O'Connor's declamation, 'Freddoso's suggestion is just wrong, for there is not anything "there" in the world which is its grounds'[28] reveals that he is presupposing the same naïve under-standing of truth-makers exposed earlier. Facts or states of affairs such as Fred-doso mentions routinely serve as perfectly respectable truth-makers. Perhaps one could try to exclude Freddoso's truth-makers by putting a nominalistic spin on facts and states of affairs, but the anti-Molinist can hardly think that an objection based on so controversial a metaphysical thesis as that will have more warrant than the affirmation that there are true future tense statements and counter-factuals of creaturely freedom.

O'Connor also argues that Freddoso's view spawns a vicious infinite regress of grounds of truth. For a true future-tense proposition *Fp* is said to have grounds of its truth just in case there will be grounds of the truth of *p* at some future time. Here the grounds of the truth of *Fp* are stated by means of another statement which is also of the form *Fp*. We are off on an infinite regress, O'Connor insists, which is vicious because no statement has unconditional grounds of its truth.[29] But O'Connor has conflated the truth-maker of *Fp* with the truth-conditions of the statement that *Fp* has a truth-maker. On Freddoso's view the truth-maker of any proposition *Fp* is the fact that *there will be a truth-maker of p*. Facts do not themselves have truth-makers, so there is no regress.

Nevertheless, O'Connor's objection is helpful in that it draws attention to the fact that even Freddoso's account of the truth-makers of future-tense propositions requires the existence of tensed facts, a point which is insisted upon independ-ently by advocates of a dynamic theory of time,[30] which, it will be recalled, is

---

[28] O'Connor, 'Impossibility,' p. 155.

[29] Ibid., pp. 155–6.

[30] See discussion in my *The Tensed Theory of Time: a Critical Examination,* Synthèse Library 293 (Dordrecht: Kluwer Academic Publishers, 2000), subject index: 'facts, tensed.' Michael Tooley would be a rare exception.

presupposed by this version of truth-making for tensed sentences. That raises the question whether we might not as well just let the relevant tensed facts be the truth-makers of tensed propositions. The regress spotted by O'Connor concerns the truth-conditions of the sentence 'There are now grounds for the truth of Fp,' and this regress is benign, since it is simply a series of entailments of one future-tense proposition by another.

Indeed, O'Connor had better hope that such a regress is benign, since on his *own* view Freddoso's formula does successfully give the truth-conditions of any future-tense proposition Fp, viz.:

$Fp \equiv p$ will have grounds at some future time t.

Since the right-hand side of the equivalence has itself the form Fp, one embarks on an infinite regress. In agreeing that Freddoso's formula does successfully give the truth conditions of a future-tense proposition despite the infinite regress involved, O'Connor tacitly agrees that such a regress is benign. O'Connor protests that he does not face the same problem as Freddoso because 'this biconditional is not intended to prescribe a procedure by which it may be determined whether a future contingent is *grounded*—it is simply indicating that it . . . is in fact true.'[31] This alleged difference, however, is rooted in O'Connor's confusion noted above concerning the truth-maker of Fp and the truth-conditions of 'Fp has a truth-maker'; there is on his own view still a (benign) infinite regress because the right-hand side of the above equivalence has itself the form Fp. O'Connor also defends himself by saying that his adaptation of Freddoso's formula is not a prescription of 'how one may determine whether such propositions are true.'[32] But, of course, neither is Freddoso intending to provide a prescription for determining in O'Connor's epistemic sense whether Fp does have a truth-maker or not.

Similarly, when we turn from future-tense propositions to counterfactual propositions and consider Freddoso's proposed truth-makers for counterfactuals of creaturely freedom, we see that O'Connor's denial that 'there is something "there "objectively" to be known" '[33] is rooted in the same crude understanding of truth-makers already exposed. As for the supposedly vicious infinite regress, it is again a benign regress of entailments generated by the truth-conditions of the statement '$F\,{}^{t}(p)$ on H has a truth-maker.'

That the regress concerns truth-conditions, not truth-makers, is especially evident in Flint's defense of Freddoso's position. Flint proposes the following formula to give the truth-maker of a counterfactual of creaturely freedom $c \,\square\!\!\rightarrow z$:

> F. 'It *would be* the case (if c were true) that z' is now grounded iff 'z is grounded' *would be* the case (if c were true).[34]

[31] O'Connor, 'Impossibility,' pp. 164–5 (this volume, pp. 60–1 n. 32).   [32] Ibid.
[33] Ibid., p. 160 (this volume, p. 64).   [34] Flint, *Divine Providence*, p. 133.

It is evident that what is provided here are truth conditions for the claim that '$c \,\Box\!\!\rightarrow z$ is now grounded,' not a truth-maker for $c \,\Box\!\!\rightarrow z$. In fact, ironically, Flint never really does tell us what the truth-maker of $c \,\Box\!\!\rightarrow z$ is! He misconstrues his own account when he says, for example, that a person's activity in a nearby possible world is what grounds a counterfactual of creaturely freedom which is true in the actual world.[35] Such an interpretation conjures up ghostly images of merely possible agents doing things in their worlds which produce causal effects in ours, surely a bizarre and untenable picture! Rather on the Freddoso-Flint view, the truth-maker of $c \,\Box\!\!\rightarrow z$ is something like the fact that *the statement 'z has a truth-maker' would be true (if c were true)*. This fact or state of affairs exists or obtains as robustly in the actual world as any other actual fact or state of affairs and is an unobjectionable truth-maker. Thus it is a misconceived worry to wonder how merely possible activities ground actual truths, just as it is a misconceived worry to puzzle over how non-existent past or future activities could ground present truths. They do not.

For my part, I should say that if true counterfactuals of creaturely freedom have truth-makers, then the most obvious and plausible candidates are the facts or states of affairs disclosed by the disquotation principle. Thus, what makes it true that 'If I were rich, I would buy a Mercedes,' is the fact that if I were rich I would buy a Mercedes. Just as there are tensed facts about the past or future which now exist, even though the objects and events they are about do not, so there are counterfacts which actually exist, even though the objects and events they are about do not. If counterfactuals of creaturely freedom require truth-makers, then it is in virtue of these facts or states of affairs that the corresponding propositions are true. And since these counterfacts are not the result of God's decree, the relevant states of affairs must obtain even logically prior to God's decree to create any concrete objects.

In his development of the grounding objection, Hasker does seem to countenance states of affairs as truth-makers. But, he insists, 'In order for a (contingent) conditional state of affairs to obtain, its obtaining must be grounded in some categorical state of affairs. More colloquially, truths about 'what *would be the case...if*' must be grounded in truths about what *is in fact* the case.'[36] For example, the truth of counterfactuals like 'If the glass were struck, it would shatter' is grounded 'in the natures, causal powers, inherent tendencies, and the like, of the natural entities described in them.'[37]

Hasker's claim is, however, very muddled. An obtaining state of affairs just is the ground or truth-maker of some truth and so is not itself 'grounded' in the relevant sense. Moreover, truths do not have other truths as their grounds or

[35] Ibid.
[36] William Hasker, *God, Time, and Knowledge,* Cornell Studies in the Philosophy of Religion (Ithaca, N.Y.: Cornell University Press, 1989), p. 30.
[37] Ibid.

truth-makers, but rather states of affairs. With respect to counterfactuals concerning instances of natural kinds like the glass, the truth of the counterfactual is
arguably grounded in a dispositional property of the object, such as in this case
the glass's fragility. Such a dispositional property may be plausibly taken to be the
truth-maker of the relevant counterfactual and even to ensure its necessary
truth.[38] Moreover, it is correct to say that dispositional properties have a causal
basis in the categorical properties of a natural object, such as the molecular
structure of the glass. But it is a *non sequitur* to conclude that the causal basis of a
disposition is the truth-maker of the relevant counterfactual. For if there were
different laws of nature, that same molecular structure might not serve to make
glass fragile. It is the glass's fragility which is the truth-maker of the counterfactual at issue, and the causal basis of the disposition is at most responsible, not
for the glass's fragility, but for the manifestation of that fragility, that is to say, for
the actual shattering of the glass. Thus, in Armstrong's analysis the truth-maker
for the categorical statement 'The glass is fragile' is the glass's having a certain
molecular structure plus the laws of nature.[39] But the rub is that laws of nature, as
Plantinga observes,[40] are equivalent to various counterfactual propositions, like
'If x were cooled to $0°$, it would expand,' so that one might just as well have said
that the truth-maker of 'The glass is fragile' is the glass's having a certain
molecular structure plus certain counterfacts of nature. Thus, even a categorical
statement concerning dispositional properties of a natural object arguably has
among its truthmakers certain counterfacts, not to speak of a counterfactual
statement grounded in the dispositional properties of an object. Thus, Hasker's
claim that counterfactuals must be purely categorically grounded is unwarranted.

How much more dubious is Hasker's claim when it comes to personal agents
endowed with freedom of the will! For free choice is not a matter of natural
dispositions involving causal bases. Indeed, as I have elsewhere charged,[41] the
grounding objection seems implicitly to reject libertarian freedom, for on a
libertarian view there is no further 'grounding' to be sought for why there
obtains a certain counterfactual state of affairs about how some agent would
freely act under certain circumstances. To seek an answer to the question 'Why is
F a fact?' or 'What makes *F* a fact?' is implicitly to deny libertarian freedom. It is
simply a fact that that is how that agent would freely choose to act under those
circumstances.

---

[38] See Frank Jackson, Robert Pargetter, and Elizabeth W. Prior, 'Three Theses about Dispositions,' *American Philosophical Quarterly* 19 (1982): 251–8; Robert Pargetter and Elizabeth W.
Prior, 'The Dispositional and the Categorical,' *Pacific Philosophical Quarterly* 63 (1982): 366–70.

[39] Armstrong, *States of Affairs*, pp. 70–3, 129.

[40] Alvin Plantinga, *The Nature of Necessity*, Clarendon Library of Logic and Philosophy
(Oxford: Clarendon Press, 1974), p. 178.

[41] William Lane Craig, *Divine Foreknowledge and Human Freedom: The Coherence of Theism:
Omniscience*, Brill's Studies in Intellectual History 19 (Leiden: E. J. Brill, 1991), pp. 261–2.

CONCLUSION

In conclusion, I think that it is evident that anti-Molinists have not even begun to do the necessary homework in order for their grounding objection to fly. They have yet to articulate their ontology of truth, including the nature of truth-bearers and truth-makers. Nor have they yet presented a systematic account of which truth-bearers require truth-makers. Neither have they applied their theory to counterfactuals of creaturely freedom, much less shown its superiority to competing theories. Of course, it is open to grounding objectors to abjure a theory of truth-makers altogether and to assert that in construing their talk about grounds of truth for counterfactuals of creaturely freedom in terms of truth-makers I have misunderstood or misrepresented them. Perhaps grounds of truth are different from truth-makers. But if that is the case, then anti-Molinists owe us all the more a careful account of what they are talking about. Until they provide that, their grounding objection cannot even hope to get off the ground.

In short, I agree with Plantinga that I am far more confident that there are true counterfactuals of creaturely freedom than I am of the theory which requires that they have truth-makers.[42] And if they do require truth-makers, no reason has been given why their truth-makers cannot be the facts or states of affairs which are disclosed by the disquotation principle.[43]

[42] Cf. The remark of Mulligan, Simons, and Smith, 'Truth-Makers,' p. 299: it is 'perfectly rational for us to know *that* a sentence is true and yet not know completely *what* makes it true.'

[43] I am indebted to Thomas Flint, Peter Simons, and Barry Smith for stimulating discussion and comments on this paper.

4

Divine Providence and Simple Foreknowledge*

David P. Hunt

While the scriptural evidence alone is doubtless subject to more than one interpretation, there are at least a couple of reasons why most theists have thought it
important to attribute complete knowledge of the future to God. The first is
simply that divine omniprescience makes God *smarter* than He would be otherwise. This justification can be elaborated into an argument as follows: (i) God, as
St. Anselm put it in a famous formula, is a 'being than which none greater can be
conceived;' but (ii) we can conceive a being possessing omniprescience; (iii) such a
being would be greater than one that lacked omniprescience; therefore (iv) God
cannot lack (and so must possess) omniprescience. We might think of this first
argument as setting forth the *ontological* basis for God's complete foreknowledge.

The other major argument for divine omniprescience is that it is required by
any adequate conception of divine *providence*. This point is less amenable than
the first one to expression as a formal argument, but the basic idea can be set forth
as follows. Belief in God loses much (if not all) of its point if the world makes no
more sense in light of this belief than it does in its absence. Now if it is the mere
existence of a world that is thought to require explanation, then nothing stronger
than deism is needed for the job; but if God is also relied upon to make sense out
of human history and the individual lives that make it up, then it is necessary to
move from the remote *primum movens* of deism to the Heavenly Father of
theism. Since the theistic God is called upon to guarantee the meaningfulness
of life and the final triumph of good over evil, it looks like He will have to reserve
to Himself ultimate control over the course of events. But divine control will be
hamstrung and God's purposes jeopardized if events can ever catch Him by
surprise, or find Him *unprepared*, or force Him to *react* after the fact to patch
things up. This means that God must have the ability to anticipate where events
are headed. Since the world includes voluntary agents possessing the power to
initiate new directions in the stream of events, the future cannot be anticipated
simply by understanding the present tendencies of things. It would appear, then,

* © *Faith and Philosophy*, vol. 10 (1993). Reprinted by permission of the publisher.

that the kind of providential control expected of a theistic God is possible only on the assumption of foreknowledge.

Unfortunately, the ontological and providential arguments for divine foreknowledge are matched by powerful arguments on the other side. One kind of opposing argument maintains that foreknowledge is logically *impossible*, on the grounds that there are no truths about the future to be known; another holds that the attribution of foreknowledge to God, while innocent of logical incoherence, is nevertheless *too costly*, since it is incompatible with the existence of voluntary agents; and yet another, while granting both the possibility and affordability of divine omniprescience, insists that foreknowledge is providentially *useless*, since a proper analysis of the providential appeal to foreknowledge shows such knowledge to be subversive of the very control it is supposed to be enhancing. Of course, logical impossibility and prohibitive costliness are far more compelling grounds for rejecting a divine attribute than is uselessness, and the attention paid to the first two arguments in the literature is a reflection of this. Nevertheless, the conclusion of the last argument is damaging enough: it would be a hollow victory indeed if the defenders of the traditional conception of God succeeded in establishing divine foreknowledge via the ontological argument only to find that such knowledge cannot be used by Him in the way presupposed by the providential argument.

It is the last of these challenges to foreknowledge—the practical challenge arising from objections to its providential utility—that I wish to examine in the pages ahead. The position that divine foreknowledge may contribute toward the providential governance of the world (which I shall refer to henceforth as 'the traditional view') seems to have fallen on hard times lately. Indeed, there appears to be something of a consensus forming around the idea that 'there are [only] two accounts compatible with a libertarian view of freedom which stand a real chance of offering a coherent account of God's providential activity within the world': the 'Molinist' account, according to which divine providence and foreknowledge are both dependent on God's middle knowledge, and the 'Free-Will Theist' account, according to which both middle knowledge and foreknowledge are objectionable and God must therefore embark on providential endeavors without any precognitive guarantees.[1] If Molinism (which offers God even more providential control than the traditional view) and Free-Will Theism (which offers considerably less) really are the only coherent positions, the middle ground occupied by the traditional view is excluded, and anyone seeking more providential control than can be found in Free-Will Theism must accept the fact that 'Molinism is the only game in town.'[2] If this assessment is correct, however, the

---

[1] Thomas P. Flint, 'Hasker's *God, Time, and Knowledge*,' *Philosophical Studies* 60 (Sept.-Oct. 1990), p. 103; I borrow the term 'Free-Will Theism' from William Hasker, 'Providence and Evil: Three Theories,' *Religious Studies* 28 (March 1992), pp. 91–105.

[2] William Hasker, 'Response to Thomas Flint,' *Philosophical Studies* 60 (Sept.-Oct. 1990), p. 118.

coherence of a robust doctrine of divine providence rests on a theory which itself has been widely rejected as incoherent. I will not add to that discussion here;[3] but I do wish to suggest that this dismissal of the traditional view from the playing field is premature. My purpose in the present paper is to make a case for resisting the new consensus on the providential uselessness of foreknowledge.

I

In a story told by Richard Taylor, a character named 'Osmo' discovers a book recounting the future course of Osmo's own life, including his death in the crash of an airplane flying to Fort Wayne. The unerring accuracy with which the book's forecasts come true, one after the other, instills in Osmo a growing confidence in its pronouncements; indeed, it is soon clear that Osmo, through consulting the book, *knows* in advance what is going to happen to him. When events conspire to place him on the appointed flight at the appointed time, he desperately attempts to divert the plane away from Fort Wayne, only to have it crash as a result of those very efforts.[4]

Let us use the term 'providential control' simply to denote an agent's capacity for affecting the future in an intentional way, thus disengaging the concept from any necessary connection with the Deity and ignoring for present purposes any normative connotations the term may have. Then Osmo is clearly engaging in an attempt at providential control—namely, control over the time and circumstances of his death—and this attempt is inspired by foreknowledge. The sorry results of his mid-air intervention appear to illustrate the problematic nature of the providential use of foreknowledge. But what exactly *are* the problems that this episode is supposed to illustrate?

One problem, it might be thought, is that Osmo's appeal to foreknowledge is directed toward the logically incoherent task of changing a future that is unchangeable because it is fixed by the truth of the statements in the book. The first thing that needs to be said about this identification of the problem is that changing the future—that is, acting in such a way that something that will in fact happen does not in fact happen—is indeed incoherent. But this incoherence has nothing to do with whether the future is fixed or known (ignorance of the future would not make Osmo any more successful in changing it). If the future includes the predicted plane crash, Osmo's actions on board the plane might help *bring about* this future event (as they do in the story), or they might have *no effect at all* on this future event; what is impossible is that they should *prevent* this future event.

---

[3] I have expressed theoretical doubts about Molinism in 'Middle Knowledge: The "Foreknowledge Defense,"' *International Journal for Philosophy of Religion* 28 (August 1990), pp. 1–24, and practical doubts in 'Middle Knowledge and the Soteriological Problem of Evil,' *Religious Studies* 27 (March 1991), pp. 3–26.

[4] *Metaphysics*, 3rd edition (Englewood Cliffs: Prentice-Hall, 1983), pp. 54–6.

It is a mistake, then, to make *changing the future* the criterion for providential success, and then identify the inevitability of failure under this criterion as the fundamental problem with the providential use of foreknowledge. Providential success, whether guided by foreknowledge or not, should be judged instead by whether one's actions help bring about a future that matches one's intentions. By this standard, Osmo could avoid failure through the simple expedient of changing his intentions (e.g., to acceptance of his impending death). Indeed, we can easily imagine other incidents from Osmo's life in which his providential employment of the foreknowledge available through the book is successful in just this sense. We might suppose, for example, that Osmo comes across the following sentence while reading chapter 28 of the book: 'On May 8, while walking past 7th and Elm on his way to work, Osmo finds a lottery ticket bearing the winning numbers.' Osmo rejoices at his pending good fortune, but reflects that he has never before taken that particular route to work. With the intention of finding the winning ticket, Osmo remembers as he leaves home on May 8 to follow a route that takes him by the corner of 7th and Elm; the ticket is there, and Osmo cashes it in for five million dollars. In this episode, unlike the one aboard the plane, Osmo makes successful use of the foreknowledge that is available to him through the book: it is *because* he foreknows his finding the ticket at 7th and Elm that he decides to take that route to work; it is *because* he decides to take that route to work that he finds the winning ticket; and his finding the ticket accords with his *intentions*.

Clarifying the notion of providential success does nothing to alleviate the other aspect of the problem, which stems from the apparent fixity of the predicted events; for if the plane crash and the discovery of the ticket are fixed, Osmo's actions (whether successful or not) can't make any difference to what happens. This worry really consists of two parts: (1) that there *is* nothing that would make a difference; and (2) that even if there is something that would make a difference, Osmo can't do it. But neither of these concerns has any foundation in the facts of Osmo's story. Regarding (1), an action presumably 'makes a difference' if the results of performing that action would be different from the results of not performing it. But clearly, if Osmo does not board a plane that day, he will not die in a plane crash; and if he takes his usual route to work, he will not find the lottery ticket on the corner of 7th and Elm. There are no grounds, then, for maintaining that nothing could make a difference to what happens. As for (2), this concern seems to arise from the view that the plane crash and the discovery of the winning lottery ticket are 'locked in' by Osmo's foreknowledge of them—since knowledge is never false, these events are bound to occur, and Osmo cannot do anything to prevent them from occurring (such as avoiding planes and keeping away from 7th and Elm). But this concern rests on a simple modal fallacy endemic to arguments for fatalism. All that follows from the fact that Osmo will die on the plane, or win the lottery, is that he *won't* do anything to prevent these things; it does not follow that he *can't*. A world in which Osmo fails to walk by 7th and Elm on May 8 is not an impossible world containing a false knowledge-claim, but a possible world in which a belief that constitutes knowledge in the actual world does *not* constitute knowledge (because it is false).

Few critics of the providential use of foreknowledge would consciously make the mistakes embodied in this first statement of the problem. I have gone into them only because a fatalistic analysis of Osmo's situation is very seductive (Taylor himself being a notable victim), and we need to be on our guard against it. Once we have rejected this red herring it is easier to see where more credible threats to Osmo's use of foreknowledge might lie. Two of these are of particular importance.

The first of these problems presupposes a certain understanding of how Osmo's beliefs are connected to the future through the book. As Taylor tells the story, the connection begins with God's foreknowledge of events; God then conveys this information to a scribe who collects it in the book that later comes into Osmo's possession. Taylor says nothing about how God comes to have such knowledge, but it will be helpful in setting up this first problem if we suppose God to be equipped with what is called 'simple foreknowledge.' Simple foreknowledge is distinguished by its origin in a direct noninferential apprehension of the future. This capacity may be thought of as analogous to ordinary vision, except that its object lies in the future. The significance of this point is that 'previsional' awareness, like ordinary vision, is *dependent* (counterfactually, at least) on its (future) object. Now if God's knowledge that Osmo will find the winning lottery ticket at 7th and Elm is of this type, then it is dependent on the actual future event which is Osmo's finding of the ticket; Osmo's belief, too, is dependent on this future event, since it is dependent on God's knowledge. But not only is Osmo's belief dependent on the discovery of the ticket—in the story, Osmo's decision to walk by 7th and Elm is dependent on his belief, and his discovery of the ticket in turn is dependent on his decision. It looks like Osmo's discovery of the ticket involves a circle of dependence in which his foreknowledge helps bring about the very future that he foreknows. But the assumption that such a metaphysical 'loop' is possible might well be incoherent. The principle at stake—call it the 'Metaphysical Principle'—can be stated as follows:

> (MP) It is impossible that a decision depend on a belief which depends on a future event which depends on the original decision.[5]

I shall call the conflict between the Metaphysical Principle and the providential use of foreknowledge the 'Metaphysical Problem.'

---

[5] (MP) may itself be an instance of a more general principle—e.g., 'It is impossible that an event e_2 depend on an event e_2 which depends on an event e_2 which depends on the original event e_1.' But given that I do not examine or challenge the principle in the present paper, it seems best to leave it in the more specific form that is directly relevant to the issue of divine providence. I hope to take up the truth of (MP) and related principles on another occasion.

The second problem afflicting Osmo's providential use of foreknowledge is this. Osmo has come to believe what the book says, and what the book says is that he *will* (unconditionally) find the winning lottery ticket—a considerably stronger claim than the conditional, '*If* Osmo walks by the corner of 7th and Elm on May 8, *then* he will find the winning ticket.' This unconditional belief is already in place when it comes time for Osmo to decide whether to deviate from his usual route to work on May 8. But this belief which precedes his decision is (in part) a belief about what he is going to decide. This conflicts with the maxim that 'one cannot deliberate over what one already knows is going to happen,' or as I shall phrase it,

> (DP) It is impossible to hold the belief that *p* while deciding to bring it about that *p*.

I shall call this the 'Doxastic Principle,' and the threat it poses to the providential use of foreknowledge the 'Doxastic Problem.' Osmo can escape the Doxastic Problem, despite his antecedent knowledge of what is going to happen, only if his walking by the corner of 7th and Elm is not the result of a decision, or if he forgets the information imparted to him by the book prior to his making the decision. In either case he would be escaping the problem only by failing to make providential use of his foreknowledge.

We have identified two distinct problems with Osmo's exercise of providential control. Supposing for the moment that these problems are genuine, what implications do they have for providential control in general? More to the point, what implications do they have for the kind of control exercised by God?

The answer depends in part on the kind of foreknowledge that God possesses. Suppose God's foreknowledge involves projections from present or past conditions (call this 'projective foreknowledge'). Then it is not metaphysically dependent on future events, and the Metaphysical Problem does not arise. Neither does the Doxastic Problem. If God's inference from past to future is based on a contingent connection between events, then His inference must always be accompanied by the proviso, 'so long as I do nothing to interfere.' But then God cannot rely on the inference to yield foreknowledge unless He has already decided not to interfere; thus His decision not to interfere cannot be informed by His foreknowledge. If, on the other hand, God's inference is based on a necessary connection which is beyond the scope of His omnipotence to contravene, the future event which He knows on the basis of this necessary connection cannot be an object of providential control. In either case, other problems with projective foreknowledge undermine its providential employment, so that the conditions triggering the Doxastic Problem never arise.

Another kind of foreknowledge is based on inferences from middle knowledge (call this 'subjunctive foreknowledge'). Subjunctive foreknowledge clearly has the wrong parentage to trigger the Metaphysical Problem, and in any event, there is no occasion for it ever to be used providential. Since middle knowledge is a far more potent resource for providential control than foreknowledge,[6] a rational agent in command of this resource would surely base her providential decisions directly on middle knowledge, rather than first inferring subjunctive foreknowledge and then appealing to this inferior providential resource for guidance. Thus the beliefs that make up God's subjunctive foreknowledge would never stand to the objects of His providential decisions in the way required by the Doxastic Problem.

In sum, projective and subjunctive foreknowledge are providentially useless for reasons that have nothing to do with the Metaphysical and Doxastic Problems. This leaves simple foreknowledge as the only form of prescience that could contribute to divine providential control.[7] But since simple foreknowledge consists of beliefs that are dependent on future events and are available prior to providential decision-making, the possession of simple foreknowledge makes God's providential position at least potentially prone to both the Metaphysical and Doxastic Problems. For critics of the traditional view, God is in no better (if not an even worse) position for avoiding these problems than is Osmo. William Hasker, for example, claims that 'simple foreknowledge is *entirely useless* for the doctrine of providence,' and justifies this claim by appealing to a version of the Metaphysical Principle: 'since the decision's *actually having been made* is presupposed by God's *knowledge* of the future,' Hasker writes, 'he cannot possibly *use* that knowledge in deciding how to *influence* that decision.' He then adds: 'In the logical order of dependence of events, one might say, by the "time" God knows something will happen, it is "too late" either to *bring about* its happening or to *prevent* it from happening.'[8] And similarly strong claims are made on behalf of the Doxastic Problem by Richard Taylor, Richard La Croix, and Tomis Kapitan.[9]

Whether these critics are correct in implicating God along with Osmo in providential futility depends in part on what thesis about the providential use of

---

[6] How *much* more potent is a subject of some dispute. For a variety of opinions on this question, see: David Basinger, 'Middle Knowledge and Classical Christian Thought,' *Religious Studies* 22 (Sept./Dec. 1986), pp. 407–22; Alfred J. Freddoso, 'Introduction,' Luis de Molina's *On Divine Foreknowledge* (Part IV of the *Concordia*), trans., with intro. & notes, by Alfred J. Freddoso (Ithaca: Cornell U. Press, 1988); Thomas P. Flint, 'Two Accounts of Providence,' in *Divine and Human Action: Essays in the Metaphysics of Theism*, ed. by Thomas V. Morris (Ithaca & London: Cornell University Press, 1988), pp. 147–81 (this volume, ch. 1); David Gordon & James Sadowsky, 'Does Theism Need Middle Knowledge?' *Religious Studies* 25 (March 1989), pp. 75–87; and David Basinger, 'Middle Knowledge and Divine Control: Some Clarifications,' *International Journal for Philosophy of Religion* 30 (December 1991), pp. 129–39.

[7] For this reason, whenever I refer simply to *foreknowledge* in subsequent pages I should be understood to mean *simple foreknowledge*.

[8] *God, Time, and Knowledge* (Ithaca & London: Cornell University Press, 1989), pp. 59, 57–8. The Metaphysical Problem is also at work, if less explicitly, in Basinger, 'Middle Knowledge and Classical Christian Thought,' *op. cit.*, and in William Lane Craig, *The Only Wise God* (Grand Rapids: Baker Book House, 1987), ch. 12.

[9] Taylor, 'Deliberation and Foreknowledge,' *American Philosophical Quarterly* 1 (January 1964), pp. 73–80; La Croix, 'Omniprescience and Divine Determinism,' *Religious Studies* 12 (Sept. 1976), pp. 365–81; and Kapitan, 'Can God Make Up His Mind?' *International Journal for Philosophy of Religion* 15 (1984), pp. 37–47.

foreknowledge they take themselves to be refuting. We must turn now to a consideration of these theses.

II

At a minimum, the position that foreknowledge can be providentially useful should entail that there are at least some conceivable cases in which the addition of simple foreknowledge to an agent's pool of knowledge would result in an incremental gain in the agent's providential control. Let us call this the '*Weak Thesis*,' and state it thus:

> (WT) It is possible for *some* foreknowledge to contribute to *more* providential control than would be available with *no* foreknowledge.

Assuming for the moment the essential correctness of our analysis of Osmo's endeavors to make providential use of his foreknowledge, can we conclude that the Weak Thesis is unacceptable? We cannot. A striking fact about Osmo's encounters with death and the lottery is that the state of affairs over which he was endeavoring to exercise providential control was precisely the state of affairs foreknowledge of which was supposed to be contributing to that control. This feature of the cases is essential to generating the incoherence brought out in our analysis; but it is surely not a feature that is essential to the providential use of foreknowledge in general.

Suppose that I exercise control over my future liberty by *fleeing the country today* because I have precognized that *a warrant will be issued for my arrest on Monday*. Here I utilize knowledge of the future to decide how to act in the present so as to bring about a certain result in the future, and thus employ foreknowledge in the exercise of providential control. But because my exercise of control (in this case, fleeing the country) neither involves, nor is believed by me to involve, the prevention or bringing about of any future state of affairs (in this case, the issuing of the warrant) which either contributes, or is believed by me to contribute, to my decision to exercise providential control, neither the Metaphysical nor the Doxastic Problem appears to have a foothold in this case.

That this is so may be clearest with respect to the Doxastic Problem. What is significant about the Weak Thesis is that it permits different objects for foreknowledge and providential decision-making. This helps against the Doxastic Problem in the following way. Since the Weak Thesis requires only that I have knowledge of *some* future events, it allows me to be ignorant of *others*, and there is no reason why my decision and its consequences may not be among the future events of which I am ignorant at the time that I am making my decision. The possibility of different objects for foreknowledge and providential decision-making is not sufficient to ward off the Metaphysical Problem, however, since this problem may be triggered by distinct objects if they are connected in the right way. In particular, since the event which is the object of foreknowledge is later in time than any providential intervention based on that foreknowledge, this may raise the worry that it stands in the causal flow emanating from the intervention. For example, as soon as I respond to my foreknowledge of the pending arrest warrant with appropriate actions, such as purchasing a plane ticket, making large withdrawals from my savings accounts, etc., this can potentially affect the foreknown event—e.g., my suspicious activities might then be noticed by the authorities, who pick me up sooner than planned. The worry, in short, is that my decision, which assumes a future event, may in turn affect that event, thus undermining the original assumption.

This worry appears to be a version of the idea that, unless my actions are simply impotent, I should be able to change the future. This idea, as we saw, is confused. If I correctly foresee some event, then that foreseen event is a product of any interventions leading up to it, including any interventions I might make on the basis of my foreknowledge; those interventions won't *change* the event, whatever that might mean. Even if I inject into the causal stream an action which would ordinarily conduce to the quashing of the warrant, my action is nevertheless *logically* compatible with the issuance of the warrant (since they are distinct events). Thus the most that can be said is that the future might contain a miracle preventing my action from having an adverse effect on the issuance of the warrant. This, of course, is nowhere near the logical (or metaphysical) contradiction needed if the Metaphysical Problem is to refute the Weak Thesis.

It appears, then, that there is no good reason to reject the Weak Thesis. A more difficult question concerns the relevance of the Weak Thesis to divine providence. The critic might argue that, while there may be cases of the providential appeal to foreknowledge which work out better than Osmo's, it doesn't follow that any of these include God. Let us consider briefly three ways the critic might endeavor to flesh out this concern. None of them is very compelling.

The first objection is this. The Weak Thesis is satisfied even if only a minimal amount of foreknowledge is making only a minimal contribution to providential control. But on the traditional doctrine, God's foreknowledge and providential control are far from minimal—indeed, God is supposed to exercise *substantial* providential control on the basis of *complete* foreknowledge. This is precisely what generates the problem to which the critic wishes to direct our attention. In sum, the Weak Thesis is theologically irrelevant because it doesn't capture those features of the divine situation that make the providential use of foreknowledge problematic. These require a stronger thesis to bring out.

In reply to this first objection, it must be admitted that the traditional doctrine *does* ask for more than the Weak Thesis delivers; it is incumbent on us, then, to examine some stronger theses as well. But the truth of the Weak Thesis is nevertheless relevant to divine providence, since it reminds us that there is a large middle ground between the providential aspirations of the traditionalist and the deflationary challenges of the critic. Should the critic succeed in undermining some stronger thesis to which the traditionalist is committed, the Weak Thesis at least offers a place to stop before falling all the way back to zero. The traditionalist would surely want to hold onto the *most* foreknowledge and providential control possible. The success of the Weak Thesis shows that this is more than none.

A second objection is implicit in an article by David Basinger, in which he examines the adequacy of various forms of knowledge (present knowledge, middle knowledge, and simple foreknowledge) for the classical doctrine of divine providence. The crucial question that Basinger asks of each candidate is this: 'Can [God] be assured ... that his decisions concerning future states of affairs involving free choices will have the desired results? Or must he ... gamble to some extent?'[10] It is clear that for Basinger any account of divine knowledge on which God ends up a 'cosmic gambler' is to be rejected. Since God will undertake a providential intervention only when He knows that it will be successful, knowledge of the actual consequences of His action is itself a condition of His acting. This means that God makes providential use of simple foreknowledge only under conditions stronger than those set forth in the Weak Thesis.

One must ask, however, why God would require a guarantee of success before acting. Consider, for example, the providential arrangement of an *opportunity* which a person can either accept or decline. If it is ever the case that God would arrange such an opportunity even though He knew that it would be declined (and His will go unfulfilled), Basinger's requirement of a providential guarantee is too strong. It may also be unattainable, if the Metaphysical Problem is genuine and the only source of a guarantee is simple foreknowledge. For Basinger, the ideal of guaranteed success makes sense because there is another source from which it can derive, namely, divine middle knowledge (if God brings about the antecedent of a true counterfactual of freedom, it is guaranteed that the consequent will occur).[11] But given the controversy surrounding this putative cognitive capacity, it is surely legitimate (and imperative) to explore how much divine providence can be purchased without drawing on the suspect currency of middle knowledge.

The third objection to the theological relevance of the Weak Thesis comes from a recent book by William Hasker. Hasker, as we have seen, takes a hard line against the providential use of foreknowledge; moreover, he clearly intends to extend this line to the Weak Thesis, since he formulates the position he is arguing against as one according to which 'God, because he foreknows that a certain event will occur, may prearrange *other* factors in the situation in such a way as to produce the best overall result'[12]—the very scenario which is supposed to save the Weak Thesis from Osmo-like gridlock. Hasker gives the following example of

---

[10] *Op. cit.*, p. 414.

[11] For Basinger's most recent (and moderated) position on the providential resources of middle knowledge, see his 'Middle Knowledge and Divine Control: Some Clarifications,' *op. cit.*

[12] *Op. cit.*, p. 58.

such a case: God foreknows the Allied encirclement at Dunkirk and begins arranging weather patterns so that the encirclement will coincide with heavy fog and calm seas, preventing the Luftwaffe from bombing and allowing the Allies to escape across the English Channel with minimal casualties. The reason this is incoherent, according to Hasker, is that the simple foreknowledge the traditionalist attributes to God must be a knowledge of concrete events rather than mere propositions, and concrete events presuppose 'the entirety of the causally relevant past history of the universe,'[13] including any attempts at divine intervention. Since the concrete future event which is the Allied encirclement at Dunkirk is made up of innumerable lesser events (sentries peering into the night, planes returning to hangars, generals poring over maps), and the character of these events is influenced by the weather, God is basing his meteorological intervention on foreknowledge of a concrete event which is itself partly a product of that intervention. What Hasker appears to be arguing is that, once we grasp what divine simple foreknowledge really involves (namely, knowledge of concrete events rather than propositions), we will realize that God cannot satisfy the conditions of the Weak Thesis without also satisfying the conditions of some stronger thesis that triggers either the Metaphysical or Doxastic Problem (or both).

This objection is not convincing, however. In the first place, just because God *has* detailed concrete knowledge does not mean that these concrete details are providentially relevant. God intervenes to help the Allies, not because of a concrete event, but because of an abstraction from that event: the fact that the event constitutes *the encirclement of the Allies*. In the second place, Hasker has chosen for his example the kind of intervention that might not only contribute to the Allied escape but also affect the details of the encirclement. Not every intervention has this feature. Suppose instead that God, endowed with simple foreknowledge of the Allied encirclement, responds by accelerating the spoilage of a consignment of sausage which is scheduled to be served to the German troops on the eve of the evacuation, with the result that the entire Luftwaffe is immobilized with food poisoning the following morning. It's not clear how Hasker's argument would work against a case like this; and if it doesn't, the Weak Thesis survives.

Finally, even if Hasker's argument is successful, the traditionalist might respond by retaining divine prescience but rejecting Hasker's account of it (perhaps denying that God's vision of concrete future events is 20/20, or that foreknowledge of one event presupposes knowledge of the entire causally relevant past history of the universe). This may lead to a weaker thesis regarding the providential use of foreknowledge than the traditionalist may have hoped for, but partial foreknowledge combined with partial providential control is surely better

---

[13] *Op. cit.*, p. 61.

than nothing. It is precisely because the Weak Thesis is better than nothing that it is theologically significant.

III

The Weak Thesis, then, appears to be immune to the kinds of problems that afflict Osmo's attempts to avoid death and win the lottery, and also to be theologically significant in case no stronger thesis is sustainable. But the traditionalist would surely *like* more than the Weak Thesis offers, if he can get it. The next question we must consider, then, is how far the Weak Thesis could be strengthened before generating either the Metaphysical or the Doxastic Problem. Since the apparent moral of the story of Osmo is that the providential use of foreknowledge is subject to failure when the object of foreknowledge and the object of providential control coincide, the critic needs to show that defenders of the traditional doctrine are committed to a thesis that entails the coincidence of these objects.

One way to guarantee at least some coincidence in the objects of foreknowledge and of providential control is to add to the Weak Thesis the requirement that *either* foreknowledge *or* providential control be *complete*. If it is foreknowledge that is complete, then any consequence of any act of providential control is already known; and if it is providential control that is complete, then any foreknown event will be an object of providential control. Either way, any case satisfying the modified thesis would have to involve at least some Osmo-like attempt at providential control over an event whose occurrence (or the consequences of whose occurrence) is foreknown. Few defenders of the providential utility of foreknowledge, however, would endorse a thesis that requires divine control over every event, since this is generally thought to be incompatible with the existence of voluntary agents other than God. If the critic is to catch anything more than straw men (or hyper-Calvinists) in his net, he would be advised to forego an attack on this modification of the Weak Thesis and instead focus on the version that requires complete foreknowledge. This new thesis can be stated as follows:

> (ST) It is possible for *complete* foreknowledge to contribute to *more* providential control than would be available with *no* foreknowledge.

I shall call this the '*Strong Thesis*.'

Let us first consider the Strong Thesis in light of the Metaphysical Problem. This shouldn't detain us for long. If we were correct in concluding that the Weak Thesis avoids the Metaphysical Problem, the Strong Thesis must avoid it as well. The reason is that the Strong Thesis adds only the *possession* of complete foreknowledge to the provisions of the Weak Thesis; but the Metaphysical Problem depends on how foreknowledge is *used*, not on how much is *possessed*.

Consider, for example, its use in the case where I flee the country because I precognize the issuance of a warrant for my arrest—a use which we have seen to be innocent of any Osmo-like problems. Now imagine the range of my precognition to increase until complete foreknowledge is achieved. What is there in this increase in knowledge that could trigger the Metaphysical Problem? Most of what I learn along the way, such as the figures for next year's wheat harvest in the Ukraine and the name of the next Western to win an Academy Award, will be patently irrelevant to my attempts to stay out of jail. Of course, complete foreknowledge will include more relevant items as well: not only the issuance of the warrant (which was so providentially useful when I possessed only partial foreknowledge), but also the fact that next Tuesday I will be in Brazil. But so long as I don't base my decision to flee the country on my knowledge of where I will be next Tuesday, the Metaphysical Problem has no purchase on the situation. Since there is nothing in the Strong Thesis to require the providential *use* of an item of foreknowledge which happens to coincide with the object of providential control, the Strong Thesis should be no more objectionable than the Weak when it comes to the Metaphysical Problem.

The Strong Thesis may still seem pretty weak, since it does not include any requirement that the amount of providential control exceed a certain minimum. But it's not clear how any (plausible) strengthening of the providential component of the Strong Thesis would make it any easier for the critic to implicate it in the Metaphysical Problem. Consider, for example, the *Stronger Thesis*:

> (ST+) It is possible for *complete* foreknowledge to contribute to *more* providential control than would be available with only *some* foreknowledge.

There is a problem specifying which bodies of partial foreknowledge must be providentially inferior to complete foreknowledge for the thesis to be true; but it clearly *cannot* be true unless at least some of the marginal gain from complete foreknowledge is *used*, not merely *possessed*. There is no basis in the Metaphysical Problem, however, for supposing that more providential control will not result from more foreknowledge. What the Metaphysical Problem reveals is the danger of using simple foreknowledge in such a way that circles of dependence are generated. But additional foreknowledge simply gives an agent greater flexibility to combine actions with precognitive grounds for action in ways that do not generate circles. Thus the Metaphysical Problem provides no reason for rejecting the Stronger Thesis. Nor is it even clear what threat it poses to the *Strongest Thesis*:

> (ST++) It is possible for *complete* foreknowledge to contribute to *maximal* providential control.

('Maximal providential control' refers here to the strongest control compatible with there being free agents other than God.) What the critic has to show is that there is no way to set up the dependence-relations required by the Strongest Thesis without generating a circle. But since maximal providential control does not encompass all foreknown events (in particular, it excludes events which are exercises of free will), this leaves open the possibility that foreknowledge of these uncontrolled events might be utilized in the production of maximal providential control in such a way that circularity is avoided—at least it is very difficult to see how the critic would go about proving the contrary.

So none of these theses—the Strong, the Stronger, or the Strongest—appears to force the Metaphysical Problem. This doesn't mean that we can't construct theses about God's providential use of foreknowledge that *would* generate this problem. Consider, for example, the theses that would result from adding the following conditions to the Strong Thesis:

(C_1) that God must utilize *all* of His complete foreknowledge in every exercise of providential control that He undertakes (entailing that any providential act and its consequences will be not only foreknown but *used* by God in deciding to act in that way);

(C_2) that every item in God's complete foreknowledge must be used for some exercise of providential control or another (entailing that every future event is such that some providential act is metaphysically dependent upon it);

(C_3) that every future event is the object of some exercise of the providential use of foreknowledge (entailing that every future event is metaphysically dependent on some providential act).[14]

But $(C_1) - (C_3)$ are obviously absurd conditions to attach to the providential use of foreknowledge, and no theist ought to accept them. Thus their involvement in the Metaphysical Problem has no implications for the traditional position on divine omniprescience.

The Metaphysical Problem does broach issues that are worth discussing further. For example, I have left the notion of *metaphysical dependence* vague, and have refrained from questioning the Metaphysical Principle itself. Pursuing such questions might undercut the Metaphysical Problem even further. David Lewis, for one, maintains that causal loops, while *inexplicable*, are nevertheless *possible*.[15] If he is right, the Metaphysical Principle would have to be reformulated in terms of inexplicability rather than impossibility, and it's not clear what would be left of the Metaphysical Problem at that point. Nevertheless, enough has been said to warrant dismissing the Metaphysical Problem as a serious threat to the providential use of foreknowledge.

The strongest case against the Strong Thesis derives from the Doxastic Problem. The Metaphysical Problem requires that foreknowledge be *used* in

---

[14] The idea behind (C_2) and (C_3) is that the chain of dependence between acts and events must finally double back on itself, generating the circle constitutive of the Metaphysical Problem. But even this isn't clear, if the set of future events is infinite.

[15] 'The Paradoxes of Time Travel,' *American Philosophical Quarterly* 13 (April 1976), pp. 145–52.

quite specific ways, but we have failed to turn up any feature of God's providential situation that would force Him to comply with this requirement. The Doxastic Problem, on the other hand, requires only that foreknowledge (fore-belief) be *possessed*. Thus the Strong Thesis, in positing the possession of complete foreknowledge, goes beyond the Weak Thesis in a way that is relevant to the Doxastic Problem.

Let us take a closer look at the effect the Doxastic Problem would have on the providential use of foreknowledge, assuming that the problem is genuine. The critic who admits the possibility of cases in which foreknowledge can improve the degree of one's providential control (e.g., my fleeing the country in light of advance intelligence that I am to be arrested) might still insist that foreknowledge can work in this case only because certain other facts about the future (e.g., that I actually will flee the country, and any other truths from which this one could be inferred) are excluded from the decision-process—fore*knowledge* about some things requires fore*ignorance* about other things if it is to be providentially useful. This relation between knowledge and ignorance can be clarified by distinguishing two factors relevant to judging the degree of an agent's providential control: one factor is how well-informed the agent is when deliberating over what to do (call this the *quality* of control); the other is the range of states of affairs over which the agent can exercise control (call this the *quantity* of control). Foreknowledge, like knowledge in general, makes its providential contribution by increasing the quality of an agent's control. But every future state of affairs that enters into the agent's foreknowledge is a state of affairs over which the agent can no longer exercise providential control, on pain of generating the Doxastic Problem. Thus every increase in quality means a decrease in quantity. Perhaps initially the loss in quantity will be eclipsed by the sharp rise in the quality of providential control made possible by foreknowledge, and the overall degree of providential control (some product of quantity x quality) will go up; but sooner or later the arc of control must flatten out and begin a steep plummet as the agent is left with fewer and fewer decisions about the future to which her awesome foreknowledge can contribute. At the end, endowed with total foreknowledge, the agent is equipped to make maximally informed decisions—but there is nothing left open to be decided. Providential control ends up stultified by too much knowledge. And, one might add, this is precisely the situation of an omniprescient God.[16]

This is a plausible picture, and its implications for the traditional view are devastating, since it shows that the possession of complete foreknowledge would not merely stymie all providential control *based on foreknowledge* (as under the

---

[16] The curve hypothesized in this paragraph presupposes that the initial gains in simple foreknowledge as one heads away from 0 along the x-axis are weighted toward future events that are both (1) relevant to providential control (so that there are events over which my control has actually increased) and (2) themselves not within my control (so that knowledge of them doesn't stultify my control over events I would otherwise control, thus decreasing control commensurately with the increase brought about by (1)).

Metaphysical Problem), but would stymie all providential control *simpliciter*, thus leaving the erstwhile controller even worse off than with no foreknowledge at all (since at least some providential control is available even without fore-knowledge). This picture does, however, give further point to the earlier discussion of a fallback position for the traditionalist in case she is driven out of her favored position on divine providence. The rejection of complete foreknowledge, if it is warranted by the Doxastic Problem, should lead the theist to search for some optimal combination of (partial) foreknowledge with (partial) providential control. Such an optimal combination might plausibly be identified as the high point of the curve discussed in the preceding paragraph; and this high point, which corresponds to the maximum providential control available without middle knowledge, involves *some foreknowledge*.

Of course, the idea that the traditionalist might have to accept partial fore-knowledge combined with partial providential control assumes that the picture just presented is correct. There are grounds for doubting this, however.

IV

In discussing the Metaphysical Problem, I simply accepted the Metaphysical Principle and challenged instead the critic's claim that it conflicts with any thesis the traditionalist might be supposed to endorse regarding God's providential use of foreknowledge. A different strategy will have to be pursued as we examine the Doxastic Problem, however, since the principle at work here clearly *is* in conflict with the Strong Thesis. It appears that the only way to prevent the Doxastic Problem from jeopardizing any minimally robust version of the traditional doctrine is to challenge the Doxastic Principle itself.

One way to do this is to examine the kind of knowledge that is supposed to be incompatible with decision-making. As Aristotle recognized, the person who is even now correctly identifying the most famous student of Socrates and the person who hasn't a clue occupy the endpoints of a wide cognitive spectrum. Between them lie, e.g., the person who knows but isn't thinking about it at the moment (this is the usual context for knowledge-attribution); the person who has learned the answer and still retains it, but is having trouble recalling it ('Come on, you know the answer!' we might say); the person who once knew, has since forgotten, but can still be reminded by some external stimulus; and the person who doesn't have the answer, but at least knows how to get it. Adopting a computer model, we might say that knowledge can exist in either an *accessed* or (as in the examples just cited) an *unaccessed* form. But the Doxastic Principle almost certainly requires accessed knowledge if it is to be at all plausible; thus the Strong Thesis can evade this problem *if* unaccessed beliefs may be counted in determining the extent of an agent's foreknowledge.

While the traditionalist may have reason to reject this conception of divine omniprescience, the existence of this alternative shows that criticisms based on the Doxastic Problem need to be supplemented by some discussion of God's cognitive structure if they are to have any chance of success. Moreover, this model can be used to strengthen the 'optimal combination' proposal from the previous section. That proposal raises the question of how God could come by *some* foreknowledge without possessing *all* foreknowledge—in particular, how He could come by just those items of foreknowledge (and no others) that would optimize His providential control. But these questions can be answered by assuming the computer model, since God would then possess complete unaccessed foreknowledge and simply access whatever would maximize providential control without stultification. For example, suppose that God, wishing to aid the Allies, decides that the quality of His control will increase dramatically if He knows what Hitler will decide on a certain day. He then (and only then) accesses that knowledge. This limits God's actions in certain ways (e.g., He cannot know what Hitler will decide and then prevent Hitler from making that decision), but this loss is outweighed by the quality of control God can exercise over other future events.

We have seen how an appeal to 'unaccessed' knowledge might be used to defend the Strong Thesis (assuming that unaccessed knowledge can count toward divine omniprescience), and also to consolidate an attractive fallback position for the traditionalist if the Strong Thesis proves untenable. But we can do better than this, since the Doxastic Principle itself is false. This principle, I believe, owes its almost universal acceptance to thought-experiments in which one attempts to violate it. Let us look at one of these.

Suppose that a young lady named Sally is being pressed to choose between two importuning suitors, Lester and Chester. She seeks advice from a fortuneteller. Instead of advice, however, she gets a prediction: 'You will marry Chester.' On the one hand, Sally's natural credulity in the presence of fortunetellers inclines her to believe what she is told; on the other hand, the identity of her future spouse depends on what she decides, and she has not yet decided. Is it possible in these circumstances for her to believe first and decide later? Apparently not. If she yields to her credulity, she thereby pre-empts any decision she might have made. In the wake of her belief that she will marry Chester, there is simply nothing left to be decided.

If the response to this case is correct, we should be able to find something in the Doxastic Principle to explain *why* it can't be violated. What is the connection between deciding and believing that renders it impossible to believe that p while deciding to bring it about that p? If deciding were simply one way of *coming to believe*, this would give us the desired connection, since one can't *come to* believe if one *already* believes.[17] But this account of deciding must be rejected. There are

[17] Carl Ginet, for example, takes this position in 'Can the Will Be Caused?' *Philosophical Review* 71 (January 1962), pp. 49–55. The following remark, for example, may be found on p. 52: 'Yet the

other things involved in deciding, beyond simply coming to believe, and it is perfectly possible that someone who already knows what the decision will be might nevertheless persevere in deliberating in order to achieve some of these other things—for example, to secure a reassurance about the decision that comes from possessing good reasons.[18] Moreover, while foreknowledge and decision-making both lead to beliefs, what one comes to believe as a result of foreknowledge is a *propositional* belief about *what will happen*, whereas what one comes to believe as a result of deciding is a *practical* belief about *what to do*. The former does not entail the latter; even if the propositional belief is acquired first, it may still be necessary to go through the actual process of decision-making in order to achieve the practical belief.[19] Other critics have found the link between deciding and believing in the principle that deciding presupposes *believing that the future is open*, a presupposition that is violated when one holds a belief about how the future will turn out.[20] But why must Sally's belief that she will marry Chester undermine her belief in an open future? She has no grounds for supposing that she *must* marry Chester, or that she *can't* pursue another course of action. If she nevertheless looks upon her future as closed, it only proves that she is as credulous about fatalism as she is about fortune-tellers.

Once the fundamental weakness in the Doxastic Principle is exposed, it is easy to think of cases for which the principle seems false. Suppose that Sally, torn between Lester and Chester, looks in frustration for a coin to flip. 'Heads it's Lester, tails it's Chester,' she says. The fortune-teller, in whom Sally has absolute confidence, lends her a coin, predicting that she will decide in favor of Chester. Sally believes her. It is clear that Sally's belief *need not* abort the decision-process that she has initiated. She flips the coin, believing that it will come up tails (as entailed by her choice of decision-procedure together with her credence in the fortune-teller's prediction). Note that, if the coin *were* to come up heads, she would decide in favor of Lester. Thus the decision-procedure is not merely 'idling.' This is perfectly compatible with Sally holding a (corrigible) belief about the outcome of that procedure.

One objection, from an article by Tomis Kapitan, merits special comment here.[21] Kapitan's objection comes in reply to the following example offered by Philip Quinn: Smith knows that, if White invites him to a concert, he will decide to attend; he then learns that White will in fact invite him, and infers that

whole point of making up one's mind is to pass from uncertainty to a kind of knowledge about what one will do or try to do.'

[18] Robin Small points this out in 'Fatalism and Deliberation,' *Canadian Journal of Philosophy* 18 (March 1988), pp. 13–30.

[19] This response to Ginet's argument may be found in J. W. Roxbee Cox, 'Can I Know Beforehand What I Am Going To Decide?' *Philosophical Review* 72 (Jan. 1963), pp. 88–92.

[20] E.g., Tomis Kapitan, 'Deliberation and the Presumption of Open Alternatives,' *Philosophical Quarterly* 36 (April 1986), pp. 230–51.

[21] 'Can God Make Up His Mind?' *op. cit.*

he will decide to attend.[22] Kapitan argues in response that the real decision is made when Smith decides *to attend if invited*, and this decision *precedes* Smith's knowledge that he will attend—thus it does not violate the Doxastic Principle. According to Kapitan, Smith does not decide anything when the invitation actually arrives; he merely *implements* a decision taken earlier. Presumably Kapitan would offer a similar analysis of Sally's choice between suitors: the real decision is made when she decides to settle the matter by flipping a coin; the actual toss of the coin is merely the implementation of this prior decision.

While there is some initial plausibility to Kapitan's analysis (it is true, after all, that Smith and Sally have each made an important decision which *precedes* their foreknowledge), his conclusion should nevertheless be resisted. If one's assent to attend a concert does not count as a decision if one has already formulated the conditional decision *to attend if invited*, there may be few if any decisions *ever* made.

At the risk of oversimplifying, let us divide decisions into those based on *criteria* and those that are not. Take a very simple decision of the first sort— whether or not to take an umbrella—which is to be settled according to the criterion: the presence or imminent threat of rain. To employ this criterion in a particular case means that I have *already* made the following conditional decision: if rain is falling or about to fall, I will take an umbrella. Now suppose that, on the basis of this criterion, I exit with an umbrella. If Kapitan's analysis is correct, I do not *decide* anything as I pass the umbrella rack on my way to the door—I merely implement a decision that I made some time ago when I chose a certain criterion, a criterion which now happens to be satisfied. Since no decision is made as I approach the door to go out, the Doxastic Principle is not violated if it happens that I knew yesterday, on the basis of a weather forecast, that I would take an umbrella with me today. But the same argument that leads to this conclusion will work for *any* decision based on a criterion. That means that the only genuine decisions—or at least the only decisions the Doxastic Principle should be construed as governing—are criterionless. This is itself a *reductio* of Kapitan's argument; alternatively, it is proof that the Doxastic Principle is not a principle governing all decisions, but only a special class of decisions (and a rather primitive class at that). There is no reason to think that God makes such decisions—or if He does, that His providential governance would be jeopardized due to the stultification of such decisions by His complete foreknowledge.[23]

Since the Doxastic Principle cannot be used to impugn foreknowledge of decisions based on criteria, we are free to accept the following picture of how

[22] 'Divine Foreknowledge and Divine Freedom,' *International Journal for Philosophy of Religion* 9 (1978), pp. 219–40. The example is on p. 234.

[23] Traditionalists who endeavor to evade the Doxastic Problem by denying that divine agency involves decision-making are still threatened by a version of (DP) which ignores decision-making and focuses directly on intentional agency. I rebut this version of (DP) in my 'Omniprescient Agency,' *Religious Studies* 28 (September 1992), pp. 351–69.

God might satisfy the Strong Thesis. The picture begins with God formulating judgments about what it would be best for Him to do in response to every possible set of conditions He might encounter. These judgments are of the form, 'If X obtains, it would be best to do Y.' Two points about such judgments should be noted. One is that they include the blueprints for every exercise of providential control that God might undertake. The other point is that, for some sets of conditions (including those involving the free choices of other agents), the best response is to take action before the conditions actually obtain; thus at least some of these judgments will be such that the conditions set forth in their antecedents are temporally later than the actions referred to in their consequents. Because God's will is directed unshakably toward the best, He relies on these judgments as He develops criteria for divine action. These criteria yield conditional decisions of the form, 'If X obtains, I will do Y.' These conditional decisions are independent of any knowledge God might have of the actual world; but once (in the logical order) these decisions are reached, He can draw on His knowledge of the actual world to determine which of these conditionals have true antecedents. Only then does He decide what response to make, and this response always follows the criteria He has adopted (since there could be no occasion for God to change His mind about these). Of course, He cannot act to implement a conditional decision unless He knows that its antecedent is true; in particular, for conditionals whose antecedents are temporally later than their consequents and refer to the choices of free agents, He cannot act unless He has simple foreknowledge. Thus simple foreknowledge allows God to undertake providential interventions that would not otherwise have been feasible, and only *complete* foreknowledge can guarantee that no conditional decision with a true antecedent will go unimplemented. This means that a God equipped with complete foreknowledge can satisfy not only the Strong Thesis, but the Stronger and (perhaps) the Strongest Theses as well.

In conclusion, I do not pretend to have solved all the problems surrounding the traditional view that omniprescience can play a useful role in God's providential governance of the world. What I do claim to have shown is that the standard criticisms of the traditional view, based on the Metaphysical and Doxastic Problems, do not succeed. If this claim is correct, the traditionalist is entitled to decline paying the price for divine providence set by the critic: the rejection of foreknowledge, or its assimilation to middle knowledge.

5

The Place of Chance in a World Sustained by God*

Peter van Inwagen

In this paper, I want to examine a number of interrelated issues in what might be called the metaphysics of divine action: creation, sustenance, law, miracle, providence, and chance. Thus my title is rather narrow for the topics considered. But it is the topic *chance* that I shall be working toward. My discussion of these other topics is a prolegomenon to my discussion of chance. (My discussion of chance, is, in its turn, a prolegomenon to a discussion of the problem of evil; but that is a topic for another time. In the present essay I shall lay out some implications of what I say about chance for the problem of evil, but I shall not directly discuss this problem, much less suggest a solution to it.)

I will begin with a discussion of God's relation to a certain object that might variously be called 'the world,' 'the universe,' 'Creation,' 'the cosmos,' or 'nature.' It is necessary for us to have a picture of this thing. I will provide a picture that is scientifically naïve and philosophically tendentious: the world consists of a certain number of small, indivisible units of matter I shall call 'elementary particles'; there is only one type of particle, and there are always just the same particles, and they are in constant motion in otherwise empty infinite three-dimensional space ('the void').

This picture could be called a Newtonian picture, although I don't insist on the absolute space or the 'absolute, true, and mathematical time' of Newton. It is, as I have said, from a scientific point of view, a naïve picture. But if it were replaced with the sort of physical world picture provided by quantum field theories like quantum electrodynamics and quantum chromodynamics, I do not think that this replacement would affect in any essential way the philosophical points I want to make. I therefore retain the naïve picture—not that I am equipped to carry on the discussion in the terms provided by any other picture.

The picture is philosophically tendentious. It presupposes that the created world is entirely material. But that could easily enough be changed. Anyone who wants to suppose that the created world contains, for example, Cartesian egos, may simply reject my assumption that the elementary particles are all indivisible units of matter, and assume that some of them are nonspatial and are capable of thought.[1] (A similar device could accommodate angels conceived as St. Thomas Aquinas conceives angles.) The generalizations I shall make about 'elementary particles' in the sequel do not in any *essential* way presuppose that elementary particles are spatial, nonthinking things. And the generalizations I shall make about created persons do not in any essential way presuppose that no created person is a Cartesian ego.

Having given this naïve and tendentious picture of the world or nature, I relate it—in a burst of simplistic picture-thinking—to God in the following way.

God created the world by bringing certain elementary particles into existence at some particular moment—six thousand years ago or twenty billion years ago or some such figure. These particles were at the moment of their creation suspended in the void—which is sheer emptiness, and not a physical object like the modern space-time or the modern quantum vacuum—and possessed of certain initial velocities. Each, moreover, possessed certain causal powers; that is, each possessed a certain intrinsic capacity to affect the motions of other particles.

Now these particles were (and are) not capable of maintaining themselves in existence or of conserving their own causal powers. For one of them to continue to exist, it is necessary for God continuously to hold it in existence. For it to have the same set of causal powers—the same set of capacities to affect the motions of other particles—at a series of instants, it is necessary for God at each instant to supply it with that set of causal powers. For that matter, for a particle to have *different* sets of causal powers at two or more instants is for that particle to be supplied with different sets of powers at those instants. To say that God once created, and now sustains, the *world* is to say no more than this: that God once created and now sustains certain particles—for the world, or nature, or the cosmos, or the universe, is nothing more than the sum of these particles. Moreover, every individual created thing is the sum of certain of these particles, and the point that was made about the created universe as a whole can be made about each individual created thing. If, for example, God sustains a bridge in existence and preserves its causal powers—its capacity to bear a ten-ton load, for example—this action is just the sum of all the actions He performs in sustaining in existence and preserving the causal powers of the elementary particles that are the ultimate constituents of the bridge; the powers, that is, by which they so affect one another as to continue to form a configuration that exhibits a certain degree of stability.

[1] Unless this philosopher accepts the Platonic doctrine of the preexistence of the soul (as well as its immortality), he will also want to reject my assumption that there are always the same elementary particles.

And this is the entire extent of God's causal relations with the created world. He does not, for example, *move* particles—or not in any very straightforward sense. Rather, the particles move one another, albeit their capacity to do so is continuously supplied by God. Here is an analogy. Suppose that two pieces of soft iron are wound round with wires and a current passed through the wires. The two pieces of iron then become electromagnets, and, if they are close to one another and free to move, they begin to move in virtue of the forces they are exerting upon each other. It would be odd to say that the generator that is supplying the current to the wires was moving the two pieces of iron. It is more natural to say that the generator is moving only electrons, and that the pieces of iron are *moving each other*, this movement being a function of their relative dispositions and the causal powers that are (in a sense) being supplied to them by the generator.

This is everything I want to say about the way in which God acts in and sustains the created world—with one omission. We have not yet raised the question whether the causal powers of a given particle are constant over time. Let us suppose that this is at least very nearly true: Each particle always, or almost always, has the same causal powers.[2] That is, God always, or almost always, supplies it with the same set of causal powers. Now we have assumed, for the sake of convenience, that there is only one type of elementary particle. It seems reasonable to suppose that causal powers are the only relevant factor in classifying elementary particles into 'types.' It would follow that the causal powers possessed by a given particle at a given time are almost certainly identical with the causal powers possessed by any other particle at any other time. (This picture of God's action in the world has an interesting consequence. Consider again the example of God's sustaining a bridge in existence and preserving its causal powers. The particles that compose the bridge would have existed even if the bridge had not, since there are always the same particles, and—almost certainly—they would have had the same causal powers. It follows that what God does in sustaining the bridge in existence and preserving its causal powers is something He would have done even if the bridge had never existed, although, in that case, this action

---

[2] This note is addressed to those who believe that there are created rational immaterial beings. It was suggested in the text that anyone who believed in such creatures could accept most of what I say if he rejected my assumption that all 'particles' were material, and assumed that some 'particles' were immaterial and rational. If anyone avails himself of this suggestion, he must take care to except thinking, immaterial 'particles' from the generalizations about particles that are made in the following discussion of the metaphysics of miracles, since it would seem obvious that, e.g., a Cartesian ego's causal powers will hardly ever be constant over time. Such a being's causal powers will vary with time (if for no other reason) because its internal representations of its circumstances will vary. If I took Cartesianism seriously, I would try to elaborate the model of the created world presented herein to provide a more comfortable niche for immaterial human minds; but I don't and I won't. As for angels, while I take them seriously, I know nothing of their metaphysical nature and thus have no idea of what sort of elaboration of the model would be needed to provide a more comfortable niche for them.

would not have fallen under the description 'sustaining the bridge in existence and preserving its causal powers.')

Now suppose that God occasionally (and only momentarily) supplied a few particles with causal powers different from their normal powers. Such an action would cause a certain part of the natural world to diverge from the course that part of the world would have taken if He had continued to supply the particles in that part of the world with the usual complement of causal powers. Such a divergence would, presumably, spread—with decreasing amplitude—till it encompassed the entire universe. The early stages of such a divergence we shall call a *miracle*. For example, imagine that God momentarily supplies unusual causal powers to the particles composing the water in a certain pot, in such a way that those particles (in virtue of their momentarily abnormal effects on one another) follow trajectories through the void that they would not normally have followed, and that, as a consequence, they rearrange themselves into the configuration we call 'wine'—at which moment God reverts to His usual policy and continues to supply each of the particles with its normal causal powers.[3]

I like this account of miracles better than either of the two alternative accounts I know of. On one account, a miracle is an 'intervention' into the course of nature by God. But the word 'intervention' seems to imply that nature has some sort of native power, independent of God's, and that in working a miracle, God has, as it were, to *overpower* some part of nature. No theist can accept such a picture of the relation of God to nature; this account of miracles provides a better description of what the deist says God *doesn't* do than of what the theist says God *does* do.[4]

---

[3] This definition of *miracle* is tailored to fit our account of the created world and its relation to God, an account that is in many respects too simple to be satisfactory. If the account were elaborated, our definition of *miracle* might have to be modified. For example, we have assumed, for the sake of simplicity, that there are always just the same particles. If we were to assume instead that God sometimes—but very rarely—annihilated particles, or created particles *ex nihilo* subsequently to the first, great Creation, then we should want to count as miracles the initial stages of the divergences occasioned by such actions from what would have otherwise been the course of events.

If we were to assume that God sometimes moved particles otherwise than by supplying them and neighboring particles with abnormal causal powers—that He sometimes moved particles 'directly'—such episodes, too, should be counted as miracles. (It is not entirely clear to me, however, that the alleged distinction between God's moving particles 'directly' and 'indirectly' is ultimately intelligible. To adapt a remark of Frege's, sometimes I seem to see a distinction, and then again I *don't* see it.)

[4] When this paper was read to the Society of Christian Philosophers, the commentator charged the author with deism. (Talk about *odium theologicum!*) In this he claimed to be following medieval Latin authority: The position I propound, that alterations in the created world are not directly caused by God, 'is stigmatized as (in effect) a form of *deism* by almost every important medieval Christian philosopher.' Well, it would have to be 'in effect,' since the words *deista* and *deismus* occur in no medieval manuscript—or if they do, this is not known to the editors of the Oxford English Dictionary, who derive the French *déiste* directly from *deus*. Since 'deist' (when used in a dyslogistic sense; it has sometimes been used to mean 'theist') has never meant anything but 'person who believes in a Creator on the basis of reason alone, and who denies revelation, miracles, Providence, and immanence,' 'in effect' cashes out to this: Someone who denies that God directly causes alterations in the created world denies God's immanence. But a God who continuously sustains all things in existence and continuously conserves their causal powers is immanent enough for me. In such a God, 'we live and move and have our being' (Acts 17:28); 'in him all things hold together'

According to the second alternative account, a miracle occurs when God causes an event that is a 'violation of the laws of nature.' I like this alternative better than the other, but I have a rather technical objection to it. Let us call a contingent proposition a *law of nature* if it would be true if God *always* supplied the elementary particles with their normal causal powers, and would, moreover, be true under any conditions whatever that were consistent with this stipulation. For those who are familiar with the philosophical use of the concept of 'possible worlds,' here is a more precise definition: A proposition is a law of nature in a possible world *w* if it is a contingent proposition that is true in all possible worlds in which elementary particles *always* have the causal powers they *always or almost always* have in *w*. Now if the proposition L is a law of nature, then we can say that an event *violates* the law L if the particles whose joint activity constitutes that event follow, while the event is going on, trajectories that are inconsistent with the truth of L. Roughly: An event violates a law if the law says that no events of that sort happen. A *miracle*, then, is an event that violates one or more laws. (It follows from this account of law and miracle that, if there are any miracles,

(Col. 1:17). (I hold, moreover, that no created thing *could possibly* exist at a given moment unless it were at that moment held in existence by God; and no created thing *could possibly* have causal powers at a given moment unless it were at that moment supplied with those powers by God.)

The alternatives to this position are occasionalism and concurrentism. Occasionalism is one of those high-minded philosophical depreciations of God's works that come disguised as compliments to God's person. As, for example, Docetism devalues the Incarnation, occasionalism devalues the Creation. What God has made and now sustains is substance, not shadow. Concurrentism is the doctrine that God must cooperate with a created thing in order for that thing to act on another thing. I find this doctrine hard to understand. Does it credit created things with the power to produce effects or does it not? In the former case, why is God's cooperation needed to produce the effect? In the latter case, Creation is devalued.

The commentator also endorsed a curious medieval argument that is supposed to show that a certain sort of miracle requires either occasionalism or concurrentism. Consider the three young men in the fiery furnace. If fire and flesh really had intrinsic causal powers, powers that could be exercised without God's cooperation (the argument runs), then God could have preserved the three young men only by altering the powers, and hence the natures, of the fire or the flesh—in which case they would not have *been* fire or flesh. There seems to me to be little to this argument. The causal influence of the fire would have had to pass from one place to another to affect the flesh, and God could miraculously block this influence at some intermediate point in space without in any way altering the fire or the flesh. Interestingly enough, in the apocryphal 'Song of Azariah in the Furnace' (which the Jerusalem Bible inserts between Daniel 3:23 and the Song of the Three Children), just this line is taken: 'But the angel of the Lord came down into the furnace [and] drove the flames of the fire outward, and fanned in to them, in the heart of the furnace, a coolness such as wind or dew will bring, so that the fire did not even touch them or cause them any pain or distress.' The commentator does consider this sort of possibility, but suggests that it represents God as engaging in an unseemly struggle with a creature; 'resisting the power of the fire,' as he puts it. Similarly, I suppose one might argue that God would not, whatever the Psalmist might say, send His angels to support one, lest one dash one's foot against a stone. That would be 'resisting' the power of the stone or of gravity or something. Such mindedness is too wonderful for me; it is high, I cannot attain unto it. But if one must have a high-minded account of the preservation of the three young men, here is one consistent with what is said in the body of the essay (in a slightly modified version, which takes into account a little elementary physics): As the photons are on their way from the fire to the flesh, God ceases to sustain most of the more energetic ones in existence.

then some laws of nature are false propositions. Some philosophers insist that, by definition, a law of nature, whatever else it may be, must be a true proposition. I can't think why.) I said that I had a rather technical objection to this account of the concept of miracle. The *objection* is simply that this account is not equivalent to the one I favor: Some events that my account labels 'miracles' this account does not. 'Technical' comes in in explaining why. It comes down to this: The two accounts coincide only if the laws of nature are deterministic; that is, only if, given the present state of the world, the laws of nature are so strict that—miracles aside—they tie the world down to exactly one future, a future determined in every detail. For suppose that the laws are *indeterministic*. Suppose that they are sufficiently 'loose' that they permit a certain event *A* to have either of two outcomes, *B* or *C*, and they don't determine which will happen. They allow history to fork, as it were, to go down either of two roads. Suppose that *A* has happened and suppose that God wants *A* to be followed by *C* and not by *B*. Suppose that, to achieve this end, God supplies certain particles with abnormal causal powers of such a nature that *B has* to happen. (Speaking very loosely, you might say that He locally and temporarily replaces the indeterministic laws with deterministic ones.) Then *B* will be a miracle by the account I have given, but not by the violation-of-laws-of-nature account. I prefer so to use the word 'miracle' that this event counts as a miracle. If you disagree, you may regard my use of the word as idiosyncratic.

It will be convenient in what follows to have a uniform way in which to describe God's actions with respect to the created world, a mode of description that comprehends both His ordinary sustaining of particles in existence and His miraculous departures from the ordinary. I shall suppose that whenever God brings about some state of affairs involving created beings, His doing this is the same action as His issuing a certain *decree*—a pronouncement of the form 'Let such-and-such be' or 'Let the following be so: . . . .' For example, 'Let there be light' is a decree, and God's issuing or pronouncing this decree is the same action as His creating light. For technical reasons, I shall want to suppose that God's decrees are, as philosophers say, 'closed under entailment.' This means that if God issues certain decrees—say a decree that *p* and a decree that *q*—and if, as a matter of absolute or metaphysical necessity, if *p* and *q* are true then *r* must also be true, then it follows that God, in decreeing that *p* and *q*, also decrees that *r*. For example, suppose that one of God's decrees is 'Let the waters be divided from the waters'; suppose that, as many philosophers, myself included, believe, it is a matter of absolute or metaphysical necessity that if there is water, then there are protons. Then it follows that in issuing this decree, God also issues the decree 'Let there be protons.' (It will, however, be convenient to except necessary truths from the closure requirement: Let us say that if God decrees certain propositions, and these propositions jointly entail *p*, it follows that God decrees *p*, provided that *p* is a contingent proposition.)

In this 'decree' language, we may represent the action of God with respect to each elementary particle at a given moment as follows. His action consists in His then issuing a decree of the form 'Let *that* now exist and have such-and-such causal powers.' If God wished to annihilate a certain particle, therefore, He would not do something *to* the particle, as I might hit a vase with a hammer if I wished to destroy it. He would simply stop issuing such decrees. (But in our rather simple model of the relations of God to the world, we tacitly assume He never ceases to hold any particle in existence, since we assume there are always the same particles. This feature of our model is not essential to any of the points made in this essay, and could be removed at the cost of putting up with a slightly more complex model.) And for God to work a miracle is for Him temporarily to decree different causal powers for certain particles from the ones He normally decrees. God's actions with respect to the entire created world at any moment subsequent to the Creation are simply the sum of His actions at that moment with respect to all the particles composing the world.[5] Thus, God's action in the created world at any given moment consists, on this model, in His issuing a vast number of decrees—as many as there are particles—of the form, 'Let *that* now exist and have such-and-such causal powers'.[6] His issuing these decrees is identical with His sustaining the world.

[5] We shall presently discuss God's action at the *first* moment, the moment of Creation. In what follows in the text and in subsequent notes, generalizations about what God does at particular instants should be understood as referring to instants subsequent to the first.

This way of talking raises the question: What, exactly, is the relation of God and His actions to *time* in our model of God's relation to the world? Let us say the following. First, we shall assume that the existence of time, of 'before' and 'after,' is a function of the existence of the physical world: If there had been no world, there would have been no such thing as time, and one can make no sense of talk of temporal relations except in reference to the physical world. As both St. Augustine and Stephen Hawking have insisted, it makes no sense to ask what happened *before*—at least in the literal, temporal sense of the word—the world existed. (Hawking employs this analogy: You might as well ask what is happening north of the North Pole.) Secondly, we shall assume that some of God's decrees can be assigned dates (dates provided by the processes of the physical world, the only dates there are): We can ask with respect to a time *t* what decrees God *then* issues. (I shall not attempt to prove that these two assumptions are consistent.) Because of our closure condition, however, it is possible that there be decrees of God that are not issued at any particular time. (An example of such a decree can be found in n. 11.) I do not insist that the two assumptions I have made about God and time represent the ultimate metaphysical truth. Those who hold that God is entirely 'outside time' are faced with certain authoritative documents—such as the Bible—which, on the face of it, say that God does one thing at one time and another thing at another time. Such philosophers generally have some way of interpreting assertions of this sort so that these assertions are seen to be compatible with their theory of an extratemporal God. They should feel free to interpret my assertions about God's actions at particular times in the same way.

[6] But, owing to our closure condition, He does not issue *only* those decrees; He also decrees, at any given moment, any contingent proposition entailed by the totality of that vast ensemble of decrees about individual particles. Or, at any rate, this follows if we interpret our closure condition (which, as stated, does not refer to time) as having this consequence: If, at *t*, God decrees certain propositions, and these propositions together entail the contingent proposition *p*, then at *t*, God decrees that *p*. Thus, at an instant *t*, God then decrees every proposition that is true in all possible worlds in which, at *t*, there are the same particles as there are in actuality and in which each of these particles has at *t* the same causal powers it has in actuality.

Let us now turn to the question, What is the place of chance in a world sustained by God? Can chance exist at all in such a world? Or, if it does exist, must its realm not be restricted to trivial matters—say, to such matters as where a particular sparrow falls—if its existence is to be consistent with God's loving providence?

In order to approach these questions, let us ask what it would be for there to be chance in the world. There are various things that can be meant by the word 'chance.' What I shall mean by saying that an event is a 'chance' occurrence, or a state of affairs a 'matter of chance' or 'due to chance,' is this: The event or state of affairs is without purpose or significance; it is not a part of anyone's plan; it serves no one's end; and it might very well not have been. A chance event, in other words, is one such that, if someone asks of it, 'Why did that happen?' the only right answer is: 'There is no reason or explanation; it just happened'.[7] But you must treat this statement charitably. I do not mean to imply that a 'chance' event in this sense has no explanation of *any* sort. If Alice suddenly remembers that she had promised to buy a box of crayons for her son, and turns into an unfamiliar street in search of an appropriate shop, and is struck and killed by a car whose brakes have failed, her death may well be a 'chance' occurrence in the sense I mean—someone who did not believe in divine providence would almost certainly say that it was—even though in one sense her death has an obvious

We should note that the thesis that God decrees at *t* that a certain particle then exist and then have certain causal powers does not entail that He decrees at *t* that it then be at any particular place. 'Let *that* now exist and have such-and-such causal powers' is not the same decree as 'Let *that* now exist and be *right there* and have such-and-such causal powers.' (A similar point applies to velocity and the higher derivatives of displacement.) More generally: From the thesis that God at *t* is sustaining the universe, it does not follow that He then decrees the particular *arrangement* of particles that in fact obtains at that time. Here is an imperfect analogy. From the fact that a gardener is now tending the flowers in a certain garden (and is thus in a sense now sustaining them in existence) it hardly follows that he is now determining the way they are now arranged. I return to this point in n. 11.

[7] Some philosophers believe that there are impersonal but intelligible 'world-historical' processes, and that these processes somehow confer intelligibility or significance on certain of the events that issue from them. For such an event there would be an answer to the question, Why did that happen? If there are such world-historical processes, one would not want to call their products 'chance' events, despite the fact that—assuming that the world-historical processes are not instruments of God's purpose—they are not a part of anyone's plan (unless it were the plan of a personified abstraction like History). The primary purpose of the qualification 'It might very well not have been' is to deny the status of a 'chance' event to an event—as it may be, the rise of capitalism—that is a necessary product of some impersonal but intelligible world-historical process like the Labor of the Concept or the Dialectic of History. Since the idea of such processes is a vague one, I will not attempt to be precise about the meaning of 'It might very well not have been.' I will explicitly and formally exclude only metaphysically necessary events (if such there be) and metaphysically necessary states of affairs from the category 'might not have been.' (Thus, if Spinoza is right, no event or state of affairs can be ascribed to 'chance.') Readers for whom Spinozism, and historicism of the Hegel-Marx-Spengler variety, are not live options can safely ignore the qualification 'It might very well not have been.' In any case, the *theist* will say, first, that Spinozism is false, and secondly, that either there are no 'world-historical' processes, or, if there are, their existence is ordained by God and any necessary product of such processes will therefore be a part of someone's plan. The theist, therefore, may ignore the qualification 'It might very well not have been.' I shall do so in the sequel.

explanation: She was struck by a car. But if her grieving husband were to cry in despair 'Why did she die?', it would be a cruel joke to tell him that she died because she was struck by a large, heavy vehicle moving at fifty miles an hour. That is not the sort of explanation he would be asking for. By calling an event a 'chance' event, I mean that it has no explanation of the sort Alice's husband might ask for: It has no purpose or significance; it is not a part of anyone's plan.

It does seem that there are many events of this sort; some horrible, some benefic, some of no consequence to anyone. But there are people who believe that this seeming is mere seeming and that either there are no chance events in this sense, or, if there are, they are always events that are of no consequence to anyone. I have in mind those people who believe in divine providence and who take a certain view, which I shall proceed to describe, of divine providence. Such people think that God not only *knows* of the fall of every sparrow, but that the fall of every sparrow is a part of God's plan for His creation. Presumably they think that the exact number of hairs on one's head is also a part of God's plan. Other people may find the attribution of every detail of the world to providence bizarre, but say that at any rate all those events that would be accounted important by human beings—Alice's death, for example—must have a place in God's plan. A person who takes this view will say that when Alice's grieving husband asks, 'Why did she die?', there is an answer to this question, an answer that God knows even if no human being knows it. My purpose in the remainder of this essay will be to suggest that this is wrong. I want to suggest that much of what goes on in the world, even much of what seems important and significant to us, is no part of God's plan—and certainly not a part of anyone *else's* plan—and is therefore due simply to chance.

If there is chance in a world sustained by God, what are its sources? Where, as it were, does it 'come from'? Let us recall our picture of God's relation to the world: The world consists of elementary particles, and God created the world by creating these particles simultaneously at some moment in the past; God sustains each of them in existence and continuously 'supplies' each of them with its causal powers; following the Creation, the world evolved in a manner determined, insofar as it *was* determined, by the causal powers of its constituent particles; the causal powers supplied to a given particle are normally invariant, but God may, of His own good pleasure, momentarily supply certain particles with different sets of causal powers from the ones they normally receive from Him, and, if He does this, then a miracle occurs.

If God has this relation to the created universe, what is meant by His 'plan' for the created universe? I believe that we should, as a first approximation, identify God's plan with the sum total of what He has decreed. (I say 'as a first approximation' because I will presently qualify this definition). Thus, if God has issued the decree 'Let there be light,' then the existence of light is a part of His plan. If He has *not* issued the decree 'Let there be lies,' then lies are no part of His plan. We should remember that a plan—God's plan or anyone's—may take account of a certain possibility without requiring that that possibility be realized. For example, bank robbers planning their getaway may *plan for* the contingency of leaving the city by air—they have bought airline tickets—but not *plan to* leave the city by air. Leaving the city by air is not a part of their plan in the way that arriving at the bank at 3:00 P.M. is. We should also remember that the fact that God knows that something will happen does not mean that that thing is a part of His plan. God may, therefore, have known before there were any rational creatures that some of them would someday tell lies, and His plan for the world may contain measures for dealing with lies should any lies be told; but it does not follow from these things that lies are a part of His plan. Now here is the qualification of our definition of God's plan that I alluded to a moment ago. It may happen that God sometimes issues decrees in response to events that He has not decreed. For example, suppose that a young man is dying following a car wreck and that God had not decreed that that car wreck should occur. Suppose the young man's mother prays that his life be saved, and that God grants this prayer by performing a miracle in virtue of which the man recovers. We shall not count this miraculous recovery as a part of God's plan, since it was contingent on an event—the car wreck—that God had *not* decreed. We might call the decree God issued to bring about the man's recovery a *reactive* decree, since it was issued in reaction to an event that God did not bring about. We may define a reactive decree of God's as a decree He would not have issued had some event not decreed by Him not occurred. Our revised definition of God's plan is: God's plan consists of the totality of all His decrees other than reactive decrees.[8]

If this is the correct picture of God's relation to the created world and His plan for it, there would seem to be, within such a world, at least three possible sources of chance, or of events or states of affairs that are not a part of God's plan: the free will of rational creatures, natural indeterminism, and the initial state of the created world. (I call these *three* sources of chance, but I realize that proponents of various philosophical theories may hold that every instance of some one of

---

[8] Or we might call this totality 'God's unqualified plan' or 'God's eternal plan' or 'God's plan *ante omnia saecula*.' We could also speak, for any contingent proposition *p*, of 'God's plan given that *p*': If the conditional 'if *p* then *q*' is a part of God's eternal plan, and if *p* is true, then *q* is a part of 'God's plan given that *p*.' If *q* is a part of God's plan given that *p*, and if *p* is not a part of God's unqualified plan, then *q* will be a part of God's plan given that *p*, but not a part of God's unqualified plan. If *q* is a part of God's plan given that *p* (but not a part of God's plan *ante omnia saecula*) and if *p* is a proposition that we all know to be true—or which we and all of our coreligionists believe to be true—it will be natural for us to speak of *q* as being 'a part of God's plan'; in fact it would be inadvisable for anyone to speak otherwise, except (as in the present case) when engaged in highly abstract theological speculation. Thus, Christians may properly speak of the Incarnation as being 'a part of God's plan,' even if there would have been no Incarnation if there had been no Fall: for, surely, there is some contingent proposition *p* (perhaps 'Man falls from his original perfection,' or the conjunction of this and various other propositions) such that the Christian will believe that *p* is in fact true and also believe that 'If *p*, then God becomes man' is a part of God's eternal plan.

We should note that God's eternal plan is not (at least according to orthodox Christian theology) a necessary product of the Divine Nature. 'There is a created universe' is a part of God's eternal plan, but not, orthodoxy has it, a necessary truth.

these sources is also an instance of one of the other two. For example, a philosopher who holds that free will and determinism are incompatible will probably maintain that every instance of human free will is also an instance of natural indeterminism.)

Let us first consider human free will. I take it to be obvious that if God decrees (I do not mean *commands*) that a certain human being on a certain occasion behave in a certain way, then that human being loses his freedom of choice on that particular occasion. When, for example, God 'hardened Pharoah's heart,' Pharoah—at that particular moment—did not *freely* choose to forbid the Hebrews to leave Egypt. Thus, if there is such a thing as human free will, it cannot be that all of our choices are like Pharoah's. And it is certainly not obviously the biblical picture of God's relation to man that all of our choices *are* of that sort. For example, Ecclesiasticus says of God (15:4): 'He himself made man in the beginning, and then left him free to make his own decisions.' (Admittedly, Christians have to deal with some difficult passages in Romans on this point.) If we have free will, therefore, the manner in which any particular person exercises this free will is no part of God's plan, and likewise the consequences of free acts, even if they occur thousands of years after the act, are no parts of God's plan. I must point out that this is not an attempt to *absolve* God of responsibility for the consequences of the free acts of creatures. After all, that an event is not part of one's plans does not necessarily mean that one is not responsible for it. If the man who fell among thieves had died beside the road from Jerusalem to Jericho, this would not have been a part of any plan of the priest or the Levite, but they would nonetheless have been responsible for his death. Whether God should be held responsible for the evils caused by the abuse of human free will—and He could certainly prevent most of these evils, if not all of them—is not the present question. I am arguing only that they are not part of His plan for the world, which is a relatively weak thesis.

A second source of chance in the world is natural indeterminism. Indeterminism is the thesis that the distribution of all the particles of matter in the universe at a given moment, and their causal powers at that moment, do not determine the subsequent behavior of the particles. In other words, an indeterministic universe is one in which a given state of affairs can have more than one outcome. The Greek atomists held that atoms—what are now called elementary particles—could swerve in the void, and something very much like this is true according to modern physics. If God's causal relations with the world are confined to continuously holding the elementary particles in existence and continuously supplying them with their causal powers, then He does not decree the outcomes of such 'swerves in the void,' since the 'swerves' are not determined by the causal powers of the particles. And the consequences of such undetermined events can show up at the level of ordinary observation, if they are sufficiently amplified. A Geiger counter is an amplifier designed for this purpose. (Another effective amplifier can be found in the collisions of rolling spheres. Imagine a billiard table on which perfectly spherical, perfectly elastic billiard balls are in motion, without loss of kinetic energy to friction or to collisions with the sides of the table. Imagine a second billiard-table-and-balls setup that is as close to being an absolutely perfect duplicate of the first as the laws of nature allow. If the 'laws of nature' are those of nineteenth-century physics, the second table will be an absolutely perfect duplicate of the first *sans phrase*, and the behavior of the balls on the second table will—presumably—duplicate exactly the behavior of the balls on the first table forever. Suppose, however, that a rolling billiard ball exhibits the position-momentum and time-energy uncertainties predicted by Heisenberg. For an object as big as a billiard ball, these uncertainties are minuscule indeed. Nevertheless, the capacity of the collisions of rolling spheres to magnify slight deviations is astounding: Within a few minutes the arrangements of balls on the two tables will be entirely different.)

Since the actual physical world seems in fact to be indeterministic, it is plausible to suppose that there are a great many states of affairs that are not part of God's plan and which, moreover, cannot be traced to the free decisions of created beings. I very much doubt that when the universe was (say) 10^{-45} seconds old, it was then physically inevitable that the earth, or even the Milky Way Galaxy, should exist. Thus, these objects, so important from the human point of view, are no part of God's plan—or at least not unless their creation was due to God's miraculous intervention into the course of the development of the physical world at a relatively late stage. I see no reason as a theist, or as a Christian, to believe that the existence of human beings is a part of God's plan. This may seem a shocking statement. Let me attempt to palliate the shock. First, I do not claim to *know* that the existence of our species is not a part of God's plan. Secondly, I am sure that the existence of animals made in God's image—that is, rational animals having free will and capable of love—*is* a part of God's plan. I am simply not convinced that He had any *particular* species in mind. Thirdly, I do not deny God's omniscience. I do not deny that He knew from the beginning that humanity would exist; but what is foreknown is not necessarily what is planned. Fourthly, *having* come into existence, we are *now* in God's care and the objects of His love and the instruments of His purpose. Here is an analogy: When my wife and I decided to have a child, we did not decide with respect to some particular child to have *that* child, as a couple might decide with respect to some particular child to adopt *that* child. But now that our child is in existence, she, that very individual and no other, is in our care and is the object of our love. I concede that if God knows the future in every detail, then He knew before humanity existed that that particular species would exist; and my wife and I did not know of Elizabeth van Inwagen, before her conception, that she, that very individual, would exist. But if God knew from the beginning of time, or even 'before all worlds,' that humanity would exist, it does not follow that He decreed the existence of humanity; He may for all I know have issued no decree more particular than 'Let there be a species in My image and likeness.'

I now turn to the third source of chance in the world: the initial state of things. (I ignore the problem presented by the fact that, according to most of the current cosmological models, although the world has a finite age, there was no first instant of its existence—or if there was a first instant, the world was then of zero volume and infinite density, an idea that seems to make no sense.)

At the first moment of the existence of the physical universe there were, let us say, $(2.46 \times 10^{80}) + 2319$ particles,[9] each having a certain set of causal powers, a certain position in space, and a certain velocity. No doubt this 'initial arrangement' (so to call it) suited God's purposes; if it did not, of course, there would have been some other initial arrangement. But is it conceivable that this was the only one out of all possible initial arrangements that suited God's purposes? Is it conceivable that God chose this arrangement because it was better for His purposes than *any* of the infinitely many alternatives? Well, I find that very hard to believe. I don't mean to deny that God could hold all of the infinitely many possible initial arrangements before His mind at once, and then say, 'Let *that* one be.' (Of course this is mere picture-thinking, treating God as if He were just like a human being, with the minor difference that He is infinite. But picture-thinking is all we are capable of. When I say I don't mean to deny this, I am saying that I don't mean to deny that it's the best picture.) I do, however, doubt whether any *one* of the alternatives *could* be superior to all the others. To me that sounds as absurd as saying that, if an artist wants to draw a portrait in chalk, then one particular arrangement of calcium, carbon, and oxygen atoms, out of all the possible arrangements, must be the arrangement that would constitute the best possible piece of chalk for the job.

Well, suppose there are various alternative initial arrangements that would suit God's purposes equally well. Doubtless if there is more than one such arrangement there are infinitely many. But let us suppose for the sake of simplicity that there are just two, X and Y. We are supposing, that is, that for God's purposes to be accomplished, either X or Y must come into existence, but it makes no difference which; it is a matter of sheer indifference to Him. Now if God wishes either X or Y to come into existence, what decree shall He issue? There would seem to be three possibilities:

(1) 'Let X be'
(2) 'Let Y be'
(3) 'Let either X or Y be.'[10]

Leibniz, though he does not talk of things in exactly these terms, might be interpreted as saying, first, that (3) is impossible because God creates only 'complete' states of affairs, fully detailed ones, 'possible worlds'; secondly, that

---

[9] Or, better, think of a number of this order of magnitude that isn't mostly zeros.

[10] We must be careful about what we mean by calling (1), (2), and (3) *three* possibilities, since, by our closure condition, if God issues either (1) or (2) He *ipso facto* issues (3). The three possibilities I mean to call attention to are: God issues (1); God issues (2); God issues (3) *without* issuing (1) or (2).

God cannot issue either (1) or (2), because that would be for God to act without a sufficient reason for His action; and, thirdly, that there must, therefore, be a *best possible* initial state, since there in fact is a created world.

I would deny the first of these assertions. It does not seem to me to be logically or metaphysically impossible that God should decree that either X or Y should be without decreeing that X should be and without decreeing that Y should be. Suppose God does decree that *either X or Y exist*; suppose Y thereupon comes into existence.[11] Then it is no part of God's plan that Y—*as opposed to X*—exist, and the result of His decree might just as well have been the existence of X. We may therefore say that Y exists owing simply to chance, and that every result or consequence of Y that would not *also* be a result of X is due to chance. There could, therefore, be chance events even in a wholly deterministic world that was created and is sustained by God. If, moreover, we assume that God cannot, after all, decree that either X or Y exist except by decreeing that X exist or else decreeing that Y exist, this will not remove the element of chance from the world. It will

---

[11] The moment Y comes into existence, there will, of course, be a particular number of particles and each will have a determinate position and velocity and complement of causal powers. It is at *that* point that God must, if He is to sustain the world He has created, begin issuing 'a vast number of decrees—as many as there are particles—of the form "Let *that* now exist and have such-and-such causal powers".' Here is another imperfect horticultural analogy. Suppose I plant a tree in my garden. Within certain limits, it may not matter much to me where the tree is. I may, within these limits, choose a spot at random. But once I have planted the tree and it is firmly rooted at a particular spot, I must tend it where it is. It's no good watering a spot ten feet to the left of the tree, even if my purposes would have been as well served by planting the tree at that other spot.

I said in n. 6 that it does not follow from the fact that God at t issues decrees that then sustain the universe in existence that He then decrees the current arrangement of particles. I will now go further and say that, if our model of God's relation to the world is anything like right, then at at most *one* instant does He then decree the current arrangement of particles: the first. And if the decree of God that brings the universe into existence is indefinite (like 'Let either X or Y be'), then at *no* instant does He then decree the current arrangement of particles. (Moreover, the existence of a first instant of time is a consequence of the limitations of our model: A more sophisticated model would allow for the possibility that, while the temporal sequence has a greatest lower bound, it has no earliest member.) It would, however, be possible for God to decree the arrangement of particles at t without *then* decreeing it. Suppose, for example, that at t_0 (the first moment of time), God then decrees a perfectly definite arrangement of particles; suppose that at every instant in the interval having t_0 as its earliest member and t as its earliest nonmember, He then decrees the existence of the same particles that existed at t_0 and also decrees a deterministic set of laws; and suppose that at t He then decrees the existence of the same particles that existed at t_0. Only one arrangement of particles at t will be consistent with this set of decrees and it therefore follows that God decrees the arrangement of particles at t. Since, however, He does not issue all of these decrees *at t*, we cannot say that *at t* He *then* decrees the current arrangement of particles. But, of course, if the theory presented in the text is correct, God does not, even in this sense, decree the arrangement of particles at any time: There are, in fact, possible worlds in which God has issued the same decrees He has issued in actuality, and in which no particle is where it is in actuality. Nevertheless, God may have (and if any revealed religion is true, *has*) decreed many of the features the universe has at any given moment: that it then contain living creatures, for example. It should be evident from what has been said in this note and in n. 6 that we cannot validly deduce from the two premises: (i) God has decreed that at t there be living creatures, and (ii) at t, God then issues decrees that sustain in existence all the living creatures there are at that moment, the conclusion that at t God then issues the decree that there be living creatures at that moment.

simply locate the ultimate source of that chance within the internal life of God, rather than in the results of an indefinite decree. For if God must issue a decree that *X* exist or else issue a decree that *Y* exist, and if He has no reason to prefer one of these states of affairs to the other—if it is really, from God's point of view, six of one and half a dozen of the other—then there seems to be no way to avoid the conclusion that some analogue of a coin toss takes place within the Divine Nature. An analogy is provided by Buridan's Ass; this unfortunate animal, you remember, is forced to choose between two equally attractive and accessible piles of hay. If the poor creature is not to starve, it must make an arbitrary choice. And, presumably, within each animal—even within rational animals like ourselves— there exists some mechanism, some biological analogue of a coin toss, for making arbitrary choices. Occasional reliance upon such a mechanism is not beneath the dignity of an animal, even a rational animal, but I find it wholly incongruous to suppose that the Divine Nature contains anything remotely resembling a coin- tossing mechanism. To suggest this seems to be almost to suggest that the Lord of all is, as Zeus was said to be, one of the subjects of the goddess Tyche or Chance. I prefer to think that God is capable of decreeing that a certain indefinite condition be satisfied without decreeing any of the indifferent alternative states of affairs that would satisfy it. However this may be, the following result seems secure: If there are alternative initial arrangements of particles, any of which would have served God's purpose for His creation equally well, then certain features of the world must be due to mere chance. How pervasive these features may be, and how important they might seem to us, are, of course, further questions, questions that are not answered by anything that we have so far said. And this same result, the existence of states of affairs due to chance, follows from our consideration of human freedom and natural indeterminism. I do not doubt that all three sources of chance have in fact been in operation, and that many of the features of the actual universe are due to them—perhaps even features as prominent as the human race or the Local Group. I do not think that such a view of the place of chance in the formation of the universe is incompatible with the proposition that God is the Maker of all things, visible and invisible. Even if the planet Mars (say) is not a part of God's plan, it is entirely composed of particles that He made in the beginning and which exist from moment to moment only because He continues to hold them in existence and which continue from moment to moment to form a planet only because He is continuously supplying them with the causal powers by which they mutually cohere. I suppose that *we* exist only by chance, and yet it is in God that we live and move and have our being. And, as I have implied, creatures that, like us, exist by chance, may well be filling a divinely ordained *role*, and in that sense be serving God's purposes—rather as individual soldiers may be serving a general's purposes, even though the battle plan the general has drafted does not include any of their names. (But again, the analogy is imperfect, for the general, we may suppose, neither knows nor cares about individual private soldiers—even if he is concerned about their collective welfare—whereas God knows all about each of us, and loves each of us with a depth and intensity that is without human parallel.)

If what I have said so far is correct, then it seems very likely that among the events that are due simply to chance and not part of God's plan are certain evils; or perhaps even *all* evils. In the remainder of this essay I want to examine this idea and its consequences.

If much of the world is due to chance, and if much of the world is infected with evil, then it would be reasonable to suppose, on purely statistical grounds, that at least some evil is due to chance. Many theists, moreover, ascribe the very existence of evil to an abuse of the divine gift of free will by created beings. If that speculation is correct, then the very existence of evil is a matter of chance; that is, there is simply no answer to the question, Why is there evil? and it is not correct to say that God planned to create a world containing evil. Since people seem to be particularly likely to misunderstand the point of suggestions like this one, I will repeat something I have said before: This suggestion is in no way supposed to be a 'solution to the problem of evil,' since it is consistent with the proposition that before evil ever was, God knew that there would someday be evil and could have prevented it. I mention the point that (if evil is wholly due to the creaturely abuse of free will) evil is not a part of God's plan for His creation, simply to distinguish this point from the points I wish to discuss. The points I wish to discuss involve particular evils and their relation to God's plan.

What I want to say about particular evils is best made clear by illustration and example. I will consider two evils, one *very* particular—the accidental death of a particular person—and the other more general. I will discuss the more general evil first. I think that the existence of a certain disease will provide a good illustration of the point I want to make. For the sake of a concrete example, I will discuss rabies—an arbitrary choice, except that I have deliberately chosen a rather horrible disease. (A disease like rabies falls in the category that students of the problem of evil call 'physical' or 'natural' evil. But in what follows, I will make no explicit use of the distinction between natural and 'moral' evil.) I see no reason to suppose that God has decreed the existence of rabies. In my view, the rabies virus simply evolved and it might not have. If the initial arrangement of things had been slightly different, or if the indeterministic course of the natural world had taken a slightly different turning in the remote past (on any of uncounted billions of occasions), the particular disease we call rabies would never have come into existence. (But other diseases might have. If the rabies virus had never evolved, the world's catalogue of diseases might have been a bit less horrible—or it might have been a bit more horrible.) Is there any reason a theist should want to deny this? Although *I* think that there is no explanation of the existence of evil—I don't deny that there is an explanation of the fact that God *permits* evil—I can see why a theist would want to say that there must be an explanation of the existence of evil. Although I think that there is no explanation of the fact that many people die in agony—I don't deny that there is an explanation of the fact that God *allows* people to die in agony—I can see why a theist would want to say that there must be an explanation of the fact that many people die in agony. Well, suppose there were explanations of these things. Suppose there were a good explanation of the fact that there is evil. Suppose there were a good explanation of the fact that some people die in agony. Why should the theist want or expect an explanation of the fact that one of the evils is the particular disease rabies, or of the fact that some of the agonizing deaths are due to that disease? By the same token, if there is an explanation of the fact that God *permits* the existence of evil and agonizing death (even if there is no explanation of the existence of these things), why should anyone want or expect an explanation of the fact that rabies is one of the evils or is one of the causes of the agonizing deaths that God permits? I think that this point is an important one, for theists are often challenged to produce an explanation—even a *possible* explanation—of the existence of this or that evil, or of God's permitting that evil to come to be or to continue. And many theists, in their pride, construct fanciful explanations of particular evils as divine punishments. (Christians who explain particular evils—like the Bubonic Plague or the AIDS virus—as divine punishments are neglecting the story of the tower at Siloam and the story of the man born blind.) But there is no reason that the theist should believe that there are any such explanations. This point is even more important in connection with the misfortunes of individual persons, to which I now turn.

Let us consider again the case of Alice who, by sheerest chance, turned into a certain street and was killed by a car whose brakes had failed. Let us borrow a term from the law and call her death an example of *death by misadventure*. Although I think that there is no explanation of the existence of death by misadventure—I don't deny that there is an explanation of the fact that God *permits* the existence of death by misadventure—I can see why a theist would want to say that there must be an explanation of the existence of death by misadventure. Well, suppose that there were an explanation of the fact that there are deaths by misadventure. Why should the theist want or expect an explanation of the fact that *Alice,* then and there, died by misadventure? By the same token, if there is an explanation of the fact that God *permits* the existence of death by misadventure, why should anyone want or expect an explanation of the fact that God permitted *Alice* to die by misadventure? Why should there be an answer to the question, 'Why did *Alice* have to die that way'? Suppose that the driver of the car had seriously considered having his brakes checked a few days ago, when he first noticed certain ominous symptoms, that he freely decided to put it off till he was less busy, and that, if his deliberations had gone the other way, Alice would now be alive and well. Suppose that God's relation to Alice and the driver and their circumstances was confined to sustaining certain elementary particles (such as those that composed Alice and the driver and the braking system in the latter's car) in existence and supplying those particles with their normal causal powers. God would, of course, have known that the accident was to occur and could have prevented it by a miracle—one unnoticed by any human being, if He wished. If it really is true that God has a general reason for permitting deaths by misadventure, need He have a particular reason for permitting *this* death by misadventure? Why?

It is clear that many theists think that He *must* have such a reason. Every now and then, in Billy Graham's newspaper column and similar places, one finds explanations—admittedly speculative—of how a particular death by misadventure (or robbery or rape or illness) might serve God's purposes. I am not, as some are, morally offended by these explanations, but I find them singularly unconvincing, even as speculations. I certainly do not want to deny that *sometimes* particular deaths by misadventure, and other misfortunes of individual persons, may be such that God has a special reason for allowing those very misfortunes. I do not want to deny that God sometimes miraculously intervenes in the course of nature—say, in answer to someone's prayer for a loved one's safety—to *prevent* such misfortunes. I do not wish to deny that God sometimes intervenes miraculously in the course of nature to *cause* individual misfortunes. I want to deny only that there is any reason to suppose that, for every individual misfortune, God has a reason for not preventing *that* misfortune. (The English word *misfortune* is rather a milk-and-water word. My use of it *faute de mieux* should not be allowed to obscure the fact that my thesis comprehends events like the sudden death of a young woman who, had she not *happened* to turn down a certain street, might well have lived a long, happy, and useful life. Some would use the word *tragedy* for such events, but, in my usage at least, the word 'tragedy' carries the inescapable implication that the event to which it applies is, above all, a *meaningful* event, the very implication I want to avoid.)

Why should a theist deny any of this? One reason might be a conviction that there could not be a *general* explanation of God's allowing deaths by misadventure unless there were, for each such event, an explanation of His allowing *it*. A conviction, that is, that a general explanation of God's allowing deaths by misadventure could only be the sum of the explanations of his allowing this one and that one and the other one. I see no reason to believe this. After all, most theists believe that there is a general explanation of God's allowing sin—as it may be, a refusal to interfere with the free choices of creatures—that is independent of such reasons as He may have for allowing this, that, or the other sin. If this belief is correct, then, even if God had *no* special reason for allowing Cain to murder Abel, *no* reason peculiar to that act, *no* reason beyond His general policy of not interfering with the free choices of His creatures, it would not follow that He had no general reason for allowing sin. By analogy we may speculate that even if God had *no* special reason for allowing Alice to be struck by a car, *no* reason peculiar to that event, *no* reason beyond His general policy of allowing deaths by misadventure (whatever exactly the reasons underlying that policy might be), it would not follow that He had no general reason for allowing deaths by misadventure.

Or a theist may feel that it is simply not *fair* to Alice that she should die young, and that this unfairness could be acceptable only if God had a special reason for allowing her premature death. (A complication arises here. Most theists believe in an afterlife, and thus may be inclined to say that, in theory at least, an early death is not necessarily a misfortune. But this complication is due to a feature of the example that is not essential to the problem; it would not have arisen if, instead of assuming that Alice died when struck by the car, we had assumed that she lived out her normal span, but crippled and in pain.) One might point out that, if God indeed does allow people to be subject to Fortune and her wheel, then He has given everyone the same chance. Suppose, moreover, that He has a good reason for allowing us to be (to some extent) at the mercy of Fortune. If Fortune's wheel is fair, how, then, can the losers say that they have been treated unfairly? If the twins Tom and Tim both wish to propose marriage to Jane, and they take this problem to their father, and he orders them (this is in the old days) to draw straws, and Tim loses, can he say that he was treated unfairly by his father because his father had no special reason for denying him the opportunity to propose to Jane? No, the situation demanded a lottery, and Tim has no complaint unless the lottery was unfair. It will probably occur to someone to protest that *life's* lottery is *not* fair and that everyone does *not* have the same chance. (For example, someone living in Beirut has a greater chance of sudden violent death than someone living in Zurich.) But whatever problem this fact may raise for the theist, it does not seem to have anything in particular to do with chance. It is simply a special case of whatever problem is raised for the theist by the fact that life's blessings are not distributed equally. People are not equal in wealth, intelligence, native strength of character, or physical constitution. No one supposes that these inequalities are always a matter of desert. (What could one do to deserve greater native strength of character than someone else?) It may be that there are good reasons, known to God, for these inequalities. But such good reasons would not make the inequalities *fair*—not unless the reasons in some way involved desert. The theist may say all sorts of things in response to this difficulty: that the potter may do as he likes with his clay, for example, or that we deserve little from God and that no one gets less than he deserves and that it is not unfair for some to get more than they deserve provided no one gets less. But whatever the theist says about inequalities in the distribution of, say, intelligence and strength of character, I don't see why he shouldn't say the same thing about inequalities in the distribution of (for example) the probability of sudden violent death. In a nutshell: If it is fair that we should all be subject to chance in some degree, then it would seem to be unfair that we should be subject to unequal chances only if unequal distribution of any sort of advantage or disadvantage is unfair. It might be good at this point to remember the words of the Preacher (Eccl. 9:11–12):

'I returned, and saw under the sun, that the race is not to the swift, nor the battle to the strong, neither yet bread to the wise, nor yet riches to men of understanding, nor yet favor to men of skill; but time and chance happeneth to them all.'

For man also knoweth not his time: as the fishes that are taken in an evil net, and as the birds that are caught in the snare; so are the sons of men snared in an evil time, when it falleth suddenly upon them.'

If what I have said is true, it yields a moral for students of the problem of evil: Do not attempt any solution to this problem that entails that every particular evil has a purpose, or that, with respect to every individual misfortune, or every devastating earthquake, or every disease, God has some special reason for allowing it. Concentrate rather on the problem of what sort of reasons a loving and providential God might have for allowing His creatures to live in a world in which many of the evils that happen to them happen to them for no reason at all.[12]

[12] This essay owes a great deal to chap. 6, 'The Ordainder of the Lottery,' of P. T. Geach's *Providence and Evil* (Cambridge: Cambridge University Press, 1977). I doubt, however, whether Professor Geach would approve of everything I say. I do give 'real assent to the doctrine that all events however trivial fall within the ordering of Providence' (p. 116); I do not, however, take that doctrine to entail that God has chosen the number of hairs on my head, or even that He chose Matthias over Joseph Justus to fill the vacant apostolate of Judas. As to the latter case, we have not been told anything about this; what we may presume is that God was content that Matthias should hold that office. I *think* that Geach believes something stronger than this. Proverbs 16:33, which Geach cites, refers (I believe) only to the rather special case of the sacred lots, and, in any event, 'the way it falls out is from the Lord' is open to various interpretations.

This paper was read at a conference on the philosophy of religion at Cornell University in February 1987 and at a meeting of the Society of Christian Philosophers in Chicago in May 1987. On the latter occasion, the commentator was Alfred J. Freddoso, some of whose spirited animadversions I have addressed in nn. 4 and 7. (Freddoso's essay in this volume [Divine and Human Action] contains much that is relevant to n. 4 and other matters discussed herein.) Different, but equally spirited, animadversions have been communicated to me by Eleonore Stump; these have mainly to do with the implications of the paper for the problem of evil. I hope to discuss these elsewhere. I thank Norman Kretzmann, Richard Swinburne, Lawrence H. Davis, and, especially, William P. Alston for helpful criticisms.

An extremely interesting book (not yet published in the United States) has come into my hands too late to influence this essay: *God of Chance*, by D. J. Bartholomew (London: S.P.C.K., 1984). This book brings the expertise and perspective of a statistician to bear on the question of the relation of chance and God's action in the created world.

Part II
Scripture and Revelation

6

Revelation*

Richard Swinburne

Divine Revelation may be either of God, or by God of propositional truth. Traditionally the Christian revelation has involved both; God became incarnate and was in some degree made manifest on Earth, and through that incarnate life various propositional truths were announced.[1] My concern in this paper is only with revelation in the secondary sense of revelation of propositional truth. I am not concerned with all knowledge which God makes available to us, nor with all knowledge about himself, but with that knowledge which he communicates directly only to certain individuals, and they communicate to the rest of the world—where the grounds for the belief in these items of knowledge available to the first recipients are not available to the rest of the world, but the latter have to accept them, in the traditional phrase, 'upon the credit of the proposer, as coming from God in some extraordinary way of communication'.[2] Religions often claim to have minor as well as major revelations. The former are purported particular messages to individuals about matters of more immediate concern; the latter are big messages of worldshaking significance for the practice of religion. My concern will be only with the latter. I wish to examine whether we have reason to expect a Revelation of this kind, what it will be like, and what kind of historical evidence would show that we had got it.

As with all claims about particular occurrences which are to be expected on one world-view but not on another, it is crucial to take into account the other evidence for that world view. Reports of observations are rightly viewed very sceptically when the phenomena purportedly observed are ruled out by a well-established scientific theory, but believed when they are to be expected in the light of such a theory. If you have a well-established theory which says that change does not occur in the heavenly regions (regions of the sky more distant from Earth than the Moon), you will rightly discount reports of observers who claim to have observed a new star appear where there was no star before, or to

* From Kelly J. Clark, ed., *Our Knowledge of God*. © 1992 Kluwer Academic Publishers. Reprinted with kind permission from Springer Science and Business Media.

[1] The First Vatican Council declared that God revealed 'himself and the eternal decrees of his will' (Denzinger 3004); and the Second Vatican Council said much the same in *De Revelatione* 2.
[2] John Locke, *An Essay Concerning Human Understanding* IV.18.2.

have observed comets pass through those regions (as opposed to being mere sublunary phenomena). When that theory has been abandoned, you require a lot less in the way of evidence to show the flare-up of new stars or the routes of comets through the heavens. So if there is other evidence which makes it quite likely that there is a God, all powerful and all good, who made the Earth and its inhabitants, then it becomes to some extent likely that he would intervene in human history to reveal things to them; and claims that he has done so require a lot less in the way of historical evidence than they would do otherwise. I have argued in *The Existence of God*[3] that there is much evidence from other sources that there is an all-powerful and all-good God. If so, does that give us reason to suppose that he would intervene in human history to reveal things to us? I believe that it does.

A God who made men with capacities to make themselves saints would think it good that they should do so, and might well help them to do so. If they do become saints, he would think that that was such a good thing that it was worth preserving them after this life to pursue the supremely worthwhile life of Heaven, centered on the worship of God.[4] Although God could from the start have made men fitted for Heaven, it is obviously a good thing that men should have the opportunity to choose for themselves what kind of persons they are to be, and through deliberate exercise of that choice over a period of time to form their characters, preferably so as to be suited to live the life of Heaven. The only workable solution to the problem of evil is to my mind that centered in the free will defence,[5] which has as an essential plank that God has made men who are not saints at the start but are capable, partly through their own choice of making themselves saints. If there is a God, that is the kind of world he has made. If men are to have this choice, they need information as to what kind of life is a saintly life, is supremely worth living, and how to take steps to live that life. The information which they need is of four kinds. First, they need to know such general moral truths as that benefactors deserve gratitude, wrongdoers need to make atonement (by way of repentance, apology, reparation and penance) to those whom they have wronged, holy beings deserve worship; and so on. Secondly, they need factual information which will enable them to apply those moral truths, in seeing which particular actions are good or bad, obligatory or wrong. If there is a God, the crucial factual information will be that there is a God. From that it will follow that he is to be worshipped, and thanked, and that men must make atonement to him for wrongs against him (that is, sins). But it will also follow, as I have argued elsewhere,[6] that it is very difficult for man to

---

[3] Oxford: Clarendon Press, 1979.

[4] For argument that that life would be supremely worthwhile, see my *Faith and Reason* (Oxford: Clarendon Press, 1981), ch. 6.

[5] See my *The Existence of God* (Oxford: Clarendon Press, 1979) pp. 152–60 and chs. 10 and 11.

[6] See my *Responsibility and Atonement* (Oxford: Clarendon Press, 1989) for full exposition and justification of this claim and the claims of the next few sentences, about atonement. See my *Faith and Reason*, ch. 6 about the need for true beliefs in order to pursue the Christian way.

make atonement for his sins and to help his fellows to make their atonement, as he should. God could deal with this difficulty by himself becoming man and offering on man's behalf a perfect human life culminating in a death arising from its perfection; and, in order to allow the men whom he has created access to himself, he has reason to do so. If he has done so, it must be among the items of information which men need to have—that and how he has done so. For an atonement which another makes on our behalf can only be something through which we secure forgiveness and reconciliation if we offer it on our own behalf to him whom we have wronged. So men need, thirdly, the information of how, if at all, God became incarnate and made atonement for their sins; and the information of how to plead that atonement. God needs to have revealed himself in the primary sense, and to have made available information as to how in detail he has done this. And, finally, it provides a valuable encouragement (as well as import- ant information about the goodness of God) to know that there is a goal of Heaven to be had after this life for those who have obtained forgiveness for their sins and made themselves saints and so fitted for Heaven; and (if that is how it is) that there is a Hell, for those who ignore God, to be avoided.

If there is a God who wills men to do good and to be good he needs to ensure that men have the information of the kinds which I have set out.[7] Cannot man's natural reason find out some, at least, of these things, without God needing to intervene in history to provide information in propositional form? Certainly natural reason can discover unaided the general moral truths, and there is perhaps enough evidence that there is a God without God needing to tell us so by a verbal communication. But even in these cases revelation helps—if an apparently knowledgeable person tells you that what you have concluded tentatively from your private investigation is true, that rightly gives you much more confidence in its truth. If God tells us basic moral truths, and assures us verbally that he is there, and makes it fairly clear to us that he is telling us these things, our confidence in their truth justifiably increases. I have claimed that we have some *a priori* reason to suppose that God will become incarnate and make atonement for us. But it is by no means certain that, if there is a God, he will do this. (Maybe, despite the difficulty of man making his own atonement, God judges it no better to make atonement for him than to leave him to try to make his own atonement.) And, anyway, mere *a priori* reasoning cannot tell us how and where the atonement will

---

[7] The need for revelation in order to convey to us moral truths, and to encourage us to live morally by offering us the hope of Heaven (and the risk of Hell) was brought out by John Locke in his *The Reasonableness of Christianity* sections 238–46 (Abridged edition, I. T. Ramsey (ed.) London: A. and C. Black, 1958). But like so many other liberal Protestants of the seventeenth and eighteenth centuries, he seems to have no serious doctrine of the Atonement. The point of Christ's coming to Earth was supposed to be simply to reveal things otherwise hard to discover. However, like all others in this empiricist tradition, Locke stressed the need for miracles in order to authenticate claims to revelation. He described miracles as 'that foundation on which the believers of any divine revelation must ultimately bottom their faith' (*A Discourse of Miracles,* p. 86 of the abridged edition of *The Reasonableness of Christianity*).

be made. We need historical information to show us this, and it is hard to see how it would do this without God, either himself or through another, telling us what was happening. And the goal of Heaven and the danger of Hell are things at which we can only guess without God telling us more. To strengthen some of these beliefs needed for our salvation, and to provide others of them, we need propositional revelation.[8]

So there is some *a priori* reason to suppose that God will reveal to us those things needed for our salvation. How will he reveal them? If, as I have urged, the major purpose of such revelation is to enable us, by showing us what it is, to choose whether to pursue the way to Heaven or to neglect to do so, it would be consonant with that purpose that we should also have the opportunity to choose whether to find out by investigation what the way to Heaven is or to neglect to do so—and so that the revelation should not be too open, but something to be looked for and found. Also, since it is good that men should have the opportunity to help each other towards material and spiritual wellbeing, it is good that the revelation be something which they can help each other to find. That men have the opportunity to make or mar each other's character is evident in the natural world. It might be expected that the availability of revelation in part or more fully only to some should reinforce that opportunity—two could cooperate in discovering the revelation, or one could tell another about it. Thirdly, however, while it is good that revelation should be available and discoverable, it is good that it should not be too evident, even to those who have discovered it, that they have discovered the revelation. For in that case they can manifest their commitment to the goals which it offers, by pursuing them when it is not certain that those goals are there to be had. If it is on balance probable, but no more than probable, that a man has discovered the way to Heaven, then he will manifest his belief that Heaven is a thing worth having above all things by pursuing it when there is some doubt whether his quest will be successful. Such pursuit will involve a more total commitment to Heaven and so be more worthy of reward; and, since by pursuing some goal steadfastly we often come to desire to pursue it, it may well make such a man one who desires Heaven alone above all things. Hence such pursuit may well make the pursuer fitted for Heaven; happiness comes from doing and having what you most desire, and the more a man desires Heaven, the happier he will be when he gets there.

So there is *a priori* reason for supposing that the revelation which God provides will be such as requires searching out with the help of others, and

---

[8] 'God destines us for an end beyond the grasp of reason. Now we have to recognize an end before we can stretch out and exert ourselves for it. Hence the necessity for our welfare that divine truths surpassing reason should be signified to us through divine revelation' (St. Thomas Aquinas, *Summa Theologiae* 1.1.1, London: Blackfriars, Vol. 1, translated by T. Gilby, 1964). It is for this reason, of course, that we cannot predict in advance the content of Revelation. See J. Butler, *The Analogy of Religion* (London: George Bell and Sons, 1902) Part II, ch. 3, part of the heading of which is 'Of our Incapacity of Judging What were to be expected in a Revelation'.

such as not to be completely evident even to those who have found it. I am not arguing that it must have such a character—there is a point in not making my salvation too much influenced by what you or I bother to do about it. All I am arguing is that, although it *might* be good that God reveal himself in other ways, the way which I have described *would* be good. Butler emphasised the value of investigation in discovering the content of revelation and of uncertainty about it:

If a prince desires to exercise, or in any sense prove, the understanding or loyalty of a servant, he would not always give his orders in such a plain manner. . . . Ignorance and doubt afford scope for probation in all senses. . . . Men's moral probation may also be, whether they will take due care to inform themselves by impartial consideration, and afterwards whether they will act as the case requires upon the evidence which they have, however doubtful.[9]

But he did not bring out the value of mutual help in this respect.[10]

How is the revelation to be made to different centuries and cultures? Of course, God could ensure that, subsequent to his revelation, there was only one century and culture on Earth, but there would seem to be no reason for him to restrict so narrowly the possibilities for human diversity. But, given that he is concerned to reveal himself to different centuries and cultures, he could make a separate revelation to each culture and century. Hinduism and other religions have claimed that he has done just that. But any division between cultures and centuries is a highly arbitrary one, as any historian will tell us. Men are too similar to each other, too much in contact with each other, capable of understanding each other's ideas and adopting each other's customs. Men of one culture are capable of transmitting a revelation to men of another culture, and it is good that they should have the opportunity of doing so. Further, if I am right in supposing that man needs not only revelation but atonement and that God might well become incarnate in order to make that atonement, then, if he does so, either there have to be many atonements, or at most one of many revelations can be associated with the one atonement. Atonements are costly, and God would not make many atonements unless one would not suffice for the whole human race. But, if God living on Earth a perfect human life would be an adequate atonement for a few million humans, surely it would avail for the whole human race. It trivializes the notion of a perfect atoning life to suppose otherwise; what atones is the quality of one life, not the number of lives. One perfect atonement must suffice for the whole human race. So any revelation of that atonement must have enough connection with the century and culture in which it took place for the report of it to be comprehensible. And that means that there cannot be totally separate revelations for different centuries and cultures. Or at least it is an argument for one *final* major revelation, reporting that atonement. Before that

---

[9] J. Butler, *The Analogy of Religion*, Part II, ch. 6 (pp. 273ff. of London 1902 edition).
[10] For a fuller and more satisfactory development of the point see David Brown, *The Divine Trinity*, (London: Duckworth, 1985), pp. 70–5.

atonement and to others who have not heard of it there is perhaps more scope for lesser revelations of the non-historical parts of what subsequently becomes the final revelation, partially inter-communicable between cultures.

But now we come to a serious problem. We need in any one culture a revelation accessible to old and young, male and female, the clever and the stupid, the uneducated and the learned. And this revelation must be transmittable to men of another culture with totally different backgrounds of religion, ethics, theoretical science, philosophy and technology. What *could* such a revelation be like?

God could provide a revelation of one or other or two simple extreme kinds. The first kind of revelation is a culture-relative revelation, one expressed in terms of the scientific, historical and even perhaps theological presuppositions (false as well as true) of the culture to which it is addressed, and giving moral instruction applicable to the situation of members of that culture. Thus the doctrine of creation might be expressed on the assumption that the world was as described by the current science—e.g. a flat Earth, covered by a dome, above which was Heaven—'God made the Heaven and the Earth'.[11] On the assumption that the world came into existence 4,000 years ago, it would teach that it was then that God caused it to be. It would teach that God had made atonement, using the analogies of sacrifice and law familiar to those in the culture. It would teach the moral truths which those living in that culture needed to know—e.g. those concerned with whether one ought to pay taxes to the Roman Emperor, or to obey the Jewish food laws; but it would contain no guidance on the morality of artificial insemination by donor, or medical research on embryos. It would offer the hope of Heaven to those who lived the right life; and it would express this hope, using such a presupposition of the culture as that Heaven was above the Earth.

Such a revelation would be perfectly adequate for providing its immediate recipients with guidance as to how to live their lives on Earth, have the right attitude to God, plead an atonement for the forgiveness of their sins, and aspire to Heaven; it would, that is, provide enough information of the kind earlier described, for the men of that culture to live saintly lives. The limitation of its moral instruction to that relevant to that community would hardly matter, and its metaphors and analogies would be comprehensible there. False scientific presuppositions would make no difference to the religious content of the message, i.e. to the kind of life and worship which it sought to encourage. A mistaken view of what God had created, or where Heaven was, would not affect the praiseworthiness of God, or the desirability of Heaven. The problem is that it could not be transmitted, as it stood, to those of another culture. Such a revelation would be of little use to the philosophers who met on Mars' Hill,

---

[11] Genesis 1.1.

Athens, in the first century A.D.; let alone to literate and numerate and numerate Anglo-Americans of today.

What I have just said about a revelation being clothed in the presuppositions of a certain culture presupposes a distinction between a message and the presuppositions in terms of which it is cast. In order to say anything we do normally take for granted a lot of fairly irrelevant things; these are the presuppositions of our particular group or wider culture. Within a context of common assumptions, we make our detailed claims, commands, requests, and questions. One way in which this happens, highlighted by recent philosophical discussion, is that we use such assumptions in order to make clear to whom we are referring, in order to say something about them. Thus, to modify a well-known pholosophical example,[12] suppose a society which normally drinks only drinks of two kinds—martini and beer, easily distinguishable by their visual appearance. I am at a party and see someone drinking what looks like martini; and I say 'the man over there drinking martini is enjoying himself'. The message which I want to convey is that a certain man is enjoying himself. That he is drinking martini is irrelevant to my claim, but I use the supposed fact that he is drinking martini to enable my hearers to know to whom I am referring, in order to make my claim. Suppose now that the man isn't drinking martini, but a drink unusual in that society, sherry—is what I have said false? In view of the fact that there are public criteria about to whom I am referring (there may be only one martini-looking drinker in the vecinity), and that my claim is not about what he is drinking, I suggest that what I have said is not false. It is true; or if we want to be more careful, we may say that it is true, given the presuppositions of the society. I add that I may even make my claim in the same way if I know that the man is drinking sherry, if my hearers do not know what sherry is, because the use of the false assumption enables me to communicate my message with minimum trouble. This distinction between message and presupposition can however only be made if there are clear public criteria for what I am trying to do with my words—e.g. to get you to worship your creator, as opposed to have a certain belief about what he created. Study of the context in which utterances are made will often enable a clear distinction to be made. A useful criterion for this purpose is that utterances are seldom made in order to convey information already believed by the speaker to be known to the hearer. Once we know what is taken for granted by a society (e.g. that the world consists of a flat Earth covered by a dome, above which is Heaven), we can resonably assume that a purported revelation does not have such common assumptions as its message, although it may have them as its presuppositions.

So, to repeat, God could provide such a culture-relative revelation, but it would be of no use outside the culture unless it could be translated into the vocabulary of another culture. That could only be done by someone who could

---

[12] Originating in Keith S. Donellan, 'Reference and Definite Descriptions', *Philosophical Review* 75 (1966): 281–304.

think away the presuppositions of the two cultures, and make the distinction between the presuppositionless message and presuppositions in terms of which it may be clad. An intellectual can to some extent perform this exercise, but in so far as he can he has a grasp of the message expressible by presuppositionless sentences. Can then be such a person? Only if there could be a culturally independent revelation. To this issue I now turn.

The second kind of revelation which God could provide would be a culturally independent one. In a way this could be done. God could give us a creed formed of sentences which make no scientific or historical presuppositions. But such a creed would not necessarily serve the purpose for which it had been devised—to provide sentences translatable into other languages and usable by other cultures, to provide for them clear guidance of the kind described above. We could get rid of the presupposition of the flat Earth covered by a dome, but any way in which we do this is open to possible misunderstanding, especially when it is translated into other languages and different questions are raised about it by other cultures. We could avoid more and more such misunderstandings by making the creed more and more rigorous, but there is no maximum degree of rigour, and the possibility of misunderstanding will always remain. (By 'misunderstanding' I mean being understood in a way in which God did not intend it to be understood).

Thus suppose God gives us the doctrine of creation by means of the sentence 'God created everything'. That could be understood as implying that God created God, which is self-contradictory. Perhaps God would do better with the sentence 'God created everything other than God'. But that might seem to have the consequence that God created logical truths, e.g. God made it the case that for all propositions p, not both p and not-p (the law of non-contradiction). But that doesn't seem true (surely the law of non-contradiction would hold, even if there was no God); and in any case hardly seems what the doctrine of creation was getting at. Let's try 'God created everything logically contingent other than God'. But since unicorns are things logically contingent other than God, this might seem to have the consequence that God created unicorns. So it had better be phrased 'God created everything which exists, and whose existance is logically contingent, other than himself'. I could go on improving this sentence for a long time—indeed much of my book *The Coherence of Theism*[13] was an exercise in spelling out coherently and rigorously the claim that there is a God, along the lines which I have begun to pursue in this paragraph for the doctrine that God is creator. I was trying to spell out with considerable philosophical rigour, avoiding the scientific assumptions of my culture, what the claim that there is a God amounted to. But I would have been deluding myself if I had supposed that I had achieved maximum rigour. There isn't such a thing. At best I could have provided a spelling out which gave a clear answer to the main concerns of our culture about

---

[13] Oxford: Clarendon Press, 1977.

that doctrine. But I did not phrase it and could not have phrased it in such a way that it would be clear what were the consequences of the doctrine with respect to questions which might interest any other culture. Even God could not have chosen a sentence of a human language which would do that job.

There is a simple philosophical reason for this. It is the nature of human language that we learn and manifest our understanding of the meaning of words and sentence forms by using them in a publicly agreed way in ordinary circumstances. We learn and show our understanding of the terms by which 'God' is defined—'person', 'able to do everything', 'knows everything' etc., and the other terms used in exposition of the doctrine of creation—'create', 'logically contingent'—by seeing them or terms by which they are defined used in mundane situations, and by using them ourselves. That gives us a grasp of their meaning which allows us to use them in new and often different situations. But an understanding of how to use terms in ordinary situations will not give clear guidance how to use those terms in situations providing borderline cases for their application of a kind not previously envisaged. 'God created everything' is a satisfactory account of the doctrine of creation given an understanding of 'thing' derived from being told that trees and humans and lakes are 'things'. But once a culture considers quite different possible cases of things, e.g. logical truths, it is unclear what 'God created everything' has to say about these—Is it committed to holding that God created logical truths? We can improve the formulation to make the answer clear. Other possible 'things' are then brought to our attention, e.g. unicorns; we then legislate that really there are no such 'things'. And so we go on. New cultures always raise new questions of interpretation, and the consequences of unreformed old sentences for their concerns become unclear. The explicit mention of the presuppositions of the culture may have been eliminated from the sentences of a creed. The sentences may no longer make explicit reference to 'Heaven and Earth'. But the presuppositions operate in a different way—to determine for what areas of inquiry (i.e. those of which the culture is well aware), the sentences have clear consequences. Sentences of a human language only have meaning to the extent to which its speakers can grasp that meaning; and as (being only human) they cannot conceive of all the possible concerns of future cultures, they cannot have sentences whose consequences for the concerns of those cultures are always clear. If God chooses to reveal his message in human language, he chooses a tool too feeble to convey an unequivocal message to all nations and generations—unless backed up in some way.

Two further empirical considerations add to this formal logical difficulty standing in the way of God conveying his revelation by means of presuppositionless sentences, which can be handed on from one culture to another. The first is that the more presuppositions are removed from the sentences of a creed, and they are made logically rigorous, the less accessible they will be to the relatively uneducated majority of members of that culture, who will then need an élite to translate to them the message in terms which they can understand. The second

further difficulty is that if the revelation involves a demanding morality, then
those who hear it have all sorts of bad reasons for forcing upon it an interpretation of their own. If correctly translated, it may demand too much of them in
the way of time, energy, and change of perspective.

Other examples in the history of Christian theology illustrate in a more
striking way than does the doctrine of creation, the general point that it is
often unclear what are the consequences of some credal formula for some new
concern—either because there is no true answer (the original formula being too
vague for there to be a right answer), or because, although there is a right answer,
many people are too biased or unsophisticated to draw it out. If Christ has two
natures, does it follow that he has two wills? And, more generally, what does the
Chalcedonian doctrine of the Incarnation commit us to, if we try to avoid stating
it in terms of the Greek words ὑπόστασις and φύσις?[14]

So the message of a revelation will inevitably become less clear as it is passed
from one culture to another. There are a number of ways in which God could
make the original such that the process of obscuration was slower. He could provide both a culture-relative and a culturally independent revelation, such that
each could provide a check on the interpretations drawn from the other—a New
Testament as well as a Denzinger. And he could perhaps even provide simultaneously, together with a revelation in terms of one culture, a translation of it in
terms of another culture. If you have, as well as an original literary work, one
translation of it into one foreign language, authorized by the author, you will
then be able to see far better how to translate it into different foreign languages.
For you will be helped to see from the example provided what has to be preserved
in translation, and what can be altered. But all of this would still not be enough
to counter the processes of obscuration which I have described. The content of
the message still would not be guaranteed always to be evident to other cultures
with new interests and concerns. Not even God can give unambiguous culturally
independent instructions accessible to men limited not merely by the knowledge,
but by the concerns and interests of their own culture.

An effective revelation cannot consist solely of original documents or other
proclamations. *Continuing* guidance is required; a mechanism which helps
translators of the original revelation to get their translation correct. There need
to be documents containing statements of the revelation in one or more cultures.
For given that obscurity will infect even a culturally independent revelation, there
is everything to be said for an initial revelation which is at any rate accessible to

[14] That new formulations of doctrine applicable to new situations (e.g. to deal with issues raised
by a new heresy) was simply a matter of deducing the consequences of previous formulations by
clear rules of unambiguous logic was a scholastic view. For its development in seventeenth-century
Catholic theology, see O. Chadwick, *From Bossuet to Newman. The Idea of Doctrinal Development.*
Cambridge: Cambridge University Press, 1957) ch. 2. This view did at any rate have an advantage
that it allowed the discovery (by deduction) of previously ill-recognized aspects of doctrine: that
possibility was hardly allowed by Bossuet's account of revelation—see Chadwick, ch. 1.

most people in an original culture. Perhaps also there could be a more culture-free statement as to how the revelation is to be translated so as to make it accessible to other cultures. But, as well, there must be such a thing as (in *some* sense) a Church in which translations have a better chance of success than they would otherwise. There are various ways in which God could effect that result through a Church. There could be an infallible authority in the Church which pronounced from time to time on which interpretations were correct. In his *An Essay on the Development of Christian Doctrine*, Newman argued that

In proportion to the probability of true developments of doctrine and practice in the Divine Scheme, so is the probability also of the appointment in that scheme of an external authority to decide upon them, thereby separating them from the mass of mere human speculation, extravagance, corruption and error, in and out of which they grow. This is the doctrine of the infallibility of the Church.[15]

This infallibility could be mediated through an individual or through the majority vote of some Council chosen by a certain procedure. Alternatively, God might ensure that, while no one mechanism guaranteed truth, truth would emerge in the long run by consensus within the Church, distinguished as such by some organizational continuity and continuity of doctrine with the original revelation. The consensus would be obtained by moral, scientific and philosophical reflection in the light of experience on the original content of revelation, and the way in which it had been developed and expounded in intervening centuries. There would be no one stopping point to controversy, but a general direction by God of interpretation, compatible with some error by individuals, groups, or even generations. God could have provided either of these methods for guaranteeing the preservation of his revelation for new centuries and cultures. *A priori* the former method might seem to grant an all-or-nothing status to some written documents—you believe that or nothing; there is little scope for an individual to work out for himself which parts of revelation fit best with other parts and with what his natural reason tells him about God. At least, that is so in so far as it is fairly certain what (if there has been a revelation) is the infallible authority for interpreting it; otherwise, of course, the individual will have plenty of work to do to work out if there is an infallible authority—and part of that work will consist in considering whether the 'interpretations' proclaimed by a given purported authority are plausible interpretations of the original revela-tion.[16] All the same, it gives much less scope than the consensus method for the

[15] (First published 1845) 1878 edition, London: Longmans, Green and Co, 1906, p. 78. Newman held that process of doctrinal evolution consisted in developing, by a process more intuitive than deduction, ideas which were implicit in an original formulation. See the *Essay* and Chadwick, *op. cit.*.

[16] As Newman urged, asking rhetorically 'What is inconsistent' in the idea of 'a probable infallibility'? (*op. cit.* p. 81). And he went on to claim: 'We have, then, no warrant at all for saying that an accredited revelation will exclude the existence of doubts and difficulties on the part of those whom it addresses, or dispense with anxious diligence on their part'. And after the qualifying clause, 'though it may in its own nature tend to do so', he boldly added, 'Infallibility does not interfere with moral probation: the two notions are absolutely distinct' (*op. cit.*, pp. 82ff).

individual to sort things out for himself, to take individual doctrines seriously
and reflect upon them. On the other hand, the consensus method of guaranteeing the preservation of revelation could prove rather weak. The existence of a
consensus may itself be by no means evident. *A priori* considerations do not seem
to me to give much greater prior probability to one over the other method of
ensuring the preservation of a revelation. But some method there must be if the
revelation is not to die out.[17] If the Bible were finished in 100 A.D., and buried in
the sands of Egypt by the last living Christian who was then executed in the
persecutions, and then dug up again by the Reformers in 1500 A.D., they would
have produced far far more diverse theologies than ever they did.

So far I have been arguing that if there is a God there is good *a priori* reason for
expecting a propositional revelation, perhaps in connection with an atoning
incarnation; and for expecting some means to be provided for preserving and
rightly interpreting that revelation for new centuries and cultures. I have not yet
considered what form the original revelation might take, except to suggest that, at
any rate in part, it will be formulated in terms of the presuppositions of the
original culture. Again there are various possibilities. At one extreme is a Koran, a
book dictated by the original revealer, or prophet, as I shall call him. Alternatively, the original prophet might talk and various others record some of the
things which he said; and the kind of life he led, and the recorders described him
as having led, might help us to understand the kind of life which he was
commending us to lead. The former method would have the disadvantage that
it might encourage excessive literalism of observance, making it difficult for
future generations to have the courage to apply an original command, appropriate to a particular culture, to a new culture. If the prophet (who was God
Incarnate, or at least his very special messenger) wrote that it was wrong to
take money on usury, or laid down rules for the right way to treat slaves, and
these were his *ipsissima verba*, then future generations would find it difficult to
introduce a system of lending money on interest for commercial investment, or
to abolish slavery—thinking that God himself had forbidden taking interest and
had commended slavery, for all time. A little distancing of any accessible version
of the revelation from the prophet, and plenty of versions of it on which new
generations can get to work to apply it to new circumstances, has much to be
said for it.

So perhaps a New Testament (itself teaching how to interpret an earlier Old
Testament) rather than a Koran; many books written by many authors, each
recording and applying the teaching of the prophet; overlapping, stressing
different aspects of revelation, and occasionally appearing to contradict each
other. Plenty of scope to ferret out the original teaching, plenty of examples to
see how it applies thirty years later. Among the tasks of the later community will

---

[17] It was a major deficiency in my account in *Faith and Reason*, ch. 7, of the tests of a genuine
revelation that I gave no consideration to the need to ensure that a revelation is correctly interpreted.

be to say which historical documents contain the original revelation; and that too is something on which they might change their view—but only marginally—over the years.

The later community will have to make the distinction between the presup-positions of the original documents and their informative content. As we noted earlier, one help here will be if there are examples in the original revelation of that revelation cast into different philosophical or scientific moulds—and, of course, the New Testament, with its Palestinian Jewish, Pauline, and Johannine tradi-tions contains just that. Another help is if the intervening centuries have reinter-preted the message into the terms of their own culture. The many (neglected) examples of how the Fathers and Scholastics sought to express the message of creation in terms of the science, no longer of Israel many centuries B.C, but of Aristotle and Ptolemy, are examples of such reinterpretation. Scientific presup-positions which they had reason to believe false (for reasons derived from Greek science) are to be discarded, they taught. The creation story in Genesis was to be seen as a message expressed in terms which 'an ignorant people' could under-stand.[18] Other examples of such reinterpretation came when the Copernican revolution forced the men of the sixteenth and seventeenth centuries to see Genesis as telling the story of the creation of the world, but a world which we now knew to be very large, indeed, possibly infinite, and certainly not earth-centred. Such examples made easier the task for later generations of prising off other scientific presuppositions from the biblical message. The Fathers and scholastics also provide us today with examples of what they regarded as false theological presuppositions in terms of which some biblical passages are cast, which we can learn to recognize as such through other more explicit revealed doctrine, and so prise off from these passages. Some Old Testament talk about God seems to speak of him as embodied and subject to emotions such as anger and jealousy; other biblical teaching reveals that God is not like that.[19] Finally, the later community may acquire historical information about the beliefs and circumstances in which the original revelation was proclaimed; and that may enable it to see what was taken for granted at the time (and so was plausibly a presupposition) and what was contested (and so may plausibly be seen as the message of the revelation).

---

[18] See Augustine's *De Genesi ad Litteram*; and Aquinas' comment (*Summa Theologiae* Ia.68.3) that 'Moses was speaking to an ignorant people' and needed to make scientific assumptions that were, strictly, false, in order for his basic point to be conveyed.

[19] Novatian (*De Trinitate* 6) claims that the Old Testament uses anthropormorphic language about God (talks of him as having hands, feet, etc.) 'not because God was like that, but because in that way the people could understand'. Aquinas writes with respect to such cases that 'Holy Scripture is intended for us all in common without distinction of persons . . . and fitly puts forward spiritual things under bodily likenesses; at all events, the uneducated may then lay hold of them, those, that is to say, who are not ready to take intellectual truths neat with nothing else' (*Summa Theologiae* Ia.1.9, Blackfriars translation, 1964).

So *a priori* we might expect a revelation, and among possible kinds of revelation, some are more to be expected than others. How can we recognize that some purported revelation is genuine? I argued in *Faith and Reason*[20] that the teaching of the prophet must be true and deep. In so far as we have moral and philosophical views which seem fairly evidently correct, the teaching of the prophet (as distinguished from the presuppositions in terms of which his teaching is cast) must to some extent coincide with our views and in no way contradict them. Some parts of his teaching which initially seem to us doubtful must seem to us after subsequent investigation and reflection more likely to be true. The purported revelation must also contain things too deep for us to find for them any adequate independent check. The fact that his teaching proves correct in areas where we can check it is some evidence, though not as such very strong evidence, that it is reliable in areas where we cannot. What we need also is evidence that the prophet was in a position to know the truth of the message which he proclaimed (other than direct evidence that that message is true). God would need to bring about some public effect which would be obviously his act (since no one else could bring it about) and which, given the conventions of that culture, would be understood by them as the sign of his approval on the prophet's teaching. Since God keeps the laws of nature going, God alone (or someone else with his consent) can violate them, make things in the world behave contrary to the way they behave in accord with the natural laws. A clear marked violation of natural laws which was the all important cause of the promulgation of that teaching, (and would also be understood by the people of that culture as God's acceptance of the prophet's atonement, if he claimed to make an atonement) would manifest God's approval of that teaching, and so be evidence that God had communicated that teaching specially to the prophet (since it was not discoverable by ordinary men). The evidence that this was so would be further reinforced if the prophet had foretold that God would violate natural laws in this way, for that would show that he had in this crucial respect knowledge of God's purposes, and would thus be evidence that he had such knowledge in other respects also. What better symbolic act could there be than the Resurrection to life of the prophet clearly dead for teaching what he taught, when the prophet had forecast that resurrection, and when it was the cause of the success of the Church which the the prophet founded explicitly to carry on his work and which claimed to interpret that revelation and mediate the atonement which, the revelation claimed, the prophet had wrought?[21]

[20] pp. 183–93.
[21] The tradition of Christian theology has been fairly unanimous until the nineteenth and twentieth centuries in finding the primary evidence of a revelation in the miracles and, above all, the miracle of the Resurrection which sealed it. Among British writers see Paley and Locke (W. Paley, *A View of the Evidences of Christianity* 1794, republished in *Works*, vol I, Derby: Henry Mozley, 1825; and J. Locke, 'A Discourse on Miracles' in I. T. Ramsey (ed.), J. Locke *The Reasonableness of Christianity*). For development of the point, see W. Abraham, *Divine Revelation and the Limits of Historical Criticism* (Oxford: Clarendon Press, 1982), ch. 2.

If a revelation has taken a particular form and a particular means has been provided for its later interpretation, one would expect the original revelation to say so. I believe that the New Testament does contain a particular view of revelation, which I shall illustrate in general terms, without commenting on points of particular denominational difference. The revelation which God provides will not be that evident, it will need searching out—such is the teaching of the parables of the pearl of great price (Mt. 13.45ff) or the treasure hid in the field (Mt. 13.44). Indeed, so much of Jesus' teaching was by parable, and by showing what he did, in order to get others to see things which he did not state—'But who say ye that I am?' (Mt. 16.15). His answer to the disciples of John 'Art thou he that cometh, or look we for another?' was 'Go your way and tell John the things which ye do hear and see' (Mt. 11.3ff). The revelation is to be spread by some telling others about it—'The harvest truly is great, but the labourers are few; pray ye therefore the Lord of the harvest that he would send forth labourers into his vineyard' (Mt. 9.38). The presence of Christ to later disciples is associated with a grouping of them—'where two or three are gathered together in my name, there am I in the midst of them'; which suggests (though it certainly does not state) that the understanding of Christian truth will be a communal activity. Even after we have learnt what we can of the Gospel, we shall not be certain of it—'we walk by faith, not by sight' (2 Cor. 5.7). And we have a vague and confused vision—'Now we see in a mirror darkly; but then face to face: now I know in part; but then shall I know even as also I have been known' (1 Cor. 13.12).

And no one better than the author of the Fourth Gospel expounded the view that understanding of revelation grows in the community through reflection. Christ had spoken to his disciples the message of the Father. 'The words that I say unto you I speak not from myself' (John 14.10); 'all things that I have heard from my Father I have made known unto you' (John 15.15). And not merely had Christ given the orders of the Father, he had lived to explain the point of them—'The servant knoweth not what his Lord doeth; but I have called your friends' (John 15.15). To quite an extent the message had been received—'The words which thou gavest me I have given unto them and they received them, and knew of a truth that I came forth from thee, and they believed that thou didst send me' (John 17.8). Yet even then the message had been imperfectly understood—'Have I been so long time with you, and dost thou not know me, Philip?' (John 14.9). And indeed, there was more to come, which simply could not be understood at that time and place—'I have yet many things to say unto you, but ye cannot bear them now' (John 16.12). There was a need of future guidance—'When he, the Spirit of truth, is come, he shall guide you into all truth' (John 16.13). But the Spirit's witness will be combined with the historical witness of the disciples—'The Comforter... shall bear witness of me; and ye also bear witness, because ye have been with me from the beginning' (John 15.26ff). The Spirit will reinforce the disciples' witness to Christ. And he will help them to remember and understand what Christ did—'He shall teach you all things and bring to your remembrance all that I said unto you' (John 14.26). However, the Spirit's witness will not be public—'The world cannot receive' the Spirit of Truth (John 14.17). The manifestation of Christ through the Spirit is for those who love Christ and keep his commandments—'He that hath my commandments, and keepeth them, he it is that loveth me; and he that loveth me shall be loved of my Father, and I will love him and will manifest myself to him' (John 14.21). In other words, that is in my words, the revelation spoken by and the deeds acted by Christ will be interpreted by human witnesses who keep the commandments of God under the guidance of the Spirit of God. The revelation goes on; it is their witness and yet their witness to an original source which forms the revelation.

On the whole, later Catholic and Protestant tradition has maintained that the revelation ended with the death of the last apostle;[22] it consisted of words of Christ and words about Christ which the Spirit told the apostles. The rest is interpretation. But, as we know well from other fields, where to put the line between a datum and its correct interpretation can be a somewhat arbitrary matter.

Evidence of the kind outlined earlier, that the original revelation was true, may be reinforced by evidence that that later interpretation of the kind suggested by the original revelation is true and a plausible interpretation for the later century and culture for which it was provided.

So much for the prior probability of a revelation and the kind of historical evidence which we would need to show that it had occurred. The issue now becomes one for historical investigation. Has there been a purported revelation (perhaps associated with an atonement), founded on a great miracle, containing (as far as we can judge) deep truth, interpreted by a community whose foundation was part of that revelation deriving from that miracle? Is there enough historical evidence to have a reasonable belief that such a revelation has occurred, given what *a priori* we can expect in the way of revelation?

I suspect that you may guess what my own (inexpert) answer to this question is. The point of this paper is to argue that we need to approach it, having sorted out beforehand two crucial issues. The first is—what sort of a revelation are we looking for? A golden tablet thrown down from the sky, preserved in a sealed glass case from all interference, including radioactivity, containing an eternally true message, unambiguous, with all consequences clear for all generations, expressed without any cultural presuppositions? Or a whole way of looking at things, embedded in documents and in a community with a tradition of how to interpret those documents and continually being worked out by them? And the second is—which general theory of the world (e.g., theism or materialism) do we

---

[22] For the Catholic Tradition, see the listing as a Modernist error, in the 1907 decree of the Holy Office *Lamentabili,* the view that Revelation was not brought to completion 'with the apostles' (Denzinger 3421).

think is best supported by other evidence? For general theory is crucial for assessing particular claims. If we think it vastly improbable that there is a God able and willing to intervene in history, then we will rightly ask a lot more of historical evidence (thousands of witnesses rather than tens of witnesses, of a resurrection; the tomb certified as the one in which Jesus was buried by a certificate signed by Pontius Pilate himself, and so on), than we will if we think that there is quite a chance that there is a God able and willing to intervene in history. I suspect that too many New Testament scholars of recent years have approached their evidence with deep secular presuppositions in a search for the wrong kind of Revelation.[23]

[23] The material of this paper was subsequently used in the full-length account of the Criteria of Divine Revelation given in my *Revelation*, Oxford: Clarendon Press, 1992.

7

The Concept of Inspiration*

William J. Abraham

If there is one mistake in recent theories of inspiration which deserves to be singled out for special attention, that mistake is at root conceptual. Rather than pause to reflect on divine inspiration, Evangelical theologians have built their theories around the idea of divine speaking. This is simply a basic category mistake. It is essential to identify and remove this mistake if there is to be progress or hope for any future account of inspiration. Virtually all the theories that we have examined are defective at this point. Indeed so widespread and all-pervasive is the conceptual confusion here that I have some sympathy with those who feel that it is impossible to rebuild or repair the concept for today. However, once my main point is grasped there can be a radical shift of vision that is liberating and refreshing to those who can accept it. Let me approach the matter from a general angle.

The fundamental conception of God that informs the Christian tradition is that God is a transcendent, personal agent. As some recent theologians have insisted, God is first and foremost the one who acts. But this very general account of who God is must be filled out by specifying more exactly what God has actually done. Otherwise all we have is a general, if not abstract, concept that fails to relate God to the world of both everyday life and religious experience. Christians have not hesitated to execute this task, although they have always recognized that this generates sophisticated and specialist philosophical and theological discussion. Thus Christians have said that God created the world *ex nihilo* and that he continues to sustain it by his power. God liberated the Hebrew slaves from Egypt and he spoke to the people of Israel and Judah through the prophets. God became incarnate in history in Jesus of Nazareth. He performed miracles; for example, he raised Jesus from the dead. He sent the Holy Spirit to the waiting disciples on the day of Pentecost and guided the early missionary efforts of the Church. And so one could continue to list the various acts and activities that God has done and one could add to that list by specifying what God continues to do and what he will do in the future. Without the fundamental

* From W. J. Abraham, *The Divine Inspiration of Holy Scripture.* © 1981 Oxford University Press. Reprinted by permission of the publisher.

category of agency we have ceased to be theists, for theism by definition is belief in a personal God who is analogous in crucial respects to human agents. Without some specification of what God has done and is doing we would be left with a very general concept that would be too far removed from life and experience to be religiously satisfying. We fill out and elaborate our fundamental picture of God by spelling out in detail what God has done, is doing, and will do.

As one might expect, philosophers and theologians have been puzzled by the idea of a divine agent. This is not surprising, for it is part of their job to examine such concepts as agency, event, revelation, persons, causation, etc. Sometimes they have been interested in the particular acts attributed to God by Christians. Thus the miraculous acts of God have for centuries been a source of analysis and controversy. In more recent days fundamental questions have been raised by the very idea of a divine agent, although these questions are not entirely new. Thus theologians have turned to other categories such as 'being' and 'process' instead of agency as a means of understanding God. Philosophers, on the other hand, have seriously wondered whether the idea of an incorporeal agent is coherent or not. To many philosophers the idea of a body is constitutive of the concept of an agent, so to talk of a divine agent is sheer nonsense, for God by definition does not have a body. For my part I am entirely happy with the idea of God as an agent. I find no insuperable logical dificulties in this notion and I see no need to substitute other fundamental categories for it. Moreover I find no insurmountable philosophical problems in assenting to such a miracle as the resurrection. Indeed I find traditional Christian thinking both religiously and intellectually enriching and exciting in both these areas. That God is a bodiless agent and that he has performed miracles in the past pose no insuperable conceptual, historical or religious difficulties for me; on the contrary they are central to my whole conception and experience of God.

What has been more of a puzzle to me is how we are to construe those predicates that ascribe particular actions to God. For example, how are we to understand the claim that God spoke to the prophets? It is far from easy to determine how exactly we are to explain the logic of such expressions as 'God spoke to Moses on Mount Sinai' or 'God spoke to Paul on the road to Damascus'. Within this enquiry there are two distinct questions. On the one hand we need to know what function these expressions are intended to have. Are they splendid poetry or factual prose? Are they intended to induce religious feelings of a special kind or to report an ineffable religious experience or to inform us of certain significant religious facts? Let us for the moment suppose that their function is primarily informative rather than, say, emotive. Let us say that they are intended as serious factual discourse, and in so doing let us leave aside the delicate and difficult matter of why this is so. For the moment let us simply accept that this is a plausible answer to our query. Having gone thus far we notice that we have a further question to answer: how are we to interpret 'speaking' when predicated of God? Are we to imagine that God spoke in an audible voice, in a fashion very similar to human speaking? Or are we to think of the speech of God as something unique and interior, something that involved an inner voice but no outer noises, say, rather like a form of telepathy? Whatever our answer to this question we can readily identify it as being logically quite distinct from the first one mentioned above.

Recent philosophical theology has been much concerned with questions of this kind. This concern is legitimate and absorbing. Such questions about the meaning of religious discourse are the most important posed by religion in our day. They are inescapable for the contemporary theologian, and how we answer them will determine the whole foundation and structure of our thinking about God. For the most part our concentration has focused on the first kind of question I identified. Since the challenge of logical Positivism in the 1930s much effort has been spent on clarifying the logic of religious discourse but to date there is no agreement in the answers given. My own view is quite simple: much fundamental religious language is intended to inform us about the way things are, and it succeeds in this respect.[1]

However, we also need to attend to the second sort of question identified. We need to clarify how we are to understand the verbs that attribute certain specific actions or activities to God. The traditional answer has involved a doctrine of analogy. When we use the verb 'speak' for example, in relation to God, it does not carry all the meaning that it has in everyday discourse when it is used of human agents, but only some of it. 'Speak' as predicated of God is neither univocal nor equivocal; it is analogous to 'speak' as predicated of human agents. As I see it, some doctrine of analogy is indispensable in any coherent account of the meaning of religious language. Without it we slide into either empty equivocation or radical agnosticism in our thinking about God. But our doctrine must be less formal and mathematical than that traditionally developed by Aquinas and his followers. That is, we have to rely on sensitive conceptual judgement in determining how analogous language is to operate. There is an irreducible element of mystery and personal linguistic judgement in our use of religious discourse for which we need make no apology. This position has been expounded with characteristic grace by Basil Mitchell. In general terms he puts it in this way:

. . . a word should be presumed to carry with it as many of the original entailments as the new context allows, and this is determined by the other descriptions which there is reason to believe also apply to God. That God is incorporeal dictates that 'father' does not mean 'physical progenitor', but the word continues to bear the connotation of tender protective care. Similarly God's 'wisdom' is qualified by the totality of other descriptions which are

---

[1] It would take me too far afield to defend this conception of religious language. I touch on the issue in 'Some Trends in Recent Philosophy of Religion', *The Theological Educator*, ix (1979), 93–102. See Richard Swinburne, *The Coherence of Theism* (Clarendon Press, Oxford, 1977), Part I, for an excellent treatment of this issue.

applicable to him; it does not, for example, have to be learned, since he is omniscient and eternal.[2]

This general proposal has crucial implications about our understanding of discourse about divine inspiration. It entails that we must first consider the word 'inspire' as it applies to human agents, if we are ever to understand it as applied to God. It is precisely this that the theologians we examined earlier failed to do. They made two fatal mistakes, first of all they ignored the need to begin with human agents; instead they began, continued, and ended with God. Secondly, they failed to focus on inspiration; they focused instead on speaking. As a result the whole character of divine inspiration was misread from the outset. They failed to attend to the root meaning of the word 'inspire' and failed in turn to exercise sensitive conceptual judgement in applying it to God. To grasp this point is to lay hold of one of the pivotal considerations that led me to develop a revised account of inspiration.

To avoid any misunderstanding here let me hasten to insist that this is a fundamental procedural consideration that demands attention in its own right. I am not at this point engaging in exegesis; this will come later. Nor am I suggesting that we reduce divine inspiration to human inspiration, for this is an absurdity that ignores the need to specify how divine inspiration differs from human inspiration, and I will do this shortly. My contention concerns the logic of the term 'inspire' as applied to God. In the case of other words we instinctively employ the procedure I am advocating. When we say that God loves us or that God knows that London is the capital of England or that God forgives us our sins, we grasp what these expressions mean by unconsciously drawing on the meaning that the terms 'love', 'know', 'forgive' possess in everyday language when applied to human agents. In the case of 'inspire' it is precisely this that we have failed to do. Instead we have focused on divine speaking, and even then we have failed to specify, if only in broad terms, how such speaking is to be related or compared to those human situations in which we first learn the meaning of our language. We need to retrace our steps and re-examine the concept of divine inspiration in the light of the principles we follow in other cases of divine action.

The term 'inspire' as developed theologically derives from its use in 2 Tim. 3: 16. The Greek word here is θεόπνευστος, which literally means 'God-breathed'. Virtually all translations express the sense of this by means of the phrase 'inspired by God'. This is entirely correct in that it is in keeping with the etymology of the English verb 'inspire', which is, in fact, derived from the Latin verb *spirare*, 'to breathe'. Our English verb 'inspire' therefore supplies quite neatly what is required by the Greek. Indeed Sanday points out that 2 Tim. 3: 16 is the only passage 'in which a direct equivalent for our word 'inspired' occurs in the Bible.'[3]

[2] *The Justification of Religious Belief* (Macmillan, London, 1973), p. 19.
[3] W. Sanday, p. 88.

This insight provides the clue to the first stage of a proper account of divine inspiration. Divine inspiration, I suggest, must be rooted in an adequate conception of what it is for one agent to inspire another. In other words, we must concentrate on the meaning of 'inspire' as used in everyday contexts before we turn to what it means as applied to God. By so doing we shall be attending to the root meaning of the concept.

The best way to begin this is to look closely at a paradigm case of inspiration as it operates in the common world of human agents. Out of this we can specify some important and necessary features of the meaning of the term 'inspire'. That done, we need to declare how the term is to be qualified when it is applied to God. Beyond this we can pause to answer some objections to our positive proposals about divine inspiration.

Our choice of a paradigm case of inspiration is always a delicate affair. There is no rigid set of procedures to determine our decisions at this level. We need to be sensitive and look for an example that will be illuminating rather than one that will be perfect in some absolute sense. A familiar case that I find helpful is furnished by a good teacher inspiring his students. Imagine for a moment a situation where we would naturally say that a teacher had inspired his students. Think of the light that this throws on the meaning of inspiration. We should note the following features as being essential to the description of the process.

First, since the students will vary in ability, temperament, and interests, and since the intensity of their relationship may also vary, it is perfectly in order to speak of degrees of inspiration. There is no guarantee that inspiration will be uniform, flat, or uneven in its effects. Indeed it should surprise us if it were so. Secondly, there is no question of the students remaining passive while they are being inspired. On the contrary: their natural abilities will be used to the full and as a result they will show great differences in style, content, and vocabulary. Their native intelligence and talent will be greatly enhanced and enriched but in no way obliterated or passed over. Thirdly, as there will be other influences and sources of inspiration at work upon them, there need be no surprise if, from the point of view of the teacher, they make mistakes. Commonly students in acknowledging the assistance and inspiration of their teachers dissociate them from any mistakes they may have made.

On the actual activity of inspiring there are two interesting points to be made. First, inspiring is not something that is done independently of other acts performed by the teacher. 'Inspiring', that is, is a polymorphous concept. It is not something that an agent does independently of other specifiable activity. One inspires someone in, with, and through other acts that one performs. Compare at this juncture another polymorphous concept—farming. One farms by ploughing fields, driving tractors, milking cows, tending sheep, going to market, etc. Farming is not something one does over and above such activity; it is done through them. Similarly with inspiring. A good teacher inspires through his supervision, teaching, lecturing, discussing, publishing, etc. He does not inspire independently of such activity. As a result—and here we arrive at the second point—the actual inspiring will generally be quite unconscious and unintentional on the part of the teacher. He may be quite unaware that his activity has this extra dimension to it, and that his students are being inspired by his routine work and example.

Finally we can note certain points about the effects of inspiration in the work produced by the students. To begin with, there are no hard and fast rules for detecting such effects. Normally we are persuaded by several strands of evidence taken together. The testimony of the students themselves will usually count for a lot. But there will probably be other considerations like continuity of interests, outlook, and perhaps even style of approach to the issue in hand. As to the actual content of the inspired work, we can make two comments with a reasonable degree of assurance. Where several people are inspired by the same agent, there will be some degree of unity in it, although how much will be difficult to specify in advance. Secondly, there will not be too radical a divergence from the views of the teacher, although again there can be no predictions in advance.

Given this description of a paradigm case of inspiration we can summarize the key features of the concept. I suggest that there are at least two that are constitutive. First, inspiration is a unique, irreducible activity that takes place between personal agents, one of whom, the inspirer, makes a definite objective difference to the work of the other, the inspired, without obliterating or rendering redundant the native activity of the other. Secondly, inspiration is a polymorphous concept in that it is achieved in, with, and through other acts that an agent performs. Both these features are surely minimal requirements in any analysis of inspiration. Therefore when we talk of the inspiration of God both these elements must be preserved. Without them the connections with the non-theological employment of the word have been so whittled away that one says nothing at all about God. With them the term is given substantial content.

The next task is a delicate and difficult one. We need to outline how far the other features identified can be presumed to apply when the term is used of God in his relation to those who gave us the Bible. In other words we must determine how far the term has to be qualified when it is predicated of God.

Very generally we should note immediately that the analogy has its limitations. the analogy between teacher and student is a highly intellectualist analogy. There is some virtue in this, for the divine inspiration of the Bible has traditionally been associated with instruction and teaching. The Bible certainly does have this rôle and deserves to have it. However, the analogy has its limits and short-comings. It is heavily cerebral in its connotations. More particularly it does not do adequate justice to the diversity and cruciality of the acts through which God has inspired the writers of the Bible. I propose that we correct this by noting that God principally but not exclusively inspired the writers of the Bible in, with, and through that sequence of his actions which reveals his heart and mind and saves us from our sins. Let me explain what I mean.

As we noted earlier, for Christians God is essentially a transcendent agent who has acted decisively in the world to reveal his intentions and purposes for that world and to redeem it from spiritual corruption. These special acts of God are not his only acts. He is doing and has done many other things. For example, at this very moment God sustains me as I write this sentence. If he did not do this I could not, on a Christian understanding of the world, continue to exist, nor to speak, nor think and write as I do. Yet no one would seriously suggest that this activity of God reveals anything significant about the intentions or purposes of God. The same can be said of many human activities. There is nothing necessarily or especially revealing, for example, in my scratching my ear or blowing my nose. Within the total set of acts and activity that an agent performs some are picked out as revelatory while others are not. Why and on what basis need not detain us here. All we need note is that the principle applies to both human agents and to God.

Traditionally Christians have proclaimed that there are two *loci* for God's revelatory acts, or for revelation. There is first the general revelation that God makes of his power and intelligence in creation as a whole. Through the general order, diversity, and brilliance of the created world God reveals his power and wisdom. In addition to this, however, he has intervened in the world in acts of special revelation. These acts fall into three classes. There are the acts of God in the history of Israel, especially his delivery of the Hebrew slaves from bondage in Egypt. Then there are the speech-acts of God in which he reveals his saving intentions and purposes to chosen prophets and apostles. Finally there are his unique and climactic acts in the life, death, and resurrection of Jesus of Nazareth. These latter acts of God constitute special revelation. As such they are at the heart of the Christian faith as it has been traditionally understood. Moreover they serve to distinguish the Christian faith from other faiths such as Deism, Judaism, or Islam.

Let it be emphasized again that these are not the only acts that God performs. God still speaks and comforts, he works in history, he brings people to new life, he forgives prodigals their sins, he promises the humble eternal life, he meets the meek in worship and in nature, he guides and directs his pilgrim people, etc. But such claims as these are made against a background wherein it is agreed that God has revealed himself uniquely in certain acts in the past and these acts serve as a criterion of what is to count as his acts today. What I am suggesting with respect to inspiration is simply this. It is through his revelatory and saving acts as well as through his personal dealings with individuals and groups that God inspired his people to write and collate what we now know as the Bible. Inspiration is not an activity that should be experientially separated from these other acts that God has performed in the past. As a matter of logic, inspiration is a unique activity of God that cannot be defined in terms of his other acts or activity, but as a matter of fact he inspires in, with, and through his special revelatory acts and through his personal guidance of those who wrote and put together the various parts of the Bible. This is the heart of my positive proposal.

In what other ways should our original analogy be qualified? Perhaps there are two. First, because God is omniscient he will be aware that he is inspiring in a way that human agents are not, therefore inspiration on his part will be fully intentional. God knows the nature and consequences of his acts in a way and to a degree that transcends human knowing, so all that he does is done intentionally rather than accidentally or without his knowledge. Secondly, because God is not an agent who can be located in the world of space and time, claims about the operation of his inspiration will be difficult to justify. We cannot, for example, show that God is active in the life of individuals or groups and thus is inspiring them with the same degree of ease as we do with human examples. This is not to say that we should be sceptical or diffident about claims to divine inspiration. It simply means that the process of justification must of necessity be more complex and indirect. Nor should this in itself surprise us, for the justification of claims about any divine action or activity is widely recognized to be far more complex and difficult than claims about human action or activity. And we all know how difficult the latter can be at times.

Beyond these qualifications I see no reason why the other features of inspiration identified should not be retained when we speak of the divine inspiration of the Bible. Some may need to be restated in a different way but this is a matter that need not detain us unduly. We can summarize the main points this way. When we speak of the divine inspiration of the Bible it is legitimate to talk in terms of degrees of inspiration; to insist on the full, indeed heightened, use of native ability in the creation of style, content, vocabulary etc.; to note that there is no guarantee of inerrancy, since agents, even when inspired by God, can make mistakes; and finally to infer that inspiration will result, first, in some kind of unity within the biblical literature and secondly in the committal to writing of a reliable and trustworthy account of God's revelatory and saving acts for mankind.

Perhaps a brief explanation of this last point is needed. It may well be wondered why it should be said that inspiration will result in a reliable account of God's saving acts. The answer is very simple. It stems from God's unique status as the agent of inspiration in question. With human agents there can be no guarantee that the content of what they inspire will be reliable or trustworthy, for human agents are by nature fallible and therefore quite as liable to inspire falsehood as truth It is very different with God, for he by definition, is omniscient and infallible. Therefore what he inspires will bear significant marks of truth and reliability. When this is added to what Christians maintain about the acts of God in the past, this has obvious consequences for the content of the Bible as inspired by God. This point was well made by John Baillie in a comment he made some years ago on the Bible as a witness to those events that constitute revelation.

... we cannot believe that God, having performed His mighty acts and having illumined the minds of prophet and apostle to understand their true import, left the prophetic and apostolic testimony to take care of itself. It were indeed a strange conception of the divine providential activity which would deny that the biblical writers were divinely assisted in their attempt to communicate to the world the illumination which, for the worlds sake, they had themselves received. The same Holy Spirit who had enlightened them into their own salvation must also have aided their efforts, whether spoken or written, to convey the message of salvation to those whom their words would reach.[4]

One has only to reflect on the foregoing analysis of inspiration to recognize how far removed divine inspiration is from divine speaking. The two are related, of course. It is partly through speaking to various significant individuals that God inspires them and others to write, edit, collate and preserve the various traditions that go to make up the Bible. But the relation between speaking and inspiration is contingent; there is no necessity for divine inspiration to be accomplished through divine speaking. Thus the relation cannot be one of identity, as so much writing on inspiration either states or presumes.

Once one grasps the full content of this analysis of inspiration it is a liberating experience, especially for anyone reared on the standard orthodoxy of the last generation. For a start, this account is compatible with what is generally known about the origin and character of the biblical writings. It lacks the artificiality that was prevalent in previous views. It is genuinely at home with differences in style and viewpoint, with differences of emphasis and vocabulary and with the existence of borderline books in the canon, i.e. books that were almost excluded from the Bible. It also allows a substantial role for critical historical investigation. Not only do we need sensitive historical judgement to engage in exegesis and the understanding of the various genres of literature to be found in Scripture, we also need it to fill out the degree to which this or that part of the Bible can be said to be historically reliable. Within the general framework sketched there is room for diversity of opinion on this or that part of the biblical tradition. We cannot tell in advance what parts are reliable and to what degree; historical study will have a genuine role to play in our assurance about reliability. For example, it is an open question whether Jonah was an historical figure or not; it is an open question how far the Pentateuch derives from Moses; it is an open question as to how far the Gospel of John is chronologically accurate. Such matters as these cannot be decided in advance. We must allow a genuine freedom to God as he inspires his chosen witnesses, knowing that what he does will be adequate for his saving and sanctifying purposes for our lives. In so doing we escape the tension and artificiality of those theories that have staked everything on the perfectionist and utopian hopes that stem from a theology of Scripture that substitutes divine speaking for divine inspiration without biblical or rational warrant.

[4] John Baillie, *The Idea of Revelation in Recent Thought* (Columbia University Press, New York, 1956), p. 111.

Many Evangelicals are reluctant to recognize the need to acknowledge openly and explicitly that this evaluative process is entirely legitimate. To be sure, as I argued earlier, it is difficult to avoid engaging in such evaluation, for history is too important and indispensable a subject to be ignored today. As a matter of actual fact therefore Evangelicals have gone along with this process and some have even sought in a determined, if not exaggerated manner, to make apologetic advantage out of this necessity. However, this evaluative process has had strict limits built into it from the outset in that under no circumstances was it allowed that true, critical evaluation of the Bible had discovered any errors or mistakes. At this point the commitment either to dictation or to acts of God that are in substance identical with dictation reveals itself with a vengeance. Consider it this way.

Evangelicals tend at times to picture the evaluative process as the purely negative one of finding mistakes. A frantic panic can set in as they conjure up the image of the Christian scholar going through his Bible destructively striking this verse and that verse from the canon. Added to this is the conviction that the critical process must be subjective in the worst sense of that term. This in turn generates the fear that there will be no end to the process. If this verse is mistaken in the slightest degree then who is to assure us that the whole lot is not mistaken. The proverbial camel, we are told, will not be content merely to put his nose into the tent, he will insist on taking over the whole tent and thus raising it to the winds.

We are all familiar with this outlook and it helps to explain the genuine attraction that inerrancy can have for both scholar and student. As such it deserves to be treated with both pastoral sensitivity and with intellectual sympathy. But it must not be allowed to coerce us theologically into an inadequate analysis of inspiration. Not only does such an outlook forget that the critical process is positively enriching and illuminating, for it has brought countless riches to our faith and understanding. Not only does it trade on a massive failure of nerve which overlooks the fact that the canons of evaluation are not viciously subjective. Not only does it ignore the fact that we gladly engage in such evaluation every time we read a newspaper, listen to a conversation, or study a learned article. Principally such an attitude trades on a theory of divine dictation. Why is the historian not allowed to find mistakes in the Bible? Because on this view every word of the Bible has been given by God. God being omniscient and infallible obviously does not make mistakes, therefore it is impertinent if not blasphemous for anyone, be he scholar or not, to challenge the word of God. The logic is impeccable but the minor premise of the argument is mistaken. It has never been shown that God spoke or dictated every word of the Bible. This is a hangover from writers like Gaussen and others who had simply failed to distinguish inspiration from speaking or dictation. This pervasive confusion continues to surface when we examine the central objections that are liable to be made against my proposal. . . .

The account of inspiration developed above allows us to make use of this term outside the confines of the writing and production of the Bible. Many Christians have felt it odd to suppose that inspiration should have suddenly dried up and stopped with the closing of the canon; as if God suddenly called a halt to his inspiring activity. In this they are surely correct. Our analysis of inspiration can accommodate this insight without strain or artificiality. Given what I have suggested about inspiration we can see how it applies to various situations. We can talk of the ordinary Christian who is coping heroically with the burdens of life as being inspired by God. We can say the same for the faithful preacher and pastor persistently building up the people of God in the faith, for the extraordinary saint giving up all in self-sacrifice for the poor and the needy, and for the persuasive evangelist proclaiming the good news of the Gospel to the outsider. I see no reason why we cannot today be inspired by God just as people of old were inspired by God. By exposure to his saving and revelatory acts in the past, by radical openness to the work of the Holy Spirit, and by diligent, sincere, and regular use of the classical means of grace, God will inspire us in the present to proclaim the Gospel, to live out its demands in the world, and think out its implications for our understanding of the issues and problems of our day and generation. In all these cases talk of divine inspiration is entirely appropriate; it is intellectually satisfying and spiritually liberating. Through his mighty acts of the past and through his continued activity in the present God continues to inspire his people.

It is at this point that many contemporary Evangelicals will be tempted to call an abrupt halt to my proposals. Were it not radical enough to suggest that inspiration does not guarantee total historical reliability, it will certainly be felt that the extending of inspiration to cover the lives of ordinary Christians is far beyond the bounds of acceptability. By this point, it might be said, the term has become so stretched and diluted as to be unworthy of significant use.

I have great sympathy with those who would raise this kind of objection. I can only hope that they will pause and ask themselves why exactly they feel this way. Their objection should not trouble us unduly. On the contrary we should be concerned if it was not raised with some force. I see in it, in fact, a reassertion of the view that divine inspiration is to be understood primarily in terms of divine speaking and divine revelation. For why do people feel uneasy about seeing inspiration at work today? The main reason is that they associate divine inspiration exclusively with the Bible. It is inspiration that safeguards for them the uniqueness and authority of the Bible. If we ask further why the Bible is inspired, we shall be told it is because it embodies God's true word to the world. But this simply confuses revelation and inspiration. It is one thing to say that the Bible contains God's special revelation to mankind and that it is the record of God's saving and revelatory acts and therefore authoritative for faith and practice.

This is quite correct, as I see it. It is another thing entirely to say that the Bible was written and produced under divine inspiration. It is only because the two are confused that people are reluctant to recognize genuine cases of divine inspiration outside the Bible.

Mark carefully that in the objection considered it is nowhere denied that God still speaks to individuals or groups today. Devotional and biographical literature is full of situations where Christians speak of God telling them to do this or that. Christians pray that God will speak to them afresh to guide them in their choice of vocation or in their solution to a particular problem that is a burden to them. Moreover they humbly ask God to speak to them through the preaching when they meet for worship. But, of course, these cases do not constitute new or special revelation in the classical sense. There is no thought, for example, of these cases of divine speaking finding their way into the canon of Scripture. This is correct, for decisions about what constitutes this kind of personal speaking are taken within a conceptual and theological framework which already pre-supposes the logical primacy of special revelation. This special revelation is believed to be unique and once-for-all in classical Christian thinking. There is no question of it being repeated in the present. I think it is this conviction that lies behind the objection that there can be no divine inspiration in the present. But this in turn can only happen if divine inspiration is identified in thought and concept with divine revelation. The tacit assumption that divine inspiration, divine revelation, and divine speaking are one and the same activity has reappeared in a new guise.

A similar process is in operation when it is objected that my account of inspiration as applied to cases outside the Bible does not leave room for propositional revelation, i.e. the possibility that revelation can take the form of the communication of religious truths capable of being expressed in propositions. This is a nagging worry that makes many wary of theological proposals that do not confine inspiration to the Bible. This objection is quite unfounded. I have no antipathy to propositional revelation; in fact I believe that revelation is in part though not in whole propositional. Again what is emerging is the view that divine inspiration and divine speaking are identical. Propositional revelation, as I see it, is one kind of divine speaking that is an integral part of special revelation. Naturally, because this special revelation is contained in the Bible, there is an understandable and proper concern to see propositional revelation uniquely related to the Bible. This concern is carried over and merges with a native antipathy to alleged cases of inspiration outside the canon. But this standpoint presupposes an assumption that divine inspiration and divine speaking are identical, which is needed as a bridge from antipathy to propositional revelation outside the Bible to antipathy to divine inspiration outside the Bible. Here is fresh confirmation that many have simply failed to abandon the view that the two are in fact and in meaning identical.

Another issue that has been closely connected in the past to the topic of inspiration, is that of authority. They are like theological Siamese twins, which theologians invariably discuss in relation to each other. The point where they join is once again at the concept of revelation. In general terms Scripture is authoritive because it contains special revelation. It provides us with knowledge of God which cannot be furnished from elsewhere. It is therefore normative for Christian theology. But because inspiration has been closely related to divine speaking and this in turn has been related to special revelation, inspiration gets carried over into the area occupied by the issue of authority and vice versa. Once the meaning of revelation is prised apart from the meaning of inspiration then we no longer feel so acutely the need to explore the issue of authority when exploring the meaning of inspiration. The issue of authority belongs in fact elsewhere; it belongs to a discussion of the place of special revelation in Christian theology. Hence it will not be pursued here.[5] That I need to mention it at all is due indirectly to the confusing of divine inspiration with divine speaking.

A further and final form of this unjustified assimilation of divine speaking and divine inspiration emerges in the suspicion and hostility that is shown towards any idea of degrees of inspiration. As I argued above, it is entirely appropriate to hold that divine inspiration is a matter of degree. God can and does inspire some people more than he inspires other people. But with divine speaking it is very different. Speaking is by nature an all or nothing affair. It makes no sense to say that some-one spoke to me to a greater or lesser degree. He either does speak or he does not speak; there are no degrees about it. This applies to God as much as man. It is therefore not a matter for surprise if those committed to a theology of inspiration that has failed to distinguish divine inspiration from divine speaking instinctively feel uneasy with talk of degrees of inspiration. What is happening is that their commitment to this confusion is surfacing in a new guise. Older views of inspiration are once again taking their revenge even though they have been verbally rejected.

In the course of this chapter I have attempted to provide and defend a positive account of divine inspiration. If the substance of this analysis is correct, then a coherent and serviceable doctrine has been furnished for the contemporary theologian. This doctrine preserves a concept that has a long and honourable standing in the Christian tradition. It does so by going back to the root meaning of the term and interpreting its meaning in a way that is fruitful, if not necessary, in any analysis of divine activity. Also, although by no means exclusively developed to harmonize with the nature and findings of responsible historical study of the bible, it is clearly compatible with what is generally known about the origin and content of Scripture. It is thus doubly satisfying to the Christian mind. In addition it is religiously significant and satisfying in that it permits and encourages us to seek divine inspiration for our own lives today. On this account the Christian may rightly pray that God will inspire him in meeting the varied needs of his generation just as fully as he inspired the great prophets, preachers, saints, and scholars of the past.

---

[5] As already indicated I hope to take up the whole question of revelation on a future occasion.

8

'Men Moved By the Holy Spirit Spoke From God' (2 Peter 1.21): A Middle Knowledge Perspective on Biblical Inspiration*

William Lane Craig

INTRODUCTION

The Church has traditionally affirmed that the Bible is inspired by God and is therefore God's Word to mankind, authoritative in all that it teaches. The deeper appreciation of the role of the human authors in the composition of the books of the Bible which dawned during the Enlightenment put a question mark behind the claim that the Bible is God's Word. How could the Scriptures be at once the Word of God and the word of man? In this paper I shall argue that the doctrine of divine 'middle knowledge' (*media scientia*) provides the key to the resolution of this conundrum. I shall first show that it has, indeed, been the historic position of the Church that Scripture is characterized by plenary, verbal inspiration. This demonstration is important because post-Enlightenment scepticism concerning Scripture's inspiration runs so deep that some have attempted to deny that the Church ever embraced so faulty a doctrine. I shall then explain the challenge posed to the traditional doctrine by incipient biblical criticism, which won a new appreciation of the human side of Scripture. Finally, in conversation with contemporary philosophers of religion, I shall defend the coherence of the traditional doctrine of inspiration by means of the doctrine of middle knowledge.

THE DIVINITY OF SCRIPTURE

On the basis of biblical texts like 2 Pet. 1.21 and 2 Tim. 3.16 ('All Scripture is inspired by God'), Church Fathers from the earliest time on unanimously

* © *Philosophia Christi* Series 2 Vol.1, No.1 (1999). Reprinted by permission of the publisher. http://www.epsociety.org/

regarded the Scriptures as 'holy,' 'sacred,' and 'divine' and therefore as absolutely authoritative, being the very words of God Himself.[1] Thus Clement of Rome advised the Corinthian church, 'Look carefully into the Scriptures, which are the true utterances of the Holy Spirit.'[2] The Sacred Scriptures are 'the oracles of God.'[3] Clement can thus introduce his quotations from Scripture with the simple formula, 'The Holy Spirit says....'[4] Even Paul's recent Corinthian correspondence is regarded as written 'under the inspiration of the Spirit.'[5]

The fact that it is God Who speaks in Scripture is especially evident in the case of prophetic utterances. According to Justin Martyr, 'the prophets are inspired by the divine Word.'[6] Thus, 'when you hear the utterances of the prophets spoken as it were personally, you must not suppose that they are spoken by the inspired themselves, but by the Divine Word who moves them.'[7] So Justin, commenting on Deut. 10.16–17, remarks, 'God Himself proclaimed by Moses' and on Is. 7.14, 'God predicted by the Spirit of prophecy' what should come to pass.[8] But even when people speak in answer to God in Scripture, it is the Divine Word which speaks.[9] No doubt this conviction lies at the base of Justin's confidence that 'no Scripture contradicts another.'[10]

Clement of Alexandria emphasizes both the breadth and the depth of Scripture's inspiration. With respect to the former he asserts, 'I could adduce ten thousand Scriptures of which not "one tittle shall pass away" without being fulfilled; for the mouth of the Lord the Holy Spirit hath spoken these things.'[11] And of the latter, he declares, 'For truly holy are those letters that sanctify and deify; and the writings or volumes that consist of those holy letters and syllables, the same apostle consequently calls "inspired of God...."'[12]

---

[1] For a survey of relevant texts, see *Dictionnaire de théologie catholique*, ed. A. Vacant and E. Mangenot (Paris: Librairie Letouzey et Ané 1922), vol. 7, pt. 2, s.v. 'L'inspiration de l'Écriture' by E. Mangenot, cols. 2068–2266; William Sanday, *Inspiration* (London: Longmans, Green, & Co.. 1914); *Religion in Geschichte und Gegenwart*, 3d ed., s.v, 'Inspiration: II. Inspiration der hl. Schrift, dogmengeschichtlich,' by O. Weber; John F. Walvoord, ed., *Inspiration and Interpretation* (Grand Rapids, Mich.: Wm. B. Eerdmans, 1957); J. N. D. Kelly, *Early Christian Doctrines*, 2d ed. (New York: Harper & Row, 1958), 60–4; Bruce Vawter, *Biblical Inspiration*, Theological Resources (Philadelphia: Westminster, 1959), 20–42; John D. Woodbridge, *Biblical Authority*, with a Foreword by Kenneth S. Kantzer (Grand Rapids, Mich: Zondervan, 1982).

[2] Clement 45. Translation from *Ante-Nicene Fathers* (hereinafter abbreviated as *ANF*), 10 vols, ed, Alexander Roberts and James Donaldson (rep. ed.: Peabody, Mass.: Hendrickson, 1994), 1: 17.

[3] Ibid., 53 (*ANF* 1: 19).

[4] Ibid., 13; cf. 22 (*ANF* 1: 8,11).

[5] Ibid., 47 (*ANF* 1: 18).

[6] Justin. *Apologia prima pro Christianis* 33 (*ANF* 1: 174).

[7] Ibid., 36 (*ANF* 1: 175).

[8] Justin, *Dialogus cum Trypone Judaeo* 16 (ANF 1: 202); idem *Apologia prima* 33 (*ANF* 1: 174).

[9] Justin, *Apologia prima* 36 (*ANF* 1: 175). Thus, in Ps. 24 it is the Holy Spirit who speaks (Idem *Dialogus* 36 [*ANF* 1: 175]).

[10] Justin, *Dialogus* 65 (*ANF* 1: 230).

[11] Clement of Alexandria, *Exhortatio ad gentes* 9 (*ANF* 2: 195).

[12] Ibid.

The great Church Father Irenaeus puts this same conviction into practice when he indicts the Gnostics for accepting part of the Gospel of Luke without accepting all of it[13] and when, in refutation of the Gnostic distinction between Jesus (the Son born of Mary) and Christ (the Father who descended upon Jesus), he bases his argument on the Holy Spirit's use of a single word:

> Matthew might certainly have said, 'Now the birth of *Jesus* was on this wise;' but the Holy Ghost, foreseeing the corrupters [of the truth], and guarding by anticipation against their deceit, says by Matthew, 'But the birth of *Christ* was on this wise;' and that He is Emmanuel, lest perchance we might consider Him as a mere man....[14]

Irenaeus is so bold as to declare that 'the writings of Moses are the words of Christ' and 'so also, beyond a doubt, the words of the other prophets are His.'[15] In sum, 'the Scriptures are indeed perfect, since they were spoken by the Word of God and His Spirit....'[16]

The Fathers did not engage in an extensive analysis of the means by which Scripture was inspired, but contented themselves with similes and analogies. Athenagoras seems to think of a sort of Spirit-possession akin to the Hellenistic model of the Sibylline oracles, the human spokesmen being mere instruments of the Spirit:

> I think that you . . . cannot be ignorant of the writings either of Moses or of Isaiah and Jeremiah, and the other prophets, who, lifted in ecstasy above the natural operations of their minds by the impulses of the Divine Spirit, uttered the things with which they were inspired, the Spirit making use of them as a flute-player breathes into a flute....[17]

Athenagoras is willing to grant that pagan poets and philosophers have 'an affinity with the afflatus from God,' but whereas they are moved by their own souls, 'we have for witnesses of the things we apprehend and believe, prophets, men who have pronounced concerning God and the things of God, guided by the Spirit of God.'[18] Similarly, Athenagoras's contemporary Theophilus states that the Spirit of God 'came down upon the prophets and through them spoke of the creation of the world and of all other things.'[19] Thus, 'Moses . . ., or, rather, the Word of God by Him as by an instrument, says, "In the beginning God created the heavens and the earth".'[20] Like Athenagoras, Theophilus

---

[13] Irenaeus, *Adversus haeresis* 3. 4. 3–4 (*ANF* 1: 438–9).

[14] Ibid., 3. 16.2 (*ANF* 1: 441). Cf. 3. 11. 1; Tertullian, *De monogamia* 11–12 (*ANF* 4: 69) for similar reliance on single words.

[15] Irenaeus, *Adversus haeresis* 4. 2. 3 (*ANF* 1: 464).

[16] Ibid., 2. 28. 2 (*ANF* 1:399).

[17] Athenagoras, *Legatio pro Christianis* 9 (*ANF* 2: 133). Kelly associates a similar view of inspiration with Alexandrian Judaism on the evidence of Philo's account of prophecy (Kelly, *Early Christian Doctrines*, 62).

[18] Athenagoras, *Legatio* 7 (*ANF* 2: 132).

[19] Theophilus, *Ad Autolycum* 2. 10 (*ANF* 2: 98).

[20] Ibid. Cf. 2. 9, where prophets inspired by the Holy Spirit are said to become 'instruments of God.'

considers this sufficient to set the 'divine writing' apart from the works of the philosophers, writers, and poets, for while they all have 'a mixture of error' in them, the prophets, possessed by the Holy Spirit of God, wrote what is accurate, harmonious, and 'really true.'[21]

The author of the pseudo-Justinian tractate *Cohortatio ad Graecos* also employed the simile of musical instruments to characterize the sacred writers:

> For neither by nature nor by human conception is it possible for men to know things so great and divine, but by the gift which then descended from above upon the holy men, who had no need of rhetorical art, nor of uttering anything in a contentious or quarrelsome manner, but to present themselves pure to the energy of the Divine Spirit, in order that the divine plectrum itself, descending from heaven, and using righteous men as an instrument like a harp or lyre, might reveal to us the knowledge of things divine and heavenly.[22]

The analogy of musical instruments is an interesting one. It might appear to depreciate the human role in the production of Scripture. However, it does, in fact, succeed in emphasizing both the divine and human aspects of Scripture, since the type of instrument selected by the musician will determine the character of the musical sounds produced by his playing. But there is no denying that the analogy does reduce the role of the human spokesmen as free agents.

For example, although Pseudo-Justin emphasizes the simple and artless diction of the prophets, still their role as human instruments is subsumed under the controlling influence of the Holy Spirit; they 'use with simplicity the words and expressions which offer themselves and declare to you whatever the Holy Ghost, who descended upon them, chose to teach through them. . . . '[23] In a similar fashion, Irenaeus, in trying to correct the inference that 2 Cor. 4.4 teaches that there is a second 'God of this world,' explains that 'according to Paul's custom . . . he uses transposition of words,' thereby seemingly emphasizing the role of the human author in the production of Scripture.[24] But then the left hand takes back what the right hand has given: 'the apostle frequently uses a transposed order in his sentences, due to the rapidity of his discourses, and the impetus of the Spirit which is in him.'[25]

Hippolytus continues to employ the simile of the divine plectrum playing the human instruments, but there is no trace of the Athenagoran idea that the prophets' natural faculties have been transcended.[26] Rather the indwelling Spirit

---

[21] Ibid., 2. 12, 22; 3. 17 (*ANF* 2: 99, 103, 116).

[22] Pseudo-Justin, *Cohortatio ad Graecos* 8 (*ANF* 1: 276). A plectrum is a sort of pick used to play the lyre.

[23] Ibid., 35 (*ANF* 1: 287).

[24] Irenaeus, *Adversus haeresis* 3. 7. 1 (*ANF* 1: 420).

[25] Ibid., 3. 7. 2 (*ANF* 1: 421).

[26] It is often suggested that the eclipse of the motif of ecstatic possession is due to the church's reaction to Montanism, which featured such prophetic experiences. See Epiphanius, *Panarion* (*Haeresis*) 48.

is conceived to enlighten and empower their faculties to speak the truths revealed to them by God:

> For these fathers were furnished with the Spirit, and largely honored by the Word Himself; and just as it is with instruments of music, so had they the Word always, like the plectrum, in union with them, and when moved by Him the prophets announced what God willed. For they spake not of their own power (let there be no mistake as to that), neither did they declare what pleased themselves. But first of all they were endowed with wisdom by the Word, and then again were rightly instructed in the future by means of visions. And then, when thus themselves fully convinced, they spake those things which were revealed by God to them alone, and concealed from all others.[27]

Although the spokesmen are here compared to instruments, Hippolytus's conception of God's working through them is more personalistic than what such a comparison might at first seem to suggest.

Jerome also employed a more personalistic model, styling inspiration along the lines of dictation. The Epistle to the Romans, he says, was dictated by the Holy Spirit through the Apostle Paul.[28] Since God is the author of Scripture, 'every word, syllable, accent, and point is packed with meaning.'[29] Augustine had a similar conception of the composition of Scripture. Christ, he explains, stands in relation to his disciples as does the head to the body.

> Therefore, when those disciples have written matters which He declared and spake to them, it ought not by any means to be said that He has written nothing Himself; since the truth is, that His members have accomplished only what they became acquainted with by the repeated statements of the Head. For all that He was minded to give for our perusal on the subject of His own doings and sayings. He commanded to be written by those disciples, whom He thus used as if they were His own hands. Whoever apprehends this correspondence of unity and this concordant service of the members, all in harmony of the discharge of diverse offices under the Head, will receive the account which he gets in the Gospel through the narratives constructed by the disciples, in the same kind of spirit in which he might look upon the actual hand of the Lord Himself, ... were he to see it engaged in the act of writing.[30]

Here Scripture is understood to be the product of a concordance of human and divine agents, the human authors writing what Christ commanded them to, so that He is ultimately the author of what they wrote. Little wonder that Augustine should therefore insist that Scripture is uniquely authoritative and 'completely free from error'![31]

---

[27] Hippolytus, *De Christo et antichristo* 2 (*ANF* 5: 204–5). Cf. idem. *Contra haeresim Noeti* 11 (*ANF* 5: 227), where the prophets' speaking by the Holy Spirit is a matter of their being gifted with the inspiration of God's power.

[28] Jerome, *Epistola* 120. 9.

[29] Jerome, *Commentariorum in epistolam ad Ephesios* 2.3.

[30] Augustine, *De consensu evangelistarum* 1. 35. 54. Translation from *Nicene and Post-Nicene Fathers,* first series (herein after abbreviated as *NPNF*[1]) 14 vols., ed. Philip Schaff (rep. ed.: Peabody, Mass: Hendrickson, 1994), 6: 101.

[31] Augustine, *Epistola* 82. 3. 24 (*NPNF*[1] 1: 350, 358); cf. idem, *Epistola* 28. 3 (*NPNF*[1] 1: 251–2); idem, *De civitate Dei* 21. 6 (*NPNF*[1] 2: 457).

The view that God is the author of Scripture in all its breadth and depth and that it is therefore authoritative and errorless was the common prepossession of the Church Fathers.[32] However the inspiration of Scripture was conceived to be brought about, the human authors of Scripture were regarded as instrumental causes only, doing what the Spirit moved them to do. Origen thus spoke for all the Fathers when he asserted, 'the sacred books are not the compositions of men, but . . . they were composed by the inspiration of the Holy Spirit, agreeably to the will of the Father of all things through Jesus Christ.'[33]

Precisely because of this unanimity, the inspiration and inerrancy of Scripture did not achieve creedal expression. As Cadoux points out, 'The fact that Biblical inerrancy was not incorporated in any formal creed was due, not to any doubt as to its being an essential item of belief, but to the fact that no one challenged it.'[34] Medieval theologians continued in the conviction of the Church Fathers. In his review of this period Sasse remarks, 'during all these centuries no one doubted that the Bible in its entirety was God's Word, that God was the principal author of the Scriptures, as their human authors had written under the inspiration of God the Holy Spirit, and that, therefore, these books were free from errors and contradictions, even when this did not seem to be the case.'[35] Thus, for example, Thomas Aquinas affirms, 'The Spirit is the principal author of sacred Scripture; and inspired man is the instrument.'[36] The Holy Spirit never utters what is false;[37] therefore, nothing false can underlie even the literal sense of Scripture.[38] Augustine, says Thomas, was right in affirming that the authors of Scripture have not erred.[39]

The Protestant Reformation brought a renewed emphasis on Scripture's authority. Committed as they were to the principle of *sola scriptura*, the Protestant Reformers were champions of the doctrine of biblical inspiration and authority. Luther dared to stand against the authority of the Catholic church because he believed that the Bible, which he took to support his teachings, is the true Word of God.[40] The Holy Scriptures, he declared, are 'the Holy Spirit's

---

[32] See A. Bea, '*Deus auctor Sacrae Scripturae*: Herkunft und Bedeutung der Formel,' *Angelicum* 20 (1943): 16–31. Vawter concludes, 'the language of the Fathers both in the East and in the West, as well as their habitual handling of the Scripture, leaves little doubt that for many if not most of them God was, altogether simplistically, the *literary* author of the Bible. He had, through men, 'written' the Biblical work; He had 'dictated' it' (Vawter, *Biblical Inspiration*, 96).

[33] Origen, *De principiis* 4. 9 (*ANF* 4: 357).

[34] C. J. Cadoux, *The Case for Evangelical Modernism* (New York: Clark, 1939), 66–7.

[35] Herman Sasse, 'The Rise of the Dogma of Holy Scripture in the Middle Ages,' *Reformed Theological Review* 18 (1959): 45.

[36] Thomas Aquinas, *Quaestiones quodlibetales* 7. 16.

[37] Thomas Aquinas, *Summa theologiae* 2a. 2ae. 172. 5 *ad* 3.

[38] Ibid., 1a. 1. 10 *ad* 3.

[39] Ibid., 1a. 1. 8.

[40] Martin Luther, 'Kleine exegetische Schriften: Auslegung vieler schöner Sprüche heiliger Schrift,' in *Sämmtliche Schriften*, 23 vols., ed. Joh. Georg Walsch, vol. 9: *Auslegung des Neuen Testaments* (St. Louis: Concordia Publishing House, [1892]), col. 1818.

book.'[41] Thus, in his comment on Ps. 90 Luther states that 'we must, therefore, believe that the Holy Spirit Himself composed this psalm.'[42] Quoting David's words in 2 Sam. 23. 2 'The Spirit of the Lord has spoken by me, and His word is upon my tongue,' Luther marvels,

What a glorious and arrogant arrogance it is for anyone to dare to boast that the Spirit of the Lord speaks through him and that his tongue is voicing the Word of the Holy Spirit! He must obviously be sure of his ground. David, the son of Jesse, born in sin, is not such a man, but it is he who has been called to be a prophet by the promise of God.[43]

Though David was a sinner, he spoke the very words of God because he was a prophet through whom the Holy Spirit spoke. Luther remarks, 'Neither we nor anyone else who is not a prophet may lay claim to such honor.'[44] Luther thus portrays David as in effect saying, ' "My speech is not really mine, but he who hears me hears God." '[45] The entirety of the canonical Scriptures are God's inspired Word: 'Thus, we attribute to the Holy Spirit all of Holy Scripture.'[46] Even the trivialities in Scripture (the *levicula*) are inspired. Commenting on an incident in Gen. 30.14–16, Luther remarks,

this is ridiculous and puerile beyond measure, so much so that nothing more inconsequential can be mentioned or recorded. Why, then is it recorded? I reply: One must always keep in view what I emphasize so often, namely, that the Holy Spirit is the Author of this book. He Himself takes such delight in playing and trifling when describing things that are unimportant, puerile, and worthless; and He hands this down to be taught in the church as though it redounded to the greatest education.[47]

Luther affirms that the very words of Scripture are divinely inspired. Thus, in defending the interpretation of Is. 7.14 as a prophecy of the Virgin Birth, Luther asserts, 'Even though an angel from heaven were to say that *almah* does not mean virgin, we should not believe it. For God the Holy Spirit speaks through St. Matthew and St. Luke; we can be sure that He understands Hebrew speech and expressions perfectly well.'[48] Because the Holy Scriptures are God's Word,

[41] Ibid., col. 1775.
[42] Martin Luther, 'Commentary on Psalm 90,' in *Luther's Works*, vol. 13: *Selected Psalms II*. ed. J. Pelikan (St. Louis: Concordia Publishing House, 1956), 81.
[43] Martin Luther, 'Treatise on the Last Words of David (2 Sam. 23: 1–7),' trans. Martin Bertram, in *Luther's Works*, 55 vols., ed. J. Pelikan and H. C. Oswald (St. Louis: Concordia Publishing House, 1972), 15: 275.
[44] Ibid., 275–6.
[45] Ibid., 275.
[46] Ibid.
[47] Martin Luther, *Luther's Works*, vol. 5: *Lectures on Genesis: Chapters 26–30*, ed. J. Pelikan and W.A. Hansen (St. Louis; Concordia Publishing House, 1968), 352. For similar citations see E. F. Klug, *From Luther to Chemnitz* (Grand Rapids, Mich.: Wm. B. Eerdmans, 1971), 20.
[48] Martin Luther, 'That Jesus Christ Was Born a Jew,' in *Luther's Works*, vol. 45: *The Christian in Society II*, ed. H. T. Lehmann (Philadelpia: Muhlenberg Press, 1962), 208.

inspired by the Holy Spirit, Luther, citing Augustine's letter to Jerome, could therefore affirm, 'The Scriptures . . . have never erred.'[49]

In the era of Protestant scholasticism following the Reformation, the Lutheran theologians insisted forcefully on the inspiration of the very words of Scripture. Abraham Calov, commenting on 2 Pet. 1.21 wrote,

> The φορα embraces both an inner enlightenment of the mind and communication of what was to be said and written, and an external urge of such a nature that the tongue and pen no less than the intellect and mind acted by that impulse. The result was that not only the *forma*, or content was suggested, but the words also, which are placed in their mouth and dictated to their pen by the Holy Spirit, were committed to the original amanuenses, or men of God.[50]

Or again, in the words of J. A. Quenstedt:

> The Holy Spirit not only inspired in the prophets and apostles the content and the sense contained in Scripture, or the meaning of the words, so that they might of their own pleasure clothe and furnish these thoughts with their own style and their own words; but the Holy Spirit actually supplied, inspired, and dictated the very words and each and every term individually.[51]

As for Aquinas, so for these Protestant scholastics, God is the *causa efficiens principalis* of Scripture; human authors are the *causae instrumentales*. They are compared to quills used by the Holy Spirit, who dictates each and every word they write. Inspiration involves not only an *impulsus ad scribendum* and a *suggestio rerum* from the Holy Spirit, but also a *suggestio verborum* as well. Now of course these divines were aware of the stylistic differences and peculiarities of the authors of Scripture, but these were explained as a sort of condescension on God's part whereby He accommodates Himself to speak in the vocabulary and style appropriate to each respective author.

The Reformed Protestant tradition took an equally strong stand on the doctrine of inspiration. Calvin's favorite characterization of the means by which Scripture was inspired is dictation.[52] Thus, he affirms, 'Whoever then wishes to profit in the Scriptures, let him, first of all, lay down this as a settled point, that the Law and the Prophets are not a doctrine delivered according to the will and pleasure of men, but dictated by the Holy Spirit.'[53] He calls the human

[49] Martin Luther, 'Wider die Papisten,' in *Werke*, vol. 15: *Reformationsschriften*, cap. 6, Abschn. 3, §448, col. 1481.

[50] Abraham Calov, *Biblia Novi Testamenti Illustrata* 2: 1547 (Citation from Robert D. Preuss, *The Theology of Post-Reformation Lutheranism*, 2 vols. [St. Louis; Mo.: Concordia Publishing House, 1970], 1: 283).

[51] J. A. Quenstedt, *Theologia didactico-polemica, sive systema theologiae* 1. 4. 2. 4 (Citation from Preuss, *Theology*, 1: 281).

[52] For many references, see Kenneth S. Kantzer, 'Calvin and the Holy Scriptures,' in *Inspiration and Interpretation*, 138.

[53] Jean Calvin, *Commentaries on the Epistles to Timothy, Titus, and Philemon*, trans. W. Pringle (Edinburgh: Calvin Translation Society, 1856), 249.

authors 'amanuenses' of the Holy Spirit; they are His 'organs' and 'instruments.'[54] Calvin goes so far as to assert that the prophet brings 'forth nothing from his own brain,' but merely delivers what the Lord commands.[55] Thus, commenting on Jeremiah's prophecies, Calvin states that while 'the words were his,' Jeremiah 'was not the author of them,' since 'he only executed what God had commanded.'[56]

Paradoxically, Calvin combined with the dictation theory of inspiration the affirmation that the biblical authors wrote freely in their own styles:

The Spirit of God, who had appointed the Evangelists to be his clerks, appears purposely to have regulated their style in such a manner, that they all wrote one and the same history, with the most perfect agreement, but in different ways. It was intended, that the truth of God should more clearly and strikingly appear, when it was manifest that his witnesses did not speak by a preconcerted plan, but that each of them separately, without paying any attention to another, wrote freely and honestly what the Holy Spirit dictated.[57]

Despite the affirmation of the authors' freedom, the weight of the passage falls on the divine sovereignty which determined that four differing accounts should be dictated.

Like their Lutheran counterparts, the Reformed scholastic theologians emphasized the inspiration and authority of Scripture. According to T. R. Phillips, 'That God is the author of all Scripture; and thus inspired not only the substance but even the words, was unquestioned within seventeenth-century Reformed scholasticism.'[58] Three emphases characterized Reformed thought on Scripture. First, 'Everything within Scripture was regarded as being free from the "peril of error" and thus absolutely certain.'[59] On this basis the statements of Scripture could serve as the authoritative premises for the deduction of theological conclusions. Second, inspiration of the Scriptures by God was conceived as the basis of the Bible's authority. Third, 'because inspiration . . . has become the ground for Scripture's authority, the nature of this authority assumes more externalistic and legalistic qualities. Scripture is viewed as a book of authoritative sentences: what

[54] John Calvin, *Institutes of the Christian Religion*, 3 vols., trans. Henry Beveridge (Edinburgh: Calvin Translation Society, 1845), 3: 166 (IV. viii. 9); idem. *Commentaries on the Twelve Minor Prophets*, vol. 3: *Jonah, Micah, Nahum*, trans. John Owen (Edinburgh: Calvin Translation Society, 1847), 197.

[55] Calvin, *Minor Prophets*, vol. 1: *Hosea*, trans. John Owen (Edinburgh: Calvin Translation Society, 1846), 42; cf. 325. See also Calvin, *Second Epistle to Timothy*, 249: 'we owe to the Scripture the same reverence which we owe to God; because it has proceeded from him alone, and has nothing belonging to man mixed with it.'

[56] Jean Calvin, *Commentaries on the Prophet Jeremiah and the Lamentations*, trans. and ed. John Owen (Edinburgh: Calvin Translation Society, 1854), 1: 34.

[57] Jean Calvin, *Commentary on a Harmony of the Evangelists: Matthew, Mark, and Luke*, trans. and ed. W. Pringle (Edinburgh: Calvin Translation Society, 1845), 1: 127; cf. 1: xxxviii, xxxix.

[58] Timothy R. Phillips, 'Francis Turretin's Idea of Theology and its Bearing upon his Doctrine of Scripture,' 2 vols. (Ph.D. dissertation, Vanderbilt University, 1986), 2: 748.

[59] Ibid., 1: 86.

Scripture says, God says.'[60] Reformed theologians, while continuing to employ terms like 'dictation' and 'amanuenses' when explicating the means of inspiration, did not, according to Phillips, intend such terms to be taken literally, since they conceived of inspiration as a *habitus* or charism, a special divine gift of knowledge and volition which inwardly supplies the human author with the capacities for carrying out God's mandate to write. Nevertheless, some Reformed theologians like Voetius could speak straightforwardly of a *suggestio verborum* in the process of inspiration:

> The Holy Spirit has spoken immediately and extraordinarily all that was to be written and has been written, either the things or the words... The Holy Spirit has provoked them, and has suggested to them so that they were writing this rather than that... the Holy Spirit ordered, arranged and constructed all of their concepts and sentences namely so that they deployed this sentence at the first, that at the second, and another at the third place, and so on in succession and as a result they are being sealed and authenticated by having been written down: in the strict sense to produce and to compose a book entails this.[61]

Other Reformed thinkers like Rivet, Thysius, and Ames denied that the process of inspiration involved a *suggestio verborum*, but all were one in the belief that the extent of inspiration in the final product included the very words of Scripture.

For their part, Catholic theologians of the Counter-Reformation also insisted on the inspiration and authority of Scripture. In the fourth session of the Council of Trent, the Catholic Church declared that the Old and New Testaments have God as their author, having been dictated by the Holy Spirit (*a Spiritu Sancto dictatas*).[62] Protestants and Catholics alike were thus united in seeing God as the author of Scripture who employed human scribes to write down what He by His Spirit dictated. In so doing, they were reaffirming what the Christian Church had always believed and taught.

THE HUMANITY OF SCRIPTURE

Although Christian theologians had always recognized the idiosyncrasies of the human authors of Scripture, the role of human agents in the writing of Scripture was undeniably minimalized. In the latter half of the sixteenth century, rumblings of discontent with the classical doctrine of inspiration began to be heard among Catholic theologians. But these misgivings broke into public view with Benedict de Spinoza's publication of his *Tractatus theologico-politicus* in 1670.

---

[60] Timothy R. Phillips, 'Francis Turretin's Idea of Theology and its Bearing upon his Doctrine of Scripture,' 2 vols. (Ph.D. dissertation, Vanderbilt University, 1986), 1: 87–8.

[61] Voetius, *Selectorum Disputationum Fasciculus*, 24 (Cited in Phillips, *Turretin's Idea of Theology*, 2: 758).

[62] Heinrich Denzinger, *Enchiridion Symbolorum*, 33d ed. (Freiburg in Breisgau: 1965) 1501 (364).

In addition to denying Mosaic authorship of the Pentateuch, Spinoza attacked the traditional doctrine of inspiration. The prophets, he observes, were only inspired when speaking directly the words of God; when they spoke in ordinary conversation as private individuals, their words were not inspired. Although the apostles were prophets, it is evident when we read their writings that they were not speaking as inspired prophets in those writings. For their style of writing and their use of argumentation is incompatible with direct revelatory utterances:

> Now if we examine the style of the Epistles, we shall find it to be entirely different from that of prophecy. It was the constant practice of the prophets to declare at all points that they were speaking at God's command, as in the phrases, 'Thus saith the Lord,' 'The Lord of hosts saith,' 'The commandment of the Lord,' and so on . . . , But in the Epistles of the Apostles we find nothing like this; on the contrary, in I Cor. 7 v. 40 Paul speaks according to his own opinion. Indeed, there are numerous instances of expressions far removed from the authoritativeness of prophecy. . . .

> Furthermore, if we examine the manner in which the Apostles expound the Gospel in their Epistles, we see that this, too, is markedly different from that of the prophets. For the Apostles everywhere employ argument, so that they seem to be conducting a discussion rather than prophesying. . . .

> Therefore the modes of expression and discussion employed by the Apostles in the Epistles clearly show that these originated not from revelation and God's command but from their own natural faculty of judgment. . . . [63]

By associating inspiration only with revelatory, prophetic utterances, Spinoza undercuts the inspiration of the non-prophetic portions of Scripture, including the bulk of the New Testament. Far from being dictated by the Holy Spirit, 'the Epistles of the Apostles were dictated solely by the natural light. . . . '[64] The Gospels fare no better:

> There are four Evangelists in the New Testament; and who can believe that God willed to tell the story of Christ and impart it in writing to mankind four times over? . . . . Each Evangelist preached his message in a different place, and each wrote down in simple style what he had preached with a view to telling clearly the story of Christ, and not with a view to explaining the other Evangelists. If a comparison of their different versions sometimes produces a readier and clearer understanding, this is a matter of chance, and it occurs only in a few passages. . . . [65]

Scripture is called the 'Word of God' only in virtue of its prophetic passages, and God is understood to be the author of the Bible only because 'true religion' is taught therein.[66]

Spinoza's *Tractatus* sparked an eruption of controversy throughout Europe. In effect Spinoza was insisting that one must take seriously the humanity of

---

[63] Baruch Spinoza, *Tractatus theologico-politicus*, trans. Samuel Shirley (Leiden: E. J. Brill, 1989), 197–9 (11).

[64] Ibid., 201 (11).   [65] Ibid., 211 (12).   [66] Ibid., 209 (12).

Scripture and argued that doing so is incompatible with the traditional doctrine of inspiration. There was no denying the human element in Scripture to which Spinoza had drawn attention; the question was whether his inference followed that inspiration must therefore be circumscribed to direct prophecy. The Dutch theologian Jean Le Clerc, shaken by Spinoza's critique, advocated abandonment of the classical doctrine of inspiration, while insisting on the general reliability of the non-inspired portions of the Bible. Le Clerc distinguishes prophecies, histories, and doctrines within Scripture. The doctrines taught by Christ and the apostles he takes to be divinely inspired. But he claimed that even prophecies need not be inspired. For example, a prophet may report visions or voices from God by giving back in his own words the sense of what he heard or saw. The fact that the various prophets differ in their style of writing disproves the dictation theory of inspiration. In the same way with respect to histories: since the Evangelists differ in precise wording of Jesus's teaching, they are merely giving back the sense of what Jesus said, for which task they needed only good memory and honesty, not divine inspiration. Citing Lk. 1.1–4 Le Clerc comments, 'You may observe in these words a Confirmation of what I have been saying, and a full Proof that St. Luke learn'd not that which he told us by Inspiration, but by Information from those who knew it exactly.'[67] Le Clerc maintains that his position does not undermine Scripture's authority because we are rationally obliged on the basis of the evidence to believe that the historical narratives of the New Testament are substantially true. Thus, in response to Spinoza he grants 'that the Sacred Pen-Men were not inspired, neither as to the Stile, nor as to those things which they might know otherwise than by revelation,' but insists 'that the Authority of the Scriptures ought not for all that to be esteemed less considerable.'[68]

Richard Simon, an early French biblical critic, attacked Le Clerc's concessions to Spinoza in *Réponse au Livre intitulé Sentimens de quelques Theologiens de Hollande* and in his epochal *Histoire Critique du Texte du Nouveau Testament.*[69] The central presupposition of Spinoza and Le Clerc attacked by Simon is their assumption that biblical inspiration is to be understood woodenly in terms of dictation. *'Il n'est pas nécessaire qu'un Livre pour être inspiré ait été dicté de Dieu mot pour mot.'*[70] Instead Simon proposes to understand inspiration in terms of God's *direction* of the authors of Scripture. Elsewhere he explains,

[67] Jean Le Clerc, *Five Letters Concerning the Inspiration of the Holy Scriptures* (London: n.p., 1690), 34, this book being a translation of his *Sentimens de quelques théologiens de Hollande sur l'Histoire critique du Vieux Testament* (1685).

[68] Ibid., 126.

[69] Le Prieur de Bolleville, *Réponse au Livre intitulé Sentimens de quelques Théologiens de Hollande sur l'Histoire Critique du Vieux Testament* (Rotterdam: Reinier Leers, 1686), 122–32; Richard Simon, *Histoire critique du Texte du Nouveau Testament* (Rotterdam: Renier Leers, 1689; rep. ed.: Frankfurt: Minerva. 1968), chap. 23.

[70] Simon, *Histoire critique*, 192.

Immediate revelation takes place when the Holy Spirit reveals to a sacred author what he writes in such a way that this author does nothing but receive and give us what the Holy Spirit has dictated to him. It is thus that the prophets were inspired concerning things of the future, which they learned directly from God. This inspiration can also extend to words, should it happen that the Holy Spirit suggests to a writer the words he uses.

One speaks of special direction when the Holy spirit does not reveal directly to an author what he puts into writing, but when he stirs him to write simply what he already knew, having learned it before, or understood it through his own perception. The Spirit assists and directs him in such a way that he will choose nothing that will not conform to the truth and the purpose for which the Sacred Books were composed, to know how to edify us in faith and charity. It is for that reason that Luke wrote in the Acts several incidents which he heard from the Apostles, and from those who were witnesses to them, as the preaching and miracles of St. Peter; or those he saw himself, as the arrival of St. Paul at Malta. It was not absolutely necessary that the facts he knew by himself be revealed to him.[71]

Spinoza and Le Clerc's objections are predicated entirely on a false understanding of the nature of inspiration, which they took to exclude human reasoning. But if inspiration is understood in terms of direction, not dictation, then there is no incompatibility between inspiration and the human phenomena noted by Spinoza. The Evangelists, for example, were not divested of memory and reason when composing the Gospels, but they were assisted by God in such a way as to prevent them from falling into error. Simon writes,

God has guided their pen in such a way that they do not fall into error. It is men who write; and the Spirit who directs them has not robbed them of their reason or their memory in order to inspire in them facts which they know perfectly well. But He has in general determined them to write instead of certain facts rather than others which they know equally well.[72]

Simon thus denies that 'the Evangelists were sheer instruments of the Holy Spirit, who dictated to them word for word what they wrote.'[73]

Le Clerc responded to Simon's critique by falling back to a more modest position: 'My argument proves not directly that there was no Inspiration on these occasions, but only that there was nothing in the thing itself to induce us to believe that there was any. . . .'[74] As for Simon's idea of inspiration as direction or guidance, this is unobjectionable so long as the direction extends no further than the selection of the subject matter. With respect to Simon's contention that divine inspiration and human reasoning are not mutually exclusive, Le Clerc maintains

---

[71] R. S. P., *Nouvelles Observations sur le Texte et les Versions du Nouveau Testament* (Paris: Jean Boudot, 1695), 35. (Citation from James Tunstead Burtchaell, *Catholic Theories of Biblical Inspiration since 1810* [Cambridge: Cambridge University Press, 1969], 49–50).

[72] Le Prieur de Bolleville, *Réponse au Livre intitulé Sentimens*, 127–8.

[73] Ibid., 128.

[74] Le Clerc, *Letters*, 158; cf. idem, *Defense des Sentimens de quelques Théologiens de Hollande sur l'Histoire Critique du Vieux Testament contre le prieur de Bolleville* (Amsterdam: Henri Desbordes, 1686), 245.

that either the Holy Spirit gave the apostles fully framed arguments or only general principles. If He gave complete arguments, then there was no need for the author's reasoning. But if He gave only general principles, then the apostles were still dependent on fallible reasoning to make their deductions, and nothing has been gained.

In his counter-response to Le Clerc Simon defended the inspiration of all Scripture on the basis of 2 Tim. 3. 16.[75] But he agrees that inspiration does not extend to the words of Scripture: 'it is not at all necessary to extend it to the words or to the style of each sacred author; it is enough that the substance be inspired.'[76] There is no need to fear that the apostle's use of fallible reasoning renders their writings errant, for God's direction will prevent this. 'The Holy Spirit guided them in such a way that they never made a mistake in what they have written; but one need not therefore believe that there is nothing in their expressions other than the divine and supernatural.'[77] As we shall later see, whether Simon meant to deny verbal inspiration will depend upon some very subtle issues arising out of the tradition of Jesuit theology in which Simon operated.

These seventeenth century debates over the nature of biblical inspiration awakened the Church to the human side of Scripture. It now seemed altogether implausible to suppose that the means of biblical inspiration was divine dictation to human authors. The authors' variety of styles, their divergence in narrating identical events, their evident effort in gathering information, their trivial remarks and grammatical mistakes all seemed to point to a more important role for them to play than that of mere scribes. Thus, free human agency had to be an essential element of any adequate doctrine of biblical inspiration. Together with the Church's historic commitment to the full breadth and depth of biblical inspiration, the element of human agency implies, in Pinnock's words, that 'Divine inspiration is plenary, verbal, and confluent.'[78] By *plenary* inspiration it is meant that all of Scripture, not just portions of it, is inspired. Along with the great doctrines, even the *levicula* are God's Word. This does not imply that all parts of Scripture are equally important or equally relevant at various times and places, but all of it is God-breathed. By verbal inspiration it is meant that the very words of Scripture are inspired. The Bible, as a linguistic deposit, is God's Word. Hence, not merely the thoughts expressed, but the very language of Scripture is God-breathed. Finally, by confluent inspiration it is meant that Scripture is the product of dual authorship, human and divine. The human authors wrote freely

[75] Le Prieur de Bolleville, *De l'Inspiration des Livres Sacrez; Avec une réponse au livre intitulé Defense des Sentimens de quelques Théologiens de Hollande sur l'Histoire Critique du Vieux Testament* (Rotterdam: Reinier Leers, 1699), 167–8.

[76] Ibid., 160.

[77] Ibid., 3.

[78] Clark H. Pinnock, *Biblical Revelation* (Chicago: Moody Press, 1971), 66; see 86–95 for exposition.

and spontaneously, and yet God somehow was also at work through them to produce His Word. Hence, the writers of Scripture were not mere stenographers, but real authors, whose individuality shines through their works. At the same time, God is the author of Scripture, so that it can truly be affirmed, 'The Holy Spirit said by David ...,' thereby guaranteeing Scripture's authority and inerrancy.

THE APPARENT INCOHERENCE OF PLENARY, VERBAL, CONFLUENT INSPIRATION

But the obvious difficulty is that the above properties of inspiration seem to constitute an inconsistent triad. John Cardinal Newman wrestled aloud with the tension they present:

In what way inspiration is compatible with that personal agency on the part of its instruments, which the composition of the Bible evidences, we know not; but if any thing is certain, it is this,—that, though the Bible is inspired, and therefore, in one sense, written by God, yet very large portions of it, if not far the greater part of it, are written in as free and unconstrained a manner, and (apparently) with as little consciousness of a supernatural dictation or restraint, on the part of His earthly instruments, as if He had had no share in the work. As God rules the will, yet the will is free,—as He rules the course of the world, yet men conduct it,—so He has inspired the Bible, yet men have written it. Whatever else is true about it, this is true,—that we may speak of the history, or mode of its composition, as truly as of that of other books; we may speak of its writers having an object in view, being influenced by circumstances, being anxious, taking pains, purposely omitting or introducing things, supplying what others had left, or leaving things incomplete. Though the Bible be inspired, it has all such characteristics as might attach to a book uninspired,—the characteristics of dialect and style, the distinct effects of times and places, youth and age, or moral and intellectual character; and I insist on this, lest in what I am going to say, I seem to forget (what I do not forget), that in spite of its human form, it has in it the spirit and the mind of God.[79]

One will look in vain among the classical defenders of plenary, verbal inspiration for a resolution of this difficulty. Of the Lutheran dogmaticians, Robert Preus confesses frankly,

The Lutheran doctrine of inspiration presents a paradox. On the one hand it was taught that God is the *autor primarius* of Scripture, that He determined and provided the thoughts and actual words of Scripture and that no human cooperation concurred *efficienter* in producing Scripture. On the other hand it was maintained that the temperaments (*ingenia*), the research and feelings (*studia*), and the differences in background (*nationes*) of the inspired writers are all clearly reflected in the Scriptures; that there is nothing docetic about Scripture; that God's spokesmen wrote willingly, consciously,

[79] John Henry Newman, *Lectures on the Scripture Proofs of the Doctrines of the Church*, Tracts for the Times 85 (London: J. G. F. & J. Rivington, 1838), 30.

spontaneously, and from the deepest personal spiritual conviction and experience; that psychologically and subjectively (*materialiter et subjective*) they were totally involved in the writing of Scripture. These two salient features of the doctrine of inspiration must be held in tension. . . .

Now it may seem utterly inconsistent that the Spirit of God could in one and the same action provide the very words of Scripture and accommodate Himself to the linguistic peculiarities and total personality of the individual writer so that these men wrote freely and spontaneously. But this is precisely what took place according to the Biblical evidence and data. And if Scripture does not inform us how both of these facts can be true, we must not do violence to either or try to probe the mystery of inspiration beyond what has been revealed. The Lutheran teachers are well aware that there is a lacuna in their theology at this point . . . ; and they are content to retain this logical gap and accept the paradox.[80]

We should not sell the doctrine of accommodation short. After all, in choosing to inspire the biblical books at all, God has already accommodated Himself to speaking in the languages of Hebrew and Greek and has thus limited His expression to what the grammar and vocabulary of those languages permit. Having stooped so low, is it incredible that He should also take account of the further limitations and idiosyncrasies of each individual author, so that through one He speaks in the language of a shepherd, through another in the language of a civil servant, and so on? To achieve truly idiomatic speech, perhaps God even deigns to speak ungrammatically on occasion. Perhaps, as Aquinas believed, God's instruction might be so subtle and mysterious that the human mind could be subjected to it without a person's knowing it, so that one is unable to discern whether his thoughts are produced by the divine instinct or by one's own spirit.[81] Whether accommodation plausibly explains the *levicula* in Scripture is more doubtful. But the salient point is that accommodation still falls short of confluence: if the author's thoughts and sentences are the product of either the divine instinct or his own spirit, rather than both, then Scripture is not the product of dual authorship. There is then one author of Scripture, God, and one stenographer, man, to whom God dictates Scripture in a vernacular that makes it indistinguishable from the writer's own expression. Inspiration is not confluent. How inspiration can be confluent as well verbal and plenary is admitted to be a paradox.

Nor will we find much help *chez* the Reformed divines. B. B. Warfield of the old Princeton school maintains that the classical doctrine of inspiration 'purposely declares nothing as to the mode of inspiration. The Reformed Churches admit that this is inscrutable. They content themselves with defining carefully and holding fast the effects of the divine influence, leaving the mode of divine action by which it is brought about draped in mystery.'[82] But what about Calvin's

---

[80] Preus, *Post-Reformation Lutheranism*, 1: 290–1.

[81] Thomas Aquinas, *Summa theologiae* 2a. 2ae. 171. 5.

[82] Benjamin Breckinridge Warfield, 'Inspiration and Criticism,' in *The Inspiration and Authority of the Bible*, ed. Samuel G. Craig with an Intro. by Cornelius Van Til (Philadelphia: Presbyterian & Reformed, 1970), 420–1. See also Phillips, *Turretin's Idea of Theology*, 744–75, who states that the Reformed scholastics only vaguely characterized the mechanics of inspiration.

heavy use of the notion of dictation with respect to Scripture's inspiration? Warfield admits that Calvin 'is somewhat addicted to the use of language which, strictly taken, would imply that the mode of their [*i.e.*, the Scriptures'] gift was 'dictation'.'[83] But he contends that 'dictation' refers to the result or the effect of inspiration, not to its mode. The Scriptures have, in virtue of their inspiration, the quality of a dictation from God; but they were not dictated by God. 'It is by no means to be imagined,' declares Warfield, that the classical doctrine of inspiration 'is meant to proclaim a mechanical theory of inspiration. The Reformed Churches have never held such a theory: though dishonest, careless, ignorant or overeager controverters of its doctrine have often brought the charge.'[84] The assertion that Calvin's notion of dictation is not 'mechanical' is frequently made by Reformed thinkers. Taken literally, mechanical dictation would be dictation involving only one agent, the speaker, such as would take place when one utilizes a machine like a dictaphone or tape-recorder to register one's words. Non-mechanical dictation would then involve two agents, not only a speaker but also a secretary, who freely writes down the speaker's words and perhaps concurs with what the speaker is saying. Unfortunately, this sort of non-mechanical dictation is still insufficient for true confluence because while the secretary exercises freedom in agreeing to write or not, he exercises no freedom at all with respect to content or style: the words are not truly his. As Warfield rightly emphasized, 'the gift of Scripture through its human authors took place by a process much more intimate than can be expressed by the term "dictation".... '[85] Kenneth Kantzer believes that such an intimate process may be found in Calvin's own conception of inspiration:

In ordinary dictation...the secretary is active only to recognize and to copy words originating outside the mind of the secretary. This sort of dictation is by no means consistent with Calvin's view of the method of inspiration. As he interprets the facts, the sacred authors are active with their minds and whole personalities in the selection both of ideas and words. Scripture really originates in the mind of God, who is its ultimate author in the sense that He controls the mind and personality of the men He has chosen to write Scripture. By this means, God inspires the writers of Scripture (better breathes out through them as instruments) to speak to man exactly His chosen words as He wills. When, in Calvin's thought, the prophet is referred to as an instrument, he is by no means an instrument which simply passes on words mechanically given to him. Rather, because of God's sovereign control of his being, he is an instrument whose whole personality expresses itself naturally to write exactly the words God wishes to speak. Only in this large and comprehensive sense are the words of Scripture dictated by God.[86]

[83] Benjamin Breckinridge Warfield, *Calvin and Calvinism* (Oxford University Press, 1931; rep. ed.: Grand Rapids, Mich.: Baker, 1981), 62.
    [84] Warfield, 'Inspiration and Criticism,' 421. So also Phillips, *Turretin's Idea of Theology*, 2: 752.
    [85] Benjamin Breckinridge Warfield, 'The Biblical Idea of Inspiration,' in *Inspiration and Authority of the Bible*, 153.
    [86] Kenneth S. Kantzer, 'Calvin and the Holy Scriptures,' in *Inspiration and Interpretation*, 140–1.

The difficulty of Kantzer's account is that while it seems to express the *desideratum* of confluence, it does not explain how this is achieved. How is it that God 'sovereignly controls the mind and personality' of a biblical author so that his 'whole personality expresses itself naturally to write exactly the words God wishes to speak'? Given Calvin's strong views on divine providence, the answer would seem to be that a very rigid determinism is in place whereby God, through the use of all causes under His control, shapes the biblical author like clay in such a way that he writes what God has pre-determined. But this is worse than secretarial dictation; it is, in fact, strict mechanical dictation, for man has been reduced to the level of a machine. God's causally determining Paul to write his Epistle to the Romans is incompatible with Paul's freely writing that epistle, on any plausible account of freedom.[87] Absent human freedom, we are not only back to mechanical dictation, but also to mere accommodation as the ultimate account of the humanity of Scripture, since God is the only agent who determines what an author shall write. Genuine confluence, then, requires human freedom, such that there are at least two authors of any book of Scripture. That inspiration is plenary prevents confluence's being understood as the divine and human authors each writing different portions of Scripture; that inspiration is verbal precludes confluence's being interpreted to mean that God is the author of the ideas and a man the author of the words. The whole of Scripture, down to its very words, is the freely written word of both God and man. How can this be?

The tension in the classical doctrine of inspiration has in our own day been more precisely formulated by Randall and David Basinger.[88] They are concerned to show that the traditional affirmation of biblical authority and inerrancy is inseparably wedded to the dictation theory of inspiration. If God alone were the author of Scripture, its inerrancy would be unproblematic; but given that the human authors write freely, how can God guarantee that they write what He desires? The defender of the classical doctrine of inspiration must argue along the following lines:

1. The words of the Bible are the product of free human activity.
2. Human activities (such as penning a book) can be totally controlled by God without violating human freedom.
3. God totally controlled what human authors did in fact write.
4. Therefore, the words of the Bible are God's utterances.
5. Whatever God utters is errorless.
6. Therefore, the words of the Bible are errorless.

---

[87] See Harry Frankfurt, 'Alternative Possibilities and Moral Responsibility,' *Journal of Philosophy* 66 (1969): 829–39; Thomas V. Morris, *The Logic of God Incarnate* (Ithaca, N.Y.: Cornell University Press, 1986), 151–2.

[88] Randall Basinger and David Basinger, 'Inerrancy, Dictation and The Free Will Defence,' *Evangelical Quarterly* 55 (1983): 177–80.

This argument is as much an argument for the verbal, plenary inspiration of Scripture on the assumption of confluence as it is an argument for inerrancy. The key premiss is (2). Detractors of plenary, verbal inspiration will regard (2) as self-contradictory. The only way God could have totally controlled (an expression Basinger and Basinger take to be synonymous with 'infallibly guaranteed') what the human authors wrote would have been to take away their freedom. The defender of classical inspiration, on the other hand, must affirm (2) if he is not to fall into a dictation theory of inspiration. Although Basinger and Basinger go on to argue that the defender of classical inspiration cannot, in view of his endorsement of (2), utilize the Free Will Defense with respect to the problem of evil, I think that the price of 'placing direct responsibility on God for each instance of moral evil in the world'[89] is so great that their appeal to the problem of evil is more perspicuously understood in terms of evil's constituting evidence against (2). Given the reality of human evil and the fact that God cannot be the author of evil, (2) must be false. Accordingly, one can then argue:

1. The words of the Bible are the product of free human activity.
2'. Human activities (and their products) cannot be totally controlled by God without violating human freedom.
7. The doctrine of the verbal, plenary inspiration of the Bible entails God's total control of the words of the Bible.
8. Therefore, the doctrine of the verbal, plenary inspiration of the Bible is false.

If one persists in affirming the doctrine of verbal, plenary inspiration, then, since (7) is true virtually by definition, one must deny (1); that is to say, verbal, plenary inspiration implies dictation. The bottom line is that the doctrine of the plenary, verbal, confluent inspiration of Scripture is incoherent.[90]

The response to Basinger and Basinger on the part of defenders of classical inspiration has not been encouraging. New Testament scholar D. A. Carson agrees that their argument that 'is valid,'[91] by which he evidently means 'sound,' since he does not dispute the truth of their premises. Carson agrees that the

---

[89] Ibid., 180.

[90] It is intriguing that this is the conclusion to which Pinnock, quoted above, was eventually driven. He says, 'A text that is word for word what God wanted in the first place might as well have been dictated, for all the room it leaves for human agency' (Clark H. Pinnock, *The Scripture Principle* [San Francisco: Harper & Row, 1984], 101). The problem is that God is said to have 'controlled the writers and every detail of what they wrote' (Ibid.). 'To hold that God predestined and controlled every detail of the text makes nonsense of human authorship and is tantamount to saying God dictated the text. It is quibbling over words to deny it so vigorously' (Ibid.). 'If God is really in total control of all things, then he must have willed all the tragedies and atrocities that have happened . . . God is the one responsible for everything that happens if he willed it so completely, and he must take the blame' (Ibid., 102). I hope to show that none of these inferences is correct.

[91] D. A. Carson, 'Recent Developments in the Doctrine of Scripture,' in *Hermeneutics, Authority, and Canon*, ed. D. A. Carson and John D. Woodbridge (Grand Rapids, Mich: Zondervan, 1986), 45.

classical doctrine of inspiration is incompatible with the Free Will Defense. But he does not see this as in any way problematic. On the one hand, the notion of divine/human confluent activity lies at the very heart of the Christian faith, since the major redemptive acts of history were wrought by both God and man:

> ... the conspirators did what God Himself decided beforehand should happen. Yet the conspirators are not thereby excused: they are still regarded as guilty. Any other view will either depreciate the heinousness of the sin or render the Cross a last minute arrangement by which God cleverly snatched victory out of the jaws of defeat, rather than the heart of His redemptive purposes.[92]

If we permit divine human *concursus* in redemptive history, Carson asks, why not also in biblical inspiration? This line of response seems to indicate that Carson would accept (2) and reject the Free Will Defense. In fact, he does go on to dismiss that defense; but he does so in such a way as to call into question his commitment to (2). For he says, 'human responsibility can be grounded in something other than "free will," where free will is understood to entail absolute power to the contrary' and footnotes Jonathan Edwards and other defenders of a compatibilist view of freedom.[93] But if one is a compatibilist about human freedom, then (wholly apart from the difficulties this occasions for theodicy) the sort of freedom envisioned in (1) seems inadequate to secure confluence. One has advanced no further than a deterministic doctrine of providence which turns the authors of Scripture into robots. One has not lived up to the charge of Carson's co-editor John Woodbridge that 'We must spell out unequivocally our full commitment to the human authorship and full freedom of the biblical writers as human authors'[94] nor have we stayed true to what Carson himself calls 'the central line of evangelical thought . . . : God in His sovereignty . . . super- intended the freely composed human writings we call the Scriptures.'[95] Rather we have simply watered down the concept of freedom so as to be able to affirm determinism and, hence, God's total control.

Norman Geisler, on the other hand, argues that the Basingers' argument is not sound.[96] Unfortunately, his critique is not as clear as it could be, and the Basingers are able to point out a number of misunderstandings in their reply to Geisler.[97] These misunderstandings notwithstanding, there are, I think, a couple of points in Geisler's critique to which Basinger and Basinger have not

---

[92] D. A. Carson, 'Recent Developments in the Doctrine of Scripture,' in *Hermeneutics, Authority, and Canon*, ed. D. A. Carson and John D. Woodbridge (Grand Rapids, Mich: Zondervan, 1986), 45.

[93] Ibid.

[94] Woodbridge, *Biblical Authority*, 9.

[95] Carson, 'Recent Developments.' 45.

[96] Norman L. Geisler. 'Inerrancy and Free Will: A Reply to the Brothers Basinger,' *Evangelical Quarterly* 57 (1985): 347–53.

[97] David Basinger and Randall Basinger. 'Inerrancy and Free Will: Some Further Thoughts,' *Evangelical Quarterly* 58 (1986): 351–4.

given due attention. First, Geisler, in effect, challenges (3). He observes that a purely human utterance may be inerrant; if, then, a true statement is made by both God and man, God need not totally control the human author in order for the statement to be without error. By extension all the statements of Scripture could be errorless and have both God and human beings as their authors, yet without God's exercising total control over what the human authors wrote. If (3) is false, then the defender of biblical inerrancy does not assume (2) in defense of his doctrine; rather he defends his position on the basis of (4–6) alone. Now Geisler is obviously correct that total divine control of human authors is not a necessary condition of the inerrancy of their writings. Nonetheless the denial of (3) is so outrageously improbable that (3) is doubtlessly true. Otherwise we should be forced to say that the biblical authors of their own free will just happened to write exactly the sentences which God wanted as His own utterances. In any case, if I am correct that what is at stake here is not so much inerrancy as plenary, verbal inspiration, then (7) tells us that the truth of that doctrine entails (3). For God and man did not merely concur in tokening separately the same Scriptural sentence-types; rather the doctrine of inspiration holds that the human author's sentence-tokens are identical with God's sentence-tokens; God tokens the sentences through the human author; his words are God's words. Thus, God must in some way so control the author as to speak through him. The control is 'total' in that it extends to the very words of Scripture. Hence, Geisler's first objection fails to show why the defender of inspiration is not committed to (3) and, if he wishes to avoid dictation, therefore (2).

But Geisler has a second line of attack.[98] He exposes a hidden assumption in Basinger and Basinger's reasoning, to wit,

9. If God can infallibly guarantee what some men will do, then He can do the same for all,

an assumption which Geisler rejects as false, Geisler is quite correct that the Basingers make this assumption, for (2) may be taken in the sense of

2*. Some human activities (such as penning a book) can be totally contolled by God without violating human freedom, *i.e.*, $(\exists x)(Hx \cdot Cx \cdot \sim Vx)$

or

2**. All human activities (such as penning a book) can be totally controlled by God without violating human freedom, *i.e.*, $(\forall x)(Hx \supset [Cx \cdot \sim Vx])$.

The Basingers require (2**) for their argument to be sound. But one could maintain that while it is within God's power to control the writing of Scripture without violating human freedom, that does not imply that God can so control human activity in general that no one ever freely does evil. In order for the classical doctrine of inspiration to be incompatible with the Free Will Defense, (2) must be taken as universally quantified rather than as existentially quantified.

---

[98] Geisler, 'Inerrancy and Free Will,' 351.

But now a familiar move in the Free Will defense may be turned against Basinger and Basinger: (2), so understood, is neither necessary nor essential to Christian theism nor a logical consequence of propositions that are; nor is the person who fails to see that (2) has these qualities intellectually deficient in some way.[99] Therefore, no incompatibility has been demonstrated between the classical doctrine of inspiration and the Free Will defense. Basinger and Basinger's reply at this point is faltering:

> Geisler... denies that people who believe that God infallibly guaranteed that the writers of Scripture freely produced an inerrant work must also believe that God can infallibly guarantee that all individuals will always freely do what he wants....

> But is this true? Can God infallibly guarantee that any single human action will *freely* occur if he cannot totally control all free human action...? We believe not.... if ([2]) is false, then God can never *guarantee* that any human will freely do what he wants.[100]

But this amounts to nothing but a personal confession of belief on the Basingers' part. It needs to be remembered that Basinger and Basinger are making the very strong claim that 'Any person wanting to both use the free will defence in his theodicy and, at the same time, defend inerrancy against dictation is attempting the impossible.... One cannot have it both ways'[101] But in order to show these doctrines to be broadly logically incompatible, they must come up with a proposition whose conjunction with the propositions formulating each doctrine is logically inconsistent and which meets the above stipulated conditions, and (2) is definitely not it.

A MIDDLE KNOWLEDGE PERSPECTIVE

But where does this leave us? I suggested that Basinger and Basinger's argument might be more perspicaciously understood as claiming that human evil constitutes evidence against (2). That is to say, given (2^*), (2^{**}) is highly probable. For if God can control human activities in such exquisite detail as to produce through free agents a Scripture which is verbally and plenarily inspired, then there seems no reason why He could not control human activities such that people always freely refrain from sin. Given, then, the evil in the world, $(2')$ is probably true. But if $(2')$ is probably true, then, as argued, the doctrine of verbal, plenary inspiration is probably false.

To defeat this argument what is needed is some plausible, positive account of how God can control free human activities in such a way as to yield inspired

---

[99] On these conditions, see Alvin Plantinga, 'Self-Profile,' in *Alvin Plantinga*, ed. James Tomberlin and Peter Van Inwagen, Profiles 5 (Dordrecht: D. Reidel, 1985), 39–40.

[100] Basinger and Basinger: 'Inerrancy and Free Will,' 353–4.

[101] Basinger and Basinger, 'Inerrancy, Dictation, and the Free Will Defense,' 179; cf. 180.

Scripture wihout being able simultaneously to control free human activities in such a way as to prevent evil. Here Geisler is less helpful. He suggests,

The way God 'can' guarantee that some do not perform evil (or err) is by knowing infallibly that they will freely do good. It does not follow that God can do this for those who freely choose to do evil. For in this case God would have to force them to do contrary to their free choice.[102]

On Geisler's view, 'since God knows (and so determines) which men will utter truth and when, then God can also affirm these truths as his infallibly true Word.'[103] There are two problems with this suggestion: (1) It appears to endorse an untenable theological fatalism springing from the fact of divine foreknow-ledge. The suggestion seems to be that future acts, whether good or bad, are somehow fixed in virtue of God's infallible foreknowledge of them. But as numerous thinkers have shown, such an inference is simply logically falla-cious.[104] Since God's foreknowledge is counterfactually dependent upon future contingents, they can fail to happen until they do happen; were they to fail to happen, then God would have foreknown differently than He does. (2) Divine foreknowledge is insufficient for providential control of the authors of Scripture. Foreknowledge only informs God of what the authors of Scripture will freely write; but such knowledge comes too late in the order of explanation for God to do anything about it. The problem is not that God would have to 'force them to do contrary to their free choice.' Rather it is logically impossible to change the future. Geisler in effect misplaces the divine creative decree later in the order of explanation than divine foreknowledge, rather than before. Thus on his view God must consider Himself extraordinarily lucky that He finds Himself in a world in which the writers of Scripture just happen to freely respond to their circumstances (including the promptings of His Spirit) in just the right ways as to produce the Bible. This is incompatible with a robust view of divine providence.

Geisler does, however, hint at the account we are looking for. In asking why some men were providentially preserved from error while others were not kept from error (or evil) at every time, he suggests,

It may have been because only some men freely chose to co-operate with the Spirit so that he could guide them in an errorless way. Or it may have been that the Holy Spirit

[102] Geisler, 'Inerrancy and Free Will,' 351.
[103] Ibid., 352.
[104] See Alvin Plantinga, 'On Ockham's Way Out,' *Faith and Philosophy* 3 (1986): 235–69; Jonathan L. Kvanvig, *The Possibility of an All-Knowing God* (New York: St. Martin's, 1986); Alfred J. Freddoso, 'Introduction,' in *On Divine Foreknowledge*, by Luis Molina, trans. with Notes by Alfred J. Freddoso (Ithaca, N.Y.: Cornell University Press, 1988), 9–29; Edward R. Wierenga, *The Nature of God: an Inquiry into Divine Attributes*, Cornell Studies in the Philosophy of Religion (Ithaca, N.Y.: Cornell University Press, 1989); William Lane Craig, *Divine Foreknowledge and Human Freedom: The Coherence of Theism 1: Omniscience*, Studies in Intellectual History 19 (Leiden, The Netherlands: E. J. Brill, 1990); Thomas Flint, *Divine Providence*, Cornell Studies in the Philosophy of Religion (Ithaca, N.Y.: Cornell University Press, 1998).

simply chose to use those men and occasions which he infallibly knew would not produce error.[105]

Here we are speaking not of simple foreknowledge, but of God's counterfactual knowledge. It involves His knowledge of what some creature would freely do, were he to be placed in a specific set of circumstances. If God has such knowledge explanatorily prior to His creative decree then such knowledge is what theologians have called middle knowledge (*media scientia*). Largely the product of the creative genius of the Spanish Jesuit of the Counter-Reformation Luis Molina (1535–1600), the doctrine of middle knowledge proposes to furnish an analysis of divine knowledge in terms of three logical moments.[106] Although whatever God knows, He has known from eternity, so that there is no temporal succession in God's knowledge, nonetheless there does exist a sort of logical succession in God's knowledge in that His knowledge of certain propositions is conditionally or explanatorily prior to His knowledge of certain other propositions. That is to say, God's knowledge of a particular set of propositions depends asymmetrically on His knowledge of a certain other set of propositions and is in this sense posterior to it. In the first, unconditioned moment God knows all *possibilia*, not only all individual essences, but also all possible worlds. Molina calls such knowledge 'natural knowledge' because the content of such knowledge is essential to God and in no way depends on the free decisions of His will. By means of His natural knowledge, then, God has knowledge of every contingent state of affairs which could possibly obtain and of what the exemplification of the individual essence of any free creature could freely choose to do in any such state of affairs that should be actual.

In the second moment, God possesses knowledge of certain true counterfactual propositions, including counterfactuals of creaturely freedom. That is to say. He knows what contingent states of affairs would obtain if certain antecedent states of affairs were to obtain; whereas by His natural knowledge God knew what any free creature *could* do in any set of circumstances, now in this second moment God knows what any free creature *would* do in any set of circumstances. This is not because the circumstances causally determine the creature's choice, but simply because this is how the creature would freely choose. God thus knows that were He to actualize certain states of affairs, then certain other contingent states of affairs would obtain. Molina calls this counterfactual knowledge 'middle knowledge' because it stands in between the first and third moment in divine knowledge. Middle knowledge is like natural knowledge in that such knowledge does not depend on any decision of the divine will; God does not

[105] Geisler, 'Inerrancy and Free Will,' 352.

[106] For Molina's doctrine see Ludovici Molina, *De liberi arbitrii cum gratia donis, divina praescientia, providentia, praedestinatione et reprobatione concordia* 4. This section has been translated as Luis Molina, *On Divine Foreknowledge*, trans, with an Introduction and Notes by Alfred J. Freddoso (Ithaca, N.Y.: Cornell University Press, 1988).

determine which counterfactuals of creaturely freedom are true or false. Thus, if it is true that

> If some agent S were placed in circumstances C, then he would freely perform action a,

then even God in His omnipotence cannot bring it about that S would refrain from a if he were placed in C. On the other hand, middle knowledge is unlike natural knowledge in that the content of His middle knowledge is not essential to God. True counterfactuals of freedom are contingently true; S could freely decide to refrain from a in C, so that different counterfactuals could be true and be known by God than those that are. Hence, although it is essential to God that He have middle knowledge, it is not essential to Him to have middle knowledge of those particular propositions which He does in fact know.

Intervening between the second and third moments of divine knowledge stands God's free decree to actualize a world known by Him to be realizable on the basis of His middle knowledge. By His natural knowledge, God knows what is the entire range of logically possible worlds; by His middle knowledge He knows, in effect, what is the proper subset of those worlds which it is feasible for Him to actualize. By a free decision, God decrees to actualize one of those worlds known to Him through His middle knowledge. According to Molina, this decision is the result of a complete and unlimited deliberation by means of which God considers and weighs every possible circumstance and its ramifications and decides to settle on the particular world He desires. Hence, logically prior, if not chronologically prior, to God's creation of the world is the divine deliberation concerning which world to actualize.

Given God's free decision to actualize a world, in the third and final moment God possesses knowledge of all remaining propositions that are in fact true in the actual world. Such knowledge is denominated 'free knowledge' by Molina because it is logically posterior to the decision of the divine will to actualize a world. The content of such knowledge is clearly not essential to God, since He could have decreed to actualize a different world. Had He done so, the content of His free knowledge would be different.

Molina's doctrine has profound implications for divine providence. For it enables God to exercise providential control of free creatures without abridging the free exercise of their wills. In virtue of His knowledge of counterfactuals of creaturely freedom and His freedom to decree that certain circumstances exist and certain free creatures be placed in those circumstances, God is able to bring about indirectly that events occur which He knew would happen as a direct result of the particular decisions which those creatures would freely make in those circumstances. Plantinga has provided an analysis of such providential control in terms of what he calls strong and weak actualization.[107] God is said to strongly actualize a state of affairs S if and only if He causes S to be actual and also causes

---

[107] Plantinga, 'Self-Profile,' 48–9.

to be actual every contingent state of affairs S^* included in S (where S includes S^* if and only if it is impossible that S be actual and S^* not be actual). God is said to weakly actualize a state of affairs S if and only if He strongly actualizes a state of affairs S^* that counterfactually implies S (that is, were S^* to obtain, then S would obtain). Then God can weakly actualize any state of affairs S if and only if there is a state of affairs S^* such that (i) it is within God's power to strongly actualize S^*, and (ii) if God were to strongly actualize S^*, then S would be actual. Weak actualization is clearly compatible with human freedom, since the actualized state of affairs S obtains in virtue of the counterfactual of creaturely freedom which connects S to S^*. Thus, God knew, for example, that were He to create the Apostle Paul in just the circumstances he was in around AD 55, he would freely write to the Corinthian church, saying just what he did in fact say. It needs to be emphasized that those circumstances included not only Paul's background, personality, environment, and so forth, but also any promptings or gifts of the Holy Spirit to which God knew Paul would freely respond.

The theological application to the doctrine of inspiration is obvious. By weakly actualizing the composition of the books of the Bible, God can bring it about that biblical inspiration is in the fullest sense confluent. The Epistle to the Romans, for example, is truly the work of Paul, who freely wrote it and whose personality and idiosyncrasies are reflected therein. The style is his because he is the author. The words are his, for he freely chose them. The argument and reasoning are the reflection of his own mind, for no one dictated the premises to him. Neither did God dictate *levicula* like the greetings ('Greet Asyncritus, Phlegon, Hermes,' *etc.*); these are spontaneous salutations which God knew Paul would deliver under such circumstances; so also the interjection of his amanuensis Tertius (Rom. 16.22). Paul's full range of emotions, his memory lapses (I Cor. 1.14–16), his personal asides (Gal. 6.11) are all authentic products of human consciousness. God knew what Paul would freely write in the various circumstances in which he found himself and weakly actualized the writing of the Pauline corpus. Perhaps some features of Paul's letters are a matter of indifference to God: maybe it would not have mattered to God whether Paul greeted Phlegon or not; perhaps God would have been just as pleased had Paul worded some things differently; perhaps the Scripture need not have been just as it is to accomplish God's purposes. We cannot know. But we can confess that Scripture as it does stand is God-breathed and therefore authoritative. The Bible says what God wanted to say and communicates His message of salvation to mankind.

Some of the statements of the defenders of the classic doctrine of verbal, plenary, confluent inspiration fairly cry out for such a middle knowledge perspective. Here is what Warfield, for example, has to say about the inspiration of Paul's letters:

So soon, however, as we seriously endeavor to form for ourselves a clear conception of the precise nature of the Divine action in this 'breathing out' of the Scriptures—this 'bearing' of the writers of the Scriptures to their appointed goal of the production of a book of Divine trustworthiness and indefectible authority—we become acutely aware of a more deeply lying and much wider problem, apart from which this one of inspiration, technically so called, cannot be profitably considered. This is the general problem of the origin of the Scriptures and the part of God in all that complex of processes by the interaction of which these books, which we call the sacred Scriptures, with all their peculiarities, and all their qualities of whatever sort, have been brought into being. For, of course, these books were not produced suddenly, by some miraculous act—handed down complete out of heaven, as the phrase goes; but, like all other products of time, are the ultimate effect of many processes cooperating through long periods. There is to be considered, for instance, the preparation of the material which forms the subject-matter of these books: in a sacred history, say, for example, to be narrated; or in a religious experience which may serve as a norm for record; or in a logical elaboration of the contents of revelation which may be placed at the service of God's people; or in the progressive revelation of Divine truth itself, supplying their culminating contents. And there is the preparation of the men to write these books to be considered, a preparation physical, intellectual, spiritual, which must have attended them throughout their whole lives, and, indeed, must have had its beginning in their remote ancestors, and the effect of which was to bring the right men to the right places at the right times, with the right endowments, impulses, acquirements, to write just the books which were designed for them. When 'inspiration,' technically so called, is superinduced on lines of preparation like these, it takes on quite a different aspect from that which it bears when it is thought of as an isolated action of the Divine Spirit operating out of all relation to historical processes. Representations are sometimes made as if, when God wished to produce sacred books which would incorporate His will—a series of letters like those of Paul, for example—He was reduced to the necessity of going down to earth and painfully scrutinizing the men He found there, seeking anxiously for the one who, on the whole, promised best for His purpose; and then violently forcing the material He wished expressed through him, against his natural bent, and with as little loss from his recalcitrant characteristics as possible. Of course, nothing of the sort took place. If God wished to give His people a series of letters like Paul's He prepared a Paul to write them, and the Paul He brought to the task was a Paul who spontaneously would write just such letters.[108]

Divine middle knowledge illumines such an interpretation, since God knew what Paul would write if placed in such circumstances and knew how to bring about such circumstances without extinguishing human freedom along the way. Warfield comments that when we give due weight in our thinking to the universality of providence, to the minuteness and completeness of its sway, to its invariable efficacy, then we may wonder that anything 'is needed beyond this mere providential government to secure the production of sacred books, which should be in every detail absolutely accordant with the Divine will.'[109] Revelation will be needed in some cases for truths not accessible through natural reason. Moreover,

[108] Warfield, 'Biblical Idea of Inspiration,' 154–5.
[109] Ibid., 157.

we must never forget that the circumstances known to God include, not exclude, all those movements of the Holy Spirit in an author's heart to which God knew the writer would respond in appropriate ways.

Given the doctrine of middle knowledge, then, we see how plenary, verbal, confluent inspiration can, *pace* Spinoza, Le Clerc, and Simon, be coherently affirmed. The distinction between strong and weak actualization reveals how the control described in (2) by Basinger and Basinger is possible.[110] We can understand how the divine/human confluence in the events of redemptive history as insisted on by Carson is possible without falling into determinism. Finally, we can see why Geisler was right to maintain that God's ability to control the free composition of Scripture does not imply His ability to so control the free actions of all persons that a world containing as much good as the actual world but with less evil would be actualized. God might well have requisite control of the authors of Scripture to ensure that Scripture would be freely written without having requisite control of all human beings to ensure that less evil, but the same amount of good, would be freely wrought. In fact, God's placing a premium on actualizing a world in which the requisite counterfactuals of creaturely freedom are true for the free composition of Scripture might require Him to forego worlds in which counterfactuals requisite for an otherwise better balance of good and evil are true. Indeed, the existence of Scripture in the world might actually serve to increase the amount of evil in the world by exacerbating sinful desires (Rom. 7.7–8)! It all depends on which counterfactuals of creaturely freedom are true, a contingency over which God has no control. A world in which Scripture is freely composed and in which the balance between good and evil is more optimal than it is in the actual world may not be feasible for God. Basinger and Basinger are in effect claiming that

>   10. A world in which an inspired, inerrant Scripture is freely written is feasible for God

and

>   11. A world containing as much good as the actual world without as much evil is not feasible for God

are broadly logically incompatible or, at least, improbable each with respect to the other. But such claims are pure speculation; we are simply not in an epistemic position

---

[110] This also helps us to see that the notion of 'infallibly guaranteeing' is really a red herring. Weak actualization does not infallibly guarantee the result in the sense that there are possible worlds in which the strongly actualized state of affairs does not counterfactually imply the weakly actualized state of affairs, since counterfactuals of freedom are true/false relative to a possible world. Thus, there may be a possible world relative to which a world with a freely composed Bible and a more optimal balance of good and evil is feasible for God. The verbal, plenary, confluent inspiration of Scripture thus does not require that God's guarantee be infallible, but merely that He in fact has the requisite control of free creatures to weakly actualize Scripture's composition. He can guarantee inerrancy without infallibly guaranteeing it.

to make responsibility such pronouncements. Thus, in the area of biblical inspiration, as in so many other areas of theology, the doctrine of divine middle knowledge proves to be a fruitful resource in shedding light on seemingly irresolvable old conundrums.[111] The doctrine is, of course, controversial and has many detractors, but the objections lodged against that doctrine are far from compelling.[112]

HISTORICAL PRECEDENTS

When one hits upon what one takes to be an original idea, it is somewhat deflating (but nonetheless encouraging) to discover that one is retracing largely forgotten paths explored by previous thinkers. When I conceived the idea of enunciating a middle knowledge perspective on biblical inspiration, I was unaware that it, or something rather like it, had been done before.[113] Indeed,

---

[111] For applications of middle knowledge to such issues as Christian exclusivism, divine sovereignty and human freedom, perseverance of the saints, infallibility, and creation/evolution see William Lane Craig, '"No Other Name": A Middle Knowledge Perspective on the Exclusivity of Salvation through Christ,' *Faith and Philosophy* 6 (1989): 172–88; idem, 'Middle Knowledge: a Calvinist-Arminian Rapprochement?' in *The Grace of God, the Will of Man*, ed. C. Pinnock (Grand Rapids, Mich: Zondervan, 1989), 141–64; idem, '"Lest Anyone Should Fall"; a Middle Knowledge Perspective on Perseverance and Apostolic Warnings,' *International Journal for Philosophy of Religion* 29 (1991): 65–74; Thomas P. Flint, 'Middle Knowledge and the Doctrine of Infallibility,' *Philosophical Perspectives*, vol. 5: *Philosophy of Religion*, ed. J. E. Tomberlin (Atascadero, Calif.: Ridgeway Publishing, 1991), 373–93; Del Ratzch, 'Design, Chance, and Theistic Evolution,' in *Mere Creation* (Downer's Grove, Ill.: Inter-Varsity, 1998), 289–312.

[112] See Alvin Plantinga, 'Reply to Robert Adams,' in *Alvin Plantinga*, 372–382; Kvanvig, *Possibility of an All-Knowing God*, 121–48; Freddoso, 'Introduction,' 62–81; Wierenga, *Nature of God*, 116–65; Craig, *Divine Foreknowledge and Human Freedom*, 237–78; Flint, *Divine Providence*, 75–176.

[113] Moreover, I discovered since writing the initial draft of this paper that it, or something like it, has been done again in our own day by Nicholas Wolterstorff, *Divine Discourse: Philosophical Reflection on the Claim that God Speaks* (Cambridge: Cambridge University Press, 1995). In his chapter 3, 'The Many Modes of Discourse,' Wolterstorff has a fascinating discussion of what he calls 'double agency,' which obtains when one person says something with words which he himself has not uttered or incribed (38–57). Exploiting examples reminiscent of those employed by the seventeenth century Jesuits, Wolterstorff focuses on what he calls 'appropriated discourse' as a model for Scripture: human discourse appropriated by God and thus divine discourse (51–4). 'All that is necessary for the whole [Bible] to be God's book is that the human discourse it contains have been appropriated by God, as one single book, for God's discourse' (54). Such an understanding of Scripture is entirely consonant with the position defended in this paper. Unfortunately, Wolterstorff makes the same category mistake as did Lessius, equating inspiration with the movement of the Holy Spirit in or on the authors of Scripture rather than as a characteristic of the text itself (54; cf. 301). This leads him to the view that the Scripture may not be in whole or in part inspired even though it is God's Word. But a providentially produced piece of discourse can be inspired, in the proper sense of that term, even in the absence of any special moving of the Spirit of God upon the human author. The question of how Scripture came to be produced exposes the greatest weakness of Wolterstorff's discussion, when in chapter 7 he asks whether God can cause the events generative of Scriptural discourse. This is the same issue raised by Warfield, which called for a middle knowledge solution. Intriguingly, Wolterstorff does consider ever so briefly a middle knowledge position, though without identifying it as such (121–2). Tragically, he rejects such a solution because he is inclined to think that there are no true counterfactuals of freedom. Eager to discover what would

I was chagrined to learn from Burtchaell that it was, in fact, 'the most venerable' of those 'discredited views from which practically every writer [in the nineteenth century] took comfort in disassociating himself in his footnotes.'[114]

In 1588, the same year that saw the publication of Molina's *Concordia*, a papal brief was issued declaring a moratorium on a controversy involving a young Jesuit theologian of the University of Louvain Leonard Leys (Lessius) concerning a long list of theological charges which had been brought against him.[115] The previous year, the theological faculty had extracted from his students' notes 34 propositions which they publicly condemned. Three of these dealt with the subject of biblical inspiration. They read:

i. For anything to be Holy Scripture, its individual words need not be inspired by the Holy Spirit.
ii. The individual truths and statements need not be immediately inspired in the writer by the Holy Spirit.
iii. If any book...were to be written through purely human endeavor without the assistance of the Holy Spirit, and He should then certify that there was nothing false therein, the book would become Holy Scripture.[116]

The theological faculty of the University of Louvain censured Lessius for these propositions, stating that Sacred Scripture is not the word of man, but the Word of God, dictated by the Holy Spirit. The University of Douay joined in the censure, explaining that dictation is not just a suggestion in general, but of the words themselves: there is not a syllable or accent in Scripture which is trifling or superfluous.

Now among the other propositions condemned were statements concerning grace and free will which indicated that Lessius was groping for the doctrine of middle knowledge which Molina first succeeded in formulating clearly and accurately. According to Burtchaell,

---

incline Wolterstorff to such a position, one turns to his attending endnote and is stunned to discover that no better reason is given for this scepticism than the misconceived and oft-refuted objections of William Hasker! In the end Wolterstorff is left without any explanation of how God, even given divine interventions in history, can bring about the writing of Scripture in the absence of divine middle knowledge—a weakness which draws bitter criticism on the part of Michael Levine. 'God Speak,' *Religious Studies* 34 (1998): 14, whose critique on this score is unfortunately skipped over in the interests of space in Wolterstorff's 'Reply to Levine,' *Religious Studies* 34 (1998): 22.

[114] Burtchaell, *Catholic Theories of Inspiration*, 44. He pronounces the theory 'dead and buried.'
[115] On the Lessius affair see *Dictionnaire de théologie catholique*, s.v. 'Inspiration de l'Écriture,' vol. 7, pt. 2, cols. 2135–45; Burtchaell, *Catholic Theories of Inspiration*, chaps. 2 and 3.
[116] (i.) Ut aliquid sit Scriptura sacra, non est necessarium singula ejus verba inspirata esse a Spiritu Sancto.
(ii.) Non est necessarium ut singulae veritates et sententiae sint immediate a Spiritu Sancto ipsi scriptori inspiratae.
(iii.) Liber aliquis...humana industria sine assistentia Spiritus Sancti scriptus, si Spiritus Sanctus postea testetur ibi nihil esse falsum, efficitur Scriptura sacra.

The crux of the Louvain-Jesuit dispute was this issue of grace and free-will. The three censured propositions on inspiration formed but a small part of a total of thirty-two which bore on this larger problem. The faculty rightly saw that Lessius's inspiration hypotheses were the logical application of the general Jesuit idea of grace: they provided for both divine authorship and human literary freedom by making divine intervention only indirect.[117]

Whether we regard Lessius as, in Woodbridge's epithet,[118] a 'slippery' theologian or a subtle dialectician will probably depend on our openness to the Molinist point of view. Claiming that he had been misunderstood, Lessius wrote an *Apologia* in which he explained how he interpreted the disputed propositions.[119] By (i) and (ii) he meant that the authors of Scripture did not need a new and positive inspiration or new illumination from God to write down each word of Scripture. As he later explained,

We are teaching that, for anything to be Holy Scripture, its every word and statement need not be positively and absolutely inspired in the author, with the Holy Spirit supplying and forming in his mind the individual words and statements. It is enough that the sacred writer be divinely drawn to write down what he sees, hears, or knows otherwise, that he enjoy the infallible assistance of the Holy Spirit to prevent him from mistakes even in matters he knows on the word of others, or from his own experience, or by his own natural reasoning. It is this assistance of the Holy Spirit that gives Scripture its infallible truth.[120]

He gave two reasons in support of his position: (1) The Evangelists did not need a new revelation to record the life of Jesus, since they either were witnesses themselves or had historical tradition of it. (2) The Holy Spirit chose competent

---

[117] Burtchaell, *Catholic Theories of Inspiration*, 91. 'Indirect' is not technically correct; better would be 'non-deterministic.' His complete neglect of this context vitiates the adequacy of Vawter's exposition of this controversy (Vawter, *Biblical Inspiration*, 63–70). Quoting Suarez to the effect that 'although everything in Scripture has been written by the Holy Spirit, nevertheless the Spirit left it to the writer to write everything in a manner accommodated to himself and according to his own talents, education, and language, although under his direction,' a befuddled Vawter protests, 'It may be asked whether such a sentence is not logically meaningless: the Spirit has "written" words that he "left to" the human writer to discover from his own resources' (Ibid., 66). But given a middle knowledge perspective, such dual authorship becomes perspicuous. Similarly, one can only smile at Vawter's allegation that Suarez, a great champion of middle knowledge, was 'confused' because he affirmed both verbal inspiration and only negative assistance by the Holy Spirit: 'Suárez was trying to harmonize into one system what were basically opposed conceptions of inspiration' (Ibid., 67). It is precisely the beauty of the doctrine of middle knowledge that it succeeds in reconciling seemingly opposed positions with respect to divine sovereignty and human freedom.

[118] Woodbridge, *Biblical Authority*, 70.

[119] See Livino de Meyer, *Historia controversiarum de divina gratia*, 6 vols., 2nd ed. (Venetiis: Nicolaum Pezzana, 1742), Appendix III: *Apologia a R. P. Leonardo Lessio e Societate Jesu scripta adversus censuras Lovaniensem & Duacensem Responsio ad Censuram Facultatis sacrae Theologiae Lovaniensis*, 756–7.

[120] Letter of Lessius to the archbishop of Machlin, in Joseph Kleutgen, 'R. P. Leonardii Lessii Soc. Iesu Theologi de Divina Inspiratione Doctrina,' in Gerardus Schneemann, *Controversiarum de Divinae Gratiae Liberique Arbitrii Concordia Initia et Progressus* (Friburgi Brisgoviae: Herder, 1881), 466 (cited in Burtchaell, *Catholic Theories of Inspiration*. 45).

instruments, gifted with the ability to express themselves, whom He then stirred to write of what they knew and whom He assisted to keep [them] from error.

Mangenot observes that taken literally Lessius's propositions (i) and (ii) would be incompatible with the inspiration of Scripture; but it is evident from the above that what he was really exercised to do was to deny the dictation theory of inspiration.[121] Lessius insisted that the impulse and assistance of the Holy Spirit were compatible with the human author's recalling things from memory, organizing his material, utilizing his peculiar style of expression, and so on. He affirmed that the entire Scripture is the Word of God and was even, in a certain sense, dictated by the Holy Spirit. We have seen that even so redoubtable a champion of verbal inspiration as Warfield affirmed that dictation has reference to the result, not the mode, of inspiration, and Lessius seems to affirm the same.

According to Burtchaell, Lessius's three propositions reduce God's role in the production of Scripture to (i) the supplying of ideas, but not words, (ii) the protection from error, and (iii) the *post factum* guarantee of inerrancy.[122] Eventually these became the official party line of the Jesuits. But it seems to me that these inferences arise from misunderstandings of the nature of inspiration which are no part of a middle knowledge perspective. Lessius seems to be guilty of two confusions: (1) He conflates the notions of inspiration and revelation, and (2) he thinks of inspiration as a property of the authors, rather than of the text, of Scripture. Both of these are common mistakes which were gestating since the time of the Church Fathers and would finally find their ugly issue in Spinoza's *Tractatus*. With respect to (1) the mistake arises by treating all Scripture on the model of prophecy. As a direct revelation from God, prophecy communicates information which transcends natural knowledge; things naturally known by the human authors of Scripture have not, therefore, been directly revealed to them by God.[123] Thus, if inspiration is co-extensive with revelation, then when the authors of Scripture write of matters which they already know, it follows that they are not inspired. But since 'all Scripture is inspired by God' (2 Tim. 3.16) this conflation is clearly a mistake, for not all Scripture is of the genre of prophecy. Even Scripture which does not involve the direct revelation of supernatural knowledge by God is inspired. Thus, Lessius's point that the Evangelists did not need a new revelation to record Jesus's life is no proof that the gospels are not inspired. With respect to (2), the Scripture states that it is the text, not the authors, of Scripture which is inspired (2 Tim. 3.16). True, the prophets were moved by the Holy Spirit to speak (1 Pet. 1.21), but it is a mistake to equate inspiration with this movement, so as to imply that because Scripture is verbally inspired therefore the authors were moved immediately by the Holy Spirit to

---

[121] *Dictionnaire de théologie catholique*, s.v. 'Inspiration de l'Écriture,' vol. 7, pt. 2, col. 2144.

[122] Burtchaell, *Catholic Theories of Inspiration*, chapter 2.

[123] Wolterstorff likewise distinguishes between Scripture and revelation; this is a concept which needs more careful analysis than is usually given by defenders of biblical authority.

write that or this particular word.[124] It is the Scripture which is God-breathed, not the authors. Thus, it is wholly erroneous to think that use of memory, research, effort, borrowing, and so forth, on the part of the author is incompatible with the final result of his labors, the text, being inspired. Thus, to speak, as Lessius does, of the authors' having no need of new and positive inspiration for writing what they did is to misconstrue inspiration as a sort of illumination of the author's mind—which, he rightly observes, seems unnecessary for much of Scripture—rather than as a quality of the final text, the quality of being God's Word. When Lessius denies that the Holy Spirit inspired Paul to write, 'Luke alone is with me; Trophimus I left ill at Miletus' (2 Tim. 4.20), he is tilting at windmills.

Once we understand that inspiration is a property of the text, not the authors, then we shall not be tempted to embrace the view, popular among Lessius's successors until its condemnation at Vatican I, that inspiration consists merely in a sort of watchdog role for the Holy Spirit of preventing the biblical authors from falling into error.[125] Such a role is compatible with human freedom[126] and no doubt is part of the Spirit's superintendence of the composition of Scripture along with the providential preparation of the authors; but it is not what inspiration is. Nor shall we be tempted to embrace another vestige of Lessius, what is known in German theology as *Realinspiration*, the theory that God inspired the propositional content of Scripture and the human authors supplied its linguistic expression.[127] Under the influence of the Jesuit tradition, this seems to have been the position adopted by Simon. This theory again misconstrues inspiration as a work of God in the authors' minds, providing them with propositional content which they clothe with words. A little reflection reveals that such a theory, besides misconstruing the nature of inspiration, actually constricts the authors' freedom, since they are not free to express whatever propositions they wish but only those God gives them. Moreover, the propositional content of Scripture may be so specific as to require certain words and expressions in a given language, so that we again approach dictation. The theory does nothing to explain the *levicula*. And it remains mysterious how God could communicate His propositional truth to someone wholly without linguistic formulation. Thus, once we distinguish inspiration from revelation and understand inspiration to be a property belonging to the text, we see that a middle knowledge perspective in no wise denies that the very words of Scripture are

---

[124] See the particularly severe criticism by Phillips, 'Turretin's Idea of Theology,' 2: 761, who calls it a 'blatant category mistake' to equate the description of inspiration's extent (*viz.*, verbal inspiration) with a description of its procedure.

[125] See discussion in Burtchaell, *Catholic Theories of Inspiration*, 45–52.

[126] See references in note 83. See also Thomas P. Flint, 'Middle Knowledge and Infallibility.' Although Flint's analysis concerns Papal infallibility, he rightly notes that it would apply to biblical infallibility as well.

[127] See Burtchaell, *Catholic Theories of Inspiration*, chap. 3.

inspired nor does it limit the Spirit's role to the merely negative role of protection from error.

Lessius's third proposition and the inference drawn from it raise the issue of what distinguishes Scripture as God's Word, if it is not dictated by the Holy Spirit. The proposition presents a clear *non sequitur* in implying that a book would become Scripture merely in virtue of the Spirit's certifying it to be inerrant. Inerrancy is a necessary, but not a sufficient, condition of being God's Word. Lessius qualified his position by saying that a statement later certified to be true by the Holy Spirit would be as authoritative as if the Spirit had uttered it through a prophet. I see no reason to object; but again there is no reason to think that such a true statement should then be incorporated into the canon of Scripture. The real question raised by Lessius's third proposition is whether some book of Scripture might not have been written without any special assistance by the Holy Spirit and yet still be inspired in virtue of the Spirit's ratification of it as His Word. Lessius gives the very intriguing illustration of a King who by approving and signing a document his secretary has drawn up makes it his own royal decree. Now from a middle knowledge perspective, there is no question of God's later ratifying a document which He did not foreknow or did not providentially bring about. Rather the question is whether God could be confronted with counterfactuals of creaturely freedom which are such as to permit Him to produce a book of Scripture by means of His providence alone without His acting as a primary cause influencing the act of writing itself. I see no reason to think that this is impossible. But then what, we may ask, would distinguish such a book as Scripture as opposed to any other product of human effort equally under the general providence of God? Presumably the answer would lie in God's intent to bring about a book designed to make us wise unto salvation and ultimately by His ratification of that book as His Word to us.

Now if such a middle knowledge perspective on biblical inspiration found expression, however inchoately, in the sixteenth and seventeenth centuries, why was it abandoned? Burtchaell mentions three reasons: (1) If the minimal requirement for biblical writing were divine preservation from error, then the Scriptures are not distinguished from official Church proclamations which also enjoy this protection. Part of the answer to this objection, from a Protestant viewpoint, is that Scripture alone has this special protection and hence alone is authoritative (*sola Scriptura*). More fundamentally, what distinguishes a writing as Scripture is God's intent that that writing be His gracious Word to mankind. (2) Infallibility is insufficient to make a human utterance into the Word of God. I readily agree. Even if some book of Scripture were written without any special promptings or assistance of the Holy Spirit, it is Scripture, not in virtue of its inerrancy, but because God in His providence prepared such a book to be His Word to us. (3) The theory is too conservative and so was eclipsed. But it is not a middle knowledge theory of inspiration which is too conservative; rather what is deemed too conservative is the theory of verbal, plenary, confluent inspiration, since it implies the inerrancy of Scripture. That issue is not under discussion here; rather the question we have been exploring is whether the doctrine of the verbal, plenary, confluent inspiration of Scripture is coherent. Given a middle knowledge perspective, the coherence of the classical doctrine becomes perspicuous.

CONCLUSION

In conclusion, it seems to me that the traditional doctrine of the plenary, verbal, confluent inspiration of Scripture is a coherent doctrine, given divine middle knowledge. Because God knew the relevant counterfactuals of creaturely freedom, He was able to decree a world containing just those circumstances and persons such that the authors of Scripture would freely compose their respective writings, which God intended to be His gracious Word to us. In the providence of God, the Bible is thus both the Word of God and the word of man.

9

Accepting the Authority of the Bible:
Is It Rationally Justified?*

James A. Keller

A central role for the Bible as a standard for Christian belief and practice is one of the most widespread features of the Christian tradition. Yet that generalization, true though it is, does not indicate anything of the wide variation in the ways the Bible has been used as a standard. These different ways are related to different answers to questions such as the following:

1. Is the Bible alone the standard, or is it one standard along with others—e.g., church tradition, reason, experience, etc.?
2. Is the Bible a standard only in matters of faith and practice, or is it a standard for beliefs on all matters to which it refers?
3. In virtue of what is the Bible a standard—e.g., in virtue of its doctrines, its concepts, its stories, its images, its symbols?[1]
4. What are the correct hermeneutical principles to use in interpreting the Bible?

The answers to these questions should not be assumed to be independent; in general they will be interrelated in various complex ways. In addition to these normative questions, there are also various historical questions about the role which the Bible has in fact played in the life and thought of individuals and groups. If one grants to church tradition a normative role for Christian thought, the answer to these historical questions may also be thought to have some relevance for the answer to the normative questions. Thus we find that the seeming agreement on the general principle of the authority of the Bible is, upon closer examination, liable to fracture into a mosaic of conflicting views, which are probably entangled in various complex ways with other aspects of one's theological and philosophical views.

---

* © *Faith and Philosophy*, vol. 6 (1989). Reprinted by permission of the publisher.
[1] Something of the variety of answers to this question and their implications for theology has been insightfully discussed by David H. Kelsey, *The Uses of Scripture in Recent Theology* (Philadelphia: The Westminster Press, 1975).

Thus, any attempt to discuss, in less than a full book, the rationality of using the Bible as a standard can be nothing more than an investigation of some normative issue which presupposes answers to various other important, and controversial, issues. In this paper I shall be focusing on this topic: is the Christian of today rationally justified in using the views expressed in the Bible as a (or the) standard for what she should accept for her own beliefs and practices. I should say explicitly that I am referring to her beliefs about the matters on which a biblical writer expressed a view, not to her beliefs about what the views of a biblical writer were. That is, I am interested, e.g., in whether the Christian is rationally justified in adopting as her own the beliefs about God which Paul expressed in his letters because he expressed them, not in whether she is rationally justified in taking Paul's letters as a standard for determining what certain of Paul's beliefs about God were.

One might wonder what is meant by the term 'Christian.' In light of the person-relativity of the rationality of at least many of our beliefs, some answer to my question might follow from the very definition of the term. It would be possible to define the term to give such a result, but I wish to try to avoid doing so. I want to use a very minimal definition of 'Christian'—something like 'one who has faith in the God who acted in Jesus Christ as identified in the Bible.' Because this God is identified in the Bible, I shall also take it that the Bible in some way (perhaps in any one of a variety of ways) plays some special role in awakening, sustaining, and/or interpreting faith in this God. Perhaps we shall find on reflection that even on these deliberately minimal assumptions, being a Christian makes it rational to give more authority to the Bible than a non-Christian typically gives it or than the Christian herself gives similar writings from other religious traditions.

THE BIBLE AS AN ABSOLUTE AUTHORITY

Some thinkers attempt to derive an answer to our question from some thesis about the nature of the Bible. For example, some hold that the biblical writers were in some special (perhaps unique) sense inspired by God. Others hold that the Bible is (or contains) the word of God or that it is God's special revelation. They combine such a thesis with the claim that God knows all truths and is sovereign, and they conclude that God would not permit the Bible to contain any errors. But as a way to answer our question, such an approach faces at least three serious problems. First, the thesis about the nature of the Bible (as well as the other premises) would itself have to be rationally justified. What this would require would, of course, depend on exactly what the thesis claims. In this paper I shall not evaluate any of the particular theses about the nature of the Bible, for I think that the other problems I shall mention are sufficient to show that this way will not enable us to answer our question. But for the sake of completeness, here I merely note that this is a problem which must be faced if one were going to use this approach to answer our question.

But even if the thesis is rationally justified, there is a second problem: premises about God's knowledge and power are not sufficient to justify the conclusion; one needs also some premise about what God wanted to accomplish in inspiring the authors. Unfortunately, we have no detailed knowledge about this and about what consequences this purpose would have for the views expressed by biblical writers. To assume that this purpose would require that these views contain no errors (or no errors of a certain kind, say on matters of doctrine and practice) or to assume that the honor of God would be impugned if any views expressed in the Bible were erroneous—all such assumptions are instances of *a priori* theorizing about the Bible which we would do well to avoid. On similar grounds, one might argue that God would not permit the Bible to contain grammatical errors or inelegant writing (for these are flaws of a sort), but it clearly contains both. Or one might argue that if inerrancy were important, God would ensure that the text remained inerrant, but it plainly has not, for errors in transmission have certainly occurred.[2] Or one might argue that God would make every important matter so clear that there would be no significant disagreement on it, but obviously God has not done so—or the church would not be divided on the role of Peter and his successors or on the mode and proper recipients of baptism, etc. So this sort of *a priori* theorizing is clearly not reliable in general. And in light of examples to be given in this paper of inconsistent, erroneous, and historically relative views expressed by many biblical writers, it also seems unjustified to draw the proposed conclusions about the implications of various divine perfections for the inerrancy of the views expressed in the Bible.

A third problem with this proposal as a way of answering our question is that even if the conclusion of the argument were true and rationally justified, it would not enable today's Christian to determine what she should believe. I say this because even proponents of the argument insist that the Bible must be correctly understood and applied if we are to derive from it what our views today should be. Therefore, to answer our question, hermeneutical issues must be faced. These prevent the view under discussion from delivering the clear-cut norm for our views which it seems to promise. I shall mention five of these issues. (1) Not every

---

[2] These are not just empty speculations. Deductions like these have been drawn by important Christian thinkers. One commentator wrote:

Quenstedt declared that Luke did not write from memory or from what others related to him, but by dictation of the Holy Spirit, who suggested to his mind the thoughts and words which he should use. In 1659 the theological faculty of Wittenberg condemned Beza's view that New Testament Greek contained barbarisms and solecisms. Gerhard argued that the Hebrew vowel points were inspired. John Owen thought that the Holy Spirit had kept the Greek and Hebrew texts pure throughout all textual transmission. (Daniel P. Fuller, 'Evangelicalism and Biblical Inerrancy' [unpublished], p. 17, cited in Stephen T. Davis, *The Debate about the Bible: Inerrancy versus Infallibility*, [Philadelphia: The Westminster Press, 1977], p. 63.)

view expressed in the Bible should be taken as one we should adopt today, but only a restricted group of these. Obviously, one should not necessarily regard as true some view which is just reported; the view must at least be in some way endorsed by the writer. Making this distinction requires a hermeneutical principle enabling one to distinguish which is which. Sometimes this is easy. If an idea is clearly attributed to some person, then it is that person's view. But is every view not expressly attributed to some person a view the author endorses? Conversely, on the other side, if a view is attributed to a godly person, should it therefore be accepted as a norm for the beliefs and practices of Christians today? (For example, should the Christian of today accept as true the conclusions about the obligations of Christians attributed to speakers at the Jerusalem Council [Acts 15] because these men expressed these conclusions?)

The other hermeneutical issues all apply to views not expressly attributed to some person. (2) Should one distinguish between views which are endorsed by the author and views which are merely employed or alluded to, but not endorsed, by the author? I think that one must and that everyone does. The hermeneutical categories of allegorical, parabolic, hyperbolic, and poetical language all refer to ways of expressing views which, in their literal sense, are not endorsed. It sometimes is difficult to determine whether or not such language is being used and, if it is, what the literal meaning is. Another hermeneutical category which employs the distinction between a view which is endorsed and one which is employed for another purpose is the category of accommodation (or speaking phenomenologically). For example, according to Joshua 10:12–13, Joshua caused a long day by ordering the sun and moon to stand still. Both the words attributed to Joshua ('Sun, stand thou still....') and the author's description ('The sun stayed....') employ locutions about the sun's standing still. These texts were among the reasons why some churchmen supported geocentrism against Galileo. Later when geocentrism had been universally abandoned, the texts were reinterpreted. It was claimed that the wording of the text employed the author's accommodation to the beliefs of the people of his day or that the author was speaking phenomenologically (speaking in terms of the way things looked, but not necessarily in terms of the way things really were). But the admission of this hermeneutical category introduces a great complexity into the attempt to use views apparently endorsed by biblical writers as a norm for the views which Christians today should hold. For the occasions when accommodation is used are not explicitly labeled in the Bible. Rather, it seems that the basis on which interpreters identify a view as an accommodation is that they, on other grounds, think it false but do not want to attribute error to the writer. In any event, they are not in fact using a view apparently endorsed by the writer as the norm for their own view on the subject; instead, they are using a view derived from non-biblical sources.[3]

---

[3] The example in the text illustrates the way in which the thesis of biblical inerrancy disposes (critics would say, forces) a proponent to seek some interpretation of the text which does not seem in

(3) Another hermeneutical issue concerns the distinction between commands which are still binding on Christians today and those which are not. Christians generally agree that this distinction must be made in relation to portions of the Old Testament law. Certain parts of that law have been explicitly set aside by Christian writers (cf. the account of the Jerusalem council, with the conclusion in Acts 15:29—assuming, of course, that one is correct in taking that conclusion as normative). Moreover, much of that law is no longer adhered to on the grounds that the Christian is not under the law. But some parts—notably the ten commandments—are still widely regarded as binding. On whatever basis this distinction is made, those who make it are plainly not adopting everything that any biblical writer said on matters of doctrine and practice as binding for them today. But the discrepancies are not limited to the applicability of Old Testament law. For example, Paul commands that men have short hair and have their head uncovered when they pray, while women are to have long hair and to wear a veil when they pray.[4] Most Christians today do not feel obligated to obey these commands, with the possible exception of men praying with their heads uncovered. Should they? If not, why not? Paul's injunctions have not been explicitly contradicted by any other biblical writer. I imagine that most Christians today would see such practices as culturally conditioned expressions of appropriate ways to show reverence and would judge that our obligation today is to show reverence in ways understood in our culture. But once we admit the difference between some basic principle and its culturally conditioned expression, can we avoid asking about any matter of practice enjoined by a biblical writer whether it is still binding on us or whether it too is some culturally conditioned expression of a more basic principle? This point is no small matter. On certain issues today the church is deeply torn by the division between those who conclude that the

error. To achieve this goal, proponents sometimes adopt interpretations which seem unlikely, to say the least, and which are guided by information which the interpreter has from non-biblical sources; moreover, the procedure causes the apparently more natural sense in which the text has been taken to be judged a misinterpretation. In such cases it is only the non-biblical information which makes possible a 'correct' interpretation of the text; thus the interpreter is not genuinely using the text itself to guide his beliefs. One example of this is the interpretation of Matt 13:31–2, where Jesus is represented as saying that the mustard seed is the smallest of all seeds. Biologists, however, inform us that the mustard seed is not the smallest seed. So inerrantists (who typically do not want to attribute error to Jesus) must look for some other way to interpret Jesus' words. They suggest that perhaps Jesus meant that the mustard seed is 'one of the smallest seeds' or 'the smallest seed of which you know.' But any such strategy has the result that today's Christian should not accept, on the basis of the 'correct' interpretation of the text, that the mustard seed is truly the smallest seed, yet it is only non-biblical sources which enable one to know this. Therefore, it seems that even the inerrantist is in fact not using a view expressed by a biblical writer to guide his own belief on this matter. (I owe this example to Davis, *op. cit.*, pp. 100–2, though the conclusions drawn about it are my own, not his.)

[4] I Cor 11:2–15. Paul's reasons are worth noting: (1) certain theological considerations—man is the image and glory of God, while woman is the glory of man; and woman was made from man, not *vice versa*; and (2) appeals to what 'nature itself' teaches. *Prima facie*, at least, none of these reasons seem limited in applicability to Paul's day; they seem to have as much validity today as they did then, despite the fact that few Christians today would consider Paul's injunctions binding today.

practice is still binding and those who do not. To cite only one issue, are the New Testament practice of ordaining only males and statements like those in I Tim 2:11–12 still binding today?

(4) A fourth hermeneutical issue is that analogous questions can be raised about matters of doctrine. New Testament writers speak of God as the father but not as the mother. Is this a culturally conditioned form of expression, reflecting the patriarchal thinking of the time, or is it a permanently valid way of speaking of God, binding on us today? The Christian hope after death was expressed by some New Testament writers as a hope for resurrection. Historically speaking, the idea of the resurrection of the dead came into Palestine and Jewish thought from non-biblical sources. (Note that the earlier books of the Old Testament contain no hint of it, and the Jewish biblical conservatives of Paul's day—the Sadducees—denied it for that very reason.) Is it therefore only a culturally conditioned expression of the Christian hope, so that we should not feel bound to express that hope in the same way today, or is this way of speaking of and understanding that hope one we must still accept today?

(5) A fifth hermeneutical issue is the problem of determining what view one should hold when different biblical writers express apparently inconsistent views. For example, there is an apparent inconsistency over whether or not unchastity is a legitimate grounds for divorce (Mk 10:11–12 and Lk 16:18 *vs.* Matt 5:32 and 19:9), and on a more minor note whether or not the disciple is to take a staff with him on his travels (Matt 10:9 and Lk 9:3 *vs.* Mk 6:8). In these cases the apparent inconsistency is explicit. In other cases it is implicit, resting on implications drawn from views expressed in one or more passages. For example, the apparently unjust commands attributed to God in some Old Testament passages seem inconsistent with the justice attributed to God elsewhere in the Bible, as does the vengeful attitude exemplified in some Psalms with the commands to love and forgive given elsewhere in the Bible.[5] Paul's affirmation of the equality of all Christians in Gal 3:28 seems inconsistent with certain writers' insistence on various sexual inequalities.[6] Of course, the implications drawn may be incorrect, but if we are to use the Bible as the norm for our views today we cannot avoid drawing implications, and the approach under discussion does not eliminate this task.

[5] The apparently unjust commands I have in mind are the commands given to Israel to destroy all the inhabitants of Canaan (Joshua 10:38–40 and 11:19–20). The inhabitants included children, and it is hard to see how ordering their deaths could be just. One place in the Psalms where a vengeful attitude is expressed is 137:9, where the Psalmist pronounces a blessing on him 'who takes your little ones and dashes them against the rocks.' I know of no Christian today who takes these as proper norms for his behavior.
[6] Among these inequalities are the wife's being subject to her husband (Eph 5:22) and a woman's not being permitted to teach or have authority over a man (I Tim 2:12). It is well known that the Christian of today must decide what stance to take on a variety of issues regarding the relation between men and women, such as whether to support ordination for women or to oppose it. Views expressed in various passages can seemingly be—and in fact are—cited in support of both stances.

The arguments and questions in the three previous paragraphs exemplify a pattern which I use several times in this paper. I begin with a fairly trivial example of something on which it would be widely agreed that a Christian today is not required to adopt some view endorsed by some biblical writer. My point in doing this is to show with a variety of examples that (virtually) no one today accepts every view endorsed by some biblical writer as something which is binding on him today. Then whatever the reason for not adopting some biblical writer's view today, I push that reason, asking why we should restrict it to fairly trivial matters. In no case do I see any principled (non-arbitrary) answer to that question. But even if there were some principled answer to this question, the trivial examples alone would establish that Christians should not adopt every view endorsed by some biblical writer.

It is not an adequate defense of the approach under discussion to say something like the following: 'Of course, the Christian of today should not adopt every view expressed by a biblical writer. The Christian should adopt only those views which the biblical writer meant to teach.' This defense is not adequate both because it assumes that all such views are those God preserved from error and because all the hermeneutical issues discussed above recur in trying to distinguish, among the views which a biblical writer expressed, those which he meant to teach. Nor is it much help to propose that we should accept as the author's meaning what we arrive at by interpreting the text in its natural sense, interpreting history as history, poetry as poetry, etc. While this proposal is unobjectionable as a principle, we still have to identify each type of writing. Debates about whether the book of Jonah is a parable and whether the Song of Songs is an allegory suggest that this may not always be easy. Moreover, once we have done this and interpreted what the author meant, we still face at least the last four hermeneutical issues mentioned above.

Some defenders of the approach under discussion may object that I am confusing matters of interpretation of the text with matters of application. I don't think I am *confusing* the two, but I would say that both are involved in answering our question. For if we are concerned with what our views today should be (in other words, with what we today should believe and do), we must not think that determining what views the biblical writers expressed (or endorsed) will by itself answer our question. If Christians of today are to take the Bible as their authority, then they must consider questions of application as well as questions of interpretation. Perhaps no one would explicitly deny this, but I think that it is often overlooked or not sufficiently appreciated in discussions about the role which the Bible should play in determining the views of Christians today.

If we look at the way Christians of today actually employ the Bible as a (or the) norm for their views, we find that they may draw on any area of their knowledge and beliefs in determining both matters of interpretation and matters of application. One might think that Christians should use only their knowledge of such areas as biblical languages and of the culture of biblical times in interpreting the text, but in fact they use far more. For example, determinations of whether a particular text is meant literally or not—a matter of interpretation, not application—are often based at least in part on the interpreter's theology. When Jesus said that it is easier for a camel to go through the eye of a needle than for a rich man to enter the kingdom of heaven, did Jesus mean this literally? When Jesus said that the bread and wine at the last supper were his body and blood, did he mean this literally? As I have suggested, the interpreter also draws on her general knowledge in deciding that an author used accommodation in a particular text. I do not object to the Christian's employing whatever of her knowledge and beliefs seem relevant in deciding matters of interpretation and application; indeed, I shall argue that this is appropriate. But so far I have merely tried to suggest that everyone does it and that it is unavoidable. My argument has been directed against those who do not exhibit sufficient awareness of it and its implications for questions about how the Bible should be used as a norm for the beliefs of Christians today.

THE BIBLE AS A DEFEASIBLE AUTHORITY

The problem raised by the sort of hermeneutical issues discussed in the previous section will, I believe, plague any attempt to state a simple rule for the way Christians should use the Bible as a norm for their views today. I can illustrate this problem by looking at another approach, which might be described as a proposal that the Bible be taken as a defeasible authority on all matters. This proposal was made by Stephen T. Davis in a recent book.[7] He states his view as follows: 'The Bible is or ought to be authoritative for every Christian in all that it says on any subject unless and until he encounters a passage which after careful study and for good reasons he cannot accept' (p. 116). This proposal raises a hermeneutical issue not raised by the earlier approach: in speaking of what 'the Bible says,' is Davis referring to what a particular author says in some particular passage or to some kind of overall view derived from the Bible? If the latter, he should tell us how to derive an overall view; and the reference to a 'passage' as well as some of Davis' detailed discussion suggests the former. So I take him to be referring to particular passages. Such a locution also glosses over the differences among expressing, employing, and endorsing a view. Which of these must an author be doing if the view is to be one which 'the Bible says'? More generally, Davis needs to clarify the relation between what particular authors say and what 'the Bible says.'

An even more serious problem with Davis' proposal is that what we learn about an author or his work may give us good grounds not to accept anything he

---

[7] *Op. cit.* Page references in this section of the text are to Davis' book.

says on a particular topic, thus obviating the passage-by-passage approach which he seems to suggest. For example, suppose that a Christian finds (after careful study and for good reasons) that an author did not intend to give an account which is historically accurate in our sense. (Some scholars think that the entire book of Jonah is an extended parable; some think this of the book of Job.) If the Christian concludes this, is it then proper for him not to give defeasible acceptance to any seeming historical detail in the entire book? Or to take a more important and controversial example, suppose that a Christian concludes (as some New Testament scholars claim) that the Evangelists were not concerned to distinguish their accounts of what Jesus did prior to his crucifixion from their insights into what he said and did which were gained in light of his crucifixion and resurrection. Would this be good reason not to give defeasible acceptance to anything the Evangelists say about historical matters involving the life of Jesus?

If (as Davis admits) the biblical writers did write with 'their cultural and historical frames of reference intact' (p. 64), is there any justification in according them even defeasible authority on any scientific matter? Given the vast changes in scientific beliefs since the days of the biblical writers and given our scientific method (which did not even exist then), does today's Christian have 'good reason' not to accept as authoritative (even defeasibly) anything which biblical writers said on any scientific matter? This is not to say that they could not describe ordinary observable situations as well as we can today. And it is not to say that what they said on some scientific matter must be in error. But it is to ask whether the Christian should feel obligated to accept even only defeasibly what a biblical writer says on some scientific matter just because the author is one of the biblical writers. Since the biblical writers in general did not employ careful historical research techniques, could not—indeed, should not—one raise similar questions about giving defeasible acceptance to everything they said about various historical events?[8]

---

[8] It might be wondered whether here I am doing just what I criticize others for doing: lumping all biblical writers together. Why might one not conclude that some biblical writers should be taken as authoritative on historical matters—or on scientific matters—even though perhaps others should not be? Am I not painting all of them with the same brush? I think not. For in everyday life we do not regard any author as an authority until he has proved himself; that is, we do not with confidence even defeasibly accept what he says as true without some reason to think that that author is an authority on that topic. In the case of the biblical writers we are considering as a reason the fact that they are writers whose work was included in the Bible. But if being such a writer does not guarantee an approach to the recounting of events which we would regard as consistent with good historiography (or with good science), then someone's being a biblical writer is not an adequate basis for us to accept him as an authority on matters of history (or science). So then we must determine whether to accept a particular author as an authority on that kind of matter by considering details peculiar to that author, not a feature which he shares with all the biblical authors. But if we must use other knowledge about particular authors to determine whether to accept what they say as authoritative, then there is no reason, prior to a detailed investigation of them, to give their views even defeasible acceptance. (Again, I point out that I am not denying that we might, by checking certain statements, discover that a particular author has been remarkably accurate on certain kinds of matters and *therefore* give a defeasible acceptance to everything he says on them. But then the author is accepted as authoritative because he has passed certain tests, not because he is a biblical writer.)

This question becomes all the more pressing if it is true (as many biblical scholars claim) that the biblical writers' purpose in their narratives often was something other than to give what we would think of as a historically reliable account. For example, if one were to conclude that the Evangelists' purpose in some places was to express Jesus' significance rather than to give what we would consider a historically reliable account, one must seriously consider the possibility that this was everywhere their purpose, for one should presume consistency of purpose; if that were so, it would preclude even a defeasible acceptance of their representation of the details of the life of Jesus. Of course, it would not necessarily imply that all (or even most) of the details were not historically accurate, but it would be grounds to give critical scrutiny to everything they say if one wishes to use it to recover historical details of the life of Jesus. Note how different this consequence is from the consequence of finding an error in some historical detail. Finding one error is not by itself grounds to refuse to give defeasible acceptance to the rest of what an author wrote. (How many even good textbooks do contain a few errors?) But an error is something the writer himself would repudiate if it were brought to his attention, for an error is a failure to achieve a standard the writer accepts for himself. If, however, one discovers that in some places the writer has some purpose or standards other than those one has in one's work, this must affect how one uses everything the author says. (The point made in this paragraph is admittedly conditional, based upon possible findings. But my point is to indicate how particular findings could give us grounds not to grant defeasible acceptance to an entire class of things a writer says. Claims about the purpose of various biblical writers are admittedly often controversial, but surely everyone would grant the claim, made in the previous paragraph, that in general they did not employ techniques of critical historical research.)

We could press this point beyond the historical and scientific issues to issues of doctrine and practice. There might be reasons to refuse to give blanket defeasible acceptance to everything any biblical writer says on matters of doctrine or practice. One such reason is that the grounds for not giving even defeasible acceptance to what the biblical writers say (or appear to say) about historical matters may in some cases also apply to matters of doctrine and practice. (For example, since even details about the actions and words of Jesus are often thought to have great significance for matters of doctrine and practice, any grounds not to give even defeasible acceptance to the Evangelists' representations of Jesus' career might also be grounds not to give it to the consequences for doctrine and practice which are drawn from these representations.) A second is that perhaps the writers were so influenced by outdated beliefs or by other aspects of their culture as to express their convictions even on matters of doctrine and practice in ways which may no longer be appropriate. (We have seen that this is likely on scientific and historical matters. Not only are there no grounds for ruling it out *a priori* on matters of doctrine and practice, but there are also positive reasons to think that it has occurred.[9]) A third reason is that it is possible that other biblical writers might have different views on this topic, thus suggesting that there might be a range of views—and not just one—compatible with Christian faith.[10] To whatever extent these reasons apply, the Christian should not grant even defeasible acceptance to every view on matters of doctrine and practice expressed by any biblical writer. Of course, it is possible that with careful checking we might find that none of these possible reasons apply. But it would seem that we have to consider them as possibilities and that even that consideration should give pause to those who would urge a blanket, even if only defeasible, acceptance of every view of every biblical writer on these matters.

I am uncertain how Davis would respond to the questions I have raised. Because he describes himself as an evangelical, I am sure that he does not believe that the possible reasons which I have suggested for not granting even defeasible acceptance to broad categories of things said by many biblical writers would be found to apply if they were carefully investigated. But would he admit that these questions should be investigated? I find nothing in his book to indicate that the questions are illegitimate questions, and it is hard to see on what basis they could be ruled out *a priori*. But if they are legitimate questions, one might wonder in what sense his proposal gives any special authority to the Bible. It does to this extent: it says that the Christian should accept what the Bible says unless she has reason not to; unless she has specific reason to the contrary, the fact that the Bible says something is reason enough for the Christian to accept it, regardless of the topic. But our typical attitude toward a work (other than one narrating personal observations and experiences) is that we need a positive reason to accept what it says—e.g., that the author is a recognized expert or that the work is

---

[9] The example of Paul's injunctions regarding hair length and head covering for women would seem a case in point. So too might his advice against marriage given in I Cor 7:1–31, which seems based at least in part on a belief in the imminent end of the world (cf. especially 31b). Perhaps other moral advice and injunctions were also, though less clearly, influenced by such a conviction. Still another possible example would be the employment of pseudonymous authorship by some biblical writers. Certainly their secular contemporaries used pseudonymity, and most contemporary New Testament scholars hold that the writers of certain New Testament books did so as well—e.g., the writer(s) of the Pastorals and perhaps certain other letters bearing the name of Paul. (I include this as a matter of doctrine because some conservatives hold that the literal accuracy of the attributions of authorship is such a matter.) A still more controversial example is the claim of some scholars that the stories of the Virgin Birth were intended only as a way to highlight Jesus' significance, rather than as the literal truth about the causal antecedents of Jesus' birth. (This seems to have been the intention behind the attribution of divine intervention in the conception of certain other notable figures in the classical period. This practice even spread to Judaism, for Philo spoke of divine intervention in the conception of certain Old Testament figures, such as Samson and Samuel.)

[10] In an earlier note I pointed out that according to Mark and Luke, Jesus denied any grounds for divorce, but according to Matthew, he accepted unchastity as a grounds. Paul also accepted the desire of the unbelieving spouse for separation as a grounds for divorce (I Cor 7:15). (Of course, Old Testament law accepted divorce.) No matter how one reconciles these disagreements, one has the result that one is not accepting as authoritative for oneself today every view approved of by every biblical writer.

approved by a recognized expert or that the author employed appropriate research techniques.[11] How one would justify according the Bible this special status on all matters is, of course, a crucial issue for our question (though not for Davis in the work referred to). And as I pointed out earlier, there are hermeneutical issues which someone who followed Davis' proposal must address. For all these reasons, I do not think Davis' approach looks like a promising way to answer our question.

A PROPOSAL REGARDING BIBLICAL AUTHORITY

Despite their differences, the two types of approaches we have considered share two important features. One is that they give every passage equal initial authority for one's beliefs today (to be accepted as inerrant or until defeated by good reasons). In so doing, these proposals function as though the locus of authority were the biblical passage and as though the Bible itself were basically a collection of passages. But any rationally justified use of the Bible as an authority for our beliefs today will have to take account of the diversity of purposes, literary techniques, etc. among the authors (a diversity which no one denies) and will have to recognize that, if the whole Bible is to function as an authority, not every view in every passage should be regarded as equally authoritative for us today. Indeed, my earlier discussion gives reason to think that every Christian in fact recognizes these factors in the way she uses the Bible, regardless of what her theory of biblical authority may be. Many of the most significant theological differences among Christians today turn not on whether these factors ever apply, but on the *extent* to which they apply and on the results for our beliefs of differing conclusions in applying them.

The second feature shared by these types of approaches is that they give the impression that one can determine what the Bible says independently of consideration of what one should believe on the basis of what the Bible says. While the two are not identical, I have given reasons for thinking that they cannot even in principle always be separated—e.g., in determining whether something in the Bible was meant literally, in determining when (if ever) the writer was using accommodation, and in determining whether what the author says is meant as a formulation binding on all Christians or as an appropriate expression in his day of a more basic idea which is binding on all Christians. Such determinations are made in part on the basis of one's theology and other beliefs, not simply on the

---

[11] In our society, before they will accept what a writer says on such matters as events in the Middle Ages or the structure of the atom, careful thinkers check the credentials of the writer (e.g., his university degree or the inclusion of his work in the bibliography of an encyclopedia.) Indeed, perhaps we tend to accept without any 'positive reason' what a person says about her direct experience because we believe that most people are competent to report their experience; this belief may provide (or replace) the 'positive reason' in such cases. I would claim that such procedures are rationally justified, though I cannot here argue for that claim.

basis of exegesis construed in a more narrow sense (as, roughly, a literary-philological enterprise).

These two features underlie many of the problems connected with the hermeneutical issues which I raised about these approaches. And as noted earlier, both types of approaches face the problem of justifying their basic thesis regarding the nature of biblical authority. In the rest of this paper I intend to sketch a theory, which does take account of these factors, of how the Bible should be used as an authority and of why such use is rationally justified.

To do so, I must first outline a view of the relation between faith on the one hand, and beliefs and practices, on the other. As Christians we have faith in God who acted decisively for humankind in Jesus Christ. Associated with that faith are certain beliefs and practices by means of which we understand and express that faith. But the nature of that association is different for different beliefs and practices. At least four different possible relations can be distinguished. Certain beliefs and practices may be essential or indispensable for faith in that God—e.g., presumably, the belief that God exists.[12] Other beliefs and practices may be one of a closed disjunctive set such that some member of this set is essential, but not any particular member—e.g., that God is omniscient either in the sense that God knows everything that has happened and everything that will happen or in the sense that God knows everything that has happened but not those future events which are not already determined by events which have occurred. Still other beliefs and practices may be one of a disjunctive set such that some member of this set is necessary but the set has no well defined limits—e.g., the elements which might be used in celebrating the Eucharist (or the Lord's Supper). Some churches today use wafers that are not really bread. And I remember hearing a discussion by some missionaries to certain Indians in Ecuador about the suitability of using bananas instead of bread in such celebrations because bananas were the food staple of these people and bread was unknown. Finally, some beliefs and practices may be purely contingent in the sense that they do not even belong to any (obvious) disjunctive set of which the adoption of some member is necessary, yet they may play roles in the faith of particular believers which vary from very important to peripheral. For instance, one may have chosen his career because he believes that God called him to that career at a particular time and place; and one may believe that God has done certain particular things, yet recognize that one's more general beliefs about God would change very little if this particular belief were to be given up. I do not claim that these four types exhaust the possibilities, but they do seem to be four different sorts of association. (It is also possible that, despite the best intentions of those who hold them, some beliefs and practices may be inadequate or erroneous expressions of faith.)

---

[12] For each of the four types of association, I have tried to give some clear and relatively uncontroversial example. Nothing, however, hinges on any particular example, as long as there is at least one example for each type—i.e., as long as no type is an empty set.

If beliefs and practices can be associated with faith in all these (and perhaps other) ways in our lives, there is no reason to think that the same would not be true of the biblical writers. Thus, when we find them expressing (or even endorsing) a belief or practice, we must recognize that it could be associated with their faith in any of these ways. And of the four ways, only the first would be absolutely binding on all Christians as something they must accept; for all the other ways, either there are alternatives or the belief or practice is completely optional. So if a belief or practice falls into any of these categories except the first, it should not necessarily be given even defeasible acceptance. Unfortunately, however, beliefs and practices do not come labelled as to the way in which they are associated with faith. Thus we must construct (or adopt[13]) a set of beliefs and practices associated with faith and an understanding of how they are associated with faith. In doing this, we will be guided by the biblical writers, for they identified for us the God in whom we have faith. But in this construction we will have to be aware of the issues and questions mentioned in our discussion of the approaches which we have already rejected. How shall we do this?

I suggest that for each biblical writer we try to become clear regarding what views he was expressing and how they related to his faith.[14] In doing this, we shall have to consider such issues as how central they seem to be to his faith, how they were related to other beliefs and practices in his community and in his culture, and how much they reflected perspectives distinctive to his faith as opposed to perspectives which he shared with persons of his time who did not belong to the community of faith.[15] We shall have to be open to the possibility that different writers endorsed different views on the same topic; if we found this happening, it would be strong (but not conclusive) evidence that any of these views is a legitimate expression of faith. It is not conclusive because we also have to consider

[13] For most people on most issues, it is probably more accurate to speak of adopting rather than constructing a set of beliefs and practices by which to express their faith. I do not wish to suggest or imply otherwise, nor to suggest that adopting is inferior to constructing. But I shall continue to speak of constructing in order to remind us of two things. First, even if one simply adopts the view of some biblical writer, that writer himself was expressing a view that someone constructed. Second, our lives are lived and our faith is expressed by these beliefs and practices; adopting a set rather than constructing it does not free us from the risk of adopting a set which results in our living somewhat less fully Christian lives than we might otherwise have done.

[14] This first suggestion might seem to run afoul of my earlier claim that it is not always possible to determine what the writer says independently of what we think it is appropriate to believe on the basis of what the writer says. I would deny neither the claim nor its applicability to my proposal. But I would point out that it is not nearly so damaging to my proposal as it was to the earlier ones. For I am not proposing that we conform our views to what we have antecedently determined to be the views of the biblical writers. So I can admit that we may not be able to determine, independently of our other beliefs, whether a writer meant something literally; then I can add that on the basis of other considerations we today should (or should not) believe literally what he said.

[15] For example, the contents of the book of Proverbs reflect a wisdom tradition common to many of Israel's neighbors; conversely, distinctive biblical themes—Abraham, Exodus, covenant, etc.—are absent. Presumably the material contained in this book was considered consistent with Israel's faith at the time, but it could hardly be claimed to be peculiarly expressive of that faith.

the possibility that biblical writers expressed (and even endorsed) views which are not consistent with faith in God as known in Jesus Christ.[16] In doing all this we shall have to draw on everything which we can learn about the biblical writers from various secular sources as well as religious sources. And finally in constructing the set of beliefs and practices by which we express our faith, we will be guided and constrained also by our other beliefs from religious and secular sources. The very existence of the Society of Christian Philosophers testifies to its members' conviction that philosophical analysis, drawing on a multitude of considerations, can assist us in formulating a more accurate understanding of the beliefs and practices involved in Christian faith. What one is doing in this process is nothing less than constructing a total theology in which the Bible plays a central role but in which one uses all the knowledge, justified beliefs, experiences, and techniques of reasoning of which one is aware.

Thus, we have to look as honestly and objectively as possible at each biblical writer, to see what he was deliberately expressing and, more subtly, what he was expressing unconsciously or without trying. (Sometimes we may be unsure which category a view falls into.) Then if there is some particular topic (e.g., Jesus' relation to God or the acceptability of divorce) in which we are interested, we should look in particular at the way every biblical writer who touched on the subject understood it. At this point we are taking it as data for our theological construction that certain biblical writers expressed certain views, but we are not giving these views either complete or defeasible acceptance. Our aim is to understand how their views related to their faith in order to be guided in constructing our views by which to express our faith. But we are not committed to adopting all of their views as our own. If on some matter we find a range of views expressed by biblical writers, we cannot say that faith in God (as Christians understand God—a qualification which I intend in what follows but which I shall not continually repeat) requires a particular position. But should we at least adopt the requirement that the Christian is bound to adopt a view within the range of those expressed by biblical writers?

There are at least two problems with imposing such a requirement. First, as we have seen, the biblical writers spoke as men of their times, and what they said was affected by their culture as well as by their faith. Surely we are not bound to accept views which are just a reflection of their culture, even if there is unanimity among the writers who expressed them. Thus, we should use what we can learn of the culture of the biblical writers to discern the faith which is refracted through that culture. It may well be impossible to be certain in all cases that we are correctly distinguishing between the faith and the culture, but we cannot ignore the distinction as though it did not exist. I will illustrate this in connection with the second point.

---

[16] Even an evangelical like Davis can admit that this has occurred. He claims that the writer who said that God commanded that all the Canaanites be killed when Israel entered the land was wrong. (Davis, *op. cit.*, pp. 96–8.)

Second, imposing this requirement would give us results which in some cases seem very dubious, to say the least. To recur to a previous example, Paul says that it is a disgrace for a woman to have short hair, and no biblical writer explicitly expresses any other view. Thus, there is only one position expressed in the Bible on this matter. Is today's Christian bound to accept this view too? I think most Christians would say no. They would probably give largely the same reasons: Paul's view reflects something in his culture; moreover, making something like this into a requirement on all Christians violates the liberty we have as children of God. These responses suggest (though they certainly do not certify) two important questions to be used in determining whether some view of a biblical writer is binding on us today: (1) does the view seem to be primarily a reflection of something in the writer's culture and (2) how is the view related to what seem to be central considerations in the understanding of the God, faith in whom has brought us salvation. Unfortunately, we have no access to these 'central considerations' free of the writer's cultural influences, nor have we any reason to think that our own understanding of them is free of the influences of our culture.

The upshot of all this is that we have to construct for ourselves (or to accept from someone else) an understanding of what Christian faith involves. In doing this we will be guided very importantly by what the biblical writers express and teach. (But the unit to which we should look for guidance is never simply the passage; rather it is the faith of the biblical writers as expressed in various views contained in certain passages.) Our overall task is to work out a view of what our faith in God involves or implies about the various matters which we face in life—matters of belief and practice. Some of these matters will seem more central than others to our faith—e.g., that God is the creator seems a more central belief than that God caused the sun to stand still for Joshua, and that we are to love one another seems more central than that women are to wear their hair short. The more central some item seems to be to the faith, the more cautious a Christian should be about adopting a view outside the range of views (perhaps a 'range' of only one) expressed by the biblical writers. But since there is no declaration in the Bible supported by all (or even a great many) of the writers regarding what is central and what is not, even our view of what is central is our own construction based on a particular way of putting together a theology. And that way of putting things together will inescapably and properly be shaped by other beliefs which we have—beliefs about the extent to which and the ways in which the biblical writers were affected by their culture and beliefs about the world, about moral principles, etc. which we have derived from our culture. The total set of beliefs and practices which we construct (or adopt) will then serve as a standard in light of which we may reinterpret, modify, de-emphasize, or reject views expressed in particular passages in the Bible.

That the resulting beliefs and practices are rationally justified is clear provided that one is rationally justified in giving to the Bible the central place in theological construction which I have suggested. With this proviso (to be discussed below), the result is rationally justified because one is drawing on all of one's knowledge, justified beliefs, experience, techniques, etc. to arrive at one's conclusions. If such a process does not result in rationally justified beliefs and practices, nothing will. (This much seems clear regardless of what theory of rational justification one holds—foundationalist, coherentist, etc., for I have not specified any theory of rationality. But on any theory of rationality, a belief which is arrived at using in appropriate ways all the considerations one has is certainly rationally justified.)

Given the number and complexity of the considerations adumbrated above, it is very unlikely that one could show that the same set of beliefs is rationally justified for every Christian. Indeed, given that we have had somewhat different experiences and have become acquainted with somewhat different items of knowledge and belief, it seems unlikely that exactly the same theology would turn out to be rationally justified for every Christian. (This is not to say that inconsistent theologies could all be true, but only that different people could all be rationally justified in holding theologies inconsistent with each other.) It should be apparent too that in principle the rationally justified theologies (sets of beliefs and practices) that emerge from this process might vary greatly, from what would be considered conservative to what would be considered liberal. For the content of the theology would depend on one's conclusions about such matters as how much the views of the biblical writers were influenced by their culture, how much they accommodated, with what purpose(s) they wrote, etc. Thus, though this approach to the authority of the Bible is not that typical of theological conservatives, there is no reason in principle why the results of applying it might not turn out to be theologically conservative, both in overall doctrine and in the doctrine of the extent to which the biblical writers were correct in what they said. On the other hand, not every set of beliefs and practices would be rationally justified, for any that did not use the considerations available to a person in an appropriate way would not be rationally justified.

But is the Christian rationally justified in giving the Bible the central place in her theological construction which my proposal calls for? Yes, for two reasons. First, because the biblical writers have identified for her the God through faith in whom she has found new life. This new life and its connections with faith are matters of present experience; thus, she is justified in believing that she has it and that she has it as a result of her faith in this God. Moreover, she came to this faith through response to something—perhaps preaching, perhaps the lives of others, perhaps the way she was raised—which is grounded in a community which looks to the Bible as a central source for its understanding of that God. That is, only through the community which takes these writings as its standard for identifying God has she come to faith in her God, and faith in that God has brought her salvation. Moreover, faith in that God was born and nurtured in the community(ies) which produced these writings. Thus, it is rationally justified to look to these writings for guidance regarding how to understand that God and what the life of faith involves.

Second, the set of beliefs and practices which she has constructed giving the Bible this central role is rationally justified in light of everything she knows, believes, etc. If she could not construct a rationally justified set of beliefs and practices giving the Bible this central role, that would be serious grounds for questioning whether she was rationally justified in giving it this role; that she can do so at least indicates that giving the Bible this role is not rationally unjustified. And unless she (and those from whom she adopts her beliefs and practices) could arrive at and hold these beliefs without using the Bible at all, it is positive confirmation for the rational justifiedness of giving the Bible this sort of authority.

My approach contrasts with the two which we looked at earlier in that it does not begin with a thesis regarding the extent to which everything said in the Bible should be accepted by Christians today as a norm for what they should believe. In those approaches, the justification of the authority of the Bible would be based on the justification of that thesis. But in my approach the justification of the authority of the Bible is its role in mediating for us the salvation which is our present experience. The most basic thing which we share with the biblical writers is faith in the same God, not acceptance of the same beliefs by which to express that faith.[17] While faith cannot be completely divorced from the beliefs by which it is expressed, there is no simple relation between them either. Faith in the same God can be expressed by one person in beliefs which are inconsistent with those by which another person expresses faith in the same God. By making faith in the same God, rather than acceptance of the same doctrines, the basic item which we share with the biblical writers (and with other Christians), my approach leaves for further determination the beliefs which we ought to hold in common.

Let me try to summarize my conclusions. The faith through which we have found salvation is faith in the God identified for us in the writings which were gathered in the Bible. Since we have experienced salvation and new life through that faith, we are rationally justified in accepting that faith. And since the God in whom we have faith is identified for us in the writings in the Bible, we are rationally justified in taking these writings as our best guide to what that faith involves. Taking them as our best guide means using them as the primary basis for constructing an overall understanding of the God in whom we have faith, an understanding which has implications for what we believe and do in all areas of our life. But though they are the primary basis for constructing this overall view, they are not the only basis (as I have argued throughout this paper). That overall understanding of God in turn serves as a standard in light of which we may reinterpret, modify, de-emphasize, or reject views expressed in particular passages in the Bible.

[17] My approach assumes that God is identified not as the instantiation of a definition (e.g., the all-perfect being) but in terms of someone else's identification of God (e.g., the God whom Jesus proclaimed). For a fuller discussion of the application of this causal theory of reference to making reference to God, see Richard B. Miller, 'The Reference of God,' *Faith and Philosophy*, vol. 3, no. 1 (January, 1986), pp. 3–15.

10

The Bible Canon and the Christian Doctrine of Inspiration*

Albert C. Sundberg, Jr.

In Protestant thought the concepts of Bible canon and of inspiration are virtually synonymous. Thus the criteria and history of canonicity rightly have been inextricably related to the issue of biblical inspiration. Since the Reformation, Protestant doctrine on biblical inspiration has been a corollary consequent to the accepted circumstances of canonization, whether of Old Testament or of New. The purpose of this essay is not to question the doctrine that the Bible is inspired; that is a universal Christian doctrine. Nor is it to question the inter-relatedness of the history of the canon and the Christian doctrine of inspiration. It is rather to suggest that clarification in our understanding of canonical history entails concomitant and commensurate revision of the doctrine of inspiration.

Revisions in our understanding of the criteria and history of the Old and New Testament canons are in the wind. Indeed, a revision of the canonical history of the Christian Old Testament, put forth by this author a decade and a half ago,[1] has gained substantial acceptance among biblical scholars, though as yet it is largely unknown in the church. In this revision it was shown that the Alexandrian or Septuagint canon had erroneously become the commonly accepted solution to the problem of how the Old Testament of the church came to differ in content from the Jewish canon of scriptures. Though it was already present in Augustine,[2] an Alexandrian canon hypothesis was first proposed in modern times by John Ernest Grabe (1666–1711)[3] and again independently by John Salomo Semler in his *Abhandlung von freier Untersuchung des Canons* (Halle: 1771). It was Semler's formulation that came into general acceptance following the

* From *Interpretation* 29 (1975): 352–71. Reprinted by permission of the publisher.

The Nils W. Lund Lecture, North Park Theological Seminary, March 28, 1973. Read also to the Fifth International Congress on Biblical Studies, Oxford, September 3–7, 1973.

[1] 'The Old Testament of the Early Church,' HTR, 51: 205–26 (1958).

[2] *City of God* 18.42–3.

[3] *Prologomena to the Septuagint*, cited in William Ralph Churton, *The Uncanonical and Apocryphal Scriptures* (London, 1884), p. 12.

work of Abraham Kuenen[4] which made it no longer possible to defend the closing of the Jewish canon by Ezra and the Great Synagogue. Until then the exclusion of the books Protestants call 'Apocrypha' from their Old Testament had been Protestant dogma since Luther.

In his debates with Johann Maier of Eck at Leipzig in June and July of 1519, Martin Luther had backed himself into a difficult corner. His colleague at Wittenberg Andreas Bodenstein of Karlstadt had argued against Eck in 1518 that the text of the Bible was to be preferred above the authority of the church.[5] A year later Luther continued this position in his debates at Leipzig.[6] It was while debating the doctrine of purgatory that Luther was hoisted on his own petard. Eck confronted Luther with the text of II Maccabees 12:46, 'Therefore he made atonement for the dead, that they might be delivered from their sin.' This text was the scriptural basis upon which the Roman church had largely based its doctrine of purgatory. Luther could neither avoid the reading nor deny that the church had accepted this book. Thus pressed, Luther launched into an argument of desperation. He denied the right of the church to decide matters of canonicity; canonicity, he argued, is determined only by the internal worth of a book.[7] Moreover, while Luther recognized that the church used this and other books not included in the Jewish canon of scriptures, he argued that Jerome had denied canonical status to these books. Jerome held that only the books of the Jewish canon are canonical and so now did Luther. While recognizing the validity of Eck's argument that Augustine and the tradition of the church accepted these books, Luther chose Jerome's position that the Jewish canon was the canon of Jesus and the apostles. Previously Luther had used and cited the books of the wider Christian usage, but the position he argued against Eck became hardened so that, following Jerome's example[8] of segregating these books from the Old Testament in his Old Testament lists,[9] Luther placed these books in a separate

[4] 'Over der mannen des Groote Synagogue,' *Verslagen on mededeolingan der Koninklijke Akademie van Wetenchoppen* (Amsterdam, 1876), pp. 207–48; Ger. trans., 'Über die Männer der gossen Synagogue,' trans. K. Budde, *Gesammelte Abhandlungon fur biblischen Wissenschaft von Dr. Abraham Koener* (Freiberg i.B., 1894), pp. 125–60.

[5] Cf. Henry Hoyle Howorth, 'The Bible Canon of the Reformation,' *The International Journal of the Apocrypha,* 15 (1908), 10f.

[6] Cf. Howorth's twelve articles 'The Bible Canon of the Reformation,' *Int. J. of Apoc.,* 14 (1908) to 51 (1917); *idem,* 'The Origins and Authority of the Bible Canon according to the Continental Reformers,' JTS, 8 (1907), 9 (1908), and 10 (1909); Edward Wilhelm Reuss, *History of the Canon of the Holy Scriptures in the Christian Church,* 2nd ed., trans D. Hunter (New York, E. P. Dutton, 1884), pp. 320–38; Joachim Karl Friedrich Knaake, *et al.,* eds., *D. Martin Luthers Werke* (Weimar, H. Böhlaus, 1883–1939), 2, 275–9, 328ff.

[7] Knaake, op. cit, 2, 328ff.

[8] *Epistola* 53.8; *Praef. in Lib. Sam. et Mal.,* J. P. Migne, *P.L.,* 22, 545–8; 28, 552–4, respectively, and *Praef. in Lib. Sol.,* Migne, *P.L.,* 28, 1242f.

[9] It is an anachronism to say, as often is done, that there are no quotations from the books of the Apocrypha in the New Testament. No collection of Apocrypha was in existence when the books of the New Testament were written. The books Protestant Christians call Apocrypha and Roman Catholics call deuterocanonical are the Jewish religious books that were included in the Christian Old Testament of the western church but that were not included in the Jewish canon of scriptures. Thus the Apocrypha was not a distinguishable group of writings until the Christian Old Testament of the west was being formed.

section following the Old Testament in his German translation of the Bible.[10] He titled them 'Apocrypha: these are not held to be equal to the sacred scriptures and yet are useful and good for reading.'[11] Most of the Protestant translations of the Bible into the languages of Europe followed Luther's lead, relegating the Apocrypha to a segregated section between the testaments. Until Kuenen, Luther's authority and his dependence on Jerome served as the Protestant dogmatic bulwark against all arguments and evidence for a larger Old Testament usage in the church. With Kuenen, however, that bulwark was breached; the case for a closed Jewish canon since Ezra was destroyed, and the Alexandrian canon hypothesis came to be generally accepted.

While Protestant scholars came to accept the Alexandrian canon hypothesis as the explanation of how the early church came to use a wider collection of Jewish religious books than the Jewish list, that canon was treated with disdain. Hellenistic Judaism, it was argued, had produced an abortive, sectarian canon which was, therefore, without authority. The early church had made a mistake, being largely Gentile, in using this Hellenistic canon of diaspora Judaism.[12] As late as 1962 Robert Henry Pfeiffer could still argue for a *de facto* Hebrew canon in Palestine in the days of Jesus and the apostles, which canon was simply rubber-stamped at the Council of Jamnia about A.D. 90.[13] Even Hans von Campenhausen's recently translated into English *The Formation of the Christian Bible* tacitly assumes this stance when he asserts that for more than a century the church and the synagogue used the same canon.[14] However, the new circumstance is that we can no longer differentiate between Palestine as Hebrew and Alexandria as Greek in the matter of canon.[15] Indeed, each of the bases upon which the Alexandrian

[10] *Biblio. das ist: dis ganes heilige Schrift altes und neues Testaments, &$$$;ubessetzung d. M. Luthers* (Gennanton, L. B. F. Gegel, 1763).

[11] This segregation in Luther's translation of 1534, was preceded by Karlstadt in his *De Canonicis Scripturis Libellus* (1520), reprinted in Karl August Credner, *Zur Ceschichte des Kanons* (Halle, Waisenhaus, 1817), pp. 316–412.

[12] Cf. C. F. Schmidt, *Historia Antiqua st Vindicatio Canonis* (Leipzig, 1775); Heinrich Corrodi, *Versuch siner Beleuchtung der Ceschichte des jüdischen und christlichen Bibelkanons* (Halle, 1792); Archibald Alexander, *The Canon of the Old and New Testaments Ascertained Testament Canon* (Andover, Allen, Morrill and Wardwell, 1845); Christopher Wordsworth, *On the Inspiration of the Holy Scripture: or, on the Canon of the Old and New Testament* (London, 1851); Archibald Hamilton Charteris, *The New Testament Scriptures, their Claims, History, and Authority* (London, J. Nisbet and Co., 1882); Philip Friederick Keerl, *Dis Apocryphen des Alten Testaments, sin Zeugniss wider dieselbes auf Grund des Wortes Cottes* (Leipzig, Cobhardt und Reisland, 1852); *idem, Das Wort Gottis und die Apokryphen des Alten Testaments* (Leipzig, Cobhardt und Reisland, 1853); *idem, Die Apokryphenfrage* (Leiprig, Cobhardt und Reisland, 1855); E. Klage, *Dis Stellung und Bedeutung der Apokryphen* (Frankfurt, 1852); L. Gaussen, *The Canon of the Holy Scriptures*, trans E. N. Kirk (Boston, 1862, Fr., Lausanne, 1860).

[13] 'Canon of the Old Testament,' IDB, I (Nashville, Abingdon Press, 1962), 510–14, written 1957–8. Pfeiffer served on my thesis committee, but let his article stand to permit me to publish my findings.

[14] Trans., J. A. Baker (Philadelphia, Fortress Press, 1972, Ger., Tübingen, 1968), p. 63.

[15] Sundberg, *The Old Testament of the Early Church*. Harvard Theological Studies 20 (Cambridge, Harvard University Press, 1964), pp. 60–2, 86–94. Joseph Augustine Fitzmyer, 'The Languages of Palestine in the First Century,' CBQ, 32: 507–18 (1970). Jan Nicolaas Sevenster, *Do You Know Greek?* (Leiden, E. J. Brill, 1968). M. Baillet, *et al.*, *Las 'Petites Grattes' de Qumran* (Oxford, Clarendon Press, 1962), pp. 142–7.

canon hypothesis had been set have proven wrong.[16] We now know that a significant number of diaspora Jews had settled in Palestine, Jews whose mother tongue was Greek, and that the Septuagint circulated in Palestine widely enough and long enough to have undergone a Palestinian revision.[17] This apparently is the Greek text used by Justin.[18] That Philo was unaware of the theory limiting inspiration to antiquity, from Moses to Ezra, is no indication of his separation from Palestinian Judaism since that theory is first encountered only in Josephus.[19] Moreover, the law received special reverence throughout Judaism, in Palestine as well as in Alexandria, and in Alexandria the collections of Law and Prophets, and additional books not yet defined into a collection, were known not only by the translator of Sirach into Greek but also by Philo.[20] Second Maccabees (15.9), like the Gospels and Paul, divides the scriptures into the Law and the Prophets. And we now know that not only the diaspora but Palestinian Judaism as well, beside the Law and the Prophets, used a wide, undifferentiated group of scriptures that included the later defined collections of the Writings, the Apocrypha, the Pseudepigrapha, and other books known to us only by name (exclusive, of course, of post-A.D. 70 writings). Both the sectarian writings from Qumran[21] and the early Christian writings of the New Testament reflect this wider usage. We are not now able to distinguish between the way in which the books of the later defined Jewish canon and those belonging to the wider group were used either at Qumran or in the early church.[22] Thus we now know that there was neither an Alexandrian canon nor an early *de facto* Hebrew list closely paralleling the Jewish canon of circa A.D. 90.[23] The church, arising in Judaism and becoming separated from it before the revolt against Rome in A.D. 66–70, received from Judaism the Law and the Prophets as closed collections and the

[16] Sundberg, *op. cit.*, pp. 51–79.

[17] *Ibid.*, pp. 88–91.

[18] *Ibid.*, pp. 91–4.

[19] *Contra Apion.* 1.8.41. Cf. Sundberg, *op. cit.*, pp. 71f.

[20] *De Vita Contemp.* 3.25.

[21] Sundberg, *op. cit.*, pp. 94–100; Bleddyn J. Roberts, 'The Dead Sea Scrolls and the Old Testament Scriptures,' BJRL, 36:84 (1953/54); Jean Carmignac, 'Les citations de l'Ancien Testament dans 'la Guerre des Fils de Lumiere contre les Fils de Tenebres,'' RB, 63: 234–60, 375–90 (1956); James Alvin Sanders, 'Cave 11 Surprises and the Question of Canon,' McCQ, 12:284–98 (1968).

[22] Sundberg, *op. cit.*, pp. 113–28.

[23] The relevance of the Council of Jamnia for the closing of the Jewish canon has been questioned: Harold Henry Rowley, *The Growth of the Old Testament* (London, Hutchinson University Library, 1950), p. 170; Raymond Abba, *The Nature and Authority of the Bible* (Philadelphia, Muhlenberg Press, 1958), p. 33 n; George Wishart Anderson, *A Critical Introduction to the Old Testament* (London, G. Duckworth, 1959), pp. 12f.; Jack Pearl Lewis, 'What do We Mean by Jabneh?' JBR, 32:125–32 (1964). Nahum Mattathias Sarna appears right in saying, 'More probably, decisions taken on that occasion came to be widely accepted and thus regarded as final in succeeding generations' ('Bible,' *Encyclopaedia Judaica*, 4 [Jerusalem, Keter Publishing House, 1971], 825); cf. Sundberg, *op. cit.*, pp. 127f. The canon of scriptures in Josephus, *Apion* 1.39–41, the apparent protest against a closed canon in 4 Ezra 14:41–6, and the Old Testament list in Melito (Eusseb., *H.E.* 4.26.14), in all probability obtained from Palestinian Jews, are hardly explainable apart from some canonical decision in Judaism about the end of the first century A.D.

wider,' undifferentiated scriptures circulating in Judaism before A.D. 70 as its scriptures. But the church did not receive a canon; Judaism had not yet a canon to bequeath when the church arose and became separated from it. Only after A.D. 70 do we see movement in Judaism toward the narrowing of their scriptures until a canon, to which nothing could be added and nothing subtracted, was formed about A.D. 90. All subsequent Jewish lists attest to this canon by the uniformity of their contents.[24]

Thus the church received 'scriptures' from Judaism, but not a canon. And if we are to be able to write an accurate history of the canon in the church, we cannot continue to use the terms 'scripture' and 'canon' as synonyms, as has been the practice. This only leads to confusion. Rather, in describing the history of the canon these terms should be differentiated. My proposal is that the term 'scripture' should be used to designate writings that are regarded as in some sense authoritative, and the term 'canon' used to designate a closed collection of scripture to which nothing can be added, nothing subtracted.[25] When the church became aware that the Jews had a canon, that the Jews employed only a restricted number of the scriptures the church had received from Judaism, the church sensed the *a priori* claim of Judaism to know what the canon was. This awareness is first noticed in Melito (c. A.D. 170) and then with increasing vividness in and following Origen.[26] Caught between the anvil of church usage—Justin's comment to Trypho, 'not your scriptures but ours,' was characteristic of the church—and the hammer of the *a priori* claim of Judaism to know what the canon was, the church was forced to define the content of her Old Testament for herself. Initially I attempted to describe this process with considerable tentativeness.[27] The want of challenge in the interim decade and a half tends towards squatter's-rights confidence. In the East, where Jewish influence was most felt, the Jewish canonical list was most closely followed. There the church included in its Old Testament only those books outside the Jewish canonical list for which they knew a tradition of authorship relating the book to an author of the Jewish list. Thus I Esdras was associated with Ezra-Nehemiah, Baruch and the Epistle (of Jeremy) with Jeremiah, and Daniel and Esther were used in their expanded Greek

[24] Henry Barclay Swete, *An Introduction to the Old Testament in Greek* (Cambridge, The University Press, 1900), p. 200, where the Jewish lists are collected. Herbert Edward Ryhe, *The Canon of the Old Testament* (London, Macmillan and Co., 1914), pp. 280f. Cf. Sundberg, *op. cit.*, pp. 56–58, 133–38.

[25] Willem Cornelis van Unnik, 'De la Regle Mēta prostheinai mēts ephalein dans l'Histoire du Canon,' *Vigiliae Christianae*, 3:1–36 (1949).

[26] Sundberg, *op. cit.*, pp. 129–69. Terms such as 'open canon' and 'flexible canon' confuse the issue, enabling us to suppose that what we now mean by 'canon' was in existence before a canon was actually formed.

[27] *Ibid.*, pp. 58, 133–48. Canon 60 of the Council of Laodicea (between 343 and 381) was probably supplied later from Athanasius. The text history of the Council strongly suggests that Canon 60 did not stand in the original text. However, Canon 59 is authentic, proscribing the reading (probably in church) of private psalms and noncanonical (*ekanoniste*) books, and permitting the reading only of the canonical books of the New and Old Testaments. Migne, *P.G.*, 33, 640; cf. B. F. Westcott, *Survey,* 7th ed. (1896), pp. 439–47.

forms. The eastern Old Testament canon appears to have reached a common ground about the middle of the fourth century. Books most dearly loved but thus excluded from the Old Testament, such as Ecclesiasticus and Wisdom of Solomon, thereafter sometimes came to appear in not yet so sharply defined New Testament lists dating subsequent to that time.[28] In the West, not only books thus agglomerated under authors of the Jewish list but books for which there is evidence that they continued to circulate in Judaism after A.D. 90 were also included: Maccabees, Ecclesiasticus, Wisdom, Judith, Tobit. With them the list of the Apocrypha is completed, that is, the books included in the Old Testament canon of the Western church but not included in the Jewish canon. The Old Testament canonical list was substantially settled in the West with the councils in North Africa at the end of the fourth and the beginning of the fifth centuries.[29]

The Apocrypha has been on the losing side of the Protestant struggle with its Old Testament. But now the issue is raised again.[30] That question is not only a matter of so and so many books. It now can be seen as much more a question of the Christian doctrine of inspiration. The historical circumstance is now unequivocal: In a time when access to the relevant historical material and methodology was unavailable, Luther appealed to a theory propounded by Jerome with respect to the Jewish canon that we now know was wrong. Furthermore, it is evident that Luther's rubric that 'Scripture is its own attester' is a camouflage statement. It seems to place the criteria of canonicity upon the internal self-witness of a writing to its own worth; whereas, in fact, the judgment

---

[28] Sundberg, 'Canon Muratori: A Fourth-Century List,' HTR, 66:15–18 (1973). Eusebius, illustrating Irenaeus' use of New Testament books, mentions Irenaeus' quotations from Wisdom among them (*H.E.* 5:8.1–8): Epiphanius includes Wisdom and Sirach in his New Testament list (*Adv. Hear.* 76; Migne, *P.G.*, 47, 560f.); Canon Muratori includes Wisdom in its New Testament canon (Ludovico Antonio Muratori, *Antiquitates Italicae Medii Aevi* [Mediolani, 1740], 3, 809–80); and the table of contents in Codex Alexandrinus concludes the New Testament with Psalms of Solomon (Edgar Johnson Goodspeed, *The Formation of the* New Testament list (*Adv. Hoer.* 76; Migne. *P.G.*, 47, 560f.).

[29] Council of Hippo (A.D. 393), Canon 36 (Giovanni Domenico Mansi, *Secrorum conciliorum nova et amplissima collectio* [Florentiae, 1759–92], 3, 850), is from the abridgement of the canons of Hippo sent in a letter from the Byzacene bishops to Aurelius at the Third Council at Carthage (397), which reenacted them. It is through these reenactments at Carthage that the canons of Hippo are known, Canon 36 of Hippo being reenacted as the 47th of Carthage. Cf. Charles Joseph Hefele, *A History of the Councils of the Church* 2, trans. H. N. Oxenham (Edinburgh, 1876), 394ff, 407, 471; Mansi, *op. cit.*, 3, 891. And again this canon was reenacted as Canon 39 of the Carthaginian Council in A.D. 419. Cf. Charles Joseph Costello, *St. Augustine's Doctrine of the Inspiration and Canoxicity of Scripture* (Washington, D. C., The Catholic University of America, 1930), p. 68; Hefele gives this as the first canon of Carthage (397), and the 47th of Carthage (419). It is clear that there were local councils, not carrying the authority of an ecumenical council. However, the unanimity of the decisions together with the proviso of concurrence with Rome leaves little doubt but that the decisions on the canon were representative of the Western church.

[30] Cf., Floyd V. Filson, *Which Books Belong to the Bible* (Philadelphia, The Westminster Press, 1956); Bruce Manning Metzger, *An Introduction to the Apocrypha* (New York, Oxford University Press, 1957); Sundberg, 'The Protestant Old Testament Canon: Should It Be Reexamined?' CBQ, 28: 194–203 (1966).

is made by the person arguing the case. Canonicity is thus made to depend entirely upon subjective judgment. If canonicity is thus to be determined, then, as Howorth has said, 'everyone must in fact either become an infallible pope to himself or else accept Luther as an infallible pope.'[31]

Beginning with our earliest Christian documents, the letters of Paul, a consistent Christian teaching has been that the inspiration that enlightened Judaism through Moses and the Prophets was now poured out upon the church. Paul argued that the meaningful ancestry of Abraham was a spiritual ancestry of faith, in which ancestry Christians now stand as inheritors.[32] The first fruit of that faith is the Spirit[33] which inspired and enlivened the subsequent life of the church. I know of no one who questions but that the inheritance of the church was from pre-A.D. 70 Judaism. But that was Judaism without a canon. The church inherited scriptures from Judaism but not a canon, the Jewish canon not being defined until about A.D. 90. Thus, in view of the Christian doctrine of inspiration, it is no longer possible for Protestant Christians to argue for the validity of the Jewish canon for the Christian Old Testament;[34] we now know that the Jewish canon was not the scriptures of Jesus and the apostles. Thus Protestant Christianity, in maintaining its practice of limiting its Old Testament to the Jewish canon, controverts the teaching of its own New Testament scriptures that the Spirit of God is to be found in the church. It is evident that both in content and doctrine, Protestantism, in its view of Old Testament canon, has broken away from its spiritual heritage. If Protestant Christianity is to continue its custom of restricting its Old Testament to the Jewish canon, an entirely new rationale and doctrine of canon will have to be described. But any Christian doctrine of canonization that takes seriously the Christian doctrine of inspiration will lead ultimately to the Christian Old Testament as defined in the Western church since that Western church is our spiritual lineage.

At the beginning of this essay I said that the winds of revision are being felt also in the history of the New Testament canon. When the process of modern historiography began to be applied in biblical studies, one of its more comforting contributions was the demonstration of an early core New Testament, relatable to apostles, apostolic men, and the hearers of apostolic men. This brought us down only to the times of Irenaeus. And the church, since the canonical histories of Brooke Foss Westcott[35] and Adolf von Harnack,[36] has been confident that the

[31] 'Bible Canon of the Reformation,' 24:5 (1911).

[32] Rom. 4: 1–17; Gal. 3: 1–4, 7; cf. Acts 2:1–21.

[33] Rom. 5:5; 7:6; 8:1–17, 23.

[34] Sundberg, 'The Prot. OT Canon,' pp. 200–3.

[35] *Survey*, eds. 1–7 (Cambridge, 1855–96), and especially *idem*, 'The Canon of Scripture.' *Dr. William Smith's Dictionary of the Bible* (New York, Hurd and Houghton, 1871), pp. 368–76, first published in 1860. This is the first statement of New Testament by the end of the second century hypothesis.

[36] *Das Neue Testament Um das Jahr 200* (Freiburg I. B., J. C. B. Mohr, 1889); *idem, Die Enstehung des Neven Testaments und die wichtigsten Folgen den neuen Schopfung, Beitrage zur Einleitung in das Neue Testament*, 6 (Leipzig, Hinrichs, 1914).

bulk of the New Testament writings—a core New Testament—were already recognized as canonical by the end of the second century. All that remained for subsequent time was the mopping-up exercise. Both Henneche and Cullmann have stated the assurance felt all around that this history of the New Testament canon is one of the more assured results of New Testament scholarship.[37]

Now that assured result is also being brought under question.[38] The foundational criteria for New Testament canon in modern studies has been authority like that of the Old Testament. In the latest major history of the New Testament canon, Von Campenhausen puts the matter thus:

> To make my own position clear, [he says,] by the beginnings of the canon I do not understand the emergence and dissemination, nor even the ecclesiastical use and influence of what were later the canonical writings. One can, in my view, speak of a 'canon' only where of set purpose such a document or group of documents is given a special, normative position, by virtue of which it takes its place alongside the existing Old Testament 'scriptures.'[39]

However, our present circumstance is, as I have discussed above, that we now know that the church had no Old Testament canon until mid-fourth century in the East and until the end of the fourth and beginning of the fifth century in the West. Thus, when Christian writings came to be used in the church with like authority to that of the scriptures inherited from Judaism, we are able to say that we have Christian scriptures but not Christian canon.[40] Similarly, the corollary to the 'parallel to the Old Testament' standard for canon, that the introductory formulas, 'as it was written (*gegraptai*) and 'the scripture' (*hē graphē*), have come unstuck. In 1948, John Lawson noticed that Irenaeus uses 'the scripture' of writings that are definitely not scripture;[41] Richard Patrick Crosland Hanson has shown that the same is true for Origen.[42] And in my 1968 article, 'Towards a Revised History of the New Testament Canon,'[43] I have shown that a case that

[37] Edgar Hennecke and Wilhelm Schneemelcher, *The New Testament Apocrypha*, in R. McL. Wilson, ed. (Philadelphiz, The Westminster Press, 1963), 1, 29: Oscar Cullmann, 'Die Pluralitat der Evangelien als theologisches Problem in Altertum,' ThZ, 1 (1945), 23.

[38] Sundberg, 'Towards a Revised History of the New Testament Canon,' StEv, 4:452–61 (1968).

[39] Remembering that Von Campenhausen uses 'Scripture' as a synonym of 'canon.' *Op. cit.*, p. 103.

[40] Sundberg, 'The Making of the New Testament Canon.' *The Interpreter's One-Volume Commentary on the Bible* (Nashville, Abingdon Press, 1971), pp. 1216–20.

[41] *The Biblical Theology of Saint Irenaeus* (London, Epworth Press, 1948), pp. 501. Cf., Johannes Werner, *Der Paulinismus des Irenaeus. Texts and Untersuchung*, 6.2 (Leiprig, J. C. Hinrichs, 1889), 36–8.

[42] *Origen's Doctrine of Tradition* (London, S. P. C. K., 1954), p. 140 n. 6.

[43] pp. 454–7. Dwight Moody Smith. 'The Use of the Old Testament in the New,' in James M. Efird, ed., *The Use of the Old Testament in the New and Other Essays* (Durham, Duke University Press, 1972), p. 5, n. 4, has quite misstated my conclusions in saying, 'all the instances of *graphē* which are usually cited as carrying the meaning of "canon" can be shown to carry instead the meaning of "specific writings" or "books." ' What I have shown is that *graphē* is sometimes used of individual writings and the uses of *Biblos/biblion* are not restricted to individual books. Hence *graphē* is not a technical term in the New Testament designating canon.

these formulas designate canon cannot be derived from the New Testament materials, as had previously been held.

The second step in the traditional development of a so-called core New Testament by the end of the second century has been based on the fourfold Gospel collection and the New Testament list of Canon Muratori together with the usage of Irenaeus and Tertullian. Scholars, such as Caspar René Gregory,[44] Alexander Souter,[45] and Robert McQueen Grant,[46] have seen in Tatian's use of our four Gospels evidence that these four Gospels were already regarded as canonical in Tatian's day. However, Tatian used our four Gospels in constructing his *Diatessaron* in a way similar to that in which Mark was used by the authors of Matthew and Luke in writing those Gospels, that is, as resource materials. No one has argued that the Gospel according to Mark was already canonical when Matthew and Luke were written since it was used as a source by the authors of these Gospels. Moreover, Gilles Quispel has attractively argued that Tatian's *Diatessaron* was actually composed from five gospels, the fifth being the Gospel of the Hebrews.[47] These considerations and the fact that the *Diatessaron* was 'the gospel' for three centuries in the Eastern church speak against the presumed canonical status of the Four when *Diatessaron* was written. Similarly, Jürgen Regul has shown that the old Latin prologues to the Gospels cannot be used to support an early canonization of the Four Gospels.[48]

Two stunning developments have arisen with respect to Canon Muratori. Canon Muratori is a Latin list of New Testament books that was found by Ludovico Antonio Muratori (1672–1750) in the Ambrosian Library at Milan, being contained in a codex dating from the eighth or possibly seventh century, which codex belonged previously to Columbian's Monastery at Bobio. The canon is fragmentary since the beginning is lost and the end is abrupt, showing that it was copied from a mutilated and presumably ancient exemplar. Also, some bits of the Muratorian canon have been found in four eleventh or twelfth century manuscripts of St. Paul's epistles at Monte Casino.[49] A Greek original was suggested by Muratori when he first published the list in 1740.[50] The Monte Casino fragments and Julio Campos' demonstration that the Latin text of the list discloses close acquaintance with the Vulgate[51] confirm Muratori's widely accepted suggestion. The fragment has been dated as early as the middle of the

---

[44] *Canon and Text of the New Testament* (Edinburgh, T. and T. Clark, 1907), pp. 124–9.

[45] *Text and Canon of the New Testament*, 2nd ed., rev. C. S. C. Williams (London, Duckworth, 1954), p. 148.

[46] *The Formation of the New Testament* (New York, Harper and Row, Publishers, 1965), p. 138.

[47] 'L' Evangile selon Thomas et le Diatessaron,' *Vigiliae Christianae*, 13:87–117 (1959).

[48] *Die antimarcionitischen Evengelienprologe* (Freiburg, Herder, 1969).

[49] *Fragmentum Muratorianum iuxta Code, Gasinenses, in Miscellanea Cassinese*, 2, 1 (1897), 1–5, cited by Adolf von Harnack, 'Excerpta aus dem Muratorischen Fragment (saec. xi et xiii,' TLZ, 23 [1898], 131–4).

[50] *Op. cit.*, pp. 809–80.

[51] 'Época del fragmenta Muratoriano,' *Helmantica, Revista de Humanidades Clasicas* 2 (1960), 486–96.

second century but is now commonly dated in the last decades of that century and placed in Rome. In our time Canon Muratori has been the handsome keystone to the 'core New Testament by the end of the second century' hypothesis. As the history of the New Testament canon has been constructed, the Muratorian list at the end of the second century was followed by a list by Origen in the third century, preserved in Euscbius,[52] bridging the gap to the multiple lists of the fourth century, thus presenting a plausible, coherent history.

One stunning shock to this coherent history is that Hanson has shown that Origen neither had a New Testament list nor a concept of a New Testament canon.[53] Eusebius made Origen's list for him. (It should be noticed that Eusebius also constructed a rudimentary New Testament canon for Irenacus.)[54] The list Eusebius gives for Origen he has collected from four separate writings of Origen's which, in their original contexts, refer not to a canonical list but to collections.[55] Origen certainly knows the letters of Paul, but he gives only a sketchy list (which actually commences with Ephesians!).[56] What Hanson has not noticed is that in thus destroying a canonical list for Origen, Canon Muratori as commonly dated is left without a parallel for nearly a century and a half. If Canon Muratori indeed is to be dated from the end of the second century, then it is an isolated list, created before there was any interest in the church for such, and done in a corner where, beyond its chance preservation, it left no discernible impact upon the church for more than a century. Thus, in no way could Canon Muratori have played the important role in the history of New Testament canonization that has been ascribed to it.

The other shock to the established place of Canon Muratori is that its early date and Roman provenance have come into question, the fourth century and the Eastern church being suggested as preferable.[57] The case is too long to detail here; I give only a brief summary. As to place of writing: the meaning of the term *urbs* (city) as Rome in line 38 does not depend upon the place of writing of the fragment, but upon the place designated in Acts 28:30f., and Romans 15:24, 28 to which the Muratori passage refers. Hugo Koch has shown that the term *catholica* (*ecclesia*) could not have the restricted meaning 'Rome,' since Cyprian, in the third century, uses the term in writing to bishops of other than the Roman see when referring to their individual bishoprics and uses *catholicae* (*ecclesiae*)

[52] *H.E.* 6.25.3–14.   [53] *Op. cit.*, pp. 133–45.   [54] *H.E.* 5.8.1–8.

[55] Cf. Vincent Henry Stanton, 'New Testament Canon,' James Hastings, *A Dictionary of the Bible*, 3 (New York, C. Scribner's Sona, 1900), 541; Joseph N. Sanders, 'The Literature and Canon of the New Testament,' *Peake's Commentary on the Bible* (London, Thomas Nelson and Sons Ltd., 1962), pp. 676–82; Paul Feine, Johannes Behm, Werner Georg Kümmel, *Introduction to the New Testament*, trans. A. J. Mattill, Jr. (Nashville, Abingdon Press, 1966), p. 384, etc. But cf., Hanson, *op. cit.*, pp. 149f.

[56] *Contra Celsum* 3.20: Eph., Col, Thess., Phil, Rom. Above, in 3.19 there is a quotation from I Cor. but that letter is not named in the list and the introduction to the list follows this quotation.

[57] Cf., Sundberg, 'Canon Muratori: A Fourth-Century List,' HTR, 66:1–41 (1973).

when more than one bishopric is involved.[58] With this the case for locating the list in Rome is lost. As to date: traditionally this has been based on what proves to be a dogmatic interpretation of what the list has to say about the Shepherd of Hermas, especially the phrase *nuperrime temporibus nostris*.[59] This phrase has been translated 'very recently, in our own time,' taking *nuperrime* as a diminished superlative, and interpreted to mean within a generation of Pius of Rome. However, another viable translation is, 'most recently,' with reference to the previously named books, 'in our own time,' that is, not apostolic times. Here a close parallel is had in Irenaeus, who, in discussing the time of writing of the Book of Revelation, says, 'For it was not seen long ago, but almost in our own generation, at the end of Domition's reign (*oude gar pro pollou chronou heōpathē. alla schedon epi tēs hēmeteras geneas, pros tō telei tēs Dometiamou archēs*).[60] Thus, since the meaning of this phrase is equivocal, it cannot be used in a determinative fashion for the date of the list. The list must be dated and placed by the location of parallels to other information contained in the list. The parallels are as follows: (1) James Donaldson has identified significant vocabulary items in the list which find no parallels in the second century, some of which find no parallel before Cyprian.[61] (2) The presence of Wisdom of Solomon within the New Testament list, previously an enigma, now is recognized as an attempt in the Eastern church to preserve books loved by the church but which could not be included in the Jewish canonical list by agglomeration, there being no tradition in the Eastern church relating them to authors of the Jewish list. The impact of the Jewish canon in the east dates from Athanasius. Parallels to Muratori's inclusion of Wisdom are had in Eusebius, who included Wisdom in the partial New Testament list he constructed for Irenaeus,[62] Epiphanius, who included Wisdom and Sirach in his New Testament list,[63] and the index of Codex Alexandrinus, which concludes the New Testament list with the Psalms of Solomon.[64] (3) Eusebius marks the transition point from the acceptability of Hermas in the church. Tertullian, the only previous father to exclude Hermas, is a special case since his rejection of Hermas dates from his conversion to Montanism and, therefore,

[58] '*Zur A. v. Harnacks Beweis für den amplichen romischen Ursprung des Muratorischen Fragments*,' ZNW, 24:154–63 (1925). Cf., Sundberg, 'Canon Muratori,' pp. 5f., and n. 22.
[59] Cf. Bernhard Weiss, *An Introduction to the New Testament* 1, trans. A. J. K. Davidson (London, 1887, Ger., 1886), p. 104, etc.
[60] Haer. 5.30.3; Euseb., H.E. 5.8.6. Cf., Weiss, *op. cit.*, p. 104; Burnett Hilhnan Streeter, *The Primative Church* (New York, The Macmillan Company, 1929), p. 313; Gottfried Kuhn, *Das Muratorische Fragment* (Zurich, S. Höhr, 1892), p. 25 n. 1: Gustav Koffmane-Kuntz, 'Das wahre Alter und die Herkunft des sogenannten Muratorischen Kanons,' *Neue Jahrbucher fur deutsche Theologie*, 2 (1893), 276ff.
[61] *A Critical History of Christian Literature and Doctrine*, III (London, Macmillan, 1866), 212; cf., Sundberg, 'Canon Muratori,' p. 12, n. 32a.
[62] *H.E.* 5.8.1.8.
[63] *Adv. Haer.* 76, Migne, P. G. 47, 560f.
[64] In Westcott, *op. cit.*, 493f. Cf. Sundberg, *OT of the Church*, p. 144; *idem*, 'Canon Muratori,' pp. 15–18.

is not representative of the church. The attitude of Muratori exactly parallels that of Athanasius so that, in this respect, the list falls between Eusebius and Athanasius.[65] (4) The questionable place of John's Apocalypse, on the very fringe of canonicity following Wisdom, and the equivocal status of the Apocalypse of Peter in the list are both distinctly Eastern features and find their parallels at the end of the third and in the fourth centuries. Therefore, far from being a Roman list from the end of the second century, Canon Muratori is probably an Eastern list dating from the fourth century. Its associations are closest to those of Eusebius of all other New Testament lists.[66]

Finally, in the traditional history of the New Testament canon, the status of those books that came nearest to being included in the New Testament but were not is either ignored or passed over as of so little significance as to be immaterial to canonical history. Think for a moment about the concept of a core New Testament at the end of the second century if it were to include I Clement, the Letters of Ignatius, the Epistle of Barnabas, the writings of Polycarp, the Shepherd of Hermas, and perhaps others. But that is just where our literature leaves us. One cannot distinguish in usage and authority between these writings and the writings collected into our New Testament in the church fathers at the end of the second century and on until the fourth.

In my view, a core New Testament canon at the end of the second century is no longer a viable hypothesis. I will not describe here the configuration I see as a more accurate and realistic history of the New Testament canon. The outline of that configuration is readily available in my articles, 'Towards a Revised History of the New Testament Canon,' *Studia Evangelica* 4; and 'The Making of the New Testament Canon,' *The Interpreter's One Volume Commentary* (1971). I wish rather to turn my attention to the Christian doctrine of inspiration as it becomes evident in the configuration of canonical history there described. This doctrine of inspiration is not different from that which obtained in the church at the close of the second century. But, when the history of the New Testament canon was thought to culminate then, criteria of canonization were too narrowly related to apostolicity to recognize it.

The Christian doctrine had its origins in earliest Christianity and is taught throughout the documents of the New Testament. It is the doctrine that God has poured out the Holy Spirit upon all believers in Jesus. Paul taught that 'no man can say, "Jesus is Lord" except by the Holy Spirit.'[67] In Acts, Luke related the promise of the prophet Joel, 'And in the last days it shall be, God declares, that I will pour out my Spirit upon all flesh,'[68] to all believers in Jesus.[69] I know of no teaching in the New Testament that in any way restricts that doctrine to particular persons or to particular times. The church into the fourth century,

---

[65] *Ibid.*, pp. 12–15.   [66] *Ibid.*, pp. 18–41.   [67] I Cor. 12:3*b*.
[68] Joel 2: 28ff.   [69] Acts 2: 14–21, 38f.

throughout the history of the canonization of the New Testament (and the Old), also knew of no restriction of that doctrine, neither to apostles, not to apostolic times, nor to apostolic men. Quite independently Krister Stendahl and I, about the same time, came to a similar conclusion that the Christian doctrine of inspiration could not serve as a criterion of canonization, certainly not because the inspiration of the scriptures was in any doubt, but because the doctrine of inspiration was so broad in the church as not to be limitable to the canon of scripture.[70] One of Stendahl's students, Everett Roy Kalin, collected an over-whelming abundance of evidence from the writings of the church fathers into an unpublished doctoral dissertation entitled, 'Argument from Inspiration in the Canonization of the New Testament,'[71] in which he shows incontrovertably that this is the case. I give here illustrative examples, mostly from his collection but also from mine.

Just as we would expect, one of our earliest Christian writings outside the New Testament, First Clement, written from the church at Rome to the church at Corinth about A.D. 95, says of Paul's letter to Corinth, 'Take up the epistle of the blessed Paul the apostle. What did he first write to you at the beginning of his preaching? With true inspiration (*ep' alētheias pneumatikōs*) he charged you concerning himself and Cephas and Apollos.'[72] This shows that Paul's own sense of inspiration was also attributed to his letters by his earliest Christian readers. But the traditional doctrine of the inspiration of the Bible[73] hardly prepares us for what the writer of First Clement has to say about his own writing. He writes, 'You will give us joy and gladness if you are obedient to the things written by us through the Holy Spirit' (*tois huph' hēmōn gegrammenois dia tou hagiou pneumatos*).[74] In 59.1 one reads, 'But if some be disobedient to the words which have been spoken by him [i.e., Jesus Christ] through us (*tois hup' autou di' hēmōn eirēmenois*), let them know that they will entangle themselves in trans-gression and no little danger.' Ignatius, bishop of Antioch in Syria wrote in his letter to the Magnesian Christians, 'for you have Jesus Christ in yourselves' (*Iēsoun gar Christon echete en heautois*),[75] 'I know that you are full of God' (*hoti theou gemete*).[76] And Ignatius wrote of having a similar inspiration himself, saying, 'I have many thoughts in God' (*polla phronō en theō*),[77] 'I write to you not according to the flesh, but according to the mind of God' (*ou kata sarka*

---

[70] 'The Apocalypse of John and the Epistles of Paul in the Muratorian Fragment,' William Klassen and Greydon Fisher Snyder, eds., *Current Issues in New Testament Interpretation* (New York, Harper, 1962), pp. 239–45; Sundberg, 'Making the NT,' pp. 1217, 1224.

[71] Harvard University, 1967.

[72] 47:1–3.

[73] Dewey Maurice Beegle, *The Inspiration of Scripture* (Philadelphia, The Westminster Press, 1963): Walter R. Bowman, 'Bible as God's Word,' *The Encyclopedia of the Lutheran Church*, 1, ed. Julius Bodensieck (Minneapolis, Augsburg Publishing House, 1965), 229–36; J. T. Forestell, 'Bible, II (Inspiration),' *New Catholic Encyclopedia*, II (New York, McGraw-Hill, 1967), 381–6.

[74] 63.2.   [75] 12.1.   [76] 14.1.   [77] *Trall.* 4.1.

humin egrapsa, alla kata gnōmēn theou),[78] 'I cried out while I was with you; I spoke with a great voice, with God's own voice. . . . the Spirit was preaching and saying this' (*elaoun megalē phōnē, theou phōnē . . . to de pneuma ekērussen legon tade*).[79] That Polycarp, Bishop of Smyrna martyred circa A.D. 155, was regarded as inspired is evident from what is said in the Martyrdom of Polycarp: 'For every word which he uttered from his mouth both was fulfilled and will be fulfilled.'[80] The angelic Shepherd, the Spirit, seized Hermas,[81] revealing to him the material of his book. The Shepherd told him, 'First write my commandments and the parables, and the other things you are to write as I show you.'[82] And again, 'For every spirit which is given from God is not asked questions, but has the power of the Godhead and speaks all things of itself, because it is from above, from the power of the Divine spirit' (*hoti anōthen estin apo tēs dunameōs tou theiou pneumatos*),[83] 'Guard this flesh of yours, pure and undefiled, that the spirit which dwells in it may bear it witness and your flesh may be justified.'[84] The author of the Epistle of Barnabas writes that the Lord put 'the gift of his teaching in our hearts,'[85] and says of himself, 'Being persuaded of this, and being conscious that since I spoke among you I have much understanding because the Lord has traveled with me in the way of righteousness.'[86] The Epistle to Diognetus reads, 'For in all things which we were moved by the will of him who commands us to speak (*hosa gar thalēmati tou keleuontos logou ekinēthēmen exeipein*) with pain, we become sharers with you through love of the things revealed to us' (*tōn apokaluphthentōn hēmin*).[87]

Justin Martyr speaks frequently of the activity of the inspiring Spirit in the Old Testament prophets. But concurring with the Jewish doctrine of canon, that inspiration had ceased in Judaism,[88] Justin asserts that the prophetic inspiration is now found in the church. He writes,

The scripture says that these inumerated powers of the Spirit have come upon him [i.e., Christ], not because he stood in need of them, but because they would rest in him, i.e., would find their accomplishment in him, so that there would be no more prophets in your nation after the ancient custom: and this fact you plainly perceive. For after him no prophet has arisen among you. . . . it was requisite that such gifts should cease from you; and having received their rest in him, should again, as had been predicted, become gifts which, from the grace of his Spirit's power, he imparts to those who believe in him, according as he deems each man worthy thereof.[89] For, [he says], the prophetical gifts remain with us, even to the present time. And hence you ought to understand that [the gifts] formerly among your nation have been transferred to us.[90]

---

[78] Ignatious, *Rm.* 8.3b.   [79] Ignatious, *Phil.* 7.1b–2.
[80] 16.2.   [81] *Vis.* 1.1.3; 2.1.1.   [82] *Vis.* 5.5.
[83] *Mand.* 11.5b.   [84] *Sim.* 5.7.1.   [85] 9.9.
[86] 1.4.   [87] 11.8.   [88] *Dial.* 51.
[89] *Dial.* 87, cf., 88.   [90] *Dial.* 82.

Kalin concentrated his interests especially upon Irenaeus, Origen, and Eusebius. I pass over his discussion of the vocabulary used by these writers to describe the presence of the Spirit for inspiration of the Old Testament authors, citing only examples illustrating the belief of these authors in their own and their contemporary Christians' inspiration by the Spirit. Irenaeus comments, 'We hear of my brethren in the church who have prophetic gifts and who through the Spirit...' (*kathōs kai pollōn akoumen adelphōn en tē Ekklēsia prophētika charismata echontōn, kai... dia tou pneumatos...*),[91] showing his belief in the Spirit's inspiration in his own day. He writes of 'the divinely inspired elder and preacher of the truth' (*divinae aspirationis senior et et pracco veritatis*)[92] who composed a poem against the heretic Marcus. He describes the Spirit-inspired activity of Christians, saying, 'For some really and truly drive out devils, ... others even have knowledge of things to come, visions, and prophetic utterances. Others heal the sick... and now, as I have said, the dead even have been raised and remained with us for many years.'[93] In Heresies 3.11.8, he remarks that the symbol of the Gospel according to Mark—the flying eagle—points out the gift of the Spirit hovering over the church,[94] and in the following section deplores the excesses of some of the anti-Montanists. He says,

Others, again, that they may set at nought the gift of the Spirit, which in the latter times has been, by the good pleasure of the Father, poured out upon the human race, do not admit that aspect [of the evangelical dispensation] presented by John's Gospel, in which the Lord promised that he would send the Paraclete; but set aside at once both the gospel and the prophetic Spirit. Wretched men indeed! who wish to be pseudo-prophets, forsooth, but who set aside the gift of prophecy from the church.[95]

Origen speaks of his own sense of being inspired:

And as Moses heard God [he writes], and then gave to the people the things which he heard from God, so we need the Holy Spirit speaking mysteries in us, so that by our prayers we might be able to listen to the scriptures and again to proclaim what we have heard to the people (*Et quomodo Moyses audiebat Deum, et deinde ea quae a Deo audierat, proferebat ad populum; sic nos indigemus Spiritu sancto laquente in nobis mysteria, ut orationibus nostris scripturam passimus audire, et rursum quod audivimus populus intimare*).[96] [Again he remarks], For if I sell for reward the things that have been spoken to me by the Holy Spirit, what else do I do but sell for reward the Holy Spirit?[97]

Origen affirms the identity of the Spirit of truth who revealed the spiritual interpretation of the apostles[98] with the Spirit who reveals the spiritual

[91] *Haer.* 5.6.1. Kalin, *op. cit.,* p. 27.
[92] *Haer.* 1.15.6 (Gr. text: Epiphanus, *Haer.* 34.11.10, Kalin, *op. cit.,* p. 16.
[93] Haer. 2.32.4: cf. 5.6.1. Kalin, *op. cit.,* p. 27.
[94] Cf. *Haer.* 5.8.1. Kalin, *op. cit.,* p. 27.
[95] *Haer.* 3.11.9. Kalin, *op. cit.,* p. 27.
[96] *Hom.* 7.10 *in Erech.*; Kalin, *op. cit.,* p. 53.
[97] *Hom.* 38 *in L.c.;* Kalin, *op. cit.,* p. 53.   [98] *Contra Celsum* 2.2.

interpretation to the church.[99] And Origen prays that just as the Lord put words in the mouth of Jeremiah, so God might give words also to him.[100]

The matter of inspiration, however, is more intricate in Origen than in any of his predecessors. Like Justin, Origen was aware of the Jewish canonical doctrine of inspiration, holding that the Spirit had forsaken Judaism and was now active in the church. However, formerly, following the ascension of Jesus, many more manifestations of the Spirit were evident than in his day. 'Nevertheless, even in this day,' he wrote, 'there are traces of a few people whose souls have been purified by the logos.'[101] But Origen also introduced the concept of non-inspiration. On the one hand he notes that here are things written in the prophets and in Paul that are not by inspiration, Moses having commanded some things by his own authority[102] as similarly Paul in his letters.[103] On the other hand, Origen also refers to the writings of the Greek philosophers[104] and of some Christian writings[105] as being written without inspiration. Elsewhere Origen speaks of philosophers and heretical Christians as having what Stendahl has called 'negative inspiration' inspiration by Satan or the demons.[106] This negative inspiration is commonly attributed to the heretics by Origen's predecessors, going back to Hermas.[107] Since, in Origen's contrast between inspired and noninspired gospels, he is contrasting the four accepted Gospels with heretical gospels (of the Egyptians, of the Twelve, of Basilides, of Thomas, of Matthias, and others), Kalin is probably correct in concluding that Origen does not employ the distinction inspired/non-inspired as a means of division or separation among orthodox writings but, similar to the inspired-negative inspiration demarkation, as a division between orthodox and heretical or pagan writings.[108]

Eusebius speaks readily of the activity of the Spirit in his own day. In his sermon for the dedication of the church built by Constantine at the site of Christ's tomb, he says that not all know the cause of the building of a church at this place, 'but those enlightened about divine matters by the power of the inspiration of the Holy Spirit (*hoi men ta theia dunamei pneumatos entheou pephōtismenoi*) both know and understand.'[109] Eusebius regarded the Spirit

[99] *Hom.* 5.8 *in Lev.;* Kalin, *op. cit.,* pp. 53f.
[100] *Contra Celsum* 4.1; Kalin, *op. cit.,* p. 54.
[101] *Contra Celsum* 7.1–11; Kalin, *op. cit.,* p. 113.
[102] Possibly with Malt. 19:8 in mind.
[103] I Cor. 7:10, 12; Orig., *Hom.* 16.4 *in Num.*
[104] *Contra Celsum* 3.68, 81; *Hom.* 2 *in Cant.,* etc.
[105] *Hom.* 1 *in Lc.; Princ. Pref.* 8.
[106] *Mand.* 11.2–3. Stendahl, *op. cit.,* p. 245.
[107] That Hermas is now probably to be dated about the end of the first century A.D., cf., Sundberg, 'Canon Muratori,' p. 12 n. 33a; W. Coleborne, 'A Linguistic Approach to the Problem of Structure and Composition of the Shepherd of Hermas,' *Colloquium,* 3:133–42 (1969); William J. Wilson, 'The Career of the Prophet Hermas,' HTR, 20:21–62 (1927).
[108] Kalin, *op. cit.,* pp. 79–109.
[109] *De laud, Const.* 11.3; Kalin, *op. cit.,* p. 135.

as having been miraculously present at the choice of Fabian as Bishop of Rome (*c.*A.D. 236).

For when the brethren were all assembled for the purpose of appointing him who was to succeed to the episcopate, [writes Eusebius], and very many notable and distinguished persons were in the thoughts of many, Fabian, who was there, came into nobody's mind. But all of a sudden, they relate, a dove flew down from above and settled on his head, in clear imitation of the descent of the Holy Ghost in the form of a dove upon the Saviour; whereupon the whole people, as if moved by one divine inspiration (*hōsper huph' henos pneumatos theiou kinēthenta*), with all eagerness and with one soul cried out 'worthy,' and without more ado took him and placed him on the episcopal throne.[110]

For aid in his composition of his Church History, Eusebius writes, 'We pray God to give us his guidance, and that we may have the help of the power of the Lord' (*sheon men hodēgon kai tēn tou kuriou sunergon schēsein euchomenoi dunamin*),[111] and speaks of his own inspiration for writing the Life of Constantine.[112] Eusebius writes of revealed directions to the martyrs at Lyons,[113] of the frequent indications of the continuing activity of the Spirit in the times of Ignatius and Polycarp,[114] of the prophetic charismata present in the church in Justin's age,[115] and to the time of Irenacus.[116] Early in the third century Narcissus, bishop of Jerusalem, miracuously changed water into oil.[117] The power of God was present even in Eusebius' own time, especially in the witness of martyrs.[118]

Examples such as these can be multiplied in the church writers throughout the period of the formation and canonization of the Christian Bible. As Kalin observes, the concept of inspiration is not used in the early church as a basis of division between canonical and non-canonical orthodox Christian writings.[119] In forming the list of the Christian Old Testament, the criteria of inspired/not-inspired is not used to divide between the included and excluded books. When the Shepherd of Hermas, the Christian writing that came closest to being included in the New Testament of all excluded books, came to be excluded from the developing New Testament canon in Eusebius' time, it was not attacked as non-inspired.[120] Throughout the entire period of canonization, discussion in the fathers over the question of inspiration or non-inspiration or negative inspiration has to do, virtually without exception, with orthodoxy versus heresy.

[110] *H.E.* 6.29.3; Kalin, *op. cit.*, p. 135.
[111] *H.E.* 1.1.3; cf., 1.5.1.
[112] *v. Const.* 1.11.2; Kalin, *op. cit.*, p. 137.
[113] *H.E.* 5.3.2f.; Kalin, *op. cit.*, p. 137.
[114] *H.E.* 3.37.3; Kalin, *op. cit.*, p. 138.
[115] *H.E.* 4.18.8; Kalin, *op. cit.*, p. 138.
[116] *H.E.* 5.3.4; 5.7.1–6; Kalin, *op. cit.*, pp. 138f.
[117] *H.E.* 6.9.1; Kalin, *op. cit.*, p. 139.
[118] *H.E.* 8.7.1ff.; Kalin, *op. cit.*, p. 140.
[119] *Idem.*
[120] Sundberg, 'Making the NT Canon,' p. 1224; *idem.* 'Canon Muratori,' pp. 12–15.

The question of inspiration, thus, does not function as a criteria of canonization; the common view of the church throughout this period is that inspiration is broadly and constantly present in the church.

The import of this material for the question of the Christian doctrine of inspiration is obvious since it describes a circumstance in the early church that is far different from the commonly accepted doctrine that the books of the Bible are different from all other writings because they are inspired, that inspiration is determinative for canon, that inspiration is synonymous with canon. It is this doctrine of the exclusivity of inspiration to the Bible canon that caused historians of the canon to use the terms 'scripture' and 'canon' as synonyms. If by 'scripture' we mean inspired books, and if all inspired books are in the canon, then 'scripture' and 'canon' are synonyms. But Kalin has now made it abundantly evident that this doctrine did not inform the early church in the process of canonizing its Bible.

We are now able to trace the history of the doctrine of the exclusivity of inspiration to canonical books. Its origin is in Judaism. When the Jewish canon was being settled about the end of the first century A.D., a doctrine of canon was propounded at the same time. It is first found in the writings of Josephus[121] and appears to have been protested by IV Ezra.[122] It is found also in the Talmud.[123] This doctrine states that inspiration existed only from Moses to Ezra; thus only the canonical books are inspired. The function of this doctrine was not that of a criteria of canonization, but appears more probably to have been to drive out of circulation those books that were not included in the canon. When the early church became aware of this Jewish doctrine, it immediately agreed with it. The church concurred that the Spirit of inspiration had ceased in Judaism; 'God now pours his Spirit upon the church' was the Christian response.

Following the rise of humanism, when Christians became cognizant of the content of Jewish literature, not John Calvin, but early Calvinists found this Jewish doctrine, first propounded in Judaism after the church had arisen and become separated from Judaism, and appropriated it to the Protestant canon which excluded the Apocrypha, and used it dogmatically against the Roman Catholic decision at Trent. Thus, for example, the Westminster Confession of 1647 reads, 'The books commonly called Apocrypha, not being of divine inspiration, are no part of the Canon of Scripture.' It is this doctrine, appropriated by early Calvinists from Judaism, that spread virtually throughout Protestantism, strengthening its dogmatic stance against Catholicism, that we have learned to accept as the Christian doctrine of the inspiration of the Bible. This

---

[121] *Contra Apion.* 1.8.

[122] 14.451.

[123] George Foot Moore (*Judaism, I* [Cambridge, Harvard University Press, 1927], 237, 243, 421) who cites Tos. Sotah 13.2; cf., Sotah 48b and Yoma 9b; Tos. Shabbat 13 (14).5; Sanhedrin 11a; cf. Tos Yadim 2.13.

is what Protestants traditionally have meant when affirming that the Bible is inspired. Now we are able to know this doctrine for what it is. It is not a Christian doctrine. It arose in Judaism subsequent to the church's separation from Judaism. And it counters the plain teaching about inspiration of the canonical books it purports to defend.

The Christian doctrine of inspiration is that taught in the New Testament itself and held in the early church throughout the period of canonization of the Christian Bible, that God pours out his Spirit upon Christians and the church. In Christian thought throughout the period of canonization there is no doctrine restricting inspiration either to a particular period or to particular persons, except that inspiration is denied to heretics. The consequent meaning of canonization and the function of the canon in the church was in keeping with the meaning of the term the church used to designate its list, 'the canon' (ho kanōn), 'the measure' or 'the standard.' Thus, in forming the canon, the church acknowledged and established the Bible as the measure or standard of inspiration in the church, not as the totality of it. What concurs with canon is of like inspiration; what does not is not of God. Thus the Christian doctrine of inspiration describes the unity of Christians with their canon; the Spirit of God that inspires these books dwells in and enlivens them. Christian inspiration, therefore, is seen not to be a derivative from the New Testament; it comes from God. But Christian inspiration parallels biblical inspiration, complementing it, and opening every Christian age to theological verisimilitude, like the books of the Bible and the periods in which they were written are verisimilar. The Christian doctrine of inspiration encourages the Christian, to paraphrase Henry Cadbury, neither to run the peril of modernizing Jesus nor of archaizing ourselves.[124] Rather, the Christian doctrine of inspiration, drawn from the New Testament and Christian thought from the period of Bible canonization, is that the Christian embodies the living and enlivening Spirit of God in every age for that age, the Bible canon being the standard, the measure in all things. 'The letter kills, but the Spirit makes alive.'[125]

---

[124] Henry Joel Cadbury, *The Peril of Modernizing Jesus* (New York, Macmillan Co., 1937); *idem,* 'The Peril of Archaizing Ourselves,' *Interpretation,* 3 (1949), 331–42.
[125] II Cor. 3:6b.

11

The Unity Behind the Canon*

Nicholas Wolterstorff

I

In this chapter I propose to explore what I shall call 'the unity behind' the Christian canon, in contrast to 'the unity within'. I think the best way to introduce the issues I have in mind is to present a brief narrative of a certain part of the history of modern hermeneutics.

In Wilhelm Dilthey's narrative of the origins of modern hermeneutics, Friedrich Schleiermacher is the great hero; in Hans-Georg Gadamer's narrative, Schleiermacher is the principal culprit. There is very little difference in the chronicle of their tellings; Gadamer follows Dilthey, for example, in assigning to Schleiermacher a decisive role in the origins of modern hermeneutics. What makes their narratives nonetheless strikingly different is the difference in their evaluation of Schleiermacher's role. The creative moves by Schleiermacher that Dilthey praises are regarded by Gadamer as fatefully mistaken.

Let it be said that Gadamer happily echoes Dilthey's praise of Schleiermacher for having finally posed the fundamental question, 'What is interpretation?' It is Schleiermacher's answer to that question which Gadamer disputes. Or more precisely, it's the answer that Gadamer, following Dilthey, *interprets* Schleiermacher as having offered that he disputes. Among the charges Gadamer lodges against Schleiermacher is that Schleiermacher proposed replacing interpretation of the text with exploration into the psyche of the author. I think Schleiermacher proposed no such thing. He did not, indeed, share Gadamer's insistence that it is for the *meaning of the text* that we interpret. He proposed that we interpret for the *discourse*, the *speech acts*, that the author used the text to perform; and authorial discourse is not to be identified with the meaning of a text. But neither is it to be identified with the psyche of the author.[1] On this occasion I must set

---

* From C. Helmer and C. Landmesser, eds., *One Scripture or Many? Canon from Biblical, Theological, and Philosophical Perspectives.* © 2004 Oxford University Press. Reprinted by permission of the publisher.

[1] I develop these points in detail in my *Divine Discourse: Philosophical Reflections on the Claim that God Speaks* (Cambridge: Cambridge University Press, 1995).

this important issue off to the side, however, along with most other parts of Gadamer's critique, so as to focus on a point in Gadamer's criticism where I think he is correct—correct both in the view he attributes to Schleiermacher and in the criticism he makes of that view.[2]

At the heart of Schleiermacher's hermeneutic, so says Gadamer, is the proposal that we replace all forms of dogmatic interpretation with the so-called 'hermeneutic circle'. Rather than interpreting a text in the light of certain convictions we already have that we bring with us to the text, we should interpret the text in terms of itself, said Schleiermacher. What that comes to, concretely, is that after arriving at a tentative interpretation of the parts, we then, in the light of that tentative interpretation of the parts, proceed to a tentative interpretation of the whole; that done, we reverse direction and, in the light of our tentative interpretation of the whole, refine our interpretation of the parts, and so forth, back and forth, constantly adjusting our tentative interpretations of parts and whole until, finally, we arrive at interpretative equilibrium, that is, at an interpretation that is stable at all levels. This strategy, when applied to the interpretation of Christian scripture, has the obvious implication, for the relation between interpretation and dogma, that rather than perpetuating the traditional practice of interpreting scripture in the light of dogmatic convictions brought *to* the interpretation, we allow dogma to emerge *from* our interpretation.

For all his praise of Schleiermacher, Dilthey thought there was one point on which Schleiermacher failed to carry through on this programme of allowing dogma to emerge from our interpretation of scripture rather than employing it in the conduct of our interpretation. In his biblical interpretation, Schleiermacher took for granted the unity of Christian scripture. That must be seen, said Dilthey, as the last remaining point at which dogmatic conviction is allowed to guide and shape interpretation. Rather than assuming unity in advance and then interpreting in the light of that conviction, we must allow such unity as there may be in these writings to emerge from our interpretation of the whole in the light of the parts and the parts in the light of the whole.

Whereas Dilthey chastised his hero, Schleiermacher, for having thus stopped just short of carrying through his project of dogma-free interpretation, Gadamer repudiated the project itself—the project of emptying one's head of all preconceptions about the text and, by the employment of the hermeneutic circle, simply interpreting the text in terms of itself. Impossible, says Gadamer. Schleiermacher is here reflecting his Enlightenment historicist background. We always and unavoidably approach texts with 'prejudices'—that is, prejudgements—

---

[2] The relevant text of Gadamer is of course Part II of his *Truth and Method*, trans. Joel Weinsheimer and Donald G. Marshall, 2nd rev. edn. (New York: Continuum, 1993). Currently the best collection and English translation of the relevant writings by Schleiermacher is Friedrich Schleiermacher, *Hermeneutics and Criticism, And Other Writings*, ed. and trans. Andrew Bowie, Cambridge Texts in the History of Philosophy (Cambridge: Cambridge University Press, 1998).

concerning verbal meaning and propositional content. In that regard, interpretation is always and unavoidably 'dogmatic'.

This is not some sad lamentable fact about interpreters. Quite to the contrary; prejudgements are a condition of interpretation, they make interpretation possible. Interpretation requires that one approach the text with more or less appropriate prejudgements (*praejudicia*) concerning verbal meaning and propositional content. In the actual process of interpretation the text then talks back. It allows this prejudgement here to stand, while saying about that one there that it is mistaken. Having received this negative assessment, we discard that prejudgement there and replace it with a new and—so we hope—improved prejudgement. If the text now allows this replacement to stand, we move on to another prejudgement that the text tells us is mistaken. We correct that one. And so it goes until, in the ideal case, the text has nothing but affirmative things to say concerning our prejudgements. The back-and-forth between whole and part in Schleiermacher's theory is replaced, in Gadamer's theory, by a back-and-forth between the prejudgements of the interpreter and the talking back of the text.

I am myself of the view that Gadamer's attempt to free himself from the objectivist assumptions of the Enlightenment in his description of how interpretation does and must work is considerably less thoroughgoing than he and his followers suppose. For consider that process whereby the text tells us whether our prejudgements concerning verbal meaning and propositional content are correct or incorrect. It is a process that Gadamer, strangely, never discusses in its own right. But presumably it consists of an engagement of the interpreter with the text whereby a belief is produced in the interpreter concerning some point of verbal meaning or propositional content, that belief then being compared by the interpreter with the belief on the matter that he holds as a prejudgement. Nowhere does Gadamer suggest that the interpretative engagement with the text, whereby beliefs are produced concerning verbal meaning or propositional content, *is itself* in any way shaped by prejudgements on the part of the interpreter. He talks about that belief-forming process as if it were immune in its workings to one's immersion in tradition.

I make these comments about Gadamer so as to provide a context for my calling attention to a type of interpretative prejudgement that Gadamer never takes note of, namely, an interpretative prejudgement concerning the unity behind the text. But before I get to that, let me observe that modern biblical scholarship strikes me as fundamentally Schleiermacherian in its self-understanding, rather than Gadamerian. I speak here as someone who reads around in biblical scholarship but is himself not a member of the guild of biblical scholars; I am, accordingly, subject to correction by specialists. But it is my clear impression that the great majority of leading biblical scholars regard interpretation conducted in the light of dogmatic convictions as a fundamental violation of proper interpretative practice. They often put the point in terms of not 'violating the text': to interpret in the light of dogmatic convictions is to violate the text. There is nothing per se wrong with interpreting a biblical text *for* its doctrinal content, assuming it has such; but it would violate the text to interpret it *in the light of* doctrinal convictions that one brings *to* the text. If doctrine is to put in its appearance anywhere in our interpretation, it must emerge *from* the interpretation. Convictions about the unity of some book of scripture would be included among doctrinal convictions; the modern inter-preter accepts Dilthey's criticism of Schleiermacher's practice. Rather than interpreting *in the light of* one's prior convictions about some book's unity, let such unity as it may have *emerge from* one's interpretation.

The relative unity and disunity of individual biblical books has in fact been a matter of major concern for biblical scholars in the modern period; it is, after all, the perceived disunity of some biblical books that motivates the claim, made over and over in the modern period, that the text we have is a collage of pre-existing units. This intense concern with unity and disunity does not carry over to the Bible as a whole, however. Most biblical scholars are pretty much indifferent to whether or not the Christian canon has unity as a whole. Perhaps the canon seems to them on the face of it to lack any unity worth talking about; or perhaps there is nothing in their background convictions that makes the issue of any interest or significance to them one way or the other.

There are important exceptions. Some scholars, out of whatever motivation, have engaged in the project of trying to discern unity *within* the canon—not to impose it but to discern it. That attempt has taken three main forms. And let me say, here, that in all that follows I will confine myself to speaking of the Christian canon and its interpretation; the canonical texts of Judaism, along with the history of their interpretation, are different in important ways. There was, for some time, a *biblical narrative* movement, according to which the writings comprising the Christian canon are united by the connected narrative they offer of God's mighty acts. A second development was the *biblical theology* movement, according to which these writings are united by a shared theology. And thirdly, there has been the movement of so-called *canon criticism*, spurred by my Yale colleague Brevard Childs. I am not fully confident that I understand this last movement; but it is my impression that it consists, for the most part, of emphasizing the ways in which the writings comprising the Christian canon contain intertextual references, allusions, quotations, and so forth.

One might wonder whether we should mention, as yet a fourth way of trying to discern unity within the canon, Karl Barth's suggestion that what principally unites the Christian canon is that all its parts, each in their own way, are a witness to Jesus Christ. I think not. Barth's suggestion was never meant as a thesis concerning a unity that emerges inductively but as a proposal for a unifying dogmatic interpretation of scripture. Let me add, lest there be any misunder-standing, that I myself do not regard this as a flaw in Barth's approach; my point is rather that Barth's proposal belongs to a different species from the others.

It would distract from my purpose in this paper were I to offer an evaluation of these three proposals. Let me confine myself to two observations. First, we should resist the rigid insistence that each and every book in the canon fully exhibit the unity proposed; no text except the very briefest would ever count as unified on that insistence. And secondly, it is my judgement that each of the three proposals has succeeded in calling to our attention interesting and important modes of unity in the Christian canon. I myself continue to think, for example, that the canon as a whole exhibits the interlocking themes of divine creation, redemption, and consummation; the fact that the book of Ecclesiastes, for example, says nothing about redemption and consummation, but speaks only of God as creator and of our human existence within creation, seems to me to count not at all against that interpretation.

II

One assumption that all of us bring to most of our interpretative endeavours, whether or not it be scripture that we are interpreting, is that what we have in hand is *a work*. Not always. Sometimes we have no idea, one way or the other, whether that is the case. And sometimes we conclude that what was presented to us as a work, and what we initially assumed to be that, is not really a work. The conclusion of many biblical interpreters about the biblical book of Isaiah is an example of this last point. Though it is presented in our canon as a work, most biblical interpreters are of the view that it is really *two* works—or perhaps even three. When I spoke above of a species of prejudgement that eludes Gadamer's attention, I had in mind the prejudgement that one is dealing with something that has the unity consisting in its being a work.

What makes something *a work*? That strikes me as an exceedingly important question for the theory of interpretation. Unfortunately, it is also one to which neither I nor anyone else—to the best of my knowledge—has ever worked out a satisfactory detailed answer. Paul Ricoeur comments in various places about the concept of a work, his main point always being that a work is a very different sort of entity from a sentence.[3] A sentence belongs to the language in a way in which a work does not; conversely, a work is a product of labour in a way in which a sentence is not. That's true; but it doesn't get us very far. I judge that the main question we want answered is what individuates and differentiates works. For example, what determines whether the component in the Bible called 'Isaiah' is one work, two works, three works, or more? Ricoeur gives no help in answering that question—other than the suggestion that the answer may just

---

[3] See for example, chapters 5 and 8 in his *Hermeneutics and the Human Sciences*, trans. John B. Thompson (Cambridge: Cambridge University Press, 1981).

possibly have something to do with the labour that resulted in the writing that our Bibles call 'Isaiah'.[4]

Clearly contradiction within what one has in hand is not proof that it's not a single work; many among those of us who have written lengthy works have suffered the indignity of some critic pointing out that we contradicted ourselves within the course of our discussion—or if not quite contradicted ourselves, wrote passages that are in one and another sort of logical tension with each other. Nor do repetitions establish that we're not dealing with a single work. I mean absent-minded repetitions; it's obvious that repetitions which play a literary or rhetorical function do not establish that it's not a single work. Many among those of us who have written lengthy works have also suffered the indignity of some critic pointing out that we have needlessly repeated ourselves at various points. Nor does the fact that at certain points the writing in hand is a collage of words taken verbatim from some other work establish that the writing does not constitute a single work. My own *Lament for a Son* is a collage of this sort. Mainly it consists of sentences that I myself composed. But there are also passages taken from scripture, a passage from Augustine's *Confessions*, one from a sermon of John Donne, another from Maria Dermoût's *The Ten Thousand Things*, and yet another from Henri Nouwen's *A Letter of Consolation*. The totality is me speaking, even though I did not myself compose all the sentences. I would reject out of hand the suggestion that, because I did not myself compose all the sentences, the text as it stands does not constitute a single work.

That which determines whether the writing one has in hand is *a work* is something that lies *behind* the text, rather than being a discernible feature of the text itself. Discernible features of the text may provide some evidence, one way or the other; but as will be clear from the points made in the preceding paragraph, the use of discernible features as evidence for whether or not one has *a work* in hand is a tricky matter.

More specifically, it appears to me that what determines the identity and diversity of works is an intentional act of a certain sort. Yes, that old bug-bear of modern hermeneutics: intention! Though it would not be a misuse of English to call it 'authorial intention', nonetheless, given the standard use of 'authorial', it would be misleading. 'Authorial' is standardly connected with our English verb, 'to author'. I did not author those passages that I just mentioned in my work *Lament for a Son*; I incorporated them into my work without having authored them. I recall reading somewhere that Walter Benjamin once contemplated composing a work that would consist entirely of passages taken from other writers. Had he done so, that would then have been a work of Benjamin no

---

[4] An interesting and important question, for the answering of which I have no expertise, is when the concept of *a work* emerged. A highly esteemed scholar of antiquity to which I put the question replied that it had definitely emerged in Greek culture by 500 B.C.; it was his impression that it had emerged even earlier in Hebraic (or Semitic) culture.

part of which he would have authored. Whether or not Benjamin did contemplate composing such a work, one can imagine someone doing it—though unless it were very brief, it would be staggeringly time-consuming. Far more efficient oneself to compose the sentences for what one wants to say, rather than finding all of them somewhere else!

In addition to our verb 'to author', we also have the verb 'to authorize'. It is that verb which expresses the relevant idea. Whether or not the words one has in hand constitute *a work* is not determined by authoring but by *authorizing*. The issue is whether someone *authorized* this totality as a work. The origin of the sentences in our present book of Isaiah is neither here nor there with respect to the determination of whether it is a work; what matters is whether someone *authorized* the totality of these words *as a work*. If so, they constitute a work, no matter where the sentences came from; if not, they do not constitute a work. Of course, even if our present book of Isaiah was authorized *as a work*, it's possible that there are two or three parts of our present book each of which had itself previously been authorized *as a work*. Works can come in layers: works within works within works.

And what is it to authorize something *as a work*? That's the central question! I have done it. That is, I have authorized something as a work—this present essay being one example of that. No doubt everyone reading this chapter has done so as well. But I confess to not having a very firm reflexive grip on what it is that I did.

Authorizing a text as a work presupposes one's judgement that it satisfies one's demands for completeness. That final chapter, that final section, that final sentence, finishes it, makes it complete, ready to be sent out into the world as a unit. But what sort of completeness? After all, a paragraph also has a certain sort of completeness, as does a section of a chapter and a chapter. As does a sentence. I agree with Ricoeur, however, that the unity of a sentence is significantly different; sentences belong to the language in a way that paragraphs, sections, chapters, and books do not.

III

Perhaps the best way to understand what's going on in our authorization of something we have written *as a work* is to borrow and adapt a line of thought that is regularly used in musical analysis. Those who analyse music standardly think of musical works as multi-layered structures of relative tension and relaxation.[5] Tension is the property notes have of, as it were, calling for other notes to follow them; relaxation is the property notes have of answering that call. In 3/4 meter, for example, the first beat in a measure calls for two following weak beats. When

[5] An excellent presentation of this way of thinking, along with references to the primary literature, can be found in Jeremy Begbie's *Theology, Music, and Time* (Cambridge: Cambridge University Press, 2000).

one superimposes rhythm on meter, when one adds the intervallic relationships inherent in melody and harmony, when one adds the dynamic contrasts characteristic of music of the modern West, and so forth, one then gets layer upon layer of tension–relaxation structures, with the final note finally bringing all these dynamic structures to the halt that the composer wanted. Of course one can play individual movements of a work separately, and individual sections of movements; often there is value in that. But the composer judges that something of worth is missed if one does only that; something important in the multi-layered tension–relaxation structure of the whole will be missed if the entire work is not played and listened to. No doubt most of us have listened to one and another of the individual variations making up Bach's *Goldberg Variations* by itself, and found it worth doing so. But most of us also know that to listen to the work piecemeal is to miss out on a quite incredible spiritual experience that can only be achieved by listening to the whole work at one sitting.

I suggest that it is along such lines that we should also understand written works. To authorize a sequence of words *as a work* is to declare that one wants one's readers to read it as a totality, on the ground that only thus will they experience the kind of completeness—of tension and relaxation—that one was aiming at. Sometimes one judges that they will not even adequately understand the parts without reading the whole. But that's not always the issue. Sometimes, for example, one adds a certain chapter because one wants to say something about questions that will naturally and properly have occurred to the reader in the course of the discussion, even though no misunderstandings threaten if the chapter is not included. It was this sort of consideration that led me to compose and include, as the final chapter in my *Divine Discourse*, what I called 'Historical and Theological Afterword'. It was not the aim of the chapter to forestall and preclude misinterpretations. Rather, I judged that the preceding discussion would have raised in the mind of virtually every reader a question that, if I said nothing at all by way of addressing it, would leave them feeling unsatisfied with the entire discussion. It was in that way that the book would have been incomplete without the final chapter. Ignoring that question would have been acceptable for an article, but not for a book. An implication of that last point is this: not only are tension–relaxation structures of different sorts; they also come in different magnitudes. The magnitude of an article contributes to determining what need not be included.

To authorize a sequence of sentences *as a work* is to declare that it has a good and proper tension–relaxation structure, and to invite the reader, for that reason, to experience it as a totality. To experience it only in fragments and not in its totality would be to miss out on something of worth in its multi-layered tension—relaxation structure. Correspondingly, for us, the readers, to interpret it *as a work* is to accept that invitation of the authorizer and to read and interpret it as a whole. Of course it is sometimes a struggle to discern why the authorizer made the judgement that he did. We fail to see how a certain part contributes to the tension–relaxation structure of the whole; it seems an interference. Or we feel strongly that something is missing. The fault may not be ours; authorizers make mistakes on such matters. But the more we esteem the authorizer, the harder we try. Add that authors sometimes grow weary and publish what is not, even in their own judgement, a completed work.

There is another mode of unity in the region that I shall mention but discuss only briefly; namely, the unity among works constituted by the fact that they are all works by the same author. They all belong to the same *corpus*. A book that comes to hand with the title *Lectures on Philosophical Theology* will be interpreted rather differently depending on whether or not we take its author to be Immanuel Kant.

There are interesting differences between interpreting sentence-sequences as together constituting a single work, and interpreting them as constituting distinct works belonging to a single corpus. To mention just one example: what we would regard as regrettable contradictions if they occurred in a single work will be understood as changes of mind, or perhaps forgetfulness, if they occur in a corpus. Werner Jaeger's way of treating Aristotle's *Metaphysics* was, in effect, to treat it as works of a single corpus rather than as a single work; so too for Norman Kemp-Smith's way of treating Kant's *Critique of Pure Reason*.

One sort of work that is an important exception to what I have been saying about the role of tension–relaxation structures is the work which is a collection, a good example of such a work being a dictionary. The judgement that the composer of a dictionary—or any other sort of collection—makes as to whether his work is complete has nothing to do with tension–relaxation structures. The author simply has in mind to collect all examples of a certain sort; when she judges that she has done that, she authorizes the totality *as a work*.

With this sort of exception in mind, along with the standard case, my thesis then is this: what determines whether the text in hand is a single work is something that lies behind the text itself, in the presence or absence of a certain intentional action. It is determined by whether or not someone authorized the text *as a work*. A corollary, present in my discussion more by implication than by explicit argumentation, is that the judgement of the reader that the text in hand was authorized as a work will and should in various ways shape her interpretation of the text (collections being the exception). The reader may be mistaken in that judgement—just as the authorizer may be mistaken in thinking that his collection is complete or that his text has the tension–relaxation structures that he thinks it has. But if the reader is mistaken in her prejudgement that what she has in hand is a work, the text will not talk back in anything like the way that Gadamer thinks happens when texts tell us whether our pre-judgements about verbal meaning and propositional content are correct or incorrect. For, as I have argued, the unity of the text *as a work* is a mode of unity that lies *behind* the text.

IV

It seems all but certain that a good many of the books in the Hebrew and Christian scriptures were assembled by editors from pre-existent texts and/or oral traditions. I have argued that such origins do not prevent the resultant text from being a single work; there may well have been some person, or group of persons, who authorized it as a work. This observation naturally suggests to those of us who are Christians the question as to whether we should regard the Bible as a whole as one work with sixty-plus chapters, the exact number depending on which canon one favours. If what I have said about that mode of unity which is *a work* is correct, then there is nothing in principle against this highly diverse collection of texts all together constituting a single work; the question is just whether there has been the requisite intentional act of authorizing it as a work. And even that question comes to something less than the reader might think, given what I have said thus far. There is nothing to prevent an *interpreter* of some text, or a community of interpreters, from performing the requisite authorization: 'Be it hereby resolved that these texts be interpreted as a single work.' The authorizer need not be either author or editor.

I anticipate that some biblical scholars will reply that *there is* something in principle against interpreting the Christian Bible as a single work. What's against it is that to treat it thus is to violate the integrity of its constituent books. A variant on this objection is the insistence of some Jewish scholars that the inclusion by Christians of the Hebrew Bible within their canon is a violation of their Hebrew Bible.

Given the point I made earlier, that there may be works within works, I fail to see that this protest has any solid basis. To argue for the legitimacy of interpreting the book of Isaiah as a component within that large work which is the Christian Bible is not thereby to question the legitimacy of interpreting it as a work in its own right, thereby fully honouring its own integrity. As I mentioned earlier, not only is there worth in listening to the entire *Goldberg Variations*; there is worth in listening to individual variations by themselves. Let it be added, though, that when one knows the entire *Variations*, it is almost inevitable that that knowledge will shape, in subtle ways, how one hears an individual variation; the tension–relaxation structure that one hears and feels in the individual variation will be different from what it would be if one knew nothing but that variation. Of course it would be possible to insist that some variations are best heard with no echoes whatsoever in one's mind of the entire set. Correspondingly, it would be possible for a Jewish interpreter to insist that 'listening to' Isaiah with echoes in mind of the entire Christian canon is a decisively inferior way of 'listening to' it. But that then is the issue: the *worth* of 'listening to' it thus, not the legitimacy.

What, if anything, is the worth of Christian interpreters treating the Christian canon as having that mode of unity constituted by its being a single work? That, as I see it, is the decisive question. And let me say yet one more time that concluding that there is worth in such interpretation does not imply the worth-lessness of interpreting individual biblical books as distinct works; surely there is worth in that. The question is whether there is *also* significant worth in interpreting individual books as chapters in one single work—a work whose opening chapter speaks in narrative form of God's work as creator and whose closing chapter speaks in apocalyptic form of God's work of consummation, with most (though not all) of what lies between speaking of God's work of redemption.

Given the way the Christian canon is typically presented to us, namely, as so-called 'books' bound together in a fixed order in a single binding, I think it is virtually inevitable, for the Christian who knows the totality, that that knowledge will shape a good deal of her interpretation of the constituent books. I think it is all but impossible not to have the gospels echoing in one's ear as one reads the messianic passages in Isaiah, and vice versa; not to have the passages in Paul about the creative activity of Christ echoing in one's ear as one reads the opening of Genesis, and vice versa; not to have the prologue of John's Gospel echoing in one's ear when one reads certain passages in the Wisdom literature, and vice versa—and so forth. It is almost impossible for those who know the whole Christian Bible to not, in practice, treat it as a single work.

The overall structure of the Christian canon, in its long-ago-fixed sequence, is clear. There is a New Testament consisting of five narratives concerning Jesus and the spread of the news about him by the apostles, followed by a number of letters concerning the significance of Jesus, presented for the most part as coming from one and another apostle, with the whole package then culminating in an apocalyptic sketch of human consummation. This package is preceded by an Old Testament which, though much more diverse, nonetheless exhibits two interacting story lines: a story line of creation and providence, and a story line of redemption. In both cases, the phrase 'story line' is a bit misleading; but I don't know of a better. The creation–providence theme sometimes becomes minimally narrative in its mode of presentation; not much narrative in Ecclesiastes or Proverbs! And though the theme of redemption is, overall, far more narrative in its mode of presentation, it too sometimes becomes rather minimally so; witness some of the prophets. Once one has this overarching thematic or story-line structure of the Christian canon in mind, be it acquired intuitively or theoretically, then, so it seems to me, it becomes all but impossible for that structure not to influence in subtle ways one's reading and interpretation of individual books, sections, pericopes, and the like. It is all but impossible not to interpret the various books as belonging to a huge tension–relaxation structure beginning with the opening of Genesis and not finally resolved until the conclusion of the Apocalypse.

The reader will have noticed that I have said nothing about the ways in which interpreting a biblical book as a chapter within that large work which is the Christian canon, rather than as an independent work, influences what one takes to be the *propositional content* of the individual books; I have said nothing, for example, about a christological interpretation of the messianic prophecies. I regard the issues here as exceedingly important. Jesus already both offered interpretations of the Hebrew Bible—the 'scriptures'—and appealed to the Hebrew Bible as the interpretative context for the understanding of himself. The apostles continued this two-way appropriation of the Hebrew Bible, apparently going well beyond anything that Jesus himself offered in the details of their interpretations. The church has continued this pattern of two-way appropriation, in its details going well beyond, in turn, anything that we find in the apostles.

In many cases the interpretation offered, by Jesus, apostles, or church, of what is expressed by a passage in the Hebrew Bible, is definitely different from what the original authorizer of that passage would have meant by it. This gives the modern interpreter pause: the New Testament appears to him full of misinterpretations of the Hebrew Bible, and later interpreters seem to him even worse offenders. But that's how it goes when extant texts are incorporated within new, more comprehensive, works: some of the words of the extant text will now have to be interpreted as expressing something different from what they expressed originally. I mentioned that I had incorporated a brief passage from Maria Dermoût's *The Ten Thousand Things* within my work *Lament for a Son*. In the context I gave it, the passage definitely expressed something different from what it expressed in its original context of her novel about Indonesia. Are those who interpret the passage within the context I gave it thereby *mis*interpreting it? That seems to me not the right way to describe what is going on in such interpretation.

Let me say again that this issue is important: the ways in which certain passages from individual books of the Bible acquire new propositional content when treated as components of that single work which is the entire Christian canon. I spent some time discussing the matter in my *Divine Discourse*. But I have come to think that it is a mistake to let what we say on this issue become all-determinative for our decision as to whether or not the church should treat its canon as a single work. It is only one aspect of the larger issue.

What led me to see this was reflecting on my own experience of deciding when a book of mine was a finished work, and my discovery that I had to resort to an adaptation of the categories of musical analysis to understand fully what went into my own decisions. The musical analogue released me from what I now see as my fixation on propositional content. In music there usually isn't any propositional content; nonetheless, there are works, and we perform and hear passages as parts of works. The relevant overarching categories, so I have suggested, are those of tension and relaxation.

V

Those readers of this chapter who have read my *Divine Discourse* may well have expected from me a quite different treatment of the unity of the canon from that which I have presented here. They will have expected me to talk about that unity of the canon which consists of God being its ultimate authorizer. But in my book I not only explored the suggestion that God is scripture's ultimate authorizer; I also claimed that if one does regard God as related to scripture in that way, one will regard scripture as God's *work*, not as God's *collected works*. I now see that regarding God as the authorizer of what stands in the Christian scriptures does not settle, one way or the other, whether those scriptures should be regarded as one work or many—God's single *opus* or God's *opera omnia*. I continue to find attractive the idea I developed in *Divine Discourse*, that God is scripture's ultimate authorizer. Here I have gone beyond that to reflect on what is at stake in the issue of whether, in authorizing scripture as his own speech, God authorized sixty-six-plus works, or one single work.

12

Visits to the Sepulcher and Biblical Exegesis*

Eleonore Stump

INTRODUCTION

In a recent article describing an innovative interdisciplinary project of some magnitude now underway at the University of Chicago,[1] Francisca Cho Bantly and Frank E. Reynolds express a view rapidly gaining currency among both philosophers of religion and historians working in religious studies, namely, that 'the traditionally rigid dichotomy in religious studies between philosophy of religion on the one hand and strictly "empirical" studies on the other must be challenged' (p. 3). What philosophers of religion need to do, in the view of Bantly and Reynolds, is to pay more attention to the nature and the history of particular religions in order to learn 'lessons drawn from the "historicity of reason"' (p. 4). It is certainly true that philosophers of religion have sometimes tended to talk about 'mere theism' and to ignore the rich and complicated details of individual religions and the history of their interpretation. Having granted this, however, I would like to suggest that, paradoxically enough, historians of religion can benefit from this very same prescription. In particular, the historical approach to biblical studies which until quite recently has held a virtual monopoly on studies of biblical texts in secular universities puts enormous emphasis on the importance of history in biblical studies, and yet it has generally been carried on in unreflective isolation from approaches to biblical exegesis in other periods.

In this paper I want to add to the incipient incursions into the isolation of the historical approach by juxtaposing a representative sample of contemporary historical biblical scholarship, namely, Raymond Brown's well-regarded interpretation of the empty tomb stories in the Gospel of John, with an example of biblical exegesis drawn from the middle ages. The medieval period, of course, abounds in intellectually sophisticated biblical commentaries produced by philosophers and theologians, such as the work by Saadya Gaon or Gregory the

* © *Faith and Philosophy,* vol. 6 (1989). Reprinted by permission of the publisher.

[1] 'Hedgehogs and Foxes: Rethinking the Philosophy and History of Religions,' *Criterion* (1988), 2–6. I am grateful to Philip Quinn for calling this article to my attention.

Great on the book of Job. But for my purposes here, the salient features of medieval biblical exegesis can be shown most graphically not by considering the lengthy and detailed exposition of a medieval philosopher or theologian but rather by looking at the summary presentation of such exposition in a typical medieval play, the *Visitatio Sepulchri*, an Easter play from the twelfth century. Furthermore, in endorsing the prescription laid out by Bantly and Reynolds, I do not mean to subscribe to the cultural relativism (epistemological or ethical) sometimes associated with such prescriptions. From the fact that it is detrimental to understanding to be ignorant of the thought of other cultures or other periods of history, it doesn't follow that the epistemological or moral norms of any and every period are correct (for that period—or with whatever other qualifier relativism may find suitable), or that there is no objective standard of truth or moral goodness by which practices can be judged. So in this paper I want to do more than just compare approaches to biblical texts from two different cultures, the contemporary academic and the medieval religious. I want also to reflect philosophically on the presuppositions on which these approaches are based, to ask what they commit us to and whether they must or even can be acceptable to everyone.

BROWN'S INTERPRETATION OF THE EMPTY TOMB STORIES IN THE GOSPEL OF JOHN

It will help at the outset to have before us the story of the empty tomb from the Gospel of John. Here it is in Brown's translation:[2]

(1) Early on the first day of the week, while it was still dark, Mary Magdalene came to the tomb. She saw that the stone had been moved away from the tomb; (2) so she went running to Simon Peter and to the other disciple (the one whom Jesus loved) and told them, 'They took the Lord from the tomb, and we do not know where they put him!' (3) Peter and the other disciple started out on their way to the tomb. (4) The two of them were running side by side; but the other disciple, being faster, outran Peter and reached the tomb first. (5) He bent down to peer in and saw the cloth wrappings lying there, but he did not go in. (6) Presently, Simon Peter came along behind him and went straight into the tomb. He observed the wrappings lying there, (7) and the piece of cloth that had covered the head, not lying with the wrappings, but rolled up in a place by itself. (8) Then, in turn, the other disciple who had reached the tomb first also entered. He saw and believed. ((9) Remember that as yet they did not understand the Scripture that Jesus had to rise from the dead.) (10) With this the disciples went back home. (11) Meanwhile

---

[2] Raymond E. Brown, *The Gospel according to John* (Garden City, NY: Doubleday and Co., 1970), pp. 978–9. Subsequent references to this work will be given by page numbers in parentheses in the text.

Mary was standing [outside] by the tomb, weeping. Even as she wept, she bent down to peer into the tomb, (12) and observed two angels in white, one seated at the head and the other at the foot of the place where Jesus' body had lain. (13) 'Woman,' they asked her, 'why are you weeping?' She told them, 'Because they took my Lord away and I do not know where they put him.' (14) She had just said this when she turned around and caught sight of Jesus standing there. She did not realize, however, that it was Jesus. (15) 'Woman,' he asked her, 'why are you weeping? Who is it you are looking for?' Thinking that he was the gardener, she said to him, 'Sir, if you are the one who carried him off, tell me where you have put him, and I will take him away.' (16) Jesus said to her, 'Mary!' She turned to him and said [in Hebrew], 'Rabbuni!' (which means 'Teacher'). (17) 'Don't cling to me,' Jesus told her, 'for I have not yet ascended to the Father. But go to my brothers and tell them, "I am ascending to my Father and your Father, to my God and your God!"' (18) Mary Magdalene went to the disciples. 'I have seen the Lord!' she announced, reporting what he had said to her.

Some people will, no doubt, be put off by the flatfootedness of this translation, evidently dead to the rhythm and nuances of English prose; and certainly comparison of the flowing King James version with the Greek makes clear that the original does not compel such awkward English. But I raise this sort of objection only to dismiss it. Brown's concern is not with the translation. He is not interested in the sort of issues which must occupy those whose main purpose is only to produce a translation, namely, what sort of English prose, what connotations and cadences, best capture the thought and manner of the original and at the same time preserve readability. Brown's manifest concern is rather with the history underlying the narrative in the story. For his purpose, he brings together an impressive battery of philological and historical skills as well as a thorough acquaintance with the secondary literature, so that his interpretation of the story is valuable not only because he presents his own historically informed judgments but also because he summarizes the secondary literature and so gives a general overview of the state of scholarly opinions about the text.

Brown begins by saying that the Gospels disagree about the visits to the empty tomb. (He summarizes the disagreements in a helpful chart on p. 974.) First, there is a disagreement, he says, about the time of the visits to the tomb. Mark claims it was very early and the sun had risen; Matthew describes it as growing light; Luke states that it was at first dawn; and John says that it was early and still dark. Next, there are disagreements over the women who went to the tomb. Mark says it was Mary Magdalene, Mary (the mother of James), and Salome; Matthew claims that it was Mary Magdalene and the other Mary; Luke says it was Mary Magdalene, Mary (the mother of James), Joanna, and others; and John mentions only Mary Magdalene. Then there is the question of what happened at the tomb. According to Mark, the stone covering the entrance to the tomb was already rolled back, and a youth was sitting inside on the right. According to Matthew, there was an earthquake and an angel descended; he rolled back the stone and sat on it outside the tomb. According to Luke, the stone was rolled back and there were two men standing inside the tomb; and John says roughly the same thing but identifies the two in the tomb as angels. There are also corresponding discrepancies concerning the conversations that take place at the tomb between the women and the men or angels. Finally, there are disagreements about the actions of the women. Mark says that the women fled, trembling and astonished, and told no one. Matthew says that the women went away quickly with fear and great joy and told the disciples, and Luke maintains something roughly similar. John says that Mary ran to Peter and the Beloved Disciple and told them that the body had been taken away. There are also disagreements about the appearances of Jesus to the women, although Brown doesn't make as much of these. Luke says nothing about appearances to the women; Mark and John claim Jesus appeared first to Mary Magdalene. Matthew says that Jesus appeared to the women as they were going to tell the disciples he was risen and that they held him by the feet and worshipped him.

Besides the discrepancies between John's account and that of the other Gospels, Brown maintains that there are also inconsistencies within John's account itself. His list of such inconsistencies includes the following (995). (1) Mary Magdalene comes to the tomb alone in v. 1 but uses the expression 'we' in v. 2. (2) She concludes that the body has been taken away in v. 2 but doesn't look into the tomb until v. 11. (3) There are confusions in the account of Peter and the Beloved Disciple. The most notable of these is that in v. 9 they are said not to understand the scripture prophesying Jesus' rising, but in v. 8 the Beloved Disciple is said to believe. (4) The belief of the Beloved Disciple has no effect on others, including Mary Magdalene. (5) It is not clear how Mary Magdalene got back to the tomb after going to alert Peter and the Beloved Disciple. (6) In v. 12 Mary Magdalene apparently doesn't see the burial clothes that Peter and the Beloved Disciple saw; the text speaks only of her seeing angels in the tomb. (7) Her conversation with the angels doesn't advance the action of the story. (8) She turns to Jesus in v. 14 and then again in v. 16. Finally, although it is not included in this list of Brown's, we may add a last point which concerns him at some length in the notes: (9) Jesus tells Mary Magdalene not to cling to him (or not to touch him, as the more traditional translation has it), because he has not yet ascended, but only slightly later in the narrative he encourages Thomas to probe his wounds.

In the face of what he sees as external and internal inconsistencies, Brown is concerned to trace the historical background of this story. He wants to use the inconsistencies as a means of discovering what the primitive versions of the story were like. He is motivated in this enterprise not by antiquarian interests but by a conviction that earlier forms of the story are more likely to be historically accurate. In discussing details of the discrepancies, he makes clear what is apparently for him a general guiding assumption, namely, that developments of biblical narratives are often constructed wholesale, out of religious or political motivations. So, for example, asking about the details of a sort of narrative, Brown says,

'Some of the additional material stems from the compositional efforts of the evangelist who has made an appearance serve as a vehicle for theological emphases' (973). In ruling out a certain interpretation of the statement in v. 8 that the Beloved Disciple believed, Brown says, 'the evangelist certainly did not introduce the Beloved Disciple into the scene only to have him reach such a trite conclusion' (987). In discussing the appearance of Jesus to Mary Magdalene, he says 'Perhaps the original story contained no significant words of Jesus, a fact that forced each evangelist to fill in as he thought best' (1004). And in general, Brown considers the options for passages in the text to be either ancient tradition or 'the free composition' (997 and 1000) and 'individual genius' of the evangelist (975).[3] Given this view of his, it is understandable that he would try to discover ancient forms of the story lying behind the text as we now have it.

To find what he takes to be the underlying earlier stories, Brown employs a methodology of this sort. First, he examines the passages in which he finds inconsistencies and considers the efforts of modern historical critics to explain away the discrepancies. So, for example, in considering the apparent inconsistency of Mary's turning to Jesus twice, Brown cites (but rejects) the view of one scholar who supposes that Mary turned away, after the initial turning toward Jesus, because Jesus stood before her naked, having left his burial clothes in the tomb, and she was too modest to look at him. Similarly, in examining Jesus' perplexing injunction to Mary not to touch him, Brown mentions (but again rejects) two interpretations: that the point of the prohibition was to keep Mary from temptation since Jesus was naked, and that the prohibition is a signal to Mary letting her know that with his resurrection Jesus wants there to be an end to the intimate relationship they formerly had. On the whole, Brown shows good judgment in his review of the literature, generally rejecting the farfetched interpretations and siding with more sensible ones. He is, however, inclined to suppose that even the most acceptable interpretations leave the inconsistencies in place.

Although Brown objects to what he calls harmonistic approaches to these stories, because in his view they 'do too much violence' to the text, (972) it seems clear that his own methodology is itself a sort of harmonization. He reconciles the inconsistences he believes to be in the text by sorting the apparently inconsistent bits into different stories, each of which is internally harmonious and self-consistent. He then considers how these disparate stories might have been woven into the text as we now have it. It is not easy to discover his methodological principles in this part of his project. On the one hand, he is willing to

---

[3] In the context, on p. 997, Brown is disagreeing with another scholar and denying that a portion of text *is* the free composition of the editor, not, however, because he thinks the editor eschews free composition but because he supposes that this particular portion of text can't be accounted for with such an explanation. On p. 975, Brown is considering whether a certain narrative is the product of 'long recitation' or of the evangelist's individual genius, and he tentatively sides with the former hypothesis—thereby indicating that in his view the latter hypothesis is an acceptable sort of explanation for certain portions of the text.

attribute to evangelists or editors both the alteration of individual details in the stories they received from earlier tradition and the wholesale construction of parts of the narrative. So, for example, he sides with the view that 'the Lucan and Johannine dating of the Jerusalem appearances on Easter Sunday was probably dictated by theological interests' (972); and he holds that an evangelist 'may have adapted the story [of an appearance of Jesus, which the evangelist received from tradition] and made it fit into a locale dictated by his purpose in writing' (971). While he acknowledges that it is possible the evangelist was correct in identifying Peter's companion as the Beloved Disciple, he has no hesitation in supposing that the evangelist made up large parts of the account of Peter and John in this chapter: 'the hypothetical companion of Peter in the original form of the Johannine story was unimportant. . . . But John has changed the story by identifying him as the Beloved Disciple and giving him a major role: he runs with Peter to the tomb; he reaches it first and looks in; ultimately the sight of the burial clothes leads him to believe' (1001).

On the other hand, Brown also apparently supposes that evangelists and editors had an attitude of deference, almost slavish deference, towards the accounts they received from tradition. So, for example, Brown points to what he takes as an inconsistency between vv. 1 and 2—'Magdalene comes to the tomb alone in vs. 1, but speaks as "we" in 2'—and maintains that this instance should be added to the 'extraordinary number of inconsistencies that betray the hand of an editor who has achieved organization by combining disparate material' (995). Although Brown doesn't say so explicitly here, it seems reasonable to assume he means that if this apparent inconsistency, and others as well, 'betray the hand of an editor,' it is because the inconsistency pointed to can be best explained as a result of the work of an editor. In other words, we are to imagine the editor or evangelist having available to him two accounts (whether written or oral) involving women at the empty tomb— either two already present in the tradition, or one received from tradition plus another version of the same story produced by the editor himself. He then combines these two accounts in some way, perhaps picking a piece from each and adding them together, with or without some new material added to effect the joining. But he does this joining in such a way as to leave an inconsistency. So in the apparent inconsistency between vv. 1 and 2 here, one of the accounts the editor used included a story of several women coming to the tomb and therefore had the appropriate phrase involving the plural pronoun; and the second account had Mary Magdalene coming to the tomb alone. The editor then produces his own—inconsistent—account by combining the account of Mary Magdalene's coming to the tomb alone with the phrase involving the plural pronoun, thereby producing the inconsistency that enables Brown to infer that the hand of an editor has been at work.

Brown reasonably enough says nothing here about the psychological state of an editor which could explain his responsibility for such an inconsistency, but it seems to me plausible enough to assume there are really only two candidates: (1) the editor was stupid, to an uncommon degree, and didn't notice that he was introducing an obvious, even blatant, inconsistency; (2) the editor was aware of the inconsistency but had some reason for accepting it anyway. Since the adoption of the first hypothesis would be just an embarrassment for any scholar, the principle of charity requires that we attribute to Brown the second hypothesis instead. And if we then ask what possible reason there could be for an editor's permitting an inconsistency in his text as plain as the one supposed to appear in vv. 1 and 2, the most plausible answer would seem to be that the editor is deferential to the accounts he is working with, so deferential that he prefers slavish adherence even to the form of the words over the disrespect that would be shown to the account he is working with by changing a 'we' to an 'I.'[4]

Using this methodology Brown advances a theory of the following sort. He holds that 'behind [John] xx 1–18 [are] the traces of three narratives: two narratives of visits to the empty tomb, and the narrative of an appearance of Jesus to Magdalene. Whether these were combined by the evangelist himself . . . or came to him in whole or partial combination . . . we are unable to say. However, the evangelist made his own contribution in any case, for he adapted these stories to serve as a vehicle for his theology about faith and about the meaning of the resurrection' (998).

The first of these narratives is the story that several women came to the tomb on Sunday morning, found it opened, and told the disciples. According to Brown, an angel interpreter was added later, and still later this expanded story was joined to a story of the appearance of Jesus. The primitive narrative is preserved in vv. 1–2 and 11–13. These verses are separated because the evangelist is combining two forms of that narrative. Vv. 1–2 is an early form, and vv. 11–13 is a later, truncated form of the same story. Along the way the evangelist or editor reduced the number of women in the original story to just Mary Magdalene; he also changed the story as regards the angels, and the conversation he attributes to Mary Magdalene and the angels is 'merely a repetition of vs. 2' (999).

The second narrative Brown finds behind the text is the story that several disciples went to the tomb, found it empty, and went away puzzled. The evangelist has changed the story to assign a prominent role to the Beloved Disciple, thereby introducing some of the inconsistencies noted in the list above. The claim that the Beloved Disciple believed was not part of the original story but was introduced into the narrative for apologetic purposes (1002).

Finally, the third narrative underlying the text on Brown's view is the story of an appearance of Jesus to Mary Magdalene. According to Brown, the version of this story in vv. 14–18 is changed substantially from its ancient form. The inconsistency of describing Mary Magdalene as turning to Jesus twice is a result of the fact that the editor needed to connect this story with what preceded it.

---

[4] Whether this presupposition about the editor or evangelist coheres with the other one Brown relies on, namely, that the editor is perfectly willing to change many details in the account he received or even to add wholesale constructions of his own to the account received, is an issue that I will consider further in the last section of this paper.

Brown thinks the editor or evangelist joined this story to the preceding material simply by repeating a verse from within the story itself. To introduce the third narrative, the editor 'borrowed from [verse] 16 where it belongs' (1003) the line that Mary turned to Jesus, thus producing the apparent inconsistency of having Mary turn to Jesus immediately after she has already turned to him.[5] On the basis of this theory about the earlier narratives underlying the biblical text, Brown goes on to make some suggestions about the theological concerns of the evangelist and the religious significance of the story. Since my focus is on the approach Brown takes towards the text rather than the lessons he draws from that approach, I will omit his theological points from this summary.

VISIT TO THE SEPULCHER

Like many early medieval plays, this twelfth-century version of the *Visitatio Sepulchri* was embedded in the liturgy of the church and was performed as part of the church service on Easter morning. The exact provenance of the play is unknown, as is the playwright and composer, but the play came to be associated with the Abbey St. Benoit de Fleury in central France. The actors' lines are largely taken from scripture; they are in Latin, and they are sung rather than spoken. (The music is clearly an integral part of the play, but I will unfortunately not be able to take account of it here.) Together with some stage directions and musical notation, the play is preserved in the *Fleury Playbook*, which is one of the largest collections of medieval plays still extant. The ahistorical character of the play is made dramatically evident from the outset by the appalling anti-Semitism in the opening speech of Mary Salome and the immediately succeeding speech of Mary Magdalene. The Marys express the sort of anger and contempt towards Jews that might have characterized some short-sighted, overzealous follower of Jesus at the events leading to his crucifixion, and they portray these emotions as suitable for all Christians of any period. And they take as the objects of their anger not some particular opponent among those playing a significant role in the crucifixion of Jesus, but rather all Jewish people of any time, with the reprehensible anti-Semitism which was typical of the middle ages, as the history of the Jews in Europe makes evident. (The text of the play is presented in Appendix I.)

The play is in effect both a harmony of the relevant portions of the Gospels and a commentary on them. Without trying to take account of every detail in the

---

[5] Interpretations such as this one, which are not uncommon in Brown's work, make it unclear whether it is an appropriate use of the principle of charity to prohibit attributing to Brown the view that the editors and evangelists involved in the production of the biblical text were at least sometimes unusually stupid. Otherwise, how is one to account for Brown's proposal that an editor who, according to Brown, introduced new characters and invented dialogue for them nonetheless could find no way of joining two narratives other than by borrowing a verse from within one narrative and repeating it in a way that produces what Brown considers to be an obvious inconsistency?

Gospel narratives, the playwright has arranged the major events of the disparate accounts into what he takes to be an ordered and plausible account.[6] Furthermore, by filling in some of the sparse detail of the scriptural accounts, playwright has given a certain interpretation of the biblical story and shown how he understands its dramatic movement. In what follows, I will give an interpretation of the play in order to show the harmonization the play employs, and then I will go on to discuss the methodology of this sort of harmonization.

To begin with, unlike Brown's interpretation of the empty tomb stories, which has as its main concern the disciples' coming to faith and the theological predilections of the evangelist, the play clearly focuses on the women, and in particular on Mary Magdalene. The disciples remain at home grieving. They show no inclination to mourn at the tomb, to weep over the dead body of Jesus, or to anoint it with spices. Furthermore, their grief is assuaged by coming to believe that Jesus is risen, and so we might not unreasonably suppose that one important source of their sorrow is the wonder whether they were mistaken in believing that Jesus was sent by God or was the savior they had hoped he was. But the pain of the women is different, as their coming to the tomb at the crack of dawn suggests. It is a suffering connected more to the person of Jesus, the sort of suffering that can find some relief in caring for the battered, dead body of the one loved. The source of their grief is much less disappointment in a great theological hope and much more a personal loss, like the sorrow of a mother over her dead child. While it is no doubt some comfort to the mother to believe that the soul of her child is not dead but raised to be with God, the pain at the heart of her grief will continue unabated even in the face of such a belief because it has its source in the fact that she must continue to live in the absence of a person she was devoted to. The pain of her loss can be stemmed only to some extent by the thought that the person she loved now lives happily elsewhere.

While all three Marys come to the tomb in the grip of such a sorrow, the apparition of the angel removes two of the Marys from the scene, and only Mary Magdalene remains. The angel's announcement that Christ is risen makes no dent in her grief, precisely because her grief isn't rooted in worries about the nature of Jesus' mission or God's vindication of Jesus' claims. And her grief is so deep that not even a vision of a supernatural being at dawn in a graveyard will frighten her away. Somewhere in the canonical or apocryphal scriptures there may be another character whose reaction to the sight of an angel (even in less frightening circumstances) is indifference, but such characters are certainly not common.

Her one thought in this crisis is to enlist the help of competent males, not for the sake of provoking their sympathy or stimulating them to comfort her in some way, but for the sake of getting the body back. So she goes to the disciples to say

---

[6] I do not mean to suggest that the playwright is singlehandedly responsible for the harmony of the Gospels which his play constitutes; harmonies of the Gospels, of course, stem from as far back as the Patristic period. By speaking of the playwright's harmonization here, I mean nothing more than the harmonization the playwright accepts and weaves into his play.

that some unidentifiable villainous 'they' have taken the body away and she doesn't know where 'they' have put it. But perhaps the disciples will know or know how to find out or in some way exert themselves to get the body back. The disciples, however, are absorbed in their own kind of sorrow. At her news they run as fast as they can to the tomb, leaving her behind. After seeing the tomb, they talk together wonderingly, focused altogether on the tremulous thought that Jesus might have risen and that their hopes of him as savior will after all be fulfilled. With their minds occupied by the excitement of this possibility, they go home, without evincing any further thought or care for Mary Magdalene. There is certainly no question of their longing for the dead body of Jesus or of their remaining at the tomb, grieving for its absence; and by the time Mary Magdalene makes her way back to the tomb, they have already gone home.

As she stands there, once again alone and weeping, she sees *two* angels in the tomb, and this time instead of the unheeded annunciation that Jesus is risen, they ask her a Socratic question: 'Woman, why are you weeping?' The question is a good one, because there is something not quite rational about the intensity of her grief. If Jesus is an ordinary mortal, then she has to be prepared, at some time, to accept his death, but the depth of her sorrow suggests that such an acceptance will never be forthcoming in her. On the other hand, if the extremity of her grief is warranted, then perhaps Jesus is not an ordinary mortal; and in that case perhaps there are ways of being close to him, of coming into his presence, even if he is no longer possessed of a body. Reflection on the angels' question might thus give her pause in her pain and put her on the road to finding the kind of comfort of interest to her. But in the story the angels' question has no such salutary effect; it provokes only another repetition of her complaint: 'they have taken my Lord away, and I do not know where they have put him.' And the angels respond with the lame line the playwright gives them, the inept sort of line one might produce in the face of a woman's inconsolable weeping: 'Don't cry!,' together with another repetition of the point which has already proven futile, 'He is risen.'

Providence, which tried to relieve her grief first with one angel and then with two, now produces the only thing which it seems will ever comfort her, Jesus himself. The messengers having failed, the master himself enters the scene, but somehow unrecognizable, so that Mary at first takes him to be the gardener. (Why he does not bring it about that she knows at once who he is has to remain a matter of speculation. The story of the interaction between Jesus and Thomas (John 20:29) suggests that there is some benefit to the believer in believing in the resurrected Jesus without overwhelming physical evidence: 'blessed are they that have not seen and have believed.')[7] Still unrecognized, he asks her two Socratic questions, the first the question the angels asked her—'Why are you weeping?'— and then a follow-up question designed to prompt her in the right direction for

[7] For some philosophical discussion of this general point, see my 'Faith and Goodness,' forthcoming.

an answer to the first question: 'Whom are you looking for?' If the one you are looking for is an ordinary human being, this unwillingness to be comforted is too much; but if this inconsolable sorrow is appropriate, then the one you seek is the sort of being who can be with you always even if he is not embodied. But like the preceding speeches of the angels, these questions of Jesus have no effect on her pained preoccupation: 'Sir,' she says, 'if you are the one who has taken him, tell me where you have put him, and I myself will take him away.'

Whether out of love for her and compassion for her pain or out of a recognition that even the creator has no right to betray her love by temporizing any longer, Jesus gives up and makes himself known to her in calling her by name. And her reaction to him is one of overflowing joy; she calls to him and reaches out for him. But he avoids her touch and warns her away, on the grounds that he is not yet ascended. What this line means is controversial (to medieval commentators as well as to us today). But in the play, very shortly after this, Jesus does not rebuff the women who hold him by the feet. The immediate inference the play suggests to us, then, is that when Jesus appears to Mary Magdalene, he is in the midst of some process and that until that process is completed, he cannot be touched. If this inference is correct, then it seems that Jesus' appearance to Mary Magdalene is somehow untimely, that it interrupts this process in which he is involved, that it disrupts the appropriate timetable for his appearance to his followers. As the play presents it, then, Jesus' overriding concern in the initial events of his resurrection is not to encourage the theological beliefs of the men who are his followers but to assuage the grief of a single sorrowing woman who loves him. And it is a concern so overwhelming, the play suggests, that he is willing to alter abruptly the appropriate or natural order of some theological or metaphysical process he is engaged in.

But with the first great staunching of Mary Magdalene's sorrow, Jesus disappears; whatever else is necessary to comfort her can apparently be safely entrusted to angels. The other women come back; and in the time-honored fashion for helping people recover from a traumatic sorrow, the angels give them all a job to do, a job of some importance and prestige, namely, to carry to the disciples the sort of news that will comfort *their* grief, a grief which can apparently wait for its comfort: Jesus is risen, and they are to go to Galilee to see him. The women are preparing joyfully to bring the message when Jesus reappears. The state in which he appears this time is apparently different from the one in which he appeared to Mary Magdalene, because this time he feels obliged to begin by urging the women not to be afraid; and the stage directions for the play indicate he is to appear in glory. Having completed whatever process the pain of Mary Magdalene convinced him to interrupt, he returns to repeat the commission the angels have just given the women. Jesus adds nothing to the injunctions the angels have given the women; but by bringing them into his presence and himself repeating those injunctions, he makes sure they are secure in their knowledge of his living love for them. Furthermore, by giving them this contact with himself, he enhances the authority of the pronouncement they are about to make to the disciples, thereby adding to the prestige of the job he has given them and consequently adding to its ability to comfort them as well.

It is clear that the playwright's methodology rests on the principle that the Gospels must all be taken to be telling only the truth, but that they need not all be telling the whole truth. On the play's understanding of the biblical stories, each of the biblical accounts is incomplete but can be accommodated within the broader view of events provided by the sort of harmonization in the play. A first question to ask about this harmonization is how well it matches the textual data. Does it incorporate all the details in the biblical texts? Are the biblical texts compatible with the story as the harmonization of the play tells it? The answer to these two questions cannot be an unqualified affirmative. (For the details on the fit between the play and the Gospel accounts, see Appendix II.) Not all the particulars of the biblical stories are included; there is, for example, no representation of disbelief on the disciples' part on hearing from any of the women. Furthermore, there are apparent discrepancies between the play and the accounts in the Gospels. For example, there are more women mentioned in Luke's account than in the play. The angel who is outside the tomb sitting on the stone in Matthew has in the play the speech assigned to two angels (or men, depending on how one understands the description of these characters in Luke) in the tomb in Luke. And the message announced by one angel inside the tomb in Mark and outside it in Matthew is announced outside the tomb by two angels in the play.

It is important, however, to notice that nothing whatsoever hangs on these discrepancies between the play and the biblical accounts except our assessments of the playwright's cleverness (or our understanding of a particular tradition in medieval biblical exegesis). For, clearly, we could continue in the way the playwright began, adding episodes and weaving them into the whole story, and by that means accommodate all the biblical data in the play, though with less economy than the playwright has shown. We could, for example, get rid of a troublesome disparity between Matthew and the play simply by adding one more scene at the start of the play involving one angel seated on the stone outside the tomb.

Therefore, what is perhaps more worth asking than questions about the consistency between details in the play and in the biblical stories is whether the drama that the playwright has concocted by his method of interweaving the disparate biblical accounts has any sort of plausibility as a story, or whether it is simply a hash made of an ill-fitting assortment of episodes and motivated by a clumsy, literarily inept dogmatism. While this question obviously can't prove decisive for an evaluation of the playwright's method of dealing with the apparent discrepancies in the Gospels, it is pertinent to the issue. If the harmonization results in a narrative which is fantastically contrived or wildly disjointed, that is *some* reason for rejecting the methodology behind the harmonization. On the other hand, if the harmonization yields a plausible and dramatically consistent story, then we have *some* reason for doubting the charge Brown levels against this methodology, namely, that such 'harmonistic approaches' do violence to the text (972). This attitude towards the methodology of the play is based on the kind of intuitions we take for granted, for example, in reading detective novels. When the detective questions the witnesses to the murder, he tends to iron out the apparent discrepancies among their stories by conflating them, in the manner of this play, as long as he can do so without producing a story that is inconsistent or implausibly complex; and unless there are overriding reasons for rejecting his manner of investigation, we generally find it reasonable that he should proceed in this way. But whatever else can be said about the play's harmonization of the Gospels, and there are undoubtedly many defects in it, it seems to me without question to constitute a story which is not only unified but in fact dramatically powerful and moving.

METHODOLOGY

The play's obtuseness to any historical considerations is evident, most distress-ingly in the appalling anti-Semitism it manifests, and a clear view of the play's deficiencies in this regard will help us to appreciate the impressive historical learning and historical sensitivity Brown and scholars like him bring to their work. While no right-minded person would want to return to the blind disregard for history evinced by the play, for which Brown's sort of approach is an important corrective, I am more interested here in the kind of corrective to Brown's approach which we get by reflecting on the methodology underlying the play.

The methodology underlying the play and the methodology used by Brown can be thought of conveniently and appropriately as mirror images of each other. Each begins with a subjective perception of discrepancies or tensions within the texts under consideration. Though Brown speaks of these discrepancies as inconsistencies[8] and I adopt the terminology from him, what is at issue here is quite often not inconsistency in a philosopher's sense, in which a set of claims is inconsistent only if it entails both a proposition and the contradictory of that proposition, but something much weaker. Furthermore, Brown's belief that there is an inconsistency even of this weaker sort in the text is often entirely subjective, not based on either historical evidence or philosophical argument. Sometimes what he takes as an inconsistency is simply generated by his assumption that what a Gospel account doesn't assert it implicitly denies.[9] He sees an inconsistency among the biblical texts as regards the number of women at the tomb, for instance, because different accounts name different women. To see an inconsist-ency in this case is apparently to assume that because the Gospel of John, for

---

[8] See, for example, p. 995.
[9] I am indebted to Alvin Plantinga for this way of putting the point.

example, doesn't assert there were other women with Mary Magdalene, we must read the text as denying that other women accompanied Mary Magdalene. If this assumption were generalized, it would, of course, be not only subjective but also highly dubious. Reliance on it would obviously render the interpretation of most texts, from Shakespeare to the daily newspapers, impossible or absurd. And so, ordinarily, we reject Brown's sort of assumption. On other occasions, what Brown takes as inconsistencies are just tensions in the text. So, for example, Brown lists as an inconsistency the claim in the Gospel of John that the Beloved Disciple believed when he saw the graveclothes and the parenthetical statement in the next verse that the disciple did not as yet know (or understand) the scripture which predicted Jesus' resurrection. But, of course, we can also read these verses as complementary rather than as inconsistent. On such a reading the parenthetical remark is explaining why the Beloved Disciple believed on the basis of the graveclothes and not on the basis of the scriptures, as readers of the Gospel might perhaps expect.

Beginning with such subjective and no doubt differing perceptions of tensions within the texts, both Brown and the play try to harmonize the texts by removing the apparent discrepancies. But the harmonizations attempted are quite different and rely on significantly different presuppositions. The presupposition used in the methodology on which the play is based is simple: it takes all the biblical accounts to be true. On that presupposition, the play tries to weave all the disparate accounts into one coherent drama which reconciles the texts. Brown's presuppositions are considerably more complicated. He tries to remove the inconsistencies he believes are in the texts by sorting the inconsistent passages into different stories. Each story is then a self-consistent whole, and the inconsistencies are accounted for by attributing them to the combiner of the stories, the evangelist or editor. Brown thus presupposes (P1) that, unlike the stories found in the later tradition, the stories of the earlier tradition were all consistent, in his sense of 'consistent,' which seems equivalent to 'tension-free.' And he accounts for the current state of the text with a pair of presuppositions, (P2) that editors or evangelists freely changed details in the accounts that were passed down to them and even added wholesale construction of their own, and (P3) that editors were slavishly deferential to the accounts they received and so allowed obviously inconsistent details to remain when they combined accounts. (The alternative to (P3) is the embarrassingly implausible presupposition, namely, (P3′) that the editors were so unusually stupid as not to notice the obvious inconsistencies they introduced in their combining of accounts.) Finally, the motivating presupposition for the whole enterprise is (P4) that earlier accounts are much more likely to be accurate witnesses than later accounts.

It is important to see that Brown's presuppositions are not themselves demonstrated by historical evidence. For some of these presuppositions historical considerations cannot provide conclusive evidence for the view expressed. So, for example, history cannot show us that all early accounts are consistent—that is, without tension—because, to begin with, history cannot demonstrate conclusively that we have found all the early accounts. Even if all the accounts we have are consistent and can be dated as early by some means which does not itself rely on (P1), there might be early accounts which we have not yet found or recognized as early and which are nonetheless not consistent or tension-free. More importantly, although history gives us examples of cases in which earlier accounts are more reliable than later ones, as (P4) claims, it also gives us examples in which later accounts are as reliable as earlier ones (as we currently believe to be the case in Muslim transmission of the Koran or oral transmission of poetry in certain nonliterate cultures), or even examples in which later accounts are more reliable than earlier ones, in virtue of having had access to better informants than the earlier accounts had (as a modern historian's account of a certain period in Roman history is more reliable than Suetonius's description of that same period).[10] Though Brown in fact concedes as much when he admits that the tradition may be ancient even if the witnesses are late, this theoretical concession is not much in evidence in his practice here.[11] Finally, to have historical evidence for (P2) and (P3), we would have to uncover corresponding texts which could be dated by some means not based on these presuppositions themselves, and in the later of two corresponding accounts we would have to find discrepancies with the earlier text as well as sizable additions absent from the first text. But even then, unless the editor of the second document or some contemporary of his left us an account of how he proceeded in producing that document, it would remain more a matter of speculative inference than of historical data that the relation between the two texts is to be explained by supposing that the editor of the later text used the earlier text as his source and that in producing his own text he changed many details in the earlier text, added passages invented wholesale, and yet simultaneously clung to his source with great deference, refusing even to alter pronouns in the source text.

If historical considerations cannot warrant these presuppositions, suppose we look at them from a philosophical point of view. Considered philosophically, however, these presuppositions are not overwhelmingly plausible, taken individually, or even clearly a coherent whole, taken collectively. Consider, for example, the third presupposition. If we take it as (P3), the inconsistency between it and (P2) is much more jarring than many of the inconsistencies Brown lists for the Gospel of John; and if we take it as (P3′), we lose in plausibility whatever we gain in coherence. As for (P2), it is itself based on presuppositions which are worth trying to be clear about. To ordinary readers, Brown seems to be suggesting that the evangelists or editors were committed Christians and yet entirely easy about making up episodes involving the appearances of angels, details about when, where, and to whom Jesus appeared, and even whole speeches of Jesus.[12] This is

---

[10] I am indebted to Joel Kramer for this point.

[11] See p. 1003; see also 1001 where he says that a late addition need not be legendary.

[12] See, for example, Raymond Brown, *The Virginal Conception and Bodily Resurrection of Jesu* (New York: Paulist Press, 1973), pp. 17–18.

a practice which would be condemned by standards common in our time, as well as in times before and after the period of the Gospels, as knowingly telling untruths, and telling them, moreover, about the religious figure one is devoted to. Objectively considered, a person who would engage in such a practice seems to resemble the worst among the contemporary television evangelists: he is hypocritical and fraudulent, or else he is self-deceived in some unsavory way. Brown suggests that the evangelists themselves saw nothing wrong with this practice, but a suggestion of that sort is beside the point. Even if the television evangelists involved in recent scandals supposed that their activities were not morally objectionable, and their social and religious communities shared their view, their names would nonetheless have become bywords for moral sleaziness. Is it plausible to suppose that the persons responsible for the Gospels, whatever they may have thought about themselves, in fact had the same sort of character or the same moral habits as those particular television evangelists? Though no doubt some scholars will think it is, I find such a supposition not at all plausible and difficult to square with the moral tenor of the texts themselves.

It is, of course, customary to repudiate this sort of argument energetically. Sometimes we are told that the evangelists did not conceive of themselves as doing history at all, that our whole notion of doing history was unknown at this period, and that the evangelists were engaged in a special sort of practice found particularly in this period of history in which fabricating stories about the central figures of one's religion was morally acceptable. I find this claim very difficult to believe. We do not, however, need to consider it here because Brown's own view is not so extreme. He does take the evangelists to have understood what history consists in and to have had some concern with doing history, whatever else they meant to do as well. For example, in another context, Brown says 'Matthew and Luke apparently accepted the virginal conception as historical.'[13] And he argues that we ought to reject the suggestion that the genealogy in the Gospels attributing Davidic descent to Jesus was a construction of Hellenistic Jewish Christianity, because, he says, we can't imagine that James, the brother of Jesus, would have acquiesced 'in such a fictional affirmation about the family ancestry.'[14] Apparently, then, on Brown's own view the evangelists and other early Christians did have a sense of history, could distinguish history from fiction with regard to stories about Jesus, and would (at least sometimes) have been unwilling to countenance fiction about Jesus, even if they found it altogether acceptable to fabricate other sorts of accounts.[15]

[13] *Ibid.*, p. 31.
[14] *Ibid.*, p. 55.
[15] Brown claims that the evangelists were aware that in introducing angels they were dealing only with 'imaginative description' and not with 'historical facts' (*ibid.*, p. 123). It would be worthwhile I think, to take a closer look at the arguments available in the literature for this claim to see to what extent they rest on historical data and to what extent they are the result of ideological presupposition.

Brown himself responds to the claim that his methodological presuppositions rest on an unpalatable view of the evangelists in this way: 'Does this [the view that the evangelist Luke was wrong in claiming that the risen Jesus could eat or could be touched] imply that an inspired evangelist is employing a falsified argument? . . . [No, rather] the terminology 'true' and 'false' should not be simplistically applied here for several reasons.'[16] The list of his reasons includes some claims which seem inadequate to support a negative answer to the question whether 'an inspired evangelist is employing a falsified argument.' For example, he says that some details about Jesus 'may reflect the artistry of effective narration,' and that Luke 'has a special tendency to objectivize the supernatural.' These reasons would be decisive for the issue in question only if Brown thought the evangelist meant to be writing fiction rather than history or was unable to distinguish history from fiction or was entirely willing to countenance fiction instead of history about Jesus. But since Brown himself apparently rejects such views, it is not immediately clear why the suggestion that the evangelist was engaged in artistic narration should count as a reason for rebutting the charge that the evangelist was 'employing a falsified argument.' The most telling reason in Brown's list is that in falsely describing Jesus the evangelist is relying on a prior tradition, which is the source of the falsehood. But, of course, this reason doesn't address the issue of how we are to understand those cases in which the evangelist himself constructed his account of Jesus wholesale.

I don't want to make too much of these objections to Brown's methodology, however. Perhaps there is some way of reconciling (P2) with (P3), other than replacing (P3) with the improbable (P3′). Perhaps there is some credible and consistent explanation of the presuppositions underlying (P2) that does not imply an unpalatable and implausible evaluation of the evangelists. For that matter, perhaps there is some way of making sense of Brown's practice without supposing that it rests on the presuppositions I have presented here. It is important to see that, even if we did not have to worry about the plausibility and coherence of Brown's presuppositions, his methodology raises a different and substantial concern.

On Brown's methodology, all the stories we are left with will necessarily be fairly simple and free from tension. Any tension in a narrative will constitute an apparent inconsistency, which will be resolved by segregating the conflicting parts of the narrative into different stories. And so it is hard to see how Brown's methodology could ever leave us with a complicated story, with the sort of rich and complicated drama outlined by the play. Furthermore, in the style of exegesis Brown represents there is in general a perplexing deadness to the nuances of drama and narrative. Neurobiologists tell us that a patient with significant damage to certain areas of the right cerebral cortex is often unable to process contextual cues adequately, so that if such a patient is told by his boss at a construction site where a

---

[16] *Ibid.*, p. 88.

load of lumber has just been dumped, 'Give me a hand, Joe,' he is likely to stare at his hands in confusion and say, 'Which one?.' Our conviction, which the brain-damaged patient does not share, that the question 'which one?' is an inappropriate response in this context to the injunction 'Give me a hand' is hard to explain, but nonetheless entirely right. No doubt it depends, at least in part, on our being able to put together many bits of information about the context in which the injunction is uttered. Similarly, it may take some reflection to explain why most of us find ludicrous the suggestion Brown cites as one scholar's considered opinion, that what explains the Gospel's description of Mary as turning twice to Jesus is the fact that Jesus was naked and modesty made her turn away, at any rate initially. Perhaps this conviction of ours also has to do with the social context in which the episode takes place. In a society in which people are generally clothed in public, the public nakedness of a person is not likely to go unremarked;[17] and so most of us would find incongruous the suggestion that Jesus was naked but that the text, or the tradition, failed to remark on that fact.

Brown himself is too sensible to approve such extreme interpretations, but even in his moderate approach there is a curious absence of sensitivity to the dramatic possibilities of the text. So, for example, Brown dismisses the episode between Mary Magdalene and the angels because he says her conversation with the angels doesn't advance the action at all (995). Or in discussing the appearance of Jesus in Matthew 28:10, he supposes that it must be an insertion into an already existing narrative because in the text Jesus simply repeats what the angels have already said (1002). But both these suggestions show a remarkable blindness to the dramatic possibilities of the episodes Brown is ready to dismiss, as reflection on the play makes clear. Whether this deadness to drama makes any difference to assessments of the historical accuracy of texts is, of course, another matter. It depends entirely on our subjective assessment of whether reality is more often like the simple, tension-free narratives Brown reconstructs as the early tradition underlying the evangelist's account, or more like the subtle, complicated dramatic story the play tells. My own experience has been unequivocally on the side of the view that the reality in which human lives are embedded is rarely simple.

But what about Brown's objections against the methodology underlying the play? Such harmonistic approaches, Brown says, go beyond the text and do violence to it (972). Brown recognizes, of course, that it is quite easy to reconcile many of the passages he takes as inconsistent. For example, the apparent differences of the time at which the visit to the tomb takes place can be readily reconciled by supposing that it was the time of day at which the sun is just beginning to rise. Such a time of day may be described with equal appropriateness as 'early and still dark' (John) or 'growing light' (Matthew) or 'very early

---

[17] See, for example, Mk. 14:51–2.

when the sun was rising' (Mark).[18] (The grouchy early riser will describe the time as still dark, and the all-night reveller will say, with satisfaction or chagrin, that it is growing light or that the sun is rising.) But Brown maintains that such 'harmonistic approaches' do 'too much violence to the Gospel evidence' and 'venture beyond the evidence' (972). It is, however, difficult for me to see why he thinks so. Why should a methodology which accepts its texts as true and tries to see how they might cohere be thought guilty of going beyond the texts or doing violence to them? If any methodology is guilty of this charge, why shouldn't we rather judge that it is Brown's own methodology, which cuts out certain portions of the text as later fabrications and pastes together other portions to reconstruct hypothetical earlier, simpler accounts that allegedly underlie the text? At any rate, to take seriously Brown's objections against the methodology used by the play, we would need at least some definition, drawn from literary theory, of what it is for an interpretation to go beyond a text or do violence to a text. And then we would need an argument to show that this definition fits the methodology employed by the play but not the methodology Brown himself employs.

CONCLUSION

The juxtaposition of Brown's interpretation and the medieval play show us the importance of the prescription Bantly and Reynolds promote, that philosophers and historians need to talk to each other (philosophers and historians and literary theorists, we might add), and that these groups have a great deal to learn from each other. The naive inattention, even blithe obliviousness, to history shown by the play should render us all grateful for the learning made available to us through the researches of historically oriented biblical critics such as Brown. On the other hand, what reflection on harmonizations such as that of the play shows us is that historical critics also have something to learn from philosophers. It is important to recognize the difference between historical evidence, on the one hand, and philosophical presuppositions and methodological commitments, on the other; and once the difference is recognized, it is important to reflect on those presuppositions and commitments with philosophical sensitivity and skill. When we examine Brown's interpretation of the empty tomb story in the Gospel of John, it is clear that his conclusions are largely a construct of his methodology

---

[18] Commentators sometimes make much of the fact that the verb for rising in Mark's description of the time of the visit to the tomb is in the aorist, indicating past tense. But since the verb itself can mean 'appear above the horizon' as well as 'rise,' the tense of the verb itself will not support the claim that on Mark's account the time of the visit was after, rather than during, sunrise. (If we take the variant 'anatellontos,' found in some manuscripts, the point is only strengthened.) Even the Anchor Bible commentator on Mark, who maintains that on this score Mark is in explicit opposition to the other Gospels, nonetheless acknowledges that this expression in Mark can be taken as 'just after (or at) sunrise'; see C. S. Mann, *Mark* (Garden City, NY: Doubleday and Co., 1986), p. 664.

and presuppositions and that, in this case at least, his historical learning does not have much of a role in shaping his interpretation. Whatever the case may be in his other work, with regard to this text in the Gospel of John nothing which can be called unequivocally historical constitutes a better reason for accepting rather than rejecting either his methodological commitments and presuppositions or the conclusions which follow from them. And when we examine them from the vantage point of philosophy, they do not fare well.[19]

With regard to this text, then, I see no more reason, either historical or philosophical, for accepting Brown's methodology than for accepting that underlying the play. On the contrary, the problems with Brown's methodological commitments and presuppositions, on which his interpretation of this text largely rests, seem to me to constitute some reason to prefer the methodology underlying the play to Brown's in this case. At any rate, if we begin with the play's methodology, we will not immediately resolve any interesting tension in the texts into simple, tension-free stories. And if it should turn out that in the end there is some good historical (really historical, and not covertly philosophical) reason for abandoning the play's methodology, by at least beginning with that methodology we will have done what we can to ensure that we are not blind to the literary qualities and dramatic possibilities of the texts.[20]

APPENDIX I

Text of *Visitatio Sepulchri*

(The translation is mine; the Latin text and score can be found in Fletcher Collins, Jr., *Medieval Music-Drama: A Repertory of Complete Plays,* University Press of Virginia, 1976. I have not included stage directions.)

Mary Magdalene (MM): Alas, the godly shepherd is killed, although he was unstained by any guilt. How lamentable a thing!

Mary, [mother] of James (MJ): Alas, the true shepherd, who brought life to the dead, is perished. How mournful this death!

[19] Someone might object that Brown's interpretation is historical in a way the play is not just in virtue of being unwilling to take episodes involving angels as historical. (See note 15.) But this objection is just confused. Whether accounts without angels are more historical than accounts giving a role to angels depends on whether reality includes angels or not. And the resolution of that issue depends on whether or not there is an omnipotent, omniscient deity who wills to create not just human beings but angels as well. But, of course, this question is without any doubt a philosophical or theological one, not a historical one. At any rate, one cannot simply suppose that demythologized accounts are more historical, unless one has a philosophical or theological argument to show either that there is no omnipotent, omniscient God, or that any God of that sort wouldn't create angels.

[20] I am grateful for helpful suggestions to William Alston and to the Notre Dame Philosophy of Religion reading group, including William Anglin, David Burrell, Terry Christlieb, Robin Collins, Fred Crosson, Thomas Flint, Alfred Freddoso, Paul Griffiths, Avak Albert Howsepian, William Mann, Philip Quinn, Alvin Plantinga, and John Strand. I am also particularly indebted to Norman Kretzmann for many useful comments and questions on an earlier draft of this paper.

Mary Salome (MS): Alas, wretched race of Jews, what dreadful madness gripped you? How cursed a people!

MM: Why did you condemn that godly man to death, you fierce, envious, ungodly people? How sinful a wrath!

MJ: Did this just man deserve to be crucified? How damnable a race!

MS: What shall we do to commiserate, bereaved as we are of our sweet master? How lamentable a fate!

MM: Let us go then quickly and with a devoted mind do the only thing we can.

MJ: Let us anoint his most holy body with fragrant spices. What a priceless thing!

MS: This nard-oil mixture will keep his blessed flesh from decaying in the tomb.

All three Marys: But we cannot accomplish this without help. Who will roll away this stone from the entrance of the tomb?

Archangel (A): Whom do you seek in the sepulcher, you followers of Christ?

All three Marys: Jesus of Nazareth, who was crucified, you citizen of heaven.

A: Why, you followers of Christ, do you seek the living among the dead? He is not here, but he has risen, as he foretold to the disciples. Remember what he said to you in Galilee, that Christ had to suffer and would rise again in glory on the third day.

MM: We come to the tomb of the Lord, mourning.

MJ: We see the angel of God sitting.

MS: And saying that he is risen from the dead.

MM: Alas! Oh, sorrow! Alas! How dreadful and sad this distress is! I am bereaved of the presence of the Master I loved. Alas! Who has taken that dearly beloved body away from the tomb? [to Peter and John] They have taken away my Lord, and I do not know where they have laid him. And the tomb is found empty. And the headcloth and the shroud are left inside.

John (J): [Coming out of the tomb] What astonishing things we see! Has the Lord been secretly taken away?

Peter (P): No, I believe the Lord has risen, as he foretold while alive.

J: But why are the headcloth and the linen left in the sepulcher?

P: Because he didn't need them when he had risen.

Peter and John: In fact, they remain here as a sign of the resurrection.

MM: Alas! Oh, sorrow! Alas! How dreadful and sad this distress is! I am bereaved of the presence of the Master I loved. Alas! Who has taken that dearly beloved body away from the tomb?

First and Second Angel (AA): Woman, why are you weeping?

MM: Because they have taken away my Lord, and I do not know where they have laid him.

AA: Do not weep, Mary. The Lord is risen!

Choir: Alleluia!

MM: My heart burns with desire to see my Lord. I seek but I do not find where they have laid him.

Choir: Alleluia!

Christ: Woman, why are you weeping? Whom do you seek?

MM: Sir, if you have taken him away, tell me where you have laid him, and I will take him away.

Christ: Mary!

MM: Master!

Christ: Do not touch me! For I am not yet ascended to my Father and your Father, my God and your God.

MM: Wish me joy, all you who love the Lord, for he whom I sought has appeared to me; and while I wept at the tomb, I saw my Lord.

Choir: Alleluia!

First Angel: Come and see the place where the Lord lay.

Choir: Alleluia!

Second Angel: Don't be afraid, you [women]! Change your sad countenance now. Announce the news that Jesus lives. Go now to Galilee. Hurry, if you want to see him!

First Angel: Go quickly and tell the disciples that the Lord is risen.

Choir: Alleluia!

MJ: The Lord is risen from the sepulcher.

MS: Who for our sakes hung on the wood.

Choir: Alleluia!

MJ and MS [holding up the shroud]: See, friends, this belonged to his dear body, the shroud, which was dropped and left empty in the sepulcher.

MM: Today is risen the God of gods.

MJ: You seal the stone in vain, you Jewish people!

MS: Join now with the Christian people.

MM: Today is risen the King of angels.

MJ: The throng of the godly is brought out of darkness.

All three Marys: The entrance to the kingdom of heaven has been opened.

Christ: Do not be afraid, you [women]. Go, tell my brothers to go into Galilee. There they will see me, as I foretold to them.

Choir: Alleluia!

Angels and Marys, or Choir: The Lord is risen today! Christ, the strong lion, the son of God.

APPENDIX II

The Play and the Gospels

The play is related to the four accounts in the Gospels in the following ways, which have been numbered for ease of reference. (1) The play begins by accepting

Mark's identification of the women who came to the tomb. It then conflates the biblical stories of the angels; whereas each biblical account has one appearance of angels, the play has three appearances of angels. (2) The first appearance involves one angel, who is outside the tomb and who appears to all the women. This appearance reflects Matthew 28:2, but (3) what the angel says reflects Luke 24:5–7: 'Whom are you seeking, you followers of Christ?...Why, you followers of Christ, do you seek the living among the dead? He is not here, but has risen, as he predicted to the disciples. Remember what he said to you in Galilee, that Christ had to suffer and rise again in glory on the third day.' After the women address the audience, (4) all but Mary Magdalene leave the stage, perhaps reflecting Mark 16:8, where the women are said to leave the tomb frightened, telling no one what they saw. Left alone at the tomb and continuing to lament, (5) Mary decides to find Peter and the Beloved Disciple, and the action of the play then basically follows the story as told in John 20:2–8, though in the play unlike the biblical account, pre-eminence is given to Peter. The disciples leave before Mary manages to return; and so when she arrives at the tomb, she is once again alone and lamenting. As she weeps, (6) she looks into the tomb and sees two angels. 'why do you weep?,' the angels ask her; and when that question produces no real change in her state, they go on to say, 'Don't cry, Mary; the Lord is risen.' The angels' question stems from John 20:13; their comforting line is reminiscent of Matthew 28:5–7 and Mark 16:6–7. (7) There follow scenes in which Jesus appears to Mary, which are faithful to John 20:14–17. Jesus then leaves the scene; and after a short address to the audience by Mary Magdalene, (8) two angels appear (or perhaps the same two angels reappear). It is clear from their speeches that the other two women are meant to return to stage at this point also, because the speeches are addressed to the women as a group. 'Come and see the place where the Lord lay,' the first angel says; and the second adds, 'Do not be afraid. Change your sad countenance. Announce that Jesus lives. Go forth to Galilee now, if you wish to see him. Hurry!' These speeches of the angels reflect the second half of the angel's speech in Matthew 28:5–7 and Mark 16:6–7. After (9) a series of speeches by the women to the audience, which proclaim the resurrection with great joy and which are perhaps meant to reflect Matthew 28:8, (10) Christ appears again, saying to the women, 'Do not be afraid. Go, announce to my brothers that they should go to Galilee; there they will see me, as I predicted to them.' This appearance and speech of Jesus reflects Matthew 28:9–10, and on this note, with a last line from the women and angels or from the choir, the play ends. Presumably, after this point the women continue on their way to tell the disciples; perhaps we can add this point as (11), as the implied ending to the play.

If we look at the relation between the play and the Gospels the other way around, the empty tomb stories in the Gospels can be accommodated within the story of the play in the following way. Matthew can be contained in elements (1), (2), (8), (9), and (10) of the play. Apart from worries about the angels, Luke can be included in elements (1), (2), (3) and (11), if we take Luke 24:12 as a part of the story out of sequence in Luke. John is the most readily accommodated of the biblical accounts; it is contained in (1), (5), (6), (7), and (11). On the other hand, Mark is the most difficult of the biblical accounts to square with the play. The playwright assigns the same characters to the scene as Mark does, and Mark's description of the angels seems to fit the play's (8); but what follows in Mark's account is a scene which the playwright puts much earlier, (4) in the play. Since most of the discrepancies between the play and the biblical account are generated by my interpretation of the scene involving angels in Mark, it may be that I have simply failed to understand the way in which the playwright wanted to incorporate Mark in his play.

13

Two (or More) Kinds of Scripture Scholarship*

Alvin Plantinga

The serious and scholarly study of the Bible is of first importance for the Christian community. The roll call of those who have pursued this project is maximally impressive: Chrysostom, Augustine, Aquinas, Calvin, Jonathan Edwards and Karl Barth, just for starters. These people and their successors begin from the idea that Scripture is indeed divinely inspired (however exactly they understand this claim); they then try to ascertain the Lord's teaching in the whole of Scripture or (more likely) a given bit. Since the Enlightenment, however, another kind of Scripture scholarship has also come into view. Variously called 'higher criticism', 'historical criticism', 'biblical criticism', or 'historical critical scholarship', this variety of Scripture scholarship *brackets* or *prescinds from* what is known by faith and aims to proceed 'scientifically', strictly on the basis of reason. I shall call it 'Historical Biblical Criticism'—HBC for short. Scripture scholarship of this sort also brackets the belief that the Bible is a special word from the Lord, as well as any other belief accepted on the basis of faith rather than reason.

Now it often happens that the declarations of those who pursue this latter kind are in apparent conflict with the main lines of Christian thought; one who pursues this sort of scholarship is quite unlikely to conclude, for example, that Jesus was really the pre-existent second person of the divine trinity who was crucified, died, and then literally rose from the dead the third day. As Van Harvey says, 'So far as the biblical historian is concerned, . . . there is scarcely a popularly held traditional belief about Jesus that is not regarded with considerable skepticism.'[1] I shall try to describe both of these kinds of Scripture scholarship. Then I shall ask the following question: how should a traditional Christian, one who accepts 'the great things of the gospel', respond to the deflationary aspects of

* From *Modern Theology* 14 (1998): 243–78. © Blackwell Publishers 1998. Reprinted by permission of the publisher.

[1] 'New Testament Scholarship and Christian Belief' (hereafter 'NTS'), in *Jesus in History and Myth* (Buffalo, NY: Prometheus Books, 1986), p. 193.

HBC? How should she think about its apparently corrosive results with respect to traditional Christian belief? I shall argue that she need not be disturbed by the conflict between alleged results of HBC and traditional Christian belief.[2] Indeed, that conflict should not defeat her acceptance of the great things of the gospel—nor, to the degree that those alleged results rest upon epistemological assumptions she does not share, of anything else she accepts on the basis of Biblical teaching.

I. SCRIPTURE DIVINELY INSPIRED

At millions of worship services every week Christians all over the world hear passages of Scripture and respond by saying, 'This is the Word of the Lord.' Suppose we begin, therefore, by inquiring into the epistemology of the belief that the Bible is divinely inspired in a special way, and in such a way as to constitute divine discourse. How *does* a Christian come to believe that the gospel of Mark, or the book of Acts, or the entire New Testament is authoritative, because divinely inspired? What (if anything) is the source of its warrant?[3] There are several possibilities. For many, it will be by way of ordinary teaching and testimony. Perhaps I am brought up to believe the Bible is indeed the Word of God (just as I am brought up thinking that thousands perished in the American Civil War), and I have never encountered any reason to doubt this. But an important feature of warrant is that if I accept a belief *B* just on testimony, then *B* has warrant for me only if it had warrant for the testifier as well: the warrant a belief has for the testifiee is derivative from the warrant it has for the testifier.[4] Our question, therefore, becomes this: what is the epistemological status of this belief for those members of the community who do not accept it on the testimony of other members? What is the source of the warrant (if any) this belief has for the Christian community? Well, perhaps a Christian might come to think something like the following:

Suppose the apostles were commissioned by God through Jesus Christ to be witnesses and representatives (deputies) of Jesus. Suppose that what emerged from their carrying out this commission was a body of apostolic teaching which incorporated what Jesus taught them and what they remembered of the goings-on surrounding Jesus, shaped under the guidance of the Spirit. And suppose that the New Testament books are all either

---

[2] I therefore concur (for the most part) both with C. Stephen Evans in his excellent *The Historical Christ and the Jesus of Faith: the Incarnational Narrative as History* (Oxford: Clarendon Press, 1996), and with Peter van Inwagen in 'Critical Studies of the New Testament and the User of the New Testament', *God, Knowledge, and Mystery* (Ithaca, NY: Cornell University Press, 1995), pp. 163–90.

[3] For an account of warrant, that property which distinguishes knowledge from mere true belief (a lucky guess, for example), see my *Warrant: The Current Debate* and *Warrant and Proper Function* (New York, NY: Oxford University Press, 1993).

[4] See *Warrant and Proper Function*, pp. 34–5.

apostolic writings, or formulations of apostolic teaching composed by close associates of one or another apostle. Then it would be correct to construe each book as a medium of divine discourse. And an eminently plausible construal of the process whereby these books found their way into a single canonical text, would be that by way of that process of canonization, God was authorizing these books as together constituting a single volume of divine discourse.[5]

So a Christian might come to think something like the above: she believes

(1) that the apostles were commissioned by God through Jesus Christ to be witnesses and deputies,

(2) that they produced a body of apostolic teaching which incorporates what Jesus taught,

and

(3) that the New Testament books are all either apostolic writings or formulations of apostolic teaching composed by close associates of one or another apostle.

She also believes

(4) that the process whereby these books found their way into a single canon is a matter of God's authorizing these books as constituting a single volume of divine discourse.

She therefore concludes that indeed

(5) the New Testament is a single volume of divine discourse.

But of course our question then would be: how does she know, why does she believe each of (1)–(4)? What is the source of these beliefs?

Could it be, perhaps, by way of ordinary historical investigation? I doubt it. The problem is the Principle of Dwindling Probabilities. Suppose a Christian proposes to give a historical argument for the divine inspiration and consequent authority of the New Testament; and suppose we think of her as already knowing or believing the central truths of Christianity. She already knows that there is such a person as God, that the man Jesus is also the divine Son of God, that through his ministry, passion, death and resurrection we sinners can have life. These constitute part of her background information, and can be employed in the historical argument in question. Her body of background information B with respect to which she estimates the probability of (1)–(4), includes the main lines of Christian teaching. And of course she knows that the books of the New Testament—some of them, anyway—apparently teach or presuppose these things. With respect to B, therefore, perhaps each of (1)–(4) could be considered at least quite plausible and perhaps even likely to be true.

[5] Nicholas Wolterstorff, *Divine Discourse: Philosophical Reflections on the Claim that God Speaks* (Cambridge: Cambridge University Press, 1995), p. 295.

Still, each is only probable. Perhaps, indeed, each is *very* likely and has a probability as high as .9 with respect to that body of belief B.[6] Even so, we can conclude only that the probability of their conjunction, on B, is somewhat more than .5. In that case, *belief* that the New Testament is the Word of God would not be appropriate; what would be appropriate is the belief that it is fairly *likely* that the New Testament is the Word of God. (The probability that the next throw of this die will not come up either 1 or 2 is greater than .5; that is nowhere nearly sufficient for my *believing* that it will not come up 1 or 2.) Of course, we could quibble about these probabilities—no doubt they could sensibly be thought to be greater than I suggested. No doubt; but they could also sensibly be thought to be less than I suggested. The historical argument for (1) to (4) will at best yield probabilities, and at best only a fairly insubstantial probability of (5) itself. The estimates of the probabilities involved, furthermore, will be vague, variable and not really well founded. If the belief in question is to have *warrant* for Christians, its epistemic status for them must be something different from that of a conclusion of ordinary historical investigation.

Now, of course, most Christian communities have taught that the warrant enjoyed by this belief is *not* conferred on it just by way of ordinary historical investigation. The Belgic Confession, one of the most important confessions of the Reformed churches, gives a list (the Protestant list) of the canonical books of the Bible (Article 5); it then goes on:

And we believe without a doubt all things contained in them—not so much because the church receives them and approves them as such, but above all because the Holy Spirit testifies in our hearts that they are from God, and also because they prove themselves to be from God.

There is a possible ambiguity here; 'we believe all things contained in them not so much because the church receives them, but...'—but to what does this last 'them' refer? The teachings contained in the books, or the books themselves? If the former, then what we have here is the claim that the Holy Spirit is leading us to see, not that a given *book* is from God, but that some *teaching*—e.g., that God in Christ was reconciling the world to himself—is indeed true. If the latter, however, what we would be led to believe is such propositions as *The gospel of John is from God*. I think it is at least fairly clear that the latter is what the Confession intends. According to the Confession, then, there are two sources for the belief that (e.g.) the gospel of John is from God. The first is that the Holy Spirit testifies in our hearts that this book is indeed from God; the Holy Spirit does not merely impel us to believe, with respect to a given teaching of the gospel

---

[6] More exactly, perhaps the probability of (1) on B is as high as .9, the probability of (2) on (1)&B as high as .9, and the same for $P((3)/(B\&(1)\&(2)))$ and $P((4)/(B\&(1)\&(2)\&(3)))$. For more on this form of argument, see *Warranted Christian Belief,* chapter 8, 'The Extended A/C Model: Revealed to our Minds.'

of John, that it is from God, but also impels us to believe that the gospel of John itself is from God. The second is that the book 'proves itself' to be from God. Perhaps here the idea is that the believer first comes to think, with respect to many of the specific teachings of that book, that they are indeed from God; that is, the Holy Spirit causes her to believe this with respect to many of the teachings of the book. She then infers (with the help of other premises) that the whole book has that same status.[7]

This is only *one* way in which this belief could have warrant; there are other possibilities. Perhaps the believer knows by way of the internal invitation of the Holy Spirit that the Holy Spirit has guided and preserved the Christian church, making sure that its teachings on important matters are in fact true; then the believer would be warranted in believing, at any rate of those books of the Bible endorsed by all or nearly all traditional Christian communities, that they are from God. Or perhaps, guided by the Holy Spirit, she recapitulates the process whereby the canon was originally formed, paying attention to the original criteria of apostolic authorship, consistency with apostolic teaching, and the like, and relying on testimony for the propositions such and such books were indeed composed by apostles. There are also combinations of these ways. However precisely this belief receives its warrant, then, traditional Christians have accepted the belief that the Bible is indeed the Word of God and that in it the Lord intends to teach us truths.[8]

II. TRADITIONAL CHRISTIAN BIBLICAL COMMENTARY

Of course, it is not always easy to tell what the Lord *is* teaching us in a given passage: what he teaches is indeed true, but sometimes it is not clear just what his teaching is. Part of the problem is the fact that the Bible contains material of so many different sorts; it is not in this respect like a contemporary book on theology or philosophy. It is not a book full of declarative sentences, with proper analysis and logical development and all the accoutrements academics have come to know and love and demand. The Bible does indeed contain sober assertion; but there is also exhortation, expression of praise, poetry, the telling of stories and parables, songs, devotional material, history, genealogies, lamentations,

---

[7] Jonathan Edwards: 'And the opening to view with such clearness, such a world of wonderful and glorious truth in the gospel, that before was unknown, being quite above the view of a natural eye, but appearing so clear and bright, has a powerful and invincible influence on the soul to persuade of the divinity of the gospel.' *The Religious Affections* (New Haven, CT: Yale University Press, 1959), p. 303.

[8] I do not for a moment mean to suggest that teaching us truths is *all* that the Lord intends in Scripture: there is also raising affection, teaching us how to praise, how to pray, how to see the depth of our own sin, how marvelous the gift of salvation is, and a thousand other things.

confession, prophecy, apocalyptic material, and much else besides. Some of these (apocalyptic, for example) present real problems of interpretation (for us, at present): what exactly is the Lord teaching in Daniel, or Revelation? That is not easy to say.

And even if we stick to straightforward assertion, there are a thousand questions of interpretation. Here are just a couple of examples. In Matthew 5:17–20, Jesus declares that not a jot or a tittle of the Law shall pass away and that '... unless your righteousness surpasses that of the Pharisees and the teachers of the law, you will certainly not enter the kingdom of heaven', but in Galatians Paul seems to say that observance of the Law does not count for much; how can we put these together? How do we understand Colossians 1:24: 'Now I rejoice in what was suffered for you, and I fill up in my flesh what is still lacking in regard to Christ's afflictions, for the sake of his body which is the church'? Is Paul suggesting that Christ's sacrifice is incomplete, insufficient, that it requires additional suffering on the part of Paul and/or the rest of us? That seems unlikely. Is it that our suffering can be a *type* of Christ's, thus standing to the latter in the relation in which a type stands to the reality it typifies? Or shall we understand it like this: we must distinguish between two kinds of Christ's suffering, the redemptive suffering, the expiatory and vicarious atonement to which nothing can be added or taken away, on the one hand, and another kind, also 'for the sake of his body', in which we human beings can genuinely participate? Perhaps it is suffering which can build up, edify the body of Christ, even as our response to Christ can be deepened by our meditating on Christ's sacrifice for us and the amazing selfless love displayed in it? Or what? Do Paul and James contradict each other on the relation between faith and works? Or rather, since God is the author of Scripture, is he proposing an inconsistent or self-contradictory teaching for our belief? Well no, surely not, but then how shall we understand the two in relation to each other? More generally, given that God is the principal author of Scripture, how shall we think about the apparent tensions the latter displays?

Scripture, therefore, is indeed inspired: what it teaches is indeed true; but it is not always trivial to tell what it *does* teach. Indeed, many of the sermons and homilies preached in a million churches every Sunday morning are devoted in part to bringing out what might otherwise be obscure in Scriptural teaching. Given that the Bible is a communication from God to humankind, a divine revelation, there is much about it that requires deep and perceptive reflection, much that taxes our best scholarly and spiritual resources. Of course, this fact was not lost on, for example, Chrysostom, Augustine, Aquinas, Calvin, and the others I mentioned earlier on; between them they wrote an impressive number of volumes devoted to powerful reflection on the meaning and teachings of Scripture. (Calvin's commentaries alone run to some twenty-two volumes.) Their aim was to try to determine as accurately as possible just what the Lord proposes to teach us in the Bible. Call this enterprise 'traditional biblical commentary', and note that it displays at least the following three features.

First, Scripture itself is taken to be a wholly authoritative and trustworthy guide to faith and morals; it is authoritative and trustworthy, because it is a revelation from God, a matter of God's speaking to us. Once it is clear, therefore, what the teaching of a given bit of Scripture is, the question of the truth and acceptability of that teaching is settled. In a commentary on Plato, we might decide that what Plato really meant to say was XYZ; we might then go on to consider and evaluate XYZ in various ways, asking whether it is true, or close to the truth, or true in principle, or superseded by things we have learned since Plato wrote, and the like; we might also ask whether Plato's grounds or arguments for XYZ are slight, or acceptable, or substantial, or compelling. These questions are out of place in the kind of Scripture scholarship under consideration. Once convinced that God *is* proposing XYZ for our belief, we do not go on to ask whether it is true, or whether God has made a good case for it. God is not required to make a case.

Secondly, an assumption of the enterprise is that the principal author of the Bible—the entire Bible—is God himself. Of course, each of the books of the Bible has a human author or authors as well; but the principal author is God. This impels us to treat the whole more like a unified communication than a miscellany of ancient books. Scripture is not so much a library of independent books as itself a book with many subdivisions but a central theme: the message of the gospel. By virtue of this unity, furthermore (by virtue of the fact that there is just one principal author), it is possible to 'interpret Scripture with Scripture'. If a given passage from one of Paul's epistles is puzzling, it is perfectly proper to try to come to clarity as to what God's teaching in this passage is by appealing, not only to what Paul himself says elsewhere in other epistles (his own or others), but also to what is taught elsewhere in Scripture (for example, the gospel of John[9]). Passages in Psalms or Isaiah can be interpreted in terms of the fuller, more explicit disclosure in the New Testament; the serpent elevated on a pole to save the Israelites from disaster can be seen as a type of Christ (and thus as getting some of its significance by way of an implicit reference to Christ, whose being raised on the cross averted a greater disaster for the whole human race). A further consequence: we can quite properly accept propositions that are inferred from premises coming from different parts of the Bible: once we see what God intends to teach in a given passage A and what he intends to teach in a given passage B, we can put the two together, and treat a consequence of these propositions as itself divine teaching.[10]

[9] See, for example, Richard Swinburne (*Revelation* (Oxford: Clarendon Press, 1992), p. 192), who suggests that Paul's Christology at Romans 1:4 should be understood in terms of the 'high' Christology of the first chapter of John's gospel. We could say the same for Paul's Christology in his speech in Acts 13, where he seems to suggest that a special status was *conferred* on Jesus, as opposed to John 1, according to which Jesus is the incarnation of the preexistent Word. See also Raymond Brown, *New Testament Christology* (New York, NY: Paulist Press, 1994), pp. 133ff.

[10] Of course this procedure, like most others, can be and has been abused; that possibility in itself, however, is nothing against it, though it should serve as a salutary caution.

Thirdly (and connected with the second point), the fact that the principal author of the Bible is God himself means that one cannot always determine the meaning of a given passage by discovering what the human author had in mind. Of course, various post-modern hermeneuticists aim to amuse by telling us that in this case, as in all others, the author's intentions have nothing whatever to do with the meaning of a passage, that the reader herself confers upon it whatever meaning the passage has, or perhaps that even entertaining the idea of a text having meaning is to fall into 'hermeneutical innocence'—innocence, oddly enough, which (as they insist) is ineradicably sullied by its inevitable association with oppressive, racist, sexist, homophobic and other offensive modes of thought. This is indeed amusing. Returning to serious business, however, it is obvious (given that the principal author of the Bible is God) that the meaning of a biblical passage will be given by what it is that the Lord intends to teach in that passage, and it is precisely this that biblical commentary tries to discern. Therefore, what the Lord intends to teach us is not identical with what the human author had in mind;[11] the latter may not so much as have thought of what is in fact the teaching of the passage in question. Thus, for example, Christians take the suffering servant passages in Isaiah to be references to Jesus; Jesus himself says (Luke 4:18–21) that the prophecy in Isaiah 61:1–2 is fulfilled in him; John (19:36) takes passages from Exodus, Numbers, Psalms and Zechariah to be references to Jesus and the events of his life and death; Matthew and John take it that Zechariah 9:9 is a reference to Jesus' triumphal entry into Jerusalem (Matthew 21:5 and John 12:15); Hebrews 10 takes passages from Psalms, Jeremiah, and Habakkuk to be references to Christ and events in his career, as does Paul for passages from Psalms and Isaiah in his speech in Acts 13. Indeed, Paul refers to the Old Testament on nearly every page of Romans and both Corinthian epistles, and frequently in other epistles. There is no reason to suppose the human authors of Exodus, Numbers, Psalms, Isaiah, Jeremiah, or Habakkuk had in mind Jesus' triumphal entry, or his incarnation, or other events of Jesus' life and death, or indeed anything else explicitly about Jesus. But the fact that it is God who is the principal author here makes it quite possible that what we are to learn from the text in question is something rather different from what the human author proposed to teach.

III. HISTORICAL BIBLICAL CRITICISM

For at least the last couple of hundred years there has also been a quite different kind of Scripture scholarship variously called 'higher criticism', 'historical criticism', 'biblical criticism', or 'historical critical scholarship'; I will call it

---

[11] A further complication: we cannot simply assume that there is some one thing, the same for everyone, that the Lord intends to teach in a given passage; perhaps what he intends to teach me, or my relevant sociological group, is not the same as what he intended to teach a fifth century Christian.

'historical biblical criticism' (HBC). Clearly, we are indebted to HBC; it has enabled us to learn a great deal about the Bible we otherwise might not have known. Furthermore, some of the methods it has developed can be and have been employed to excellent effect in various studies of interest and importance, including traditional Biblical commentary. It differs importantly from the latter, however. HBC is fundamentally an enlightenment project; it is an effort to try to determine from the standpoint of reason alone what the Scriptural teachings are and whether they are true. Thus HBC eschews the authority and guidance of tradition, magisterium, creed, or any kind of ecclesial or 'external' epistemic authority. The idea is to see what can be established (or at least made plausible) using only the light of what we could call 'natural, empirical reason'. (So, of course, not everyone who uses the methods of textual criticism commonly employed in HBC is involved in the project of HBC as I am thinking of it; to take part in that project one must aim to discover the truth about Scripture and its teachings from the standpoint of reason alone.) The faculties or sources of belief invoked, therefore, would be those that are employed in ordinary history: perception, testimony, reason taken in the sense of *a priori* intuition together with deductive and probabilistic reasoning, Reid's sympathy, by which we discern the thoughts and feelings of another, and so on—but bracketing any proposition one knows by faith or by way of the authority of the church. Spinoza (1632–1677) already lays down the charter for this enterprise: 'The rule for [Biblical] interpretation should be nothing but the natural light of reason which is common to all—not any supernatural light nor any external authority.'[12]

This project or enterprise is often thought of as part and parcel of the development of modern empirical science, and indeed practitioners of HBC often drape about their shoulders the mantle of modern science. The attraction is not just that HBC can perhaps share in the prestige of modern science, but also that it can share in the obvious epistemic power and excellence of the latter.[13] It is common to think of science itself as our best shot at getting to know what the world is really like; HBC is, among other things, an attempt to apply these widely approved methods to the study of Scripture and the origins of Christianity. Thus Raymond Brown, a Scripture scholar than whom none is more highly

---

[12] *Tractatus theologico-politicus*, 14. Of course, this method does not preclude a rational argument (an argument from reason alone) for the proposition that indeed there has been a divine revelation, and that the Bible (or some part of it) is precisely that revelation: exactly this was John Locke's project.

[13] To understand historical criticism and its dominance properly, says David Yeago, one must understand 'the historic coupling of historical criticism with a "project to the Enlightenment" aimed at liberating mind and heart from the shackles of ecclesiastical tradition. In the modern context, claims to "Enlightenment" must be backed up with the claim to have achieved a proper *method*, capable of producing real knowledge to replace the pre-critical confusion and arbitrariness of tradition.' 'The New Testament and the Nicene Dogma', *Pro Ecclesia* Vol. III, No. 2 (Spring, 1994), p. 162.

respected, believes that HBC is 'scientific biblical criticism';[14] it yields 'factual results' (p. 9); he intends his own contributions to be 'scientifically respectable' (p. 11): and practitioners of HBC investigate the Scriptures with 'scientific exactitude' (pp. 18–19).[15]

But what is it, exactly, to study the Bible scientifically? As we will see below there is more than one answer to this question. One theme that seems to command nearly universal assent, however, is that in working at this scientific project (however exactly it is to be understood) you do not invoke or employ any theological assumptions or presuppositions. You do not assume, for example, that the Bible is inspired by God in any special way, or contains anything like specifically divine discourse. You do not assume that Jesus is the divine Son of God, or that he arose from the dead, or that his suffering and death is in some way a propitiatory atonement for human sin, making it possible for us to get once more in the right relationship to God. You do not assume any of these things because in pursuing science, one does not assume or employ any proposition which one knows by faith.[16] (As a consequence, the meaning of a text will be what the human author intended to assert (if it is an assertive kind of text); divine intentions and teaching do not enter into the meaning.[17]) Thus the idea, says E. P. Sanders, is to rely only on 'evidence on which everyone can agree'.[18] According to Jon Levenson,

[14] *The Virginal Conception and Bodily Resurrection of Jesus* (New York, NY: Paulist Press, 1973), p. 6.

[15] See also John P. Meier, *A Marginal Jew: Rethinking the Historical Jesus* (New York, NY: Doubleday, 1991, two volumes), p. 1.

[16] Nor can you employ a proposition which is such that the warrant it has for you comes from some proposition you know or believe by faith; we might put this by saying that in doing science you cannot employ any proposition whose epistemic provenance, for you, includes a proposition you know or believe by faith.

But is this really true? Why should we believe it? What is the status of the claim that if what you are doing is science, then you cannot employ, in your work, any proposition you believe or know by faith? Is this supposed to be true by definition? If so, whose definition? Is there a good argument for it? Or what? See my 'Methodological Naturalism?', *Facets of Faith and Science*, ed. J. van der Meer (Lanham, MD: University Press of America, 1996), pp. 177–222.

[17] Thus Benjamin Jowett (the 19th century Master of Balliol College and eminent translator of Plato): 'Scripture has one meaning—the meaning which it had to the mind of the prophet or evangelist who first uttered or wrote, to the hearers or readers who first received it.' 'On the Interpretation of Scripture', in *The Interpretation of Scripture and Other Essays* (London: George Routledge & Sons, 1906), p. 36. Quoted in Jon D. Levenson, *The Hebrew Bible, the Old Testament, and Historical Criticism* (Louisville, KY: Westminster/John Knox Press, 1993), p. 78. Jowett was not a paragon of intellectual modesty, which may explain a poem composed and circulated by undergraduates at Balliol:

> First come I, my name is Jowett.
> There's no knowledge but I know it.
> I am the master of the college.
> What I don't know isn't knowledge.

[18] E. P. Sanders, *Jesus and Judaism* (Philadelphia, PA: Fortress Press, 1985), p. 5.

Historical critics thus rightly insist that the tribunal before which interpretations are argued cannot be confessional or 'dogmatic'; the arguments offered must be historically valid, able, that is, to compel the assent of *historians* whatever their religion or lack thereof, whatever their backgrounds, spiritual experiences, or personal beliefs, and without privileging any claim of revelation.[19]

Barnabas Lindars explains that

There are in fact two reasons why many scholars are very cautious about miracle stories ... The second reason is historical. The religious literature of the ancient world is full of miracle stories, and we cannot believe them all. It is not open to a scholar to decide that, just because he is a believing Christian, he will accept all the Gospel miracles at their face value, but at the same time he will repudiate miracles attributed to Isis. All such accounts have to be scrutinized with equal detachment.[20]

And even Luke Timothy Johnson, who is in general astutely critical of HBC:

It is obviously important to study Christian origins historically. And in such historical inquiry, faith commitments should play no role. Christianity is no more privileged for the historian than any other human phenomenon.[21]

In practice, this emphasis means that HBC tends to deal especially with questions of *composition* and *authorship,* these being the questions most easily addressed by the methods employed. When was the document in question composed—or more exactly, since we cannot assume that we are dealing with a single unified document here, when were its various parts composed? How was the gospel of Luke, for example, composed? Was it written by one person, relying on his memory of Jesus and his words and deeds, or was it assembled from various reports, alleged quotations, songs, poems and the like in the oral tradition? Was it dependent on one or more earlier written or oral sources? Why did the editor or redactor put the book together in just the way he did—was it to make a theological point in a current controversy? Where traditional Biblical commentary assumes that the entire Bible is really one book with a single principal author, HBC tends to give us a collection of books by many authors. And even within the confines of a single book, it may give us a collection of discontinuous sayings and episodes (pericopes), these having been stitched together by one or more redactors. How much of what is reported as the sayings and discourse of Jesus really was said by Jesus? Can we discern various strata in the book—perhaps a bottom stratum, including the actual sayings of Jesus himself, and then successive overlaying strata? As Robert Alter says, scholarship

---

[19] Levenson, p. 109.

[20] 'Jesus Risen: Bodily Resurrection But No Empty Tomb', *Theology* Vol. 89 No. 728 (March, 1986), p. 91.

[21] *The Real Jesus: The Misguided Quest for the Historical Jesus and the Truth of the Traditional Gospels* (San Francisco, CA: HarperSanFrancisco, 1996), p. 172. The target of much of Johnson's criticism is the notorious 'Jesus Seminar'.

of this kind tends to be 'excavative'; the idea is to dig behind the document as we actually have it to see what can be determined of its history.[22]

Of course, the idea is also to see, as far as this is possible, whether the events reported—in the gospels, for example—really happened, and whether the picture they give of Jesus is in fact historically accurate. Did he say the things they say he said, and do the things they say he did? Here the assumption is that we cannot simply take at face value the gospels as we now have them. There may have been all sorts of additions and subtractions and alterations made in the interest of advancing theological points. Further, the New Testament books are written from the standpoint of faith—faith that Jesus really was the Christ, did indeed suffer and die and rise from the dead, and did accomplish our salvation. From the standpoint of reason alone, however, this faith must be bracketed; hence (from that standpoint) the hermeneutics of suspicion is appropriate here. (This suspicion is sometimes carried so far that it reminds one of the way in which the CIA's denial that Mr X is a spy is taken as powerful evidence that Mr X is indeed a spy.)

A. Varieties of HBC

Those who practice HBC, therefore, propose to proceed without employing theological assumptions or anything one knows by faith (if indeed there is anything one knows by faith); these things are to be bracketed. Instead, one proceeds scientifically, on the basis of reason alone. Beyond this, however, there is vastly less concord. What is to count as reason? Precisely what premises can be employed in an argument from reason alone? What exactly does it mean to proceed scientifically?

1. Troeltschian HBC

Here many contemporary biblical critics will appeal to the thought and teaching of Ernst Troeltsch.[23] Thus John Collins:

Among theologians these principles received their classic formulation from Ernst Troeltsch in 1898. Troeltsch sets out three principles...: (1) The principle of criticism or methodological doubt: since any conclusion is subject to revision, historical inquiry can never attain absolute certainty but only relative degrees of probability. (2) The principle of analogy: historical knowledge is possible because all events are similar in principle. We must assume that the laws of nature in biblical times were the same as now. Troeltsch referred to this as 'the almighty power of analogy.' (3) The principle of

---

[22] I do not mean to suggest, of course, that the traditional Biblical commentator cannot also investigate these questions; if she does, however, it will be in the ultimate service of an effort to discern what the Lord is teaching in the passages in question.

[23] See especially his 'Über historische und dogmatische Methode in der Theologie' in his *Gesammelte Schriften* (Tubingen: Mohr, 1913) Vol. 2, pp. 729–53, and his article 'Historiography' in James Hastings (ed.). *Encyclopedia of Religion and Ethics* Vol. VI (Edinburgh: T & T Clark, 1925), pp. 716–23.

correlation: the phenomena of history are inter-related and inter-dependent and no event can be isolated from the sequence of historical cause and effect.[24]

Collins adds a fourth principle, this one taken from Van Harvey's *The Historian and the Believer*,[25] a more recent *locus classicus* for the proper method of historical criticism:

To these should be added the principle of autonomy, which is indispensable for any critical study. Neither church nor state can prescribe for the scholar which conclusions should be reached.[26]

Now the first thing to note is that each of these principles is multiply ambiguous. In particular, each (except perhaps for the second) has a non-controversial, indeed, platitudinous interpretation. The first principle seems to be a *comment on* historical inquiry rather than a principle for its practice: historical inquiry can never attain absolutely certain results. (Perhaps the implied methodological principle is that in doing historical criticism, you should avoid claiming absolute certainty for your results.) Fair enough, I suppose nearly everyone would agree that few historical results of any significance are as certain as, say, that $2 + 1 = 3$, but if so, they do not achieve absolute certainty. (The only reasonably plausible candidates for historical events that *are* absolutely certain, I suppose, would be such 'historical' claims as that either Caesar crossed the Rubicon or else he did not.)

The third also has a platitudinous interpretation. What Troeltsch says is, 'The sole task of history in its specifically theoretical aspect is to explain every movement, process, state and nexus of things by reference to the web of its causal relations.'[27] This too can be seen as toothless if not platitudinous. Every event is to be explained by reference to the web of its causal relations—which of course would also include the intentions and actions of persons. Well then, consider even such an event as the resurrection of Jesus from the dead: according to the principle at hand, this event too would have to be explained by reference to the web of its causal relations. No problem; on the traditional view, this event was caused by God himself, who caused it in order to achieve certain of his aims and ends, in particular making it possible for human beings to be reconciled with God. So taken, this principle would exclude very little.

I say the second principle is perhaps the exception to the claim that each has a banal, uncontroversial interpretation: that is because on any plausible interpretation the second principle seems to entail the existence of *natural laws*. That there *are* such things as natural laws was a staple of 17th and 18th century science and

---

[24] 'Is Critical Biblical Theology Possible?' in *The Hebrew Bible and its Interpreters*, eds. William Henry Propp, Baruch Halpern and David Freedman (Winona Lake, IN: Eisenbrauns, 1990), p. 2.

[25] Subtitled *The Morality of Historical Knowledge and Christian Belief* (New York, NY: Macmillan, 1966).

[26] *loc. cit.*

[27] 'Historiography', p. 718.

philosophy of science;[28] what science discovers (so they thought) is just these laws of nature.[29] Empiricists have always been dubious about natural laws, however, and at present the claim that there are any such things is at best extremely controversial.[30]

So all but one of Troeltsch's principles have platitudinous interpretations; but these are not in fact the interpretations given to them in the community of HBC. Within that community those principles are understood in such a way as to preclude *direct divine action* in the world. Not that all in this community *accept* Troeltsch's principles in their nonplatitudinous interpretation; rather, those who think of themselves as accepting (or rejecting) those principles think of themselves as accepting or rejecting their nonplatitudinous versions. (Presumably *everyone* accepts them taken platitudinously.) So taken, these principles imply that God has not in fact specially inspired any human authors in such a way that what they write is really divine speech addressed to us; nor has he raised Jesus from the dead, or turned water into wine, or performed miracles of any other sorts.

Thus Rudolph Bultmann:

The historical method includes the presupposition that history is a unity in the sense of a closed continuum of effects in which individual events are connected by the succession of cause and effect.

This continuum, furthermore,

cannot be rent by the interference of supernatural, transcendent powers.[31]

Many other theologians, oddly enough, chime in with agreement: God cannot or at any rate would not and will not act directly in the world. Thus John Macquarrie:

The way of understanding miracles that appeals to breaks in the natural order and to supernatural intervention belongs to the mythological outlook and cannot commend

---

[28] Thus Descartes (part 2 of *Principles of Philosophy*) in stating something like a law of conservation of momentum:
xxvii. The first law of nature: that each thing as far as in it lies, continues always in the same state; and that which is once moved always continues so to move.

[29] An opinion preserved among such contemporary philosophers as David Armstrong (see his *What is a Law of Nature?* (Cambridge: Cambridge University Press, 1984)) and David Lewis (see, e.g., his 'New Work for a Theory of Universals', *Australasian Journal of Philosophy* Vol. 61 No. 4 (December 1983), pp. 343ff.).

[30] See, in particular, Bas van Fraassen's *Laws and Symmetry* (Oxford: Clarendon Press, 1989) for an extended and powerful argument against the exercise of natural laws.

[31] *Existence and Faith*, ed. Schubert Ogden (New York, NY: Meridian Books, 1960), pp. 291–292. Writing 50 years before Troeltsch, David Strauss concurs: '...all things are linked together by a chain of causes and effects, which suffers no interruption.' *Life of Jesus Critically Examined* (Philadelphia, PA: Fortress Press, 1972), sec. 14. (Quoted in Harvey, *The Historian and the Believer*, p. 15.)

itself in a post-mythological climate of thought . . . The traditional conception of miracle is irreconcilable with our modern understanding of both science and history. Science proceeds on the assumption that whatever events occur in the world can be accounted for in terms of other events that also belong within the world; and if on some occasions we are unable to give a complete account of some happening . . . the scientific conviction is that further research will bring to light further factors in the situation, but factors that will turn out to be just as immanent and this-worldly as those already known.[32]

And Langdon Gilkey:

. . . contemporary theology does not expect, nor does it speak of, wondrous divine events on the surface of natural and historical life. The causal nexus in space and time which the Enlightenment science and philosophy introduced into the Western mind . . . is also assumed by modern theologians and scholars; since they participate in the modern world of science both intellectually and existentially, they can scarcely do anything else. Now this assumption of a causal order among phenomenal events, and therefore of the authority of the scientific interpretation of observable events, makes a great difference to the validity one assigns to biblical narratives and so to the way one understands their meaning. Suddenly a vast panoply of divine deeds and events recorded in scripture are no longer regarded as having actually happened. . . . Whatever the Hebrews believed, *we* believe that the biblical people lived in the same causal continuum of space and time in which we live, and so one in which no divine wonders transpired and no divine voices were heard.[33]

Gilkey says no divine wonders have transpired and no divine voices have been heard; Macquarrie adds that in this post-mythological age, we cannot brook the idea of 'breaks in the natural order and supernatural intervention'. Each, therefore, is ruling out the possibility of miracle, including the possibility of special divine action in inspiring human authors in such a way that what they write constitutes an authoritative communication from God. Now, of course, it is far from easy to say just what a miracle is; this topic is connected with deep and thorny questions about occasionalism, natural law, natural potentialities, and so on. We need not get into all that, however. The Troeltschian idea is that there is a certain way in which things ordinarily go; there are certain regularities, whether or not due to natural law, and God can be counted on to act in such a way as never to abrogate those regularities. Of course, God *could* if he chose abrogate those regularities (after all, even those natural laws, if there are any, are his creatures); but we can be sure, somehow, that God will not abrogate those regularities. Troeltschian Scripture scholarship, therefore, will proceed on the basis of the assumption that God never does anything specially; in particular, he neither raised Jesus from the dead nor specially inspired the Biblical authors.

[32] *Principles of Christian Theology*, 2nd ed. (New York: Charles Scribner's Sons, 1977), p. 248.

[33] 'Cosmology, Ontology and the Travail of Biblical Language', reprinted in Owen C. Thomas, ed., *God's Activity in the World: the Contemporary Problem* (Chico, CA: Scholars Press, 1983), p. 31.

2. Duhemian HBC

Not all who accept and practice HBC accept Troeltsch's principles, and we can see another variety of HBC by thinking about an important suggestion made by Pierre Duhem. Duhem was both a serious Catholic and a serious scientist; he was accused (as he thought) by Abel Rey[34] of allowing his religious and metaphysical views as a Christian to enter his physics in an improper way. Duhem repudiated this suggestion, claiming that his Christianity did not enter his physics in any way at all and *a fortiori* did not enter it in an improper way.[35] Furthermore, the *correct* or *proper* way to pursue physical theory, he said, was the way in which he had in fact done it; physical theory should be completely independent of religious or metaphysical views or commitments.

Why did he think so? What did he have against metaphysics? Here he strikes a characteristic Enlightenment note: if you think of metaphysics as ingressing into physics, he says, then your estimate of the worth of a physical theory will depend upon the metaphysics you adopt. Physical theory will be dependent upon metaphysics in such a way that someone who does not accept the metaphysics involved in a given physical theory cannot accept the physical theory either. And the problem with *that* is that the disagreements that run riot in metaphysics will ingress into physics, so that the latter cannot be an activity we can all work at together, regardless of our metaphysical views:

Now to make physical theories depend on metaphysics is surely not the way to let them enjoy the privilege of universal consent...If theoretical physics is subordinated to metaphysics, the divisions separating the diverse metaphysical systems will extend into the domain of physics. A physical theory reputed to be satisfactory by the sectarians of one metaphysical school will be rejected by the partisans of another school.[36]

Duhem's main point, I think, is that if a physical theorist employs metaphysical assumptions or other notions that are not accepted by other workers in the field, and employs them in such a way that those who do not accept them cannot accept his physical theory, then to that extent his work cannot be accepted by those others; to that extent, furthermore, the cooperation important to science will be compromised. He therefore proposes a conception of science (or physics in particular) according to which the latter is independent of metaphysics:

...I have denied metaphysical doctrines the right to testify for or against any physical theory.... Whatever I have said of the method by which physics proceeds, or the nature

---

[34] 'La Philosophie scientifique de M. Duhem', *Revue de Métaphysique et de Morale*, XII (July, 1904), pp. 699ff.

[35] See the appendix to Duhem's *The Aim and Structure of Physical Theory*, trans. Philip P. Wiener, foreword by Prince Louis de Broglie (Princeton, NJ: Princeton University Press, 1954) (the book was first published in 1906). The appendix is entitled 'Physics of a Believer' and is a reprint of Duhem's reply to Rey; it was originally in the *Annales de Philosophie chrétienne* Vol 1 (Oct. and Nov. 1905), pp. 44ff. and 133ff.

[36] Duhem, p. 10.

and scope that we must attribute to the theories it constructs, does not in any way prejudice either the metaphysical doctrines or religious beliefs of anyone who accepts my words. The believer and the nonbeliever may both work in common accord for the progress of physical science such as I have tried to define it.[37]

Duhem's proposal, reduced to essentials, is that physicists should not make essential use of religious or metaphysical assumptions in doing their physics: in that way lies chaos and cacophony, as each of the warring sects does things its own way. If we want to have the sort of commonality and genuine dialogue that promotes progress in physics, we should avoid assumptions—metaphysical, religious or otherwise—that are not accepted by all parties to the discussion.[38]

Duhem's suggestion is interesting and important, and (although Duhem himself did not do so) can obviously be applied far beyond the confines of physical theory: for example, to Scripture scholarship. Suppose we say that *Duhemian* Scripture scholarship is Scripture scholarship that does not involve any theological, religious or metaphysical assumptions that are not accepted by everyone in the relevant community.[39] Thus the Duhemian Scripture scholar would not take for granted either that God is the principal author of the Bible or that the main lines of the Christian story are in fact true; these are not accepted by all who are party to the discussion. She would not take for granted that Jesus rose from the dead, or that any other miracle has occurred; she could not so much as take it for granted that miracles are possible, since these claims are rejected by many who are party to the discussion. On the other hand, of course, Duhemian Scripture scholarship cannot take it for granted that Christ did *not* rise from the dead or that *no* miracles have occurred, or that miracles are *im*possible. Nor, of course, could it employ Troeltsch's principles (taken non-platitudinously); not everyone accepts them. Duhemian Scripture scholarship fits well with Sanders' suggestion that 'what is needed is more secure evidence, evidence on which everyone can agree' (above, p. 275). It also fits well with John Meier's fantasy of 'an unpapal conclave' of Jewish, Catholic, Protestant and agnostic scholars, locked in the basement of the Harvard Divinity School library until they come to consensus on what historical methods can show about the life and mission of Jesus.[40] Among the proposed benefits of Duhemian HBC, obviously, are just the

---

[37] Duhem, pp. 274–5.

[38] Of course, this proposal must be qualified, nuanced, sophisticated. It makes perfect sense for me to continue to work on a hypothesis after others have decided it is a dead end; science has often benefited from such disagreements.

[39] To be sure, it may be difficult to specify the relevant community. Suppose I am a Scripture scholar at a denominational seminary: what is my relevant community? Scripture scholars of any sort, all over the world? Scripture scholars in my own denomination? In western academia? The people, academics or not, in my denomination? Christians generally? The first thing to see here is that our Scripture scholar clearly belongs to many different communities, and may accordingly be involved in several different scholarly projects.

[40] *A Marginal Jew: Rethinking the Historical Jesus*, p. 1.

benefits Duhem cites: people of very different religious and theological beliefs can cooperate in this enterprise. Furthermore, although in principle the traditional Biblical commentator and the Troeltschian Biblical scholar could discover whatever is unearthed by Duhemian means, it is in fact likely that much will be learned in this cooperative enterprise that would not be learned by either group working alone.

3. Spinozistic HBC

Troeltschian and Duhemian HBC do not exhaust HBC; one can be a practitioner of HBC and accept neither. You might propose to follow reason alone in Scripture scholarship, but think that the Troeltschian principles, taken in the strong version in which they imply that God never acts specially in the world, are not in fact deliverances of reason. Reason alone, you say, certainly cannot demonstrate that God never acts specially in the world, or that no miracles have ever occurred. If so, you would not be a Troeltschian. On the other hand, you might also reject Duhemianism as well: for you might think that, as a matter of fact, there are deliverances of reason not accepted by everyone party to the project of Scripture scholarship. (The deliverances of reason are indeed *open* to all, but impeding factors of one kind or another can sometimes prevent someone from seeing the truth of one or another of them.) But then you might yourself employ those deliverances of reason in pursuing Scripture scholarship, thereby employing assumptions not accepted by everyone involved in the project, and thereby rejecting Duhemianism. You might therefore propose to follow reason alone, but be neither a Troeltschian nor a Duhemian. Suppose we use the term 'Spinozistic HBC'[41] to denote this variety of HBC. The Spinozist concurs with the Troeltschian and Duhemian that no theological assumptions or beliefs are to be employed in HBC. She differs from the Troeltschian in paying the same compliment to Troeltsch's principles: they too are not deliverances of reason and hence are not to be employed in HBC. And she differs from the Duhemian in holding that there are some deliverances of reason not accepted by all who are party to the project of Scripture scholarship; hence, she proposes to employ some propositions or beliefs rejected by the Duhemian.

A final point: It is not of course accurate to suppose that all who practice HBC fall neatly into one or another of these categories. There are all sorts of half-way houses, lots of haltings between two opinions, many who fall partly into one and partly into another, and many who have never clearly seen that there *are* these categories. A real live Scripture scholar may be unlikely to have spent a great deal of thought on the epistemological foundations of his or her discipline and is likely to straddle one or more of the categories I mention.

---

[41] According to Spinoza, as we saw, 'The rule for [Biblical] interpretation should be nothing but the natural light of reason...' (above p. 250).

B. Tensions with Traditional Christianity

There has been a history of substantial tension between HBC and traditional Christians. Thus David Friedrich Strauss[42] in 1835: 'Nay, if we would be candid with ourselves, that which was once sacred history for the Christian believer is, for the enlightened portion of our contemporaries, only fable.' Of course, the unenlightened faithful were not so unenlightened that they failed to notice this feature of Biblical criticism. Writing ten years after the publication of Strauss's book, William Pringle complains that, 'In Germany, Biblical criticism is almost a national pursuit... Unhappily, [the critics] were but too frequently employed in maintaining the most dangerous errors, in opposing every inspired statement which the mind of man is unable fully to comprehend, in divesting religion of its spiritual and heavenly character, and in undermining the whole fabric of revealed truth.'[43]

Perhaps among Pringle's complaints were the following. First, practitioners of HBC tend to treat the Bible as a set of separate books rather than a unified communication from God. Thus, they tend to reject the idea that Old Testament passages can be properly understood as making reference to Jesus Christ, or to events in his life: 'Critical scholars rule out clairvoyance as an explanation axiomatically. Instead of holding that the Old Testament predicts events in the life of Jesus, critical scholars of the New Testament say that each Gospel writer sought to exploit Old Testament passages in order to bolster his case for the messianic and dominical claims of Jesus or of the church on his behalf.'[44] More generally, Brevard Childs: 'For many decades the usual way of initiating entering students in the Bible was slowly to dismantle the church's traditional teachings regarding scripture by applying the acids of criticism.'[45]

Second, following Ernst Troeltsch HBC tends to discount miracle stories, taking it as axiomatic that miracles do not and did not really happen, or at any rate claiming that the proper method for HBC cannot admit miracles either as evidence or conclusions. Perhaps Jesus effected cures of some psychosomatic

---

[42] The author of *The Life of Jesus, Critically Examined* (London: Sonnenschein, 1892), one of the earliest higher critical salvoes.

[43] 'Translator's Preface', *Calvin's Commentaries,* Vol. xvi, trans. the Rev. William Pringle (Grand Rapids, MI: Baker Book House, 1979), p. vi. Pringle's preface is dated at Auchterarder, Jan. 4, 1845.

[44] John D. Levenson, 'The Hebrew Bible, the Old Testament, and Historical Criticism' in *The Hebrew Bible, the Old Testament, and Historical Criticism,* p. 9. (An earlier version of this essay was published under the same title in *Hebrew Bible or Old Testament? Studying the Bible in Judaism and Christianity,* eds. John Collins and Roger Brooks (Notre Dame, IN: University of Notre Dame Press, 1990).) Of course, *clairvoyance* is not at issue at all: the question is really whether the Scripture has one principal author, namely God. If it does, then it does not require clairvoyance on the part of a human author for a passage from a given time to refer to something that happens much later. All that is required is God's omniscience.

[45] *The New Testament as Canon: An Introduction* (Valley Forge, PA: Trinity Press International, 1984, 1994), p. xvii.

disorders, but nothing that modern medical science cannot explain. Many employing this method propose that Jesus never thought of himself as divine, or as the Messiah, or as capable of forgiving sin[46]—let alone as having died and then risen from the dead. 'The Historical Jesus researchers,' says Luke Timothy Johnson, 'insist that the "real Jesus" must be found in the facts of his life before his death. The resurrection is, when considered at all, seen in terms of visionary experience, or as a continuation of an "empowerment" that began before Jesus' death. Whether made explicit or not, the operative premise is that there is no 'real Jesus' after his death' (Johnson, p. 144).

Those who follow these methods sometimes produce quite remarkable accounts—and accounts remarkably different from traditional Christian understanding. According to Barbara Thiering's *Jesus and the Riddle of the Dead Sea Scrolls,*[47] for example, Jesus was buried in a cave; he did not actually die and was revived by the magician Simon Magus, whereupon he married Mary Magdalene, settled down, fathered three children, was divorced and finally died in Rome. According to Morton Smith, Jesus was a practicing homosexual and conjurer.[48] According to German Scripture scholar Gerd Ludemann: the Resurrection is 'an empty formula that must be rejected by anyone holding a scientific world view'.[49] G. A. Wells goes so far as to claim that our name 'Jesus', as it turns up in the Bible, is empty: like 'Santa Claus', it does not trace back to or denote anyone at all.[50] John Allegro apparently thinks there was no such person as Jesus of Nazareth; Christianity began as a hoax designed to fool the Romans, and preserve the cult of a certain hallucinogenic mushroom (*Amanita muscaria*). Still, the name 'Christ' is not empty: it is really a name of that mushroom.[51] As engaging a claim as any is that Jesus, while neither merely legendary, nor actually a mushroom, was in fact an atheist, the first Christian atheist.[52] And even if we set aside the lunatic fringe, Van Harvey is correct: 'So far as the biblical historian is concerned,... there is scarcely a popularly held traditional belief about Jesus that is not regarded with considerable skepticism' (NTS, p. 193).

---

[46] 'The crisis grows out of the fact now freely admitted by both Protestant and Catholic theologians and exegetes: that as far as can be discerned from the available historical data, Jesus of Nazareth did not think he was divine [and] did not assert any of the messianic claims that the New Testament attributes to him...' Thomas Sheehan, *The First Coming* (New York, NY: Random House, 1986), p. 9.

[47] San Francisco: HarperSanFrancisco, 1992.

[48] *Jesus the Magician* (New York, NY: Harper and Row, 1978).

[49] *What Really Happened to Jesus: A Historical Approach to the Resurrection* (Louisville, KY: Westminster/John Knox Press, 1995).

[50] 'The Historicity of Jesus' in *Jesus in History and Myth*, eds., R. Joseph Hoffman and Gerald A. Larue (Buffalo, NY: Prometheus Books, 1986), pp. 27ff.

[51] *The Sacred Mushroom and the Cross* (Garden City, NY: Doubleday and Co., 1970).

[52] Sheehan, *op. cit.*

IV. WHY ARE NOT MOST CHRISTIANS
MORE CONCERNED?

So HBC has not in general been sympathetic to traditional Christian belief; it has hardly been an encouragement to the faithful. But the faithful seem relatively unconcerned; of course, they find traditional biblical commentary of great interest and importance, but the beliefs and attitudes of HBC have not seemed to filter down to them, despite its dominance in mainline seminaries. According to Van Harvey, 'Despite decades of research, the average person tends to think of the life of Jesus in much the same terms as Christians did three centuries ago ...' Harvey finds this puzzling: 'Why is it that, in a culture so dominated by experts in every field, the opinion of New Testament historians has had so little influence on the public?'[53] Are traditional Christians just ignoring inconvenient evidence? In what follows I will try to answer these questions. Obviously, HBC has contributed greatly to our knowledge of the Bible, in particular the circumstances and conditions of its composition; it has given us new alternatives as to how to understand the human authors, and this has also given us new ideas as to how to understand the divine Author. Nevertheless, there are in fact excellent reasons for tending to ignore that 'considerable skepticism', of which Harvey speaks. I do not mean to claim that the ordinary person in the pew ignores it because she has these reasons clearly in mind; no doubt she does not. I say only that these reasons are *good reasons* for a traditional Christian to ignore the deflationary results of HBC.

What might these reasons be? Well of course one thing is that skeptical Scripture scholars display vast disagreement among themselves.[54] There is also the fact that quite a number of the arguments they propose seem at best wholly inconclusive. Perhaps the endemic vice or at any rate the perennial temptation of HBC is what we might call the Fallacy of Creeping Certitude. To practice this fallacy, you note that some proposition A is probable (to .9, say) with respect to your background knowledge k (what you know to be true); you therefore annex it to k. Then you note that a proposition B is probable with respect to k&A; you therefore annex it too to k. Then you note that C is probable to .9 with respect to A&B&k, and also annex it to K; similarly for (say) D, E, F and G. You then pronounce A&B&C&D&E&F&G highly probable with respect to k, our evidence. But the fact is (as we learn from the probability calculus) that these probabilities must be *multiplied*—so that in fact the probability of A&B&C&D&E&F&G is .9 to the 7th power, i.e., less than .5! But suppose we look into reasons or arguments for preferring the results of HBC to those of traditional commentary. Why should we suppose that the former take us closer to

---

[53] Ibid., p. 194.

[54] As we have just seen. This lack of accord is especially well documented by Stephen Evans (op. cit.), pp. 322ff.

the truth than the latter? Troeltsch's principles are particularly important here. As understood in the interpretative community of HBC, they preclude special divine action including special divine inspiration of Scripture and the occurrence of miracles. As Gilkey says, 'Suddenly a vast panoply of divine deeds and events recorded in scripture are no longer regarded as having actually happened' (above, p. 280). Many academic theologians and Scripture scholars appear to believe that Troeltschian HBC is *de rigueur*; it is often regarded as the only intellectually respectable variety of Scripture scholarship, or the only variety that has any claim to the mantle of science. (And many who arrive at relatively traditional conclusions in Scripture scholarship nevertheless pay at least lip service to the Troeltschian ideal, somehow feeling in a semi-confused way that this is the epistemically respectable or privileged way of proceeding.) But why think Scripture scholarship should proceed in this specific way—as opposed both to traditional biblical commentary and varieties of HBC that do not accept Troeltsch's principles? Are there any reasons or arguments for those principles?

A. Force Majeure

If so, they are extraordinarily well hidden. One common suggestion, however, seems to be a sort of appeal to *force majeure*: we simply cannot help it. Given our historical position, there is nothing else we can do; we are all in the grip of historical forces beyond our control (this thing is bigger than either one of us). This reaction is typified by those, who like Harvey, Macquarrie, Gilkey, and others claim that nowadays, given our cultural situation, we just do not have any options. There are potent historical forces that impose these ways of thinking upon us; like it or not, we are blown about by these powerful winds of doctrine. 'The causal nexus in space and time which the Enlightenment science and philosophy introduced into the Western mind . . . is also assumed by modern theologians and scholars; since they participate in the modern world of science both intellectually and existentially, they can scarcely do anything else', says Gilkey (above, p. 280); another example is Bultmann's famous remark to the effect that 'it is impossible to use electrical light and the wireless and to avail ourselves of modern medical and surgical discoveries, and at the same time to believe in the New Testament world of spirits and miracles.'[55]

---

[55] *Kerygma and Myth* (New York, NY: Harper and Row, 1961), p. 5. Compare Marcus Borg's more recent comment: ' . . . to a large extent, the defining characteristic of biblical scholarship in the modern period is the attempt to understand Scripture without reference to another world because in this period the visible world of space and time is the world we think of as "real." ' ('Root Images and the Way We See', *Fragments of Infinity* (Dorset, UK, & Lindfield, Australia, 1991), p. 38. Quoted in Huston Smith's 'Doing Theology in the Global Village', *Religious Studies and Theology*, Vol. 13/14, No. 2/3, (December, 1995), p. 12. On the other side, note Abraham Kuyper (*To Be Near Unto God,* trans. John Hendrik de Vries (Grand Rapids, MI: Wm. B. Eerdmans Publishing Co., 1918), pp. 50–1); writing not long after the invention of the 'wireless', he saw it not as an obstacle to traditional faith but as a sort of electronic symbol of the way in which each of us can communicate instantaneously with God.

But is not this view—that we are all compelled by contemporary historical forces to hold the sort of view in question—historically naive? First, why think we proceed together in lockstep through history, all at any given time perforce holding the same views and making the same assumptions? Clearly we do not do any such thing. The contemporary intellectual world is much more like a horse race (or perhaps a demolition derby) than a triumphal procession, more like a battleground than a Democratic Party fund-raiser, where everyone can be counted on to support the same slate. At present, for example, there are many like Macquarrie, Harvey and Gilkey who accept the semi-deistic view that God (if there is any such person) could not or would not act miraculously in history. But this is not, of course, the view of nearly everyone at present; hundreds of millions would reject it. The fact is that far more people reject this view than accept it. (So even if Gilkey, *et al.*, were right about the inevitable dance of history, they would be wrong in their elitist notion to the effect that what *they* do is the current step.)

The utter obviousness of this fact suggests a second interpretation of this particular justification of Troeltschian HBC. Perhaps what the apologists really mean is not that *everyone* nowadays accepts this semi-deism (that is trivially false), but that everyone *in the know* does. Everyone who is properly educated and has read his Kant and Hume (and Troeltsch) and reflected on the meaning of the wireless and electric light knows these things; as for the rest of humanity (including, I suppose, those of us who have read our Kant and Hume but are unimpressed), their problem is simple ignorance. Perhaps people generally do not march lockstep through history, but those in the know do; and right now they all or nearly all reject special divine action.

But even if we chauvinistically stick to educated Westerners, this is still doubtful *in excelsis*. 'The traditional conception of miracle', Macquarrie says, 'is irreconcilable with *our* modern understanding of both science and history' (above, p. 280; emphasis added): to whom does this 'our', here refer? To those who have gone to university, are well-educated, know at least a little science, and have thought about the bearing of these matters on the possibility of miracles? If so, the claim is once more whoppingly false. Very many well-educated people (including even some theologians) understand science and history in a way that is entirely compatible both with the possibility and with the actuality of miracles. Many physicists and engineers understand 'electrical light and the wireless' vastly better than Bultmann or his contemporary followers, but nonetheless hold precisely those New Testament beliefs Bultmann thinks incompatible with using electric lights and radios. There are large numbers of educated contemporaries (including even some with Ph.Ds!) who believe Jesus really and literally arose from the dead, that God performs miracles in the contemporary world, and even that there are both demons and spirits who are active in the contemporary world. As a matter of historical fact, there are any number of contemporaries, and contemporary intellectuals very well acquainted with science, who do not feel any problem at all in pursuing science and also believing in miracles, angels, Christ's resurrection, the lot.

Once more, however, Macquarrie, *et al.*, must know this as well as anyone else; so what do he and his friends really mean? How can they make these claims about what 'we'[56]—we who use the products of science and know a bit about it—can and cannot believe? How can they blithely exclude or ignore the thousands, indeed millions of contemporary Christians who do not think as they do? The answer must be that they think those Christians somehow do not count. What they really mean to say, I fear, is that they and their friends think this way, and anyone who demurs is so ignorant as to be properly ignored. But that is at best a bit slim as a *reason* for accepting the Troeltschian view; it is more like a nasty little piece of arrogance. Nor is it any better for being tucked away in the suggestion that somehow we just cannot help ourselves. Of course, it is possible that Gilkey and his friends cannot help themselves; in that case they can hardly be blamed for accepting the view in question.[57] This incapacity on their parts, however, is no recommendation of Troeltsch's principles.

So this is at best a poor reason for thinking serious Biblical scholarship must be Troeltschian. Is there a better reason? A second suggestion, perhaps connected with the plea of inability to do otherwise, is given by the suggestion that the very practice of science presupposes rejection of the idea of miracle or special divine action in the world. 'Science proceeds on the assumption that whatever events occur in the world can be accounted for in terms of other events that also belong within the world', says Macquarrie (above, p. 280); perhaps he means to suggest that the very practice of science requires that one reject (e.g.) the idea of God's raising someone from the dead. Of course, the argument form

if X were true, it would be inconvenient for science; therefore, X is false

is at best moderately compelling. We are not just given that the Lord has arranged the universe for the comfort and convenience of the American Academy of Science. To think otherwise is to be like the drunk who insisted on looking for his lost car keys under the streetlight, on the grounds that the light was better there. (In fact it would be to go the drunk one better: it would be to insist that since the keys would be hard to find in the dark, they must be under the light.)

But why think in the first place that we would have to embrace this semi-deism in order to do science?[58] Newton certainly did some sensible science, but he

---

[56] We might call this the preemptive 'we': those who do not agree with us on the point in question are (by comparison with us) so unenlightened that we can properly speak as if they do not so much as exist.

[57] Some, however, might see here little more than an effort to gain standing and respectability in a largely secular academia by adopting a stance that is, so to say, more Catholic than the Pope.

[58] Here I can be brief; William Alston has already proposed a compelling argument for the claim I propose to support, namely, that one can perfectly well do science even if one thinks God has done and even sometimes still does miracles. See his 'Divine Action: Shadow or Substance?' in *The God Who Acts: Philosophical and Theological Explorations*, ed. Thomas F. Tracy (University Park, PA: Penn State University Press, 1994), pp. 49–50.

thought Jesus was raised from the dead, as do many contemporary physicists. But of course that is physics; perhaps the problem would be (as Bultmann suggests) with *medicine*. Is the idea that one could not do medical research, or prescribe medications, if one thought that God has done miracles in the past and might even occasionally do some nowadays? To put the suggestion explicitly is to refute it; there is not the faintest reason why I could not sensibly believe that God raised Jesus from the dead and also engage in medical research into, say, Usher's Syndrome or Multiple Sclerosis, or into ways of staving off the ravages of coronary disease. What would be the problem? That it is always *possible* that God should do something different, thus spoiling my experiment? But that *is* possible: God is omnipotent. (Or do we have here a new antitheistic argument? If God exists, he could spoil my experiment; but nothing can spoil my experiment; therefore...) No doubt if I thought God *often* or *usually* did things in an idiosyncratic way, so that there really are not much by way of discoverable regularities to be found, *then* perhaps I could not sensibly engage in scientific research; the latter presupposes a certain regularity, predictability, stability in the world. But that is an entirely different matter. What I must assume in order to do science, is only that *ordinarily* and for the *most* part these regularities hold.[59] This reason, too, then, is monumentally insufficient as a reason for holding that we are somehow obliged to accept the principles underlying Troeltschian Biblical scholarship.

It is therefore difficult indeed to see any reason for supposing that Troeltschian Scripture scholarship is somehow *de rigueur* or somehow forced upon us by our history.

B. A Moral Imperative?

Van Harvey proposes another reason for pursuing Troeltschian scholarship and preferring it to traditional Biblical commentary;[60] his reason is broadly *moral* or *ethical*. He begins[61] by referring to a fascinating episode in Victorian intellectual history[62] in which certain Victorian intellectuals found themselves wrestling with a serious problem of intellectual integrity. As Harvey sees it, they 'believed that it was morally reprehensible to insist that these claims [Christian claims about the activities and teachings of Jesus] were true on faith while at the same time arguing that they were also the legitimate objects of historical inquiry'.[63] Now I think this

[59] As Alston argues.

[60] I *think* the argument is intended to support Troeltschian HBC; it could also be used, however, to support Spinozistic or (less plausibly) Duhemian HBC.

[61] NTS, pp. 194ff; a fuller (if older) and influential presentation of his views is to be found in his *The Historian and the Believer.*

[62] Described with insight and verve in James C. Livingston's monograph *The Ethics of Belief: An Essay on the Victorian Religious Conscience* in the American Academy of Religion's *Studies in Religion* (Tallahassee, FL, and Missoula, MT: Scholars Press, 1978). I thank Martin Cook for calling my attention to this monograph.

[63] Harvey, NTS, p. 195.

is a tendentious account of the problem these intellectuals faced—tendentious, because it makes it look as if these intellectuals were endorsing, with unerring prescience, precisely the position Harvey himself proposes to argue for. The fact is, I think, their position was both less idiosyncratic and far more plausible. After all, why should anyone think it immoral to believe by faith what could also be investigated by other sources of belief or knowledge? I am curious about your whereabouts last Friday night: were you perhaps at The Linebacker's Bar? Perhaps I could find out in three different ways: by asking you, by asking your wife, and by examining the bar for your fingerprints (fortunately the bar is never washed). Would there be something immoral in using one of these methods when in fact the others were also available? That is not easy to believe.

It was not just *that* that troubled the Victorians. Had they been confident that both faith and historical investigation were reliable avenues to the truths in question, they surely would not have thought it immoral to believe on the basis of one of these as opposed to the other or both. Their problem was deeper. They were troubled (among other things) by the German Scripture scholarship about which they knew relatively little; but they did know enough to think (rightly or wrongly) that it posed a real threat to the Christian beliefs that for many of them were in any event already shaky. They suspected or feared that this Scripture scholarship could show or would show or already had shown that essential elements of the Christian faith were just false. They were also troubled by what many saw as the anti-supernaturalistic and antitheistic bent of science: could one really believe in the New Testament world of spirits and miracles in the era of the steam engine and ocean liner? They were troubled by the advent of Darwinism, which seemed to many to contradict the Christian picture of human origins. They were convinced, following Locke and the whole classical foundationalist tradition, that the right way to hold beliefs on these topics is by following the (propositional) evidence wherever it leads; and they were deeply worried about where this evidence was in fact leading. They were troubled, in short, by a variety of factors all of which seemed to suggest that traditional Christian belief was really no more than a beautiful story: inspiring, uplifting, perhaps necessary to public morality, but just a story. Given our scientific coming of age, they feared, informed people would regretfully have to jettison traditional Christian belief, perhaps (especially on ceremonial occasions) with an occasional nostalgic backward look.

But many of them also longed for the comfort and security of serious Christian belief; to lose it was like being thrown out of our Father's house into a hostile or indifferent world. And, of course, many of the Victorians had strong moral opinions and a highly developed moral sense. They thought it weak, spineless, cowardly to refuse to face these specters, to hide them from oneself, to engage in self-deception and double-think. All of this, they thought, is unworthy of a serious and upright person. They abhorred the weakness and moral softness of the sort of stance in which you suspect the bitter truth, but refuse to investigate the matter, preferring to hide the truth from yourself, perhaps hoping it will somehow go away. Many of them thought this was precisely what some of the clergy and other educators were doing, and despised them for it. Far better to face the sad truth with intellectual honesty, manly courage and a stiff upper lip. So it was not just that they thought it reprehensible to believe on faith what can also be addressed by reason or historical investigation. It was rather that they suspected and deeply feared that the latter (together with the other factors I mentioned) would undermine the former. And they scorned and detested a sort of willful head-in-the-sand attitude in which, out of timidity or fear or a desire for comfort, one refuses to face the facts. It is reasons such as these that account for the moral fervor (if not stridency) of W. K. Clifford's oft-anthologized 'The Ethics of Belief'.[64]

However things may have stood with the Victorians, Harvey proposes the following bit of moral dogma:

The gulf separating the conservative Christian believer and the New Testament scholar can be seen as the conflict between two antithetical ethics of belief... New Testament scholarship is now so specialized and requires so much preparation that the layperson has simply been disqualified from having any right to a judgment regarding the truth or falsity of certain historical claims. Insofar as the conservative Christian believer is a layperson who has no knowledge of the New Testament scholarship, he or she is simply not entitled to certain historical beliefs at all. Just as the average layperson is scarcely in a position to have an informed judgment about the seventh letter of Plato, the relationship of Montezuma to Cortez, or the authorship of the Donation of Constantine, so the average layperson has no right to an opinion about the authorship of the Fourth Gospel or the trustworthiness of the synoptics.[65]

'The layperson has simply been disqualified from having any right to a judgment regarding the truth or falsity of certain historical claims. . . . ' Strong words! In an earlier age, priests and ministers, often the only educated members of their congregations, would exercise a certain intellectual and spiritual leadership, hoping the flock would in fact come to see, appreciate, and of course believe the truth. On Harvey's showing, the flock does not so much as have a right to an opinion on these points—not even an opinion purveyed by the experts! Harvey complains that many students seem unreceptive to the results of Scripture scholarship.[66] But of course if he is right, the students do not have a right to believe the results of Scripture scholarship; they are therefore doing no more than their simple duty in refusing to believe them. One hopes Harvey remembers, when teaching his classes, not to put his views on these matters in an attractive and winsome fashion—after all, if he did so, some of the students might *believe*

---

[64] First published in *The Contemporary Review* (XXIX, 1877); reprinted in Clifford's *Lectures and Essays* (London: Macmillan, 1879), pp. 354ff.

[65] Harvey, NTS, p. 197.

[66] Harvey, NTS, p. 193.

them, in which case they would be sinning and he himself would be giving offense in the Pauline sense (Romans 14, not to mention I Cor. 8:9).

But suppose we sadly avert our gaze from this elitism run amok: why does Harvey think that only the historian has a right to hold an opinion on these matters? Clearly enough, because he thinks that the only way to achieve accurate and reliable information on these matters is by way of Troeltschian scholarship. And *that* opinion, obviously, presupposes the philosophical and theological opinion that there is not any *other* epistemic avenue to these matters; it presupposes that, for example, faith (and the internal instigation or testimony of the Holy Spirit) is not a source of warranted belief or knowledge on these topics. If the latter *were* a source of warranted belief, and if the 'average layperson' had access to this source (if the 'average layperson' could have faith), then presumably there would be nothing whatever wrong with her holding views on these matters on this basis. 'Just as the average layperson is scarcely in a position to have an informed judgment about the seventh letter of Plato, the relationship of Montezuma to Cortez, or the authorship of the Donation of Constantine, so the average layperson has no right to an opinion about the authorship of the Fourth Gospel or the trustworthiness of the synoptics,' says Harvey. The only way to determine the truth about the seventh letter of Plato is by way of ordinary historical investigation; the same goes, Harvey assumes, for questions about the life and ministry of Christ, whether he rose from the dead, whether he thought of himself as a Messiah, and the like. What lies at the bottom of this moral claim is really a philosophical/theological judgment: that traditional Christian belief is completely mistaken in taking it that faith is in fact a reliable source of true and warranted belief on these topics.

This view is not, of course, a result of historical scholarship, Troeltschian or otherwise; nor is it supported by arguments that will appeal to anyone who does not already agree with him—or indeed by any arguments at all. Harvey's view is rather a *presupposition*, a methodological prescription of the pursuit of Troeltschian historical criticism and proscription of traditional Biblical commentary. So it can hardly be thought of as an independent good reason for preferring the former to the latter. What we have are different philosophical/theological positions that dictate different ways of pursuing Scripture scholarship. A way to show that the one really *is* superior to the other would be to give a good argument *for* the one philosophical/theological position, or *against* the other. Harvey does neither, simply assuming (uncritically, and without so much as mentioning the fact) the one position and rejecting the other. He assumes that there is no source of warrant or knowledge in addition to reason. This is not self-evident; millions, maybe billions of Christians and others reject it. Is it sensible, then, just to *assume* it, without so much as acknowledging this contrary opinion, without so much as a feeble gesture in the direction of argument or reason?

C. HBC More Inclusive?

John Collins recognizes that Troeltschian scholarship involves theological assumptions not nearly universally shared. He does not argue for the truth of these
assumptions, but recommends them on a quite different basis. Criticizing
Brevard Childs's proposal for a 'canonical' approach to Scripture scholarship,[67]
he claims that the problem is that the former does not provide an *inclusive context*
for the latter:

> If biblical theology is to retain a place in serious scholarship, it must be...conceived
> broadly enough to provide a context for debate between different viewpoints. Otherwise
> it is likely to become a sectarian reservation, of interest only to those who hold certain
> confessional tenets that are not shared by the discipline at large. Childs's dogmatic
> conception of the canon provides no basis for advancing dialogue. In my opinion
> historical criticism still provides the most satisfactory framework for discussion.[68]

He adds that:

> One criterion for the adequacy of presuppositions is the degree to which they allow
> dialogue between differing viewpoints and accommodate new insights.... Perhaps the
> outstanding achievement of historical criticism in this century is that it has provided a
> framework within which scholars of different prejudices and commitments have been able
> to debate in a constructive manner.[69]

So why should we prefer Troeltschian Scripture scholarship over traditional
Bible commentary? Because it offers a wider context, one in which people with
conflicting theological opinions can all take part. We may be conservative
Christians, theological liberals, or people with no theological views whatever:
we can all take part in Troeltschian Scripture scholarship, provided we acquiesce
in its fundamental assumptions. This is why it is to be preferred to the more
traditional sort.

Now this would perhaps be a reason for practicing *Duhemian* Scripture
scholarship, but of course Troeltschian Scripture scholarship is not Duhemian:
the principles upon which it proceeds are not accepted by nearly everyone. They
would be accepted by only a tiny minority of contemporary Christians, for
example. And this shows a fundamental confusion, so it seems to me, in Collins's
defence of Troeltschian scholarship. The defense he offers is appropriate for
Duhemian scholarship; it is not at all appropriate for *Troeltschian* scholarship.
The principles of Troeltschian historical scholarship, so interpreted as to preclude
miracle, direct divine action, and special divine inspiration of the Bible, are

[67] See, e.g., Childs's *The New Testament as Canon: An Introduction* (Valley Forge, PA: Trinity Press International, 1994), pp. 3–53.
[68] 'Is a Critical Biblical Theology Possible?' in *The Hebrew Bible and its Interpreters,* pp. 6–7. Collins speaks here not of Troeltschian HBC but of HBC simpliciter; a couple of pages earlier, however, he identifies HBC with Troeltschian HBC.
[69] Ibid., p. 8.

extremely controversial philosophical and theological assumptions. Those who do not accept these controversial assumptions will not be inclined to take part in Troeltschian HBC, just as those who do not accept traditional Christian philosophical and theological views will not be likely to engage in traditional Biblical commentary. (If you do not think the Lord speaks in Scripture, you will be unlikely to spend a great deal of your time trying to figure out what it is God says there.) As John Levenson puts it, historical criticism 'does not facilitate communication with those outside its boundaries: it requires fundamentalists, for example, to be born again as liberals—or to stay out of the conversation altogether.' He adds that 'if inclusiveness is to be gauged quantitatively, then [Brevard] Childs would win the match hands down, for far more people with biblical interests share Christian faith than a thoroughgoing historicism. Were we historical critics to be classed as a religious body we should have to be judged a most minuscule sect indeed—and one with a pronounced difficulty relating to groups that do not accept our beliefs.'[70]

V. NOTHING TO BE CONCERNED ABOUT

We are now prepared to return to Harvey's original question: why is it that the person in the pew pays little attention to the contemporary HBC, and, despite those decades of research, retains rather a traditional picture of the life and ministry of Jesus? As to why *in actual historical fact* this is the case, this is a job for an intellectual historian. What we have seen so far, however, is that there is no compelling or even reasonably decent argument for supposing that the procedures and assumptions of HBC are to be preferred to those of traditional Biblical commentary. A little epistemological reflection enables us to see something further: the traditional Christian (whether in the pew or not) has a good reason to reject the skeptical claims of HBC and continue to hold traditional Christian belief despite the allegedly corrosive acids of HBC.

A. Troeltschian HBC Again

As we have seen, there are substantially three types of HBC. For present purposes, however, we can consider Duhemian and Spinozistic HBC together. Let us say, therefore, that we have both Troeltschian and non-Troeltschian HBC. Consider the first. The Troeltschian Scripture scholar accepts Troeltsch's principles for historical research, under an interpretation according to which they rule out the occurrence of miracles and the divine inspiration of the Bible (along with the corollary that the latter enjoys the sort of unity accruing to a book that has one principal author). But then it is not at all surprising that the Troeltschian

---

[70] Levenson, p. 120.

tends to come up with conclusions wildly at variance with those accepted by the traditional Christian. As Gilkey says, 'Suddenly a vast panoply of divine deeds and events recorded in scripture are no longer regarded as having actually happened' (above, p. 280). Now if (instead of tendentious claims about our inability to do otherwise) the Troeltschian offered some good reasons to think that in fact these Troeltschian principles are *true*, then the traditional Christian would certainly have to pay attention; then she might be obliged to take the skeptical claims of historical critics seriously. But Troeltschians apparently do not offer any such good reasons. They simply declare that nowadays we cannot think in any other way, or (following Harvey) that it is immoral to believe in, e.g., Christ's resurrection on other than historical grounds.

Neither of these is remotely persuasive as a reason for modifying traditional Christian belief in the light of Troeltschian results. As for the first, of course, the traditional Christian knows that it is quite false: she herself and many of her friends nowadays (and hundreds of millions of others) do think in precisely that proscribed way. And as far as the implicit claims for the superiority of these Troeltschian ways of thinking go, she will not be impressed by them unless some decent arguments of one sort or another are forthcoming, or some other good reason for adopting that opinion. The mere claim that this is what many contemporary experts think will not and should not intimidate her. And the second proposed reason (Harvey's reason) seems to be itself dependent on the very claim at issue. Clearly the critic thinks it immoral to form beliefs about historical facts on grounds other than historical research because he believes that the only reliable grounds for beliefs of the former type is research of the latter type. Again, however, he offers no argument for this assumption, merely announcing it as what those in the know believe, and perhaps also adopting an air of injured puzzlement about the fact that the person in the pew does not seem to pay much attention.

To see the point here, consider an analogy: suppose your friend is accused and convicted of stealing an ancient and valuable Frisian vase from the local museum. As it happens, you remember clearly that at the time this vase was stolen, your friend was in your office defending his eccentric views about the gospel of John. You have testified to this in court, but to no avail. I come along and offer to do a scientific investigation to see whether your view here is in fact correct. You are delighted, knowing as you think you do that your friend is innocent. When I explain my methods to you, however, your delight turns to dismay. For I refuse to accept the testimony of memory; I propose to ignore completely the fact that you *remember* your friend's being in your office. Further, my method precludes from the start the conclusion that your friend is innocent, even if he *is* innocent. Could I blame you for losing interest in my 'scientific' investigation? But the traditional Christian ought to view Troeltschian HBC with the same suspicion: it refuses to admit a source of warranted belief (the testimony of Scripture) the traditional Christian accepts, and is precluded in advance from coming to such conclusions as that Jesus really did arise from the dead and really is the divine Son of God.

B. Non-Troeltschian HBC

Troeltschian HBC, therefore, has no claim on a serious Christian; it is wholly reasonable for her to form and maintain her beliefs quite independently of it. How about non-Troeltschian (Duhemian and Spinozistic) HBC? This is, of course, a very different kettle of fish. The non-Troeltschian proposes to employ only assumptions that are clearly deliverances of reason (or accepted by everyone party to the project). She does not (for purposes of scholarship) accept the traditional Christian's views about the Bible or the life of Christ, but she also does not accept Troeltsch's principles. She does not assume that miracles did or could not happen; but of course that is quite different from assuming that they did not or could not, and she does not assume that either. She does not assume that the Bible is in fact a word from the Lord and hence authoritative and reliable; but she also does not assume that it is not.

Of course, that may not leave her a lot to go on. The non-Troeltschian is handicapped in this area in a way in which she is not in such areas as physics or chemistry. In the latter, there is little by way of theological controversy that seems relevant to the pursuit of the subject. Not so for Scripture scholarship; here the very foundations of the subject are deeply disputed. Does the Bible have one principal author, namely God himself? If not, then perhaps Jowett—'Scripture has one meaning—the meaning which it had to the mind of the prophet or evangelist who first uttered or wrote, to the hearers or readers who first received it'—is right; otherwise, he is wrong.[71] Is it divinely inspired, so that what it teaches is both true and to be accepted? If it reports miraculous happenings—risings from the dead, a virgin birth, the changing of water into wine, healings of people blind or lame from birth—are these to be taken more or less at face value, or dismissed as contrary to 'what we now know'? Is there an entry into the truth about these matters—faith or divine testimony by way of Scripture, for example—quite different from ordinary historical investigation? If we prescind from all these matters and proceed responsibly (remembering to shun the Fallacy of Creeping Certitude, for example), what we come up with is likely to be pretty slender.

A. E. Harvey, for example, proposes the following as beyond reasonable doubt from everyone's point of view, i.e., Duhemianly: 'that Jesus was known in both Galilee and Jerusalem, that he was a teacher, that he carried out cures of various illnesses, particularly demon-possession and that these were widely regarded as miraculous; that he was involved in controversy with fellow Jews over questions of the law of Moses: and that he was crucified in the governorship of Pontius

---

[71] see note 17 above.

Pilate.'[72] It is not even clear whether Harvey means that the *conjunction* of these propositions is beyond reasonable doubt, or only each of the conjuncts;[73] in either case what we have is pretty slim.

Or consider John Meier's monumental *A Marginal Jew: Rethinking the Historical Jesus*.[74] Meier aims to be Duhemian, or anyway Spinozistic: 'My method follows a simple rule: it prescinds from what Christian faith or later Church teaching says about Jesus, without either affirming or denying such claims'.[75] (I think he also means to eschew assumptions incompatible with traditional Christian belief.) Meier's fantasy of 'an unpapal conclave' of Jewish, Catholic, Protestant and agnostic scholars, locked in the basement of the Harvard Divinity School library until they come to consensus on what historical methods can show about the life and mission of Jesus, is thoroughly Duhemian. This conclave, he says, would yield '. . . a rough draft of what that will-o'-the-wisp "all reasonable people" could say about the historical Jesus.'[76] Meier sets out, judiciously, objectively, carefully, to establish that consensus.[77] What is striking about his conclusions, however, is how slender they are, and how tentative—and this despite the fact that on occasion he cannot himself resist building occasional towers of probability. About all that emerges from Meier's painstaking work is that Jesus was a prophet, a proclaimer of an eschatological message from God, someone who performs powerful deeds, signs and wonders, that announce God's kingdom, and also ratify his message.[78] As Duhemian or Spinozist, of course, we cannot add that these signs and miracles involve special or direct divine action; nor can we say that they do not. We cannot say that Jesus rose from the dead, or that he did not; we cannot conclude that Scripture is specially inspired, or that it is not.

Now what is characteristic of non-Troeltschian HBC is just that it does not involve those Troeltschian principles: but of course it also rejects any alleged source of warranted belief in addition to reason (Spinozistic) and any theological assumptions not shared by everyone party to the discussion. Traditional Christians, rightly or wrongly, think they do have sources of warranted belief in addition to reason: faith and the work of the Holy Spirit, or divine testimony in Scripture, or the testimony of the Spirit-led church. They may of course

---

[72] *Jesus and the Constraints of History* (London and Philadelphia: Westminster Press, 1982), p. 6.

[73] It could be that each of the conjuncts is beyond reasonable doubt but that their conjunction is not. Suppose (just to choose arbitrarily a number) what is probable to degree .95 or higher is beyond reasonable doubt. Then if each of the above is beyond reasonable doubt, their conjunction might still be little more than twice as probable as its denial.

[74] New York, NY: Doubleday, 1991, 1994. The first volume has 484 pages; the second has 1,055 pages; a third volume is currently expected.

[75] Meier, *A Marginal Jew*, p. 1.

[76] Ibid., p. 2.

[77] 'Meier's treatment, in short, is as solid and moderate and pious as Historical Jesus scholarship is ever likely to be. More important, Meier is a careful scholar. There is nothing hasty or slipshod in his analysis; he considers every opinion, weighs every option.' Johnson, p. 128.

[78] See Johnson, pp. 130–1.

be *mistaken* about that; but until someone gives a decent argument for the conclusion that they *are* mistaken, they need not be impressed by the result of scholarship that ignores this further source of belief. If you want to learn the truth about a given area, you should not restrict yourself to only *some* of the sources of warranted belief (as does the Spinozist), or only to beliefs accepted by everyone else (with the Duhemian); maybe you know something some of the others do not. Perhaps you remember that your friend was in your office expostulating about the errors of postmodernism at the very time he is supposed to have been stealing that Frisian vase; if no one else was there, then you know something the rest do not.

So the traditional Christian need not be fazed by the fact that non-Troeltschian HBC does not support her views about what Jesus did and said. She thinks she knows some things by faith—that Jesus arose from the dead, for example. She may concede that if you leave out of account all that she knows in this way, then with respect to the remaining body of knowledge or belief the resurrection is not particularly probable. But that does not present her with an intellectual or spiritual crisis. We can imagine a renegade group of whimsical physicists proposing to reconstruct physics, refusing to use belief that comes from memory, say, or perhaps memory of anything more than one minute ago. Perhaps something could be done along these lines, but it would be a poor, paltry, truncated, trifling thing. And now suppose that, say, Newton's Laws or Special Relativity turned out to be dubious and unconfirmed from this point of view: that would presumably give little pause to the more traditional physicists. This truncated physics could hardly call into question physics of the fuller variety.

Similarly here. The traditional Christian thinks she knows *by faith* that Jesus was divine and that he rose from the dead. But then she will be unmoved by the fact that these truths are not especially probable on the evidence to which non-Troeltschian HBC limits itself. Why should that matter to her? So this is the rest of the answer to Harvey's question: if the HBC in question is non-Troeltschian, then the fact it does not verify traditional Christian beliefs is due to its limiting itself in the way it does, to its refusing to use all the data or evidence the Christian thinks he has in his possession. For a Christian to confine himself to the results of non-Troeltschian HBC would be a little like trying to mow your lawn with nail scissors or paint your house with a tooth-brush; it might be an interesting experiment if you have time on your hands, but otherwise why limit yourself in this way?

More generally, then: HBC is either Troeltschian or non-Troeltschian. If the former, then it begins from assumptions entailing that much of what the traditional Christian believes is false; but then it is no surprise that its conclusions are at odds with traditional belief. It is also of little direct interest to the traditional Christian. It offers her no reason at all for rejecting or modifying her beliefs; it also offers little promise of enabling her to achieve better or deeper insight into what actually happened. As for non-Troeltschian HBC, on the other hand, this variety of historical criticism omits a great deal of what she sees as relevant evidence and relevant considerations. It is therefore left with little to go on. But again, the fact that it fails to support traditional belief will be of little direct interest to the traditional believer; that is only to be expected, and casts no doubt at all upon that belief. Either way, therefore, the traditional Christian can rest easy with the claims of HBC; she need feel no obligation, intellectual or otherwise, to modify her beliefs in the light of its claims and alleged results.[79]

CONCLUDING CODA

But is not all of this just a bit too sunny? Is not it a recipe for avoiding hard questions, for hanging onto belief no matter what, for guaranteeing that you will never have to face negative results, even if there *are* some? 'HBC is either Troeltschian or non-Troeltschian: in the first case it proceeds from assumptions I reject; in the second it fails to take account of all of what I take to be the evidence; either way, therefore, I need not pay attention to it.' Could not I say this *a priori,* without even examining the results of HBC? But then there must be something defective in the line of thought in question. Is not it clearly *possible* that historians should discover facts that put Christian belief into serious question, count heavily against it? Well, maybe so. How could this happen? As follows. HBC limits itself to the deliverances of reason; it is possible, at any rate in the broadly logical sense, that just by following ordinary historical reason, using the methods of historical investigation endorsed or enjoined by the deliverances of reason, someone should find powerful evidence against central elements of the Christian faith;[80] if this happened, Christians would face a genuine faith-reason clash. A series of letters could be discovered, letters circulated among Peter, James, John and Paul, in which the necessity for the hoax and the means of its perpetration are carefully and seriously discussed; these letters might direct workers to archeological sites in which still more material of the same sort is discovered.[81] The Christian faith is a *historical* faith, in the sense that it essentially depends upon what did in fact happen: 'And if Christ has not been raised, your faith is futile' (I Cor. 15:17). It could certainly happen that by the exercise of reason we come up with powerful evidence[82] against something we

---

[79] *Alleged* results: because of the enormous controversy and disagreement among followers of HBC, it is very difficult to find anything one could sensibly call 'results' of this scholarship.

[80] Or, less crucially, evidence against what appear to be the teaching of Scripture. For example, archeological evidence could undermine the traditional belief that there was such a city as Jericho.

[81] See Bas van Fraassen, 'Three-sided Scholarship: Comments on the Paper of John R. Donahue, S. J.', in *Hermes and Athena,* eds. Eleonore Stump and Thomas Flint (Notre Dame, IN: University of Notre Dame Press, 1993), p. 322. 'Finish it [the depressing scenario] yourself, if you have the heart to do it', says van Fraassen.

[82] Or *think* we come up with it; even if we are mistaken about the evidence in question, it could still precipitate this sort of problem for us.

take or took to be deliverance of the faith.[83] It is conceivable that the assured results of HBC should include such evidence. Then Christians would have a problem, a sort of conflict between faith and reason.

But, of course, nothing at all like this has emerged from HBC, whether Troeltschian or non-Troeltschian; indeed, there is little of any kind that can be considered its 'assured results', if only because of the wide-ranging disagreement among those who practice HBC.[84] We do not have anything like assured results (or even reasonably well-attested results) that conflict with traditional Christian belief in such a way that belief of that sort can continue to be accepted only at considerable cost; nothing like this has happened. What would be the appropriate response if it *did* happen, or rather if I came to be convinced that it had happened? Would I have to give up Christian faith, or else give up the life of the mind? What would be the appropriate response? Well, what would be the appropriate response if I came to be convinced that someone had given a wholly rigorous, ineluctable disproof of the existence of God, perhaps something along the lines of J. N. Findlay's alleged ontological disproof?[85] Or what if, with David Hume (at least as understood by Thomas Reid), I come to think that my cognitive faculties are probably not reliable, and go on to note that I form this very belief on the basis of the very faculties whose reliability this belief impugns? If I did, what would or should I do—stop thinking about these things, immerse myself in practical activity (maybe playing a lot of backgammon, maybe volunteering to help build houses for Habitat for Humanity), commit intellectual suicide? I do not know the answer to any of these questions. There is no need to borrow trouble, however: we can think about crossing these bridges when (more likely, if) we come to them.[86]

[83] See my 'When Faith and Reason Clash: Evolution and the Bible' in *Christian Scholar's Review*, Vol. XXI No. 1 (September, 1991), pp. 9–15.

[84] Thus Harold Attridge in 'Calling Jesus Christ' in *Hermes and Athena*, p. 211: 'There remains enormous diversity among those who attempt to describe what Jesus really did, taught, and thought about himself. For some contemporary scholars he was a Hellenistic magician; for others, a Galilean charismatic or rabbi; for yet others, a prophetic reformer; for others, a sly teller of wry and engaging tales; for some he had grandiose ideas; for others he eschewed them. In general, the inquirer finds the Jesus that her historical method allows her to see. It is as true today as it was at the end of the liberal quest for the historical Jesus catalogued by Albert Schweitzer that we moderns tend to make Jesus in our own image and likeness.' The Schweitzer reference is to his *Von Reimarus zu Wrede* (1906), translated by W. Montgomery under the title *The Quest of the Historical Jesus: A Critical Study of its Progress from Reimarus to Wrede* (New York, NY: Macmillan, 1956).

[85] 'Can God's Existence be Disproved?' *Mind* Vol. 57 No. 226 (April, 1948), pp. 176–83.

[86] My thanks to Mike Bergmann, John Cooper, Kevin Corcoran, Ronald Feenstra, Marie Pannier, Neal Plantinga, Tapio Puolimatka, David Vanderlaan, James VanderKam, Calvin Van Reken, and Henry Zwaanstra. A longer version of this paper appears as chapter 12 of *Warranted Christian Belief* (New York, NY: Oxford University Press, forthcoming).

14

Reformed Epistemology and Biblical Hermeneutics*

Evan Fales

Jesus loves me, this I know
For the Bible tells me so.

So goes a familiar song. But what does the Bible in fact say?

And is what it says true? How do we know what it says, and whether those things are true? One might initially think that, respecting the first question if not the second, a straightforward reading of the text should settle the matter. But when it comes to the Bible—and sacred texts generally—we all know that matters are very far from so simple as that. One might hope that, in the course of the centuries, we have managed to eke out a few stable insights. But perhaps not.

On both the question of proper interpretation and that of truth, Christians have traditionally fallen (broadly speaking) into two camps. According to one view, understanding and evaluation of the Canon are properly mediated by the Church, its designated authorities, and the traditions it preserves. According to the other, these matters rest ultimately with individuals, guided (of course) by the literal content of the text but also by some special perceptivity supplied by God—a special grace or insight provided by the Holy Spirit. Much of what was at stake in the battles fought during the Reformation concerned which of these two views was correct.

During the Enlightenment matters took a new turn. Reason asserted its independence of both tradition (cum institutionalized authority) and divine inspiration. The Bible came increasingly under the scrutiny of scholars who, though for the most part Christians, accepted the principles and procedures of a developing scientific historiography grounded in common sense, ordinary inductive canons, and certain specialized techniques of historical research—that is, the procedures found proper to the evaluation of non-sacred texts and to the sacred texts of the 'heathen.' Some localized squabbles aside, the techniques developed by modern historiography were not themselves particularly controversial: except when

* © *Philo*, vol. 4 (2001). Reprinted by permission of the publisher.

applied to the sacred texts of the 'home' religion, texts that appear to make quite striking historical claims. Putting matters bluntly, the debate focussed on the Enlightenment demand that the historian cannot countenance special pleading on behalf of Christianity's foundational texts.

Of course therefore, the new methods were not adopted lightly or with open arms, but after much struggle. Contemporary apologetes sometimes write as if modern Bible critics just *assumed* some sort of ontological or methodological naturalism because it suited them, and not because they had read, e.g., Spinoza or Hume or Kant, and found in them arguments carrying conviction.

But maybe those arguments shouldn't have convinced them; maybe they rely upon a fundamentally misconceived conception of how religious knowledge (at least) is acquired. That is, indeed, what a number of contemporary philosophers would have us believe. The philosophers I shall be discussing usually help themselves to a trend in current epistemology that rejects the internalist foundationalism characteristic of the Enlightenment in favor of externalism. Perhaps the most prominent of these is Alvin Plantinga, who sees in externalism an echo of the view of religious knowledge that can be found in Calvin.[1]

But Plantinga is not alone, and what I have to say about his Reformed hermeneutics will apply in large measure to others such as Stephen Evans and Peter van Inwagen.[2] All of them reject the methodological constraints that characterize modern historiography, and though they welcome some of the results of research conducted within that framework, they argue for what is in

---

[1] Because I am a committed internalist, I must face the question whether to engage the issue by attacking Reformed epistemology, or whether to argue on my opponent's turf. As I proceed, it will become evident that I do both: I shall bring out internal difficulties that a Reformed hermeneutic must face; and I shall challenge the background epistemology on second-order grounds, by bringing forward evidential challenges to the claim that the interpretive traditions to which Plantinga *et al.* appeal have indeed been reliably informed or inspired by the Holy Spirit.

I shall be discussing primarily Plantinga's view as articulated in his recent *Warranted Christian Belief* (New York: Oxford University Press, 2000) but also make reference to C. Stephen Evans, *The Historical Christ and the Jesus of Faith: The Incarnational Narrative as History* (Oxford: Clarendon Press, 1996), and to Peter van Inwagen, *God, Knowledge, and Mystery: Essays in Philosophical Theology*, part II (Ithaca, NY: Cornell University Press, 1995).

[2] It is not clear that van Inwagen is committed to anything like a Reformed account of religious knowledge. See, e.g., 'Genesis and Evolution,' in van Inwagen *God, Knowledge, and Mystery*, 159, where he says,

it may be that there are certain people who know that a Creator exists and know this because of their mystery [*sic*!] of a vast range of data too complex to be summarized in anything so simple as a single argument.

My own guess is that [this] sort of knowledge [does not] exist. If there are people who *know* that there is a Creator, this must be due to factors other than (or perhaps in addition to) the inferences they have drawn from observations of the natural world....

Van Inwagen goes on to say (180–1) that the reasons he himself has for accepting Christianity being inarticulable, such reasoning as can be given voice will be no more probative than that to which the defense of, e.g., many philosophical positions can appeal. This sounds like a kind of mute evidentialism. Whatever it is, it is worth noting that one could replace it with Plantinga's claim that the essential propositions of the faith are properly basic, without damage to the rest of van Inwagen's argument against Critical Studies.

effect a return to the hermeneutical approaches of an earlier era: roughly, the sixteenth century. That, I shall argue, is a serious mistake.

REFORMED EPISTEMOLOGY

According to Plantinga, Christians (or more carefully, some Christians) know what he calls the Great Things of the Gospels—the essential salvific message of the New Testament (complete with a story about why salvation is needed and how it must be effected)—in a properly basic way. They do not reason to these truths—for example, by using the Biblical text as evidence—but are directly led to know them by the 'internal instigation' of the Holy Spirit (hereafter, HS). As Plantinga sees it, reading or hearing the Bible might serve as an *occasion* for one's coming to believe these things, but this belief-forming mechanism is not to be understood as a matter of performing overt or covert inferences from evidence. It is rather that reading or hearing these words may open one's heart to the promptings of the HS.[3]

A bit more fully, on Plantinga's A/C (Aquinas/Calvin) model of Christian knowledge, human beings are endowed with a *sensus divinitatis* (SD), which, properly functioning, enables them to enter into a right relationship with God. Because original sin degraded the ability of the SD (and of our cognitive and affective faculties more generally) to function properly, we cannot by our own efforts restore that relationship. But because God has sent His HS to assist us, and sent His Son to atone for sin, we (or some of us) can regain sanctification. Because the HS instills in Christians *directly* the Great Things, and because this is a reliable belief-forming mechanism, Christians know these things in a properly basic way—provided that belief is accompanied by sufficiently strong conviction.

Well, what do they thus know? What are these Great Things? Here, Plantinga does some rather careful (carefully vague) gerrymandering. He suggests that they comprise, roughly, those doctrines agreed upon by the various historically major Creeds. They include the doctrines that our proper relationship to God was destroyed by original sin, that God, via a virgin birth, sent Jesus, who is His only begotten Son, to rectify matters, and that Jesus atoned for our sins on the cross, rose from the dead after three days, and will one day return to judge the quick and the dead, saving some to eternal life with God.[4]

The above list is offered with considerable hesitation. The object of Christian faith, says Plantinga, is the Great Things, 'the whole magnificent scheme of salvation. . . . The content of faith is just the central teachings of the gospel; it is contained in the intersection of the great Christian creeds.' Now Plantinga cannily does not tell us which are the 'great' creeds. Perhaps we should include at least the

---

[3] In do not think Plantinga's account is remotely adequate to the phenomenology of the formation of religious beliefs. But that is a topic I cannot pursue here.

[4] Moreover, we are to believe that these things are quite *literally* true—whatever that may exactly mean.

Ecumenical Creeds—the Apostles', Athanasian, Chalcedonian, and Nicene Creeds. But that won't do: inspection reveals that the intersection of their doctrines is the null set. To make matters worse, there are literally hundreds of Christian creeds, and thousands of declarations in which one group or denomination anathematizes the creedal doctrines of another.[5] I shall return to this; for the moment, let us set it aside and use the list of doctrines I proposed above.

A properly basic belief that is generated by a sufficiently reliable cognitive process in favorable circumstances, and that is accompanied by the right kind of doxastic experience—strong confidence—has sufficient warrant to constitute knowledge. But it is only prima facie warrant: it can be defeated, e.g., by evidence that counts against the belief or against the reliability of its means of acquisition, if that evidence sufficiently undermines confidence.[6]

HISTORICAL BIBLICAL CRITICISM: METHODS

Is Christian faith subject to defeat? Plantinga discusses several potential defeaters; the one we are examining is the findings of what he calls Historical Biblical Criticism (HBC). To this enterprise, Plantinga opposes Traditional Christian Biblical Commentary (TBC). Let us first set out some central commitments of TBC.[7]

1. TBC holds that Scripture is *perspicuous*. In its main lines, it can be correctly 'understood and grasped and accepted by anyone of normal intelligence....'
2. TBC holds that Scripture is divinely inspired. This means that the Bible—all of it—is really one book, whose author is God. It is therefore authoritative for Christians. Moreover, the unity of the Bible licenses using one part to interpret another part. This is so even though the human amanuensis—e.g., Isaiah—may not have understood that what he was writing foreshadowed the coming of Jesus of Nazareth.[8]

---

[5] Perhaps Plantinga meant to suggest that the Great Truths encompass the union, rather than the intersection, of the 'great' creeds. That would certainly yield a richer set of doctrines. But dangerously rich: absent a careful selection of which Christian creeds are the great ones, this strategy risks generating a set that is multiply inconsistent.

[6] Plantinga's characterization of defeaters is given in *Warranted Christian Belief*, 359–66. There are a few niceties that need not detain us here.

[7] Van Inwagen has the same enterprise in mind when he describes what he calls Critical Studies as those historical studies which either deny the authority of the New Testament or else maintain a methodological neutrality on the question of its authority, and which attempt, by methods that presuppose either a denial or neutrality about its authority, to investigate such matters as authorship, dates, histories of composition, historical reliability, and mutual dependency of the various books of the New Testament. (*God, Knowledge, and Mystery*, 163)

[8] Wouldn't God have whispered *that* rather important piece of information into Isaiah's ear? Well, maybe He did; maybe He also told Isaiah not to write it down. Or maybe He judged that it was best for Isaiah not to understand this. Yet Plantinga thinks it highly improbable that God wouldn't want us to know these things.

3. The way in which a believer comes to *know* that the Canon is divinely inspired is not by way of historical investigation, but by being so informed by the HS (which either implants just this belief or one entailing it—e.g., that the HS has ensured that the Church was founded upon, and has preserved, the essential truths about salvation).[9]
4. Nevertheless—and in contrast with point (1)—Plantinga concedes that there is much in Scripture that is opaque, much that resists easy interpretation. (With this we may emphatically agree. It is *one* of the factors that necessitated the development of HBC.)

As we might expect, Plantinga's attack on HBC moves primarily at the level of an assault upon the *methodology* of HBC; his taking issue with the *results* of HBC is confined primarily to some disparaging remarks about what he takes to be some of the more outlandish claims made by HBC scholars. This is not insignificant. While the methodological issues are certainly on the table and need to be examined, much of the conviction that HBC findings carry derives from familiarity with the empirical details. Nor is this an accident: skillful play does not require ability to articulate the rules of the game.

HBC, as Plantinga says, undertakes an assessment of the meaning and historical reliability of Scripture from the perspective of reason (and sense) alone. It refuses the assistance of faith; it eschews the authority of creed, tradition, and magisterium. In so doing, it understands itself to adhere to the conditions of a scientific method. And in so doing, it begins by construing Scripture as a series of books (or shorter passages), composed and pasted together by human authors and redactors, whose meaning is the messages intended by those human individuals.

Still, it would be overly sanguine to suppose that the defenders of HBC have been able to formulate a unified account of their methodological commitments. Rather, there are at best several such accounts. In the face of these disparate accounts, Plantinga's strategy is to divide and conquer. So, let's look at the accounts Plantinga considers and ask what is to be made of them. Plantinga discerns within HBC three methodological positions: Troeltschian HBC, Duhemain HBC, and Spinozistic HBC (as he dubs them). Let us proceed by considering in order the central tenets of these positions and Plantinga's commentary on them. I shall then offer some general reflections upon Plantinga's treatment of HBC, turning from this to a comparison of the methods and fruits of HBC with those of TBC. Finally, I shall suggest some conclusions that we should draw from this study concerning the workings of the HS and the prospects for the A/C model of Christian knowledge.

---

[9] By way of comparison, van Inwagen holds that he knows for inarticulable reasons these Great Truths, and takes it to be a historical fact that the early Church preached, understood, and preserved the Gospel narratives *as* historical fact, reliable on essential matters. Van Inwagen does not tell us how he knows what the early Church's understanding of the Gospel narratives was, nor how, absent HBC, one can know the historical claim his case rests on.

Troeltschian HBC (TrHBC)[10] is characterized by four principles:

1. The principle of methodological doubt: historical inquiry can never attain absolute certainty, but only relative degrees of probability.
2. The principle of analogy: historical knowledge is possible [only] because all events are similar in principle, i.e., subject to uniform laws of nature.
3. The principle of correlation: no event can be isolated from the sequence of historical cause and effect [history is a causally closed system].
4. The principle of autonomy: no secular or sectarian authority can dictate to the historian which conclusions he or she should reach.[11]

Though these principles have an innocuous interpretation, Plantinga takes TrHBC to understand them specifically in such a way as to exclude miracles. I shall return to this.

The essential prescription of Duhemian HBC (DuHBC) is that historical research must proceed on assumptions upon which all parties to the discussion can agree, so as to make possible genuine dialogue and progress.[12] Plantinga suggests that this ban on partisan presuppositions would leave Bible scholars with little indeed by way of either substantive claims or methodological principles, there being so little upon which the interested parties can agree.[13]

Finally, Spinozistic HBC (SpHBC) proposes what might seem an improvement on DuHBC; it allows just those conclusions to be drawn by historians that are legitimated by reason alone.[14] Plantinga's animadversions on the human faculty of reason are well known; reason is allegedly not in general less frail than our other cognitive faculties, and in particular, should surely not be given priority over such a reliable and authoritative source of knowledge as the HS if the A/C model is correct.

Now Plantinga's treatment suggests in the first place that these three types of HBC represent different methodological schools of thought within HBC, ones that might lead to opposing historical conclusions. Indeed, though Plantinga does not explicitly say so, one might get the impression that the widely differing opinions among scholars who practice HBC can in significant measure be traced to disagreements over which methodology is correct. In any event, Plantinga,

---

[10] Which Plantinga attributes to such scholars as John Collins, Van Harvey, Jon Maquarrie, and Langdon Gilkey. Plantinga sees A. E. Harvey, E. P. Sanders, Barnabas Linders, and Jon Levenson as more or less Duhemian; and John Meier as at times Duhemian and at times Spinozistic.

[11] See *Warranted Christian Belief*, 391–3 [cf. this volume, pp. 277–9].

[12] Ibid., 396–7 [cf. this volume, pp. 281–2].

[13] Oddly enough, elsewhere in *Warranted Christian Belief*, Plantinga defines epistemic possibility in terms of what is 'consistent with what we know, where "what we know" is what all (or most) of the participants in the discussion agree on.' This definition—crucial to his claim that the A/C model is epistemically possible—suffers exactly the same infirmity.

[14] See *Warranted Christian Belief*, 398 [cf. this volume, p. 283]. Plantinga would have done better to refer to the formulation given by John Locke; Locke argues that our ultimate appeal must be to reason and sense experience. See *An Essay Concerning Human Understanding*, bk. IV, chap. XVIII. I shall be defending this claim of Locke's.

Evans, and van Inwagen agree that what they see as the disarray within HBC scholarship is an independent reason for Christians not to be overly concerned about the implications of HBC for the faith.

I believe there is a better explanation for what is going on here. Are there deep methodological differences that divide HBC scholars? Or do we have what is more nearly a familiar phenomenon: the practitioners of an empirical science attempting, often rather ineptly, to perform the task that even philosophers of science find vexingly difficult, viz., to formulate abstractly and generally the principles that guide their research? If you ask any dozen historians or physicists to articulate such principles, you may be sure of getting a dozen more or less different—and usually clumsy—formulations.

Naturally, HBC scholars do have differences over matters of both methodology and actual historical findings. But there is little reason to attribute this to ill-conceived global principles. The genuine debates, I suggest, occur closer to ground level: they are debates over historical matters—e.g., over the significance of certain Jewish and pagan ideologies in the formation of early Christian views about resurrection; or over specialized tools—e.g., the significance and security of conclusions that can be reached by paleographic analysis or source criticism.

So far as the more global issues go—the correct assessment of testimony for miracles, or the proper way to judge the revelatory claims of ancient texts—it would be more nearly fair to say that HBC grew out of (and its partisans were convinced by) the arguments of Spinoza, Locke, Hume, Paine, and Kant. Surely such a compressed and popularizing characterization of this critical sensibility as Bultmann's much-maligned comment that we moderns can no longer believe in miracles once we avail ourselves of the fruits of modern technology, is properly to be understood by situating it within this intellectual context. So, ineptitude in formulating the operative methodological principles goes almost no distance toward convicting HBC scholars of incompetence in their historical research or toward undermining their conclusions.

But perhaps we should judge HBC by its fruits, and haven't those fruits presented the spectacle of wildly different interpretations of Scripture and historical judgments about those momentous events that took place in ancient Galilee and Judea? What are we to make of this chaos of conclusions?

Well, one thing to make of it—and Plantinga, for one, will agree—is that the evidence we have (the ordinary evidence, that is) is dismayingly thin on many matters of paramount religious importance. That—together no doubt with the fact that many of these matters *are* of paramount religious importance—has tempted scholars to explore a wide variety of possibilities, some quite speculative, that seem to make sense of at least some significant stretch of the data we do have. But that is what creative scholarship is supposed to do, and we are asking for false security if we demand firm consensus where data are scanty and inferences difficult.

HISTORICAL BIBLICAL CRITICISM: FINDINGS

Still, it is germane to ask whether HBC has supplied reasonably firm historical conclusions about anything concerning the Biblical narratives. And, of course, it has. A serious listing of such established results is out of the question; but a few bear mention that illustrate the issues before us.

1. We know that the creation account given in the first three chapters of Genesis owes a large debt in style, imagery, and content to the creation myths of the Sumerians and other Ancient Near Eastern (ANE) pagan religions.

2. We have good reason to believe that the seven-headed dragon mentioned in Revelations is derived from a similar beast who inhabits the myth-world of the Sumerians.[15]

3. There appears to be not a single Biblical prophecy that meets minimal conditions for being genuinely prophetic, and whose fulfillment can be independently confirmed.[16] Indeed, the two prophecies attributed to Jesus that are surely of most central concern to Christians—Matt. 12:39–40 and Matt. 16:27–28—have on the face of it been falsified. These failures, and others, are in themselves evidence for HBC scholars that the HS was not at work—certainly not consistently so—in providing correct prophecy to the Biblical authors, and that therefore all Biblical prophetic texts, including those whose fulfillment is Biblically attested, are to be viewed with suspicion.

4. There is a general consensus within HBC that the Gospels were composed later than the collapse of the Jewish revolt in 70 c.e. There are multiple lines of evidence for this, but Evans rejects the claim as illustrating HBC prejudice against the 'prophetic anticipation' of the Roman suppression of the revolt. In support of earlier dates of composition, Evans reverts narrowly to the familiar— and lame—argument that Acts (hence Luke, hence Mark) must have been written prior to 64 c.e. because it ends abruptly prior to the martyrdom of Paul in Rome around that date.

That argument presupposes that there is no other plausible explanation for this feature of Acts. But there is another explanation: in fact, there are two. The first is that the rest of Acts has simply been lost. The second points out that the early Church had enormous hopes pinned on Paul's mission to Rome. They (Paul especially) were engaged in a calculated effort to win over Roman officials, and much was riding on the success of that effort. This concern for a Pauline

---

[15] See Simo Parpola, 'From Whence the Beast?' *Bible Review* (Dec. 1999), 24. Parpola also has linked the Christian notions of Jesus as a perfect Son of God and as savior to similar notions in Assyrian kingship ideology (see his 'Sons of God,' *Archaeology Odyssey* (Nov./Dec. 1999): 18 *passim*.

[16] See Fales, 'Can Mystics See God?' in *Contemporary Debates in the Philosophy of Religion*, ed. Michael L. Peterson (forthcoming) for a more detailed discussion.

success story in Rome led even to the circulation of an early Christian forgery—admiring letters to Paul, purportedly from the Roman statesman Seneca. It would hardly be surprising if the Roman execution of Paul was such a severe embarrassment to the Church that the author of Acts felt it best to omit it—and hence to terminate his history by portraying Paul's stay in Rome in decidedly positive terms.

5. Both HBC and ANE archaeology widely concur that the Exodus story is a myth.[17] There remains speculation that there may have been Canaanitic slaves in Egypt who escaped and made their way, via Midian perhaps, into the hill-country of Palestine to join with refugees from other areas to form a proto-Israelitic confederation.[18]

6. It is generally acknowledged that an understanding of the Gospel passion narratives cannot proceed in isolation from an examination of the large body of ANE literature and cultic practice that deploys the notion of death and resurrection, and links it to other themes that pervade the lore of the Hebrew Bible and a wide range of ANE religious traditions—e.g., the theme of descent into, and rescue from or control over, the chaos-waters of the deep (the *tehom*), which appears repeatedly in the Hebrew Bible (the original parting of the waters, the Noachic flood, the crossing of the Red Sea and Jordan River, the descent into Sheol of the king in numerous of the Psalms, the ritual of baptism, and much more).[19]

MIRACLES?

In this debate, a perennial lightning-rod issue is the question of miracles. Plantinga has rather little to say about the possibility of God's performing

---

[17] See Baruch Halpern, 'The Exodus from Egypt: Myth or Reality?' in ed. Hershel Shanks, *The Rise of Ancient Israel* (Washington, D.C.: Biblical Archaeological Society, 1992); the articles by Ze'ev Herzog and Itzhaq Beiut-Arieh in section A of *Archaeology and the Bible: Vol. One, Early Israel*, eds. Hershel Shanks and Dan P. Cole (Washington, D.C.: Biblical Archaeological Society, 1990); and Nadav Na'aman, 'The "Conquest of Canaan" in the book of Joshua and in History,' in *From Nomadism to Monarchy: Archaeological and Historical Aspects of Early Israel*, eds. Israel Finkelstein and Nadav Na'aman (Jerusalem: Yad Izhak Ben-Zvi, 1994).

[18] See ed. Hershel Shanks, *Frank Moore Cross: Conversations with a Bible Scholar* (Washington, D.C.: Biblical Archaeology Society, 1994).

[19] The literature is very large. The *locus classicus* is, of course, James Frazer's *The Golden Bough*. More recent work includes *Myth, Ritual, and Kingship: Essays on the Theory and Practice of Kingship in the Ancient Near East and in Israel*, ed. S. H. Hooke (Oxford: Clarendon Press, 1958); Sigmund Mowinckel, *The Psalms in Israel's Worship*, trans. D. R. Ap-Thomas (New York: Abingdon Press, 1962); George Nickelsburg, *Resurrection, Immortality, and Eternal Life in Intertestamental Judaism* (Cambridge: Harvard University Press, 1972); and Adela Yarbro Collins, 'The Empty Tomb in the Gospel according to Mark,' eds. Eleonore Stump and Thomas P. Flint, *Hermes and Athena: Biblical Exegesis and Philosophical Theology* (Notre Dame, Ind.: University of Notre Dame Press, 1993).

miracles; Evans says just a bit more. The issue is vexed, unfortunately, by the deep disagreements among philosophers concerning the very notions of causation and laws of nature. Because of this, my own remarks will have to be quite cursory.

It is helpful to divide up the question about miracles. If miracles are understood to be departures from the regular operations of nature, there are first the metaphysical questions to be faced: in what sense must miracles 'violate' the laws of nature (if at all), and just how does God accomplish them? Second, there are a number of epistemic issues. Can an instance of divine causation or intervention be scientifically investigated? Can an event's claim to reveal the hand of God be given strong scientific credentials? If not, can there be any other reason to credit divine intervention? And then Hume's question: can the occurrence of a miracle be reasonably believed on the strength of testimony?

As to the metaphysical question, Plantinga and Evans concur that we cannot just assume that the physical universe is a closed system, immune from supernatural interventions. So, when the miraculous occurs, no physical law need actually be violated; it could just be that, in addition to normal physical causes, some divine force is present. Unfortunately, this way of understanding miracles (though, I think, the best account available) does not avoid the difficulty in making miracles intelligible, for virtually any sort of divine intervention would violate the laws of conservation of energy and momentum.[20] Moreover, theists must face the 'how' question: just how does God manage it?

On the first two epistemic questions, I shall just have to be dogmatic. I cannot find any principled reason why, *if* supernatural causation is metaphysically possible, its presence could not be detected. A central mission of science is to discover the causes of things, and if an event cannot be sufficiently explained by appeal to natural causes, an eligible hypothesis is a non-natural one—though that leaves much open concerning the nature of that cause. There would however be a burden on theists to formulate more rigorously than they have, hypotheses about the mechanisms of divine causation.

But the real epistemic issue, of course, is the Humean one. Here I want to direct attention to just two fundamental issues. The first has received considerable attention from Reformed epistemologists, but the second is regularly overlooked. First, from where does testimony get its epistemic credentials? And second, what are the significant options to which HBC can appeal to explain miracle reports?

---

[20] Plantinga adds (*Warranted Christian Belief*, 395 [cf. this volume, p. 280]) that God could, if need be, abrogate the laws of nature, and could do so (*Warranted Christian Belief*, 406 [cf. this volume, p. 290]) in temporary and limited ways that would not systematically undermine our understanding of the world (including historical understanding). But this is very far from evident. On at least some views—e.g., that laws are grounded in metaphysically necessary connections between universals—'abrogation' would amount to wrecking—or rather exchanging for another one—the entire scheme of laws.

THE EVIDENTIAL CREDENTIALS OF TESTIMONY

Classical foundationalists typically restrict the cognitive processes that yield knowledge to two: a priori intuition and experience (with memory perhaps as a distinct third faculty). In contrast, Reformed epistemologists characteristically suppose that a much wider variety of irreducibly distinct processes can yield knowledge—including testimony. Evans argues that Hume and his followers are mistaken that the initial or prima facie credentials of testimony require to be established inductively from sense experience; and he takes this to have significant bearing upon assessment of Biblical miracle reports. Evans depends upon an allegedly decisive refutation of Hume's 'reductionist thesis' by C. A. J. Coady.[21]

Here I need to draw attention to two points central to Coady's attack on Hume's thesis. The first concerns Coady's argument that reliance upon testimony is an ineliminable and irreducible component of our knowledge in general, because any attempt to justify such reliance by induction from personal verification of testimony will inevitably itself rely upon further testimony. Coady writes:

> We are told by Hume that we only trust in testimony because experience has shown it to be reliable, yet where experience means individual observation . . . this seems plainly false and, on the other hand, where it means common experience (i.e., reliance on the observations of others) it is surely question-begging.[22]

Coady proceeds to reprimand Hume for *himself* relying on communal experience to establish such general propositions as, e.g., that dead men don't rise—on the grounds that this has '*never* been observed in any age or country.' Not only is Hume using testimony, but surely he is tendentiously privileging favorable testimony over the NT reports.

This is a needlessly uncharitable reading of Hume; but to see why, we need a look at Coady's second principle argument. This is a carefully developed version of the argument that a general practice of truth-telling is a necessary condition for the existence of any public language. So it is an a priori condition on the possibility of testimony—and not an inductively arrived at conclusion—that it is in general truthful. Now this is correct, but it is not strong enough to serve Evans' purpose; nor does it show that Hume was fundamentally mistaken about the epistemic bona fides of testimony.

We may put the matter as follows. It is true that the possibility of radical interpretation (or learning one's first language) presupposes that the assertoric use of language by informants is not steeped in ignorance and fraud. So, *if* the

---

[21] C. A. J. Coady, *Testimony* (Oxford: Oxford University Press, 1992). Coady's nuanced discussion deserves much closer treatment than I can devote to it here.

[22] Ibid., 80.

sounds made by others constitute a system of linguistic communication, it must be the case that they generally say what they believe, and generally believe what is true—at least with respect to features of the world more or less straightforwardly detectable by common observation. This is not an empirical matter. But *that* the noises others make are interpretable as a language—and of course, what given stretches of language can plausibly be taken to mean—those certainly *are* empirical matters; and it is hard to see what recourse an individual speaker could have in determining this, other than to his or her sensory faculties and reasoning.[23] So, we can construe the hypothesis that what we are told has a prima facie claim to truth as the empirical hypothesis that we are in fact being given testimony—which carries with it the (weak) implication of truth.

In this sense, Coady's second argument, while containing an important observation, does not show that Hume's reductionist thesis is false. Evans, however, thinks that the interpretive charity mandated by the argument does help to establish the autonomy of testimony as an irreducible source of knowledge. I shall now argue that, on the contrary, it counts *against* Evans, and also against Coady's uncharitable reading of Hume.

Evans recognizes that the proper way to frame the question about miracle reports is to bracket skeptical doubts of the most general sort, doubts that would undermine empirical knowledge claims *tout court*. Given what has just been said, this means that in addressing the present issue, we must accept the ordinary inductive procedures that permit the learning of a language. We can think of this process as involving two intercalated kinds of induction: inductions that, operating with a provisional principle of charity, confirm semantic hypotheses and thereby enable us to identify the content of testimony, and further inductions that enable us to 'fine-tune' the principle of charity itself, as we search for hypotheses that best accommodate our entire range of relevant data—including testimony that contradicts first-hand knowledge of the facts or other testimony, folk-psychological observations informing us of the circumstances under which people are least prone and most prone to utter falsehoods, and contextual cues signalling figurative use of language.

Thus considered, our mastery of linguistic communication can be seen to imbed a ground-level principle of interpretive charity that applies especially to the domain of the familiar and easily recognizable, *together with* inductively based wisdom concerning the factors that promote error and fraud. Thus, when Hume refers to the 'uniform experience of mankind' respecting the permanence of death, I suggest that he is implicitly appealing to testimony and experience respecting which there is no prima facie reason for doubt—including doubt

---

[23] It might be that we are somehow 'hard-wired' to acquire language without making explicit to ourselves either the general presuppositions required by a rational reconstruction of this process, or the inductions to specific word-meanings. It remains true that *justification* for one's semantic beliefs must be understood in terms of such inductions by the autonomous individual.

raised by the very fact of disagreement with a large preponderance of other testimony or experience. This is entirely in order. It is just a matter of finding the hypothesis most strongly confirmed by the total data to suggest that testimony out of step with uniformities we have reason to accept (on the basis of large bodies of independent data) is more likely false than true—*even* if special motives for fraud such as those associated with religious propaganda are not in play.[24]

For all that, I would insist that our principle of charity cannot be lightly overthrown in favor of an imputation of folly or fraud to the Biblical authors. Far from it: giving due weight to the apparent intelligence, conviction, and sincerity of the NT writers counts strongly against either of those explanations. But on the other side, we *do* have the improbability of the events themselves. What to do?

It would be a mistake of the first order to be drawn into the false dilemma of supposing that we must decide between miracle and fraud.[25] For there is a third possibility, and because of it Evans' defense of a charitable reading of Scripture is quite compatible with a Humean rejection of miracles. We need only to reject the assumption that the NT authors intended to engage in historical reportage. How obvious is it, then, that this was their intent?

TESTIMONIES OF THE SPIRIT

As we have seen, Reformed epistemologists like to make heavy weather over disagreements among HBC scholars, while at the same time doing careful editing when it comes to saying what the HS teaches. Being externalists, they can, of course, insist that if the HS is a reliable guide to truth, then an individual who has been guided by the HS to believe (a correct version of) the Christian story will have knowledge. But *which* version of the Christian story? Just which Christians are those whose beliefs have been arrived at in this way?

I earlier remarked that Reformed epistemology would, in effect, return us to the Biblical hermeneutics of the sixteenth century. That century, after all, experienced perhaps above all others the heyday of the Spirit—for, phenomenologically speaking at least, evidence of the indwelling Spirit haunted nearly every hamlet in Europe; and never were claims to have been taught by the HS made more stridently or with greater conviction.

---

[24] Independent congruent testimonies make, of course, a much stronger case for an event than a single source, just because plausible skeptical explanations for the congruence are typically hard to come by. Evans and other apologetes often suggest that the NT authors provide such congruent independent witnesses for miracles. But of course we know no such thing; indeed, the evidence weighs heavily in favor of dependence. What is therefore really astonishing, if we assume an intent to report historical events, is the level of *discrepancy* between the NT accounts.

[25] A classic example (Evans, *This Historical Christ and the Jesus of Faith*, 236 and 351, following C. S. Lewis) is the argument that either Jesus was the Son of God, or else a fraud or mad for asserting it. Since neither mendacious nor mad (as portrayed by his disciples!), he was divine. This simply ignores the semantic import of 'Son of God' as a royal title.

Did these voices achieve greater unanimity over Christian doctrine and the proper interpretation of Scripture than HBC scholars have? They did not; and produced rather less gentlemanly ways of settling their doctrinal disputes to boot: from this period date, e.g., Calvin's execution of Michael Servitus, Luther's anathematization of Jews and Anabaptists, and the Synod of Dordt's expulsion of Arminians—to say nothing of the Inquisition and the Thirty Years' War. So, evidently, Christians themselves have had—and continue to have—a rugged hard time discerning who is Spirit-taught.

Plantinga does not trouble to enter these lists,[26] and van Inwagen speaks globally of the teachings preserved by 'the Church.' But Evans does make an attempt to provide some criteria for inspiration. Evans is rightly suspicious of *phenomenological* criteria for the indwelling of the HS; given the history just alluded to, this should come as no surprise. His primary criteria are a) that the doctrines thus received should conform to Scripture, and b) that the alleged revelations should yield good 'fruits' in the life of the believer—a sense of peace, humility, and sanctity.

Now as Evans recognizes, these criteria are starkly question-begging. They are so on multiple counts. As to (a), there has been no lack of disagreement among those putatively guided by the HS *precisely over what Scripture does teach*. More dramatically, some Anabaptists went Calvinist hermeneutics one better. Observing that Scripture itself could claim authority only on the strength of having been received from God, they held that the direct teaching of the indwelling Spirit can trump any doctrine mediated by the written word.[27]

As to (b), we may observe that the fruits reflect values accorded criterial standing on the strength of a prior commitment to certain Christian doctrines. Even if a *necessary* concomitant of true inspiration, they are clearly not sufficient: the supposition that good fruits are the effects of the HS ignores the much more mundane and familiar explanation in terms of social reinforcement by a community of peers who affirm and reward such behaviors.

LEVELS OF KNOWLEDGE

Externalists characteristically distinguish between knowledge that *p* and knowledge that one knows that *p*. One can possess the former without the latter. So, one might know the Great Things in a properly basic way, courtesy of the HS, but not realize that this is so—of course, one might also falsely suppose it to be

---

[26] Though he does accuse HBC scholars of just assuming without argument that faith (the inspiration of the HS) is not a reliable source of knowledge: 'This view is not, of course, a result of historical scholarship . . . (*Warranted Christian Belief*, 410 [cf. this volume, p. 293]). This ignores the historical point just made. Plantinga (in conversation) has said that faith in the Great Things is phenomenologically distinguishable from other doctrinal beliefs in the way a conviction that $2 + 2 = 4$ is firmer than belief that, say, $2^{20} > 10^6$. The evidence regarding religious conviction simply does not support Plantinga's suggestion.

[27] See Steven E. Ozment, *Mysticism and Dissent: Religious Ideology and Social Protest in the Sixteenth Century* (New Haven, Conn.: Yale University Press, 1973), 85–6.

so. In view of the cacophony of Christian voices claiming inspiration, this should be cold comfort to believers. To steal a phrase of Alston's, we are offered bread but given a stone.[28]

Perhaps a believer can know, in a properly HS-induced basic way, that the HS himself has delivered the Great (or other) Things. But that strategy invites vicious regress or circularity. Nor will it do to fob off the problem of circularity that threatens second-level justification or warrant by appeal to the ultimate circularity of all justification.[29] For we have agreed to bracket *general* skepticism, and as testimony is epistemically less fundamental than sense experience and induction, demand for a second-level justification of testimonial evidence that makes noncircular appeal to direct experience is entirely in order. Moreover, mystical experience—and by parity appeals to the help of the HS—are not epistemically on a par with sense experience, because not independently checkable.[30]

But matters are considerably worse than this. The cacophony of putative leadings of the HS counts as evidence *against* Plantinga's A/C model and van Inwagen's appeal to the magisterium of 'the Church.' Either the HS has been unaccountably capricious and selective in its election of some subclass of Christians, allowing many others to be misled by pseudo-inspirations, or else there is simply no HS.[31]

It will hardly answer to try to soften the corrosive implications of HBC scholarship and of the confusion of Christian 'revelations' to select out some set of Christian doctrines, vaguely enough understood, that command widespread agreement among Christians and that are the supposedly essential doctrines of the faith, making allowance that non-central Biblical passages might actually be false. Van Inwagen, for example argues that the false passages are such as 'do no harm.' But surely, major contradictions (to mention just one difficulty among many) *do* harm the intelligibility of Scripture and foment Christian strife—to say nothing of general and reasonable distrust of the texts. But worse: to distance oneself from the *details* of the Biblical texts would be to miss most of their richness and much of their message. One of the enormous advantages of understanding these texts by using the tools of myth analysis is that many of the difficulties, e.g., with contradictions, simply vanish.[32] Here, then, is *one* reason to doubt that a primary purpose of Scripture is recording history.

[28] William Alston, *Perceiving God: The Epistemology of Religious Experience* (Ithaca, NY: Cornell University Press, 1991), 148.

[29] Ibid., chap. 3; Plantinga *Warranted Christian Belief*, 125; and Evans (*The Historical Christ and the Jesus of Faith*, 306) all make this appeal.

[30] See Fales, 'Mystical Experience as Evidence,' *International Journal for Philosophy of Religion* 40 (1996): 19–46.

[31] For further evidence that disconfirms the A/C model, see Fales, 'A Critical Study of Alvin Plantinga's *Warranted Christian Belief*,' *Noûs* (forthcoming).

[32] That is a topic I cannot pursue here. Some hints can be found in Fales, 'Truth, Tradition, and Rationality,' *Philosophy of the Social Sciences* 6 (1996): 97–113; 'The Ontology of Social Roles,' *Philosophy of the Social Sciences* 7 (1997): 139–161; and 'Review of Douglas Geivett and Gary Habermas, *In Defense of Miracles*,' *Philosophia Christi* 3 (2001): 7–35.

PERSPICUOUS OR PERPLEXING?

One of the signature doctrines of Traditional Biblical Commentary, as Plantinga understands it, is the perspicuousness of Scripture. This has some plausibility: it is entirely plausible that Scripture would have been comprehensible by an intended audience—by ancient Jews and Gentiles—with the recognition that there may have been levels of meaning directed to *hoi poloi* and others meant for sophisticates. It is another matter altogether to claim that Scripture is perspicuous *for us now*. The difficulties besetting HBC and enormous disagreements within TBC are in themselves sufficient to make it entirely clear that Scripture is *anything but* perspicuous for lay Christians.

It should hardly be necessary to belabor this point. Even within the ambit of TBC, how easy is it to understand the nature of original sin by reference to the Genesis story? Why should we consider it possible to understand NT talk of death and resurrection without recourse to scholarly knowledge of the ANE context for such talk? (Is 1 Cor. 15 a model of perspicuous prose? Is Paul's meaning transparent when he claims to die every day?) It takes hardly any reflection to recognize that similar problems arise with understanding the meaning of claims about heaven and Sheol, or angels and demons. Yet these are hardly matters peripheral to Christian soteriology. Indeed, it is telling that one can ask almost any lay Christian a few probing questions regarding the nature of the soul, and reveal an almost complete conceptual whiteout.

I want, in conclusion, to suggest that adoption of the hermeneutical approaches recommended by Plantinga, Evans, and van Inwagen would represent not only a cognitively disastrous step backwards in Bible studies, but a dangerous one. The Reformation era, permeated by the spectral whisperings of the HS, is one whose religious hostilities echo worrisomely in the shrill 'culture-wars' rhetoric of contemporary right-wing ideologues.

Though he never actually defends the A/C model, Plantinga offers on behalf of it something like the following argument:

1. Christians know the Great Things of the Gospels.
2. If Christians know the Great Things, then in all probability something like the A/C model is correct.
3. Therefore, in all probability, something like the A/C model is correct.

I believe we should take Plantinga's *modus ponens* as our *modus tollens*.

Part III
Materialism and the
Resurrection of the Dead

15

The Possibility of Resurrection*

Peter van Inwagen

It has been said that the Christian doctrine of the Resurrection of the Dead faces the following philosophical difficulty: There is no criterion that anyone could use to determine whether a given post-Resurrection man was Caesar or Socrates or anyone else who had long ago lived and died and returned to the dust. But the real philosophical problem facing the doctrine of the Resurrection does not seem to me to be that there is no criterion that the men of the new age could apply to determine whether someone then alive was the same man as some man who had died before the Last Day; the problem seems to me to be that there *is* such a criterion and (given certain facts about the present age) it would, of necessity, yield the result that many men who have died in our own lifetime and earlier will not be found among those who live *after* the Last Day.

Let us consider an analogy. Suppose a certain monastery claims to have in its possession a manuscript written in Saint Augustine's own hand. And suppose the monks of this monastery further claim that this manuscript was burned by Arians in the year 457. It would immediately occur to me to ask how *this* manuscript, the one I can touch, could be the very manuscript that was burned in 457. Suppose their answer to this question is that God miraculously recreated Augustine's manuscript in 458. I should respond to this answer as follows: The deed it describes seems quite impossible, even as an accomplishment of omnipotence. God certainly might have created a perfect duplicate of the original manuscript, but it would not be *that one*; its earliest moment of existence would have been after Augustine's death; it would never have known the impress of his hand; it would not have been a part of the furniture of the world when he was alive; and so on.

Now suppose our monks were to reply by simply asserting that the manuscript now in their possession *did* know the impress of Augustine's hand; that it *was* a part of the furniture of the world when the saint was alive; that when God

* Peter van Inwagen, 'The Possibility of Resurrection.' in *The possibility of Resurrection and Other Essays in Christian Apologetics.* © 1998 by Westview Press. Reprinted by permission of Westview Press, a member of the Perseus Books Group.

re-created or restored it, he (as an indispensable component of accomplishing this task) saw to it that the object he produced had all these properties.

I confess I should not know what to make of this. I should have to tell the monks that I did not see how what they believed could *possibly* be true. They might of course reply that their belief is a mystery, that God had *some* way of restoring the lost manuscript but that the procedure surpasses human understanding. Now I am sometimes willing to accept such answers; for example, in the case of the doctrine of the Trinity. But there are cases in which I would never accept such an answer. For example, if there were a religion that claimed that God had created two adjacent mountains without thereby bringing into existence an intermediate valley, I should regard any attempt to defend this doctrine as a 'mystery' as so much whistle-talk. After all, I can hardly expect to be able to understand the Divine Nature, but I do understand mountains and valleys. And I understand manuscripts, too. I understand them sufficiently well to be quite confident that the monks' story is impossible. Still, I wish to be reasonable. I admit that one can be mistaken about conceptual truth and falsehood. I know from experience that a proposition that seems to force itself irresistibly upon the mind as a conceptual truth can turn out to be false. (If I had been alive in 1890, I should doubtless have regarded the Galilean law of the addition of velocities and the unrestricted comprehension principle in set theory as obvious conceptual truths.) Being reasonable, therefore, I am willing to listen to any *argument* the monks might have for the conclusion that what they believe is possible. Most arguments for the conclusion that a certain proposition is possibly true take the form of a story that (the arguer hopes) the person to whom the argument is addressed will accept as possible and which (the arguer attempts to show) entails the proposition whose modal status is in question.

Can such a story be told about the manuscript of Augustine? Suppose one of the monks is, in a very loose sense, an Aristotelian. He tells the following story (a version of a very popular tale): 'Augustine's manuscript consisted of a certain parcel of matter upon which a certain form had been impressed. It ceased to exist when this parcel of matter was radically deformed. To re-create it, God needed only to collect the matter (in modern terms, the atoms) that once composed it and reimpress that form upon it (in modern terms, cause these atoms to stand to one another in the same spatial and chemical relationships they previously stood in).'

This story is defective. The manuscript God creates in the story is not the manuscript that was destroyed, since the various atoms that compose the tracings of ink on its surface occupy their present positions not as a result of Augustine's activity but of God's. Thus what we have is not a manuscript in Augustine's hand. (Strictly speaking, it is not even a *manuscript*.) (Compare the following conversation: 'Is that the house of blocks your daughter built this morning?' 'No, I built this one after I accidentally knocked hers down. I put all the blocks just where she did, though. Don't tell her.')

I think the philosophical problems that arise in connection with the burned manuscript of Saint Augustine are very like the problems that arise in connection with the doctrine of the Resurrection. If a man should be totally destroyed, then it is very hard to see how any man who comes into existence thereafter could be the *same* man. And I say this not because I have no criterion of identity I can employ in such cases but because I have a criterion of identity for men and it is, or *seems* to be, violated. And the popular quasi-Aristotelian story that is often supposed to establish the conceptual possibility of God's restoring to existence a man who has been totally destroyed does not lead me to think that I have got the wrong criterion or that I am misapplying the right one. The popular story, of course, is the story according to which God collects the atoms that once composed a certain man and restores them to the positions they occupied relative to one another when that man was alive; thereby (the storyteller contends) God restores the man himself. But this story, it seems to me, does not 'work.' The atoms of which I am composed occupy at each instant the positions they do because of the operations of certain processes within me (those processes that, taken collectively, constitute my being alive). Even when I become a corpse— provided I decay slowly and am not, say, cremated—the atoms that compose me will occupy the positions relative to one another that they do occupy *largely* because of the processes of life that *used* to go on within me: or this will be the case for at least some short period. Thus a former corpse in which the processes of life have been 'started up again' may well be the very man who was once before alive, provided the processes of dissolution did not progress too far while he was a corpse. But if a man does not simply die but is totally destroyed (as in the case of cremation) then *he* can never be reconstituted, for the causal chain has been irrevocably broken. If God collects the atoms that used to constitute that man and 'reassembles' them, they will occupy the positions relative to one another they occupy because of God's miracle and not because of the operation of the natural processes that, taken collectively, were the life of that man. (It should also be willing to defend the following theses: The thing such an action of God's would produce would not be a member of our species and would not speak a language or have memories of any sort, though, of course, he—or it—would *appear* to have these features.)

This much is analogous to the case of the burned manuscript. Possibly no one will find what I have said very convincing unless he thinks very much like me. Let me offer three arguments against an 'Aristotelian' account of the Resurrection that have no analogues in the case of the manuscript and which will perhaps be more convincing to the generality of philosophers. Arguments (a) and (b) are ad hominems, directed against Christians who might be inclined toward the 'Aristotelian' theory. Argument (c) attempts to show that the 'Aristotelian' theory has an impossible consequence.

A. The atoms of which I am composed cannot be destroyed by burning or the natural processes of decay, but they *can* be destroyed, as can atomic nuclei and even subatomic particles. (Or so it would seem: The principles for identity through time for subatomic particles are very hazy; physical theory has little if anything to say on the subject.) If, in order to raise a man on the Day of Judgment, God had to collect the 'building blocks'—atoms, neutrons, or what have you—of which that man had once been composed, then a wicked man could hope to escape God's wrath by seeing to it that all his 'building blocks' were destroyed. But according to Christian theology, such a hope is senseless. Thus, unless the nature of the ultimate constituents of matter is different from what it appears to be, the 'Aristotelian' theory is inimical to a central point of Christian theology.

B. The atoms (or what have you) of which I am composed may very well have been parts of other people at some time in the past. Thus, if the 'Aristotelian' theory is true, there could be a problem on the day of the Resurrection about *who* is resurrected. In fact, if that theory were true, a wicked man who had read his Aquinas might hope to escape punishment in the age to come by becoming a lifelong cannibal. But again, the possibility of such a hope cannot be admitted by any Christian.

C. It is possible that none of the atoms that are now parts of me were parts of me when I was ten years old. It is therefore possible that God could collect all the atoms that were parts of me when I was ten, without destroying me, and restore them to the positions they occupied relative to one another in 1952. If the 'Aristotelian' theory were correct, this action would be sufficient for the creation of a boy who could truly say, 'I am Peter van Inwagen.' In fact, he and I could stand facing one another and each say truly to the other, 'I am you.' But this is conceptually impossible and therefore the 'Aristotelian' theory is *not* correct.

No story other than our 'Aristotelian' story about how it might be that a man who was totally destroyed could live again seems even superficially plausible. I conclude that my initial judgment is correct and that it is absolutely impossible, even as an accomplishment of God, that a man who has been burned to ashes or been eaten by worms should ever live again. What follows from this about the Christian hope of resurrection? Very little of any interest, I think. All that follows is that if Christianity is true, then what I earlier called 'certain facts about the present age' are *not* facts.

It is part of the Christian faith that all men who share in the sin of Adam must die. What does it mean to say that I must die? Just this: that one day I shall be composed entirely of nonliving matter; that is, I shall be a corpse. It is not part of the Christian faith that I must at any time be totally annihilated or disintegrate. (One might note that Christ, whose story is supposed to provide the archetype for the story of each man's resurrection, became a corpse but did not, even in his human nature, cease to exist.) It is of course true that men apparently cease to exist: those who are cremated, for example. But it contradicts nothing in the creeds to suppose that this is not what really happens, and that God preserves our corpses contrary to all appearance. Perhaps at the moment of each man's death, God removes his corpse and replaces it with a simulacrum, which is what is burned or rots. Or perhaps God is not quite so ~~wholesale~~ as this: Perhaps he removes for 'safekeeping' only the 'core person'—the brain and central nervous system—or even some special part of it. These are details.

I take it that this story shows that the Resurrection is a feat an almighty being could accomplish. I think this is the *only* way such a being could accomplish it. Perhaps I'm wrong, but that's of little importance. What *is* important is that God can accomplish it this way or some other. Of course one might wonder why God would go to such lengths to make it look as if most people not only die but pass into complete nothingness. This is a difficult question. I think it can be given a plausible answer, but not apart from a discussion of the nature of religious belief. I will say just this: If corpses inexplicably disappeared no matter how carefully they were guarded or inexplicably refused to decay and were miraculously resistant to the most persistent and ingenious attempts to destroy them, then we should be living in a world in which observable events that were *obviously* miraculous, *obviously* due to the intervention of a power beyond nature, happened with monotonous regularity. In such a world we should all believe in the supernatural: Its existence would be the best explanation for the observed phenomena. If Christianity is true, God wants us to believe in the supernatural. But experience shows us that if there is a God, he does not do what he very well *could* do: provide us with a ceaseless torrent of public, undeniable evidence of a power outside the natural order. And perhaps it is not hard to think of good reasons for such a policy.

POSTSCRIPT (1997)

If I were writing a paper on this topic today, I should not make the definite statement, 'I think this is the *only* way such a being could accomplish it.' My goal in 'The Possibility of Resurrection' was to argue for the metaphysical possibility of the Resurrection of the Dead. My method was to tell a story, a story I hoped my readers would grant was a metaphysically possible story, in which God accomplished the Resurrection of the Dead. But I was, I now think, too ready to identify the possibility of the Resurrection with the story I told to establish it. I am now inclined to think that there may well be other ways in which an omnipotent being could accomplish the Resurrection of the Dead than the way that was described in the story I told, ways I am unable even to form an idea of because I lack the conceptual resources to do so. An analogy would be this: A medieval philosopher, or even a nineteenth-century physicist, could have formed no idea of the mechanisms by which the sun shines, not because these mechanisms are a mystery that surpasses human understanding but simply because some of the concepts needed to describe them were not available before the twentieth century.

This analogy can be pressed a bit. Despite overwhelming evidence (provided by the fossil record) that there had been life on the earth for hundreds of millions of years, the great nineteenth-century physicist Lord Kelvin insisted that the sun had been shining for at most 20 million years. He maintained that the only conceivable mechanism of solar radiation was this: The sun is undergoing very gradual gravitational contraction, and solar radiation is due to the resulting gradual transformation of gravitational potential energy into radiant energy. When you plug the sun's mass, radius, and surface temperature into the appropriate equations (Kelvin contended), you will find that the sun cannot have been putting out radiant energy at anything like its current level for more than 20 million years. So (he concluded) the geologists and paleontologists—who are, after all, mere 'stamp collectors' and not real *scientists*—have, demonstrably, drawn a false conclusion from their fossils and sedimentary layers.

Lord Kelvin's calculations were (I understand) correct: Given his premise about the mechanism of solar radiation, his conclusion follows. Twentieth-century nuclear physics, however, has supplied the real mechanism of solar radiation, and we now know that Kelvin's premise and conclusion were both wrong and that the conclusion the despised 'stamp collectors' drew from the fossil record was right. Even in the nineteenth century, however, it would have been possible to show that Kelvin's premise and conclusion were not indisputable. Even within the confines of classical physics, it would have been possible to tell 'just-so stories' according to which the sun has been shining for hundreds of millions of years. Here is the beginning of one: The sun is made up of rapidly spinning atoms; continual collisions between these atoms result in their kinetic energy of rotation being gradually transformed into radiant energy.

If one continues the story by specifying (for some particular moment in the past) the right average rotational kinetic energy for the solar atoms and the right average linear velocity and mean free path of the atoms between collisions and the right average loss of rotational kinetic energy in each collision, the resulting filled-out story will have the consequence that the sun has been producing light and heat at its present level for hundreds of millions of years—or for any period one likes.

This is, of course, a 'just-so story': Although it serves to establish a possibility, it isn't *true*. In fact—as Kelvin would certainly have been quick to point out—it's a preposterous story, for no imaginable physical mechanism could have produced the initial conditions (the enormous rotational kinetic energy of the solar atoms) the story postulates. And yet, in a way, the story *is* true. There is one very abstract—and very important—feature that the sun-in-the-story shares with the real sun: Most of the energy that the sun gives off in the form of light and heat was not stored before it was radiated as gravitational potential energy, but rather was stored in the inner dynamics of the atoms of which the sun is composed (in the story, as kinetic energy of rotation; in the real world, as nuclear binding energy).

I am inclined now to think of the description that I gave in 'The Possibility of Resurrection' of how an omnipotent being could accomplish the Resurrection of the Dead as a 'just-so story'; Although it serves to establish a possibility, it probably isn't true. (And it is easy to see why someone might think it was preposterous, although it might be questioned whether any of us is in an epistemic position to make a judgment of this sort.) But I am also inclined to think that even if the story is not true, even if it gets the 'mechanism' of Resurrection wrong, it nevertheless *is* true—in a way. That is, I am inclined to think that even if the story is wrong about the specifics of the Resurrection, the Resurrection-in-the-story, like the sun-in-the-story, nevertheless shares some important but very abstract feature of the real thing. My inclination is to believe that God will somehow—in the way I have imagined or in some way I lack the conceptual resources to imagine, 'in this way or some other'—preserve a remnant of each person, a *gumnos kókkos* (a naked kernel: 1 Cor. 15:37), which will be sown in corruption and raised in incorruption.

16

The Compatibility of Materialism and Survival: The 'Falling Elevator' Model*

Dean W. Zimmerman

1. INTRODUCTION: PETER VAN INWAGEN'S PROBLEM FOR MATERIALIST SURVIVAL

Suppose that the materialist is right about me: I am a physical object, namely the living human body sitting here at my desk. Now consider the fact that this particular physical object would appear to be doomed. It will suffer decay, cease to exist, its parts probably ending up spread all around the world. Do not these two suppositions together imply that *I* am doomed? That I will suffer decay and cease to exist? If I and the body in question are not two things but one, then whatever fate awaits my body awaits me.

The Christian—at least the Christian who affirms, say, the Nicene creed—is one who 'looks for the resurrection of the dead, and the life of the world to come.' Can such a one be a materialist? Can she accept the conclusion of the preceding argument, judging that she will suffer decay and cease to exist—for a time, until 'the life of the world to come' begins?

Well, why not? What is supposed to be the big problem about ceasing to exist for a time and then coming back into existence again? Perhaps, at the general resurrection, God collects all the parts of me that are left (or some portion of them if a few have found their way into other people's bodies to be resurrected with them) and reconstitutes me more or less as I was at my death. Isn't that enough to bring me back onto the scene?

The primary problem with this and similar scenarios is not that there are obvious objections to the possibility of 'gappy existence'. Locke's principle, that nothing could have two beginnings of existence, is trivially true if taken to mean that nothing could have two earliest moments at which it exists; but it is not at all obvious if taken to rule out the possibility of something's ceasing to be for a time and then coming back into existence again. The real problem is that it is hard to see how a living body could come back into existence after *this sort* of temporal gap.

* © *Faith and Philosophy,* vol. 16 (1999). Reprinted by permission of the publisher.

For the gap described is one over which there appear to be no causal connections— or at least no very direct ones—passing from the body as it was at death to the body as it will be in the world to come. For God to create a 'new me' at that late date— even if He uses mostly old parts salvaged from the wreck of my body—is not for Him to bring *me* back, but to create a mere *replica* of me, a doppelgänger.

Peter van Inwagen makes the point succinctly and forcefully:

The atoms of which I am composed occupy at each instant the positions they do because of the operations of certain processes within me (those processes that, taken collectively, constitute my being alive). . . . [I]f a man does not simply die but is totally destroyed (as in the case of cremation) then *he* can never be reconstituted, for the causal chain has been irrevocably broken. If God collects the atoms that used to constitute that man and 'reassembles' them, they will occupy the positions relative to one another they occupy because of God's miracle and not because of the operation of the natural processes that, taken collectively, were the life of that man.[1]

I find van Inwagen's basic contention extremely plausible. In order that a given material object—or any other individual thing, for that matter—persist throughout a period of time, there must be appropriate causal relations between the object as it is at earlier times and the object as it is at later times. Exactly what relations are 'appropriate' is, of course, a vexed question. But most metaphysicians seem to agree with van Inwagen that there must be a causal element in any adequate 'criterion of identity' for persisting material objects.[2] Later states of a persisting body must be causally dependent, at least in part, upon its earlier states.

But not just any sort of causal dependence seems sufficient to give us the kinds of causal relations that are crucial to the persistence of a living body. It is not enough, says van Inwagen, that the way my body was at death serve as a mere *blueprint* for God's creation of a new one at the general resurrection. That is causal contribution of a sort; but here the causal chain passes through God's mind; it doesn't remain at all times 'immanent' with respect to processes going on inside a living human body. The case is analogous to that of van Inwagen's monks who claim that God 'recreated' an original manuscript in Augustine's own hand.[3] If the original was destroyed in a fire, no document brought into existence later on, by God or anyone else, could literally *be* the original—no matter how precisely similar the two might be.

Does the Christian materialist have any options left? It might seem that she has none, that she is forced either (a) to deny van Inwagen's thesis about the necessity

---

[1] Van Inwagen, 'The Possibility of Resurrection,' *International Journal for Philosophy of Religion* 9 (1978), pp. 114–21; reprinted (with postscript) in *Immortality*, ed. by Paul Edwards (New York: Macmillan, 1992), pp. 242–6; reprinted again (with longer postscript) in van Inwagen, *The Possibility of Resurrection and Other Essays in Christian Apologetics* (Boulder, Colorado: Westview Press, 1998), pp. 45–51. My references are to this last volume; the passage quoted in the text is from p. 47. [This volume, p. 323.]

[2] The arguments producing this agreement, due to David Armstrong and others, are discussed in the sequel.

[3] Cf. van Inwagen, 'The Possibility of Resurrection,' pp. 45–6. [This volume, pp. 321–2.]

of direct causal dependencies of the appropriate, 'immanent' sort for her persistence, or (b) to deny that she is identical with her body. But I think there are options left—as does van Inwagen.[4] Abstractly, the only other way out is to deny the second, empirical premise in the problem as I stated it in the first paragraph: Namely, the premise asserting that this body is doomed. Perhaps my body's future is really not so grim; perhaps, appearances to the contrary notwithstanding, my upcoming death is not, strictly speaking, the complete and utter destruction of my body after all.

Van Inwagen has suggested one way in which this body could have a brighter future than at first appears: Granted, it seems as if the organic life of my body peters out, and appropriate causal paths end. If this were what really happens, then (van Inwagen insists) setting up some batch of simples later on in such a way that they are alive and constitute an organism resembling me as I was at death would just be starting up a new life, one that is lived by a new organism. But perhaps appearances are deceiving; perhaps God secures my survival by surreptitiously removing my corpse—or at least my brain and central nervous system—and replacing it with a simulacrum at the time of my (seeming) death. At one time, van Inwagen thought this was the only way (consistent with empirical facts) for God to effect my survival.[5]

But the Christian materialist would surely do well to look for a better story than this. I once helped a friend with some of the more laborious steps in the process of taking a human corpse apart.[6] Opening a human skull and finding a dead brain is sort of like opening the ground and finding a dinosaur skeleton. Of course it is in some sense possible that God takes our brains when we die and replaces them with stuff that looks for all the world like dead brains, just as it is possible that God created the world 6000 years ago and put dinosaur bones in the ground to test our faith in a slavishly literal reading of Genesis. But neither is particularly satisfying as a picture of how God actually does business.

And that provides the motivation for this paper: My goal here is to tell a better 'just so' story (consistent with van Inwagen's version of materialism) according to which God ensures that this very body escapes the deadly powers that would otherwise destroy it—and does so without 'body-snatching' (that is, without

---

[4] Cf. van Inwagen, 'Dualism and Materialism: Athens and Jerusalem?,' *Faith and Philosophy* 12 (1995), pp. 475–88; and the 'Postscript (1997)' to 'The Possibility of Resurrection,' pp. 49–51 [this volume, pp. 325–7.].

[5] 'The Possibility of Resurrection,' p. 246 [this volume, p. 325.]. More recently (in a postscript added in 1997), van Inwagen has said that 'there may well be other ways in which an omnipotent being could accomplish the Resurrection of the Dead apart from literal 'body-snatching'—'ways I am unable even to form an idea of because I lack the conceptual resources to do so' ('The Possibility of Resurrection,' p. 50 [this volume, p. 325.]). The present essay can be seen as an attempt to augment van Inwagen's conceptual resources in such a way that he *is* able to form an idea of one or two of the ways God might do this.

[6] The friend was not a mobster, but a student of anatomy. Saddled with a lazy lab partner, she recruited my wife and me to assist.

spiriting away any of my body's parts and leaving behind different matter so that the miracle goes unnoticed). The escape is by a hair's breadth, effected by a miraculous last minute 'jump' that takes me out of harm's way. So I am tempted to call this story 'the falling elevator model of survival'—for you'll recall that, according to the 'physics' of cartoons, it is possible to avoid death in a plummeting elevator simply by jumping out in the split second before the elevator hits the basement floor. I argue that it is consistent with the rest of van Inwagen's materialistic metaphysics that our bodies do something like that when we die.

And we needn't add anything too wildly implausible in order to allow for this possibility—at least, nothing implausible that isn't already present in or required by van Inwagen's materialism. To establish this last point, I shall have to discuss problems of fission at some length. The goal will be to show that a materialism such as van Inwagen's cannot avoid a 'closest continuer' account of the persistence conditions for persons—that is, van Inwagen must deny what is sometimes called 'the only x and y principle.' This is important, since the falling elevator model requires that human persistence conditions include a 'temporally closest continuer' clause. Some will insist that adopting a closest continuer theory of personal identity is just as wildly implausible as supposing that God is a body-snatcher—and, for the record, I am inclined to agree. But, however that may be, I show that a closest continuer account of personal identity is an inevitable corollary of van Inwagen-style materialism.

Although van Inwagen's materialism provides the context in which I develop the falling elevator model of entry into the next life, I am confident that my strategy could be deployed within other theories of persistence, as long as they give pride of place to a causal element in criteria of identity over time. In particular, those who, unlike van Inwagen, accept the thesis that a human being persists by having a different 'temporal part' for each time at which she exists will have a somewhat easier time of it. I choose van Inwagen's own metaphysics because he has set the problem for us, and because his theory of persisting living things is probably one of the hardest to square with survival.

Finally, although I tell the story under the supposition of materialism, it remains of some relevance for any substance dualist, like myself, who would like to be able to say that it is this very body which will be reunited with my immaterial soul at the 'general resurrection.'

2. VAN INWAGEN'S METAPHYSICS
OF MATERIAL BEINGS

Van Inwagen's account of the nature and persistence conditions of physical objects is found in his impressive book, *Material Beings*.[7] Here's the *Reader's*

---

[7] Ithaca: Cornell University Press, 1990.

Digest condensed version: At bottom, the universe is filled with material simples—tiny particles that have no proper parts. Some of them are arranged table-wise in the center of my study; many more are arranged house-wise around me. However, contrary to what one might initially have thought, the simples arranged in a table shape here do not in fact compose anything, nor do the ceiling-shaped simples hanging over me. Simply heaping simples together is not sufficient to produce an object having them for its parts. Some simples, however, are caught up into a very special kind of event: namely, a Life. A set of objects are caught up in a Life when they are organized in such a way that they work toward insuring the continued existence of successor sets of simples organized in roughly the way they are—they possess a *conatus sese conservandi*, a knack for self-maintenance. The only events in our world that really exhibit this sort of self-sustaining activity are biological (although a particularly stable weather pattern, like a hurricane, is at least a pale imitation of a Life). When a set of objects are caught up in a Life, then there exists an object that is composed of these parts—a living organism. This organism lasts just so long as the event which is its Life continues. And, since there is no other way of organizing a collection of objects so that they compose an object, the world contains nothing but living things and the simples from which they are made.

Self-maintenance, the hallmark of Lives, is an intrinsically causal notion. And it requires a kind of 'immanent causation'. If matter is organized in one of the ways characteristic of living things, it tends to *directly* bring it about that there be matter organized in roughly the same way. A process that only *indirectly* ensures that a certain sort of structure be maintained will not count as a single Life. For instance, a process whereby I have offspring, even offspring as like me as a clone, will not count as a single Life, since it is, for a time, not an event happening to any living human organism. A process may preserve my body's structure but it won't be a single Life if, for example, it passes through the banks of a Star Trek-style teleporter or a blueprint in the mind of God. Such processes are not instances of true *self*-maintenance. Clearly, it is this component of van Inwagen's metaphysics that makes the possibility of survival so problematic. Since my Life is necessarily a self-perpetuating event, the apparently complete failure of my body to perpetuate itself at my death would seem to assure its demise; once the living structure has been completely lost, say in cremation, an attempt by God or anything else to bring my parts back together to form a living thing cannot possibly result in the continuation of *my* Life.

How does van Inwagen's materialism handle the familiar problems of fission and fusion? What is to be said, for instance, about a Life that splits when a human organism divides in two by means of some fancy brain-splitting surgery? Here I think van Inwagen, like all materialists save certain temporal parts theorists, must give up what is sometimes called the 'only *x* and *y* principle': roughly, the thesis that facts about events outside the spatiotemporal path swept out by an object could not have made any difference to the question of whether or not a single object passed along that path.[8] Van Inwagen must allow for at least the abstract possibility of cases of organic fission which break the only *x* and *y* principle. Although this will take some showing, it is important that I do so. For the falling elevator model of survival implies that the (antecedently highly plausible) only *x* and *y* principle be false. If van Inwagen's materialism should force him to reject the principle anyway, the falling elevator model does not have this implication as an *added* cost.

We know that it is possible for a person to survive the removal of an entire brain hemisphere. And it seems plausible to suppose that 'brain transplants' are at least possible in principle, and that in such a case the person goes where her brain goes. Now if my brain were only a little bit different,[9] then it would seem that I could survive not just the loss of an entire hemisphere, but the destruction of an entire half of my brain; and, given the possibility of brain transplants, the subsequent transplantation of my remaining half-a-brain into a different body. But this raises a familiar, troublesome question: What would happen were my (supposedly) symmetrical brain split in two, each of the halves being transplanted into a separate body? Each of the resulting organisms would have an equally good claim to be continuing my Life—that is, to be me. But they cannot both be me; one thing cannot become two, on pain of contradiction. Now the believer in souls can say that I went wherever my soul went—either with the one half-brain or the other or neither, as the case may be.[10] But what should the materialist say?

Those who believe in temporal parts can maintain that there were two people all along; they simply shared their earlier stages, much as two roads may share a certain stretch of pavement in common. But the opponents of temporal parts, such as van Inwagen himself, must say something else—namely, that, at least in cases of perfectly symmetrical fission, the original organism ceases to be and is replaced by two new ones. And indeed that is what van Inwagen does say.[11] But, as shall become apparent, this response leads inevitably to a 'closest continuer' theory of personal identity: the view that whether a given process is a single Life will sometimes depend upon events that are not part of that process.

---

[8] Harold Noonan introduced the expression 'only *x* and *y* principle.' David Wiggins was after something of the same sort with his 'only *a* and *b* condition.' See Noonan, 'The Only *x* and *y* Principle,' *Analysis* 45 (1985), pp. 79–83; and Wiggins, *Sameness and Substance* (Cambridge, Mass.: Harvard University Press, 1980), pp. 95–6. For related discussions, see Mark Johnston, 'Fission and the Facts,' in James Tomberlin (ed.), *Philosophical Perspectives* 3, Philosophy of Mind and Action Theory (Atascadero, Cal.: Ridgeview, 1989), pp. 369–97 (see esp. pp. 378–82); and my 'Criteria of Identity and the "Identity Mystics,"' *Erkenntnis*, 48 (1998), pp. 281–301.

[9] That is, if it were more like that of van Inwagen's Neocerberus; cf. *Material Beings*, pp. 202–3.

[10] Richard Swinburne turns the fact that the believer in souls can say this into an argument against materialism; cf. 'Personal Identity: The Dualist Theory,' [an excerpt from *Personal Identity*, by Swinburne and Sydney Shoemaker (Oxford: Blackwell, 1984)], in *Metaphysics: The Big Questions*, ed. by Peter van Inwagen and Dean W. Zimmerman (Oxford: Blackwell, 1998).

[11] Cf. *Material Beings*, pp. 205–7.

Here is what van Inwagen actually says about fissioning Lives. First, he sets up a 'best case scenario' for fission. Imagine an intelligent but amoeba-like creature—call it 'Neocerberus'—with two 'brains' corresponding rather closely to our two hemispheres. Each brain is the seat of reasoning, of the processing of sensory information, and of Neocerberus's other 'higher' mental functions. One thing these brains don't do is direct any of the homeodynamic activities of the body—they exercise no control over metabolism, antisepsis, respiration, pulse rate, and so on. These activities are governed by two 'organs of maintenance,' similarly paired. Like our two hemispheres, the two brains send messages back and forth by means of a commissure; and the two organs of maintenance are similarly linked. But unlike our hemispheres, which only imperfectly mirror one another's activity, the two brains are practically mirror images of one another, and likewise for the two organs of maintenance. Each works with its partner to stay in roughly the same state, so that each sends out the same signals to the rest of the amoeba-like body. Consequently, both conscious bodily movements and unconscious regulation of homeodynamic processes are overdetermined—each brain and each organ of maintenance sends a message which would have been sufficient by itself to bring about the bodily change in question.

Van Inwagen allows that the activities of Neocerberus's brains, organs of maintenance, and other parts, constitute a single life; Neocerberus is a living, thinking individual, while its left half and its right half are not. Given the substantial doubling up of functions in our own twin hemispheres, it would be a dangerous thing to deny the possibility of there being an individual like Neocerberus. But then van Inwagen must face the following question:

[S]uppose we surgically divide Neocerberus right down the middle. We suppose that his vital organs—pumps, glands, and so on—are symmetrically distributed, and that lesions in Neocerberus' outer integument heal almost instantly. When this is done, we shall obviously have two organisms. What is their relation to Neocerberus? You [i.e., van Inwagen], I think, must say that neither is Neocerberus. You must hold that two new organisms have come into existence, and that Neocerberus ceased to exist at the moment it became true that the simples that had composed him began to compose two organisms. Call the two new organisms Alpha and Beta. Brain 1 is a part of Alpha ... and brain 2 is a part of Beta.[12]

And van Inwagen accepts this conclusion: fission would mean the death of Neocerberus; its Life is over, and two new Lives begin.

Does this automatically make van Inwagen a closest continuer theorist, a denier of the only *x* and *y* principle? Not necessarily. For he could say that, even if brain 2 and its corresponding organ of maintenance had been simply 'removed by destruction,' as it were, that would have ended Neocerberus's life. He could then claim that it is not the mere presence of a competitor that keeps

[12] *Material Beings*, p. 203.

Neocerberus's Life from following the spatiotemporal path traced out by Alpha (or Beta). And this is just what van Inwagen does say.

So what is so bad about the removal by destruction of Neocerberus's right or left half? Why could it not survive such a loss? The event which Neocerberus could not survive is not, on van Inwagen's view, the loss of one of the *brains*. That, he thinks, is perfectly possible—just as we humans can survive the loss of a hemisphere. What Neocerberus cannot survive is the loss of one of the *organs of maintenance*. Destroy one, or separate the two, and Neocerberus dies.

But why would the destruction of one of these organs automatically 'kill' Neocerberus? After all, the rest of the organism could get along just fine without it, since all its signals are duplicated by the other organ. Destruction of the Beta organ of maintenance, says van Inwagen, 'ends Neocerberus' life because it destroys one of the two "organs of maintenance" that had been directing that life. The resulting life is a new event, distinct from Neocerberus' life because it had different causes from Neocerberus' life. It is in fact Alpha's life, and the resulting organism is... Alpha.'[13]

This strategy for avoiding the closest continuer theory ceases to be feasible, however, as soon as a broader range of possible organisms is considered. Take Leftycerberus, for example, an organism only slightly different from Neocerberus. Both of its organs of maintenance are more or less in synch, but the left one is a little faster than the right in sending electrical impulses to the rest of the body; and the first signal to arrive always preempts the slower signal, preventing it from causing changes in respiration, pulse rate, and so on. In this case, the right-hand organ of maintenance *isn't* among the causes of Leftycerberus's Life; and so, according to van Inwagen's reasoning, it can be removed without bringing Leftycerberus's Life to an end. But let's tinker a bit with Leftycerberus. What if, its right organ were sometimes successful and sometimes not? What if, for each electrical impulse sent, there were a fifty-fifty chance that the one and not the other would succeed? Perhaps the most 'realistic' scenario would be something like this: Leftycerberus's dual organ system has evolved in order to provide the organism with a 'backup' in case one of its organs of maintenance runs into trouble. Then switching off might be common; when one becomes tired, the other picks up speed and wins all duels for awhile.

What would van Inwagen say about such a creature? To be consistent with what he says about Neocerberus, it would seem that he must say something like this: whenever one organ of maintenance is, for a time, the sole cause of the changes it tries to direct, then it cannot give up any of its control to the other organ of maintenance without one Life coming to an end and a new one beginning. To pass on control would be to produce a Life with 'different causes.' But how plausible is that? Control of my heart rate can be taken over by a pacemaker without my ceasing to be. Why couldn't Leftycerberus's heart rate

[13] *Material Beings*, p. 208.

alone, say, be taken over by its right organ of maintenance without the poor thing's ceasing to be? For that matter, couldn't I survive the artificial control, at least for a short time, of all sorts of bodily functions—the systolic being only the most obvious example? If so, why couldn't the left organ pass some or even all of its duties to the right organ for a while? There seems no reason to deny that an organism such as Leftycerberus could survive such shifting of control. Only a desperate resolve to save the only *x* and *y* principle at any cost could motivate such a denial.

But if van Inwagen were to allow the possibility of a Leftycerberus, he would have to admit that such a creature *could* survive the removal of one of its organs of maintenance. Suppose the left organ has passed on its duties to the right. Then we remove the left organ, leaving the right one to carry on by itself. Leftycerberus's Life need not come to an end, at least not for the reason van Inwagen originally gave—that is, because the post-op Life now being directed by the right organ has different causes. Removing the left organ doesn't change the causes of the Life that's going on in this situation. So Leftycerberus can survive the destruction of one organ of maintenance and (van Inwagen has already allowed) the destruction of the corresponding brain. Suppose it's the left organ of maintenance and brain 1 that are destroyed. In that case, there's a Life which involves both of these for a time (along with brain 2 and the right organ), and then is continued by brain 2 and the right organ on their own. Call this process 'Life 1.' Now what happens in true fission? What happens if brain 1 and the left organ are removed not by destruction, but by their breaking away to constitute a mirror-image organism? I have argued elsewhere that the materialist who eschews temporal parts has no choice but to regard a perfectly symmetrical fission as the end of the original individual;[14] and van Inwagen seems to agree. So Leftycerberus can't survive this episode. And yet, the process I called 'Life 1' is still there, just as it was before—or at least, a process intrinsically just like Life 1, involving all the same particles doing all the same things. This process was, in the absence of competitors, sufficient for Neocerberus's survival. But, when a competitor is present, it is not. And so, to retain its plausibility, van Inwagen's account of organism identity is forced into the denial of the only *x* and *y* principle.

I am convinced that *any* materialism concerning human beings that eschews temporal parts can be driven in similar fashion toward a closest continuer account of human persistence conditions. Such materialists cannot avoid saying that, if there are two simultaneously existing and equally good candidates for being involved in the same Life as some earlier person; then the original person ceases to exist, her Life ends, and two new Lives begin. But if one of the two candidates had been completely absent (destroyed at the point of fission instead

<hr/>

[14] Cf. 'Immanent Causation,' in James Tomberlin (ed.) *Philosophical Perspectives* 11, Mind, Causation, and World (a supplement to *Noûs*) (Oxford: Basil Blackwell, 1997), pp. 433–71; cf. esp. pp. 454–5.

of being preserved alive), then the original Life would have continued and the original person would have persisted through the loss of half her brain.

I shall shortly need a little more information about how to trace Lives through branchings. The principle I will appeal to is this: If you are looking for the next event in a given Life, and the present event is causally connected in the appropriate, immanent way to two nonsimultaneous later events, but one is earlier than the other, go to the earlier of the two—it is the earlier one that represents the continuation of this Life, and the subsequent appearance of the later one does not turn this into a case of fission. I shall be assuming, then, something like a 'temporally-closest continuer' theory of persistence conditions.

3. LIVES WITH SPATIOTEMPORAL GAPS

Suppose that van Inwagen's notion of a Life does constitute the proper way to trace the careers of human beings; and that, when there is branching, it is the temporally-closest branch (if there is one) that continues the original Life. I think we can still make sense of an afterlife without having to suppose that God is a secret body-snatcher—someone who invisibly removes bodies or body-parts at death, replacing them with lookalikes. Here's one way:

On van Inwagen's view of human persistence, as on many others that emphasize a causal component in personal identity, if someone has persisted into the present, then his existence in the immediate past must not be causally irrelevant to his having lasted until now. For instance, the fact that I am presently standing here must be at least partly causally explicable in terms of the fact that I was standing here a moment ago; for if the body standing here then had no causal connections with the body here now, then the latter is not a continuation of the old one but a replacement that just happens to resemble the old one a good deal. This follows from van Inwagen's thesis that Lives are self-sustaining events; but it is often advanced as part of a larger metaphysical thesis, one that is sometimes put in this way: it is necessary that the stages of a single individual thing (animate or inanimate) be connected by 'immanent causality.'[15]

The role of immanent-causal relations among the stages of a persisting thing is most often discussed within the context of a metaphysics of temporal parts. David Armstrong, for instance, notes that 'preceding phases of a thing are a necessary part of the total cause which brings the succeeding phases to be.'[16] For Armstrong, the 'phases' in question are temporal parts; but one may emphasize the importance of immanent causation without accepting the doctrine of

[15] The *locus classicus* on immanent causation is W. E. Johnson, *Logic*, Part III (Cambridge: Cambridge University Press, 1924), Chapters 7–9. For a more recent discussion, cf. my 'Immanent Causation.'

[16] D. M. Armstrong, 'Identity Through Time,' in Peter van Inwagen (ed.), *Time and Cause* (Dordrecht: D. Reidel, 1980), pp. 67–78; quoted passage occurs on p. 75.

temporal parts. This can be seen most clearly by considering different views about the nature of causal relata. Let us assume, for simplicity, that conditions, states, and events together constitute one big category of causal relata, all of which may—with some stretching of ordinary usage—be called 'events'. It is generally agreed that objects only enter into causal relations derivatively by having causally efficacious events happen to them. For instance, the baseball's breaking the window is really a matter of a set of events C causing another event e—where C will include the event of the baseball's hitting the window with such-and-such a velocity, the 'event' of the window's being made of a certain kind of glass, etc., and e is the window's breaking.

Although Armstrong's way of describing immanent causation seems to pre-suppose a theory of events according to which (at least some) events are temporal parts, surely it is possible to agree with Armstrong about the importance of causal connections in persistence conditions while withholding commitment to a metaphysics of temporal parts.[17] The target thesis about immanent causation can be put in metaphysically neutral terms. First, we define 'temporal stage of an object' as a kind of complex, comprehensive event:

> (D1) s is the temporal stage at t of an object $x =_{df}$ there is a set R of all the intrinsic properties x has at t, and s is the event of x's exemplifying R at t.

If a property-exemplification theory of events is correct, then temporal stages as defined by (D1) are not temporal parts.[18] But if some of the friends of temporal parts are correct, then such comprehensive exemplifications of properties may in fact be identified with the temporal parts of things; in which case temporal stages *are* temporal parts. However this dispute about the correct theory of events turns out, (D1) can be used without prejudice to either view to express Armstrong's thesis about immanent causation.

Formulating a more precise statement of Armstrong's claim about immanent causation is complicated by the fact that, since time is a continuum, for any momentary stage which has previous stages among its partial causes, there is no *single* previous stage. What one should say, I think, is that, for an object that persists throughout a given period of time, the way the object is at any moment

---

[17] Both sides in the dispute over temporal parts are willing to agree that, for instance, 'a dog at an earlier moment will be "structurally similar to and play a significant role in the production of" the dog at a later moment' (Frederick Doepke, 'Identity and Natural Kinds,' *Philosophical Quarterly* 42 (1992), pp. 89–94; Doepke is quoting Andrew Brennan, *Conditions of Identity* (Oxford: Clarendon Press, 1988), pp. 26–7—Doepke is an opponent of temporal parts, Brennan a proponent).

[18] On property exemplification accounts of events, an event is the having of a property by a thing at a time (for property exemplification theories, compare Jaegwon Kim, 'Events as Property Exemplifications,' reprinted in his *Supervenience and Mind* (Cambridge: Cambridge University Press, 1993), pp. 33–52; and Roderick M. Chisholm, 'Events without Times: An Essay on Ontology,' *Noûs* 24 (1990), pp. 413–28; to identify such an entity with a temporal part would imply that temporal parts *happen to* some more fundamental substance. And this is something temporal parts theorists would be unlikely to accept—unless the thing to which the events happen is, perhaps, a region of space-time.

in that interval must be partially determined by the way it was during the interval leading up to that moment. This yields the following sort of principle:

(IC) Necessarily, if a physical object *x* persists throughout an open temporal interval *T*, then for every instant *t* in *T* there is an open interval of time *T** with *t* as its point-limit such that the sum of *x*'s temporal stages that exist during *T** is a partial cause of *x*'s temporal stage at *t*.[19]

Many metaphysicians seem to agree that something like (IC) must be true, and that immanent-causal relations among stages are much more central to the persistence conditions of physical objects than relations of spatiotemporal contiguity among stages.[20] Furthermore, the notion that spatiotemporal continuity of stages is not even necessary for persistence is a natural enough view. Why suppose that things cannot jump discontinuously from one place to another, or flicker out of existence for a while only to re-emerge elsewhere and elsewhen?[21] Armstrong sums up the relationship between spatiotemporal continuity and immanent causation succinctly: 'Spatiotemporal continuity of phases of things appears to be a mere result of, an observable sign of, the existence of a certain sort of causal relation between the phases.'[22]

(IC) does not rule out the possibility of discontinuous spatiotemporal jumps for objects, or even of 'temporally gappy' objects; it merely describes a condition that applies to periods of time *throughout which* an object exists. If immanent-causal connections are indeed necessary for persistence, then if it is possible for an

---

[19] I offer an analysis of the notion of 'partial cause' in 'Immanent Causation,' pp. 445–9.
[20] Cp. the discussions in D. M. Armstrong, 'Identity Through Time,' pp. 74–6; Sydney Shoemaker, 'Identity, Properties, and Causality,' in his *Identity, Cause, and Mind* (Cambridge: Cambridge University Press, 1984), pp. 234–60; and Chris Swoyer, 'Causation and Identity,' *Midwest Studies in Philosophy* 9, Causation and Causal Theories, ed. by Peter A. French, Theodore E. Uehling, Jr., and Howard K. Wettstein (Minneapolis: University of Minnesota Press, 1984), pp. 593–622. Armstrong and Shoemaker both propose thought-experiments designed to show that tracing a continuous spatio-temporal path is neither necessary nor sufficient for something's being a persisting object (cf. D. M. Armstrong, 'Identity Through Time,' p. 76; and Sydney Shoemaker, 'Identity, Properties, and Causality,' pp. 241–8). Imagine demons (Shoemaker introduces annihilation and creation machines, while Armstrong prefers deities) who can annihilate or create human beings at will. If one destroys me at *t* (i.e., makes *t* the first moment of my non-existence), while another creates a physical and psychological duplicate that takes my place at *t* (i.e., makes *t* the first moment of my duplicate's existence), then the series of stages traces a spatio-temporally continuous path. But suppose the demons are not working in concert, so that the duplicate appears in just that spot with just my physical and psychological make-up utterly by chance. In this case my temporal stages before *t* have absolutely no causal relevance to the stages of my replacement. He would have come into being there at *t* whether or not I had ever existed, we may suppose. Clearly, in this situation, I died and something else took my place. So spatio-temporal continuity by itself is not sufficient for persistence. Eliminate immanent-causal connections among stages, and all you have are distinct objects replacing one another.
[21] Some scientists talk as though certain sub-atomic particles *actually* move discontinuously, and some suggest that matter absorbed by a black hole may emerge at a distant location in space-time without having traversed any intervening locations. Whatever we think of the evidence for such claims, there seems nothing straightforwardly unintelligible or utterly impossible about them. (Chris Swoyer mentions the black-hole example ('Causation and Identity,' p. 598)).
[22] D.M. Armstrong, 'Identity Through Time,' p. 76.

object to persist through temporal gaps during which it has no stages, there must be suitable immanent-causal relations which cross the temporal gap between earlier and later stages. The statement of a more general condition allowing for this possibility is complicated, once again, by the fact that (time being continuous) an intermittently existing thing would seem capable of having an 'existence gap' that is either open or closed on both ends, or else open on one end and closed on the other.[23] In the case of a thing x that goes out of existence for an open interval T between t and t^*, we should say that it is a necessary condition of x's persistence over this gap that x's temporal stage at t is a partial cause of x's temporal stage at t^*. And we should add that at no time during the gap is there a set of conditions sufficient by itself for the occurrence of x's temporal stage at t^*. To allow that would be to allow that immanent-causal connections could pass through the circuitry of the *Enterprise*'s transporter or the mind of God; and, on van Inwagen's account of Lives, such causal connections are not sufficiently 'immanent' to preserve sameness of Life (and, with it, sameness of living body). Similar conditions may be formulated for the three other sorts of existence-gaps.

Assuming, then, that the kind of immanent-causal connections that normally preserve a Life could cross spatial and temporal gaps, there's no reason to think that one and the same Life could not contain spatial jumps or temporal gaps. As long as the causal processes from earlier stages to later stages are of the right sort, preserving the self-sustaining structure peculiar to the living thing in question, one has the same Life. If, for instance, every particle in my body were disposed at a given time to (discontinuously) 'jump' precisely one yard in a certain direction, then my body would sustain itself over a discontinuous jump of one yard as well.

Of course the supposition that causal processes can be spatiotemporally gappy in this way is contentious. But it should be much less so than it once was, for the following reasons: there is no a priori reason to think it is impossible, and some a posteriori reason to think it happens; the theories of causation which imply that it is impossible have been exploded; and the most promising theories still in the water can accommodate it. I can give only the briefest survey of these points here.

One species of gappy causal process is what Russell called 'mnemic causation'—'that kind of causation... in which the proximate cause consists not merely of a present event, but of this together with a past event.'[24] He concludes that there is 'no a priori objection to a causal law in which part of the cause has ceased to exist.'[25] But what *are* the supposed a priori objections to causally direct action at a spatial or temporal distance? The traditional one was just that 'a thing

[23] For a discussion of similar problems, cf. Philip Quinn, 'Existence Throughout an Interval of Time and Existence at an Instant of Time,' *Ratio* 21 (1979), pp. 1–12.

[24] *The Analysis of Mind* (London: George Allen & Unwin, 1921), p. 85.

[25] *The Analysis of Mind*, p. 89.

cannot act where it is not'; and so an event cannot cease to be before its effect comes into existence or directly bring about an effect at some spatial distance. But this line of reasoning quickly leads to the conclusion that all causation must be simultaneous, and that a cause and its effect must occupy the very same spot—and how, then, is the propagation of causal processes possible? This result constitutes a near reductio of the primary source of the a priori objections to mnemic and otherwise gappy causation.

On the a posteriori side in favor of direct causation across spatiotemporal gaps, there is Bell's inequality, verified by Aspect's experiments, which suggests that either there is faster-than-light signaling at the quantum level, or else there are nonlocal causal influences at work. Of course I cannot pretend to know how the paradoxes of quantum mechanics will ultimately be resolved (if indeed they ever will be, to everyone's satisfaction). But all I wish to point out here is this: nonlocal causal processes are a serious contender for explaining certain very mysterious physical phenomena; and many of those who have thought hardest about these matters take the possibility seriously. Unless we metaphysicians have some very powerful a priori arguments against gappy causal processes (and, as I said, I think we don't), we had better stop insisting that they're impossible.

True, some philosophical theories about the nature of causation straightforwardly imply that cause and effect must be at least spatiotemporally contiguous, if not coincident. Most notably, contiguity of cause and effect is built into the theories of Hume and C. J. Ducasse. But, by my lights, the critics of these views have won: causation is more than just constant conjunction and spatiotemporal contiguity; and the cause of a given effect cannot be defined in Ducasse's way, either—as, roughly, the sole change occurring right before the effect and in its immediate environment.[26] What theories of causation are still afloat? There is a bewildering variety, but most of the real contenders have room for gappy causal processes. There are purely singularist accounts, like Elizabeth Anscombe's,[27] that simply take the causal relation as fundamental and unanalyzeable; given the simplicity of the causal relation on such a view, the impossibility of causation over gaps could hardly *follow* from the thesis. There are counterfactual analyses, like David Lewis's;[28] and nothing in such accounts prohibits counterfactual dependencies of the right sort between events that (a) have spatiotemporal gaps between them, and (b) have no other events between them capable of taking up the causal slack. A number of theories posit some sort of intrinsically causal persisting process or thing as a primitive notion, and use it in the analysis of

---

[26] For Ducasse's theory, see his 'On the Nature and Observability of the Causal Relation,' reprinted in Ernest Sosa and Michael Tooley (eds.), *Causation* (New York: Oxford University Press, 1993); for some of the standard criticisms of Humean analyses and Ducasse's theory, see the editors' introduction.

[27] 'Causality and Determination,' reprinted in Sosa and Tooley, *Causation*.

[28] 'Causation,' reprinted in Sosa and Tooley, *Causation*.

causal relations among events. Wesley Salmon, for instance, takes 'causal processes' as basic—causal processes being spread out in space-time, and (unlike mere 'pseudo-processes') capable of transmitting signals or bearing a mark.[29] Most recently, Douglas Ehring has suggested that the 'singularist element' that links a cause to an effect is the persistence of a 'trope,' a property-instance that is part of the cause and endures as part of the effect.[30] Like the simpler singularism of Anscombe, theories like Salmon's and Ehring's cannot in any straightforward way *imply* the spatiotemporal continuity of causal processes, or the contiguity of cause and effect. Since the notion of a causal process or a persisting trope is taken as a primitive, there can be no analytic requirement that such things exhibit spatiotemporal continuity.

These are, in brief, the reasons it seems to me to be sensible to suppose that mnemic or otherwise gappy causation is possible. And given that it's possible, then, whatever the likelihood of its occurrence in the ordinary course of nature, gappy causation remains a tool that God might use to effect the preservation of this living body. Is such causation *necessary* in order for God to secure my body's survival without body-snatching? Perhaps not; for, in the final section, I shall suggest that, even if there be some sort of hidden impossibility here, there remains a less problematic sort of 'quasi-causal' dependence that could cross spatiotemporal gaps and be used by God to ensure my survival.

If we can make sense of immanent-causal connections over spatiotemporal gaps, then we are well on our way to an account of survival without body-snatching. Suppose my body were to undergo an extraordinary and discontinuous case of fission: every particle in my body at a certain time *t* is immanent-causally connected with two resulting particle-stages after that time. The two sets of resulting particles appear at some later time *t** in disjoint spatial regions, and each is arranged just as the set of 'parent' particles that produced it; what's more, they are so arranged *because* the original particles were so arranged—for each particle produces its 'offspring' at precisely the same distances and directions as every other particle, ensuring duplication of my body's overall structure. My body, in this case, replicates itself over a temporal gap. Given the solution to fission cases advocated above, we must say that this event brings my life to an end. But now suppose that the same sort of fissioning of each particle occurs, but that only *one* set constitutes at *t** a living human body structured just like mine; the other set appears at *t** as an unstructured pile of dead matter. Perhaps many of the particles failed to 'send' one set of 'offspring' to the right place, so that the particles that appear on one side are not arranged just like the original set of particles. Then, thanks to the failure of one body to 'take,' my life is continued by the successful candidate that appears after a temporal interval.

[29] 'Causality: Production and Propagation,' reprinted in Sosa and Tooley, *Causation*.
[30] *Causation and Persistence* (New York: Oxford University Press, 1997).

Now we have a model for how God may resurrect this very body: He does so by, just before it completely loses its living form, enabling each particle to divide—or at least to be immanent-causally responsible for two resulting particle-stages. One of the resulting particle-stages is right here, where the old one was; another is either in heaven now (for immediate resurrectionists), or somewhere in the far future. But in any case, since the set of particle-stages on earth that are immanent-causally connected with my dying body do not participate in a Life, there is no danger of my 'fissioning out of existence' due to competition with my corpse. My corpse is not even a *candidate* for being me, since it does not participate in a Life. In fact, on van Inwagen's view, there *is* no such object—it's just a collection of particles that doesn't add up to anything. But whether or not the corpse is a single thing, it could not be identical with the living organism that was here just prior to my death, since organisms are essentially *living* things. Furthermore, if the ultimate simples in my body are the kinds of things that can last through time (some talk as though quantum mechanics rules this out), it will turn out that each simple which God 'zaps' with this replicating power in fact does not *itself* divide, but simply remains right here—as a part of my corpse. Each particle x is immanent-causally connected to two streams of later particle-stages; one of them—the one in the here and now—includes stages of x itself; the other, the one in the hereafter, consists of stages of a different particle. Unlike a case of fission in which the fission-products co-exist, the case of the future-replicating individual particle involves only one resultant particle now; so, in the present there is no other candidate to threaten the continued existence of the original particle—there is only one 'temporally-closest continuer' for each particle.

The diversity of the particles I'll have after death from the particles in my dying body does not, however, prevent the *bodies* from being the same. All that matters for the continuation of my Life is that the right kind of life-sustaining causal continuity obtain among person-stages. In fact, if I'm made entirely of particles that are bosons or fermions (as seems to be the case), then there is reason to doubt whether my body can *ever* be said, strictly speaking, to consist of the same particles from one moment to the next. For fermions and bosons obey statistical laws which lead many to say that they 'lack individuality.'[31] But whether or not the ultimate simples in my body persist, the atoms and molecules in my body as I die will all still be here, heaped up on the floor as parts of my corpse. For the causal relations normally sufficient to preserve atoms and molecules will obtain between the pre- and post-death atoms and molecules; and, as long as the only competitor for being this or that molecule is something that appears in the future, there are no competitors here and now.

Thus we have a story that includes everything we want: The heap of dead matter I leave behind is made of stuff which really was a part of my body (it is not

---

[31] For a simple-minded discussion of the quantum-statistical reasons for thinking such particles don't persist, see my 'Immanent Causation,' pp. 459–61.

a simulacrum; God is not a body-snatcher), and the resurrected body is really identical with this present one—it is causally continuous with it in just the way adjoining stages of my present body are causally continuous, except that in this case there is a spatial or spatiotemporal gap which my poor body was given the power to cross by means of God's intervention.

4. OBJECTIONS AND REPLIES

Objection: What if God had given my particles this replicating power back at the end of my 20th year, so that at that time they were immanent-causally connected both with a living duplicate in the hereafter as well as with succeeding spatio-temporally continuous 21-year-old body-stages in the here-and-now?

Reply: I answer just as in the particle case. Since there is no rival candidate for me in existence immediately after the last 20-year-old person-stage, my life continues in the ordinary way—the ostensibly 20-year old 'resurrected' replica of me is just that, a replica of 'the me that used to be.' One only faces fission when a life divides into two co-existing (and therefore competing) streams.

Objection:[32] If my body reappears exactly as it was right before my death, then the first thing I will do when I get to heaven is die. And that's not much to look forward to!

Reply: The simplest response is to point out that, right up to the moment of my death, it remains possible for God to miraculously heal my body, preserving my life by fixing an organ that isn't functioning, kick-starting a process that has stopped, or holding together bits of me that are flying apart. As long as His miraculous interference is not too extreme (not, for instance, the instantaneous replacement of every cell in my body with a new cell specially created on the spot), He would be *healing my body* and not just *replacing it* with a simulacrum. If He could have worked such a miracle at any point up to the moment of my death, then He could surely do it as soon as my body reappears—so quickly, in fact, that neither I nor any other (normal human) witness would notice that my body was, for a moment, in bad shape. But there are sure to be other ways around this problem; for instance, the extraordinary causal powers given to the particles of my dying body could be tampered with slightly, so that some of their results in the hereafter are not *precisely* what one would have expected given their organization at my death.

Objection: You have spoken blithely of God 'zapping' material particles to give them replicating power; but I suspect there is a deep impossibility lurking here. On my view, it is *essential* to an object that it have all of the most fundamental causal powers it actually has, *and no more*. But then the replicating

---

[32] This objection was put to me by David Lewis.

power you posit could not be foisted on a thing from 'outside'—to do so would be to violate its very nature.

Reply: Although I am suspicious of your rigid theory of causal powers, I can respond to your objection without denying your theory. Particles in the here-and-now can mnemically-cause—or at least mnemically-'quasicause'—particles in my resurrected body without the introduction of foreign powers. The chief difficulty to be avoided in a materialist theory of survival is the severing of direct causal dependence between the heavenly person-stages and the dying person-stages. If the body appearing in the hereafter is the way it is *not* primarily because of the way my body was at death, but as a direct result of God's creative act, then the required immanent-causal connection is broken. The important question here is whether, at the time of resurrection, there are causally sufficient conditions in existence for the appearance of a body of precisely this sort; or whether the causally sufficient conditions must be extended back to include the state of my body at death. In the former case, survival is in jeopardy. But in the latter case, the falling elevator model is off the hook.

Fortunately, it is fairly easy to see how God could issue a decree that would produce a body just like mine was at my death, without at the same time precisely determining the characteristics of the body that appears. God's part in resurrecting me—His decree—could be extremely limited in its content. If his decree is appropriately limited, the particular structure exemplified by the resurrected body will depend directly upon a past existent: Namely, the temporal stage of my body at the time of my death.

I propose that we think of God's creative acts on the order of the carrying out of a king's commands. There are, of course, big differences. A king has authority to issue decrees; but his orders (at least the significant ones) can only be carried out by means of causal intermediaries, whereas God need only give the command and it is so. Still, the comparison proves illuminating. Consider Frederick the Great, issuing one of his whimsical decrees: 'Let the tallest man in the kingdom be brought before me!' And his messengers scour the kingdom measuring people, in search of a man taller than all the others. Assuming there are not two or more equally tall men taller than all others, there is a certain state of affairs that would represent the fulfillment of Frederick's decree. If Jones happens to be the tallest man in the kingdom, it is: Jones's standing before the king. But if Robinson had been an inch taller, or Jones an inch shorter, a different state of affairs would have satisfied the king's order. Clearly, the result of the king's command in this case depends on more than just its content; it also depends upon facts about the heights of the men in his kingdom.

Now suppose God's command at the general resurrection is limited in something like the way Frederick's 'Find the tallest man' is limited. Suppose God says: 'Let there be a body which is just like Zimmerman's was at his death.' The precise nature of the body that appears will *not* be determined by the content of God's decree—or by any other set of conditions that exist then.[33] There is no blueprint in God's mind specifying my body's former states, a blueprint that figures in his act of creation. Rather, the nature of the body depends entirely upon what my final bodily stage was like. This seems to me to represent, if not genuine mnemic causation, at least a kind of mnemic quasi-causal dependence. In particular, it is, I believe, sufficient to address van Inwagen's worry that the particles in any ostensibly resurrected body 'will occupy the positions relative to one another they occupy because of God's miracle and not because of the operation of the natural processes that, taken collectively, were the life of that man.' What the new body is actually like in its details depends upon what the original body was like, and not upon the will of God—at least not upon the particular act of will that is involved in this particular miracle.

The bite of van Inwagen's original dilemma comes from our feeling that a body put together in such a way that its every feature depends entirely upon God's action at the time he creates it could only be a *replica* of me. But the details of the body that results from the very limited divine decree I've described would *not* depend upon the particular activity God engaged in then; they would depend instead upon the states of my body at death. The fact that the dependence in question is not ordinary causal dependence is, I think, beside the point—what's needed is simply a way for the intrinsic states of the heavenly body to depend upon those of the earlier one *directly*, that is, without passing through intermediate conditions sufficient themselves to explain the heavenly body's structure. And this has been done. There is no causal process that passes outside every living human body and provides a sufficient explanation for the heavenly body's existence and intrinsic nature. The chain of dependence (in this case, quasi-causal dependence) going backwards from the initial state of the heavenly body remains 'immanent' with respect to a living, human organism—namely, my body.[34]

[33] One factor that does exist then and is in danger of helping to determine the details of my heavenly body-stages is God's (necessarily infallible) beliefs about how my body was at death. But these beliefs are what they are because of how my body was, and not the reverse; and, let us suppose, they do not determine the content of God's decree or in any other way figure causally in bringing me back.

[34] Portions of this paper appear under the title 'Materialism and Survival' in *Philosophy of Religion: The Big Questions*, ed. by Eleonore Stump and Michael Murray (Oxford: Basil Blackwell, 1998). Ancestors were read at the Pacific Meeting of the APA (1995) and at Franklin and Marshall College. I received good criticism and advice on both occasions. I thank Trenton Merricks, Andrew Cortens, David Lewis, and David Armstrong for particularly helpful comments. Two referees for this journal (one has since identified himself as Bill Hasker) also supplied me with useful criticisms, which I have tried to take into account; as a result, the paper is, I hope, much better organized than it once was, and now addresses worries about immanent causation which many readers may share—although I suspect I have not done enough to fully satisfy at least one of the referees on this last score.

17

Need a Christian be a Mind/Body Dualist?*

Lynne Rudder Baker

Dualism of body and soul, or of body and mind, permeates Western thought. Many prominent Christian theologians have assumed the truth of mind/body dualism: Augustine, Anselm, Luther, Calvin, and in a different respect, apparently Thomas Aquinas.[1] So, in addition to its distinguished philosophical lineage—through Plato and Descartes—mind/body dualism has venerable credentials in the history of Christian thought. Nevertheless, even while respecting the tradition, we can go on to ask: Does Christian doctrine entail mind/body dualism? *Need* a Christian be a mind/body dualist?

The answer partly depends, of course, on what is meant by 'mind/body dualism,' and by what is meant by 'Christian.' As I am using the terms here, a Christian affirms traditional Christian doctrines—such as the two-natures doctrine of Christ and the doctrine of the resurrection of the body. And mind/body dualism is the thesis that human persons have non-bodily parts—immaterial souls—that can exist independently of any body. According to mind/body dualism, if Jane is a human person living in Canada, she has a body, but Jane's existence does not depend on her having the body that she has or on her having any body at all: If mind/body dualism is correct, even though she is now embodied, Jane could exist as a purely immaterial being.

Very tentatively, I shall offer some reasons to deny that a Christian need be, or even should be, a mind/body dualist. I shall sketch a picture of mind, and of human persons, that is not a form of mind/body dualism; then, I shall argue not only that the nondualistic picture is consistent with Christian doctrine, but also that it fits quite comfortably within a Christian outlook and is philosophically superior to mind/body dualism. Finally, I shall conclude with some methodological reflections.

---

* © *Faith and Philosophy*, vol. 12 (1995). Reprinted by permission of the publisher.

[1] Aquinas's view is nuanced and not easy to pin down. 'Therefore, since the human soul, insofar as it is united to the body as a form, also has its existence raised above the body and does not depend on it, it is clear that the soul is established on the borderline between corporeal and separate [i.e., purely spiritual] substances.' Thomas Aquinas, *Disputed Questions on the Soul IC*, quoted by Norman Kretzmann, 'Philosophy of Mind,' in *The Cambridge Companion to Aquinas*, Norman Kretzmann and Eleonore Stump, eds., (Cambridge: Cambridge University Press, 1993): 136.

PERSONS AND THEIR BODIES

Materialism dominates contemporary philosophy. On the standard materialistic view in the philosophy of mind, mental states are brain states. The only alternative, it is assumed, is to construe mental states as states of a nonbodily entity, an immaterial soul, and this is to endorse mind/body dualism—a doctrine now widely regarded as untenable. A little reflection, however, shows the dichotomy—mental states as brain states or mental states as immaterial-soul states—to be a false one. For there is another alternative, which elsewhere I call 'Practical Realism,' that stands in contrast to the Standard View: According to Practical Realism, mental states—like beliefs, desires, and intentions—are rather states of the whole person—person-states, as it were, not states of any particular organ or proper part of a person.[2]

Persons have beliefs; brains have neural states. Having certain neural states is (presumably) a necessary condition for persons to have beliefs; but it does not follow that for each belief that a person has, there is a neural state that is identical to (or that constitutes) that belief. Compare: Beavers build dams; jaws have mandibular states. Having certain jaw states is (presumably) necessary for beavers to build dams; but it does not follow that for each dam a beaver builds, there is a mandibular state that is identical to (or that constitutes) the building of the dam.

What believing is, I am convinced, cannot be described or explained in terms free of reference to intentional states; nonetheless, illuminating things may be said about belief. Whether or not S believes that p depends solely on what S would do, say and think in various circumstances. (Doing and saying cannot be understood by anyone who doesn't already understand belief.) Although S may not always manifest her belief in behavior, if S believes that p, there must be circumstances in which S's belief that p would make a difference to what S would do, say or think—where what S does, says or thinks may be specified by ordinary descriptions of actions, such as 'answer the letter,' 'invite the neighbors,' 'buy the blue one,' and so on. Conversely, if relevant counterfactuals are true of S, then S believes that p—whether or not S acknowledges having that belief, or even realizes that she has it. Even if there is no noncircular account of belief in general, a particular person's having a particular belief is explainable in terms of the counterfactuals relevant to that person's having that belief. (There are complex issues about identifying the relevant counterfactuals for S's having a certain belief, but these are beyond the scope of this paper.)[3] A person believes that foxes have tails if and only if relevant (intentionally specified) counterfactuals are true—independently of how the brain is organized. Perhaps the

[2] See my *Explaining Attitudes: A Practical Approach to the Mind* (Cambridge: Cambridge University Press, 1995).
[3] See *Explaining Attitudes*, Chapter 6.

relevant counterfactuals are true only of those with certain kind of brain functioning in a certain way, but it does not follow that beliefs *are* brain states. Since the term 'belief' is just a nominalization of 'believes that,' we should not think of beliefs as particular internal states of an organ like the brain.

Someone may object that to have the relevant counterfactuals true of one simply is to be in a certain state; and the only candidates for such states are brain states or soul states. I think that the objection is misguided. For the kind of state required for the counterfactuals to be true is not any particular internal state, but a state in an extended sense. My 'state' in virtue of which it is true that I would lend you money for lunch if you asked me depends on my being embedded in a certain social and linguistic environment. There is no good reason to identify such a state with particular state of one's brain. Similarly for belief states. The reality of belief does not depend on the term 'belief''s denoting a kind of spatiotemporal entity or of a particular internal state. One's state of believing that p depends on global properties (including relational properties, and properties about what would happen in various counterfactual circumstances) of whole organisms.

The reason, I think, that it is appropriate to construe mental states as global states is that it is the person, the whole person and not just her brain, who is an agent.[4] Having attitudes enables persons to do things that otherwise could not be done. In a world without attitudes, there would be no such thing as befriending, or insulting, or obeying, or paying bills, or having parties, or many of the other things that make up human life. Beliefs and desires are on a par with the actions that they make possible. Just as Joan's promising to pick up a colleague's mail is a property of a person, not of a mouth, so too is her believing that she will be able to find the colleague's mailbox a property of a person, not of a brain. In short, beliefs and desires are not spatiotemporal entities that have causal powers; rather, persons have causal powers in virtue of having beliefs and desires. The relevant entities are person, not attitudes.

If beliefs and desires are not spatiotemporal entities, yet believing and desiring are real properties of persons, then it might seem that I have exchanged substance dualism, as found in Descartes and Plato, for a more up-to-date property dualism. I resist this description, because I think that property dualism is in the same philosophical camp as both substance dualism and mind/brain identity theories. For according to property dualism, there are two fundamental kinds of properties—mental and physical—that in some way determine all other properties. I no more think that there are two kinds of fundamental properties than I think that there is one kind of fundamental property. There are many kinds of properties (social, legal, moral, aesthetic, artifactual, and on and on), and it seems

---

[4] The ways in which actions are related to motions of various parts of the body are complicated; and I cannot deal with that topic here, except to say that what is morally, legally, socially important are intentional actions, not bodily motions. For philosophers of mind, bodily motions hold philosophical interest only insofar as they serve action.

to me highly unlikely that there is a single relation—supervenience, reduction, or anything else—in terms of which all properties are connected to one or two kinds of fundamental property. Hence, I reject property-dualism along with substance-dualism and mind/brain identity theories. But my main point in this section is that beliefs and desires are not states of brains or of souls, but of persons. This point makes acute the question: What is a person?

In the first instance, a person (human or not) is a being with a capacity for certain intentional states like believing, desiring, intending, including first-person intentional states. A first-person intentional state requires that one think of oneself in a first-person way—typically, in English, with the pronouns 'I,' 'me,' and 'mine.'[5] To use an example from Castañeda, who brought this point to the fore, when Castañeda thinks that he (himself) is the Editor of *Soul*, he expresses his thought by 'I am the Editor of *Soul*,' where this though is distinct from the thought that he would express by 'Castañeda is the Editor of *Soul*,' or 'The author of *Thinking and Doing* is the Editor of *Soul*,' (Castañeda may not know that he {himself} is the author of *Thinking and Doing* or even that he {himself} is Castañeda.) First-person intentional states are irreducible to third-personal intentional states. In order to be a person, any being must have first-person intentional states.[6]

A *human* person is (at least for part of its existence) a biological entity—a member of the species *homo sapiens*—with a capacity for first-person intentional states. As a *homo sapiens*, a human person—Smith, say—must have a biological body that she can think of in a first-person way assuming that there is a biological body of which Smith can think in a first-person way, and that it is metaphysically impossible for anyone who is not Smith to think of that body in the first-person way, the capacity to think of that biological body[7] in a first-person way individuates Smith and distinguishes her from every other metaphysically possible person.

Let me elaborate a little on the idea of having the capacity to think of a biological body in the first-person way. Smith thinks of a biological body in the first-person way if she can distinguish that body from all other bodies without aid of a name or description or third-personal pronoun. When Smith thinks of the pain in her head in the first-person way, she needs no name (e.g., 'Smith') or description (e.g., 'person with the biggest head in the room') or third-person

---

[5] First-personal states do not require what might be called 'Cartesian privacy.' Philosophers such as Dewey, Sartre, and George Herbert Mead construe first-personal states as dependent on social context.

[6] Hector-Neri Castañeda argued for the irreducibility of the first-person perspective to a third-person perspective in several publications, beginning with 'He: A Study in the Logic of Self-Consciousness' *Ratio* 8 (1966): 130–57. See also his 'Indicators and Quasi-Indicators' in the *American Philosophical Quarterly* 4 (1967): 85–100. For a study of philosophy from the first-personal point of view, see Gareth B. Matthews, *Thought's Ego in Augustine and Descartes* (Ithaca NY: Cornell University Press, 1992). In 'Why Computers Can't Act,' (*American Philosophical Quarterly* 18 (1981): 157–63), I argued that a first-person perspective was required in order to form intentions.

[7] Or at least some part of it, in the case of Siamese Twins.

pronoun (e.g., 'her') to identify the person whose head is in question. Smith's wishing that the pain in her head would go away is not the same as wishing that the pain in Smith's head would go away, or that the pain in the largest head in the room would go away. Although 'capacity' is a vague term, in saying that human persons must have the *capacity* to think of themselves in the first-personal way, I mean not to exclude, say a person in an irreversible coma: If one has ever thought of her body in the first-person way (and has not yet died), she has the capacity of think of her body in the first-person way. (If there is no life after death, then the capacity to think of one's body in the first-person way is forever extinguished at death.) Hereafter, I'll drop reference to the *capacity* for intentional states, and say that one 'has' a particular intentional state if she has ever had it.

x is a human person in virtue of having intentional states, some of which make first-person reference to a biological body. (I am not claiming that all of a human person's first-person intentional states make reference to a body. The thoughts that a human expressed by saying, 'I'm lonely,' or 'I'm in debt,' or 'I just cannot stop thinking of you' do not refer to a body; rather, there would be no human to think those thoughts without a body.) x is the particular person she is—Smith, say—in virtue of a whole cluster of properties peculiar to her. Some of these properties are psychological (for example, having certain memories, desires, fears, and other attitudes); some are moral (being generous, refusing to pay taxes); some are—for want of a better word—behavioral (being introverted, being a braggart); some are more-or-less physical (having a limp, being allergic to nuts). Many of these properties can be exemplified only by someone in a particular linguistic, social and physical environment. They are manifested in the ways that she behaves in various circumstances, in the ways that she presents herself, in what she takes for granted, in her self-deceptions, her habits, preferences, and attitudes; her nervous tics, gait, gestures, and so on through the motley of features that make her the person she is and allow others to recognize her as Smith. Smith's features may be construed in a fine-grained way: It is not only that Smith is considerate, but that she consistently remembers Old Lady Jones's birthday; not only that she wants to project an image of success, but that she buys all her clothes from Eileen Fischer. Of course, Smith's features can change radically, while Smith remains Smith: Perhaps she starts buying all her clothes at L. L. Bean, or converts to Christianity, or she wins the lottery, or she discovers that she has cancer—and she is deeply altered—but she can never completely escape her past. (As Faulkner said, 'The past is not dead. It's not even past.')

The features in virtue of which a particular human person is Smith can be instantiated only by a bodily being. Smith's peculiar smile, for example, depends on Smith's having a certain kind of body. Moreover, the features in question are, for the most part, intentional and relational. The way that Smith treats her less able students, the way that she responds to appeals from charities, the precautions she takes when she travels abroad—these and many more of Smith's defining features cannot be exhibited by any being (even a bodily being) in splendid isolation. So, even apart from consideration of first-person reference to her body, there is no question of Smith's being a disembodied soul. In the absence of a body, there would be no Smith.

It is necessary that Smith have a body, but is not necessary that Smith have the particular body that she actually has. Although the question of personal identity over time is a vexed one, it is clear that a person's body changes continually. Smith's body today may have no cells in common with Smith's body twenty years ago, but Smith remains Smith. Although I cannot say what the relation is between Smith's body now and Smith's body twenty years ago, I do think that we allow that Smith can persist through great bodily changes—perhaps even gradual replacement of her organic parts with bionic parts—provided that her intentional states remain intact.[8] To allow for this possibility, let me amend my characterization of a human person: Rather than requiring that some of Smith's intentional states make first-person reference to a biological body, let me say that Smith's intentional states make first-person reference to a biological body, *or to some body suitably related to a biological body*, where I leave it empty just what the suitable relation is. The point of this rather uninformative amendment is to leave open the possibility that Smith could exist without having the body that she now has, without leaving open the possibility that Smith could exist without any body at all.

If a human person is not identical to an immaterial soul, nor is a human person a composite of a material body and an immaterial mind, what, then, is the relation between a human person, Smith, and the biological body, b, to which she makes first-person reference? The answer, which I share with certain so-called nonreductive materialists, is that persons are constituted by bodies, but are not identical to bodies.

Consider an analogy: In certain respects, Smith is to her biological body, b, as Michelangelo's *David* is to a particular hunk of marble, h. Is the relation between David and h (or between Smith and b) one of identity? No. *David* is not identical to h. h could have existed in a world without art; in such a world, *David* would not have existed. For there are no statues or any other artwork in such a world. *David* could not exist without having certain intentional properties; but h could exist without having those intentional properties. Similarly, Smith could not exist without having certain intentional properties; but b could exist without having those intentional properties. As already noted, many of the properties that make Smith the person she is depend on her being embedded in a linguistic, social and physical environment. So, the relation between Smith and her body is not one of identity.

Let me contrast this 'constitution' view of persons and bodies with alternative views. The 'constitution' view is not a form of mind/body dualism. A statue is not a hunk of marble plus some other entity. Both persons and statues are particulars constituted by material objects; but each is the thing it is (a person, a statue) in

---

[8] Bruce Aune makes a similar point in *Metaphysics: The Elements* (Minneapolis: University of Minnesota Press, 1985): 94–5.

virtue of its intentionally-specified relational properties.[9] Smith is no more a composite of two kinds of entities than is Michelangelo's *David*.

Nor is the relation between Smith and her body one of supervenience. Supervenience is a relation between (families of) properties. Again, the example of the statue and the hunk of marble is instructive: What makes something a statue are not the intrinsic properties of the hunk of marble that constitutes it, but rather its relations, intentionally specified, to other things—perhaps to the artist's intentions, perhaps to an artworld, perhaps to something else. So, since instantiation of all the intrinsic properties of the hunk of marble does not guarantee instantiation of the property of being a statue, the property of being a statue does not supervene on the (intrinsic) physical properties of the hunk of marble—any more than the property of being a contract supervenes on the (intrinsic) physical properties of the paper in which it is written. Similarly, the property of being a human person does not supervene on the intrinsic physical properties of the body.

Let me emphasize that this rejection of supervenience does not rest on any theological considerations. For theism is compatible with metaphysical theories of supervenience. One could even hold that all properties supervene on microphysical properties in Jaegwon Kim's strong sense and still be a theist. As long as all of God's interventions in the natural order remained at the level of microphysical properties—basic properties, which, according to supervenience views, determine all other property instantiations—supervenience is not violated.[10] My rejection of person/body supervenience rather concerns the fact that relational and intentional properties are required for a person to be a person, but not for a body to be a body.

Finally, contrast the view that persons are constituted by their bodies to the view that persons are identical to their bodies. A person/body identity theorist may say, '*David* is identical to h. Since h could exist in a world without art, and h is *David*, then *David* could exist in a world without art. Of course, in a world without art, *David* would not be a statue, but *the very thing* that is a statue in our world, h, exists in a world without art.' The person/body identity theorist may continue: 'Now let b' be Smith's body b after Smith's death; b' could exist in another possible world in which there were no persons at all (nothing in that world had ever had intentional states), and hence in that world, b', had never been a person. So, assuming that Smith is identical to b, in a world without persons, *the very thing* that in our world is (or was) a person, b', exists but is not a person.'[11] Hence, the identity of Smith and her body still holds, and, the person/

---

[9] This formulation leaves open the possibility of reducing intentional properties to nonintentional properties.

[10] This point emerged in a conversation with Richard Boyd.

[11] The argument that I am putting in the mouth of the person/body identity theorist has affinities with arguments given by Fred Feldman. Feldman focuses on the property of being alive, which he argues is only a contingent property of the things (bodies) that have it. See his *Confrontations with the Reaper: A Philosophical Study of the Nature and Value of Death* (New York: Oxford University Press, 1992).

body identity theorist may claim, the argument that Smith is not identical to her body, but is only constituted by it, should be rejected.

I have several responses to the person/body identity theorist here. First, the argument that I have put into the mouth of the person/body identity theorist should not convince anyone to hold the identity theory since its force depends on having already accepted the identity theory. For 'Smith is identical to b' (as well as '*David* is identical to h') occurs as a premise in the argument. Second, the person/body identity theorist's argument has, to my ears at least, highly counterintuitive consequences—about the referents of names and about the first-person perspective.

In the first place, the person/body identity theory requires that *David* name the hunk of marble (whether it is a statue or not); for according to the person/body identity theorist's argument, *David* and Smith both exist in worlds without, respectively, statues and persons. Of course, they would not be called '*David*' or 'Smith' in such worlds, but on the identity theory, those very individuals exist in such worlds. It seems to me, on the contrary, that '*David*' names a particular statue, not the marble that constitutes it; and 'Smith' names a particular person, not the body that constitutes it—just as '*The Mona Lisa*' names a particular painting and not the canvas that constitutes it. Therefore, I do not think we should say that Smith exists in a world without persons, or that *David* exists in a world without statues. In our world, we need not distinguish between the statue and h as the referent of the name '*David*,' or between the person and b as the referent of the name 'Smith.' But, in other possible worlds, I think that the names '*David*' and '*Smith*' should 'track' the statue and the person, respectively—and not the material objects that constitute them in the actual world. So, the first counterintuitive consequence of the person/body identity theorist's argument concerns the referents of names.

The second counterintuitive consequence of the identity theorist's argument can be seen by considering the first-person point of view. If the person/body identity theorist is right, then Smith (or any of us) could truly say, 'Being me (this very thing) does not require that I be a person. I could have existed—me, the very individual that I am—without ever having had any intentional states at all. That individual, who never had any intentional states, could have been me.' This consequence is hard for me to swallow. I can imagine myself to be otherwise than I am in many ways—I could have been homeless, I could have been a lawyer, I could have been deaf, and so on—but I cannot imagine myself as having no intentional states at all. I can imagine that my life had been quite different, but I cannot imagine that I existed without having any conscious life at all.

The person/body identity theorist will accept these consequences—that names track bodies (not persons) across worlds, and that you could have existed without ever having been a person—but the rest of us need not. The difference between the person/body identity theorist and me here can be seen as an example of one philosopher's *modus ponens*' being another philosopher's *modus tollens*. Both the person/body identity theorist and I agree on this conditional:

> If the person/body identity theory is correct, then it is *not* the case that persons are essentially persons.

The person/body identity theorist holds that persons are not essentially persons, and accepts the consequences. Since I think that persons are essentially persons (i.e., if *x* is a person, then it is impossible that *x* exist and not be a person), I conclude that the person/body identity theory is incorrect. In any case, there is no reason to be moved by an argument for rejecting the 'constitution' view of persons and bodies in favor of the 'identity' view that takes the person/body identity theory to be a premise.

To sum up this nondualistic conception of a human person: If Smith is a human person, then Smith has intentional states, some of which make first-person reference to a biological body, or to a body suitably related to a biological body, where the relation between Smith and the body to which she makes first-person reference is constitution. This nondualistic conception is not a denial that there are souls. 'Soul' is the name given to the properties that make someone the person she is. Just as a belief is not an inner state of some organ, so a soul is not an inner entity. To know oneself is to know a human person in her full concreteness in a first-person way; it is not to know a private entity 'inside,' inaccessible to others. You know your own mind when you have correct second-order beliefs about your first-order intentional states. To be self-interested is not to care excessively about a private object, but to act on behalf of the interests of a certain person. Of course, I think that you have a soul; otherwise, I wouldn't think that you are a person. It is just that to say that you have a soul is not to say that your soul is a concrete particular: You—in your full bodily being—are the concrete particular; your soul is that cluster of properties that makes you the person you are.

This conception of a human person is 'naturalistic' in a broad sense: it neither invokes nor presupposes the existence of immaterial souls or supernatural beings. The intentional states and the first-person perspective required for something to be a person are just as likely to be products of natural selection as is the organization of human brains. This conception of a human person rests comfortably with materialism about the natural order; and if the natural order is all that there is, then it rests comfortably with materialism *tout court*. The conception avoids mind/body dualism, but should it be acceptable to a Christian?

THE CHRISTIAN DOCTRINE OF RESURRECTION

It is undeniable that natural human life is bodily existence. We are earthy, of dust. The question is whether Christian belief requires that a human person also have an immaterial part that is detachable from any constituting body. I now want to focus on a traditional Christian doctrine—the doctrine of the Resurrection of the dead—and show that the nondualistic conception of human persons is consistent with several interpretations of the doctrine. I have never swum in theological waters before, and I fear that I am already over my head. But here goes.

Christians who recite the Apostles' Creed say: 'I believe in . . . the resurrection of the body and the life everlasting.' Explicit Christian doctrine concerns resurrection of the body, not immortality of an immaterial soul.[12] Nevertheless, we may ask whether the doctrine of resurrection of the body entails that human beings have immaterial souls that can exist independently of any body. Matters of entailment are tricky here, because on any interpretation, resurrection can be accomplished only through divine agency. Indeed, Christian doctrine is different from the Greek conception of immortality (e.g., in the *Phaedo*) on just this point; on the Greek conception, the soul is naturally immortal; on the Christian conception, everlasting life is a gracious gift of God. So, to refer to divine agency in the doctrine of resurrection is not to import a *deus ex machina*. Rather, divine agency lies at the heart of the doctrine. This is what makes matters of entailment tricky. For the infinite attributes that make possible divine agency cannot be understood in the same way as finite attributes. Since I have little confidence in my ability to understand what is 'required' for divine agency, I approach the topic of whether the doctrine of resurrection entails that there be an immaterial soul with great tentativeness.

Before exploring the question of whether the doctrine of resurrection entails mind/body dualism, let me make explicit some assumptions: (i) The doctrine of resurrection does entail that an individual can exist without the biological body that she was born with, and, indeed, without any 'fleshly' body at all. (But the flesh/spirit distinction, so prominent in Pauline writings, is decidedly not a mind/body distinction. Sometimes Paul subsumes the whole person under the 'flesh' side of the distinction, and other times under the 'spirit' side of the distinction.)[13] (ii) The doctrine of resurrection asserts a personal afterlife (not some merging with the infinite, in which one's individuality is extinguished); if the doctrine is correct, then Smith herself—that very person—lives after death. If Smith's life after death—a life of that same individual, not a replica—entailed that Smith have an immaterial soul that can exist apart from any body, then Christian doctrine, as I understand it, would require mind/body dualism. And

---

[12] See Oscar Cullman, 'Immortality of the Soul or Resurrection of the Dead? The Witness of the New Testament,' in Terence Penelhum, ed., *Immortality* (Belmont CA: Wadsworth Publishing Company: 1973): 53–85. (I am grateful to Thomas Senor for bringing this work to my attention.)

[13] E.g., 'For those who live according to the flesh set their minds on the things of the flesh, but those who live according to the Spirit set their minds on the things of the Spirit. To set the mind on the flesh is death, but to set the mind on the Spirit is life and peace. For this reason the mind that is set on the flesh is hostile to God; it does not submit to God's law—indeed, it cannot, and those who are in the flesh cannot please God.' Romans 8:5–8.

the answer to the question—Need a Christian be a mind/body dualist?—would be 'yes.'

Now the question of reidentification of the person is a serious philosophical problem: In virtue of what is a future individual Smith, and not just a replica of Smith? I confess that I cannot say; but let me offer two considerations to mitigate criticism of my ignorance. First, the problem of reidentification is a serious general problem about personal identity, apart from theological considerations. Even concerning identity in the here and now, there is no consensus among materialists. Personal identity over time is a problem for everyone, not just for Christians. Second, mind/body dualism offers no illumination on the problem of reidentification. There is a least as much difficulty in coming up with criteria for reidentifying immaterial souls as for reidentifying bodies. So, a dualist would have no advantage over a nondualist with respect to reidentification of Smith. Since my aim is to show that a Christian need not be a mind/body dualist, and since nondualism fares no worse than dualism vis à vis the problem of reiden-tification, and since there is no consensus on reidentification of persons even in the pre-resurrection world, I shall put aside the issue here.

Finally, let me distinguish two ways that we use the term 'alive.' Restricting the domain of discourse to persons, if we construe 'x is alive' to entail that x has biological properties (e.g., has DNA), then a believer in a personal afterlife can agree that being alive is a contingent property of persons. If we construe 'x is alive' to entail nothing about biological properties per se, but only to entail that x has whatever properties are required for x to enjoy, say, conscious experience, then the believer in a personal afterlife should take being alive to be an essential property of persons—but, since corpses abound, being alive would not be an essential property of human bodies. If we construe 'being alive' in this latter sense of having whatever properties are required for conscious experience, and if there is a personal afterlife, then the property of being alive is realized in two different ways for human beings—in natural properties before death and in supernatural properties after death.[14]

Now I want to try to show that the nondualistic conception of human persons just sketched is compatible with various interpretations of the doctrine of resurrection.

I. First, consider the doctrine that takes a general resurrection to be a temporal event—an historical event that has not yet occurred, but will occur in the future—perhaps as the last temporal event. On this interpretation, what happens to Smith between the time of Smith's death and the general resurrection when Smith will be raised? There seem to be two possible answers: either Smith exists in the interim in an 'intermediate state,' or Smith goes out of existence at

---

[14] I say 'Natural' rather than 'biological' here to allow for the replacement of Smith's biological body by a bionic body.

death, and then, by God's grace, is brought back into existence at the general resurrection.

Suppose, as many Christians do, that Smith exists in the interim between death and resurrection in an intermediate state. A number of Christian philosophers take such an intermediate state to be a disembodied state. In that case, presumably, what exists during the interim is an immaterial soul that is Smith.[15] Hence, Christians have supposed that the doctrine of the intermediate state entails mind/body dualism. But there is no reason to suppose that the intermediate state (if there is one) is one of disembodiment: an intermediate body is appropriate as the bearer of the properties that make Smith the person she is. (A person with a postmortem but pre-resurrection body intuitively could be said to be 'asleep in Christ.' It is difficult {for me} to see how an immaterial soul could be asleep.) The possibility of an intermediate body shows that the doctrine of the intermediate state does not entail mind/body dualism.

Still considering the general resurrection to be a future historical event, the other apparent alternative is that there is no intermediate state, but that Smith (temporarily) does not exist in the interim. One version of the 'temporal gap' view is that at the general resurrection, God reassembles the atoms that constituted Smith and restores the relationships that they bore to one another during Smith's natural life, and thereby 're-creates' Smith. This view is clearly compatible with a nondualistic conception of the human person. During the time that Smith does not exist, some of Smith's atoms still do, and they provide the basis for Smith's resurrection body to be a continuant of Smith's biological body. (We can trust in God's goodness not to make a plethora of bodies spatiotemporally continuous with Smith's biological body.)

Peter van Inwagen has argued powerfully against a 're-assembly' version of the temporal-gap view, on both logical and theological grounds. I can only discuss one example here. Van Inwagen argues that if an original manuscript of Augustine's had burned in 457, then nothing we have today could be that original manuscript by Augustine; God could have made a perfect duplicate of it, but the result of God's handiwork would not, could not, be the original manuscript. By analogy, if Smith's natural body were entirely destroyed, no reconstituted body could be Smith's. I agree about the original manuscript, for the property of having been inscribed by Augustine cannot obtain without the causal intervention of Augustine, but the 're-created' manuscript has its inscriptional properties without the causal intervention of Augustine.[16] What makes it the case that a

---

[15] A number of philosophers argue in this vein. For an extended argument for mind/body dualism based on the doctrine of the intermediate state, see John W. Cooper, *Body, Soul and Life Everlasting* (Grand Rapids, MI: William B. Eerdmans Publishing Company, 1989).

[16] I assume that we are imagining that the hypothetical manuscript was actually produced by Augustine, not merely dictated. If it were imagined to have been dictated, then Augustine's causal role in the first manuscript would not seem all that different from Augustine's causal role in God's later re-creation.

certain piece of paper is an original manuscript by Augustine is that Augustine inscribed it: it has a particular origin; without that origin (which requires Augustine's causal intervention), a piece of paper is not Augustine's original manuscript.[17] But the case of resurrection is different: Although God could not simply will that a certain manuscript have the property of having been inscribed by Augustine without involving Augustine, He could simply will (it seems to me) there to be a body that has the complexity to 'subserve' Smith's characteristic states, and that is suitably related to Smith's biological body, to constitute Smith. (The biological Smith's *de re* attitudes become the resurrected Smith's memories of *de re* attitudes. The biological Smith's timidity becomes the resurrected Smith's memory of timidity; the biological Smith's lovingkindness remains the resurrected Smith's lovingkindness, and so on.) If creation of a resurrected body is within the power of God at all, it seems to me equally in His power to produce the conditions necessary for the body to constitute Smith, where what makes Smith the person she is are her characteristic intentional states, including first-person reference to her body.[18] The fact that a certain resurrection body would not exist without the direct intervention of God is irrelevant to whether or not it was Smith's body—just as the fact that a certain bionic body would not exist without the direct intervention of scientists and surgeons is irrelevant to whether or not it is Smith's body.

Another kind of temporal-gap conception can be developed, I think, from the views of Thomas Aquinas. Suppose, as Aristotle and Aquinas held, that the soul is the form of the body; also suppose, as Aristotle held but Aquinas did not, that the soul cannot exist apart from the body. So when Smith dies, she ceases to be actual. But Smith may still exist potentially: As I understand Aquinas, he thought that Smith's soul could exist apart from Smith's body, but that Smith's soul was not Smith, but a remnant or truncated version of Smith; a disembodied soul is Smith's soul in virtue of the fact that it has the potential to be reunited to a body that would reconstitute Smith.[19] If this is Aquinas's view, then it would seem that

[17] Identity conditions for different kinds of things are different—and usually vague and unspecifiable. Identity conditions for some things do not include properties about their origin. If a licensed repairman takes my squeaky lawnmower apart, oils all the parts and reassembles them exactly as before, I think that I still have my old lawnmower. (If I asked for a replacement of my mower, the repairman would laugh and remind me that my warranty was still good on the original one that he returned to me.)

[18] For further arguments, see Peter van Inwagen, 'The Possibility of Resurrection,' in *Immortality*, Paul Edwards, ed. (New York: Macmillan Publishing Company, 1992): 242–6 [this volume, ch. 15].

[19] This interpretation is Peter Geach's: On Aquinas's conception, 'a soul is not the person who died but a mere remnant of him.:' The individuality of a disembodied soul is grounded in the claim that 'each disembodied human soul permanently retained a capacity for reunion to such a body as would reconstitute a man identifiable with the man who died.' Peter Geach, *God and the Soul* (London: Routledge and Kegan Paul, 1969): 22–3. Kenny quotes Aquinas as follows: The 'soul, since it is part of the body of a human being, is not a whole human being.' Thomas Aquinas, *Commentary on I. Cor. 15*, quoted by Anthony Kenny, *The Self* (The Aquinas Lecture, 1988) (Milwaukee: Marquette University Press, 1988): 27. Copleston comments about Aquinas's view: 'And though the human soul survives death, it is not strictly speaking a human person when it is in a state of rational nature.' F. C. Copleston, *Aquinas* (Baltimore MD: Penquine Books, 1955): 160.

in the interim between Smith's death and resurrection, Smith's soul actually exists, but Smith herself—the person—exists only potentially. What I am suggesting as a temporal-gap view is that not even a remnant of Smith is actual during the period between Smith's death and resurrection. Smith—body and soul—remains only a potential being, to be reactualized at the resurrection. (This would not violate Locke's dictum that nothing can begin to exist at two different times: the resurrection is not a beginning of Smith's existence but a resumption or restoration of it.)[20] I'm not sure whether such a view is coherent; but if it is, then it too would be compatible with a nondualistic conception of the human person.

Even if the nondualistic conception of human persons is compatible with temporal-gap versions of the doctrine of resurrection, temporal-gap versions may themselves be theologically unacceptable. Temporal-gap versions, according to which there is some interval between Smith's death and resurrection during which Smith herself does not exist, may raise problems for the doctrine of purgatory (this is a difficulty only for those who hold a doctrine of purgatory, of course). The intermediate-state versions, by contrast, make room for purgatory between death and final resurrection. My point here, however, is only this: A nondualistic conception of the human person is compatible with the doctrine of resurrection in either an intermediate-state version or a temporal-gap version.

II. There is yet another way to construe the doctrine of resurrection, and that is to deny that the general resurrection is a temporal event at all. In that case, it would not be a future event—an event that will occur at some future time—but rather it would reside in the realm of eternity. If the general resurrection is eschatological in the sense of being out of the temporal realm altogether, there need be no period of 'wait-time' between Smith's death and her resurrection, and hence no intermediate state or temporal gap in a person's existence. At death, perhaps, a person would pass over into eternity. Perhaps supernatural bodies are to natural bodies as eternity is to physical time (whatever that relation is).[21] I take prominent Protestant theologians, like Karl Barth, to have held this view. Although Barth himself may have been a mind/body dualist, his view of resurrection does not compel him to be one.

Suppose that a nondualistic conception of the human person is logically consistent with acceptable interpretations of the doctrine of resurrection. So what? Nonphilosophers, in my experience, don't give a fig for logical possibility. Nonphilosophers, and even some philosophers, want to know what the truth actually is, not just what it could be. And for all that I have said about the doctrine of resurrection, mind/body dualism may still be true. Right. But there are other, to my mind compelling, reasons not to be a mind/body dualist. So,

---

[20] John Locke, *An Essay Concerning Human Understanding*, II.

[21] See, for example, Eleonore Stump and Norman Kretzmann, 'Eternity,' *Journal of Philosophy* 78 (1981): 429–58.

I think that if a Christian need not be a mind/body dualist, she should not be a mind/body dualist.

AGAINST MIND/BODY DUALISM

I think that there are both theological and philosophical reasons to oppose mind/body dualism. Since philosophical reasons to reject mind/body dualism are well-known, I shall mention only theological or quasi-theological reasons to affirm nondualism about human persons. It seems to me that a nondualistic conception of human persons best accords with the picture of human persons presented throughout the Jewish and Christian Bibles. If mind/body dualism were Scriptural, I would expect the doctrine to be suggested in accounts of the resurrection of Christ. But the resurrection appearances of Christ are all bodily, with no hint of mind/body (or soul/body) dualism. After death, Christ underwent some kind of bodily transformation—He was not recognized by those closest to him right away; but was recognized eventually—but not loss of body altogether. Although I take ordinary humans to be essentially bodily (created that way by God), and I take it that the Word became flesh, I do not think that God is a material being. I understand Christ's resurrection appearances to be the model for understanding the resurrection of human person, not for understanding God in His divinity. Hence, for a Christian, the fact that Christ appeared bodily is significant for the conception of human persons. On the whole, the picture of human nature afforded by both the Old and New Testaments, seems to me best understood as nondualistic: a human is a psychosomatic unity.[22] But I am not an authority on the Bible and shall not pursue this matter here.

A second at least quasi-theological reason for rejecting mind/body dualism concerns the character of God's creation. Nature, as I see it, is a unified whole with its own internal integrity; and human persons are a part of nature. According to Christian belief, human beings (by nature, of dust) are capable of redemption (and in this respect made in the image of God); but redemption comes from outside the realm of nature through God's grace. Nature may be perfected and fulfilled by grace, but grace is not a component of nature. Mind/body dualism introduces an unneeded bifurcation into the realm of nature. The real dualism—the theologically important dualism—is not internal to nature at all. It is the dualism between nature and grace, between creation and the Creator, between the natural and the supernatural. A Christian who rejects mind/body dualism need not, and should not, reject this larger dualism.

A materialist will note gleefully that I have just endorsed dualism with a vengeance: I have merely traded mind/body dualism for a supernatural/natural

---

[22] See Stephen T. Davis, *Risen Indeed: Making Sense of the Resurrection* (Grand Rapids MI: William B. Eerdmans, 1993): 47.

dualism. After all, resurrected bodies are as mysterious to us as immaterial souls. So the apparent gain in rejecting mind/body dualism, an atheist may urge, is only a terminological mask. To this objection, I should reply: The philosophically important difference is that resurrected bodies are not part of the natural order; but if mind/body dualism were true, natural phenomena, here and now, would be mysterious: resurrection may be tolerable as a mystery, but Smith's deciding not to shoplift should not be. Indeed, on mind/body dualism, natural phenomena would become mysterious in ways that most contemporary people think that they are not.

By conceiving of the natural world as an integrated whole, and not as a conjunction of two fundamentally different kinds of things—mind and matter—the nondualist conceives of nature as susceptible to human investigation. Nothing in the natural order, not even mentality, is inherently unsuitable for natural inquiry.[23] Perhaps the natural world is too complex for human beings ultimately to comprehend—perhaps, perhaps not. But we cannot tell a priori. This nondualistic view of nature accords theologically and philosophically with the way that I take the natural order to be. So, a human person is essentially a bodily being. It is in virtue of the instantiation of certain intentional properties that a human person exists—whether instantiation of those properties came about through natural selection or not. A Christian need not claim that these properties are any more supernatural than biochemical properties.

CONCLUSION

It may seem the height of presumption to go against the dualistic strains in the Christian tradition. Let me plead that I am not simply rejecting the tradition; there are many matters on which the wisdom of ancients—Augustine, say, on moral psychology—is unsurpassed. On the other hand, I do not think that philosophy, even Christian philosophy, should be elevated to a matter of faith. And I think that what we now know about nature renders untenable the idea of a human person as consisting, even in part, of an immaterial soul capable of independent existence.

I would like to conclude with some remarks on method: Although I think that philosophy and theology are extremely difficult, I think that it is relatively easy to have philosophical positions that square with Scripture, because I think that many different philosophical positions are consistent with the scant clues to be found in the Bible. Depending on how one understands sleep, to say that people are 'asleep in Christ' is consistent with an intermediate state, with a temporal gap

---

[23] I say 'natural inquiry' rather than 'science,' because, for reasons unrelated to this paper, I believe that scientific inquiry is played out against a common-sensical background that is not itself regimentable into scientific theory.

(nonexistence which is thought of as dreamless sleep) and with disembodied existence accompanied by vivid experiences as in dreams. To say that 'We shall all be changed' is likewise consistent with a variety of views on the resurrection. Augustine was a great philosopher; Aquinas was a great philosopher, but I do not think that Paul (or Jesus) was a philosopher at all. The Bible can be used by Christian philosophers as a test against which to measure their views, and it can be used to suggest topics for philosophical discussion. But I do not think that there is a unique Christian philosophy that is authoritative for all Christians. Philosophers, perhaps most of all, should not forget that now we only see through a glass darkly.[24]

[24] I owe a great debt to Katherine Sonderegger and to Gareth B. Matthews for helping me with this work. I was helped by discussions with Edmund Gettier and Fred Feldman. Thanks also are due to Ted Warfield and to Eleonore Stump, who commented on versions of this paper read at the Notre Dame Conference on the Philosophy of Mind, November 4, 1994, and at the meeting of the Society for Christian Philosophers in Boston, December 27, 1994, respectively.

18

The Resurrection of the Body
and the Life Everlasting*

Trenton Merricks

But your dead will live; their bodies will rise. You who dwell in the dust, wake up and shout for joy. Your dew is like the dew of the morning; the earth will give birth to her dead.

Isaiah 26:19

I. INTRODUCTION

Those who accept the closing line of the Apostles' Creed believe in 'the resurrection of the body and the life everlasting.' Similarly, the Nicene Creed closes with 'I look for the resurrection of the dead, and the life of the world to come. Amen.' The Athanasian Creed tells us that, at Christ's coming, 'All men shall rise again with their bodies.' Below I will present and discuss some of the central passages in the Bible that deal with the resurrection. The Christian tradition has always affirmed—in addition to the resurrection of Jesus Christ—the resurrection and victory over death of all believers.

There are puzzling philosophical questions associated with this doctrine. Consider, for example, the resurrection of the believer whose body was cremated, and whose ashes were then spread on the four winds. Does God gather all the ashes together and *then* resurrect the body? What if some of the ashes were, after death but before that Great Day, annihilated? And does it even make sense to say that one gets the *same*, the *original*, body back on the Day of Resurrection, while at the same time saying that one's body is *changed* and glorified?

Even if these questions can be answered, another, more fundamental question remains. What, if anything, does the resurrection of the body have to do with eternal life? I think that most Christians (indeed, most people) think of themselves as souls—nonphysical, spiritual entities—that inhabit bodies. Most Christians believe that when their *bodies* are placed in the grave, *they* are not. They are souls, and while their bodies may be buried in the ground at their death, they are off to be with God. Absent from the body, present with the Lord. (In support of this view, one might cite near-death experiences of 'leaving one's body behind' as one proceeds down a dark tunnel to a light at the far end.) If all this is correct, then life after death is possible, indeed actually occurs, without a body. Why, then, do the creeds and some scriptures seem to mention our hope for everlasting life and our hope for resurrection in the same breath?

The goal of this chapter is to address these sorts of questions. Of course, this will not show that the doctrines of the resurrection and the life everlasting are *true*. I think that we know this only by way of scripture. But it will help us to *defend* these doctrines against objections rooted in the puzzles we will discuss. And, more importantly, it should help us to have a deeper understanding of what it is we believe when we believe in the resurrection and the life of the world to come.

II. IMMORTALITY AND PERSONAL IDENTITY OVER TIME

> *It is a serious thing to live in a society of possible gods and goddesses, to remember that the dullest and most uninteresting person you can talk to may one day be a creature which, if you saw it now, you would be strongly tempted to worship, or else a horror and a corruption such as you now meet, if at all, only in nightmare.*
>
> C. S. Lewis, 'The Weight of Glory'

Let's begin, not with questions of my (presumably) far-off post-resurrection existence in glory, but with my comparatively recent *past* existence as a little child. When I was one year old, I had a different personality and different beliefs, memories, attitudes, desires, and opinions from those I now have. Not only was I different psychologically, but I was different physically: I was shaped differently, had a different height and weight, had less hair, and so on. Merricks of today is vastly different from Merricks as a one-year-old child. Yet there is, of course, only one person in question. That is why I can truthfully assert such commonplaces as 'I was once a one-year-old child.' In other words, I am the *same person* as the one-year-old child in question. Yet because of the great differences between the way I am and the way the child was, I am *not the same person* as that child.

Despite initial appearances, there is no contradiction here. There is, instead, an *ambiguity* in the expression 'is the same person as.' Compare: 'There is a bank beside the James River' and 'There is not a bank beside the James River.' If the word 'bank' means riverbank in the first sentence, but financial institution in the second, then these sentences—because 'bank' is ambiguous—do not contradict each other.

Sometimes we use the expressions 'is the same person as' and 'is not the same person as' when we are comparing the way a person is at one time to the way that (same!) person is at another. This is what is going on if one says, for example, 'she is not the same person she was before she became famous.' This does not mean that one person literally ceased to exist and was replaced by a new (and famous) person. What is normally meant by sentences like 'she is not the same person she was before she became famous' is that the person in question used to have certain salient and central qualities or features, and now has very different qualities or features. So perhaps she was friendly and approachable before becoming famous, but now is aloof and distant. And, conversely, when we say 'he's just the same person he was in college' we mean that the way he was in college is, in important respects, very much like the way he is now. Because this sort of sameness is a sameness in a person's features or 'qualities,' it is called 'qualitative sameness' or 'qualitative identity.'

But we do not always use the expressions 'is the same person as' and 'is not the same person as' in this way. For instance, suppose the prosecuting attorney asks you in court whether the man being tried is the same person that you saw rob the bank. It would not do to think to yourself 'well, while robbing the bank he was friendly and approachable, but now he is aloof and distant' and then to answer 'no.'

The reason this would not do is that the prosecutor is *not* asking you whether the man before you now has undergone any deep and extensive changes; she is *not* asking about qualitative sameness. The prosecutor is asking about another sort of sameness associated with persons, the second sort of sameness associated with the expression 'is the same person as.' This sort of sameness is called 'numerical sameness' or 'numerical identity.'[1] We presupposed facts of numerical sameness throughout the discussion of qualitative sameness. For example, in the case of the woman who became famous, we assumed that one person—the very same person—can undergo, over a stretch of time, change in qualities, such as a change from being approachable to being aloof.

We can now see that there is no contradiction in saying that, in one way, I am the same person as the one-year-old Merricks, but in another, not. All this means is that while I am numerically identical with that one-year-old—there is just one person in question—the qualities I had then are not the same as the qualities I have now.

Besides being used to refer to numerical and qualitative identity, there are a number of other ways that the expression 'personal identity' is used in everyday

---

[1] This sort of sameness or identity is called 'numerical' because it is associated with counting. For if the man who stands before you in court is numerically identical with the man who committed the crime, then there is only *one* man in question. If the accused man is not numerically identical with the guilty man, then there are *two* men in question—the accused and the guilty.

conversation. For instance, we can imagine a great ballerina saying that if she could no longer dance, she would lose her 'identity.' Or we might say that an avid athlete's 'identity' is all tied up in his ability to play sports. I once told a woman that I was writing an article on personal identity, and she began to explain to me how her husband strayed while trying to 'find his identity.' And when I made a comment about personal identity on another occasion, I was asked 'How do you know that there is any personal identity? Is there really a self?'

So there are many ways in which the expressions 'identity' and 'personal identity' are used in everyday English. And more than one of these might be relevant to our future existence in Heaven. One might argue that in Heaven, it matters to me not only that I exist, but that I exist with my 'self' intact. (This is something people say—though I admit I'm not sure I understand what they mean by 'self' in this context.) But no matter what else I want in Heaven, at least *part* of what I want is that someone there is numerically identical with me.[2] For it cannot be that *I* have my self intact in Heaven if *I* am not there. Again, I cannot exist in Heaven complete with whatever other features matter to me unless, obviously, I exist in Heaven. And it is this last part—the future existence in Heaven of a person numerically identical with me—that I am concerned with here. Whenever I talk about personal identity over time (or, for short, personal identity) in this paper, I am talking about the numerical identity over time of a person.

There is more at stake here than mere terminology. For the point is not that I shall use the expression 'personal identity' in a certain way. The point is that there are a number of separate, distinct topics that people sometimes mistakenly lump together, and I want to disentangle them. Progress has been made in our discussion if we can see that claims about qualitative sameness of a person, about numerical identity of a person, and about a person's 'identity' being wrapped up in playing football are all *different* claims.

They are all different claims, but at least some of them are interrelated in interesting and important ways. For instance, a central philosophical question about numerical personal identity over time is just how much, and what kind of, qualitative change a person can experience. To see some of the issues involved here, ask yourself whether you think it is possible that *you* could continue to exist but turn into a single speck of dust. Most of us would say 'no': you could not exchange all the features or qualities you now have for all the qualities of a speck of dust. So—although numerical sameness is not always threatened by qualitative

[2] I think that it is obviously true that part of what one should want when one wants future survival is that someone numerically identical with oneself exists in the future. But this has been denied by Derek Parfit in 'Personal Identity,' *The Philosophical Review* 80 (1971): 3–27 and *Reasons and Persons* (Oxford: Oxford University Press, 1984), Part III. For my response to Parfit's arguments, see 'Endurance, Psychological Continuity, and the Importance of Identity,' *Philosophy and Phenomenological Research* (forthcoming).

differences—certain very special or very extreme qualitative differences seem to imply that you would cease to exist.

It seems that we cannot survive just any sort of qualitative change. But what is most interesting here, I think, is not the sort of changes that we *cannot* survive, but the deep and radical changes that we *can* and *do* survive. For instance, you were once a one-year-old child. (Even more strikingly, there is the fact—as I take it—that you were once a fetus.) So the answer to the question 'can a person continue to exist through a process of radical and deep psychological and physical change?' is 'yes.' The proof is that you, yourself, have already done it.

It is part of the Christian hope that we will one day, in Heaven, be perfectly conformed to the image of Christ. We will one day actually be what it is we have been created to be. For all of us, this will involve deep and radical change. If you were able to 'peer into the future' and see yourself as you will be millions of years from now, glorified and united with God, you would not, I imagine, recognize yourself. This might cause you to worry about how that person could really be *you*. But you should not worry. As a one-year-old child you would not, presumably, have been able to recognize yourself as you now are. As a one-year-old child, you could not have even *imagined* what it would be like to be the adult you now are. You could not have imagined, for example, many of the things that occupy your thoughts as an adult.

The promise of eternal life in Heaven is really two promises. The first is that we shall enjoy personal identity over time forever—far into the future, for ever and ever, there will always exist a person who is numerically identical with each one of us. In less complicated terminology, the first promise is simply that *we* shall exist for ever and ever. The second is that during our future existence, we shall undergo deep and even unimaginable changes—or, better, deep and even unimaginable improvements. These are the things we hope for when we hope for immortality. And our hopes make sense; they are coherent. For just as you can be numerically identical with someone who was once a one-year-old child, so you can be numerically identical with someone who will one day be ancient beyond imagining and glorious and holy.

III. RESURRECTION AND BODILY
IDENTITY OVER TIME

Where be all the splinters of that Bone, which a shot hath shivered and scattered in the Ayre? Where be all the Atoms of that flesh, which a Corrasive hath eat away, or a Consumption hath breath'd, and exhal'd away from our arms, or other Limbs? In what wrinkle, in what furrow, in what bowel of the earth, ly all the graines of the ashes of a body burnt a thousand years since? . . . One humour of our dead body produces worms, and those worms suck and exhaust all other humour, and then all dies, and all dries, and molders into dust, and that dust is blowen into the River, and that puddled water tumbled into the sea, and that ebs and flows in infinite revolutions, and still, still, God knows ... in what part of the world every graine of every mans dust lies ... he whispers, he hisses, he beckens for the bodies of his Saints, and in the twinckling of an eye, that body that was scattered over all the elements, is sate down at the right hand of God, in a glorious resurrection.

John Donne, 'At the Earl of Bridgewater's House in
London at the Marriage of his Daughter'

The topic of personal identity over time is really just one particular instance or example of a more general topic, that of (numerical) identity over time of *any* sort of thing. Since bodily identity over time and personal identity over time are both specific instances of the same overall topic—identity over time—we should not be surprised if some of the observations made in the previous section about personal identity were relevant to questions one might have about bodily identity over time. And they are. For instance, we can now answer directly one worry raised in the introduction: How can it be that I have this very body in the afterlife, if my body is to be glorified and made new? And how can one who is blind, lame, crippled, broken, weak, or hurting have *his* very same body in Heaven, if in Heaven he will be whole and healthy?

The answer here obviously turns on the general issue of numerical versus qualitative identity. There is no contradiction in saying that on Resurrection Day I will have the same body I now have, and, at the same time, saying that my body now is weak and flawed, but at resurrection my body will be perfect and glorified. There is no contradiction because when we say that one will have *the same* body at resurrection, we mean that one's current body is *numerically identical* with one's resurrection body. But when we say that one's resurrection body will *not be the same* as one's current body, but will be glorified, we mean that the way one's body will be at resurrection is *qualitatively different* from the way it is now.

We don't know much about the ways in which our resurrected bodies will differ from our bodies as they now are. And the few details we are given are subject to various interpretations. (There is, for example, notorious disagreement about what it means to say that the resurrected body will be 'a spiritual body.') Perhaps all we really know for sure is that the way our bodies will be at resurrection is very different from the way they are now. Perhaps the way your body will be on Resurrection Day differs from the way your body is now as much as (or more than) the way your body is now differs from the way it was when you were a fetus. Perhaps the way your body will be at resurrection differs from the way your body is now as much as a fully mature plant differs from the way it was when it was only a seed.

We don't know the details about how our bodies, at resurrection, will differ from our bodies right now. All we really know is that they will be greatly qualitatively changed (and changed for the better!). Great qualitative change, as we have seen, is consistent with numerical identity. So we know of nothing at all in the promise of glorification that threatens your earthly body's identity with your resurrection body. And that is a good thing. For if *your* body (in other words, a body numerically identical with your body) does not rise glorified on the Day of Resurrection, then, obviously, your body will not be resurrected. Just as *personal* identity over time is crucial to immortality—if you are not numerically identical with a person who exists in Heaven in the distant future, then you do not have immortality—so *bodily* identity is crucial to resurrection.

One might object that our resurrection need *not* include getting the numerically same body back. For one might claim that a person is resurrected just so long as *some glorified body or other* comes into existence on the Day of Resurrection, and is then given to that person. If this claim were right, then on the Day of Resurrection, a person might not get her old body back at all, but rather a numerically distinct one. But there are two reasons that I think this claim is not right.

First, the overwhelming majority of theologians and philosophers in the history of the church have endorsed the claim of numerical identity. Historical debates surrounding the resurrection were over *how* (not whether) a dead earthly body would secure identity with a resurrection body. We'll look more closely at some of the issues in these debates below. But for now I want only to point out that those debates *presuppose* that the very same body that dies (and perishes) will rise again.[3] Theologians and philosophers throughout the history of the church presupposed this because—and this is the second reason I think the resurrected body and the earthly body are one—this seems to be what scripture teaches.

Why do I think scripture seems to teach this? Note that the Lord's resurrected body was numerically identical with his preresurrection body, the body that was crucified on the cross. At least, this seems to be the obvious conclusion to draw from the fact that after his resurrection, Jesus bore the scars of crucifixion. Christ's resurrection was the kind of resurrection we can all hope for; Christ's resurrection was the 'firstfruits' of the general resurrection to come (1 Cor. 15:20). So each of us can expect that after his or her body dies, it too—that very body—will be resurrected.

In 1 Corinthians 15, Paul does affirm *qualitative* differences between the way our bodies are now and the way they will be at resurrection. But note also that Paul's way of presenting the qualitative differences implies that there is only one body in question; it implies the numerical identity of the earthly body with its resurrection counterpart. Consider vv. 42–44:

[3] For a fascinating study of the history of views on the resurrection, see Caroline Walker Bynum's *The Resurrection of the Body in Western Christianity, 200–1336* (New York: Columbia University Press, 1995).

The body that is sown is perishable, it is raised imperishable; it is sown in dishonor, it is raised in glory; it is sown in weakness, it is raised in power; it is sown a natural body, it is raised a spiritual body.

Paul talks of 'it'—the one body that is both sown and raised—not of 'them,' as he would were the earthly body numerically distinct from the resurrected one. It is no coincidence that the word 'resurrection' has its roots in a Latin word which literally means to rise *again*—if the body that is resurrected is rising again, it has risen before, and so is not coming into existence for the first time on the Day of Resurrection.

The body you will be given at resurrection is none other than the body you have in this life. This claim seems to be supported by the Bible, and is about as historically uncontroversial as any point of philosophical theology. This claim, as we have seen, is not threatened by the great qualitative changes of glorification. But it is threatened in another way. To begin to see the worry, note that not all dead bodies remain well-preserved from death to resurrection. Indeed, because of decay or cannibals or cremation, some bodies, probably most bodies, actually pass out of existence at some point in time after death. Corpses dissolve into dust and then are no more. So it appears that the doctrine of the resurrection commits us to the claim that after a body has ceased to exist, it can, at a later date—the Day of Resurrection—come back into existence.

Many philosophers balk at the claim that a thing that has ceased to exist can come back into existence at some later date. To see why, imagine the following scenario. A terrible fire sweeps through the Louvre, destroying the *Mona Lisa*. You read about this in the newspaper. A month later, a friend tells you that she has just returned from Paris, adding that she saw the *Mona Lisa* hours before her flight home. You ask 'Ah, so it escaped the fire after all?' and your friend responds 'No; it was destroyed completely, burned to ashes. And the ashes themselves were even dissolved in water from the fire hoses. But a crack team of curators got the painting back. I had to pay a lot to see it, though, what with all the restoration costs.'

You would rightly suspect that your friend was duped. For, so you would reasonably think, once the *Mona Lisa* has been totally destroyed, it cannot possibly be 'restored' by any team of curators. You know, although your gullible friend does not, that she saw a mere copy of the *Mona Lisa*, not the original. Again, you know that while the painting your friend saw might have been *qualitatively* identical with the *Mona Lisa*, it could not have been *numerically* identical with Da Vinci's masterpiece. And you know this without having ever examined the copy, without having discovered, for example, some telltale flaw. You know your friend saw a copy *simply because you know that the original was destroyed*. For you know that because the original was destroyed, it, the original, is gone for good.

So much seems right, even obviously right. But as it goes with great master-pieces, many philosophers have thought, so it goes with all physical objects, including human bodies. Once they are gone, they are gone for good. And these philosophers have thought that getting the same body back is not merely impossible for curators or other human beings, but is *absolutely impossible,* impossible even for God.[4] This claim seems to undermine the doctrine of resurrection. For, as we have seen, the doctrine of the resurrection implies that a body can cease to exist and then—on the Day of Resurrection—that very same body can come back into existence again.

Whether ceasing to exist and then coming back into existence is absolutely impossible is something philosophers debate. In my opinion, there are no conclusive philosophical arguments one way or the other on this issue. So, if all we have are the tools of philosophy, perhaps we ought to say we have no idea whether a thing can utterly cease to exist and then come back into existence later. But we have more than the tools of philosophy at our disposal. We have divine revelation. And, as we have already seen, given the fact that at least some bodies decay and cease to exist, scripture teaches that a body which has ceased to exist will come back into existence on the Day of Resurrection. And, since what will happen must be possible, scripture implies that it is possible for a thing which has ceased to exist to come back into existence. So we know that this *is* possible. (This is one nice example of how our philosophical views can be informed by scripture.)

But even those Christian philosophers who believe that long-gone bodies *will* come back into existence have puzzled over *how,* exactly, this is supposed to happen. Indeed, it is no exaggeration to say that a historical survey of philosoph-ical discussions of the resurrection would, in large part, be a survey of discussions about how a body that has been destroyed could possibly be numerically identical with a body that exists long after the destruction.[5] So let's dig a little deeper.

To understand better the issues here, let me ask you to imagine something rather fanciful. Imagine that you build a time machine that can 'take you to the future.' You push the 'start' button. Observers see you and the machine disappear here in 1998. You (and your machine) then reappear in the year 2030. Now there are easier ways to travel to the future. Just sit there for a minute, and

[4] For a defense of the claim that even God cannot do what is absolutely impossible, see Scott Davison, "Divine Providence and Human Freedom," pp. 217–37 in Michael J. Murray, ed., *Reason for the Hope Within* (Grand Rapids, MI: Wm. B. Eerdmans, 1999).

[5] Such discussions go on even today. One contemporary Christian philosopher, Peter van Inwa-gen, is so sure that a body which has ceased to exist could not come back into existence that he suggests that perhaps corpses do not really decay and cease to exist, but rather are stored (somewhere) for Resurrection Day by God, while clever replicas decay in their place. See his 'The Possibility of Resurrection,' *International Journal for Philosophy of Religion* 9 (1978): 114–21 [this volume, Ch. 15].

The fact that a corpse can cease to exist has convinced the authors of two contemporary books that deal with the resurrection to deny the numerical identity of the resurrection body with the earthly one. See Bruce Reichenbach *Is Man the Phoenix?* (Grand Rapids: Eerdmans, 1978), 182, and John W. Cooper, *Body, Soul, and Life Everlasting* (Grand Rapids: Eerdmans, 1989), 188ff.

you'll move ahead a minute in time. The whole purpose of the time machine, of course, is to allow you to get to the future—in this case, to 2030—while 'skipping' all the times in between.

One way to describe what the time machine does is to say that it allows you to travel to future times, skipping the years in between. But there is another, equally accurate description. We could say that, because of the machine, you cease to exist at 1998 and come back into existence in 2030, even though *you fail to exist at any of the times in between*. The machine—and this is the point of introducing the time machine into our discussion of resurrection—causes a 'temporal gap' in your life. This is just what the resurrection seems to cause when it comes to the career of (at least some) human bodies. For the doctrine of the resurrection seems to imply that a body which has decayed or has been cremated or for some other reason has gone out of existence can, on Resurrection Day, come back into existence; in other words, it seems to imply that it is possible that a body 'jump ahead' in time.[6]

Thinking of ceasing to exist and then coming back into existence as 'jumping ahead' in time makes it seem more plausible that, possibly, a destroyed object could come back into existence. And the possibility of temporal gaps can be made to seem even more plausible if we consider—not the burning *Mona Lisa*— but a watch that is disassembled, perhaps for cleaning, and then reassembled. It seems that, once disassembled, the watch no longer exists. And it seems that reassembly brings the original watch back into existence. So this seems to be an example of a genuine temporal gap in the watch's career.[7]

The watch example seems to show that temporal gaps in an object's existence are possible. Moreover, it is pretty clear *how* the watch comes back into existence after having ceased to exist. It comes back into existence because all of its original parts are reassembled in just the way that they were before disassembly. One might think that, as it goes with watches, so it goes with human bodies. So one might hold that if a body that has been destroyed is to come back into existence,

---

[6] The way in which we probably imagine the time machine causing your body to jump ahead in time is a little different from the way in which your body will jump ahead to Resurrection Day. We probably imagine that when someone pushes the 'start' button in the time machine, not only the passenger's body ceases to exist, but, in addition, so do all the body's parts. In contrast, when a body ceases to exist at death or decay, some of its parts—atoms, for example—usually remain. (Of course, it is plausible that some of a body's other parts, such as its organs, do cease to exist when the body does.)

[7] I hedge my comments here with the word 'seems,' because there are many assumptions underlying the claim that disassembling and reassembling a watch provides a genuine temporal gap in an object's career. I will note just one in order to illustrate why the watch example is controversial—the assumption that, when disassembled, the watch actually ceases to exist. Some philosophers claim that, when disassembled, the watch *still exists* but is spread out all over the jeweler's workbench. (Philosophers would call a watch spread out like that a 'scattered object.') Obviously, if the watch continues existing all through the process of disassembly and reassembly, the process of disassembly and reassembly is not an example of a temporal gap in the watch's existence.

then all of its parts—such as the atoms—that composed it at death must be gathered back together and reassembled.[8]

This 'reassembly of last parts' view was the dominant view of resurrection for a very long time—for all I know, it may *still* be the dominant view. And it seems to have at least one obvious benefit. For while a body may decay and rot and pass out of existence, it could be that the very smallest things that compose that body—such as atoms or electrons or quarks—do not pass out of existence. While my body may not be around in a thousand years, perhaps its smallest parts will. And if those smallest parts still exist, then the 'reassembly' view of resurrection can explain how my body can, just like the watch, come back into existence after it has been very efficiently 'disassembled' by decay or cremation or being eaten by a tiger.

But there are three problems with the view that resurrection of the body consists in God's reassembling the still-existing parts that composed the body at death. First, it is not obvious that all of the atoms that composed, say, Noah when he died, exist today. Maybe they do. Or maybe the atoms themselves are gone, but all the parts of all those atoms, like electrons or quarks, still exist. But maybe some of them do not. And maybe some of my parts, even some of the smallest ones, will have somehow passed out of existence in a thousand years. If so, then they won't be around for reassembly. And so reassembly of all my still-existing smallest parts cannot secure my resurrection in a thousand years.

The second problem with 'resurrection as reassembly' has its roots in the fact that the atoms that compose a body at death can eventually find their way into another body. Cannibalism offers a striking and clear illustration of this problem, and so worries about cannibalism occupied Christian thinkers from very early on. So let's suppose that you are eaten by a cannibal. The cannibal then digests your body, and some of the atoms that composed your body at death then compose the cannibal's body. The cannibal then dies. Resurrection Day comes, and God sets out to reassemble both your body and the cannibal's body from the atoms that composed each body at its last moment. But some of the atoms that composed you at death also composed the cannibal at death. If the shared atoms go to you, then they cannot go to the cannibal; if they go to the cannibal, they cannot go to you. God cannot, therefore, reassemble both your body *and* the body of the cannibal.

So if it is true that a body comes back into existence at resurrection only if all of the atoms that composed it at death are reassembled, it is not possible that both you and the cannibal get resurrected. But it must be possible for you and the cannibal to be resurrected. For, as the scripture passages quoted later in this paper

---

[8] More carefully, the view here is that one must gather all of a body's parts *of a certain size*. For suppose I die and my body decays. My body presumably had parts such as my liver and my heart. But these organs ceased to exist along with my body, and so cannot be 'gathered back' and reassembled. It is the small parts—the atoms, perhaps—with which the friends of reassembly are concerned.

show, *everyone* gets resurrected on Resurrection Day. Our hope in the resurrection is not—contrary to the beliefs of some early enemies of the church—held hostage to what happens to our bodies after we die.[9]

A number of moves have been suggested to make the 'reassembly of last parts' view consistent with the doctrine that every body (and so everybody) will be resurrected. My personal favorite is the claim, first defended by Athenagoras in the second century, that human flesh was simply not digestible.[10] If Athenagoras was right, when the cannibal eats you, the atoms that compose you pass right through. They *never* are parts of the cannibal. So at the Last Day, you are the only one with a claim to those atoms. (After they had passed through a cannibal, would you want them back?) Of course, Athenagoras' solution won't wash; he had the facts wrong; human flesh is digestible.

In addition to the question of just how long atoms survive, and in addition to puzzles about cannibalism—and in general puzzles about the fact that atoms that compose one body at death can in a variety of ways eventually find their way into another person's body—there is a third and more fundamental worry about the reassembly view. To start to see the worry, suppose, again, that you take a watch to be cleaned; when you return later, the jeweler hands you a watch that he *says* is yours, although he adds that he replaced *every single part*. You would rightly insist that the jeweler has got it wrong—he's not returned your old watch with new parts; rather, he's given you a new watch. Considerations such as these lend plausibility to the general claim that a watch cannot continue to exist after every single one of its parts is replaced.[11] Conversely, it seems that just so long as you have all the original parts of the watch, in all their original positions, you have the original watch. A watch's numerical identity over time seems to be tied very closely to the numerical identity of its parts.

But these facts are not true of organisms like human bodies. Human bodies can—and *do*—survive the replacement of all their parts. All, or nearly all, of the atoms that composed me twenty years ago no longer compose me today. (To illustrate this point, only about half of the atoms that composed your liver just *five days ago* are in your liver today.)[12] Moreover, getting all the parts that compose a human body at one time, and reassembling them, does not necessarily bring that very same human body back. To see this, suppose God were to find all

[9] In a second-century persecution, the Romans thought they could extinguish the Christians' hope of resurrection by burning and scattering the bodies of martyrs. See Bynum, *The Resurrection of the Body*, 49.

[10] Bynum, *The Resurrection of the Body*, 33.

[11] But this is controversial. Suppose that you replaced the watch's parts, one by one, over a very long period of time. Then maybe the watch would survive. Philosophical puzzles are lurking close by, since you could then gather all the original parts and reassemble *them* into a watch. Which watch—the product of the gradual replacement or the one that is made of all the original parts—is the original watch?

[12] I ran across this fun fact in van Inwagen's *Material Beings* (Ithaca: Cornell University Press, 1990), 93–4.

the atoms that composed you when you were five years old and reassemble them into a living five-year-old child, and then set that five-year-old child next to you. Would that child have *your body?* Certainly not; you are standing (and so your body is standing) right *next to* the five-year-old's body. We have two bodies here, one numerically distinct from the other.

So we can see that a human body's numerical identity over time is not tied to the numerical identity of its parts in the simple and straightforward way that the numerical identity of an inanimate object like a watch seems to be. This should make us cautious about the reassembly view of resurrection. And we can press this point a bit more. We have seen that the fact that some group or set or collection of atoms composed your body at some time in history—such as on your fifth birthday—does not imply that those atoms, when reassembled, would compose your body. If this is right, then we should worry that the fact that some collection of atoms composes your body at the time in history at which you happen to die might not imply that *those* atoms, when reassembled, would compose *your* body.

Since the parts that compose a human body constantly change throughout life, there seems to be something arbitrary in insisting that the human body at resurrection must be composed of the parts that composed that body *at death.* And reassembling the parts that compose the person at any other particular time during the person's life would be arbitrary in the same way. So the problem here is with resurrection as reassembly in general, not just resurrection as reassembly of *last* parts.

Defenders of the reassembly view of resurrection were aware of this charge and have offered responses (this charge was made as early as the second century by Origen, one of the first to reject explicitly the reassembly view).[13] Athenagoras, for instance, claimed that a human body neither loses nor gains any parts throughout one's life; he thought that one never exhales nor excretes any atoms that ever composed one's body, and that no new atoms are ever added to one's body by eating and drinking.[14] So, Athenagoras could claim, there is nothing arbitrary about focusing on the *last* parts after all, since the parts you have at your last moment of life are the very same parts you had at every moment of life. But this defense won't work since, again, Athenagoras had the facts wrong.

I think the above points suggest that there is good reason to reject the 'reassembly of last bits' description of how resurrection occurs. But if it is not in virtue of reassembly, then *in virtue of what,* one might ask, is the resurrected body numerically identical with the body that has died?[15] There have been other

---

[13] Bynum, *The Resurrection of the Body,* 64.

[14] Bynum, *The Resurrection of the Body,* 69.

[15] My own answer to this question, which I won't develop here because it is both complicated and controversial, is that the resurrection body is identical with the earthly one *just because it is,* and this does not need to be explained by anything else. To better understand why I say this, see my 'There Are No Criteria of Identity Over Time,' *Noûs* 32 (1998): 106–24.

answers to this question. The most well-known, after reassembly, is the ancient rabbinical tradition that just so long as the resurrected body is composed around an indestructible bone from the earthly body's spinal column, the identity of the earthly body with the resurrected one is fixed.[16] But this answer has even more problems than reassembly. For one thing, there is no totally indestructible bone in the spinal column.

Suppose that we have *no* satisfactory account of what makes for the identity of the earthly body with the resurrection one. All that follows is that none of us has any clear idea *how* resurrection will work. That, however, is no threat at all to the doctrine that it *will* work. What *would* be a genuine threat to the doctrine of resurrection would be some sort of proof or argument that temporal gaps in the career of a body are *impossible*. But the fact that we cannot see how resurrection is supposed to go, that we cannot explain what God does to bring an annihilated body back into existence, does not imply that God's doing this is impossible; it implies only that we are ignorant.

Indeed, since the resurrection of a no-longer-existing human body is contrary to the normal way nature proceeds, it would be no surprise if our models of how a physical thing enjoys numerical identity over time in everyday life suggest no plausible account of how a human body that dies and decays could be identical with a body that is resurrected. Resurrection of the body may not be impossible, but it will take a miracle.

IV. IMMORTALITY AND RESURRECTION AND PERSONS AND BODIES

The LORD God formed the man from the dust of the ground and breathed into his nostrils the breath of life, and the man became a living being.
By the sweat of your brow you will eat your food until you return to the ground, since from it you were taken; for dust you are and to dust you will return.

Genesis 2:7; 3:19

The previous two sections of this paper have dealt with two topics: The life everlasting and the resurrection of the body. As we shall see below, scripture often speaks of these two topics in the same breath, seeming to treat them as two sides of a single coin. A similar point holds of the creeds mentioned at the start of this chapter. This should strike many of us as puzzling. Life after death is one thing, so many of us think, and the resurrection of the body is something else altogether. In this final, more speculative section of this chapter, I shall explain one way of thinking about human persons—I shall call this way of thinking

[16] See Bynum, *The Resurrection of the Body*, 54, and Cooper, *Body, Soul and Life Everlasting*, 188.

'physicalism'—according to which the resurrection of one's body and one's life after death are, in fact, two ways of describing the very same thing.

We shall see that the fact that physicalism links everlasting life to resurrection in the most direct way possible is a powerful reason to think physicalism is true. I want to concede right from the start, however, that this reason, although powerful, is neither a proof nor a full-scale defense of physicalism.[17] A full defense would consider all the arguments for and against physicalism, taking into account all of physicalism's rivals. But such a project—besides being enormously difficult and involved—would take us too far from the focus of this section, the relation of resurrection to life after death.[18]

Although we will not take all of physicalism's rivals into account, we will consider its chief rival, dualism. For comparing and contrasting physicalism to dualism will allow us better to understand physicalism itself. Most Christians—or at least most Christians who have a clear and consistent opinion on the matter—are dualists. (Please read carefully my explanation of how I will use the word 'dualism.')[19] Dualists believe in the existence of nonphysical souls. To say that a soul is *nonphysical* means, at least, that a soul does not have standard physical properties such as color or weight or visibility or spatiality. So it is impossible for a soul to weigh an ounce or to be seen. Although a soul lacks physical properties, it has mental properties. This means, among other things, that a soul can be thinking about the weather, a soul can be confused, and a soul can accept or reject the claims of the gospel.

---

[17] And this is a topic that Christians can quite reasonably disagree on. There is, of course, a true view. If physicalism is false, then I am wrong in believing it. If physicalism is true, then those who reject it are themselves mistaken. But the true view is not obvious. Although I will use scripture to defend physicalism about human beings, I do not mean to accuse those who disagree with me of being 'soft on scripture' or otherwise suspect.

[18] That said, two theories of personal identity that I won't discuss in the text, two theories which fail to unite immortality and resurrection in the direct way that physicalism does, are at least worth noting:

Some people think that human beings are souls, but deny that souls are non-physical. Instead, they seem to think of a soul as a very thin and wispy physical thing like a cloud or fog; a soul is—just barely—visible after death and perhaps weighs just a little bit. A soul is like a ghost. For good or for ill, philosophers do not take this position seriously. I mention it only because this view (as opposed to standard dualism) seems to be implicit in the story of the Witch of Endor when the witch says that Samuel's spirit *looks like* an old man wearing a robe (1 Samuel 28:14).

Some philosophers deny that a person is a physical object like an organism and also deny that a person is a nonphysical object like a soul. This is because they think that a person is no sort of object at all, but rather a series of mental events or thoughts. This view was presupposed by a recent newspaper story I read which claimed that we will one day achieve immortality by storing our thoughts and memories on a computer chip. Just so long as our 'thoughts' continue to exist, we continue to exist, for we are just our thoughts. I do not really understand this view.

[19] The word 'dualism' has been used in many different ways and in many different contexts. I mean by 'dualism' exactly the view I explain in the text, and nothing else at all. So, after reading my discussion in the text, it should be obvious that dualism (as I understand it here) has nothing to do with, for example, the doctrine that there are two forces in the universe, one for good, the other for evil. Nor does it imply, to offer a second example, that matter is evil and that having a body is a bad thing.

Dualists believe that, in this life, each soul is intimately associated with a body. They might say that in this life a soul 'has' a body. Very roughly, a soul's 'having' a body amounts to that soul's exercising direct causal control over a body and receiving sensory input directly from that same body. An example of direct causal control: When a soul has the mental property of intending to move a left arm, the left arm of 'its' body moves.[20] An example of sensory input: When someone pinches a body, the associated soul feels pain. While dualists think that souls 'have' bodies in this life, they don't think that having a body is essential to a soul's existence. For they think that upon death, the soul continues to exist without a body.

And not just the *soul* continues to exist after death without a body, but so does the *person herself*. In fact, dualists think that after death (and before resurrection) a person *just is* a soul. This leads many dualists to conclude that a human person is numerically identical with a soul in *this* life, *before* death. For they reason that since a person can survive the destruction of her body, and since only the person's soul can survive the destruction of her body, the person must be nothing other than a soul. These dualists do not deny, of course, that in this life, the person (who is a soul) is intimately associated with a body. They just don't think that the body is really a part of the person herself. Other dualists agree that a person survives death as only a soul, yet somehow maintain that, in this life, a person is *not* identical with a soul, but rather is identical with a composite of both body and soul. (Just as a person's body is composed of a left half and a right half, but is identical with neither, so the person herself, according to some dualists, is in this life composed of a soul and a body, but identical with neither.)

The above comments should give us a good idea of what the dualist believes, and they also set the stage for an explanation of physicalism. The physicalist rejects dualism. The physicalist, at least the sort of physicalist I have in mind, agrees that something has mental properties; she just thinks that that something is a physical human being rather than a nonphysical soul. The physicalist does not think that the relation of you to your body is one of merely direct causal control and sensory input. Nor does she think that your body is just one part of you and your soul another. Rather, she thinks that there are *no* souls and that you are the *very same thing as* your body. So anything true of the physical human organism that is your body is true of you; anything true of you is true of that organism.[21]

---

[20] I call this *direct* causal control to distinguish it from *indirect* causal control. *My* soul could have indirect causal control over *your* arm if I could cause your arm to move, but could not do so simply by intending it. I might do so, instead, by moving your arm with my hand. The dualist insists that one's soul exerts *direct* causal control over one's own body; it controls it simply by intending to do so.

[21] As with 'dualism,' the word 'physicalism' has been used in a variety of ways. In this chapter, it means only and exactly the claim that a human person is identical with the organism that is his or her body. It does *not* mean, in this chapter, that *everything* is physical. The Christian physicalist will insist, for example, that God is nonphysical.

It should be clear that in the debate between the dualist and the physicalist, the word 'soul' has a very specific meaning. In less philosophical contexts, the word 'soul' often has other meanings. For example, a die-hard Notre Dame football fan might say 'My soul is blue and gold.' She probably doesn't mean that she is or has a nonphysical, yet colored, object—that would be absurd. Rather, she is probably using the word 'soul' only to testify, in a picturesque way, to her commitment to the Fighting Irish. Indeed, in *this* sense of the word 'soul,' someone who is a physicalist could say—without contradicting his physicalism—that *his* soul is blue and gold.

Along similar lines, the physicalist should have no problem with saying that one should 'love God with all of one's heart, all of one's soul, and all of one's strength.' She will just insist that 'soul'—in this context—does not mean 'nonphysical entity with mental properties.' To love God with all of one's soul, she might insist, is nothing other than to love God deeply and with great passion and in one's 'innermost being.' Likewise, the physicalist can be enthusiastic about saving souls, although she will be careful to explain that this means nothing more and nothing less than being enthusiastic about saving people. The physicalist might even grant that she *has* a soul, in contexts where the word 'soul' means something like mind or personality.

So when the physicalist denies that she has (or is) a soul, she is denying only the dualist's very specific claim that she has (or is) a nonphysical mental entity. She is not denying that the word 'soul' can be used in other contexts and in other ways, and when used in these other ways, she might affirm that she has a soul, that she wants to see souls saved, or that she likes soul food. Because of this, I do not think that we need to worry about an attack on physicalism that does no more than simply point out a Bible verse that has the word 'soul' in it; for the physicalist might well agree that in the sense of 'soul' at issue there, she *does* have a soul.[22] Indeed, it might be better to say that the physicalist and the dualist agree that people *have souls*, they just disagree about what a person's *soul is like*. Nevertheless, I will follow standard *philosophical* usage in this paper, and use the word 'soul' to mean the sort of nonphysical mental entity that the dualist believes in. Given this very special and philosophical usage of the word 'soul,' it is correct to say that the physicalist does not believe that people have souls.

As we shall see in the verses below, the Bible treats the resurrection as very important. But if dualism were true, it is hard to see why our resurrection would be a big deal. Now the dualist might object that a soul in Heaven without a body is somehow mutilated or incomplete, and so the dualist might therefore insist that resurrection is a blessing. But it is hard to know just how much stress she should put on the value of resurrection, since stress on what we gain in

---

[22] Along similar lines, the physicalist can claim that human persons are 'spiritual' beings, but that this means (for example) that they can have a certain kind of relationship with God. She can also agree that we should worship God in spirit and in truth. And so on.

resurrection is, by its very nature, stress on what we lack before resurrection. Preresurrection existence united with God in Heaven is not supposed to be *too* bad; indeed, it is supposed to be *very good*.

And however the dualist might deal with this problem, one thing is certain: The dualist cannot say that resurrection is *necessary* for eternal life. After all, Christian dualists often claim that an advantage of their theory—even *the* advantage of their theory—is that it allows humans to live on after death but before the general resurrection. And, obviously, one cannot maintain both that life after death occurs *before* resurrection and also that life after death *requires* resurrection.

If, on the other hand, we are physical organisms, then our resurrected bodies coming back into existence on that Great Day just is *our* coming back into existence. If we are physical organisms, the resurrection of the body is the whole ball game as far as life after death goes. If we are physical organisms, then our hope for life after death and our hope for resurrection of the body are one and the same thing. If we are physical organisms, death is defeated in, and only in, the resurrection.

With these thoughts in mind, note—along with the passage from Isaiah that opened this paper—the following scriptures:

At that time Michael, the great prince who protects your people, will arise. There will be a time of distress such as has not happened from the beginning of nations until then. But at that time your people—everyone whose name is found written in the book—will be delivered. Multitudes who sleep in the dust of the earth will awake: some to everlasting life, others to shame and everlasting contempt. (Daniel 12:1–2)

When you give a luncheon or dinner, do not invite your friends, your brothers or relatives, or your rich neighbors; if you do, they may invite you back and so you will be repaid. But when you give a banquet, invite the poor, the crippled, the lame, the blind, and you will be blessed. Although they cannot repay you, you will be repaid at the resurrection of the righteous. (Matthew 14:12–14)

I tell you the truth, whoever hears my word and believes him who sent me has eternal life and will not be condemned; he has crossed over from death to life. I tell you the truth, a time is coming and has now come when the dead will hear the voice of the Son of God and those who hear will live. For as the Father has life in himself, so he has granted the Son to have life in himself. And he has given him authority to judge because he is the Son of Man. Do not be amazed at this, for a time is coming when all who are in their graves will hear his voice and come out—those who have done good will rise to live, and those who have done evil will rise to be condemned. (John 5:24–9)

I believe everything that agrees with the Law and that is written in the Prophets, and I have the same hope in God as these men, that there will be a resurrection of both the righteous and the wicked. (Paul, responding to his accusers at his trial before Felix in Acts 24)

Brothers, we do not want you to be ignorant about those who fall asleep, or to grieve like the rest of men, who have no hope. We believe that Jesus died and rose again and so we believe that God will bring with Jesus those who have fallen asleep in him. According to the Lord's own word, we tell you that we who are still alive will certainly not precede those who have fallen asleep. For the Lord himself will come down from heaven with a loud command, with the voice of the archangel and with the trumpet call of God, and the dead in Christ will rise first. After that, we who are still alive and are left will be caught up together with them in the clouds to meet the Lord in the air. And so we will be with the Lord forever. Therefore encourage each other with these words. (1 Thessalonians 4:13–18)

For if the dead are not raised, then Christ has not been raised either. And if Christ has not been raised, your faith is futile; you are still in your sins. Then those also who have fallen asleep in Christ are lost. If only for this life we have hope in Christ, we are to be pitied more than all men. (1 Corinthians 15:16–19)

If I fought wild beasts in Ephesus for merely human reasons, what have I gained? If the dead are not raised, 'Let us eat and drink, for tomorrow we die.' (1 Corinthians 15:32)

We will not all sleep, but we will all be changed—in a flash, in the twinkling of an eye, at the last trumpet. For the trumpet will sound, the dead will be raised imperishable, and we will all be changed. For the perishable must clothe itself with the imperishable, and the mortal with immortality. When the perishable has been clothed with the imperishable, and the mortal with immortality, then the saying that is written will come true: 'Death has been swallowed up in victory.' 'Where, O death, is your victory? Where O death is your sting?' (1 Corinthians 15:51–5)

If we take the above passages at face value, it is dead *people* that are raised to life; *hope of resurrection* is the believer's *hope of eternal life*. If that is correct, then resurrection is much more than 'getting your body back' (as good as that may be)—it is the believer's victory over death. It is the guarantor of a final judgment and entrance into eternal union with God or eternal separation from him. It is what gives us hope in God and keeps us from saying 'let us eat and drink, for tomorrow we die.' The physicalist will find the picture of resurrection painted in the verses above a very natural one. For he will insist that *life after death* and *resurrection* are, for physical organisms like us, *one and the same thing*.

While the physicalist holds that life after death and resurrection are one, the dualist does not. The dualist does not believe that dead *people* are raised to life; rather, she believes that dead *bodies* are raised to be reunited with already living people (who are, in the intermediate state at least, souls). I think that means that the picture of resurrection painted in the verses above does not sit comfortably with dualism. I do not deny that the dualist can interpret these passages in a way consistent with her view. I claim only that her interpretation of these passages will not be as natural or plausible as that of the physicalist, and so I think these passages support physicalism over dualism.

The physicalist should also take comfort in the fact, noted in the previous section of this paper, that the resurrection body is numerically identical with the body one has in this life. For if a human being is identical with her body, she cannot exist after death unless her body, that is, an object numerically identical with the very organism that was her body in this life, exists after death. So, given physicalism, it is part and parcel of the promise of eternal life that one's 'original' body will itself be resurrected. The numerical identity of the earthly body with the resurrection body is just what the physicalist who believes in life after death would expect.

But if dualism were true, one would not expect the resurrection body to be numerically identical with the earthly one. For even granting that a soul without a body is mutilated or incomplete, there is no reason to think that a soul needs the very same body it had before death. The identity of the resurrection body with the body of this life is not inconsistent with dualism, of course. But it does seem to be rather pointless, except for the fact that our original bodies might have some sentimental value to us.[23] Like the centrality of the resurrection to our hope for eternal life, the nature of the resurrection body—insofar as its identity with the earthly body is concerned—fits hand in glove with physicalism but makes little sense given dualism.

If we are identical with our bodies, then we do not exist when our bodies do not exist. Therefore, if physicalism is true, at some point between the death and total decay of one's body, one literally ceases to exist. Ceasing to exist is different from existing and being 'asleep,' and even different—if this makes any sense at all—from existing and being dead. It may be hard for you to imagine your nonexistence, but there is nothing incoherent here. (After all, you did not exist, e.g., in the year 500 B.C.). It is bad that beings like us, created for eternal life, pass away into nothingness. So I can insist on what I think the scriptures affirm. I can insist that death is a bad thing. Death is an enemy. Death is a curse. Death's doom is sealed, of course; we know at resurrection it will be conquered once and for all. But a doomed enemy is an enemy nevertheless.[24]

It is not clear that the dualist can agree that death is bad. When the Christian dies, according to the dualist, he or she goes immediately to a much better place. Death for the believer, according to the dualist, is nothing other than exchanging the travails of this life for immediate and glorious union with the Father in Heaven. Death, it would seem, is even better than quitting your job and moving to a beachfront villa in Hawaii. I think this is a problem for dualism. For I think

[23] And the whole emphasis on Resurrection Day and the bodies we get then seems to me absolutely pointless if those forms of dualism are true which insist that after death, but before resurrection, we are given 'interim' bodies.

[24] So if I am right, you will cease to exist when you die and then, on the Day of Resurrection, you will come back into existence. Some dualists might object that this requires a 'temporal gap' in a person's life. And they might object that such gaps are impossible. (They might then add that an advantage of their view is that a person is a soul and never goes out of existence, not even between death and resurrection.) But I do not think that this is a very strong objection. For I think that whether one is a dualist, physicalist, or otherwise, one ought to agree that temporal gaps in a human *body's* career are implied by the resurrection. Once that is granted, however, one cannot object to physicalism on the grounds that it endorses temporal gaps. Physicalists and dualists agree that a person's body can 'jump ahead in time' to the Day of Resurrection; physicalists just add to this that a person and her body are the same thing.

the scriptures teach that death is a bad thing, a curse, an enemy; and an enemy defeated in resurrection. If physicalism is true, it is easy to see how bad death is and also how death is defeated in resurrection. But if dualism is true, it is hard to see how death is an enemy, and harder still to see how it is overcome in resurrection.

Now the dualist might reply that death is separation from your body and that this separation is very bad. And she might add that resurrection is the end of this separation and thus very good. Fair enough. Nevertheless, death is much worse given physicalism than dualism. To see this, imagine what you would say to a mourner at a Christian's funeral if you and the mourner knew for certain that *dualism* were true. You could comfort the mourner by noting that now the deceased is in a better place and with the Lord. She is much happier than she was before death (happier, even, than she would be on the beach in Hawaii . . .). If, on the other hand, you and the mourner knew for certain that *physicalism* were true, you would have only one comfort—the resurrection. You might say 'For now, there is little to comfort you. But someday the dead will rise again.' Physicalism makes death all the worse and resurrection all the more glorious. This fits very well with scripture's attitudes toward death and resurrection.

Or at least with some of the attitudes expressed in scripture. For scripture also says 'To die is gain.' Since the dualist can understand death as immediate passage to God, without having to await resurrection, passages of scripture that seem to teach that death is gain are passages, I think, that seem to support dualism over physicalism.

What should the Christian physicalist say about these passages? Perhaps the answer is found in the story of the time machine. If I thought that I were about to take a ride on the time machine and that the very next moment at which I would exist would be the glorious Day of Resurrection, I would be quite excited. So while my dying results in my literal non-existence, I can nevertheless be comforted at my death in knowing that death's defeat is the very next thing I shall experience. With the fact in mind that to die is to jump ahead in time to the Day of Resurrection, I could say that 'to die is gain.' And I could think to myself, as I lie on my deathbed, that, so far as things seem to me—and only because of the resurrection of the body—this day I shall be with the Lord in paradise.

I have not addressed even a fraction of the passages of scripture that bear on whether or not one exists between death and resurrection or, more generally, on physicalism and dualism. This is a topic of deep controversy among biblical scholars, and for those who are interested in pursuing it, there is no end of materials to read.[25] As far as biblical interpretation goes, my aim in this final,

---

[25] One good place to start is John W. Cooper's *Body, Soul, and Life Everlasting*. Cooper's book is very accessible, presupposing no prior knowledge of theology or philosophy. Cooper defends the claim that scripture teaches some form of dualism. The book is useful not only because of Cooper's own arguments, but because of the many footnotes and references he gives to papers and books defending both sides of the issue.

more speculative, section of this chapter is fairly modest. It is to suggest one way—the best way, I think—to make sense of the picture of resurrection that the Bible seems to endorse. That picture involves the numerical identity of the earthly body with the resurrection body, a close connection between our hope for resurrection and our hope for eternal life, and the defeat of a bitter enemy—death—in the resurrection.

You may remain unconvinced. You may remain a stalwart of dualism and dualistic interpretations of scripture. I still think the above discussion ought to convince you of at least one significant thing—that the Christian's belief in life after death does not necessarily and absolutely require dualism. For in the doctrine of the resurrection, we have the resources to make sense of—and have hope for—eternal life even if physicalism is true. Because of this, the believer need not feel threatened when scientists, philosophers, or psychologists pronounce belief in the soul irrational or demonstrably false. Such pronouncements (although sadly common) are unjustified. But it is nice to know that even if, someday, someone proves that physicalism is true, nothing essential to the Christian faith would be undermined.

19

Against Materialism*

Alvin Plantinga

I propose to give two arguments against materialism—or, if you think that's too negative, two arguments for substantial dualism. 'Substantial' is to be taken in two senses: first, the dualism in question, the dualism for which I mean to argue, is substantial as opposed to trivial; some versions of property dualism seem to me to be at best wholly insubstantial. Second, according to the most popular form of dualism—one embraced by Plato, Augustine, Descartes and a thousand others— a human person is an immaterial substance: a thing, an object, a substance, a suppositum (as my Thomist colleagues would put it), and a thing that isn't material, although, of course, it is intimately connected with a material body. But there is also the view the name 'dualism' suggests: the view according to which a human person is somehow a sort of composite substance S composed of a material substance S^* and an immaterial substance S^{**}.[1] We can sensibly include this view under 'dualism'—provided, that is, that having S^* as a part is not essential to S. (I add this proviso because my first argument is for the conclusion that possibly, I exist when my body does not.)

Perhaps a better name for the view I mean to defend is 'immaterialism'; the view that a human person is not a material object. Of course it's far from easy to say just what a material object is.[2] For present purposes let's put it recursively: a material object is either an atom, or is composed of atoms. Thus atoms, molecules, cells, hearts, brains and human bodies are all material objects; we'll leave open the question whether such things as electrons, quarks, protons, fields, and superstrings (if indeed there are such things) are material objects. What I'll argue for, accordingly, is the view that human persons are not material objects. They *are* objects (substances), however; therefore they are immaterial objects. My

* © *Faith and Philosophy*, vol. 23 (2006). Reprinted by permission of the publisher.

[1] See, e.g., Richard Swinburne, *The Evolution of the Soul* (Oxford: Clarendon Press, 1987), pp. 2, 145. Aquinas' position on the relation between soul and body may be a special case of this view; see my 'Materialism and Christian Belief,' in *Persons: Human and Divine*, ed. Peter van Inwagen and Dean Zimmerman, forthcoming.

[2] See, e.g., Bas van Fraassen, *The Empirical Stance* (New Haven: Yale, 2002), pp. 50ff.

conclusion, of course, is hardly original (going back at least to Plato); my general style of argument also lacks originality (going back at least to Descartes and possibly Augustine). But the method of true philosophy, unlike that of liberal theology and contemporary French thought, aims less at novelty than at truth.

Three more initial comments: (i) when I speak of possibility and necessity, I mean possibility and necessity in the broadly logical sense—metaphysical possibility and necessity, as it is also called. (ii) I won't be arguing that it is possible that I (or others) can exist disembodied, with no body at all.[3] (iii) I will make no claims about what is or isn't conceivable or imaginable. That is because imaginability isn't strictly relevant to possibility at all; conceivability, on the other hand, is relevant only if 'it's conceivable that p' is to be understood as implying or offering evidence for 'it's possible that p.' (Similarly for 'it's inconceivable that p.') It is therefore simpler and much less conducive to confusion to speak just of possibility. I take it we human beings have the following epistemic capacity: we can consider or envisage a proposition or state of affairs and, at least sometimes, determine its modal status—whether it is necessary, contingent, or impossible—just by thinking, just by an exercise of thought.[4]

I. THE REPLACEMENT ARGUMENT: AN ARGUMENT FROM POSSIBILITY

I begin by assuming that there really is such a thing, substance or suppositum as I, I myself. Of course I'm not unique in that respect; you too are such that there really is such a thing as you, and the same goes for everybody else. We are substances. Now suppose I were a material substance: which material substance would I be? The answer, I should think, is that I would be my body, or some part of my body, such as my brain or part of my brain. Or perhaps I would be something more exotic: an object distinct from my body that is constituted from the same matter as my body and is colocated with it.[5] What I propose to argue is that I am none of those things: I am not my body, or some part of it such as my brain or a hemisphere or other part of the latter, or an object composed of the

---

[3] Although I can't help concurring with David Armstrong, no friend of dualism:

But disembodied existence seems to be a perfectly intelligible supposition.... Consider the case where I am lying in bed at night thinking. Surely it is logically possible that I might be having just the same experiences and yet not have a body at all. No doubt I am having certain somatic, that is to say, bodily sensations. But if I am lying still these will not be very detailed in nature, and I can see nothing self-contradictory in supposing that they do not correspond to anything in physical reality. Yet I need be in no doubt about my identity. (*A Materialist Theory of Mind* [London: Routledge, 1968], p. 19)

[4] See my *Warrant and Proper Function* (New York; Oxford University Press, 1993), chap. 6.

[5] See, e.g., Dean Zimmerman, 'Material People' in *The Oxford Handbook of Metaphysics* (Oxford: Clarendon Press, 2002), pp. 504ff. Zimmerman himself seems attracted to the thought that 'the mass of matter' of which one's body is composed is an object distinct from the latter, but colocated with it (although of course he is *not* attracted to the idea that a person is identical with such a mass of matter).

same matter as my body (or some part of it) and colocated with it. (I'll call these 'eligible' material objects.) For simplicity (and nothing I say will depend on this simplification) I shall talk for the most part just about my body, which I'll name 'B.' (I was thinking of naming it 'Hercules' or maybe 'Arnold,' but people insisted that would be unduly self-congratulatory.)

The general strategy of this first argument is as follows. It seems possible that I continue to exist when B, my body, does not. I therefore have the property *possibly exists when B does not*. B, however, clearly lacks that property. By Leibniz's Law, therefore (more specifically, the Diversity of Discernibles), I am not identical with B. But why think it possible that I exist when my body does not? Strictly speaking, the replacement argument is an argument for this premise. Again, I conduct the argument in the first person, but naturally enough the same goes for you (although of course you will have to speak for yourself).

So first, at a macroscopic level. A familiar fact of modern medicine is the possibility and actuality of limb and organ transplants and prostheses. You can get a new heart, liver, lungs; you can also get knee, hip, and ankle replacements; you can get prostheses for hands and feet, arms and legs, and so on. Now it seems possible—possible in that broadly logical sense—that medical science should advance to the point where I remain fully dressed and in my right mind (perhaps reading the *South Bend Tribune*) throughout a process during which each of the macroscopic parts of my body is replaced by other such parts, the original parts being vaporized in a nuclear explosion—or better, annihilated by God. But if this process occurs rapidly—during a period of 1 microsecond, let's say—B will no longer exist. I, however, will continue to exist, having been reading the comic page during the entire process.

But what about my brain, you ask—is it possible that my brain be replaced by another, the brain I now have being destroyed, and I continue to exist? It certainly seems so. Think of it like this. It seems possible (in the broadly logical sense) that one hemisphere of my brain be dormant at any given time, the other hemisphere doing all that a brain ordinarily does. At midnight, we can suppose, all the relevant 'data' and 'information' is 'transferred' via the corpus callosum from one hemisphere—call it 'H_1'—to the other hemisphere—H_2—whereupon H_2 takes over operation of the body and H_1 goes dormant. This seems possible; if it were actual, it would also be possible that the original dormant half, H_2, be replaced by a different dormant half (in the same computational or functional state, if you like) just before that midnight transfer; then the transfer occurs, control switches to the new H_2, and H_1 goes dormant—at which time it is replaced by another hemisphere in the same computational or functional condition. In a period of time as brief as you like, therefore, both hemispheres will have been replaced by others, the original hemispheres and all of their parts annihilated by God. Throughout the whole process I serenely continue to read the comics.

This suffices, I think, to show that it's possible that I exist when neither my body nor any part of it exists. What about material objects distinct from my body and its parts, but colocated with it (or one of them) and constituted by the same matter as they? I doubt very much that there could be any such things. If objects of this kind *are* possible, however, the above argument also shows or at least suggests that possibly, I exist when none of them does. For example, if there is such a thing as *the matter of which B is composed*—if that phrase denotes a thing or object[6]—it too would be destroyed by God's annihilating all the parts of my body.

Of course very many different sorts of object of this kind—objects constituted by the matter of my body and colocated with it—have been suggested, and I don't have the space here to deal with them all. However, we can offer a version of the replacement argument that will be relevant to many of them. Turn from macroscopic replacement to microscopic replacement. This could go on at several levels: the levels of atoms, molecules, or cells, for example. Let's think about it at the cellular level. It seems entirely possible that the cells of which my body is composed be rapidly—within a microsecond or two—replaced by other cells of the same kind, the original cells being instantly destroyed. It also seems entirely possible that this process of replacement take place while I remain conscious, thinking about dualism and marveling at some of the appalling arguments against it produced by certain materialists.[7] Then I would exist at a time at which B did not exist.

But is it really true that this process of replacement would result in the destruction of B? After all, according to current science, all the matter in our bodies is replaced over a period of years, without any obvious compromise of bodily integrity or identity. As a matter of fact, so they say, the matter in our brains is completely replaced in a much shorter time.[8] Why should merely accelerating this process make a difference?[9]

---

[6] See Zimmerman, loc. cit.

[7] One such argument, for example, apparently has the following form:

(a) Many people who advocate p, do so in the service of a hope that science will never be able to explain p;

therefore

(b) not-p.

See Daniel Dennett, *Darwin's Dangerous Idea* (New York: Simon and Schuster, 1995), p. 27. Another seems to have the form

(a) If you believe p, prestigious people will laugh at you;

therefore

(b) not-p

(or perhaps

(b*) don't believe p?)

See Daniel Dennett, *Explaining Consciousness* (Boston: Little, Brown and Co., 1991), p. 37.

[8] 'But on the kinds of figures that are coming out now, it seems like the whole brain must get recycled about every other month.' John McCrone, 'How Do You Persist When Your Molecules Don't?' *Science and Consciousness Review*, (web-journal, June 2004, No. 1).

[9] Here I am indebted especially to Michael Rea.

Well, as they say, speed kills. When a cell is removed from an organism and replaced by another cell, the new cell doesn't become part of the organism instantaneously; it must be integrated into the organism and assimilated by it.[10] What does this assimilation consist in? A cell in a (properly functioning) body is involved in a network of causal relations; a neuron, for example, emits and responds to electrical signals. A cell receives nourishment from the blood, and cooperates with other cells in various causal activities. All these things take time—maybe not much time, but still a certain period of time. At the instant the new part[11] is inserted into the organism, and until it has begun to play this causal role (both as cause and effect), the new part is not yet a part of the organism, but a foreign body occupying space within the spatial boundaries of the organism. (Clearly not everything, nor even everything organic, within the spatial boundaries of your body is *part* of your body: think of the goldfish you just swallowed, or a tapeworm.) Let's use the phrase 'assimilation time' to denote the time required for the cell to start playing this causal role. The assimilation time is the time required for the cell to become assimilated into the body; before that time has elapsed the cell is not yet part of the body. To be rigorous, we should index this to the part (or kind of part) and the organism in question; different parts may require different periods of time for their assimilation by different organisms. For simplicity, though, let's assume all parts and organisms have the same assimilation time; this simplification won't make any difference to the argument.

That a given part and organism are such that the time of assimilation for the former with respect to the latter is dt, for some specific period of time dt, is, I take it, a contingent fact. One thinks the velocity of light imposes a lower limit here, but the time of assimilation could be much greater. (For example, it could depend on the rate of blood flow, the rate of intracellular transport, and the rate at which information is transmitted through neuron or nerve.) God could presumably slow down this process, or speed it up.

There is also what we might call 'the replacement time': the period of time from the beginning of the replacement of the first part by a new part to the end of the time of the replacement of the last part (the last to be replaced) by a different part. The time of replacement is also, of course, contingent; a replacement can occur rapidly or slowly. Presumably there is no non-zero lower limit here; no matter how rapidly the parts are replaced, it is possible in the broadly logical sense that they be replaced still more rapidly.

---

[10] See, e.g., David Hershenov, 'The Metaphysical Problem of Intermittent Existence and the Possibility of Resurrection,' *Faith and Philosophy* (Jan. 2003), p. 33.

[11] Complaint: this new 'part' as you call it, isn't really a part, at first, anyway, because at first it isn't yet integrated into the organism. Reply: think of 'part' here, as like 'part' in 'auto parts store.' Would you complain that the auto parts store is guilty of false advertising, on the grounds that none of those carburetors, spark plugs and piston rings they sell is actually part of an automobile?

What's required by the Replacement Argument, therefore, (or at any rate what's sufficient for it) is

> (Replacement) It is possible that: the cells in B are replaced by other cells and the originals instantly annihilated while I continue to exist; and the replacement time for B and those cells is shorter than the assimilation time.

Objections and Replies

(1) Doesn't a Star Trek scenario seem possible, one in which you are beamed up from the surface of a planet to an orbiting spacecraft, both you, and in this context more importantly, your body surviving the process? This objection is relevant to the Replacement Argument, however, only if in this scenario your body survives a process in which its matter is replaced by other matter, the original matter being annihilated. But that's not how the Star Trek scenario works: what happens instead is that the matter of which your body is composed is beamed up (perhaps after having been converted to energy), not annihilated. You might think of this case as one of disassembly (and perhaps conversion into energy) and then reassembly. Perhaps your body could survive this sort of treatment; what I claim it *can't* survive is the rapid replacement of the matter in question by other matter, the original matter being annihilated.

(2) I've been assuming that you and I are objects, substances; but that assumption may not be as innocent as it looks. Might I not be an *event*[12]— perhaps an event like a computer's running a certain program? We ordinarily think of an event as one or more objects $O_1 \ldots O_n$, exemplifying a property P or relation R, (where P or R may be complex in various ways and, may of course entail extension over time). Perhaps what I am is an event involving (consisting in) many material objects (organs, limbs, cells, etc.) standing in a complex relation. Then, although I wouldn't be a material object, I *would* be an event involving nothing but material objects—a material event, as we might call it; and why wouldn't that be enough to satisfy the materialist?

Further: suppose I were a material event: why couldn't that event persist through arbitrarily rapid replacement of the objects involved in it? Think of an event such as a battle; clearly there could be a battle in which the combatants were removed and replaced by other combatants with extremely great rapidity. Let's suppose the commanding officer has an unlimited number of troops at his command. He needs 1,000 combatants at any given time: eager to spread the risk, he decrees that each combatant will fight for just thirty seconds and then be instantly replaced by another combatant. (Imagine that technology has advanced to the point where the obvious technical problems can be dealt with.) The battle, we may suppose, begins on Monday morning and ends Tuesday night; this one

---

[12] Here I'm indebted to Richard Fumerton.

event, although no doubt including many subevents, lasts from Monday morning to Tuesday night—and this despite the constant and rapid replacement of the combatants. Although there are never more than 1000 troops in the field at any one time, several million are involved in the event, by virtue of those rapid replacements. Of course the replacement could be much faster; indeed, there is no logical limit on the rapidity of replacement of the combatants, the same event (i.e., the battle) persisting throughout. More generally:

> (a) For any duration d and event E and substances $S_1, S_2 \ldots S_n$ involved in E, if $S_1, S_2 \ldots S_n$ are replaced by substances $S_{n+1}, S_{n+2} \ldots S_{n+n}$ during d, then there is an event E^* that persists through d and is such that at the beginning of d, E^* involves $S_1, S_2 \ldots S_n$, and at the end of d does not involve $S_1, S_2 \ldots S_n$, but does involve $S_{n+1}, S_{n+2} \ldots S_{n+n}$.

So events have a certain modal flexibility along this dimension.[13] Now suppose I were an event. Why couldn't the event which I am persist through arbitrarily rapid replacement of the material objects involved in it? Is there any reason, intuitive or otherwise, to suppose not? Perhaps a material *substance* can't survive the arbitrarily rapid replacement of its parts; is there any reason to think a material *event* suffers from the same limitation?

(3) We can conveniently deal with objection (2) by considering it together with another. According to Peter van Inwagen, human beings are material objects; a material object, furthermore is either an elementary particle or a living being. Living beings comprise the usual suspects: organisms such as horses, flies, and oak trees, but also cells (neurons, for example), which may not rise to the lofty heights of being organisms, but are nonetheless living beings. It is *living* horses, flies etc., that are objects or substances. Indeed, 'living horse' is a pleonasm. On van Inwagen's view, there aren't any dead horses; a 'dead horse,' strictly speaking, is not really a thing at all and *a fortiori* not a horse; it is instead a mere heap or pile of organic matter. Once that horse has died, its remains (as we say in the case of human beings) are a mere assemblage of elementary particles related in a certain way; there is no entity or being there in addition to the particles. A living horse, on the other hand, is a thing, a substance, in its own right and has as parts only other living beings (cells, e.g.) and elementary particles. Strictly speaking, therefore, there isn't any such thing as a hand, or arm or leg or head; rather, in the place we think of as where the hand is, there are elementary particles and other living things (cells, e.g.) related in a certain way.

But by virtue of what is this horse a thing or a substance: under what conditions does an assemblage of elementary particles constitute a thing, i.e.,

---

[13] No doubt this flexibility results from a principle of compounding for events: given any two successive events e1 and e2 occurring at roughly the same place, there is another event e3 compounded of them, an event that has each of them as a subevent. Short of such metaphysical extravaganzas as mereological universalism, clearly there is no corresponding principle for material objects. I stand in the corner from t1 to t2; then I leave and you stand in the corner from t2 to t3; it doesn't follow that there is a material object that stands in the corner from t1 to t3 and has my body and your body as successive parts.

become *parts* of a *substance*? When those particles are involved in a certain complex event: a *life*. Elementary particles can stand in many relations and be involved in many kinds of events; among these many kinds of events are lives; and when elementary particles are involved in that sort of event, then they become parts of a substance. Further, the object, that living thing, exists when and only when the event which is its life exists or occurs. Still further (and here we may be taking leave of van Inwagen) the survival and identity conditions of the organism are determined by the survival and identity conditions of that event, that life. Consider an organism O and its life L(O). The idea is that O exists in just those possible worlds in which L(O) occurs; more precisely, O and L(O) are such that for any world W and time t, O exists in W at t if and only if L(O) exists at t in W. Hence

(b) Given an organism O and the event L(O) that constitutes its life, necessarily, O exists at a time t just if L(O) occurs at t.

(We can think of 'exists' as short for 'exists, did exist, or will exist'; similarly for 'occurs.')

This elegant position certainly has its attractions. It's not wholly clear, of course, that there *are* any elementary particles (perhaps all particles are composed of other particles so that it's composition all the way down, or perhaps what there really is, is 'atomless gunk' configured in various ways[14]); perhaps electrons, etc., aren't particles at all, but perturbances of fields; and it's a bit harsh to be told that there really aren't any such things as tables and chairs, automobiles and television sets. Nevertheless van Inwagen's view is attractive. Now suppose we add (b) to van Inwagen's view; the resulting position suggests an objection to the Replacement Argument (an objection that doesn't have van Inwagen's blessing). For (again) why couldn't the event which is my life persist through arbitrarily rapid replacement of the objects it involves? Is there any intuitive support for the thought that there is a lower limit on the rapidity of replacement through which this event could persist? If not, then even if I couldn't be a material substance, I could be a material event; no doubt the materialist would find this materialism enough.

We can respond to these two objections together. According to objection (2), I can sensibly think of myself as an event: presumably the event that constitutes my life. Now perhaps the objector's (a) is true; for any replacement, no matter how rapid, there will be an event of the sort (a) suggests. But of course nothing follows about the modal properties of any particular event. So suppose I am an event: nothing about my modal properties follows from or is even suggested by (a); and it is my modal properties that are at issue here. In particular, it doesn't follow that if I were my life, then I could have continued to exist (or occur) through the sort of rapid replacement envisaged in the Replacement Argument. Now turn to (3). Suppose for the moment we concede (b): we still have no reason to think my life, that particular event, the event which is in fact my life, could

---

[14] See Dean Zimmerman, op. cit., p. 510.

have survived those rapid replacements of the objects involved in it. No doubt for any such replacement event, there is an event of the sort suggested by (a); nothing follows with respect to the modal properties of the event which is in my life. In particular it doesn't follow that it could have persisted through the sort of rapid replacements we've been thinking about.

So (a) is really a red herring. But there is a more decisive response here. Objection (3) endorses (b), the claim that there is an event—my life—such that, necessarily, I exist just when it does. Objection (2) also (and trivially) entails (b); if I just *am* my life then, naturally enough, (b) is true. Fortunately, however, (b) is false. For (b) entails

(c) I and my life are such that necessarily, I exist just when it occurs,

and (as I'll now argue) (c) is false.

Why think (c) is false? First, it's far from clear just which properties events have essentially. Some think it essential to any event that it include just those objects that it does in fact include, and also that these objects exemplify just the properties and relations they do in fact exemplify. If that were true, an event involving an object O's having a certain property could not have occurred if O had not had that property. But that seems a bit strong; surely the Civil War, for example, (that very event) could have taken place even if a particular Confederate soldier had not trodden on a blade of grass he did in fact step on. Still, there are serious limits here. Perhaps the Civil War (the event which is the Civil War) would have existed even if that soldier hadn't trampled that blade of grass; but the Civil War (that event) could not have lasted only ten minutes. There is a possible world in which there is a very short war between the states (and it could even be called 'The Civil War'); but there is no possible world in which the war that did in fact take place occurs, and lasts for only ten minutes. Similarly for my life (call it 'L'): if (b) is true, then of course L has existed exactly as long as I have. L, therefore, has by now existed for more than seventy years. Clearly enough, however, *I* could have existed for a much shorter time: for example, I could have been run over by a Mack truck at the age of six months (and not been subsequently sustained in existence by God). L, however, could not have existed or occurred for only those first few months, just as the Civil War could not have existed or occurred for only ten minutes. There is a possible world in which I exist for just those first few months, or even for just a few minutes; there is no possible world in which L exists for that period of time. Of course, if I had existed for, say, just ten minutes, there *would have been* an event which would have been my life, and which would have existed for just ten minutes; that event, however, would not have been L. We can put it like this: in any world in which I exist, there is an event which is my life; but it is not the case that there is an event which is my life, and which is my life in every world in which I exist.

(c), therefore, is false; it is not the case that I and the life of my body are such that necessarily, we exist at all the same times—that is, it is not the case that I and the life of my body are such that I have essentially the property of existing when and only when it does. But if (c) is false, the same goes for (b); since objections (2) and (3) both entail (b), both objections fail.

(4) If, as I say is possible, the replacement time for B and those parts is shorter than the assimilation time, there will be a brief period during which I don't have a body at all.[15] I will no longer have B, because all of B's parts have been replaced (and destroyed) during a time too brief for the new parts to be assimilated into B. I won't have any other body either, however; I won't have a body distinct from B, because there hasn't been time for these new parts to coalesce into a body. I therefore have no body at all during this time; there is no body that is *my* body at this time. How, then, can I continue to be conscious during this time, serenely reading the comics? Isn't it necessary that there be neurological activity supporting my consciousness during this time, if I am to be conscious then?

But is it *logically* necessary that there be neurological or other physical activity supporting my consciousness at any time at which I am conscious? That's a whopping assumption. The most I need for my argument is that it is *logically possible* that I remain conscious during a brief period in which no neurological activity is supporting my consciousness; that's compatible with its being causally required that there be neurological activity when I am conscious. My entire argument has to do with what *could* happen; not with what *would* as a matter of fact happen, if this sort of replacement were to occur.[16] So the most that argument needs is that possibly, I exist and am conscious when no neurological activity is supporting my consciousness.[17] But the fact is it doesn't require even that. For consider a time t after the end of the replacement time but before the assimilation time has ended; let t be as close as you please to the end of the replacement time. At t, the replacing elements, the new parts, haven't yet had time to coalesce into a body. Nonetheless, any one of the new elements could be performing one of the several functions it will be performing when it has been integrated into a functioning human body. It could be playing part of the whole causal role it will be playing when the assimilation time has elapsed. In particular, therefore, the new neurons, before they have become part of a body, could be doing whatever it is they have to do in order to support consciousness. Accordingly, my argument requires that possibly I am conscious when I do not have a

[15] Here I am indebted to Nicholas Wolterstorff.

[16] And hence strictly speaking, the argument doesn't require a thought experiment; it requires instead seeing that a certain state of affairs or proposition is possible. See George Bealer, 'Intuition and the Autonomy of Philosophy' in *Rethinking Intuition*, ed. Michael DePaul and William Ramsey (New York: Rowman and Littlefield, 1998), p. 207.

[17] Not strictly relevant, but of interest: could I perhaps be a *computer* (hardware), a computer made of flesh and blood? There are three possibilities here: I might be the hardware, I might be the program, and I might be the mereological sum of the hardware and the program. The first suggestion is vulnerable to the macroscopic Replacement Argument; on the other two, I would not be a material object. So no help for materialism there.

body; it does not require that possibly I am conscious when no neuronal or neurological activity is occurring.

II. CAN A MATERIAL THING THINK? AN ARGUMENT FROM IMPOSSIBILITY

The Replacement Argument is an argument from possibility; as such, it proceeds from an intuition, the intuition that it is possible that my bodily parts, macroscopic or microscopic, be replaced while I remain conscious. But some people distrust modal intuitions. Of course it's impossible to do philosophy (or for that matter physics) without invoking modal intuitions of one sort or another or at any rate making modal declarations of one sort or another.[18] Still, it must be conceded that intuition can sometimes be a bit of a frail reed. True, there is no way to conduct philosophy that isn't a frail reed, but intuition is certainly fallible. Further, some might think modal intuitions particularly fallible—although almost all of the intuitions involved in philosophy have important modal connections. Still further, one might think further that intuitions of *possibility* are especially suspect.[19] That is because it seems easy to confuse *seeing the possibility of p* with *failing to see the impossibility of p*. You can't see why numbers couldn't be sets; it doesn't follow that what you see is that they *could* be sets. Maybe I can't see why water couldn't be composed of something other than H_2O; it doesn't follow that what I see is that water could be something other than H_2O. And perhaps, so the claim might go, one who finds the replacement argument attractive is really confusing seeing the possibility of the replacements in question with failing to see their impossibility. Granted: I can't see that these replacements are impossible; it doesn't follow that what I see is that they are indeed possible.

To be aware of this possible source of error, however, is to be forewarned and thus forearmed. But for those who aren't mollified and continue to distrust possibility intuitions, I have another argument for dualism—one that depends

---

[18] Realists will say that there can't be similarity without a property had by the similar things, thus resting on an alleged intuition of impossibility; nominalists will deny this claim, thus resting on an alleged intuition of possibility. In his argument for indeterminacy of translation, Quine claims that the native's behavior is consistent with his meaning 'rabbit state' or 'undetached rabbit part' or 'rabbit' by 'gavagai,' thus (despite his animadversions) relying on an intuition of possibility. Similarly for his and others' claims about the underdetermination of theory by evidence. Further, anyone who proposes an analysis (of knowledge, for example) relies on intuition, as does someone who objects to such an analysis (by proposing a Gettier case, for example). In philosophy of mind we have Jackson's Mary example, Burge's arthritis example, twin earth arguments for *a posteriori* necessities and wide content, refutations of phenomenalism and behaviorism, and much else besides, all of which rely centrally and crucially on modal intuition. Most arguments for materialism rely on modal intuition (for example the intuition that an immaterial thing can't cause effects in the hard, heavy, massive material world). Indeed, take your favorite argument for any philosophical position: it will doubtless rely on modal intuition.

[19] See below, pp. 412.

on an intuition, not, this time, of possibility, but of impossibility. One who distrusts possibility intuitions may think more kindly of intuitions of impossibility—perhaps because she thinks that for the latter there isn't any obvious analogue of the possible confusion between failing to see that something is impossible with seeing that it is possible. Or rather, while there is an analogue—it would be confusing failure to see the possibility of p with seeing the impossibility of p—falling into that confusion seems less likely. In any event, the argument I'll now propose is for the conclusion that no material objects can think—i.e., reason and believe, entertain propositions, draw inferences, and the like. But of course I can think; therefore I am not a material object.

A. Leibniz's Problem

I (and the same goes for you) am a certain kind of thing: a thing that can think. I believe many things; I also hope, fear, expect, anticipate many things. I desire certain states of affairs (desire that certain states of affairs be actual). I am capable of making decisions. I am capable of acting, and capable of acting on the basis of my beliefs and desires. I am conscious; and conscious of a rich, kaleidoscopic constellation of feeling, mental images, beliefs, and ways of being appeared to, some of which I enjoy and some of which I dislike. Naturally enough, therefore, I am not identical with any object that lacks any or all of these properties. What I propose to argue next is that some of these properties are such that no material object can have them. Again, others have offered similar arguments. In particular, many have seen a real problem for materialism in *consciousness:* it is extremely difficult to see how a material object could be conscious, could enjoy that vivid and varied constellation of feelings, mental images and ways of being appeared to. Others have argued that a material object can't make a decision (although of course we properly speak, in the loose and popular sense, of the chess playing computer as deciding which move to make next). These arguments seem to me to be cogent.[20] Here, however, I want to develop another argument of the same sort, another problem for materialism, a problem I believe is equally debilitating, and in fact fatal to materialism. Again, this problem is not a recent invention; you can find it or something like it in Plato. Leibniz, however, offers a famous and particularly forceful statement of it:

17. It must be confessed, moreover, that *perception,* and that which depends on it, *are inexplicable by mechanical causes,* that is by figures and motions. And supposing there were a machine so constructed as to think, feel and have perception, we could conceive of it as enlarged and yet preserving the same proportions, so that we might enter it as into a mill. And this granted, we should only find on visiting it, pieces which push one against

---

[20] There is also the complex but powerful argument offered by Dean Zimmerman, op. cit., pp. 517ff.

another, but never anything by which to explain a perception. This must be sought for, therefore, in the simple substance and not in the composite or in the machine.[21]

Now Leibniz uses the word 'perception' here; he's really thinking of mental life generally. His point, in this passage, is that mental life—perception, thought, decision—cannot arise by way of the mechanical interaction of parts. Consider a bicycle; like Leibniz's mill, it does what it does by virtue of the mechanical interaction of its parts. Stepping down on the pedals causes the front sprocket to turn, which causes the chain to move, which causes the rear sprocket to turn, which causes the back wheel to rotate. By virtue of these mechanical interactions, the bicycle does what it does, i.e., transports someone from one place to another. And of course machines generally—jet aircraft, refrigerators, computers, centrifuges—do their things and accomplish their functions in the same way. So Leibniz's claim, here, is that thinking can't arise in this way. A thing can't think by virtue of the mechanical interaction of its parts.

Leibniz is thinking of *mechanical* interactions—interactions involving pushes and pulls, gears and pulleys, chains and sprockets. But I think he would say the same of other interactions studied in physics, for example those involving gravity, electromagnetism, and the strong and weak nuclear forces. Call these 'physical interactions.' Leibniz's claim is that thinking can't arise by virtue of physical interaction among objects or parts of objects. According to current science, electrons and quarks are simple, without parts.[22] Presumably neither can think—neither can adopt propositional attitudes; neither can believe, doubt, hope, want, or fear. But then a proton composed of quarks won't be able to think either, at least by way of physical relations between its component quarks, and the same will go for an atom composed of protons and electrons, a molecule composed of atoms, a cell composed of molecules, and an organ (e.g., a brain), composed of cells. If electrons and quarks can't think, we won't find anything composed of them that *can* think by way of the physical interaction of its parts.

Leibniz is talking about thinking generally; suppose we narrow our focus to *belief* (although the same considerations apply to other propositional attitudes). What, first of all, would a belief *be*, from a materialist perspective? Suppose you are a materialist, and also think, as we ordinarily do, that there are such things as beliefs. For example, you hold the belief that Marcel Proust is more subtle than Louis L'Amour. What kind of a thing is this belief? Well, from a materialist perspective, it looks as if it would have to be something like a long-standing event or structure in your brain or nervous system. Presumably this event will involve many neurons related to each other in subtle and complex ways. There are plenty of neurons to go around: a normal human brain contains some 100 billion. These neurons, furthermore, are connected with other neurons at synapses;

---

[21] *Monadology* 17. In *Leibniz Selections*, ed. Philip Weiner (New York: Charles Scribner's Sons, 1951), p. 536.

[22] Although there are speculative suggestions that quarks may in fact be composed of strings.

a single neuron can be involved in several thousand synapses, and there are some 10^{15} synaptic connections. The total number of possible brain states, then, is absolutely enormous, vastly greater than the 10^{80} electrons they say the universe contains. And the total number of possible neuronal events, while no doubt vastly smaller, is still enormous. Under certain conditions, groups of neurons involved in such an event fire, producing electrical impulses that can be transmitted (with appropriate modification and input from other structures) down the cables of neurons that constitute effector nerves to muscles or glands, causing, e.g., muscular contraction and thus behavior.

From the materialist's point of view, therefore, a belief will be a neuronal event or structure of this sort. But if this is what beliefs are, they will have two very different sorts of properties. On the one hand there will be *electrochemical* or *neurophysiological* properties ('NP properties,' for short). Among these would be such properties as that of involving *n* neurons and n^* connections between neurons, properties that specify which neurons are connected with which others, what the rates of fire in the various parts of the event are, how these rates of fire change in response to changes in input, and so on. But if the event in question is really a *belief*, then in addition to those NP properties it will have another property as well: it will have to have a *content*. It will have to be the belief that *p*, for some proposition *p*. If this event is the belief that Proust is a more subtle writer than Louis L'Amour, then its content is the proposition *Proust is more subtle than Louis L'Amour*. My belief that naturalism is all the rage these days has as content the proposition *Naturalism is all the rage these days*. (That same proposition is the content of the German speaker's belief that naturalism is all the rage these days, even though she expresses this belief by uttering the German sentence 'Der Naturalismus ist dieser Tage ganz gross in Mode'; beliefs, unlike sentences, do not come in different languages.) It is in virtue of having a content, of course, that a belief is true or false: it is true if the proposition which is its content is true, and false otherwise. My belief that all men are mortal is true because the proposition which constitutes its content is true, but Hitler's belief that the Third Reich would last a thousand years was false, because the proposition that constituted its content was false.[23]

And now the difficulty for materialism is this: how does it happen, how can it be, that an assemblage of neurons, a group of material objects firing away *has a content*? How can that happen? More poignantly, *what is it* for such an event to have a content? What is it for this structured group of neurons, or the event of

---

[23] I've been assuming that there really are such things as beliefs. A materialist might demur, taking a leaf from those who accept 'adverbial' accounts of sensation, according to which there aren't any red sensations or red sense data or red appearances: what there are instead are cases of someone's sensing redly or being appeared to redly. Similarly, the materialist might claim that there isn't any such thing as the belief that all men are mortal (or any other beliefs); what there is instead are cases of people who believe in the all-men-are-mortal way. This may or may not make sense; if it does make sense, however, a person will presumably believe in the all-men-are-mortal way only if she harbors a neuronal structure or event that has as content the proposition all men are mortal.

which they are a part, to be related, for example, to the proposition *Cleveland is a beautiful city* in such a way that the latter is its content? A single neuron (or quark, electron, atom or whatever) presumably isn't a belief and doesn't have content; but how can belief, content, arise from physical interaction among such material entities as neurons? As Leibniz suggests, we can examine this neuronal event as carefully as we please; we can measure the number of neurons it contains, their connections, their rates of fire, the strength of the electrical impulses involved, the potential across the synapses—we can measure all this with as much precision as you could possibly desire; we can consider its electro-chemical, neurophysiological properties in the most exquisite detail; but nowhere, here, will we find so much as a hint of content. Indeed, none of this seems even vaguely *relevant* to its having content. None of this so much as slyly suggests that this bunch of neurons firing away is the belief that Proust is more subtle than Louis L'Amour, as opposed, e.g., to the belief that Louis L'Amour is the most widely published author from Jamestown, North Dakota. Indeed, nothing we find here will so much as slyly suggest that it has a content of *any* sort. Nothing here will so much as slyly suggest that it is *about* something, in the way a belief about horses is about horses.

The fact is, we can't see how it *could* have a content. It's not just that we don't know or can't see how it's done. When light strikes photoreceptor cells in the retina, there is an enormously complex cascade of electrical activity, resulting in an electrical signal to the brain. I have no idea how all that works; but of course I know it happens all the time. But the case under consideration is different. Here it's not merely that I don't know how physical interaction among neurons brings it about that an assemblage of them has content and is a belief. No, in this case, it seems upon reflection that such an event could *not* have content. It's a little like trying to understand what it would be for the number seven, e.g., to weigh five pounds, or for an elephant (or the unit set of an elephant) to be a proposition. (*Pace* the late (and great) David Lewis, according to whom the unit set of an elephant *could* be a proposition; in fact, on his view, there are uncountably many elephants the unit sets of which *are* propositions.) We can't see how that could happen; more exactly, what we can see is that it *couldn't* happen. A number just isn't the sort of thing that can have weight; there is no way in which that number or any other number could weigh anything at all. The unit set of an elephant, let alone the elephant itself, can't be a proposition; it's not the right sort of thing. Similarly, we can see, I think, that physical activity among neurons can't constitute content. There they are, those neurons, clicking away, sending electrical impulses hither and yon. But what has this to do with content? How is content or aboutness supposed to arise from this neuronal activity? How can such a thing possibly be a belief? But then no neuronal event can as such have a content, can be *about* something, in the way in which my belief that the number seven is prime is about the number seven, or my belief that the oak tree in my backyard is without leaves is about that oak tree.

Here we must be very clear about an important distinction. Clearly there is such a thing as *indication* or *indicator meaning*.[24] Deer tracks in my backyard indicate that deer have run through it; smoke indicates fire; the height of the mercury column indicates the ambient temperature; buds on the trees indicate the coming of spring. We could speak here of 'natural signs': smoke is a natural sign of fire and the height of the mercury column is a natural sign of the temperature. When one event indicates or is a natural sign of another, there is ordinarily some sort of causal or nomic connection, or at least regular association, between them by virtue of which the first is reliably correlated with the second. Smoke is caused by fire, which is why it indicates fire; measles cause red spots on your face, which is why red spots on your face indicate measles; there is a causal connection between the height of the mercury column and the temperature, so that the latter indicates the former.

The nervous systems of organisms contain such indicators. A widely discussed example: when a frog sees a fly zooming by, the frog's brain (so it is thought) displays a certain pattern of neural firing; we could call such patterns 'fly detectors.' Another famous example: some anaerobic marine bacteria have magnetosomes, tiny internal magnets. These function like compass needles, indicating magnetic north. The direction to magnetic north is downward; hence these bacteria, which can't flourish in the oxygen-rich surface water, move towards the more oxygen-free water at the bottom of the ocean.[25] Of course there are also indicators in human bodies. There are structures that respond in a regular way to blood temperature; they are part of a complex feedback system that maintains a more or less constant blood temperature by inducing (e.g.) shivering if the temperature is too low and sweating if it is too high. There are structures that monitor the amount of sugar in the blood and its sodium content. There are structures that respond in a regular way to light of a certain pattern striking the retina, to the amount of food in your stomach, to its progress through your digestive system, and so on. Presumably there are structures in the brain that are correlated with features of the environment; it is widely assumed that when you see a tree, there is a distinctive pattern of neural firing (or some other kind of structure) in your brain that is correlated with and caused by it.

Now we can, if we like, speak of 'content' here; it's a free country. We can say that the mercury column, on a given occasion, has a certain content: the state of affairs correlated with its having the height it has on that occasion. We could say, if we like, that those structures in the body that indicate blood pressure or temperature or saline content have a content on a given occasion: whatever it is

---

[24] See Fred Dretske's *Explaining Behavior* (Cambridge, MA: MIT Press, 1988), pp. 54ff. See also Bill Ramsey's *Using and Abusing Representation: Reassessing the Cognitive Revolution* (presently unpublished). Materialists who try to explain how a material structure like a neuronal event can be a belief ordinarily try to do so by promoting indicators to beliefs; for animadversions on such attempts, see the appendix in my 'Materialism and Christian Belief.'

[25] Dretske, op. cit., p. 63.

that the structure indicates on that occasion. We could say, if we like, that the neural structure that is correlated with my looking at a tree has a content: its content, we could say, is what it indicates on that occasion. We can also, if we like, speak of information in these cases: the structure that registers my blood temperature, we can say, carries the information that my blood temperature is thus and so.

What is crucially important to see, however, is that this sort of content or information has nothing as such to do with *belief*, or belief content. There are those who—no doubt in the pursuit of greater generality—gloss over this distinction. Donald T. Campbell, for example, in arguing for the relevance of natural selection to epistemology, claims that 'evolution—even in its biological aspects—is a knowledge process.'[26] Commenting on Cambell's claim, Franz Wuketits explains that

> The claim is based on the idea that any living system is a 'knowledge-gaining system.' This means that organisms accumulate information about certain properties of their environment. Hence life generally may be described as an information process, or, to put it more precisely, an information-increasing process.[27]

At any rate Wuketits has the grace to put 'knowledge' in scare quotes here. Knowledge requires belief; correlation, causal or otherwise, is not belief; information and content of this sort do not require belief. Neither the thermostat nor any of its components believes that the room temperature is thus and so. When the saline content of my blood is too low, neither I nor the structure correlated with that state of affairs (nor my blood) believes the saline content is less than it should be—or, indeed, anything else about the saline content. Indication, carrying information, is not belief; indicator content is not belief content, and these structures don't have belief content just by virtue of having indicator content. And now the point here: I am not, of course, claiming that material structures can't have indicator content; obviously they can. What I am claiming is that they can't have belief content: no material structure can be a belief.

Here someone might object as follows. 'You say we can't see how a neural event can have content; but in fact we understand this perfectly well, and something similar happens all the time. For there is, after all, the computer analogy. A computer, of course, is a material object, an assemblage of wires, switches, relays, and the like. Now suppose I am typing in a document. Take any particular sentence in the document: say the sentence 'Naturalism is all the rage these days.' That sentence is represented and stored on the computer's hard disk. We don't have to know in exactly what *way* it's stored (it's plusses and minuses, or a magnetic configuration, or something else; it doesn't matter). Now the sentence

[26] 'Evolutionary Epistemology' in *The Philosophy of Karl Popper*, ed. P. A. Schilpp (LaSalle, IL: Open Court, 1974), p. 413.
[27] 'Evolutionary Epistemology' in *Biology and Philosophy*, vol. 1, No. 2 (1986), p. 193.

'Naturalism is all the rage these days' *expresses* the proposition *Naturalism is all the rage these days*. That sentence, therefore, has the proposition *Naturalism is all the rage these days* as its content. But then consider the analogue of that sentence on the computer disk: doesn't it, too, express the same proposition as the sentence it represents? That bit of the computer disk with its plusses and minuses, therefore, has propositional content. But of course that bit of the computer disk is also (part of) a material object (as is any inscription of the sentence in question). Contrary to your claim, therefore, a material object can perfectly well have propositional content; indeed, it happens all the time. But if a computer disk or an inscription of a sentence can have a proposition as content, why can't an assemblage of neurons? Just as a magnetic pattern has as content the proposition *Naturalism is all the rage these days*, so too a pattern of neuronal firing can have that proposition as content. Your claim to the contrary is completely bogus and you should be ashamed of yourself.' Thus far the objector.

If the sentence or the computer disk really *did* have content, then I guess the assemblage of neurons could too. But the fact is neither does—or rather, neither has the right kind of content: neither has *original* content; each has, at most, *derived* content. For how does it happen that the sentence has content? It's simply by virtue of the fact that we human beings *treat* that sentence in a certain way, *use* the sentence in a certain way, a way such that if a sentence is used in that way, then it expresses the proposition in question. Upon hearing that sentence, I think of, grasp, apprehend the proposition *Naturalism is all the rage these days*. You can get me to grasp, entertain, and perhaps believe that proposition by uttering that sentence. How exactly all this works is complicated and not at all well understood; but the point is that the sentence has content only because of something *we*, we who are *already* thinkers, do with it. We could put this by saying that the sentence has *secondary* or *derived* content; it has content only because we, we creatures whose thoughts and beliefs already have content, treat it in a certain way. The same goes for the magnetic pattern on the computer disk; it represents or expresses that proposition because we assign that proposition to that configuration. But of course that isn't how it goes (given materialism) with that pattern of neural firing. That pattern doesn't get its content by way of being used in a certain way by some other creatures whose thoughts and beliefs already have content. If that pattern has content at all, then, according to materialism, it must have *original* or *primary* content. And what it is hard or impossible to see is how it could be that an assemblage of neurons (or a sentence, or a computer disk) could have original or primary content. To repeat: it isn't just that we can't see how it's done, in the way in which we can't see how the sleight of hand artist gets the pea to wind up under the middle shell. It is rather that we can see, to at least some degree, that it can't be done, just as we can see that an elephant can't be a proposition, and that the number 7 can't weigh seven pounds.

B. Parity?

Peter van Inwagen agrees that it is hard indeed to see how physical interaction among material entities can produce thought: 'it seems to me that the notion of a physical thing that thinks is a mysterious notion, and that Leibniz's thought-experiment brings out this mystery very effectively.'[28]

Now I am taking this fact as a reason to reject materialism and hence as an argument for dualism. But of course it is a successful argument only if there is no similar difficulty for substance dualism itself. Van Inwagen believes there *is* a similar difficulty for dualism:

> For it is thinking itself that is the source of the mystery of a thinking physical thing. The notion of a non-physical thing that thinks is, I would argue, equally mysterious. How any sort of thing could think is a mystery. It is just that it is a bit easier to see that thinking is a mystery when we suppose that the thing that does the thinking is physical, for we can form mental images of the operations of a physical thing and we can see that the physical interactions represented in these images—the only interactions that can be represented in these images—have no connection with thought or sensation, or none we are able to imagine, conceive or articulate. The only reason we do not readily find the notion of a non-physical thing that thinks equally mysterious is that we have no clear procedure for forming mental images of non-physical things. (loc. cit.)

So dualism is no better off than materialism; they both have the same problem. But what precisely *is* this problem, according to van Inwagen? '[W]e can form mental images of the operations of a physical thing and we can see that the physical interactions represented in these images—the only interactions that can be represented in these images—have no connection with thought or sensation or none we are able to imagine, conceive or articulate.' As I understand van Inwagen here, he is saying that we can imagine physical interactions or changes in a physical thing; but we can see that the physical interactions represented in those images have no connection with thought. We can imagine neurons in the brain firing; we can imagine electrical impulses or perhaps clouds of electrons moving through parts of neurons, or whole chains of neurons; we can imagine neural structures with rates of fire in certain parts of the structure changing in response to rates of fire elsewhere in or out of that structure: but we can see that these interactions have no connection with thought. Now I'm not quite sure whether or not I can imagine electrons, or their movements, or electrical impulses; but it does seem to me that I can see that electrical impulses and the motions of electrons, if indeed there are any such things, have nothing to do with thought.

Another way to put van Inwagen's point: no change we can imagine in a physical thing could be a mental change, i.e., could constitute thought or sensation, or a change in thought or sensation. But then we can't imagine a physical thing's thinking: i. e., we can't form a mental image of a physical thing

[28] *Metaphysics* (Boulder, Colorado, 2002 (second edition)), p. 176.

thinking. And this suggests that the problem for materialism is that we can't form a mental image of a material thing thinking. But the same goes, says van Inwagen, for an immaterial thing: we also can't imagine or form a mental image of an immaterial thing thinking. Indeed, we can't form a mental image of any kind of thinking thing: 'My point,' he says, 'is that nothing could possibly count as a mental image of a thinking thing' (177). Materialism and dualism, therefore, are so far on a par; there is nothing here to incline us to the latter rather than the former.

Thus far van Inwagen. The thought of a physical thing's thinking, he concedes, is mysterious; that is because we can't form a mental image of a physical thing's thinking. But the thought of an immaterial thing's thinking is equally mysterious; for we can't form a mental image of that either. This, however, seems to me to mislocate the problem for materialism. What inclines us to reject the idea of a physical thing's thinking is not just the fact that we can't form a mental image of a physical thing's thinking. There are plenty of things of which we can't form a mental image, where we're not in the least inclined to reject them as impossible. As Descartes pointed out, I can't form a mental image of a chiliagon, a 1000-sided rectilinear plane figure (or at least an image that distinguishes it from a 100-sided rectilinear plane figure); that doesn't even suggest that there can't be any such thing. I can't form a mental image of the number 79's being prime: that doesn't incline me to believe that the number 79 could not be prime; as a matter of fact I know how to prove that it *is* prime. The fact is I can't form a mental image of the number 79 at all—or for that matter of any number; this doesn't incline me to think there aren't any numbers.

Or is all that a mistake? Is it really true that I can't form a mental image of the number 7, for example? Maybe I *can* form an image of the number 7; when I think of the number seven, sometimes there is a mental image present; it's as if one catches a quick glimpse of a sort of partial and fragmented numeral 7; we could say that I'm appeared to numeral-7ly. When I think of the actual world, I am sometimes presented with an image of the Greek letter alpha; when I think of the proposition *All men are mortal* I am sometimes presented with a sort of fleeting, fragmentary, partial image of the corresponding English sentence. Sets are nonphysical, but maybe I can imagine the pair set of Mic and Martha; when I try, it's like I catch a fleeting glimpse of curly brackets, enclosing indistinct images that don't look a whole lot like Mic and Martha. But is that really imagining the number 7, or the actual world, or the pair set of Mic and Martha? Here I'm of two minds. On the one hand, I'm inclined to think that this isn't imagining the number 7 at all, but instead imagining something connected with it, namely the numeral 7 (and the same for the actual world and the set of Mic and Martha). On the other hand I'm a bit favorably disposed to the idea that that's just how you imagine something like the number 7; you do it by imagining the numeral 7. (Just as you state a proposition by uttering a sentence or uttering certain sounds.) So I don't really know what to say. Can I or can't I imagine nonphysical things like numbers, propositions, possible worlds, angels, God? I'm not sure.

What is clear, here, is this: if imagining the numeral 7 is sufficient for imagining the number 7, then imagining, forming mental images of, has nothing to do with possibility. For in this same way I can easily imagine impossibilities. I can imagine the proposition *all men are mortal* being red: first I just imagine the proposition, e.g., by forming a mental image of the sentence 'All men are mortal,' and then I imagine this sentence as red. I think I can even imagine that elephant's being a proposition. David Kaplan once claimed he could imagine his refuting Gödel's Incompleteness Theorem: he imagined the *Los Angeles Times* carrying huge headlines: 'UCLA PROF REFUTES GÖDEL; ALL REPUTABLE EXPERTS AGREE.' In this loose sense, most anything can be imagined; but then the loose sense has little to do with what is or isn't possible. So really neither the loose nor the strong sense of 'imagining' (neither the weak nor the strong version of imagination) has much to do with possibility. There are many clearly possible things one can't imagine in the strong sense; in the weak sense, one can imagine many things that are clearly impossible.

What is it, then, that inclines me to think a proposition can't be red, or a horse, or an even number? The answer, I think, is that one can just see upon reflection that these things are impossible. I can't form a mental image of a proposition's having members; but that's not why I think no proposition has members; I also can't form a mental image of a set's having members. It's rather that one sees that a set is the sort of thing that (null set aside) has members, and a proposition is the sort of thing that cannot have members. It is the same with a physical thing's thinking. True, one can't imagine it. The reason for rejecting the idea, thinking it impossible, however, is not that one can't imagine it. It's rather that on reflection one can see that a physical object just can't do that sort of thing. I grant that this isn't as clear and obvious, perhaps, as that a proposition can't be red; some impossibilities (necessities) are more clearly impossible (necessary) than others. But one can see it to at least a significant degree. Indeed, van Inwagen might be inclined to endorse this thought; elsewhere he says: 'Leibniz's thought experiment shows that when we carefully examine the idea of a material thing having sensuous properties, it seems to be an impossible idea.'[29] But (and here is the important point) the same clearly doesn't go for an immaterial thing's thinking; we certainly can't see that no immaterial thing can think. (If we could, we'd have a quick and easy argument against the existence of God: no immaterial thing can think; if there were such a person as God, he would be both immaterial and a thinker; therefore. . . .)

[29] 'Dualism and Materialism: Athens and Jerusalem?', *Faith and Philosophy* 12:4, Oct. 1995, p. 478. That is (I take it), it seems to be necessary that material things don't have such properties. Van Inwagen's examples are such properties as *being in pain* and *sensing redly*; the same goes, I say, for properties like *being the belief that p* for a proposition p.

Van Inwagen has a second suggestion:

In general, to attempt to explain how an underlying reality generates some phenomenon is to construct a representation of the working of that underlying reality, a representation that in some sense 'shows how' the underlying reality generates the phenomenon. Essentially the same considerations as those that show that we are unable to form a mental image that displays the generation of thought and sensation by the workings of some underlying reality (whether the underlying reality involves one thing or many, and whether the things it involves are physical or non-physical) show that we are unable to form any sort of representation that displays the generation of thought and sensation by the workings of an underlying reality. (*Metaphysics*, pp. 177–78)

The suggestion is that we can't form an image or any other representation displaying the generation of thought by way of the workings of an underlying reality; hence we can't see how it can be generated by physical interaction among material objects such as neurons. This much seems right—at any rate we certainly can't see how thought could be generated in that way. Van Inwagen goes on to say, however, that this doesn't favor dualism over materialism, because we also can't see how thought can be generated by the workings of an underlying *non*-physical reality. And perhaps this last is also right. But here there is an important dissimilarity between dualism and materialism. The materialist thinks of thought as generated by the workings of an underlying reality—i.e., by the physical interaction of such physical things as neurons; the dualist, however, typically thinks of an immaterial self, a soul, a thing that thinks, as *simple*. An immaterial self doesn't have any parts; hence, of course, thought isn't generated by the interaction of its parts. Say that a property P is *basic* to a thing x if x has P, but x's having P is not generated by the interaction of its parts. Thought is then a basic property of selves, or better, a basic activity of selves. It's not that (for example) there are various underlying immaterial parts of a self whose interaction produces thought. Of course a self stands in causal relation to its body: retinal stimulation causes a certain sort of brain activity which (so we think) in turn somehow causes a certain kind of experience in the self. But there isn't any *way* in which the self produces a thought; it does so immediately. To ask 'How does a self produce thought?' is to ask an improper question. There isn't any how about it.

By way of analogy: consider the lowly electron. According to current science, electrons are simple, not composed of other things. Now an electron has basic properties, such as having a negative charge. But the question 'How does an electron manage to have a charge?' is an improper question. There's no how to it; it doesn't do something else that results in its having such a charge, and it doesn't have parts by virtue of whose interaction it has such a charge. Its having a negative charge is rather a basic and immediate property of the thing (if thing it is). The same is true of a self and thinking: it's not done by underlying activity or workings; it's a basic and immediate activity of the self. But then the important difference, here, between materialism and immaterialism is that if a material thing managed to think, it would have to be by way of the activity of its parts: and it seems upon reflection that this can't happen.[30] Not so for an immaterial self. Its activity of thinking is basic and immediate. And it's not the case that we are inclined upon reflection to think this can't happen—there's nothing at all against it, just as there is nothing against an electron's having a negative charge, not by virtue of the interaction of parts, but in that basic and immediate way. The fact of the matter then is that we can't see how a material object can think—that is, upon reflection it seems that a material object can't think. Again, not so for an immaterial self.

True, as van Inwagen says, thought can sometimes seem mysterious and wonderful, something at which to marvel. (Although from another point of view it is more familiar than hands and feet.) But there is nothing here to suggest that it can't be done. I find myself perceiving my computer; there is nothing at all, here, to suggest impossibility or paradox. Part of the mystery of thought is that it is wholly unlike what material objects can do: but of course that's not to suggest that it can't be done at all. Propositions are also mysterious and have wonderful properties: they manage to be about things; they are true or false; they can be believed; they stand in logical relations to each other. How do they manage to do those things? Well, certainly not by way of interaction among material parts. Sets manage, somehow, to have members—how do they do a thing like that? And why is it that a given set has just the members it has? How does the unit set of Lance Armstrong manage to have just *him* as a member? What mysterious force, or fence, keeps Leopold out of that set? Well, it's just the nature of sets to be like this. These properties can't be explained by way of physical interactions among material parts, but that's nothing at all against sets. Indeed, these properties can't be explained at all. Of course if you began with the idea that everything has to be a material object, then thought (and propositions and sets) would indeed be mysterious and paradoxical. But why begin with that idea? Thought is seriously mysterious, I think, only when we assume that it would have to be generated in some physical way, by physical interaction among physical objects. That is certainly mysterious; indeed it goes far beyond mystery, all the way to apparent impossibility. But that's not a problem for thought; it's a problem for materialism.

[30] But couldn't a material thing also just directly think, without depending on the interaction of its parts? According to Pierre Cabanis, 'The brain secretes thought as the liver secretes bile;' couldn't we think of this as the brain (or, if you like, the whole organism) directly thinking, not by way of the interaction of its parts? Well, if that's how a brain thinks, it isn't like the way a liver secretes bile; the latter certainly involves the liver's having parts, and those parts working together in the appropriate way. Further, the idea of a physical thing's thinking without the involvement of its parts is even more clearly impossible than that of a physical thing's thinking by virtue of the interaction of its parts. Aren't those neurons in the brain supposed to be what enables it to think? You might as well say that a tree or my left foot thinks. Consider any nonelementary physical object—a tree, an automobile, perhaps a horse: such a thing does what it does by virtue of the nature and interaction of its parts. Are we to suppose that some physical object—a brain, let's say—does something like thinking apart from involvement of its parts? Talk about appealing to magic!

III. ARGUMENTS FOR MATERIALISM

The above arguments for dualism and others like them are powerful. Like philosophical arguments generally, however, they are not of that wholly apodictic and irrefragable character Kant liked to claim for his arguments; they are defeasible. It is possible to disregard or downgrade the intuitions of possibility and impossibility to which they appeal. Further, if there were really powerful arguments *for* materialism—stronger than these arguments against it—then perhaps the appropriate course would be to embrace materialism. But are there any such powerful arguments?

No—or at least I've never seen any. There is the old chestnut according to which no immaterial object can cause changes in the hard, heavy, massive, massy (messy) physical world; there is the claim that dualism, or at least interactionistic dualism, violates the principle of Conservation of Energy; there is the charge that dualism is unscientific; there is the complaint that soul stuff is hard to understand; there is the canard that dualism is explanatorily impotent. None of these has any force at all.[31] However there is one that is perhaps not completely without promise. According to Nancey Murphy:

In particular, nearly all of the human capacities or faculties once attributed to the *soul* are now seen to be functions of the brain. Localization studies—that is, finding regional structures or distributed systems in the brain responsible for such things as language, emotion and decision making—provide especially strong motivation for saying that it is the brain that is responsible for these capacities, not some immaterial entity associated with the body. In Owen Flanagan's terms, it is the brain that is the *res cogitans*—the thinking thing.[32]

Localization studies show that when certain kinds of mental activity occur, certain parts of the brain display increased blood flow and increased electrical activity. Paul Churchland goes on to point out that mental activity is also in a certain important way *dependent* on brain activity and brain condition:

Alcohol, narcotics, or senile degeneration of nerve tissue will impair, cripple, or even destroy one's capacity for rational thought. Psychiatry knows of hundreds of emotion-controlling chemicals (lithium, chlorpromazine, amphetamine, cocaine, and so on) that do their work when vectored into the brain. And the vulnerability of consciousness to the anesthetics, to caffeine, and to something as simple as a sharp blow to the head, shows its very close dependence on neural activity in the brain. All of this makes perfect sense if reason, emotion and consciousness are activities of the brain itself. But it makes very little

---

[31] This may seem a bit abrupt; for substantiation, see my 'Materialism and Christian Belief,' (footnote 1).

[32] Brown, Murphy and Malony, *Whatever Happened to the Soul?* (Minneapolis: Fortress Press, 1998), p. 1.

sense if they are activities of something else. We may call this the argument from the *neural dependence* of all known mental phenomena.[33]

Of course it isn't true that it makes very little sense to say that activities of the immaterial self or soul are dependent in this way on the proper function of the brain; still, this argument from localization and neural dependence is perhaps the strongest of the arguments against dualism. That may not be much of a distinction; the other arguments, I believe, are without any force at all. But perhaps this argument has a little something to be said for it; at any rate dependence and localization phenomena do suggest the possibility that the brain is all there is. Taken as an argument, however, and looked at in the cold light of morning, it has little to be said for it. What we know, here, is that for at least many mental functions or actions M, there are parts of the brain B such that (1) when M occurs, there is increased blood flow and electrical activity in B, and (2) when B is damaged or destroyed, M is inhibited or altogether absent. Consider, therefore, the mental activity of adding a column of figures, and let's assume that there is a particular area of the brain related to this activity in the way suggested by (1) and (2). Does this show or tend to show that this mental activity is really an activity of the brain, rather than of something distinct from the brain?

Hardly. There are many activities that stand in that same or similar relation to the brain. Consider walking, or running, or speaking, or waving your arms or moving your fingers: for each of these activities too there is a part of your brain related to it in such a way that when you engage in that activity, there is increased blood flow in that part; and when that part is damaged or destroyed, paralysis results so that you can no longer engage in the activity. Who would conclude that these activities are really activities of the brain rather than of legs and trunk, or mouth and vocal cords, or arms? Who would conclude that your fingers' moving is really an activity of your brain and not of your fingers? Your fingers' moving is

---

[33] *Matter and Consciousness* (Cambridge: MIT Press, 1984), p 20. See also Thomas Nagel's 'The Psychophysical Nexus,' in *Concealment and Exposure and Other Essays* (New York: Oxford University Press, 2002); in the course of a long, detailed and subtle discussion, Thomas Nagel argues that there is a logically necessary connection between mental states and physical states of the following sort: for any mental state M there is a physical state P such that there is some underlying reality R, neither mental nor physical but capable of having both mental and physical states, which has essentially the property of being such that necessarily, it is in P just if it is in M. (And perhaps it would be sensible to go on from that claim to the conclusion that it is not possible that I exist when my body B does not.) Nagel concedes that it seems impossible that there be such a reality; his argument that nonetheless there really is or must be such a thing is, essentially, just an appeal to localization/dependency phenomena: 'The evident massive and detailed dependence of what happens in the mind on what happens in the brain provides, in my view, strong evidence that the relation is not contingent but necessary' (p 202), and 'The causal facts are strong evidence that mental events have physical properties, if only we could make sense of the idea' (p. 204). The particular route of his argument here is via an argument to the best explanation: he suggests that the only really satisfactory explanation of those localization/dependency phenomena is the existence of such an underlying reality. (Of course if *that* is what it takes for a really satisfying explanation, it is less than obvious that there *is* a really satisfying explanation here.)

This argument has also made its way into the popular press: See Steven Pinker's 'How to Think About the Mind,' *Newsweek* (Sept. 27, 2004), p. 78.

dependent on appropriate brain activity; it hardly follows that their moving just is an activity of your brain. Digestion will occur only if your brain is in the right condition; how does it follow that digestion is really an activity of the brain, and not an activity of the digestive system? Your brain's functioning properly depends on blood flow and on the proper performance of your lungs; shall we conclude that brain function is really circulatory or pulmonary activity? All of your activities depend upon your ingesting enough and the right kind of food; shall we see here vindication of the old saw 'you are what you eat'? The point, obviously, is that dependence is one thing, identity quite another. Appropriate brain activity is a necessary condition for mental activity; it simply doesn't follow that the latter just is the former. Nor, as far as I can see, is it even rendered probable. We know of all sorts of cases of activities A that depend upon activities B but are not identical with them. Why should we think differently in this case?

Perhaps a more promising way of developing this argument would go as follows. In science, it is common to propose *identities* of various kinds: water is identical with H_2O, heat and pressure with molecular motion, liquidity, solidity, gaseousness with certain properties of assemblages of molecules, and so on. This kind of identification, it might be argued, is theoretically useful in at least two ways; in some cases it provides explanations, answers to questions that are otherwise extremely difficult to answer, and in others finesses the questions by obviating the need for answers, showing instead that the question itself is bogus, or ill-formed, or has a wholly trivial answer. Well, why not the same here? Suppose we identify mental activity with brain activity; more precisely, suppose we identify such properties as *being in pain* and *being conscious* with such properties as *having C-fibers that are firing* and *displaying activity in the pyramidal cells of layer 5 of the cortex involving reverberatory circuits*.[34] Then first of all, we don't have to answer the otherwise difficult questions, 'Why is it that when someone is in pain, the C-fibers in her brain are firing?' Or 'Why is it that when someone is conscious, his brain is displaying activity in the pyramidal cells?' (Alternatively, they might have answers, but the answer would be pretty easy: 'Because being in pain *just is* having firing C-fibers and being conscious *just is* displaying pyramidal activity.') And second we will be able to answer some questions otherwise very difficult: for example, 'Why is it that rapping someone smartly over the head interferes with their ability to follow a proof of Gödel's Theorem?' This identification, therefore, is theoretically fruitful and hence justified by the principle of inference to the best explanation (B&S, pp. 24, 45). Still further, of course, if mental properties are really identical with and thus reduced to neurophysiological properties of the brain, then dualism will be false. So here we have another objection to dualism.

Now first, note the language involved here: the suggestion is that *we identify*, say, the property of being in pain with the property of having firing C-fibers.

---

[34] See Ned Block and Robert Stalnaker, 'Conceptual Analysis, Dualism, and the Explanatory Gap' (hereafter 'B&S'), *Philosophical Review*, Jan. 1999, p. 1

That makes it sound as if it's just up to us whether these properties are identical—we can just identify them, if we find that useful. But of course it isn't just up to us, and we can't really do any such thing. All we can do is declare, perhaps loudly and slowly, that these properties are identical; but saying so doesn't make it so (not even if your peers let you get away with so saying).

More important, what about the fact that these properties—*being in pain* and *having firing C-fibers*, for example, or *being conscious* and *displaying activity in the pyramidal cells* seem so utterly different? Pain and consciousness are immediately apprehended phenomenal properties; not so for firing C-fibers or active pyramidal cells. And as for that pyramidal activity, if that's what *being conscious* just is, then nothing, not even God, could be conscious but not have those pyramidal cells. So do we have here another shiny new argument for atheism, this time from neural science: God, if he exists, is conscious, but without a body; neuroscience shows that *being conscious* just is having active pyramidal cells; hence . . . ? On the face of it, these properties seem at least as different as *being chalk* and *being cheese*. In fact on the face of it they seem *more* different than the latter; at least any pair of things that exemplify *being chalk* and *being cheese* are clearly both material objects. How can *being in pain* be the same property as *having firing C-fibers* when it seems so utterly clear that someone could be in pain without having C-fibers that are firing, as well as have firing C-fibers without being in pain? Perhaps it's true that if these properties *were* identical, we would have answers to some otherwise difficult questions (and avoid some other questions): but isn't it obvious that the properties are *not* identical? Are not both

(1) Possibly, someone is in pain when no C-fibers are firing

and

(2) Possibly, C-fibers are firing when no one is in pain

wholly obvious?

Well, they certainly *look* obvious. Maybe identifying these properties would have a theoretical payoff; but the properties just don't seem to be identical. You might as well 'identify' Bill with his essence: concrete objects are so unruly and messy, after all. And why stop with Bill? Why not identify every concrete object with its essence, thus finessing all those annoying questions about the relation between concrete objects and abstract properties? There is a problem about how God knows future contingents: how does he know that tomorrow I will freely go for a bike ride? It hasn't happened yet, and since it will be a free action when it does happen, he can't deduce it from present conditions and causal laws. No problem, mates; just identify *truth* with the property *being believed by God*. How can we so blithely declare these properties identical when they look so different? How can we declare (1) and (2) false when they seem so obviously true?

Now here appeal will be made to Kripke and his celebrated thesis about necessary but *a posteriori* propositions. B&S and others suggest that the appearance of falsehood for (1) and (2) is like the appearance of contingency of such propositions as

    (3) Water is H_2O,

or

    (4) Gold has atomic number 79.

In these cases we have the appearance of contingency; but, so the claim goes, the appearance is shown by Kripkean considerations to be illusory. We initially think that these propositions are contingent; Kripke shows us that in fact they are necessary. As Sydney Shoemaker says in a similar context,

Kripke...argued that the class of truths deserving this label [i.e., the label of being necessary] is much larger than had traditionally been supposed. And, in his most radical departure from the traditional view, he held that many of these truths have the epistemic status of being a posteriori.[35]

Among these truths, of course, are (3) and (4). But then once we see that this is how it goes in the case of water and H_2O, and *being gold* and *having atomic number 79*, we can apply the lesson to neurophysiological and mental properties. Indeed, according to B&S,

The crucial question for the issue we have been discussing in this paper is whether a relevant contrast can be shown between the relation between water and H_2O on the one hand and the relation between consciousness and some brain process on the other (43).

But such a relevant contrast, I believe, can easily be shown. Suppose we look a bit more deeply into the relevant Kripkean considerations. Kripke's principal thesis here, of course, is that natural kind terms—'tiger,' 'water,' 'gold'—function as *rigid designators*; they are not, for example, as Frege or Russell thought, disguised or abbreviated definite descriptions.[36] While there is a certain amount of controversy about the notion of rigid designation, what is clear is that the thesis in question is a *semantical* thesis, a thesis about the meaning or function of certain terms. And that should put us on our guard. A semantical thesis about how certain terms work is not, just by itself, of direct relevance to the modal question which *propositions* are necessary or contingent; what it *is* relevant to, is the question which propositions get expressed by which *sentences*. *Pace* Shoemaker, a semantical thesis can't by itself show us that the class of necessary propositions is larger than we thought; what it *can* show us is that sentences we thought expressed contingent propositions really express necessary propositions.[37]

[35] 'Causal and Metaphysical Necessity,' *Pacific Philosophical Quarterly* 79 (1998), p. 59.
[36] Or if they are disguised descriptions, the descriptions they disguise express essences of their donotata.
[37] Not everyone is prepared to distinguish propositions from sentences. Those who do not make that distinction, however, will presumably be able to make an equivalent distinction by noting the difference between coming to see that a sentence is necessary in virtue of discovering that it doesn't mean what one thought it did, and coming to see that it is necessary without learning anything new about its meaning.

Accordingly, consider the *sentences*

(5) 'Water is H_2O'

and

(6) 'Gold has atomic number 79';

what Kripke shows us is that these sentences, contrary to what we perhaps originally thought, really express necessary rather than contingent propositions. But it wasn't that we were clear about which propositions were in fact expressed by those sentences, and Kripke got us to see that those propositions, contrary to what we thought, were necessary. It is rather that he corrected our ideas about which propositions are expressed by those sentences: we mistakenly thought (5) expressed a certain proposition P which we correctly thought to be contingent; in fact (5) expresses a different proposition Q, a proposition that appears to be necessary. We might have thought that 'water' is synonymous with something like 'the clear tasteless odorless stuff we find in lakes and streams,' in which case the sentence (5) expresses a proposition put more explicitly by

(7) The clear, tasteless odorless stuff found in lakes and streams is H_2O.

This is clearly contingent: it entails the contingent proposition that H_2O is found in lakes and streams. By way of a judicious selection of examples, however, Kripke gets us to see (if he's right) that the proposition expressed by (5) isn't (7) at all. What proposition does it express? That proposition can be put as follows.

(8) Consider the stuff actually to be found in the rivers and lakes: that stuff is H_2O.

That's the proposition expressed by (5). Alternatively, consider the stuff we do in fact find in lakes and rivers and name it 'XX'; then

(8) XX is H_2O.

(8) is at least arguably necessary:[38] it seems sensible to think that very stuff, i.e., H_2O, could not have failed to be H_2O. We are inclined to think, perhaps under the influence of mistaken views about the function of kind terms, that 'water' expresses such properties as *being clear, tasteless, odorless and filling the lakes and streams.* Kripke gets us to see that 'water' does not express those properties, which could be had by very many different substances, but is instead a rigid designator of the stuff that actually has those properties, i.e., as I would put it, expresses the (or an) essence of that stuff. The difference is between, on the one hand, the term's expressing the properties we use to fix its reference, and, on the other, the term's being a rigid designator (I'd say expressing the essence) of what it denotes when its reference is fixed in that way. By analogy, return to those thrilling days of yesteryear, when Quine asked us to consider such sentences as

[38] For the moment ignore the fact that it's contingent that there is any such thing as H_2O.

(9) Hesperus is identical with Venus.

This may look contingent: we might think 'Hesperus' expresses the property of being the evening star, i.e., of being the first heavenly body to appear in the evening. Surely it's not necessary that the first heavenly body to appear in the evening is Venus—any number of other heavenly bodies could have been (and I guess sometimes actually are) the first to appear in the evening. But what Kripke got us to see is that in fact 'Hesperus' does not express that property; it is instead a name or rigid designator (expresses an essence of) the thing that has that property, in which case (9), contrary to what we might have thought, does not express a contingent proposition after all.

How does this apply to the case in question, the case of the proposed identification of mental properties with neurophysiological properties? As follows: in the water/H_2O case, what we learn from Kripke is not that some proposition we had thought contingent is really necessary; what we learn instead is that some sentence we thought expressed a contingent proposition really expresses a necessary proposition. What we learn is a semantical fact, not a modal fact. It isn't that there is some proposition we thought to be contingent and is now seen to be necessary. It isn't that (3), the proposition, formerly appeared to us to be contingent, but then was seen, via Kripkean considerations, to be necessary; it is rather that (5) formerly seemed to express a contingent proposition and is now seen to express a necessary proposition. Our problem was not modal illusion, but semantical illusion. So what we have is not a reason for mistrusting modal intuition (more specifically, an intuition of possibility); it is rather a reason (if only a weak one) for mistrusting our ideas about the semantics of proper names and kind names.

But then there is a large, important and crucial difference between the water/H_2O case and the pain/firing C-fibers case. In the former, as I've just been arguing, the proposed identification doesn't conflict with any modal intuitions at all. Indeed, (3) does seem intuitively to be necessary: that very stuff could not have been something other than H_2O. So here there isn't so much as a hint of conflict with modal intuition. In the latter case however, the case of pain/C-fibers firing, there is a clear and wholly obvious conflict with intuition.

(10) Someone is in pain when no C-fibers are firing;

appears for all the world to be possible; similarly, of course, for

(11) Someone is conscious when there is no pyramidal cell activity.

According to the proposed identification, however, these propositions are (of course) impossible. If pain just is the firing of C-fibers and consciousness just is pyramidal cell activity, then (10) and (11) are equivalent, in the broadly logical sense, to

(12) C-fibers are firing when no C-fibers are firing

and

> (13) There is pyramidal cell activity when there is no pyramidal cell activity.

In other words, the proposed identification of water with H2O goes contrary to no modal intuition; the proposed identification of pain with C-fiber firing, and consciousness with pyramidal cell activity, on the other hand, is wholly counter-intuitive. The latter identifications go directly against strong modal intuitions; the former does not.

This objection to dualism, therefore, is no stronger than the others. No doubt splendid theoretical advantages would be forthcoming from the identification of mental with neurophysiological properties, as with the identification of concrete objects with their essences. But these theoretical advantages are surely outweighed by the fact that the proposed identifications are obviously false. Like the other objections to dualism, accordingly, this one is without any force. In conclusion, then: there are powerful arguments against materialism and none for it. Why, therefore, should anyone want to be a materialist?[39]

[39] In addition to the people mentioned in the text, I thank Michael Bergmann, Evan Fales, Trenton Merricks, William Ramsey, and the members of the Notre Dame Center for Philosophy of Religion discussion group, in particular Thomas Flint and Peter van Inwagen, as well as others I have inadvertently overlooked. I'm especially grateful to Dean Zimmerman.

Index

Abraham, W., 140n
actualization
  strong, 181–82
  weak, 182, 184n
Adams, R., 50–52, 53, 55–58, 72–73
Alston, W., 72n
Anscombe, G. E. M., 341
Anselm, 84
apocrypha, 211–12, 215
Apostles' Creed, 356, 364
Aquinas, St Thomas, 30, 130n, 139n, 146n,
  162, 347, 359–60, 386n
Aristotle, 359–60
Arminianism, 18
Armstrong, D. M., 73n, 74, 82, 337–39, 387n
Athanasian Creed, 364
Athenagoras, 159, 376
Attridge, H., 301n
Augustine, 139n, 161

Baille, J., 152n
Bantly, F. C., 242, 243
Barth, K., 232, 360
Bartholomew, D. J., 123
Basinger, D., 93, 174–78, 184
Basinger, R., 174–78, 184
Belgic Confession, 269
Bigelow, J., 72n, 73n, 77n
Bossuet, J., 136
brain transplant, 333
Brown, D., 131n
Brown, R., 242–249, 250, 254–60, 274–75
Bultmann, R., 279, 287
Burtchaell, J. T., 186–87, 188, 190
Butler, J., 130n, 131n
Bynum, C. W., 370n

Cabanis, P., 408n
Cadoux, C. J., 162
Calov, A., 164
Calvin, J., 19, 164–65, 173–74
Calvinism, 18, 35, 36
Campbell, D. T., 402
canon, 210–241
  Alexandrian hypothesis, 210–214
  as a work, 238–9
  criteria and formation, 210–21, 222, 226–7,
  228
  unity, 238–40
Canon Muratori, 218–21

Carson, D. A., 175–76
Castañeda, H. N., 350
causation
  gappy (or mnemic), 340–42, 345
  immanent, 332, 337–40
  theories of, 341–42
Chadwick, O., 136n
chance, 104–23
  and evil, 119–23
  characterized, 111–12
  sources of, 113–119
changing the future, 86, 87
Childs, B., 232, 284, 294, 295
Churchland, P., 409
circumstances of action, 22, 26n, 31–35, 37
Clement, 158, 222
Coady, C. A. J., 312, 313
Collins, J., 277–78, 294
compatibilism, 37–43
conditional excluded middle, 69–70
constitution view of persons, 348–55
counterfactual
  and divine knowledge, 23–29, 30
  and laws of nature, 49–50
  truth conditions, 45–46, 51–53
  see also counterfactuals of freedom, middle
  knowledge, *and* Molinism
counterfactual knowledge, 180–81
counterfactuals of freedom
  and divine knowledge, 30–31, 55–56,
  62–66, 180–81
  characterized, 22–23, 45
  grounding, 50–55, 57, 58–63, 64, 68–83; *see*
  also truthmaker theory
  objections to the truth of, 46–66, 68–83
  see also counterfactual, middle knowledge,
  and Molinism

Davis, S., 199–200, 202–3, 206n
death by misadventure, 120
Dilthey, G. W., 229–32
divine foreknowledge, *see* foreknowledge
divine freedom, *see* freedom
divine goodness, *see* goodness
divine inspiration, *see* inspiration
divine knowledge, *see* foreknowledge, free
  knowledge, middle knowledge, *and*
  natural knowledge
divine revelation, *see* revelation
divine sovereignty, *see* sovereignty

Made in the USA
Monee, IL
06 September 2020